D1568333

Feast of Excess

Feast of Excess

A CULTURAL HISTORY OF THE
NEW SENSIBILITY

George Cotkin

OXFORD
UNIVERSITY PRESS

OXFORD
UNIVERSITY PRESS

Oxford University Press is a department of the
University of Oxford. It furthers the University's objective
of excellence in research, scholarship, and education
by publishing worldwide.

Oxford   New York

Auckland   Cape Town   Dar es Salaam   Hong Kong   Karachi
Kuala Lumpur   Madrid   Melbourne   Mexico City   Nairobi
New Delhi   Shanghai   Taipei   Toronto

With offices in

Argentina   Austria   Brazil   Chile   Czech Republic   France   Greece
Guatemala   Hungary   Italy   Japan   Poland   Portugal   Singapore
South Korea   Switzerland   Thailand   Turkey   Ukraine   Vietnam

Oxford is a registered trade mark of Oxford University Press
in the UK and certain other countries.

Published in the United States of America by
Oxford University Press
198 Madison Avenue, New York, NY 10016

© George Cotkin 2016

Library of Congress Cataloging-in-Publication Data
is available

ISBN 978-0-19-021847-8

1 3 5 7 9 8 6 4 2

Printed in the United States of America
on acid-free paper

For Those Authors Who Inspired in Me a Desire to
Become a Better Writer

{ CONTENTS }

PART III **Cultural Commonplace, 1969–1974**

19. 1970: "I Just Love Freaks": Diane Arbus   269

20. 1971: Vegas, Baby!: Robert Venturi, Denise Scott Brown,
    Hunter S. Thompson   283

21. 1972: Erectile Destruction: Samuel R. Delany and Thomas Pynchon   297

22. 1973: Zipless Abandon: Erica Jong   311

23. 1974: Crucified and Shot: Chris Burden   323

    Conclusion: The Shock of the Old—and New   333

    Notes   339
    Index   407

{ ACKNOWLEDGMENTS }

For readings of chapter(s), advice, bits of information, words of encouragement, or simply asking how things were going, I thank: Elie Axelroth, Tim Barnes, Casey Nelson Blake, Tim Becher, Eileen Boris, Sarah Bridger, Lawrence Buell, Charlie Cohn, Kyle Cuordileone, Jimm Cushing, Richard Enfield, Christina Firpo, Cristina Giorcelli, Cindy Green, Melody Herr, Jim Hoopes, Matt Hopper, Robert Inchausti, Konstantina Karageorgous, Bruce Kuklick, Jeff Larsen, Ralph Leck, Jane Lehr, Nelson Lichtenstein, Robert Lockhart, Steven Marx, Kevin Mattson, Mike McCormick, Paul Miklowitz, Andrew Morris, Jay Parini, Giovanna Pompele, Marta Peluso, Tatiana Njosh Petrovich, Maria Quintana, Jennifer Ratner-Rosenhagen, Joan Shelly Rubin, Robert Rydell, Ann Schofield, Emanuele Scoppola, Richard Shaffer, Gary and Vallerie Steenson, Maxine Stein, Jack Sullivan, Leslie Sutcliffe, Quintard Taylor, John Thomas, Ilana Winter, and Martin Woessner. Thank you as well to the anonymous readers of the manuscript for Oxford.

My editor, Brendan O'Neill, has been unceasingly enthusiastic about this project, which has meant much to me. His reading of every chapter made this a better book. And thanks to him, as well, for recommending *Holy Motors*, a transcendently great film. Others with Oxford, Stephen Bradley and Joellyn Ausanka, have been excellent. Copyeditor Ben Sadock has been superb, earning my gratitude. My agent, John Thornton, has become a friend while helping me navigate the often choppy waters of publishing. Research was aided by archivists at a number of institutions: Columbia University (Ginsberg and Jong Papers), New York University (Gelber Papers), Stanford University (Ginsberg Papers), UCLA (Sontag Papers), and Yale University (Living Theatre Collection). Thank you, too, to Cal Poly Interlibrary Loan and to the Department of History at Cal Poly.

While working on this book, I often escaped by reading works distanced from my subject. These books left me impressed and inspired. I offer my appreciation to the following authors and urge readers to cast a glance in their direction: Sarah Bakewell, Laurent Binet, Kevin Birmingham, Lisa Cohen, Alexandra Harris, Kevin Jackson, Gilbert King, Olivia Laing, Helen Macdonald, Robert Macfarlane, D. T. Max, Maggie Nelson, Orhan Pamuk, Andrea Pitzer, George Prochnik, and the great W. G. Sebald.

Thank you to my Facebook friends for voting on potential titles for this book. As always, my deep love to Marta Peluso, who helps me to live better by urging me to turn away from my excessive nonhedonism to embrace bits of pleasure. And she is a great reader of page proofs—no easy task.

Feast of Excess

Introduction

The New Sensibility

"Don't you think that John has gone too far this time?" Lucretia Cage worried after first "hearing" her son John's piano piece *4′33″*.

A reasonable query, for nary a key had been touched nor a note sounded from the piano during the performance. But the ever sly and mischievous John Cage had created music, in a manner. The "expressive silences" of the work opened attendees to sounds aplenty in the immediate environment—creaking concert-hall rafters or the anxious whispering and fidgeting of people in their seats.[1] When the piece debuted in August 1952, boos and groans of downright hostility had greeted it. The piece was excessive in its minimalism, but also delightful in its challenge to artistic conventions.

Earlier in that sublime August of creativity, Cage had staged a "happening," a diverse-media frenzy in a dining hall at Black Mountain College in North Carolina. With a maximum of chaos, a dose of the absurd, and a desire for spontaneity, the event swirled with poetry read, a piano played, records spun, all-white paintings displayed, slides and movies shown—all as dancers wended their way through the phantasmagoria. It was a feast of excess.[2]

Jump ahead to the early 1970s in Southern California. A baby-faced artist named Chris Burden, wearing only a skimpy swimsuit, hands behind his back, slithered and crawled, body bleeding, across a fifty-foot gallery floor strewn with broken glass. In 1974, he had friends crucify him by hammering nails into his palms as he nestled against the curved back of a Volkswagen Beetle. Someone revved the engine, which screamed in contrast to Burden's own silence. As part of the piece, he would later display the gritty "stigmata" scars that had been left on his palms. Nor should we forget his infamous performance piece *Shoot* from 1971. From a distance of fifteen feet, in front of an audience of friends, Burden had himself shot. A copper-jacketed .22-caliber bullet was supposed to graze his arm; instead it hit the fleshy part full on. A couple of photographs show the artist on the verge of shock—he was bleeding for his art. He remarked later that the piece had succeeded; after all, he had experienced being shot and lived to tell of it.[3]

From silence to blood, the American cultural scene between 1952 and 1974 pushed boundaries, defied expectations, and trafficked in excess.

Many artists joined Cage and Burden in this challenging and crazed adventure. Patricia Highsmith penned unsettling novels in which amoral criminals went unpunished and enjoyed ill-gotten prizes. Norman Mailer unleashed ego and violence-drenched performances in his writing (anal rape, approval of murder, and celebration of drugs) and in daily newspaper headlines, as when he stabbed his wife; Andy Warhol embraced boredom (films that went on for seven hours without much of anything happening) and repetition in his artwork (image after image of Marilyn Monroe, with lusty red lips) to become famously famous for more than fifteen minutes; Anne Sexton, in her confessional poetry, picked at the scabs of her physical and mental pain; John Coltrane assaulted listeners with the transcendental, almost unbearably long shrieks of his saxophone; Amiri Baraka's poetry screamed with angry calls for blood in the streets (and sometimes his own flowed); Erica Jong explicitly described the delights for women of a "zipless fuck," while Samuel R. Delany wrote in exacting detail of every sexual and coprophilial act imaginable; and Diane Arbus broke down barriers between photographer and subject (sometimes by having sex with her subjects) in a manner at once honest and frightening, especially since her subjects of choice were often those considered by society to be freaks and outcasts.

All of these artists were creating a new sensibility for American culture that refused the polite and traditional while celebrating the excessive and unconventional. Acts of excess; going to extremes; focusing on violence, sexuality, and madness; blurring lines between genres, between artist and audience, had always been present in art and culture of the past. But in the period under consideration in *Feast of Excess*, they became more common, pronounced, and pervasive. In large part, they came to constitute a culture—our culture—which still enthuses and beleaguers us to this day.

"The New Sensibility," the white-suited dandy Tom Wolfe wrote in 1965, was a new cultural world. In manic, signature prose he exulted: "*Baby baby baby where did our love go*—the new world, submerged so long, invisible, and now arising, slippy, shiny, electric—Super Scuba-man!—out of the vinyl deeps."[4] A Columbus of cultural exploration, Wolfe jumped into the American landscape of demolition derbies, custom car stylization, and stock car racing. He cooed about the intensity of instant experience; he celebrated, with his usual irony, the celebrity of one Ms. Jane Holzer (a woman with great hair but no discernible talent). He was gleeful that the once traditional border between high and low culture had been trespassed. Content and style were brilliantly conjoined in his reporting on the signage of the Las Vegas strip: "Free form!

Marvelous! No hung-up old art history words...artists for the new age, sculptors for the new style....It was happening, baby!"

Susan Sontag—stunningly erudite and enticing, a young critic and novelist—was cooler in register than Wolfe. She discovered the New Sensibility in avant-garde theater, absurdist and experimental novels, and in the over-the-topness of camp style. She reveled in the experimental flourishing of American culture—in odd films such as Jack Smith's *Flaming Creatures* (1963), in which blurred figures, some naked, others swathed in flowing sheets, cavorted in dream-like revelry. She rebelled against the need to find deep meaning (historical, psycho-analytic, or otherwise) in works of culture, preferring to experience the work of art on its own terms, to skate along its surface. Sontag was no cultural stick-in-the mud. She loved to kick off her shoes and dance to the pop music of the great girl group the Supremes.[5]

The differing visions of a New Sensibility enunciated by Wolfe and Sontag shared a fascination with excess, a demand for pleasure (of various sorts), a willingness to push further into experiments in style, and an openness to new content. As with Cage's music, excess could lead in the direction of minimalism, a clearing out of the cupboards of the mundane. Burden's dismissal of the usual artistic object (the painting or sculpture) was intended to make his own body and its experiences into a work of art. Yet the New Sensibility also embodied maximalism: the cacophony of Cage's happening, the heated poetry of Allen Ginsberg, the macho musing of Mailer, the erudition gone wild of Thomas Pynchon, or the camp transvestism of Gore Vidal's *Myra Breckinridge* (1968). Could there be anything more excessive than the perfervid use of four-letter words in a performance by Lenny Bruce or tales of drug-addled Las Vegas adventures as narrated by Hunter S. Thompson?

A theatrical or performative style was central to the New Sensibility. Life and work intermingled; the artist became enmeshed in the celebrity world, often willingly—as with Ginsberg, Mailer, Baraka, Vidal, Warhol, and Jong, to name a few. Artists in all media had become hyperconscious about themselves performing for an audience—of being watched; such was the essence of Burden's thorny performances. Artists were in general, according to critic Richard Poirier, creating a new identity.[6] In contrast, Pynchon was a performance artist of hiding, shielding himself from any public presence beyond his written words. Two of Burden's pieces from 1971 played with the idea of anonymity, too, as when he once stayed for five days cramped in a school locker or when he spent three days in Kansas City with a mask always on his face—anonymity and attention at the same moment.

In the hands of less skillful artists, a mania for publicity translated into self-indulgent oversharing, confessional kitsch. But with the imperative to go far-ther, increasingly little was hidden, and much that was daring accomplished. The lines between the personal and the political, as feminists averred, grew skimpy. Confession became, in William Styron's view, "a particularly 1960s form of address."[7]

Divisions between artist and audience melted, in various ways. Since Warhol's films and silkscreens seemed to exist only on the surface and paraded themselves either as works of brilliance or insipidity, critic Lucy R. Lippard contended that viewers were forced to take a stance in relation to the work. Passivity in relation to the products of the New Sensibility was discouraged.[8] Performers of the Living Theatre tried to draw the audience into the play or take the performance into the audience. Such forms of involvement at first included actors, still in role, mingling with the audience during intermission; within the decade, cast members would encourage audience members to frolic with them in sexual acts.[9] In similar manner, the happening, a nonrepeatable ecstasy of spontaneous expression, refused to be divorced from "daily life." Happenings involved participants in its operation and critiqued, by so doing, the nature of art and its institutions. Allan Kaprow, an early proponent of happenings, imagined these new "alchemies" would define art in the decade of the 1960s.[10]

When protestors at the Democratic National Convention in the summer of 1968, amidst tear gas and beatings, intoned, "The whole world is watching," they were, in a sense, summing up the performative ethos of the New Sensibility. Everything had become theater as radicals Abby Hoffman, Jerry Rubin, and Amiri Baraka understood perfectly well. There was, as social critic Marshall Berman observed a "new intimacy between" all aspects of culture and "the life of the street."[11]

The New Sensibility aimed to obliterate the cultural divide in order to hurry forward into the territory of liberation. Mailer's *The Armies of the Night* (1968) was subtitled *History as a Novel/The Novel as History.* Not only did Mailer blur divisions between reportage and fictional depiction, he performed as a central character in the drama. Truman Capote had already forged a similar hybrid with *In Cold Blood* (1966), which he called a "non-fiction novel." The book narrated the horrific slaughter of a Kansas farm family by two ex-cons. It was a gripping tale, awash with violence and exhibiting both detachment and empathy for one of the murderers.[12] Pynchon's novel *Gravity's Rainbow* (1973) was not only a crossword puzzle of clues but also an explosion that demolished genre distinctions.

Excess defined the stylistic imperative of the New Sensibility. "Apocalyptic expression" and "overkill" became its expressive coin of the realm. Norman O. Brown caught this heightened sense in 1966 by declaring, "Only the exaggerations are true."[13] Consider in this regard how a minimalist aesthetic could meld into a maximalist obsession. In his film *Empire* (1964), Warhol's immobile camera focused on the iconic Empire State Building. Filming began at around 8:00 p.m. and ended just before 3:00 a.m. The six-hour film was later shown in slow motion, pushing it to eight hours in length. It was minimalist in conception and execution; it was maximalist in scope and audacity. The subject was less the Empire State Building than the unfolding of time, reveling in a fascination with the unexpected coming into view (birds, shifts in light, airplanes) and with the oddly dynamic interplay between boredom and attentiveness. It was, in effect, a child of Cage's 4′33″.

The New Sensibility's celebration of excess as a style, a way of seeing and presenting the world, was riveted on a common core of subjects: violence, liberation (especially sexual), and madness. Such topics had, of course, long been significant, but had often been handled with kid gloves, romanticized, or shunted to the sidelines of poor taste. No longer. Now, as critic and poet John Gruen put it in 1966, "No subject is taboo, no action forbidden."[14] Transgression was tattooed on the arm of American culture. The New Sensibility vigorously endorsed the notion of "thinking about the unthinkable," a term which had been popularized in another context by Herman Kahn, a theorist of nuclear-war survival.

If one was going to depict violence, then so be it—do so in Technicolor imagery, horrifyingly exquisite detail, or feverish prose. In the 1950s, Brando emoted a sense of violence, almost savoring its possibility in every twitch of his body and facial expression. Violence stalked with screechy footsteps in the work of such diverse figures as Highsmith, Mailer, Delany, and Baraka. Although Warhol was famous for his repetitive images of celebrities and consumer products, he did a provocative series of prints that captured this burgeoning fascination with violence. *Death and Disaster* consisted of silkscreened images, often inked in different colors, of an electric chair (the one in Sing Sing Prison that had executed atomic spies Julius and Ethel Rosenberg), automobile and plane crashes, and even newspaper stories about women that had died from eating cans of tainted tuna fish. It was everyday death staring into your face.

By the late 1960s, an aesthetics of graphic gore reigned in the cinema. In earlier films, violent death was depicted without blood spurting, body parts being severed. With four cameras running, director Arthur Penn orchestrated the filming of a "spastic ballet of death" as eighty-six bullets riddled the bodies of his antiheroes Bonnie Parker and Clyde Barrow. A couple of years later, Sam Peckinpah's *The Wild Bunch* (1969) offered a four-minute shootout orgy, with at least a hundred bloodied men twisted in agony—at once repellant and mesmerizing.

Artists (novelists, filmmakers, and painters), all supping at the table of the New Sensibility's excess, savored sexual possibility and unabashed joy. Pleasure began to challenge the tragic for a central place among the cultural elite. Drama critic Walter Kerr wanted to see the "habit of unhappiness" broken. Artist Claes Oldenburg waxed about artworks that "a kid licks, after peeling away the wrapper." Most famously, perhaps, Susan Sontag craved an "erotics of art" to displace the boring and staid that had dominated American culture and criticism. It seemed possible for viewers, if they so desired, to skip across the surface of some artworks—in the view of artist Robert Motherwell, writing in the mid-1960s, "One does not have to 'understand' wholly to feel pleasure."[15]

Erotic sexuality, once suppressed in American culture or relegated to the privacy of the bedroom, now unblushingly abounded. Raw sexuality and much more exuded in works such as William S. Burroughs's *Naked Lunch* (1959), John Rechy's *City of Night* (1963), and Hubert Selby Jr.'s *Last Exit to Brooklyn* (1964). By the late 1960s, it would be ubiquitous in American culture.

Following on the heels of heterosexual male liberation, as narrowly exemplified by *Playboy* in the 1950s, Helen Gurley Brown greeted the 1960s with sharp advice about how single women could make sexiness pay dividends. Americans would soon view Benjamin Braddock, the antihero in the film *The Graduate*, cavorting with married Mrs. Robinson, or they might ogle full frontal nudity on the stage in *Hair* or *Oh! Calcutta!* Combining sexual detail, Jewish guilt, and careening lust, Philip Roth published a bestselling novel, *Portnoy's Complaint* (1969), that charted the sex and times of one Alexander Portnoy and his female companion, affectionately known as "The Monkey." If Roth's sexuality was beholden to the *Playboy* ideal, Erica Jong's novel *Fear of Flying* (1973) upturned tables to grapple with the personal and sexual liberation of a woman. By the 1970s, pornography was no longer housed in seedy theaters but was on screens across the nation and in bestselling books, even in work by highly respected authors such as Pynchon and Delany.

Many of the early masters of the New Sensibility (Cage, Rauschenberg, Highsmith, Brando, Ginsberg, Sontag, Vidal), it bears noting, were gay or bisexual. This is hardly surprising, since the New Sensibility was about aesthetic *and* personal liberation. It did not unlock the closet but made its confines more commodious. In time, through the jaunty excess of camp, aspects of a gay sensibility increasingly entered the cultural mainstream, as with the popularity of the Batman television series of the mid-1960s. And it was only a matter of time before Vidal's fictional Myra Breckinridge proclaimed: "I broke the arms, the limbs, the balls of their finest warriors."[16]

"The exemplary modern artist is a broker in madness," announced Sontag. King Lear types romped about the culture at large. By the mid-1960s, the topic of madness had become for some a royal route to liberation. In a major assault on traditional rationality, thinkers as diverse as Herbert Marcuse, Norman O. Brown, Thomas Szasz, and R. D. Laing contended that madness freed the individual from the numbing repressiveness of normality. "Madness may not be all breakdown," wrote Laing. "It may also be breakthrough."[17] With stunning verisimilitude, Diane Arbus photographed patients in mental facilities, and Sylvia Plath wrote candidly, albeit with a fictional overlay, about her own institutionalization. This theme resounded in films, captured in the French film *King of Hearts*, which played in one Cambridge, Massachusetts, movie theater for five years straight.[18] The main character in the film, played by Alan Bates, awakens to find himself among an assortment of nutjobs. He eventually realizes that he—and they—all reside in an insane asylum. By the end of the film, this venue proves to be far more normal and humane than the killing fields of the surrounding countryside, then engulfed by the conflagration of World War I.

Poets and writers increasingly talked directly, perhaps excessively, about their own experiences with depression, abortion, madness, and suicide attempts. Plath and Sexton, no less than Ginsberg, Robert Lowell, John Berryman, and Mailer, revealed their own demons, balancing the constraint of art with the volcano of emotion. Sexton was explicit about this. "You see, I am given to excess," she wrote a friend, "that's all there is to it. I have found that I can control it best in a poem."[19]

Some readers may have some questions at this point about the concept of a New Sensibility. First, might its definition be too capacious? Is it merely a version of philosopher William James's summer home, once described as having "fourteen doors, all opening outward?" Second, what the heck is a sensibility? Third, where does the New Sensibility stand in relationship to entrenched categories such as modernism, late modernism, romantic modernism, and postmodernism?

In looking at the phenomenon of camp, Sontag noted that it was, ultimately, "ineffable." This was good, she argued, for when one draws the strings too tightly around a sensibility, its life can be choked out.[20] The New Sensibility, a term that Sontag helped to popularize, thrives when allowed to breathe. But, for the sake of clarity and emphasis, a sort of quick-study guide to the New Sensibility is necessary.

The New Sensibility was about excess, exaggeration, pushing limits, embracing the popular, and going too far in style and spirit. The New Sensibility, in opposition to much of what had come to be known as high modernism, vaulted the presumed barrier between high and low culture. Modernism was marked by an "anxiety of contamination," to use critic Andreas Huyssen's phrase.[21] True, but tricky. After all, James Joyce was a modernist of the highest order, and in his fiction he did not eschew excess or popular culture (the ordinary details of daily life).[22]

Not surprisingly, some of the figures associated with the New Sensibility— Cage and Pynchon—followed in his footsteps, demonstrating that the lines drawn between the modern and the postmodern are inexact and sometimes wrong. Perhaps modernism in general was a bit tamer, pointed toward order, or at least the illusion of order, in contrast with the New Sensibility. A quip about T. S. Eliot, a modernist saint, might drive home this distinction. Eliot's tailor, Cyril Langley, when asked about his client's suits, replied: "Remarkable man, Mr. Eliot…very good taste. Nothing ever quite in excess."[23]

The New Sensibility obsessively concerned itself with violence, madness, sexuality, confession, and liberation. The New Sensibility was a constellation of ideas, kept in orbit by the gravitational force of excess. No single cultural creator exemplified all its tensions and subjects, nor did one need apply for membership in the guild. One simply worked within its characteristic style and focused on its common themes, in the process expanding the reach of the sensibility.

Was the New Sensibility, then, a continuation of modernism or its last gasp? After all, traditional avant-gardes (itself an oxymoron, I realize) invariably sought to demolish lines between art and life, between the personal and the political, between artist and spectator—and to shake things up. Certainly, many aspects of the New Sensibility, even its excess, had resided within the castle of modernism, especially in futurism, surrealism, and Dadaism. Consider when Hugo Ball and his compatriots at Cabaret Voltaire in Zurich donned the oddest of costumes and recited the strangest of poems to protest against the greatest creative madness of all, the First World War. Or read some lines of Gertrude Stein's "An Acquaintance with Description" (1926), where an experimental excess of minimalism and maximalism intertwine: "Let it be when it is mine to be sure let it be when it is mine when it is mine," on and on.[24] High modernist critics were often unamused with such displays. In response to Dada and surrealism, for instance, art critic Clement Greenberg rejected their "anti-institutional, anti-formal, anti-aesthetic nihilism" as a stance that was empty of force and irrelevant to the times.[25]

Little is absolutely new, except the persistent call to make it new, as uttered by poet Ezra Pound in the early twentieth-century (a phrase which, according to Michael North, only became popular in the period under consideration in this book).[26] Newness itself—like measles or fads—has its outbreaks. But the styles and concerns of the New Sensibility coagulated and thickened sufficiently for a new movement to be realized and sustained over a long period of time—with connections to the earlier, but with a sustaining identity all its own. In this sense, borrowing from critic Edmund Wilson, the New Sensibility might be viewed as the "second flood of the same tide" of modernism—or as the first tide of the postmodern.[27]

How does one define or surround such elusive terms as modernism or postmodernism? Ironically, the best way to engage this concern might be with Cage's or Samuel Beckett's admonition for silence. Nonetheless, in 1970, critic Irving Howe composed a list of qualities associated with the modernist temperament: mania for the new, subjectivity, difficulty, despair, revolt, desire for purity, utopian longings, disdain for audience, a sense of historical discontinuity and the artist as heroic. But all these, he acknowledged, were peppered with internal divisions; it was unclear how to proceed, and to what destination.

Modernism continues to be placed under the microscope of analysis by legions of zealous and insightful scholars.[28] Out of this frenzy have arisen further modifications, romantic modernism, anarchistic modernism, late modernism, and, of course, the fabulously catch-all term postmodernism (presumed to be marked by pastiche, hedonism, refusal of history, demise of the subject, rejection of master narratives and celebration of theoretical discourse, gaudy surfaces, or even a "form of Free-Style Classicism"). Where does this take us?[29]

To put my own cards on the table, the New Sensibility combined aspects associated with both modernism and postmodernism. The poet David Antin once remarked wisely, "From the modernism you want, you get the postmodernism you deserve." And vice-versa. Or, better still, Ihab Hassan, who has spent as much time living in the postmodernist neighborhood as any scholar, admitted that postmodernism, no less than romanticism, and modernism, "suffer[s] from a certain *semantic* instability."[30] Definitional consensus about these terms, then, will forever be elusive; trying to reach one is a game that has its delights but never ends with victory.

Nor should one dwell on presumed contradictions within the New Sensibility, such as between its minimalism and maximalism. They existed alongside one another, as creative tensions, so long as they were taken to extremes. Writing in 1960, art critic Harold Rosenberg stated: "The new cannot become a tradition without giving rise to unique contradictions, myths, absurdities—often creative absurdities."[31] Indeed, these tensions were present at the birth of the New Sensibility in the 1950s. And this is as it should be.

Recall the famous imperative of William James's pragmatism, the value of an idea is in how well it works, how it helps us to see things in a different light, how it leads us forward. Let the value of the New Sensibility be submitted to the pragmatic test. As James always desired for pragmatism, so too let the New Sensibility become a point of departure, rather than of closure. Let it be considered a style and subject matter that began to stir in the early 1950s, got named as a phenomenon and exploded in the 1960s, and became the lingua franca for much of our culture in the 1970s, continuing to our present day. It was, and is, a culture marked by excess, an imperative to shrug off limits.[32]

A few words about what is meant by the concept of a sensibility. A sensibility, new or otherwise, allows us to encounter and create culture. A sensibility is a style or a code—both conscious and unconscious, a certain attitude or way of approaching the world. As historian Daniel Wickberg smartly notes, a "sensibility is anterior to the objects it represents in various concrete manifestations." Concepts closely related to sensibility have long been bandied about by great scholars: Raymond Williams's "structure of feeling" (the tone, codes, and presumptions of a society); Michael Baxandall's "the period eye" ("a stock of patterns, categories, methods of inference," and training) or, borrowing from Max Weber, Clifford Geertz's view that culture exists as "webs of significance" (rituals, symbols, and modes of being), or a version of Thomas Kuhn's paradigm (a way of organizing materials into a coherent whole that initially dismisses anomalies and sets the direction for research). In a Kuhnian sense, the New Sensibility certainly emerged to guide the cultural creativity of the period from the early 1950s to the present.[33]

Problems arise, certainly. Concepts can become wet blankets smothering paradox and conflict and undermining agency. As literary critic Lionel Trilling put it, culture is a "struggle, or at least a debate," marked by multiplicity.[34] The style of the New Sensibility, in its essential aspects, was capacious—able to house Cage's minimalist aesthetic as well as Lenny Bruce's impassioned comedic spleen, Mailer's monumental ego and Pynchon's waterfall of prose. As the New Sensibility became powerful in the 1960s, it helped to create and reflect the contradictions of the era. In the words of literary editor Gerald Howard, "The coolly ironic mood so characteristic of so much of Sixties art seems to contradict the heated idealism, political activism and self-exploration so equally characteristic of the Sixties."[35]

However, the New Sensibility never vanquished other cultural configurations. Restraint and tradition never exited the stage. The plurality of American culture has always been assured—if not by class, regional, and racial divisions, then by the need of commercial capitalism to increase rather than to foreclose the possibilities of consumption. As an example, American popular music in the 1960s, we need to remember, for all of the excitement and experimentation of the Beatles and the Rolling Stones, Dylan and the Velvet Underground, also had its fill of fluff. Historian George Lipsitz reminds us that the bestselling single record for 1960 was a sugary-sweet instrumental number, "Theme from A Summer Place," by the Percy Faith Orchestra, and Kenny G. has long remained a musical star. The most widely viewed television show between 1962 and 1964 was *The Beverly Hillbillies*, and today mainstream television channels have no lack of pabulum.[36]

Nonetheless, our house of culture has settled permanently in the concrete of excess.

All sensibilities exist within political, social, and economic contexts, and these contexts, in turn, are dialectically affected by the sensibility. "Ours is indeed an age of extremity," wrote Sontag in 1965. She had uncovered an "aesthetics of destruction" in science fiction films and in happenings, where the artwork had no lasting presence or, in some cases, self-destructed. Such excess and extremity mirrored the destructive power that had been birthed with the initial explosion of a hydrogen bomb in 1952 and was further heightened by the nuclear arms race of the 1950s. She also noted how excess was connected with the productivity of American culture and economy, threatening "a steady loss of sharpness in our sensory experience."[37]

An "H-bomb world" registered in the New Sensibility.[38] Sometimes this culture of destruction's artistic presence was obvious: in Mailer's philosophy of the hipster ("Our collective condition is to live with the instant death by atomic war") or in Dylan's "A Hard Rain's a-Gonna Fall" or Warhol's *Disaster* series of prints, or in Ginsberg's poetry ("weeping and undressing while the sirens of Los Alamos wailed them down").[39] Might an unconsciousness of destruction lurk behind Robert Rauschenberg's attempt in 1953 to erase a drawing by Willem de Kooning? That he failed, despite many hours of effort to remove all traces, can be taken as hinting at the survivability of art in an age of destruction. Might too the excessive devotion of camp to the ephemeral, or the wasted landscape in Delany's *Dhalgren* (1974) or the V-2 rockets hitting London in Pynchon's *Gravity's Rainbow* (1973) be indicative of a lurking fear of annihilation? And might dreams of sexual liberation be linked with potential for destruction in the voluble lyrics of Jerry Lee Lewis's 1957 song "Great Balls of Fire"?

It seems fair to anoint these years—when the "hydrogen jukebox" (to use Ginsberg's phrase in *Howl*) of destruction played loudly—as an age of extremity, a period when going too far was de rigueur. Suffice it to say a fear of annihilation was in the air, breathed deeply by all, most chokingly in 1962 with the Cuban Missile Crisis (see chapter 11). But this sense of being on the "eve of destruction," as a popular song phrased it in 1965, served as a compelling context for the New Sensibility's willingness to go as far as it could to focus upon destruction, madness, and a clearing of the decks of repression and conventionality. In an existential sense, the proximity of destruction could push individuals down previously deserted streets of creativity. The New Sensibility, then, acknowledged reality and battled to transcend it. Poet Kenneth Rexroth found Ginsberg's *Howl* to be a "confession of faith in the generation that is going to be running the world... if it's still there to run."[40]

This new culture was also connected with the explosive growth of capitalism, consumerism, and advertising in a "golden age" for the American economy.[41] "*Culture follows money*," F. Scott Fitzgerald wrote to his pal Edmund Wilson in 1921. Years later, Sontag acknowledged the cash-culture nexus as well: "There is really quite a close fit between avant-garde art and the values of the consumer society which needs products, constant turn-over, outrage, and so on."[42] A culture of excess was obviously well fitted for a burgeoning economy, one that until the late 1960s hummed along with possibility and hints of utopian satisfaction. But the push and pull between art and economics can be erratic. Historian Tom Frank has shown how creative people in business and advertising in the late 1950s began to follow culture—embracing a cultural sensibility or style as a way of selling products *and* liberating themselves from subservience to the stodgy.[43] We must keep in mind, too, that artists respond to relatively internal aesthetic challenges. As Willem de Kooning once proudly declared, "History doesn't influence me, I influence it."[44]

Even when the economy had sputtered and nosedived in the early 1970s, with the drain of the Vietnam War, smoldering urban crises, the ignominy of Watergate, and the oil crisis, the New Sensibility continued to thrive—indeed, it never absented itself from the scene. By then it had become rooted, needing little water to grow.

The survival of the New Sensibility might suggest that it has become stale and trite—reduced to excess for the sake of excess. Speaking of the once shocking gyrations of Elvis Presley, poet Tom Gunn concluded that "what starts as revolt finishes as style—as mannerism," as commonplace, shorn of revolt.[45] Certainly an argument can be made that the New Sensibility did sometimes engage with excess cheaply—in violence, confession, sexuality, and much more. Going too far to make a buck, sell a product, or inflate an empty reputation is all too common. According to filmmaker Quentin Tarantino, for whom excess in art serves as his regular diet, "Violence is a totally aesthetic subject." Nothing more, nothing less; violence denuded of meaning and reduced to style.[46] On many television series featured on cable or through streaming services like Netflix, the titillation of nudity has been rendered blasé by its ubiquity. Rather than shock, it simply confirms our pretension that we are watching something adult and sophisticated.

Has the New Sensibility, then, been appropriated by capitalism and institutions of power (art galleries and collectors, publishing conglomerates, television networks, etc.)? Who would dare to dismiss such a proposition whole cloth? But the issue, as many cultural commentators have taught us, is complicated. Capitalism has survived, albeit not unchanged. It continues to thrive on excess, although today the financial and cultural surplus seems to accumulate in fewer and fewer hands. In popular culture—indeed, in all culture—as Stuart Hall contended, there is "a double movement of containment and resistance."[47] Many critics of the New Sensibility focus excessively on the first of Hall's two movements of culture. Cooptation has its truths—the excess associated with the cultural products of the New Sensibility has not (and will not) dethrone capitalism. The logic of excess is shared by both capitalism and the New Sensibility.

Thus, some figures once associated with the New Sensibility later came to regret their apostolic roles. Looking back on her once excited reviews of campy or blood-lusty films, critic Pauline Kael lamented, "When we championed trash culture we had no idea it would become the *only* culture."[48] Even Sontag, the early cheerleader of the New Sensibility, later found some of her enthusiasm misplaced, if not downright false. Her *Against Interpretation* had once served as a sort of bible for experimental culture when it was published in 1966. Thirty years on she regretted her "evangelical zeal" in the battle "against philistinism, against ethical and aesthetic shallowness and indifference."[49]

The liberation of excess and experimentation in the New Sensibility has not been rendered moribund. It has continued to shock past the period of 1952–74 covered in *Feast of Excess*. Consider outraged citizens and puffed-up politicians agitating against the erotically overcharged images of Robert Mapplethorpe in the late 1980s and early 1990s. Around this time, the "NEA four," winners of National Endowment for the Arts grants, became national figures for ridicule or celebration with works that exuded excess. Under intense political pressure, the director of the NEA, John Frohnmeyer, rescinded the grants. That the four artists had received these grants in the first place, however, revealed how commonplace and accepted the New Sensibility had become, as well as its continued ability to rile and alienate.[50]

Punk was for many years outrageous—a screaming, sometimes bloody revolt—minimalist in song lyrics and instrumental skills, maximalist in energy and derision. By 2013 it had entered into the staid halls of the Metropolitan Museum of Art in New York City. Under bright lights and generously supported by corporate sponsorship (Versace and others), punk couture was literally placed on pedestals. The music pumped so loudly in the museum's corridors that guards were shifted to other areas every twenty minutes. Was this exemplary of punk's appropriation, of a stripping away of its original, ferocious anger? While this is a logical conclusion, it remains possible that punk's throb continues to mock high culture and offer a return to the beat of the primal, the scream of liberation that breaks through the thick walls of museums.

The New Sensibility remains valuable and viable. Perhaps now it needs to be renamed "Our Sensibility." It inspires cultural work that is fresh and complex, and naturally excessive. Listen to the repetitive spin of Philip Glass's music. Consider how writer Kate Zambreno's indefinable, genre-defying work *Heroines* (2012)—with heat and brilliance—combines scholarly acumen, feminist wrath, and personal confession to summon forth those female modernists who have been airbrushed out of history. The New Sensibility has also made possible the delightful excess and keen insight that informs Lena Dunham's popular television program, *Girls*. In the show, the "dumpy" star gallivants around in the nude; in her writings she revels in revelations about herself, tempered only by her wit and insight. If Mailer in 1959 proclaimed his desire to effect "a revolution in the consciousness of our time," then so too does Dunham aspire to be the voice of her generation. As her television character, Hannah Horvath, proclaims to her parents while she is on drugs: "I don't want to freak you out, but I think that I may be the voice of my generation—or at least the voice of *a* generation."[51]

The New Sensibility today grapples, in its best expressions, with a perennial problem which critic Roger Shattuck once referred to as the need "to reconcile liberation and limits."[52]

A few additional words are in order about the methodology and repertoire of figures in this book. *Feast of Excess* offers its tale in the form of vignettes. This allows interplay between individual artists and historical moment—hence each chapter deals with a single year. Vignettes allow cultural creators to be examined in the passion of creation, at the point when their work helped to create and solidify the New Sensibility. In their own manner, these vignettes mimic aspects of the New Sensibility, foregoing some of the conventions of traditional historical scholarship in an attempt to capture the explosiveness and drama of the moment.

The book opens with John Cage, who, as Rauschenberg fondly put it, "gave you permission" to revolt against tradition and to go as far as you might imagine.[53] Its pages are populated by musicians (Cage, Coltrane, James Brown, Jerry Lee Lewis, Dylan), artists (Warhol, Rauschenberg, Robert Frank, Arbus, Burden), figures from stage and screen (Brando, Judith Malina, Jack Gelber), writers and poets (Highsmith, Ginsberg, Mailer, Baraka, William Styron, Vidal, Jong, Pynchon, Delany), social commentators and critics (Bruce, Sontag, Wolfe, Thompson), and architects (Robert Venturi and Denise Scott Brown). All were drawn to new possibilities, to the thrill of demolishing the status quo, to a hankering for freedom—both for themselves and their art. And in their dreams and often in their actions, they tried to liberate politics and society.

Each figure in *Feast of Excess* has been chosen because he or she exemplified key elements of the New Sensibility—as defined by Sontag, Wolfe, and others in the 1960s. The apostles of the New Sensibility were numerous. Any number of substitutions of one artist for another might have been possible (Capote rather than Mailer, Albert Ayler in place of Coltrane, Roth instead of Jong). The characters in the vignettes are connected by their shared revolt against tepid conventions. And by their revelry in excess—invariably in their art, and perhaps too readily in their lives.[54] If a hint of the arbitrary covers the choice of figures discussed, that seems in keeping with the aesthetic of the New Sensibility. Moreover, as the poet Anne Carson writes, "The things you think of to link are not in your own control. It's just who you are, bumping into the world."[55]

My bumps into this world of the New Sensibility, however, are not solely contingent. Links aplenty, stylistic and content, as we shall see, existed between the creative artists covered in *Feast of Excess*. Their paths, too, often crossed. Cage and Rauschenberg were close friends; Arbus photographed Mailer and Sontag; Warhol filmed both of them, and he did silkscreens of Brando in motorcycle regalia; Ginsberg appeared in a film of Frank's, and he organized a protest against the arrest of Lenny Bruce on charges of "indecency," finding it all part of "a pattern of harassment of the avant-garde" in New York City.[56] Baraka, Malina, and Dylan admired Ginsberg; Dylan idolized Brando and was in the audience for Malina and Gelber's production of *The Connection*; Delany attended Allan Kaprow's *Eighteen Happenings in Six Parts*; Thompson and Wolfe were pals that admired one another's work; Mailer famously head-butted Gore Vidal but later reconciled with him; Cage and Ginsberg were onstage together in Boulder, the former provoking as always, the latter trying to keep the peace, in the mid-1970s; around that time, Highsmith was in East Berlin hearing Sontag and Ginsberg lecture.

The term New Sensibility has never really sunk into the vocabulary of historians and critics. But it is a valuable way of thinking about and conceptualizing the period from 1952 to 1974—and beyond to our own day. It captures an essential beat of American culture. "The sixties" is the usual derivation applied to a transformative period in American culture and society, but it is limited by association with a particular decade and overemphasis on youth rebellion. The New Sensibility was *not* strictly analogous with the 1960s counterculture. Indeed, the contours of the revolt of the sixties, as *Feast of Excess* suggests, were drawn by an older generation of rebels against convention. The term New Sensibility offers a better, fuller way to describe and order a crucial and chaotic twenty-plus-year period in the development of American culture. It allows us to think about our present cultural configuration, perhaps to the point of grasping even the twerking of onetime child star and now full-time sex symbol Miley Cyrus.

Thirty-five years ago, Morris Dickstein's marvelous *The Gates of Eden* employed the term New Sensibility in a chapter charting its role in the breakup of the late 1950s. He focused mainly on literary figures and obviously could not extend the term's relevance deep into the 1970s (aside from a chapter) or to the present. Although he did not use the phrase New Sensibility, W. T. Lhamon Jr.'s *Deliberate Speed: The Origins of a Cultural Style in the American 1950s*, dealt impressively with some of the themes central to this book and, along with Dickstein, posited that the origins of a change in sensibility went back to the earlier decade. Lhamon's volume emphasized "deliberate speed." *Feast* takes a different tack by charting excess burgeoning even in the early years of the 1950s. By the 1970s, the term New Sensibility was bandied about a bit. Both Daniel Bell and Irving Howe attacked it as exemplary of the destructiveness of culture in the 1960s; in their view, it gave birth to little of artistic value. That pejorative tradition surfaces on occasion among conservative commentators, as shown in Roger Kimball, *The Long March* (2000).[57] The New Sensibility deserves better, although its excess did not always result in magnificent art or improved lives.

Enough! It is time to harken back to a particular moment, New Year's Day 1952. Actress Judith Malina is rushing to the Cherry Lane Theater to listen to a piece by John Cage, appropriately titled *Music of Changes*. She will prove eager, along with the other figures in *Feast of Excess*, to create a New Sensibility in the darkest moments of Cold War America.

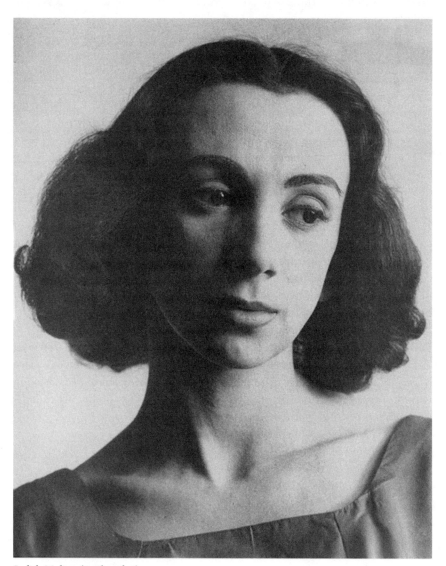

Judith Malina (© Photofest)

Prelude

A NEW YEAR: JUDITH MALINA

A bedraggled and bemused Judith Malina stumbled along the thickly fogged streets of Greenwich Village on New Year's Day 1952. The "pleasingly mournful sound" of foghorns briefly interrupted her malaise. She felt her life to be in ruins—"like a room in great disorder."

At twenty-five years of age, the exotically beautiful Malina was already a fixture in local avant-garde circles. An actress, writer, and director, blessed with nervous energy and enthusiasm, Malina, along with her husband, Julian Beck, had worked tirelessly for six years to create the Living Theatre, now housed in the Cherry Lane Theater. She was already considered something of a "taste bender" and a rebel. In 1949, Malina had confided to her journal, "My rebellion is all that I have." Now even that seemed insufficient.[1]

On New Year's Eve a disaster had occurred during the opening performance of Kenneth Rexroth's four-act play *Beyond the Mountains*, a tedious, demanding three-hour production. Malina was to perform three roles, Iphigenia, Phaedra, and Berenike (Electra). Appearing as Phaedra, fairly early in the play, Malina had just finished her sensual "Minotaur dance," with piano and cello accompaniment. She wore a flowing garment, complete with veil. Movement proceeded with Noh-like restraint. Sitting down and eyeing Hippolytus standing side stage, she recited the leaden dialogue: Hippolytus: "I have taken on the penance/ For a career of lust and blood." Phaedra stunned, replied: "I am amazed. I cannot / Believe it is you speaking. / I have loved and hated you." Then she proclaimed: "Someday they may discover the moon's held in its orbit by the menstruation of women."[2]

A young oboist in the orchestra pit "began to laugh uncontrollably." The sparse audience joined in the merriment. Malina was not amused. She ripped off her veil and rushed offstage, stunning cast and audience alike. The stage manager, Martin Macklin, warned Malina, "Get back on stage or I'll slap you." While the laughter had subsided, Malina remained frozen. Macklin's slap failed to return her to the stage. Instead, she fled into the dark of the streets and the blaring of New Year's Eve horns.

First she rushed to the apartment house of Harald Brixel, a former boyfriend, but he was not home. She sagged, weeping in the corridor. From another apartment a sculptor named Janio emerged, full of sympathy. They entered his apartment and chatted about yoga, Buddhism, and more. Mahler's Fourth Symphony played on the gramophone; in its fourth movement Malina could hear the words: "The angelic voices / gladden our senses / so that all awaken for joy." She and Janio made love. But this awakened little joy.

Malina left the apartment before midnight, en route to her favorite hangout, the San Remo Cafe, on the corner of MacDougal and Bleecker Streets. "In the San Remo Café where the tiles grow dirty…we gather to meet our loves, in this part of heaven," she wrote.[3] Malina ached for camaraderie and happiness but found the crowded bar's atmosphere forlorn. At midnight, she joined others to sing "Auld Lang Syne." After drinking too much, she took to the streets anew, this time in search of another former lover, composer Lou Harrison. She finally ended up spending night's fading hours at the house of a different friend, without sexual intercourse occurring.

The past few years had been both exciting and exasperating for Malina. Many of her days were spent hurrying to casting offices, auditioning for any available role. Rejection hurt, but so did the occasional commercial gig, which caused her to feel ashamed: "I've forgotten that I'm an artist," she admitted. In one role, on the then-popular television series *The Goldbergs*, she played a professor's wife, singing and faking it on the piano. She often found herself burdened with "stale, tenacious dreams" and felt anxious much of the time. Her life was supposed to be devoted to the goals of directing and acting in the theater— "I am intoxicated with the theater."[4] But she also busied herself with poetry (some of which was published) and wrote a play, libretto, and short stories. Her energy was as prodigious as her accomplishments were limited at this time.

She had been intoxicated with the theater from an early age. At eighteen, she had enrolled for classes at Erwin Piscator's famed Dramatic Workshop. "Visions of Paradise," she wrote, then "danced in my head." In order to afford tuition, even with a half scholarship, Malina worked two jobs. When not attending school, she counted dirty clothing in a laundry for slim pay; evenings she was a "waitress, singer and hat-check girl in Valeska Gert's Beggar Bar." At the Dramatic Workshop, Malina took classes in theater history, makeup application, voice, movement, acting, and directing. She was determined to direct plays but Piscator discouraged her, contending that women lacked force of character. But he relented after Malina confounded him by crying in his office. She respected Piscator mightily—after all, he had helped to develop the notion of "epic theater," which emphasized the connection between politics and art, as well as an intense relationship between actor and audience. Moreover, he had collaborated with the great playwright and poet Bertolt Brecht. Piscator seemed an incarnation of various European currents, ranging from Dada to Marxism. And the teenaged Malina soaked it all up.[5]

Malina felt blessed developing her life and art in "New York, city of wonders and joys." A cultural omnivore, she could never get enough of it. In the first six months of 1951, she went to many plays, Jean Cocteau's ballet *Marriage on the Eiffel Tower*, musical performances by John Cage and Virgil Thomson, art openings (at Grace Hartigan's show Malina espied filmmaker Maya Deren entering "like a wild woman"), various foreign films, and wild parties galore.[6] At such shindigs she chatted with the unworldly and handsome mythicist Joseph Campbell and his dancer wife, Jean Erdman; at another party she discussed experimental music and theater with Cage and choreographer Merce Cunningham. At yet another venue she was transfixed listening to volatile poet Chester Kallman hold forth on the libretto that he had written, along with his lover W. H. Auden, for *The Rake's Progress*, with music by Stravinsky.

Malina and Beck threw parties of their own. At one, she reported, pink champagne had been served and guests danced to the records of Marlene Dietrich and Lotte Lenya. The party proved an immense success, since "the police and the mad psychoanalysts from downstairs complained." In the midst of all this, along with caring for her two-year-old son, Garrick, Malina carved out space for eclectic reading—Herodotus and Robert Graves's *The White Goddess*. The latter, she remarked, "can make changes in the reader...and I am vulnerable."[7] She would become her own myth, incorporating ancient and new myths into the strands of the sensibility woven into her plays.

Her relationship with her husband was complicated.[8] They had been together for nearly ten years, since they had been teenagers worshipping culture and rebellion. But Julian refused to commit to her because of his homosexual orientation. A psychologist had for years been urging him to embrace women; Malina was, for him, certainly an object of love, if not of stormy desire. They married after Malina discovered that she was pregnant. Since Julian had a studio in their apartment—at the time he was pursuing a career in painting—he often minded Garrick. Beck and Malina's relationship was intense, despite, or perhaps because of, sporadic sexual relations. They anchored each other and pushed one another to dream of possibilities. Julian, in Malina's view, suffered from being too inward-oriented; he imagined the universe to be his for the taking. She, in contrast, found her passion sometimes ran too hot and effusive. Nonetheless, they had been journeying along the same path for years—toward creating a theater that would be experimental, marrying words and music, movement and art. She craved a Living Theatre that promised to "take us beyond our theatrical conventions."[9]

Many times the dream had darkened. In January 1948, Malina wrote, "I refuse to say that the Living Theatre is dead." A few months later, she was "overjoyed" at the prospect of restarting the theater project. That meant finding an affordable space, gaining rights to plays, and recruiting sponsors (who had either money or reputation—preferably both). Alas, at the end of 1949, the Living Theatre remained a distant reality—"entirely unfeasible," she noted sadly. Month after month they dreamt, bustling with plans and Malina aching to return to the stage.

They first organized plays in spacious living rooms. Both Beck and Malina threw themselves excitedly into such productions while continuing to search for a real theater space. Finally, in the summer of 1951, they leased for two months the Cherry Lane Theater, with its "musty, stale odor."[10] In addition to *Beyond the Mountains*, they planned to perform their friend (and soon to be Malina's psychotherapist) Paul Goodman's *Faustina* and Gertrude Stein's *Doctor Faustus Lights the Lights*. Perhaps John Cage, with whom Malina had a ripening friendship, might compose music for the Stein play? Carl Van Vechten, a versatile artist who had been a fixture during the great days of the Harlem Renaissance, controlled rights to Stein's play. He dismissed the Cage idea quickly. Cage would, he avowed, ruin everything by having drums beating nonrhythmically the whole time. No matter; the play was the thing, and the Living Theatre had materialized.

The long struggle for a theater coexisted with Beck and Malina's growing political consciousness. Both identified as nonviolent anarchists. They had become attached to similar souls at various meetings; some of these individuals had spent time in prison during the Second World War as conscientious objectors. Beck had avoided service in that conflict because of his professed homosexuality. Like nearly all avant-gardists, Beck and Malina wanted to bring art and life into closer proximity. This meant that they must dedicate themselves to protest at a time when the Cold War world had grown increasingly heated.

As early as 1950, they had trembled at the coming reality of hydrogen bombs—"Hell Bombs" was how Beck referred to them. Malina found it a time of "sweaty foreboding of calamity." She slept fitfully: "All night I dream of war." The outbreak of the Korean War threw them both deeper into politics and action, however futile and limited. They printed thousands of stickers with antiwar sentiments on them, sneaking around the city in quiet nighttime hours posting them on buildings and lampposts. They lucked out one night when a police officer let them go with merely a warning. But their fears about a potential nuclear holocaust had become deep dwelling. They imagined retreating to a communal life on an Indiana farm. Financial exigencies forced them to rely upon the largess of Julian's parents. But lack of money did not hogtie them politically or artistically.[11] Over time the Living Theatre would come to reflect a marriage of art and politics in the most renegade and excessive manner.

But this was still in the future. On New Year's Day 1952—"this bright morning born out of my darkest night"—Malina was in agony.[12] That afternoon she pulsed with "anger" and "shame" upon learning that she had been exiled from the cast for the remainder of the run of *Beyond the Mountains*.

Despite her sadness, she scurried back to the Cherry Lane Theater to attend a concert that evening, which featured a new John Cage piece, along with experimental music from composers Morton Feldman, Christian Wolff, and Pierre Boulez.

All day Cage had been ensconced in the box office merrily selling tickets. At age thirty-nine, he still emanated youthful vigor, enhanced by his crew cut and jovial smile. He greeted ticket buyers in a high-pitched, singsong voice. His gentle demeanor, however, masked an inner core of passion and intensity. Cage had a vision for music, art, and life that refused to be stilled.

The Cherry Lane seated a little over two hundred. Cage expected aficionados of avant-garde music to flock to the performance. Additional seats had been set up on the stage and orchestra pit to accommodate the overflow crowd. As anticipated, the place was packed for the concert.

Malina had known Cage less than a year, but she was captivated by the man and his music. In comparison with the neurotic artists whom she regularly encountered at the San Remo, Cage seemed to live in the present, with a courageous esprit. Malina admired too his refusal to draw distinctions between art and life. Even his apartment on Monroe Street, a center for artistic gatherings, bespoke the man. He made the drab space breathe by painting the walls startlingly white and punching holes in them allowing views of the East River and Empire State Building. He also hung from the ceiling mobiles that his pal Richard Lippold had created.[13] Malina was thrilled a year later when Cage revealed to her the question and answer that powered his life: "Am I alive in my work and life?" Cage answered in the affirmative.[14]

At Malina's behest, Cage prepared a "manifesto" for the program for the Cherry Lane concert. It was characteristically quirky, announcing that music must be "instantaneous" and "unpredictable." Further, it insisted, "Nothing is accomplished by writing a piece of music" or by "hearing" or by "playing" "a piece of music." Cage asserted in conclusion that "our ears are now in excellent condition."[15]

After forty-five minutes spent listening to pianist David Tudor play Cage's extremely intricate and difficult new work, Malina was enraptured and transformed. Her ears were now in excellent condition. The music had moved her as sensations rather than as thoughts. The composition announced itself with "a divine precision like a monstrous heart."[16]

A monstrous heart beat within Malina. She soon returned to the Living Theatre, as an actress, director, and guiding light. Her embarrassment from the New Year's Eve performance drifted away. She would grow ever more politically radical, getting arrested at anti-nuclear-bomb protests. She would continue as a life partner with Beck but would take on various lovers.[17] By 1959, she would direct a play about heroin addicts, integrating improvisational jazz into the heart and soul of the play. The excessive realism of the play convinced some in the audience that the actors were shooting up real heroin; that might well have been the case. Another decade later, in 1968, Malina (with Beck) would stage *Paradise Now*, more a happening than a play. The members of the Living Theatre troupe ritualistically intoned, "To be free is to be free"; they shrieked as if in an Esalen therapy session, stripped naked, groped one another onstage (with audience participation encouraged), and denounced war, racism, capitalism, and repression. The musical score was orchestrated chaos, and the play was anarchic.[18]

Thanks to *Paradise Now*, Malina would have a permanent place at the feast of excess.

But the table had yet to be set. Change was in the offing, and the title of Cage's piece that New Year's Day was appropriate: *Music of Changes*. If Malina listened attentively, she might have heard in its odd resonances and clanking tones an early stirring of a New Sensibility in American culture. As she wrote that January, "The change must come now! / Even tomorrow will be too late."[19]

PART I

Emergence, 1952–1960

Woodstock Artists Association

presents

john cage, composer

david tudor, pianist

PROGRAM

aug. 29, 1952 .... john cage
for piano .... christian wolff
extensions #3 .... morton feldman
3 pieces for piano .... earle brown
premier sonata .... pierre boulez
                              2 parts
5 intermissions ..... morton feldman
for prepared piano ... christian wolff
4 pieces .... john cage
    4' 33"
      30"
        2' 23"
          1' 40"
the banshee .... henry cowell

MAVERICK CONCERT HALL

Friday, August 29   8:15 P. M.

BENEFIT ARTISTS WELFARE FUND

Program for first performance of John Cage's 4'33" (1952) (courtesy of the John Cage Trust at Bard College)

Sounds of Silence

JOHN CAGE

1952

Going too far—as his mother realized—was Cage's point. It had long been the imperative of the avant-garde around the globe, allowing artists to transcend limits through the freedom of excess. Yet the artist also came face to face with the dangers of absolute freedom without limits. This potentially invited the devil of anarchy and disorder into work. Via some magical alchemy, order and anarchy tugged at each other in Cage's work. He managed to move the hearts of his listeners, causing them to pound faster and in unusual rhythms. That was the reaction of John Gruen, a composer, dance critic, and all-around avant-gardist in the Village. He had been at a low point in his own creative work, until he attended the New Year's Day performance at the Cherry Lane Theater. "It was a fantastic experience," he related. "It seemed that anything was possible after listening."[1]

The year 1952 proved to be Cage's annus mirabilis. That year he laid many of the foundation stones for the New Sensibility. The furor and influence of his performances evokes a comparison with the birthing of modernism thirty years earlier. Ezra Pound had declared that 1922 marked the beginning of a new artistic era, thanks to the publication of James Joyce's *Ulysses* and T. S. Eliot's *The Waste Land*. Cage was doing his part both to continue and to reject aspects of a modernist sensibility.

Cage created a stir, but many rejected his musical revolution. The reviewer for the *New York Times* was unimpressed with Cage's radically innovative composition *Music of Changes*. No doubt readers of the paper chuckled to learn that Cage's piece had featured the piano "treated like a great guitar, with its strings being strummed and plucked and its side tapped." It all seemed quite absurd.[2] The reviewer further noted that *Music of Changes* included slamming the piano lid, frenzied playing, and odd pedaling technique. The piece started and stumbled, sometimes lingering on a note, at other times offering achingly elongated silences.

If there was continuity between the notes, then it existed as mere coinci-
dence. It was true only in the Zen sense that everything is, by dint of existence,
connected with everything else. Not surprisingly, a month after the premiere,
Cage began attending classes on Zen taught by D. T. Suzuki at Columbia
University.[3]

Cage carefully orchestrated every whack and wham on the piano for *Music
of Changes*. Only a virtuoso pianist like David Tudor, who was deeply in synch
with Cage's experimentalism, could have flawlessly mastered the mixed tempi,
constant pedal changes, and strange emphases. Poet John Ashbery attended
the New Year's Day performance. He had a "fantastic experience" listening to
the "disjointed chords" which repetitiously sounded "until you sort of went not
out of your mind, but *into* your mind."[4]

Music of Changes resisted any essential interpretation. Listeners could apply
whatever meaning and perception to it that they chose—almost at random.
This no doubt thrilled Cage, who had stated in his "Lecture on Nothing" (1950):
"Our poetry now is the realization that we possess nothing. Anything therefore
is a delight (since we do not possess it) and thus need not fear its loss."[5]

An intricately developed methodology of chance powered the composition
of *Music of Changes*. Cage wanted to distance music from emotion and subjectivity, which he considered old-fashioned and uninteresting. A chance-based
compositional method rendered the piece immune to singular interpretation
and searching for authorial intent. The piece existed in its immediacy, in the
sensations that it evoked in listeners. Cage was thus exemplifying what would
become, in the opinion of Susan Sontag in the mid-1960s, a key tenet of the
New Sensibility—being "against interpretation."[6] As Cage put it, speaking of
his work and that of dancer Merce Cunningham, "We are not saying something. We are simple-minded enough to think that if we were saying something
we would use words."[7]

Could chance actually determine a musical composition? The saga of how
Cage achieved this end is familiar and perplexing. His student Christian Wolff
had presented him in 1950 with a copy of a recent translation of the *I Ching*, also
known as *The Book of Changes*. The book offered Cage a wealth of ancient wisdom
along with a method that stressed randomness. Ever open to innovation and already intrigued with Eastern philosophy, Cage was ready to employ the text to
tease out possibilities and break with the traditional standards of composition.[8]

Cage explained to his friend and fellow composer Pierre Boulez how his
compositional process decided by change worked. He began with various
charts for superpositions, tempi, durations, sounds, and dynamics. Half the
charts were "mobile," the other half "immobile." Here is Cage's description of
just part of the laborious process:

Three coins tossed six times yield sixty-four hexagrams (two trigrams,
the second written above the first) read in reference to a chart of the

numbers 1 to 64 in a traditional arrangement having eight divisions horizontally corresponding to the eight lower trigrams and eight divisions
vertically corresponding to the eight upper trigrams. A hexagram having
lines with circles is read twice, first as written then as changed.[9]

Got it? The goal of the process was, according to Cage, to compose a work
whose "continuity... is free of individual taste and memory (psychology)" and
also of the "traditions" of art. Sounds were not in service to any "abstraction"
which made "their 360 degrees of circumference free for an infinite play of interpretation." Moreover, there could be no mistakes in the work, since "once
anything happens it authentically is."[10]

Cage, as fellow composer Virgil Thomson observed, exuded a "relentless" determination, a tendency to excess, even when in the service of simplicity[11]—and
a hint of madness. Cage believed that madness was related to the "grandness of
conception." Only an Ahab—"madness maddened"—could chart new seas of
creativity. Cage recalled his friend Norman O. Brown, the philosopher of the
Dionysian, telling him that "any worthwhile activity is mad. And the only
reason it ever is taken seriously eventually is that one persists."[12]

Persistence was essential to Cage's repertoire for life and music. The origins
of *Music of Changes* and the revolutionary work that Cage composed and performed in 1952 can be traced back to his personal history and craving for
new sounds.

Cage was, in the best sense of the word, a tinkerer, an American original. He
came by this propensity naturally. His father was an inventor of great originality, if limited success; at one point, he patented a submarine that could
remain underwater for a long time but which unfortunately failed because its
motor caused bubbles to rise to the surface, undermining the concealment
that was the reason for its submersion. Cage's mother was a talented musician
and always encouraging. The parents' respective talents coalesced in their
only child.

Born in 1912, Cage grew up in Southern California. His high school year-
book noted that he was "quite radical," presumably in his politics and cultural
taste. During this time, Cage imagined himself becoming a Methodist minister. Yet he had also briefly flirted with conversion to Catholicism. Spiritual
searching was to frame much of his life and work, albeit in an untraditional
fashion. Like an ascetic monk seeking to open his soul to God, Cage strove to
enlarge his ears and ego to accommodate new sounds. "We must open up the
ego," he once explained, "open it up in the way Satie or Thoreau did! Open it
up to all experiences."[13]

After a stint at Pomona College and a joyful sojourn in France, with further
excursions around Europe and North Africa, Cage returned to depression-
ridden America in 1931. Following a year of odd jobs to support himself and

his impoverished family, Cage acted upon his determination to study musical composition. Not only was he an able student, he was assertive in pursuing his goals. When he wanted something from someone, he tracked down their home address, knocked on their door, and, with a combination of naiveté and self-interest, implored them to take him on as a student. "I've always gone, insofar as I could," Cage later remarked, "to the president of the company."[14] Although without funds, he managed to study with important teachers of music, including Henry Cowell and Arnold Schoenberg. The latter, who himself had taken modernism in new directions with his scale system, famously informed Cage that he "had no feeling for harmony," which would, Schoenberg presumed, bode poorly for his career. Unperturbed, Cage came to reject harmony, at least of a classical sort, in his composition.[15]

In 1935, in a desert ceremony, Cage married an alluring artist/model, Xenia Kashevaroff. The relationship was heated from the outset; they were two artists with rebellious temperaments and visions. They drifted about, first to Seattle (where Cage befriended and collaborated with Merce Cunningham), then San Francisco, and later stays in Chicago to New York City, all with a hint of inevitability, of pending arrival before the cognoscenti. Penniless in New York, Cage managed to place himself and Xenia in the luxury apartment of the surrealist painter Max Ernst and megarich art connoisseur Peggy Guggenheim. When the living arrangement began to fray, the couple moved downtown to stay with dancer Jean Erdman and her husband, Joseph Campbell, a specialist in mythology. Cage did indeed have a knack for knowing the right people. But he also impressed nearly everyone with his ardor, openness, and creativity.[16]

Love and its vicissitudes weighed on Cage's mind during in the early 1940s. Cunningham had relocated to New York. The two of them had fallen in love (before marrying Xenia, Cage had been involved in various homosexual relationships). For a time, Xenia joined Cage and Cunningham in a triadic relationship, but Cage's affection and energy were directed toward Cunningham. This was a period of anguish for Cage about his sexual identity and the fate of his marriage. He finally divorced Xenia in 1945 and became a partner and collaborator with Cunningham, a relationship that would continue until Cage's death in 1992.[17]

Love was probably not the emotion that *Amores* elicited from listeners at the Museum of Modern Art in February 1943. The evening's entertainment had featured Cage playing a piano with its strings rigged with nuts and bolts and "damped with rubber wedges" to transform it into a percussive sound engine. Cage or his tuxedo-clad assistants banged the piano, sometimes with gentleness, sometimes with force. Here, as in much of his work, Cage was bowing to certain streams of modernism, especially Dada, while slowly working toward his own style, with its emphasis on contingency and involvement of the audience in the work.

Cage acknowledged that he was offering audiences "noise," but as a way station on the road to a new sort of auditory comprehension. He wanted his auditors to hear the "unsuspected beauty in their everyday life." This imperative had a genealogy in the work of Joyce, Gertrude Stein, and Virginia Woolf, for example.[18] But Cage, in his manner, would in time take it farther. Attention to the clank of the mundane, Cage maintained, would expand the world of sounds and break down stodgy distinctions between life and music.[19]

Amores brought Cage to national attention. *Time* and *Life* magazines both reported on a recent performance of *Amores* at the Museum of Modern Art. The work premiered at a time when it must have appeared frivolous, if not downright disrespectful. After all, in February 1943 the Battle of Stalingrad finally concluded with millions dead, and the Battle of Guadalcanal had only recently commenced. Jolting sounds suggested bomb blasts, air raid sirens whirring, and cries of agony that filled the world at that pivotal time.

Life noted approvingly that when Chinese rice bowls had been "played," they emitted "a very pleasant tinkling."[20] Cage explained to the reporter for *Time* that his "quartet for drums, rattle, woodblocks and specially prepared piano" was "intended to arouse...feelings of love." If such was his intent, he failed to make explicit how such "feelings of love" were meant to soften the blows of war.

Three years later, in 1946, Cage showed some new experimental tricks in a concert at the Carnegie Chamber Music Hall. A reporter from the *New York Times* marveled that it took ten hours for Cage to prepare five pianos for the performance. Some of the results, at least in the view of the reporter, sounded "metallic, like the striking of a spoon on a frying pan." Other sounds were more soothing and subdued. One wag in the audience remarked that the concert was "the dividing line between the peanuts and the caviar," with the former being served. But the *New York Times* reporter admitted to being "opened up [to] all sorts of new and undreamed of rhythmic possibilities and musical effects in a fascinating world of tiny sonorities."[21]

In January 1949, apparently having been filed in some category for the odd and interesting, Cage was again fodder for a *Time* report. As before, the article on Cage's performance was certain to leave readers shaking their heads about the antics of the avant-garde. Yet the article's opening lines quoted Cage in praise of silence, as an end in and of itself and as a form of music. Then Cage, whom the article described as having a "Huck Finn" grin, remarked, "I thought of composing a piece like that. It would be very beautiful, and I would offer it to Muzak."

The performance *Time* covered had been part of a program at Carnegie Hall, full of "rhythmic, percussive 'sounds and silence.'" In Cage's usual manner, the piano had been "prepared" using all sorts of objects, ranging from the tried-and-true nuts and bolts to "pieces of rubber and plastic" designed to "short-circuit the tones." Cage wanted "sounds" rather than "tones" in his music. He scoured "junk yards, bone yards and hardware stores" to find "brake drums, pipe lengths, asses' jaws." These "instruments" joined his prepared piano to produce music. The welter of sounds evoked all sorts of associations.[22]

"My music is changing," Cage wrote to Boulez in December 1950. He had begun paying increased attention to chance and silence. It must be emphasized, however, that the desire was no sudden shift in Cage's compositional consciousness. As early as 1937, he had realized that "wherever we are what we hear is mostly noise.... When we listen to it we find it fascinating." He included among such sounds "static between stations" on the radio. He also noted in his letter a new devotion to "the flow of sound and silence."[23]

Silence fascinated Cage. Although exactly when, and under what precise conditions, he came closest to experiencing it remains unclear. Perhaps it was in the fall of 1950, when he had paid a visit to one of two labs at Harvard University where there were chambers that were almost totally soundproof and reverberation free. As a connoisseur of silence, Cage "literally expected to hear nothing." But once in the chamber Cage maintained that he "heard two sounds, one high and one low." He asked the engineer what they might be and was told, he recalled, "The high one was my nervous system in operation, the low one my blood in circulation." The experience stunned Cage, leading him to conclude, "Until I die there will be sounds. And they will continue following my death. One need not fear about the future of music."[24]

Cage's fixation on the relationship between sound and silence was strongly illustrated in his *Imaginary Landscape No. 4*, which premiered in May 1951 at Columbia University. Like *Music of Changes*, the piece relied upon a method of "unpredictability" offered by tossing coins according to instructions in the *I Ching*. The result, according to Cage, was that "value judgments" had been abolished for the "composition, performance, or listening" of the work. The piece was designed to allow anything to happen.[25]

Imaginary Landscape No. 4 featured twelve radios, each one "played" by two performers; one changed stations while the other manipulated the volume control. The twists and turns of the dial, however, were orchestrated by Cage's evolving method of chance. Thus, Cage wanted contingency and spontaneity in the composition but precision in the performance. The audience that evening was able to discern simultaneously snippets of a news broadcast or play-by-play of a baseball game, or they heard a windy sound of static, or perhaps a groan of silence. Pure Cage.

Like so much of Cage's work, the piece was avant-garde in its experimentalism and primed to outrage many of its listeners. Harold Norse, a fixture in the Village and a writer, reported that he heard many in the audience hiss, boo, and shout derogatory comments. This only seemed right and proper, Norse acknowledged, for a piece that was kooky and confrontational in a Dada mode. Two of Cage's close friends and fellow composers, Lou Harrison and Virgil

Thomson, according to Morton Feldman, disliked the piece; they "began to think that maybe he was going too far."[26]

If it was inspired by Dada (one of the many streams comprising modernism), the World War I–era movement dedicated to absurd art as a response to an absurd and violent world, then the piece was also dead serious musically. Part of what Cage desired with his cacophony of sounds was the creation of new sound combinations. And these sounds, as had been the case in earlier work, should stimulate the imagination of listeners to hear something different and challenging, requiring them to bring their own meaning to the work. Norse maintained that the "effect" of the music was to make him imagine "an automobile ride at night on an American highway in which neon signs and patches of noise from radios and automobiles flash and disappear in the silence."

This would have delighted Cage, especially since the work anticipated what in a year would become his most famous piece, his ode to silence. The long durations of silence that punctuated *Imaginary Landscape No. 4* were disturbing, signaled by Cage, serving as the conductor. They left the audience uncertain if the piece was simply suspended or ended. But uncertainty, anxiety about silence, was the musical language through which Cage was beginning to compose.[27]

Was Cage's work of the 1940s and early 1950s—with its banging and silences—intended to challenge the cultural lethargy often associated with this period—which poet Robert Lowell referred to as "tranquillized" by conformity, economic comfort, and political consensus? If so, then Cage seems an anomaly of the highest order, which attests even more to his relentless quest for creativity, under any conditions.

There is certainly truth in the view that American culture was rather lame and self-satisfied in this period. Even intellectuals who had in the 1930s upheld the ideal of Marxian revolution seemed tamed by the 1950s. In a famous symposium, "Our Country and Our Culture," in the journal *Partisan Review*, almost all of the contributors (ranging from theologian Reinhold Niebuhr to sociologist David Riesman to cultural critic Lionel Trilling), although they disdained the deleterious effects of mass culture, were largely satisfied with American politics and social life. They were pleased to be in the catbird seat, in prestigious universities and exercising cultural authority. Trilling pronounced that over the last thirty years there had been "an unmistakable improvement... in the American cultural situation."[28] Works once banished from classroom and public examination were now available. Funding, once tightly limited to works in the classical canon, now flowed into newer modes of art. Modernism had triumphed.

Some worried that victory came at a cost. Joyce and Pound were now assigned on university reading lists and celebrated as canonical. Pound had even been awarded the Bollingen Prize for Poetry in 1948, despite his pro-Fascist activities during the Second World War. Did acceptance blunt the power of modernist thought? Writing in the *New York Times Book Review*, poet Stephen Spender claimed modernism had lost its "vital spontaneity," victim to its own success and the constraints of conformity. He glimpsed nothing new and exciting on the cultural horizon.[29] But, of course, he was writing at the historical moment when the New Sensibility was only beginning to percolate.

It has been argued, with some truth, that mainstream American culture in the 1950s was maple-syrup sweet in its tastes. Doris Day starred in a new musical, *April in Paris*. It promised to burnish her reputation as America's bland, bouncy, and virginal queen of cinema. Another tepid blonde, Patti Page, wowed fans in December 1952 with a song that would become a huge hit, "(How Much Is) That Doggie in the Window."[30]

But such generalizations about the sappiness of American culture are incomplete. Culture is rarely static and singular. The landscape of popular music, for example, was not simply reserved for bland and blonde singers. A *Life* magazine story highlighted sultry singer Eartha Kitt. When she sang, the magazine reported, "Every muscle in her lithe, feline body sways in a ballet of its own." In the summer of 1952, a new film, *Affair in Trinidad*, promised viewers glimpses of Rita Hayworth's abundant cleavage. For those desiring something experimental in literary culture, Ralph Ellison's novel *Invisible Man* fit the bill, and readers eagerly anticipated publication on the first of September of Ernest Hemingway's new novel, *The Old Man and the Sea*. An early review in the *New York Times* praised the novel's existential verisimilitude. While artifice abounded in American culture, hints of authenticity and experiment were also present.[31]

In point of fact, Cage inhabited a world that was agog with creativity. And he was alive to varied experimental currents pulsating through a rich, albeit rather constrained area of Manhattan, from the Lower East Side where he lived to Greenwich Village, with occasional eruptions happening further uptown.

Cage interacted with, and learned from, artists of all types. He was friends with Robert Rauschenberg and regularly visited his studio to marvel at his white paintings (this will be discussed in chapter 2).[32] Cage associated with others devoted to experimental music. He corresponded with Boulez, and worked alongside avant-gardists Henry Cowell, Christian Wolff, Morton Feldman, and Earle Brown closer to home. They all challenged traditional practices and often appeared on the same musical programs.[33]

Cage's apartment was a veritable commune for such artists. "If there's no social life, there's no art movement," Gruen announced.[34] At the "Bozza Mansion" (so called after the building's landlord), Cage served up "sumptuous dinners"—spaghetti with many types of mushrooms, picked by his own hands—for friends such as sculptor Richard Lippold, artist Philip Guston, dancer Caroline Brown, and many others.[35]

When not entertaining at home, Cage often headed to the Cedar Tavern, a home away from home for such painters as Franz Kline, Jackson Pollock, and Larry Rivers, among others. There he discussed the exciting work of abstract expressionists, sometimes staying until 3 a.m. when the bar finally closed. Nearby, he often attended the Artists' Club on Eighth Street, a venue set up by abstract expressionists for the exchange of ideas. No doubt he appreciated one of its cardinal rules: "no politics" were to be discussed at get-togethers. Rather, artists were to mingle with philosophers (William Barrett gave a well-received chat on existentialism), while painters learned about Cage's musical ideas when he delivered two lectures at the venue, one titled "Lecture on Nothing," followed, naturally, by "Lecture on Something."[36]

Clearly, something was afoot in New York City in the early 1950s. It was, as historians have remarked, vying with Paris for the title of cultural capital of the world. Artists with reputations lived there comfortably, and every promising young artist from the provinces traveled there to seek stimulation and reputation. While the cultural landscape in America overall may have seemed bleak in the summer of 1952, things were hopping in New York. The novelist Dan Wakefield arrived in the city that fall from Indiana, and he instantly realized that the city was "the place where everything happened first."[37]

In August of 1952, John Cage was nearing forty years of age. Although he was never one to dwell on self-analysis, it is possible that this milestone event made him realize that the time had come for him to produce cultural landmarks both original and shocking. At the same moment, the new work was to be yet another examination of the relationship between sound and silence—but this time undertaken in a spirit of creative excess. There had always been a theatrical aspect to much of his earlier work—imagine the sight of tuxedoed performers playing rice bowls or whacking the side of a piano or tapping on some discard from a junkyard. But during this summer season, Cage would put it all together, taking his logic to its extreme, perhaps to a conclusive moment.

The first Cage blast happened in the unlikely space of a dining hall located beside Lake Eden, at Black Mountain College, near Asheville, North Carolina. The second occurred at the Maverick Concert Hall, not far from Woodstock, New York.

It is best to begin at Woodstock, because what actually happened there on a Friday evening in late August was etched clearly in the memories of those present. A concert of experimental music pieces by Cage, Wolff, Brown, Feldman, Boulez, and Cowell was to be staged to raise money for an Artists Welfare Fund.[38] The setting was stunning. Maverick Concert Hall sat contentedly in a heavily wooded area. It loomed like a barn or an off-kilter house of worship. Its many windows filled the space with light, and its multiple doors made it possible for those seated outside to enjoy the music.

Darkness had settled in for the premiere of Cage's second piece of the evening. Its title, *4'33"*, referred to the duration of the composition. Such a title, however, was hardly stranger than that of Cage's first piece for the concert, *aug. 29, 1952*, or Wolff's *for piano* or Feldman's *extensions 3*. Most concert attendees were probably familiar with Cage's sly humor and musical experimentation.

The history of music changed once David Tudor sat down at the piano. His considerable keyboard skill was not demanded that evening. He did follow the score, however, with devotion to detail. Over the course of the next four minutes and thirty-three seconds, he raised and lowered the piano lid to indicate start and conclusion for each movement of the piece. At precisely determined moments, as well, he turned pages of the score and touched the pedals of the piano. Nary a key was struck.

The silence of the piano, allowed audience members to hear tree branches brush up against the concert hall walls and drops of rain splatter on the roof. Carolyn Brown recalled the "restlessness" of the audience, "bodies shifting uneasily in the seats, shuffling feet, the inevitable self-conscious giggle; the nervous cough." Most auditors were unpleasantly perplexed, uncertain if they were the butt of a joke. One participant stormed out of the hall, shouting that Cage should be driven out of town.[39]

Cage considered *4'33"* his most important composition, and its influence has resounded ever since its initial performance. Cage said that he had rolled the concept of a silent composition around in his mind for four years. In the view of a recent writer on Cage, the composition might well be "the apotheosis of twentieth-century music."[40]

In many ways, once eyebrows raised in skepticism are lowered, the composition lives up to its hype. It was a hydrogen bomb of conceptual creativity that shattered musical expectations and opened up the ears of audiences to the sounds that surrounded them. It also compelled the audience to become performers, to attune themselves to the sounds they heard in the midst of their restlessness, anxiety, and stray thoughts. He was, in a way, deprogramming them of expectations—and trying to "reward" them with new possibilities.[41] Cage, like Warhol and other creators of the New Sensibility, treasured repetition and boredom. Repetition, in their view, was a fiction, since no moment was ever replicated or experienced in precisely the same manner as the previous iteration. Boredom and silence, Cage maintained, were goads to reflection and imagination. In his famous formulation:

> In Zen they say: if something is boring after two minutes, try it for four. If it is still boring, try it for eight, sixteen, thirty-two, and so on. Eventually one discovers that it's not boring at all but very interesting.[42]

Cage bristled at overinterpretation that reduced art to a formula, one connected either to the author's intentions or to a contextual reading of the work.

He felt that such cerebral approaches stopped the ears and deadened the senses. Thus, a piece on silence, without a single note sounding, resisted any deep meaning—it simply existed. And it could not be pinned down, because each time it was "performed" the audience would be in a different state of mind and the environment would offer a new set of ambient sounds.

Finally, perhaps the best take on the piece came from Cage's friend and fellow composer Morton Feldman. He argued that thanks to *4'33"* composers "must ask questions that previously were avoided, never thought about when composing a musical composition."[43]

The other crowning moment occurred earlier that August in 1952 when Cage and his partner Cunningham were teaching in Black Mountain College's summer program. Black Mountain had been founded in 1933, and it was an oasis of the sort of experimentalism and daring associated with an avant-garde modernist ethos—a perfect place for Cage's sensibility to blossom.

The piece that was to be performed at Black Mountain College came to be known as *Theater Piece no. 1*. It was a marvelous pastiche, a mixture of various art forms, an exercise in creative excess. In a sense, it was the summa for all of the eddies of art theory and practice that Cage had imbibed during long evenings at the Cedar Tavern, Bozza Mansion, and artists' studios and listening to the music of his friends.[44]

After dinner in the Black Mountain dining hall, Cage and company went to work. Chairs were organized and props set up so that no single focal point was favored. Students and faculty were then treated to *Theater Piece no. 1*, which also later came to be known as *Black Mountain Piece*, or simply "The Event."[45]

Since accounts of what transpired differ markedly, it is probably best to list those things that probably happened over a period of forty-five minutes or two hours, separately or simultaneously: Cage, positioned a few steps up a ladder, lectured, perhaps on the German mystic Meister Eckhart; Robert Rauschenberg played records (probably songs by Edith Piaf) on an old Victrola, and some of his recent all-white paintings were displayed in the dining hall; Mary Caroline Richards, a poet and translator of Antonin Artaud, read poetry; Charles Olson, the gargantuan poet of often intimidating verse, also read poetry; Merce Cunningham, with a handful of dancers, weaved through the seated audience, without paying attention to the rhythm of the music surrounding them; David Tudor played something on the piano; slides and movies were projected; and youthful servers, at some point in the evening, poured coffee into cups on the tables.

Whatever happened that evening, *Theater Piece no. 1* may have been the first multimedia event of its sort in America. Within a few years, Allan Kaprow and other artists would be staging similar events called happenings.[46] The allure of the performance piece was varied. First, it promised to resist commercialization, since it could not be bought and sold, given its temporal nature. Second, despite precise instructions from Cage about what each performer was supposed to do, the piece was chaotic, merrily bursting with miscues. And, as Cage had emphasized in regard to his musical compositions, such errors were welcomed. Third, since there was no focal point, members of the audience became part of the piece, experiencing it differently depending upon where they sat and the direction in which they gazed. Fourth, it signaled Cage's adherence to an essential element of the New Sensibility—the "confusion of realms," the mixing up of different art media.[47] Finally, the value of the performance piece was that it created a community among artists, which Cage cherished.

Cage did not single-handedly create the New Sensibility. No one person, even the monumentally creative Cage, could exemplify such a complex movement. After all, his work exhibited not a whit of sensuality (perhaps because as a gay man he was exiled to a sort of expressive closet), and it was without a hint of confessional turn (unless one takes his silence as teeming with personal meaning).[48] Although his work often shocked and surprised his listeners, Cage admitted in 1956, "I have never gratuitously done anything for shock."[49] In his openness to possibility, fascination with stylistic bravado and repetition, refusal to bow to tradition, and willful disdain for a firm division between various art forms, Cage nonetheless was a trailblazer preparing elements of the score for the New Sensibility. Other friends, such as Robert Rauschenberg, joined with Cage to go farther in other media.

Erasure and Addition

ROBERT RAUSCHENBERG

1953

In her autobiographical novel, poet Sylvia Plath aptly described the New York City summer of 1953 as "queer" and "sultry."[1] Kids cooled off under spouting fire hydrants while Marilyn Monroe sizzled in *Gentlemen Prefer Blondes*. Least surprisingly, the New York Yankees defeated the Brooklyn Dodgers in a subway World Series. And, as Plath noted, it was the summer that atomic spies Ethel and Julius Rosenberg were electrocuted at Sing Sing Correctional Facility.

Temperatures continued to reach the high double digits in late August and early September. Painter Robert Rauschenberg probably ignored the heat better than most native New Yorkers. A few months earlier, he had returned from a seven-month trip to Italy and North Africa, and he had been raised in the sticky heat of Port Arthur, Texas. He was now living in an attic studio in an "ancient derelict building" on Fulton Street in Lower Manhattan. The heat there must have been oppressive, with the discomfort compounded by the smell of fish at the nearby Fulton Street Fish Market. But the space was abundant and appealing, with cathedral ceilings, white walls, and wood-plank floors. The rent was only ten dollars a month, but there was no running water. Rauschenberg showered at friends' apartments, lived on pennies a day, slept on fish crates, employed a bucket in the yard as a sink, and scrounged the neighborhood for materials for his artwork. One imagines Rauschenberg happy, focused not only on the paintings that would be exhibited at the Stable Gallery, beginning on the fifteenth of September, but also on other art projects that would help to establish his reputation.[2]

One day that fall, Rauschenberg headed uptown to ask a huge favor from Willem de Kooning, who was then the toast of the art world. His series of paintings at the Sidney Janis Gallery had stunned and thrilled the critics. These paintings retained the passionate brushstrokes common to abstract expressionism while depicting recognizable female figures. Some of them presented women with horrific, devouring mouths, perversely based on models appearing in cigarette advertisements. Two leading art critics, Clement Greenberg and Harold Rosenberg, despite the fury of their disagreements over the nature of painting and the role of the painter, celebrated de Kooning. He was, Greenberg exulted, a genius.[3]

The "genius" resided in a rear top-floor apartment on Tenth Street. As Rauschenberg climbed the stairs, he moved slowly, hesitantly, summoning up his courage. He was more an acquaintance than a friend of de Kooning. A generation younger than de Kooning, Rauschenberg had been making a small mark on the New York art scene. In 1951, he had exhibited work at the Betty Parsons Gallery. Rauschenberg stood about six feet tall, hair cropped short and kept neat; he had gentle, southern manners that failed to paper over his intense ambition. His creativity and energy were boundless. Yet he was a contradiction, according to his friend the dancer Carolyn Brown: an artist that wanted to have fun with his work but who also was "wildly competitive."[4]

As he knocked on the apartment door, Rauschenberg "prayed the whole time" that de Kooning "might not be at home." But de Kooning opened the door, probably attired in his usual outfit of rolled up blue jeans, splattered with paint. He had a mop of light, tussled hair, with a powerful torso atop a sagging midsection.

Rauschenberg came bearing a bottle of Jack Daniel's as a welcome gift. For an enthusiastic alcoholic such as de Kooning, whiskey was like manna from heaven. Rauschenberg hesitated to bring up the startling purpose of his visit, counting on small talk and booze to ease the path. Finally, Rauschenberg came out with it: Might de Kooning give him a drawing so that he could erase it? "I know what you're doing," responded an "annoyed" de Kooning, who presumed that Rauschenberg wanted to engage in an act of symbolic patricide, declaring his own avant-garde credentials by defacing the work of an established figure.[5]

Nevertheless, de Kooning ambled over to where he kept portfolios of his drawings. Slowly, almost methodically, he pulled out one drawing after another, examining each and then finding it unsuitable. The appropriate drawing, de Kooning announced, had to be of high quality: "I want to give you one that I'll miss." And, importantly, it needed to be "very hard" to erase. After leaving Rauschenberg dangling for what seemed an eternity, de Kooning finally handed him a drawing, done in crayon, charcoal, ink, grease, and pencil.[6]

Rauschenberg headed home to work on erasing the de Kooning. One month of hard labor and many disintegrated gummy erasers (estimates vary from fifteen to forty) later, the task was completed—more or less.

Rauschenberg failed to eradicate all traces of de Kooning's drawing.[7] The master had wisely bequeathed to the upstart a work that resisted decimation. In addition, traces of another drawing on the verso managed to gently peek through. Perhaps, too, Rauschenberg desired to leave wisps of de Kooning's presence in the new work. He had his new romantic partner, the artist Jasper Johns, frame the piece in gold leaf and hand-title it *Erased de Kooning Drawing*. "I erased the de Kooning," Rauschenberg related, "not out of any negative response."[8] Both de Kooning and Rauschenberg in their drawings often included sediment from erasures in the finished work. At once an homage to an established artist and declaration of independence, *Erased De Kooning* was, as art historian Leo Steinberg put it, "a sort of collaboration."[9]

It was a realization of Rauschenberg's appreciation for diminishing the various lines, in this case literally, between original material and newly created work. When pushed to characterize this new creation, Rauschenberg referred to it, quite simply, as "poetry."[10]

As the heat of summer lingered into the fall, Rauschenberg entered into a collaboration with John Cage. The pair shared a conceptual and performative bent. Indeed, the importance of Cage to Rauschenberg's art and spirit cannot be underestimated. If nothing else, Cage allowed Rauschenberg to feel, he said, that "the way I was thinking was not crazy."[11]

Crazy or not, they rendezvoused at Rauschenberg's Fulton Street apartment building on a Sunday morning, when traffic on the busy thoroughfare would be minimal. The plan was simple. Rauschenberg had glued together about twenty sheets of drawing paper into one long train, about twenty-three feet long, which he then proceeded to lay out upon the street. Cage, in his beloved Model A Ford, drove over the expanse of paper while Rauschenberg slopped black paint on a back tire. The result was a long piece of paper covered with tire marks. The marks were not uniform, given the unevenness of the tires and surface, the differing amounts of applied paint, and other factors.

One interpreter suggested that, rather than being a conceptual artwork or even "a new formal design," *Automobile Tire Print* was actually a comment on Fulton Street, which was home to many small printing businesses. In this view, Rauschenberg captured in the print the chaos and pulse of mobility, in a form that unfolded like a Chinese scroll.[12] Ever enticingly enigmatic, Cage remarked about the work, "I know he put the paint on the tires. And he unrolled the paper on the city street. But which one of us drove the car?"[13] Perfect: Cage musing about who drove the car of creativity.

In almost all of Rauschenberg's work in 1953, and beyond, there lurked the allure of interpretation, of finding meaning in his objects, performances, quirks, and paintings. The challenge, however, was that Rauschenberg's art supported any number of equally valid interpretations—so many, in fact, that they might be so open to interpretation as to remain forever resistant to it, early examples of artworks that, in Sontag's famous phrase, were "against interpretation." These artworks sparkled with plurality and possibility.[14] In sum, exemplary of the New Sensibility then emerging.

Nowhere was this sensibility more apparent than in Rauschenberg's *White Paintings*, which were part of the Stable Gallery show that opened in September. Those paintings had played a role in Cage's *Theater Piece no. 1* at Black Mountain in September 1952. In fact, Cage later stated that the seeming emptiness of the *White Paintings* had inspired him to compose *4'33"*. More probably, Rauschenberg's *White Paintings* had nudged Cage along with his own experimental piece. Suggestions of such a turn had festered in Cage's mind for close to a decade. Rauschenberg and Cage, clearly, were riding in the same Model A car of invention and paradox.

The *White Paintings* consisted of flat white house paint applied with rollers onto canvas. Although a white painting, *White on White*, had been done by the Russian artist Kazimir Malevich in 1918, Rauschenberg was unaware of any precursor work.[15] According to one commentator at the time of the Stable Gallery show, the *White Paintings* were "worthless": "Four blank white walls the landlord provides will do as well." Rauschenberg had "committed a gratuitously destructive act."[16] Another critic declared the white canvases "beyond the artistic pale." Eleanor Ward, owner of the gallery, removed the guest book because it was filled with numerous "awful" comments.[17]

Rauschenberg obviously viewed his work differently. The *White Paintings*, he proclaimed, were "probably more beautiful than anything else I have done."[18] How are we to take such a statement? The works showed, in contrast to the abstract works then in vogue, no slashing gestural marks, few subtle changes in color tonality, and little evidence of the personal anguish of the painter translated onto the canvas. Certainly, as in *Erased De Kooning*, there was at least a hint of spoofing, an attempt to poke fun at painters' highfalutin notions about the sanctity of art.

Rauschenberg believed that the *White Paintings* were doing "something interesting."[19] The painting did not exist to call attention to itself, certainly not as a sacral object. It demanded an active response from the viewer, and he noted how flecks of dust or dirt could change its appearance—hence why Rauschenberg called these canvases "hypersensitive."[20] More important, the white canvases reflected movement as well as light and shadow. One could look at them as at a mirror, gaining more than just a turned-around reflection. Depending upon where and when one gazed and where one stood, the paintings offered different possibilities—an artistic exemplum of Einstein's concept of relativity. And democratic, too, in their pluralism and openness. "One could look at them," Rauschenberg claimed, "and almost see how many people were in the room by the shadows cast, or what time of day it was."[21]

The *White Paintings* wanted to alert viewers to more possibilities than those entombed on the picture plane. Cage called the paintings "airports for lights, shadows, and particles." The painting existed not to call attention to themselves. "Before such emptiness, you just wait to see what you will see," remarked Cage.[22] And that could be both beautiful and enlightening.

As with *Erased De Kooning*, they resisted interpretation by dismissing essentialism and fixed meaning. Rauschenberg admitted, "I would like to make a picture that no two people would see the same thing."[23] Like Cage's *4'33"* there could not be a passive response to the work; thoughts, insights, disgust, interest, and the natural environment merrily intruded into the now imaginary space between the viewer and the work.[24]

The irony of the *White Paintings* evoked another kindred spirit, a man who was the doyen of the postwar New York City avant-garde, Marcel Duchamp. Duchamp's work first alighted on American shores in 1913 when his semi-cubist work *Nude Descending a Staircase* had startled the crowds at the Armory Show in New York City. That show had combined examples of edgy modernist art from Europe with works by American artists. Duchamp's piece caused the greatest controversy. The painting depicted movement, but no matter how much viewers squinted at the piece, they failed to detect a nude—probably much to their disappointment. Duchamp seemed to be sneering at his audience, playing a joke on their sense of perception and propriety.

In another piece, Duchamp presented as a work of art an enamel urinal, which he had bought at a plumbing supply store. He signed and dated it "R. Mutt 1917." Since the early 1940s, however, Duchamp had been living quietly in Greenwich Village with his wife, spending much of his time playing chess. Although he declared that he had abandoned art, he was secretly working on a monumental piece (*Étant Donnés*, a three-dimensional assemblage) and serving as a guru to young artists and an advisor to wealthy patrons.[25]

Rauschenberg first glimpsed Duchamp's work in the winter of 1951, when a recreated version of *Bicycle Wheel* was displayed at the Janis Gallery. As with much of Duchamp's art, *Bicycle Wheel* was what it appeared to be, a bicycle wheel perched atop a mass-produced stool. The materiality and the beauty of the objects—unadorned by the artist—flowered. With Duchamp's dry wit and ironic juxtaposition, the artwork became a conceptual object that upended notions about what properly constituted art. Duchamp coyly tweaked the pretense of art, something that appealed greatly to both Cage and Rauschenberg. He was a provocateur, a conceptual jester of high seriousness whose work was always fascinating, sometimes more. Rauschenberg found *Bicycle Wheel* "more beautiful than anything in the exhibition."[26]

Rauschenberg's work echoed Duchamp's critical imperatives as much as Cage's. Duchamp was cognizant of the connection. He had attended Rauschenberg's show at Stable, where the *White Paintings* were exhibited alongside works called *Elemental Sculptures*. The sculptures were made out of found objects and detritus, pieces of wood, mossy rocks, and strands of heavy rope, all of them united by Rauschenberg's appreciation for the material world that surrounded him, indicative of what one art historian referred to as his "vernacular glance."[27] One of those structures—*Music Box*—was a rough-hewn box, studded with nails and included some pieces of rock. When he encountered the piece, Duchamp picked it up, shook it, and with characteristic wit announced: "I think I recognize that tune."[28]

Was Rauschenberg—and Cage for that matter—less than original, simply resurrecting a Dadaist/Duchampian sensibility? To a degree, certainly. All artists recycle ideas, pay homage to and rebel against their precursors. Cage and Rauschenberg, certainly, were conversant with modernist giants. They followed, in part, the rebellious spirit of modernism while also poking fun at it—taking it to extremes. In a sense, they were adherents of the view that T. S. Eliot famously presented in "Tradition and the Individual Talent": artists place themselves within traditions and by their work change the nature of that tradition.[29]

Conceiving of oneself as an avant-garde artist demanded rebellion against the established art of one's moment, as well as an embrace of newness. To question the meaning of art, to introduce serious play against uptight seriousness, to thumb one's nose at art institutions and the cash nexus, and to bring perception down to the materials involved in the artwork was, if not entirely original, then at least significant and startling within the context of American art in 1953.

To be acknowledged even narrowly as an epigone of Duchamp—the master of creativity and provocation—was, if nothing else, a high honor. And, in that spirit, Rauschenberg pushed his art ever further. He faithfully voiced the avant-garde ideal in his well-known statement "Painting relates to both art and life. Neither can be made." But he then undermined somewhat the obliteration of the lines by claiming: "I try to act in the gap between the two." What and where that gap is remained poorly clarified.[30]

Rauschenberg's work focused on the diminution of gaps. Consider another piece at the Stable Gallery show, *Dirt Painting (for John Cage)*. The work, at first glance, was Duchampian in its agonistic relation to artistic creation—it dissolved the boundary between the natural and the created worlds. *Dirt Painting* consisted of dirt mixed with an adhesive so that, in Cage's description, "it sticks to itself and the canvas." The muddle of materials was then placed in a box to be hung from the wall, just like a normal painting.[31] Mold and lichens grew on the dirt surface, giving it, as art critic Walter Hopps aptly noted, the look "of field-structured Abstract Expressionist painting." But in this case, nature itself was doing the brushwork. Similarly, Rauschenberg's *Growing Painting*, consisting of dirt and vegetation in a wood frame, which was shown at the Stable Gallery, was a living thing, and Rauschenberg returned to the gallery to water it regularly.[32]

Dirt Painting and *Growing Painting*, as art historian Branden Joseph notes, captured "temporality" and "duration." They are about how the natural world moves, quite apart from the action of artist and spectator. Another aesthetic was at work with Rauschenberg, one that would become central to the New Sensibility—an acknowledgment and embrace of boredom. Boredom hinges on repetition or long duration, as in Warhol's prints and films (chapter 12). Rauschenberg accepted willingly the unfinished, in-process, growing, never-standing-still aspects of his art. To all but the most directed of viewers, however, they were precisely the opposite, capturing in an art gallery the old saw about "watching the grass grow." The art of boredom, Rauschenberg and Cage claimed, opened the viewer up to new possibilities, to a sort of Zen of perception.[33]

Running throughout Rauschenberg's artwork in 1953 was a sense of serious play and disrespect for the cash value of the artwork. Rauschenberg was not ideologically opposed to making a living from his work; he was disappointed when works from his initial show had failed to sell. Yet he was known to be generous in giving works away. Indeed, he was also quite capable of destroying artwork as a mode of artistic expression, of his disdain for the sacralization of the artist and his or her work.

Rauschenberg had spent a good part of the first half of 1953 traveling in Europe and North Africa. He wangled a couple of shows at the conclusion of his sojourn. He had been collecting various objects—odd items from flea markets, natural materials from the North African desert, rusty metallic objects, and much more. He placed some of these objects in boxes; others, like an Italian washboard, were hung on the wall. Rauschenberg considered these objects as being "fetishes," imbued with an almost religious cast.

One of his shows, at the Galleria d'Arte Contemporanea in Florence, in March 1953, had been scathingly reviewed by a local critic. Rauschenberg, so the story goes, perhaps impressed by the insight of the critique or by the passion behind it, decided to destroy the offending artworks. He joked that in doing so he would save the expense of shipping them home. With the help of his artist pal Cy Twombly, he lugged the art to the bank of the Arno River and proceeded to dump the works into the water. A couple of the works floated to the surface, and they were saved, packed in his wicker trunk to be sent back to New York City.[34]

Rauschenberg's rather flippant attitude to his art coexisted with a devotion to creating work that allowed, as it were, the materials themselves to speak. He cherished objects and materials, as was apparent in the *White Paintings*. At this time, he began working on two sets of new paintings, either entirely in red or entirely in black, which mimicked—without the possibility of reflection—the paintings he had completed in white.

In a series of paintings done in black, Rauschenberg began his movement toward "combines," toward building up the canvas with all sorts of objects. These paintings spoke to texture, complexity, physicality, and depth. He took newspapers, sometimes a single sheet, sometimes an entire paper, sometimes pages that were crumbled, and attached them to the canvas, using them as the surface upon which he applied copious amounts of black paint. On occasion, hints of content from the newspapers unintentionally peeked through the paint: "Saturday, March 3, 1952" or "Damage 20 Jets…Battle in Korea."[35] These built-up surfaces not only gave a sculptural feel to the works; they also allowed the play of light upon them to shift colors and intensity, creating a landscape that was at once haunting and beautiful. But some viewers, as Carolyn Brown recalled, found the work "a shocker."[36]

Rauschenberg wanted the *Black Paintings* to be about nothing more than the beauty of the black pigment. He would be dismayed when a later commentator found these works suggestive of "fecal matter," in "the smeared quality of the paint, the varying degrees of viscosity, and the color—shit black and brown."[37] Such "clichés of associations," Rauschenberg responded, might lead him to erase or change the picture.[38]

Within a couple of years, all sorts of objects—ranging from electric fans to buttons to a stuffed eagle—would protrude from his paintings. All was held together in a fantastic combination of materials, design sense, and daring—with an "absence of hierarchy."[39]

Perhaps no one appreciated Rauschenberg more than Cage. In honor of the Stable Gallery show, Cage listed some key points of the artist's approach: "No subject / No image / No taste," and more. "I have come to the conclusion that there is nothing in these paintings that could not be changed," Cage continued, "that they can be seen in any light and are not destroyed by the action of shadows. Hallelujah! The blind can see again, the water is fine."[40]

Rauschenberg desired to efface himself, to reject idea, beauty, and subject in the work of art. This was striking and problematic. Art historian Moira Roth called out Rauschenberg and Cage (as well as Jasper Johns and others from their circle) for practicing an "aesthetic of indifference." How, Roth wondered, had Rauschenberg and Cage produced artworks that were so deficient, silent, and ignorant of the historical context in which they were produced? How, in a period when one was expected to be simply for or against Communism, mere months after the United States had exploded a hydrogen bomb, with the body counts from the Korean War still undetermined, had these artists employed "neutrality as their springboard"?[41]

One answer, which Roth and others have offered, was that Rauschenberg and company were well aware of their historical context, a time when McCarthyism raged, homophobia was rampant, and the H-bomb loomed.[42] In such a world, especially for gay artists such as Cage, Rauschenberg, and Johns with an anarchist or radical bent, the danger of speaking out forthrightly was apparent. They were silenced, moved to efface themselves from the artwork. A box filled with dirt adorning a gallery wall, paintings that were simply white, a long roll with tire marks upon it—all could be viewed as politically impotent, jokes without bite.

Art historians therefore easily place Rauschenberg in the same Cold War discourse as abstract expressionists. According to this hypothesis, the existential individualism and abstraction associated with painters such as Mark Rothko, Jackson Pollock, Clyfford Still, and others perfectly fit the era. Because they were ideologically neutral and artistically radical, they were easily appropriated, made into signs that exemplified American freedom without challenging American imperialism, racism, or economic inequality. Indeed, the radical nature of these works of art served—in the uses put to them by custodians of American culture and foreign policy—as proof positive that in the United States freedom of expression and unfettered creativity reigned. They became objects to be exported abroad and consumed at home for display in corporate offices or advertising.[43]

Although Rauschenberg later in his career would energetically take up political causes, in 1953 he demonstrated little political consciousness. Perhaps his sensibility had been numbed by horrible experiences he had working as a hospital orderly during the Second World War. There he had encountered human beings literally torn apart by warfare; others whose minds had been erased by the pain they had suffered or the horrors that they had witnessed. "Every day your heart was torn out," Rauschenberg grimly recalled, "until you couldn't stand it." He added, "I learned how little difference there is between sanity and insanity and realized that a combination is essential."[44]

In the face of such inhumanity and horror, in a world awash with repression and destruction, perhaps the only comfortable stance for an anarchist and gay man such as Rauschenberg was to mock slyly the possibility of erasure (of himself and the human race) in *Erased De Kooning* or *White Paintings*. His imperative was to go as far as he could with his art, to push his sensibility in new directions. It was all about, as he stated, "checking my habits of seeing, to counter them for the sake of a greater freshness."[45]

Certainly Rauschenberg in 1953 was following his muse, with muscular intensity. He was, in many ways, a determined and delightful naïf. Rauschenberg had only been aware for a decade that art could be a serious enterprise. Growing up in Port Arthur, poor but solvent, had denied him the experience of museums and highbrow cultural activities. Only after his service in the Second World War had he come into contact with Dada and surrealism, with the collage boxes of Joseph Cornell and the conceptual rigor of Duchamp. He was like a kid in a candy store, stuffing his face with all sorts of goodies, on a sort of artistic sugar high.

His openness to varied materials—apparent in *Elemental Sculptures*—expressed appreciation for the simplicity of the primitive, and hence was a critique of the present. Or the work can be read as recognizing that all civilizations end up as detritus. In the plurality of his approaches and materials, in the blurring of distinctions between high and low, Rauschenberg embraced chaos and multiplicity, offering them as potential solutions to the order imposed by an increasingly bureaucratic, instrumentalized reason.[46] The stasis or entombment of a finished work of art was also something that Rauschenberg delightfully challenged, as in works that actually grew as they hung on the wall.

Rauschenberg's willingness to dance along the edge of excess, to challenge the harrumph of satisfaction common to mainstream artists, his ability to combine ebullience and ambition, and his fervid creativity and democratic openness figured as critical features of a camp sensibility, still an underground phenomenon, until Sontag made it famous in the 1960s. Camp excess and immaturity, at least in the minds of Cold War liberals, were taken as signs of political weakness and homosexuality. Rauschenberg turned these presumed weaknesses into the stuff of an artistic sensibility that would come to dominate the art world. What is more camp, after all, than white paintings, multiple panels of them being offered for sale in a respectable art gallery?

If Rauschenberg in 1953 bore the markings of the New Sensibility, it had not yet been exhibited in full. Like Cage, he refused to go the route of confessionalism in his artwork, first, because he lacked any desire to hitch his star to that emerging aspect of the American cultural sensibility—"I don't want my personality to come out through the piece"[47]—and second, because he and his gay comrades—Cage, Cunningham, and Johns—had, each in his own manner, already subtly expanded artistic possibilities in their often ironic works of art. They were the vanguard of a New Sensibility, soon joined, as we will see, by a variety of other gay creators: Patricia Highsmith, Allen Ginsberg, and Andy Warhol for starters.[48]

In 1953, Rauschenberg was staying temporarily in Cage's apartment. On one wall was a piece of his from an earlier Parsons Gallery show that he had given to Cage as a token of respect. Cage was stunned, even angered, when he returned to his apartment and noticed that Rauschenberg had painted over the original in black. After he had calmed down, Cage came to appreciate the gesture and love the complexity of the black surface. As he once put it, "It's a joy in fact to begin over again."[49] How appropriate, given the essential perception and desire that tumbled through Rauschenberg and Cage's shared sensibility—that art was a process, the work ever open to revision, to new possibilities. And that going too far in the direction of experiment was not a crime but a requirement for the artist.

Marlon Brando in The Wild One *(1954) (© Photofest)*

The Wild One

MARLON BRANDO

1954

Brando enters the sunlit café in Nowheresville, USA. He saunters to the counter, whistling and glancing about, slowing peeling off his gloves. He wears a leather jacket with his name, "Johnny," neatly stitched on the front.[1] A second-place trophy for motorcycle racing dangles like costume jewelry from his arm, a trinket that had been heisted by one of the members of his gang, the Black Rebels. He exudes bravado, tempered by undercurrents of turmoil and weakness. Time passes, as if in slow motion, until the young woman behind the counter breaks the silence, inquiring what this beleathered mirage of a biker would care to order. "I'd like a bottle of beer," he replies, with an accent that is vaguely southern and definitely odd.

The waitress, Kathy Bleeker, a niece of the owner and daughter of the ineffectual town sheriff, informs Johnny that beer can only be served in the bar section, a shuffle of feet away. So Brando must move himself again. He interrupts the short journey to pop a nickel into the jukebox, and he begins to snap his fingers to the music, in a private reverie. Then comes a cat-and-mouse game, as he pulls the coin for the beer away from Kathy when she reaches for it. Brando eschews the politeness of a glass to drink the beer from the bottle. Additional glances are directed at the waitress; it is unclear whether Johnny is sizing her up sexually or regarding her as an alien species.[2] The silence and gestures of the scene only end with the intrusion of chaos from the street—a car accident caused by his band of thugs. Johnny will soon impose momentary order through his quiet, menacing authority.

Later in the film, while the gang carouses in the crowded bar, a local asks Johnny what he's rebelling against. His now famous answer, curt and cutting is, "Whaddya got?"[3]

As much as John Cage, Brando was a master of eloquent silences.[4] Like Rauschenberg, he was a devotee of gestures. He inscribed himself with signatures from the emerging New Sensibility. He craved a style of acting that was vibrant and spontaneous—unbeholden to staid expectations. Gender distinctions sagged under Brando's subtle assault. His acting was a form of what Susan Sontag desired, "an erotics of art"—each gesture pointing toward a potential volcanic eruption of sexuality. Brando sought a wide range of experiences, refusing to bow to the expectations of Broadway and Hollywood. And he made himself, both in his life and work, an exemplar of rebellion. There was also an aura of camp that surrounded Brando's performances and regalia.[5]

Consider the motorcycle jacket he wore in *The Wild One*. It was spanking, Sunday-best new, summing up a style, at once rebellious and ersatz. As rebellion, the jacket symbolized a sharp break from middle-class proprieties. As camp it was subversive of those same expectations. "Clothes are our weapons," wrote Angela Carter, "our challenges, our visible insults." If so, then the leather jacket that Brando brandished—along with his smirks and sneers—constituted "visible insults" that teenagers ate up.[6]

Brando almost made a fetish (camp or otherwise) of welled-up sensitivity in his acting. In a marvelous, improvised scene in *On the Waterfront*, Brando, in the role of Terry Malloy, strolls on a wintry day through a city park with a young woman, Edie, played by the angelic Eva Marie Saint. He is desperately trying to connect with her, out of both attraction and guilt over his responsibility for the death of her brother. When his words emerge, they are mumbled or hesitant. Time seems unbearably suspended. He achingly takes out a stick of gum, slowly unwrapping it and failing to offer a piece to his companion. Later, Edie drops a dainty glove. With brilliant improvisation, Brando picks it up, but he does not return it immediately. Instead, he absentmindedly plays with it, smoothing out the fingers. At one point, he puts the glove on his own hand, a gesture that feminizes his character, a morally challenged ex-boxer. Elia Kazan, the film's director, claimed, "I didn't direct that; it happened."[7] Malloy tells Edie about how the sisters of the Catholic school he had attended used to whack him. Rather than resentment and hatred, a puppy-dog look graces Brando's face; emotions at this point are subdued, kept under lock and key.

The year 1954 was a very good one for Brando. Six months after *The Wild One* had faded from screens, *On the Waterfront* opened at the end of July. Reviews about Brando's performance were glowing: "A shatteringly poignant portrait," announced the *New York Times*.[8] A cover story about the enigmatic actor appeared in *Time* magazine in the fall, and the next year Brando garnered an Oscar for his depiction of Terry Malloy, who "could've been a contender."

According to *Time*, Brando could "vanish into the character" he portrayed "like a salamander into stone—or a tiger in the reeds."[9] *The Wild One* and *On the Waterfront* did not make Brando a star; film stardom had come to him earlier ("the untamed acting prodigy"), when he recreated his Broadway role of Stanley Kowalski in the film *A Streetcar Named Desire*, based on the play by Tennessee Williams, which premiered in 1951.[10] Brando tapped into Stanley's primitive, rough-hewn nature, dripping with the ambivalent sweat of masculine power and impotency. As with most of his great roles, Brando endowed Stanley with weaknesses, with an almost childish need for Stella—culminating in his now famous guttural cry: "Stella! Stella!" As Brando recognized, in person, he said, "I was the antithesis of Stanley Kowalski."[11]

All was not garlands, however, for the thirty-year-old Brando. Unlike most of his contemporaries, who played ball with the press corps and gossip mongers, Brando was openly disdainful of celebrity, which, of course, brought him ever greater celebrity. It became de rigueur for articles about Brando to detail his manner of dress. Could a self-respecting actor traipse around publicly in soiled blue jeans and T-shirt? Could the public cotton to an actor who reportedly belched in public and scratched his private parts? Could the public accept an actor who chose to live in squalid conditions and kept a pet raccoon (named Russell)?[12] If the traditional Hollywood expectations of style demanded elegance and a certain haute glamour, then Brando defied them, gleefully.

Even more shocking were his interviews. Reputations were made—and broken—by a powerful coterie of gossip columnists. Walter Winchell, Louella Parsons, Hedda Hopper, and others served as guardians of the Hollywood tradition of glamour. During the Red Scare years, they acted as sentinels on the lookout for any sort of radical political activity, on the screen (pro-Communist subplots), in the credentials of actors and writers, and in the private lives of all connected to the entertainment industry. "Every actor," Brando later noted, "was expected to butter up the columnists" and toe the line. He generally refused.[13]

In a column, "Hollywood Shaken by Nonconformity of Marlon Brando," Hopper repeated the standard critique of Brando's poor manners and general grunginess. He was, as someone had put it, "a grubby Peter Pan."[14] Yet Brando's sex appeal and smile were sufficient to charm even Hopper; she admitted that Brando had integrity and that his nonconformity was genuine (and not, apparently, tied to any political agenda). Louella Parsons, an acid writer and wearer of outrageous hats, in contrast, resisted Brando's charm and talent. Brando, she wrote, has "the manners of a chimpanzee, the gall of a Kinsey researcher, and a swelled head the size of a Navy blimp, and just as pointed—as far as I'm concerned he can ride his bike off the Venice pier."[15] Hollywood taste mavens Sheilah Graham and Faye Emerson had suffered through his interview shenanigans of yawning, dozing, mumbling, and turning the table by posing questions to interlocutors.[16] The ultimate interview disaster occurred in 1956, when Brando was filming *Sayonara* in Japan, relaxed enough by drink to speak openly with Truman Capote.[17] Although a sensitive side was revealed in the interview, Capote depicted Brando as a brooding "monologuist." But one thing Brando got across in this interview was his disdain for the Hollywood system and its "bitch-goddess" of financial success. "The only reason I'm here [doing a film]," Brando confided, "is that I don't yet have the moral courage to turn down the money."[18]

In his personal life, however, Brando had the courage to follow his sexual convictions. *Time* magazine quoted a producer about him: "He's a walking hormone factory." Apparently, Brando was blessed, or damned, with a voracious appetite for sex. Luckily, he was a sexual hunter whose great magnetism impelled many to happily lie down before him. In the early years, he was beautiful, almost beyond imagination. The sensuous lips, the wide face and brooding smile, the extreme handsomeness made more bearable by the sloping broken nose were joined in Brando with a well-muscled body (he lifted weights and sparred often). The power was apparent but not overstated—a hint of pudginess remained that made him less threatening. Although he bedded many starlets, it was reported that he preferred young women who were waitresses, salesgirls, or from "exotic" backgrounds. In 1954 Rita Moreno, then at the start of her career, swooned to Brando's allure. He was, she recalled, "a sensitive colossus," a lover of great quality, "a walking A-bomb" when it came to the seduction of women. There was, she realized, a compulsive quality to his conquests, an almost childish need for love driving him forward.[19]

There was, however, in his personal life and on the screen, a sexual aura that challenged traditional ideals of heterosexual masculinity. The postwar years, as many historians have pointed out, were a period of gender uncertainty. Some analysts bewailed the feminization of the American male, as captured in one scene from *Rebel without a Cause* where an ineffectual father wearing an apron proves unable to offer his son a sufficiently paternal role model. Thanks to the Kinsey Report, the presence of homosexuality in American culture was revealed. But it was not applauded, as the government slapped down anyone considered any shade of pink. While earlier models of masculinity continued to abound (consider John Wayne), they seemed almost camp in their excess of testosterone. A host of film stars, led by Brando, James Dean, and Montgomery Clift, came upon the scene to present new, more nuanced models of male behavior that were rebellious and subversive—and hard to ignore. In his personal life, Brando gave off whiffs of unconventional sexual behavior, despite his oft-proclaimed macho aspects. Moreno remembered that Brando was fond of dabbing himself with Vent Vert, a woman's perfume. It was rumored that Brando was open to various homosexual experiences.[20]

The early 1950s was a perfect time for an actor to present himself as sexually charged yet gender-ambivalent—a hunk and a vulnerable individual. The Kinsey reports on human sexuality (the second volume, on women, had come out in 1952) recorded an American populace far more sexually active and varied in its sexual tastes than previously imagined by the heterosexual majority. Many rejected Kinsey's findings out of hand, prattling about its database (interviews with convicts). For instance, literary critic Lionel Trilling worried that Kinsey's conclusions reduced the complexity of relationships and love to social-scientific jargon. Further fears about the state of American popular culture were sounded when psychiatrist Fredric Wertham published his well-meaning but overwrought book *The Seduction of the Innocent* (1954); Wertham argued that gory violence and overt sexual content in comic books were warping a generation of adolescents. The United States Congress listened and concurred. The comic industry followed meekly in order to avoid sanctions; they cleaned house and started their own system of internal policing of content and graphics.[21] Yet the culture continued to be fascinated by the sexually unusual.

In February 1953, Christine Jorgenson, an ex-GI formerly known as George William Jorgensen Jr., returned to the United States after having undergone operations and taken hormones to transition from a man to a woman. She fascinated the public, calling into question gender boundaries that had previously largely been sacrosanct. *Playboy* debuted at the end of 1953, quickly becoming a palatable magazine that combined pictures of female nudes, serious literature, and a philosophy of freedom, especially when it came to sex and consumerism. Marilyn Monroe, its first centerfold, was already well positioned, thanks to two films from 1953, *Gentlemen Prefer Blondes* and *How to Marry a Millionaire*, as a voluptuous and seductive presence. She was upfront about her sexuality (how could it be ignored?), combining it with an innocence and humor that proved hard to resist. Sexuality, in all of its varieties, was beginning to bloom in public, although this should not be confused with its entering into the mainstream.[22]

America seemed to be awakening from a slumber in other ways, too. The overall economy was booming (with a growth rate for the decade at 19.1 percent). Televisions sold like hotcakes. Indeed, by 1956, twenty thousand televisions a day were being sold in the United States. By 1960, the land was home to fifty million sets.[23] The May 1954 United States Supreme Court decision in *Brown v. Board of Education of Topeka* declared unanimously that it was unconstitutional—at least in principle—to have one set of facilities for whites and another for African Americans, giving a shot in the arm to advocates of ending racial discrimination—"with all deliberate speed."[24] In June 1954, Joseph McCarthy, finally overplayed his hand and met his match in lawyer Joseph Welch, who wondered aloud if the Senator had any decency in his attacks on individuals innocent of any crimes of treason and betrayal. Six months later, the Senate voted 67–22 to censure McCarthy, effectively bringing an end to his four-year reign of terror against mainly innocent Americans. It had begun in 1950 with a theatrical speech in Wheeling, West Virginia, when he claimed to possess a list of known Communist infiltrators in the United States government, a list that McCarthy mysteriously failed to share with the American public or appropriate investigative agencies.

This is not to say that anxieties about homosexuality and Communism at home ended instantly, nor that Cold War tensions had burned out by 1954. The high stakes of the Cold War continued to play out whenever the United States tested a new, ever more immense H-bomb at Bikini Atoll in the Pacific and when the lagging-behind Soviets finally detonated a bomb more powerful than the one dropped on Hiroshima (see chapter 11). Secretary of State John Foster Dulles believed that the only way to avert nuclear war was through what he called "massive retaliatory power," a phrase which, unsurprisingly, did little to quell fears of an atomic holocaust. The defeat of the French colonial forces at Dien Bien Phu in Vietnam inaugurated American intervention in the area, as Eisenhower upheld American responsibility to halt Communism in Asia, lest the nations there fall like a row of dominoes.[25]

Brando caught these changes and anxieties brilliantly in two film roles of 1954. The biker Johnny presents himself with macho swagger, refusing to observe middle-class proprieties, more than willing to punch it out with a rival gang leader, and buzzing around the hive of waitress Kathy. But it is clear that his posturing hides an inner core of sensitivity. He drawls, "Why don't we go out and have a ball?" to Kathy in *The Wild One*. Her notion of a good time is a picnic, a scenario that he ridicules as "too square" and "cornball." Of course, over time, her resistance to Brando is worn down by her own rebellious spirit and his hidden gentleness. After Kathy is surrounded by sexually menacing bikers, Johnny, as a black knight on his motorcycle steed, saves her. Alone with Kathy in the countryside, he pulls her toward him for a passionate kiss; accordingly, she falls into his arms like a rag doll, too tired, she claims, to resist. Despite the power that Johnny has over her, he does not abuse it. In fact, he cannot violate her innocence. At one point, she realizes, "You're afraid of me." Kathy turns the table on Johnny, to the point of fondling his motorcycle and cooing that it "feels good." Johnny is now the frightened square: "I'm gonna leave."

In *On the Waterfront*, Brando's Terry Molloy is a mixture of brute and baby. As director Elia Kazan remarked, "Mature and adolescent at the same time."[26] Terry's background as a fighter—with strange eyeshadow (Brando often did his own makeup or made revisions) somehow supposed to indicate scar tissue—and his connections to the waterfront mob, along with his crude manners, place him firmly in the jungle among the beasts.[27] Although he can erupt with violence and in a bruising way take Edie into his well-muscled arms, it is clear, too, that he has a gentleness, a sexual hesitancy when in her presence. Flash back to the glove scene: it was risky because it coded Brando as feminine. Identity was becoming less defined, more fluid in the postwar period—and Brando's performances made that apparent on the screen.[28] Along with Montgomery Clift and James Dean, Brando was one of the actors who, in the words of critic Graham McCann, showed onscreen that they were "unsure of their masculinity."[29] Brando tempted the fates for the artistic grand slam, bringing out the feminine side of his character, Terry's edgy weaknesses as much as his brutal aspects in order to mine complexities, to resist reduction.[30]

It worked in the glove scene and in others. Consider how Terry Malloy caresses and cares for his pigeons on the rooftop or how he frets about his moral culpability in fingering someone for mob violence and later on his social responsibility to testify before an investigative committee. Terry has a lot on his plate, and Brando magnificently captures the full range of emotions on the menu.

In these films Brando played characters that are both givers and takers of violence. In *The Wild One*, his fighting prowess is demonstrated when he beats up a rival biker, played by the imposing figure of Lee Marvin. But later in the film, when the townsfolk rebel against the bikers and become convinced that Johnny has violated Kathy, they beat him up. In a chaotic moment, he escapes, showing not only his own physical hurt—his motorcycle is damaged as well—but his emotional pain, as he wipes tears from his eyes. In *On the Waterfront*, we know that Terry was a talented fighter, probably more of a brawler than a stylist. One on one, he proves able to beat up Johnny Friendly (the corrupt union leader, played in hulking fashion by Lee J. Cobb). But victory is snatched from him—as it was years earlier when Friendly ordered Terry to throw a fight that he could easily have won and that would have made him a "contender." A bunch of Friendly's goons, played by former prizefighters whose faces look like they have been run over with a tractor, join the fight, brutally beating Terry. Thanks to the pleadings of a priest and the ministrations of Edie, Terry manages to rise and stagger forward, to lead the workers—if not to certain victory, then, in a paean to the power of the individual to battle corruption, at least at the Hoboken dockside.

Analysts of *On the Waterfront* often battle over the film's political meaning. Was it, as Kazan and scriptwriter Budd Schulberg claimed, simply an exposé of corruption on the docks? Or was it a defense on their part for bowing to name associates to the House Un-American Activities Committee—in sum, a rationale for turning on one's friends when they presumably represented a threat to the well-being of a larger community? Was the film a work of inspired realism, with marvelous attention to setting, details, and atmosphere, or something of a clunker thanks to overused and simplistic religious symbolism? Whatever the intentions for the film, Brando owned it with his magnificent portrayal of Terry Malloy. In the words of film critic Richard Schickel, "By the end of the film one didn't really give a damn about what the film was saying"; one simply delighted in Brando.[31]

A new style of acting was emerging, one that was sometimes more daring, thanks to competition from television and to the slowly weakening power of Production Code censorship. By the 1940s, method acting had begun to transform both stage and screen. In the view of film historian Leo Braudy, the method approach was perfectly suited to postwar America, since it rejected the authority of language (especially classical rhetoric) and reason in favor of emotion and gesture; it was about tapping into reservoirs of emotion in an age when instrumental reason hovered like a menacing cloud over humanity.[32]

The method school of acting traced its roots back to Constantin Stanislavski, a Russian actor and director who developed a system for acting that was popularized by Lee Strasberg and Stella Adler in New York City. Brando's favorite director, Elia Kazan, had been trained in the method approach. But the influence and meaning of Stanislavski's approach was murky and contested. Adler, the daughter of a famous Yiddish actor, and an actress in her own right, praised strict adherence to the text of the play or film. She maintained that an actor must understand the text (which was also the position of Erwin Piscator) and time period, as well as the role, to strive for a heightened realism.[33] In her thespian bible, *The Art of Acting*, she instructed actors, "You're not speaking to the world in your own voice. You're speaking in the voice of an author who matters to the world, who's changed the world." The responsibility of the actor, then, was to prepare the scene on the stage of the imagination and then to make it truthful when acted.[34] But Brando, clearly, did not follow this imperative. He improvised without blushing. In some ways, his respect was greater for Adler as a person (she had been very helpful to him early on in his career) than as a theorist. Adler admired Brando's ability to call up emotions. With Brando, most of it ("seven-eighths") remained "underneath," so that when it exploded in acting, it became monumental—and controlled.[35]

Adler, he later wrote, taught him to examine his "emotional mechanics." Before Adler's training, according to Brando, actors had played themselves, writing their own personalities onto the role. Now the imperative had become to "*experience* a character's feelings and emotions."[36] Were such "feelings and emotions" the same as Adler's respect for the text? Or did they constitute a more open sea of possibility, wherein a creator such as Brando could develop a new sensibility? Actors needed to become receptive voyeurs, scooping up experiences and observations, and then transferring them to their roles. Brando readily admitted the pleasure he took in watching others, taking mental notes of how individuals spoke and moved in real life—with mumbles and stutters rather than with fluency, with nervous tics and affectations. As he once explained, "Actors have to observe, and I enjoy that part of it.... They have to know how much spit you have in your mouth, and where the weight of your elbows is."[37]

When the role demanded it and the spirit moved him, Brando could be obsessive in his preparation. Before filming *The Men* (1950), a drama about wounded veterans in which his character is confined to a wheelchair, Brando spent difficult weeks in a veterans' hospital learning how to do everything as if he were himself incapacitated. Yet on occasion he loyally followed Adler's admonition about worshipping words. Brando said he had played Kowalski as "a compendium of my imagination, based on the lines of the play." "I created him from Tennessee [Williams]'s words."[38] There is a wonderful tension, like that enunciated by Eliot in "Tradition and the Individual Talent," in this notion of being true to the script and yet creating out of it something new and original.

Brando's style of acting, in fact, owed more to Lee Strasberg's method style. Here the key concept was "affective memory." According to Strasberg, who helped to train such actors as Shelley Winters, Eli Wallach, and many others, the essence of good acting was drawing upon one's own emotional resources. Thus, the actor reached far into personal memories of a childhood hurt, for example, which was then translated into the emotional rhythms of the character being portrayed. Less important than the sanctity of the text was emotional realism, the inner and deeper truths to be communicated. Since emotions were rarely fluid and easily verbalized at their core, the actor summoned them forth, in part, through gesture and stammering, by jerkiness and mumbling, and by beguiling moments of improvisation.

Improvisation was a particular talent of Brando's, well displayed in both *The Wild One* and *On the Waterfront*. The entire production of *The Wild One* had been plagued with problems—a censored script, fears that the film would celebrate nihilism, and a director that was barely engaged with the production.[39] The original idea for the film grew out of a real incident that had occurred on July 4, 1947, in Hollister, California, when a gang of bikers rioted. Producer Stanley Kramer saw the tale as a cautionary one about how society was failing to curb forces that led to dissatisfaction. The film, in typical Kramer style, was against repression and in favor of understanding the sources of social rebellion.[40] Although the film now seems a tired and tame period piece, at the time of its showing it was quite daring, in part because it depicted a segment of the townsfolk as vigilantes, venting their rage on innocent Johnny. The film concluded with Johnny and his gang—at the behest of an imposing commander of the state troopers—forced to leave town in a cloud of motorcycle dust, without being convicted of any crimes. To satisfy film executives and censors, the film opened with a solemn, almost comical Brando voice-over about the social challenge presented by lost, angry young men such as Johnny.[41]

Disgusted with the script and lack of directorial passion, Brando decided to improvise and worked wonders via his silences, hesitations, and mumbles: people "are looking for words [and it] shows on their faces."[42] This often threw off the timing of fellow actors. Neophyte actress Mary Murphy, who played Kathy, barely knew how to respond to Brando's glares, silence, and unrehearsed effusion. Years before, veteran actor Paul Muni had been so frustrated with Brando's peculiar timing that he said Brando "has pauses you could drive a truck through."[43] But Kazan remarked that Brando's silences and pauses mimicked the thought process of others and indicated that he was thinking himself into a mood or sensibility, followed unerringly, it seemed, by just the right gesture. According to Kazan, however, Brando's gestures and silences were "often more eloquent than the lines he had to say."[44] Grabbing at a coin on the bar, twirling the trophy, tapping on the counter, and drumming along to the music were, no doubt, ad-libs. But they were also nods to the affectation and style of the bikers that he had hung out with in preparation for the role. Authenticity, it seemed, came via research *and* listening to one's own emotions and instincts.

This ability to sink into a role, to appear effortless in his acting and at ease with his body, made Brando a powerful presence. And it helped that Brando identified with Johnny's inchoate rebellion. "It seemed perfectly natural for me to play this role," Brando stated. "I related to Johnny, and because of this, I believe I played him as more sensitive and sympathetic than the script envisioned.... He was a rebel, but a strong part of him was sensitive and tender."[45]

Brando's improvisation reached its apex in the famous taxi scene in *On the Waterfront*. The scene—as written by Schulberg, a fine writer with a strong knowledge of boxing and investigative reporting on waterfront corruption— called for Terry's older, mob-connected brother, Charley, played by Rod Steiger, to threaten Terry with a pistol if he refused to stay mum before a commission investigating waterfront organized crime. Brando balked. He felt that the love (and guilt) that the older brother had for Terry made brandishing a gun unrealistic, emotionally tinny. As revised—"changing it completely"— Brando and Steiger played the scene brilliantly. Huddled together in the back seat, the pistol appears only as a meek accessory, allowing Brando the opportunity to tap it lightly, as if to dismiss its potential lethality. His famous soliloquy that followed, poignant if not fluent, was scripted in part, but mostly ad-libbed. In fact, he had overheard the line about the possibility of being a contender from Roger Donahue, a former boxer, then working as an extra on the set. Like a sponge, and acutely aware of what sounded authentic, Brando stored it in his memory bank and cashed it during the central scene of the film.[46]

Terry knows that the stakes are high. His life, and perhaps his brother's fate as well, his place in the community, his job, his love for Edie, and his own moral stature are all in play. After the gun incident, Charley speaks of how beautiful and talented Terry was in his boxing prime. Terry grows agitated at this reverie. He realizes that his chance for fame as a fighter had been irrevocably squandered when Charley, along with Friendly, told him to throw a bout with a pug named Wilson. "I'd of taken Wilson apart that night!...So what happens—This bum Wilson he gets the title shot—outdoors in the ball park!— and what do I get—a couple of bucks and a one-way ticket to Palookaville." Building to an emotional crescendo, Brando points the finger of blame unerringly: "It was you, Charley. You was my brother. You should have looked out for me. Instead of making me take them dives for the short-end money." Charley defends himself weakly, saying that some real bucks came Terry's way. But Terry cuts him off, with a perfect hook of dialogue: "You don't understand. I could've been a contender. I could've had class and been somebody. Real class. Instead of a bum, let's face it, which is what I am."[47] Brando liked that his revisions revealed Terry's emerging self-consciousness, his coming to terms with his responsibility to stand up to the mob while at the same time recognizing that he has lived his life like a "bum," and he refused to delude himself that he would suddenly, or easily, be redeemed.[48]

The die has been cast. Charley accepts his betrayal and pays the price: he is shot to death and hung up on a hook by his former cronies. Terry is now freed from social restraints, and temporarily from love, to seek revenge against those who have done his brother wrong. This emotional roller coaster, however, stops, thanks to various promptings which help to transform Terry into a symbol of goodness and social responsibility. The plot moves dully forward, the symbols mounting ever more obvious, but Brando transcends it all with spirited and complex acting.

Emotional expression became Brando's signature style, displayed in subtle fashion. But the summoning of the proper emotional state began with Brando mining his own experiences, selecting the one most appropriate for the character and scene. The "raising of an eyebrow, chasing a piece of food around your mouth with your tongue, or making a tiny, fleeting statement by frowning," were all parts of Brando's repertoire for capturing emotional states.[49]

It seemed an axiom for the method school notion of "affective memory" that the more emotional experience (joys and hurts) the actor would have to draw upon, the better the performance. There was no scale ranking emotions—childhood beatings versus unrequited love. And, of course, while all actors no doubt have pasts marked by unhappiness, not all actors can draw upon those memories with equal effectiveness. Brando admitted: "In hindsight, I guess my emotional insecurity as a child...may have helped me as an actor, at least in a small way. It probably gave me a certain intensity I could call upon that most people don't have."[50]

Brando's childhood had been flooded with a storm of emotional damage. When he spoke to reporters, however, he went out of his way to emphasize the normal and happy nature of his childhood. In the *Time* magazine cover story from 1954, his childhood was represented in broad, idyllic strokes—a mother at once encouraging and beautiful, talented and loving sisters, life on a farm where Marlon's empathy for animals and the downtrodden was apparent (he once brought home a sick homeless woman). Although he was exiled as a teen for a few years of discipline at a military academy—Brando referred to it as "the military asylum"—the upside of the experience was that he had begun acting in school plays. Little in his past, according to the magazine, hinted of darkness and despair.[51]

Brando in fact caressed a teething hurt about his childhood. His mother, while beautiful and encouraging, was deeply unhappy—finding escape in a liquor bottle. Many were the times, Brando later admitted, when he and his sisters had been forced to haul their mother, lost in an alcoholic haze, back home to dry out, only to find her soon repeating her disappearing act. His father had successes in business, and he could be charming, but he was restless and often on the road, hooking up with bar floozies or brawling in a barroom. When home, he was distant and competitive with Marlon, trying to make his sensitive son into the type of hardened and hearty fellow that he considered himself to be. Such plans went awry—hence the military school to discipline young Marlon, who already disdained authority. He refused to kowtow to expectations, and prized above all else displays of individuality. Nonetheless, Brando maintained that he had inherited his "instinctual traits" from his mother and his "endurance" from his father.[52]

But their legacy sometimes crippled him in private, and his personal life in 1954 was unraveling. It was written into his contract for *On the Waterfront* that he could flee the set, no matter what was happening, when it came time for regular appointments with his psychiatrist, Dr. Bela Mittelman. And he cashed in this get-out-of-jail card at the most inopportune times, for instance midway in the filming of the cab scene. Unfortunately, in many ways Mittelman was precisely the wrong psychiatrist for what ailed Brando. He wanted the love that had been denied him by his parents when he was a child. As Brando sadly admitted, Mittelman was "the coldest man I've ever known. I saw him for several years, seeking empathy, insight and guidance, but all I got was ice."[53] Even Mittelman's office, Brando recalled, was "frigid" in its furnishings.

Maybe Mittelman, paradoxically, was to thank for not resolving Brando's inner turmoil. He was allowed to draw from the well of his experiences and to translate them into complex characters, men that were uncomfortable with older tradition and sensibility, young men experimenting with their sexual identity and fretting about their moral cores. Harold Clurman, who was married to Stella Adler and a director of great ability himself, put his finger on Brando's pain and its relation to his acting: "He cannot voice the deepest part of himself: it hurts too much." But that "innermost core—secret... can find its outlet only through acting. And it is precisely because his acting has its source in suffering, the display of which he unwittingly resists, that it acquires its enormous power."[54]

Acting, especially in films like *The Wild One* and *On the Waterfront*, served as a roundabout means of Brando satisfying his need for love and for expressing his rebellious nature. Brando inaugurated a new "intensity of feeling," in the words of stage director and critic Robert Brustein. He was a risky, serious actor, upping the Hollywood ante. Now American films, Brustein predicted, might become more artful and daringly realistic, full of deep emotion, as in the films made by Italian directors Vittorio de Sica and Roberto Rossellini.[55] Brando's special talent, as critic Pauline Kael remarked, was to "convey the multiple and paradoxical meanings in a character."[56]

Brando's emotional sensibilities and style resonated with at least part of the American public. After *The Wild One*, sales of leather jackets were said to have soared, according to Brando.[57] Elvis Presley, a huge fan of that film, joined Brando's look to his blues-infused music to become a superstar. In an era when overblown fears of juvenile delinquency resounded and teenagers were looking for a screen presence that spoke (with studied hesitation—"inarticulation that was so articulate," according to one critic) to their own inner turmoil, Brando fit the bill magnificently.[58] His was an aesthetic of emotional range, rebellion, and liberation—transformed, via talent and style—into artistry of the highest order, into a new sensibility.

The Price of Salt, *lesbian novel written by Patricia Highsmith (1955) (courtesy Bantam Books/ Random House)*

Ever Mysterious

PATRICIA HIGHSMITH

1955

In 1955 a rather unusual character arrived on the scene. Tom Ripley seemed to be a pleasant fellow, agreeable in looks, demeanor, and breeding. For some poor souls who came into contact with him, however, the encounter proved fatal. Mr. Ripley was a talented killer, rather blasé in his attitude about the act, charmed more by the results. Something of a chameleon, Ripley, when required, dispensed with the baggage of his previous life effortlessly. He might be viewed as exemplary of what the sociologist David Riesman had only recently designated as the "other-directed" character—someone wanting to conform to the system, to not make waves, and to bow down to the views of others.[1] Of course, unlike the glad-handing, affable sorts that Riesman analyzed, Mr. Ripley was spooky, obsessive, and lethal.

The same might be said for his creator, Patricia Highsmith. In December 1948, Highsmith—then twenty-seven years old and fetching in an offbeat style, razor thin, tall, usually dressed in a white Oxford shirt from Brooks Brothers— was working as a temporary salesclerk in the toy department at Bloomingdale's in Manhattan. It was a rather bleak day, with showers making the mild temperatures less pleasant. In any case, it was a day that she would never forget. A tall blonde woman in her late thirties, reeking of class, wearing a mink coat, approached the counter to inquire about a toy for her daughter. Dazzled by the woman's cool beauty and presence, Highsmith struggled to focus on the simple request. A few words, no more, were exchanged. In a poof, it seemed, this vision of beauty exited the art deco store on Lexington Avenue. Only her perfume and presence lingered for Highsmith, made palpable by the fact that she had near to hand the woman's name and home address on a slip of paper for shipping purposes.[2]

The day after this fevered encounter, Highsmith wrote a plot outline for a novel. "It flowed from my pen as from nowhere," she recalled.[3] In her journal she recorded the intensity of the experience: "I see her the same instant she sees me, and instantly, I love her, . . . Instantly, I am terrified, because I know she knows I am terrified and that I love her."[4] In a chilling observation, Highsmith admitted, "Murder is a kind of love, a kind of possessing."[5]

Such was the stuff of Highsmith's art and life, dedicated as it was to turning things on their heads, to dissolving lines between madness and sanity, and to an upswell of excess.

The name of the woman who skittered into Highsmith's life that day in Bloomingdale's was Kathleen Senn. Highsmith always appreciated quality and was attracted to trouble, so she had sized up Senn perfectly. Beyond her pristine beauty, Senn was an aviatrix and a keen golfer, married to a wealthy executive. Unfortunately, she was also a raging alcoholic suffering from psychiatric problems. In 1951, prior to publication of Highsmith's novel that recounted their brief encounter, Mrs. Senn turned on the car engine in the enclosed garage attached to her home and asphyxiated herself.[6]

Highsmith spent hours huddled over her notebooks and typewriter until she had imaged Senn as the character Carol Aird in the novel *The Price of Salt*. Twice, however, Highsmith indulged her obsessive curiosity about the real Mrs. Senn. As she admitted about herself, "Obsessions are the only things that matter."[7]

In fact, Highsmith stalked Senn. On June 30, 1950, one day after completing a first draft of *Price of Salt*, Highsmith took a train from Penn Station to Ridgewood, New Jersey. She recorded in her journal: "Today, feeling quite odd—like a murderer in a novel, I boarded the train." Highsmith arrived at the Ridgewood train station, gulped down a couple of stiff drinks, then clambered aboard a bus to find the house—and perhaps steal a glimpse of the divine Mrs. Senn. Exiting the bus, she moved conspicuously along streets with tony homes. Solitary walkers along the tree-lined streets were unusual, and Highsmith feared she would be discovered and revealed as a voyeur. Highsmith failed to locate Senn's upscale Normandy Tudor home, which bustled with turrets and stonework. She liked to think, however, that a passing automobile had been driven by the object of her attention. The experience, Highsmith wrote, "shook me physically and left me limp."[8]

Patricia Highsmith's life and work existed on the edge of a moral abyss. Severe alcoholism and frenzied promiscuity complicated her private life, but she managed somehow to drag herself daily to her desk to write about her favored subjects: murder, obsession, paranoia, and the permeable boundaries of identity. And she adored perversity: "Perversion interests me most and is my guiding darkness," she recorded in her diary at age twenty-one.[9]

Everyone constructs their history by retrospectively mining it for tidbits that seem relevant. Many blame Highsmith's perversities on her mother, who was reported to have tried to abort Pat by drinking turpentine. Her mother joked later about Pat's unusual appreciation for "the smell of turpentine."[10] Highsmith survived birth, apparently none the worse. Her haughty, beautiful mother was a fashion illustrator, who often left Patricia in the care of her mother, Willie Mae Coates. Highsmith's biological father, Jay Plangman, was out of the picture early on, except for a time when, in Pat's account, as a teenager, she reunited with her father briefly enough to be shown pornographic pictures and share "some lingering kisses."[11] Highsmith's mother remarried and took the child from Texas to live in New York City, although they rarely stayed put in any domicile for too long. Patricia managed to graduate from Barnard College and dreamed of becoming a great novelist. From 1942 until 1948, she supported herself by writing volcanic stories for comic books such as *Jap Buster Johnson*, *The Human Torch*, and *Spy Smasher*.[12]

Despite natural shyness and embarrassment about her work in comics, Highsmith was well connected. By 1950, her roster of influential friends was substantial and varied: photographers Ruth Bernhard and Karl Bissinger; writers Sybille Bedford, Dorothy Parker, Chester Himes, Truman Capote, James Merrill, and Carson McCullers; and many in the fashion world. She impressed everyone with her intellect and charmed them with her eccentricities; she would tap her cigarette (Camels up until 1949; only Gauloises after a trip to Europe) on her watch face prior to lighting up. Many remarked on her impeccable manners and thoughtfulness. But she tended to avoid physical contact, preferring not to shake hands with new acquaintances.[13]

Nonetheless, Highsmith was sexually voracious. What interested her most, however, as reflected in her fiction, was the excitement of the quest, the seduction rather than the result. This sexual allure was captured in a nude photograph by Rolf Tietgens, a bisexual lover who wanted to marry her (she did have a complex life). In the photograph she appeared at once androgynous, slim, and powerful. She enjoyed being viewed as attractive, and she pursued sex mainly with women. Arthur Koestler, a writer of great talent and connections, became her friend in 1950; he liked her work but, with his vaunted lecherousness, also wanted to bed her. Highsmith allowed this to happen, after fortifying herself with "seven martinis, a bottle of wine and three gins." Suffice it to say, intercourse with Koestler was a "miserable, joyless episode." After sex with men, Highsmith confided, she was riven with "hostility, masochism, self-hatred, self-abasement."[14]

Perhaps it is best at this point to move away from the numerous potholes in Highsmith's personal life to the delicious and daunting perversities on the pages of her first novel, *Strangers on a Train* (1950). As with most of her writing, according to novelist James Sallis, Highsmith "pushed things to the very border of expectation, civility, civilization and reason—even of humanity."[15] Such qualities of the New Sensibility, sugarcoated somewhat in her initial novel, would only become more overt in subsequent works.

Paranoia and guilt eat at the main character of this novel—sometimes with good reason; Highsmith would undoubtedly have nodded in agreement with the poet Delmore Schwartz's remark that "even paranoids have real enemies." Layered with troubling themes, *Strangers* leaves readers with a shaky feeling. Although the novel is marred by artificial plot twists and stagey moments, the atmosphere is relentlessly Highsmith.[16] The novel was a perfect vehicle for her views about murder, as she confided to her journal the year it was published:

I am interested in the murderer's psychology, and also in the opposing planes, drives of good and evil (construction and destruction). How by a slight defection one can be made the *other*, and all the power of a strong mind and body be deflected to murder or destruction! It is simply fascinating.[17]

The story spins around a chance meeting on a train heading west between Guy Haines, an appealing young architect, and a rather odd fellow, Charles Anthony Bruno. When Bruno learns that Guy's wife is hindering his career and potential happiness with another woman, the conversation takes a startling and dastardly turn. Bruno asks Guy if he would like him "to dope out a perfect murder" of his wife.[18]

Amoral, drunk, and obsessive, Bruno is the character that sparkles with the daring of a new sensibility. Highsmith acknowledged as much: "I am so happy when Bruno reappears in the novel. . . . I love him!"[19]

Bruno is determined to kill for Guy. Drawing on a thimbleful of information about Guy's wife, Miriam, Bruno tracks her down and stalks her. With each glance, Bruno's repulsion for her grows. Finally, in a wooded area near a carnival, he finds her alone and attacks, choking her fiercely: "He sunk his fingers deeper, enduring the distasteful pressure of her body under his. . . . Her throat felt hotter and fatter." In a few moments, the deed was done; the killer "felt great."[20]

With more twists than a pretzel, *Strangers on a Train* piles on psychological nuances. Bruno's adoration of Guy verges on the perverse. He stalks (a key theme in Highsmith's work) Guy, slowly insinuating himself into Guy's life, at the most unexpected and inopportune moments. Guy's moral resources start to wear thin. He anxiously fulfills his half of the implicit bargain by killing Bruno's father. Bruno and Guy are now brothers in sin.[21]

The guilty are punished, at least in this novel. A dumpy detective named Shannon is a loyal and smart bulldog; he tracks down the most hidden clues, all leading to Guy's doorstep. But first comes Bruno's accounting. While drunk on board a yacht with Guy and his new wife, Anne, and a few others, Bruno slips on the deck into the water and drowns, despite Guy's brave attempt to save him.

The story concludes in even more absurd fashion. Guy has returned to Texas, to the town where Miriam was strangled. Racked with guilt, Guy feels encased in an "invisible glass cell."[22] He decides to locate Owen, his wife's former lover, and confess to him his passive, accidental role in her death. To further unburden himself, Guy intends to admit to the murder of Bruno's father. Owen could care less about any confessions or even Miriam; "Hell," he says, "I didn't love her." Undeterred by his unfeeling auditor, Guy confesses: "I—I killed someone, too! I'm a murderer, too!" Owen's response, offered with a smile, is "Live and let live."[23]

Detective Shannon has secretly been eavesdropping on Guy's confessional. Once confronted, Guy is relieved: "Take me."[24] Case closed.

Highsmith's own bundle of obsessions and identity confusions remained in the late 1940s. She was involved in a relationship with a man (disdainful of the sex and horrified at the potential of getting pregnant), yet seeing women and enjoying them briefly, laboring unhappily in the comic book trade, and writing, writing, writing. And her fraught relationship with her mother continued.

Forty-seven times Highsmith dragged herself to the office of psychiatrist Eva Klein Lipshutz. A Rorschach test for Highsmith concluded that she suffered from "raging violence" and a "weak ego." Lipshutz's recommendations were both precise and absurd: Highsmith should work toward "a condition to be married," since the therapist equated heterosexuality with normality. But until she got her bearings, Highsmith was warned to refrain from entering into any serious, obsessive relationship. Armed with this prescription, and ending therapy in May 1949, Highsmith booked passage aboard the *Queen Mary* for Europe. She would quickly violate all of Lipshutz's imperatives.[25]

In England, Highsmith succumbed immediately to the intoxicating presence of Kathryn Hamill Cohen. She was a remarkable woman: American-born, once a Ziegfeld Follies dancer, a geneticist, and a psychiatrist. Moreover, as Highsmith's biographer Joan Schenkar states, Cohen was also "beautiful, intelligent, melancholy, moneyed, and married: a combination Pat always found irresistible."[26] Kathryn and her husband, an editor for Harper & Brothers, were fabulously wealthy, no doubt thrilling the ever-materialistic Highsmith with their Rolls-Royce and magnificent house. Kathryn introduced Highsmith to London's cultural elite. Yet Highsmith soon heeded the call of the Continent, heading first to Paris, then to Italy.

During this period, Highsmith obsessively and enthusiastically frequented lesbian bars in Paris, and she had managed during her short time in London to have sex with a few women. Lonely in a Roman hotel, Highsmith wired Cohen, inquiring if she might join her on a jaunt around Italy. The two of them met up in Naples, traveling to Positano (the city that would become the setting for *The Talented Mr. Ripley*), as well as to ever romantic Capri. Mutual attraction had blossomed into a passionate romance. It was no more than a fling for Cohen; she had no intention of abandoning her London life for the strangely alluring young writer. On September 23, "the horrible day," Highsmith wrote, Kathryn returned to London. A month later, Highsmith was back in New York City, working arduously on the manuscript that would become *The Price of Salt*.[27]

Highsmith was finally accepting her lesbianism, although she would continue on occasion to sleep with men. Her infatuation with Senn in December had convinced her that lesbianism was natural and ripe with possibilities. This emerging sense of confidence about her sexuality would become apparent in the new novel. *Strangers on a Train*, which was published on 15 March 1950, was dedicated to "all the Virginias," a reference to past female lovers.[28]

Confidence in the writing of the new novel, however, coexisted with shame. The book did bear, she remarked, a "close truthfulness" to aspects of her life, but it promised little for her reputation. As the novel hurried to publication,

Highsmith drank so much that weeks in her life had dissolved into a "blank in memory." Published under the pseudonym Claire Morgan, *The Price of Salt* was reissued a year later as a Bantam paperback edition; its lurid cover captured all the tropes then common for the lesbian novel genre. A beautiful young woman sits seductively on a couch. Looming over her is a beautiful older woman, one hand holding a cigarette, the other hand placed fondly on the younger girl's shoulder. In the distance, rushing to put a stop to the seduction is a handsome young man. "Bad" girls were meant to get caught and punished, according to historian Jaye Zimet: "The lesbian gets her due...marriage, insanity or...suicide."[29]

Being a lesbian in the United States in the late 1940s and 1950s was, as Zimet makes clear, difficult and dangerous. The pressure was great from family and friends to conform to the heterosexual norm. And the consequences of refusal could be immense. Gay men and women were considered not only perverts but security risks; thousands of government workers were dismissed from service during the "lavender scare" for being presumed to be gay. Women in the postwar years were expected to marry and raise a family, to anchor their existence within the happy confines of the home.[30]

In some ways, however, lesbianism in this period was emerging from the shadows. The Kinsey Report on women's sexuality, published in 1952, found that 6 percent of women between the ages of twenty and thirty-five were lesbian in inclination. As more young women with such an orientation gravitated to urban centers in search of careers and liberation, they discovered lesbian bars, where a culture of freedom was tempered by fear of harassment.[31] Highsmith gained entry into a world of wealthy lesbians who threw lavish parties in their homes. This rich environment teemed with talented and wealthy women. For those unwilling or unable to enter into either of these worlds, some titillation might be gained from pulp fiction depicting female relationships.

The Price of Salt centered on a lesbian relationship. But it went beyond expectations of pulp fiction. Lesbians invariably bowed to the heterosexual demands of society—or, if unrepentant, experienced its wrath. Highsmith's novel was remarkable both for its tender depiction of lesbian love and for its sensitivity to shifting balances and power relations between lovers. Most of all, as Highsmith wrote later, "It had a happy ending for its two main characters, or at least they were going to try to have a future together."[32] This emphasis on pleasure, without guilt or punishment, was part of the New Sensibility that was central to writers such as Allen Ginsberg, Gore Vidal, and Samuel R. Delany.

After that magic moment with Kathleen Senn at Bloomingdale's (Frankenberg's in the novel), nineteen-year-old salesgirl Therese sends a thank-you Christmas card to Mrs. Carol Aird. She coyly signs it with her employee number, 645-A—secretly hoping that Carol will be tickled and respond positively.

She does, and they meet. Therese swoons in Carol's perfume, admires her beauty, and marvels at her confidence. Therese is in the tight arms of an infatuation, a love that had never gushed so high with her boyfriend, Richard Semco. But Therese remains childlike, alienated from the larger world (experiencing life "secondhand"), and "anxious." As Carol puts it at one point, Therese is "a strange girl…flung out of space."[33]

Carol assumes the role of a mother to Therese—pampering her, trying to get her to be more realistic about the vicissitudes of life and love. But Therese craves more than mothering (although she does enjoy the "hot milk" that Carol provides her at night). She wants a passionate relationship; nothing less will suffice. For Therese is obsessed: "There was not a moment when she did not see Carol in her mind."[34]

At Carol's behest, they embark on a road trip west. They are in search of metaphorical freedom, but also, as it turns out, going "westward into the darkness." Finally, in Waterloo, Iowa, sharing a single bed in a hotel room, their bodies touch and cling, their lips lock, and their desire for one another is satisfied. It is a victory on the one hand but also a harbinger of suffering.[35]

Highsmith stories always brim with problems (real and anticipated), scattered like litter along the highway. It develops that their first night of sexual bliss in Waterloo has been discovered. Therese had noticed earlier that they were being followed by a detective "with creases on either side of the mouth." He has been hired by Carol's estranged husband to gather evidence of promiscuous perversity, to use in court to gain full custody of their child, Rindy. And he has managed to wire the Waterloo hotel room to record the delighted moans of their first coupling.[36] Will this Waterloo rendezvous be the scene of Napoleon's defeat or Wellington's victory?

The plot thickens. An armed Carol confronts the detective but is forced to return east to deal with divorce issues. Therese feels isolated. But abandonment has a hidden silver lining, since Therese, now living on her own in the west, achieves maturity and independence. In typical Highsmith fashion, Therese nurtures resentment for Carol, who has betrayed her by caring more for Rindy than for her.[37]

When they meet anew, Carol tells Therese: "I was hoping you might like to come and live with me, but I guess you won't." Upon hearing these words, Therese's heart leaps, but it is quickly brought back to earth by her seething resentment at Carol's presumed betrayal: "No, I don't think so," responds Therese.[38]

Yet the seed has been planted. Therese realizes in a flash that "it was Carol that she loved and would always love." She flees a party and rushes along New York streets to the restaurant where she knows Carol is having dinner. Carol sees her coming and seems to acknowledge in a subtle glance their future together, as "Therese walked toward her."[39] So ends Highsmith's novel, without a single murder or suicide taking place. And no punishment for the lesbians, only the prospect of a life together.

"My personal maladies and malaises," Highsmith confided in her journal, "are only those of my own generation and of my time, heightened."[40] This was a surprising admission; the novels she published between 1950 and 1955 seem disconnected from the historical moment. There is nary a mention of the Cold War, Red Scare, Korean War, or civil rights movement. But, in a sense, like Ginsberg and other exemplars of the New Sensibility, such as Norman Mailer (chapter 9), Highsmith had placed her finger on one aspect of the historical pulse of the time: the existential challenge of living in an age of anxiety. What moral constraints existed to stop an individual from going too far—apart from empty traditions or prohibitive legalisms?

Highsmith was familiar with the giants of existentialism—Kierkegaard, Kafka, Nietzsche, Sartre, de Beauvoir, and Camus. She was writing in the heyday of the initial wave of American enthusiasm for existentialism. Translations of key existential texts cascaded from presses; books explaining existentialism were common, and even in popular culture existential motifs became de rigueur for almost anyone claiming to be aware of social and intellectual currents. W. H. Auden had captured the "groans of grief" well in his long poem *The Age of Anxiety* (1946), while psychologist Rollo May plumbed the depths of such grief—and its transcendence—in *The Meaning of Anxiety* (1950).[41]

Highsmith read such works selectively. She exulted in the existential emphasis on alienation, on contingency (think of how it plays in *Strangers on a Train*), and the problematic nature of identity. The (perhaps overly) famous line from one of Sartre's plays about hell being other people became a sort of mantra for Highsmith. For Sartre, the problem of the age was bad faith, failing to accept responsibility for making the world a place devoid of exploitation, racism, and anti-Semitism. Alas, on the latter two issues, Highsmith's prejudices could cut deeply. She had many Jewish friends and lovers, but when they crossed or disappointed her, they were immediately reduced to disgusting stereotypes. Highsmith was more of a curmudgeonly existentialist in the fashion of Nietzsche—freedom was about power and creativity, about being above morality. She ignored how Camus and Beauvoir grasped for a common humanity, realizing how since everyone is thrown into this world, each individual has the responsibility to develop an ethical stance which can accommodate competing visions.[42]

Without such an understanding, the world becomes a place of power struggles, deceit, and murder. A fine description, of course, for the universe that Highsmith created in her novels.

Cold War secrecy, confession, and paranoia were mirrored in Highsmith's fiction. Secrecy, of course, became a paramount concern in the postwar years—especially with revelations of atomic spy rings and Communist agents infiltrating the government. In the name of national security, the United States government and its political representatives increasingly sought to penetrate the personal lives of Americans, looking for any hint of subversive activity. In fact,

Highsmith had once been intrigued with the Communist Party, at least in the early 1940s. She was drawn more to its machinations than to its politics, however: "This business of dodging and bulldozing the authorities has limitless opportunities for clever remarks."[43]

The postwar years also brought forth a new sort of literature—heralded most compellingly by Whittaker Chambers's bestselling *Witness* (1952). Much of the book detailed Chambers's secret life as a Communist spy; he revealed how Alger Hiss, a high-level government official, had worked closely with him in Communist espionage. The book, however, went beyond detailing spy networks and various modes of secrecy; it was a cri de cœur, a masterful work of confession. Having exchanged his Communism for a sort of existential Christianity, Chambers was pushed as strongly by his harrowing sense of guilt to confess as Guy had been in *Strangers on a Train*. Rejecting his earlier hints of sexual deviance, Chambers worked to find refuge in faith, marriage, fatherhood, and life on a farm.[44] None of those options interested Highsmith.

As usual, high drama marked Highsmith's personal life. In her journal entries she obsessively kept lists of the women she slept with (she rated them as lovers), her medical information, and much else. Her relationships with women were volcanic. Joan Schenkar nicely captured why this was so: Highsmith "could live *for* love, but she couldn't live *with* love."[45] For four years—during composition of *The Talented Mr. Ripley*—Highsmith was in an open relationship with Ellen Hill (a woman who sought to dominate Highsmith—no easy task).[46] One night Hill threatened to commit suicide if Highsmith went out on a scheduled date. Highsmith stormed out of the apartment—later to find Hill in a hospital, having almost made good on her threat. Hill and Highsmith returned to their fraught, constantly squabbling relationship. Depression, excessive drink, and fears of madness plagued Highsmith's life in this period of the early 1950s—and yet she pecked away at the typewriter, managing to write her first Ripley novel, completing it in six months and publishing it in December 1955.[47]

Tom Ripley captured Highsmith's devotion to a handful of themes and her penchant for taking things too far. His life revolves around contingent situations, chance encounters (as with the characters in *Strangers on a Train*). Ripley's identity (like that of Therese in *The Price of Salt*) is malleable. He is a stalker. First he imagines being connected with the target; then he actually seeks to attach himself to those who have struck him as appealing. In turn, he will adopt their identities while retaining the option of shifting back to his own original presentation of self.

Lest we forget, Ripley is a murderer. Much like Charles Bruno, he kills without remorse. And he gets away with his murders—both of others and, in a sense, of himself. Ripley is, then, the exemplification of a dream that Highsmith had once experienced. She had dreamt of immolating a figure in a bathtub that was herself as well. Highsmith interpreted this dream thusly: "I had two identities: the victim and the murderer."[48] Further proof of the closeness between Ripley and Highsmith is found in how she sometimes signed copies of the Ripley books, "Pat H, alias Ripley."[49]

The Talented Mr. Ripley opens on a typically Highsmithian furtive note. Tom Ripley believes he is being followed and about to be arrested. He has, after all, committed mail fraud—although for various reasons he has not cashed in on any of his ill-gotten gains. Ripley's stalker, it turns out, is a Mr. Herbert Greenleaf, the father of Dickie, who is living a lush and listless life in Italy. Presuming Tom to be an old pal of Dickie's, he tries to enlist him to bring his wayward son home. At this point, the novel promises to be an updated version of Henry James's *The Ambassadors*. The prospect of going to Europe offers Ripley freedom—an opportunity to shift his identity and possibilities for seduction, of varied kinds.[50]

Tom Ripley is a bit of a scoundrel, unanchored in his plans, unmoored in his relationships. There is a blankness about him, although he is not totally bereft of emotions, but he does have a particular soft spot for material objects; he appreciates value—be it in a fine watch or a particularly impressive floral gift. He is convinced that by donning an outfit, speaking in a certain manner, effecting certain gestures, he becomes that role. Hardly surprising, then, that Tom had once imagined himself becoming an actor. But he lacks gumption: "He had never stuck to anything."[51]

Tom finds Dickie in Mongibello, a town modeled on Positano, which Highsmith had visited during her tryst with Kathryn Cohen. She had at that time espied a young man who made an indelible impression upon her, and she based Dickie on his physical appearance and style. In some ways, Dickie is much like Tom, someone who skips from one thing to another without achieving much. At this moment he is serious about painting. Unlike Tom, however, Dickie is blessed with plenty of money and social savoir faire; he has a rather lovely existence in Mongibello.

Under false pretenses and with imaginative effort, Tom enters into Dickie's lavish daily life. To make the alluring Dickie like him was what Tom "wanted ... more than anything else in the world."[52] But in Highsmith's world, to have someone like or love you is to court disaster, to depend on affection which comes from a well that will quickly run dry.

Tom clings to Dickie. He studies him closely, like a method actor, and begins to ape him. Gazing in the mirror one day, he realizes that their physical differences are minimal, distinctions of hair shade, slightly more pudginess on Tom's part. One time Tom goes into Dickie's bedroom, dons his clothing, mimics his gestures, and realizes "he could become Dickie Greenleaf."[53]

Spurned by Dickie, who grows bored with him, and no longer of any use to Dickie's parents, Tom realizes that his stay in Shangri-La will soon end. With equal parts jealousy and fear, he decides to kill Dickie and assume his identity. Traveling together through Italy, they rent a boat to go out on a placid lake. But

Tom's mind roils with murder. Highsmith's passage at this key moment is notable for its phallic undertone: "He picked up the oar, as casually as if he were playing with it between his knees, and when Dickie was shoving his trousers down, Tom lifted the oar and came down with it on top of Dickie's head."[54]

With Dickie dead, Tom transforms himself into Dickie. Tom begins wearing his clothes, adopting his gestures, impersonating his speech. He writes long letters to the Greenleafs, scamming for additional funding. He enjoys the emoluments of wealth and confidence. When his ruse is discovered by Freddie, an old pal of Dickie's, Tom is forced to kill him. Things get complicated, as the Italian police and an American private investigator enter the picture, trying to solve two murders which may be connected. A bank questions the signature that Tom has forged on a check made out to Dickie, which adds another piece to a muddled puzzle. With dizzying skill, Tom manages to elude his pursuers, but at a cost:

> This was the end of Dickie Greenleaf, he knew. He hated becoming Thomas Ripley again, hated being nobody, hated putting on his old set of habits again, and feeling that people looked down on him and were bored with him unless he put on an act for them like a clown, feeling incompetent and incapable of doing anything himself except entertaining people for minutes at a time. He hated going back to himself as he would have hated putting on a shabby suit of clothes, a grease-spotted suit of clothes that had not been very good even when it was new.[55]

Tom has gotten away with murder but finds himself in need of money. In an audacious appendix to his crimes, Tom claims that he has found an envelope in his suitcase that Dickie had given him prior to his demise. It is a last will and testament—neatly forged—that grants Dickie's trust funds to Tom Ripley. With surprisingly little fuss, the Greenleafs accept the veracity of the will.

"It was his! Dickie's money and his freedom." Mr. Ripley, talented and amoral, has emerged victorious. As Highsmith noted, "I find the public passion for justice quite boring and artificial, for neither life nor nature cares if justice is done or not."[56]

And in a sense, so had Highsmith emerged victorious. She had created a killer with few redeeming features, a protean figure living without guilt, enamored of material objects and heaving with homosexual desire. Ripley was a man who played roles, an actor no less skilled than Brando, as much in rebellion against what the fates had decreed for him as the biker Johnny was against staid conventions. But Ripley takes it further; his sensibility refuses limits, resides in the territory of extremes. He is a monster of sorts, destroying the lives of those around him, his only concern his own pleasure.

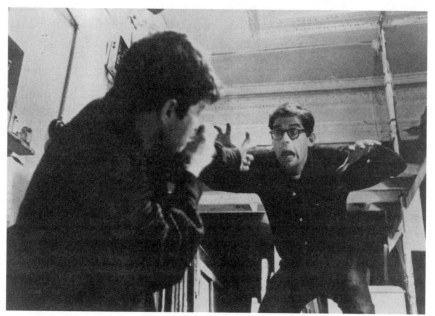

Allen Ginsberg and Gregory Corso in Robert Frank's film Pull My Daisy *(1959) (© Photofest)*

Howling in the Wilderness

ALLEN GINSBERG

1956

Allen Ginsberg was aboard a merchant marine ship during the summer of 1956 trying to earn money to travel to Morocco. The vessel sometimes anchored close to the Alaskan shoreline, offering Ginsberg views of Eskimos going about their daily chores. His duties were undemanding, and he was delighted watching the ice floes and thrilled to be within a thousand miles of the North Pole. But he encountered turbulence when contemplating his confused reality and Kafkaesque dreams. His beloved and mentally ill mother had died in June while she was confined to the Pilgrim State Hospital on Long Island. "I see a part of my childhood in the grave," he wrote to a friend in San Francisco, "a piece of my own life gone and the rest surely to go."[1]

Such churning of the soul had long been a staple for Ginsberg. It would reach artistic heights in his poem *Howl*. While Ginsberg was at sea physically and mentally, City Lights Press in San Francisco was readying publication of the slim volume, after many revisions and mishaps by the printer in England. Potential problems loomed in getting the book through customs. For a book born of such deep angst and joyful release, its debut in 1956 was certain to be both controversial and monumental.[2]

Part of the poem had its public debut on a Friday evening in early October 1955. That night, around 11:00 p.m., Ginsberg was sitting on a toilet when he was called to the Six Gallery stage. The gallery, once an auto parts store, was located in a seedy section of San Francisco. Pulling up his jeans, Ginsberg walked a bit unsteadily, thanks to large amounts of cheap wine— "I was *very* drunk."[3]

Some of Ginsberg's closest friends were crowded around the stage, ready to participate in what would prove to be a "mad," historic night.[4] Jack Kerouac was sprawled on the floor, drunk and excitable, his back to the stage. Beat muse Neal Cassady, in a brakeman's uniform with vest and pocket watch, eagerly waited to hear Ginsberg read his new poem in progress.[5] Also among the throng were poet Gregory Corso and dancer Yvonne Rainer, along with Ginsberg's new boyfriend, Peter Orlovsky, and Ruth Witt-Diamant, the doyenne of the Bay Area poetry scene. Kenneth Rexroth, outfitted in what was described as formal pinstripe diplomat garb, bought in a thrift store, served as master of ceremonies. Reading that night as well were poets Michael McClure, Gary Snyder, Philip Lamantia, and Phil Whalen. The audience was studded, McClure recalled, with "anarchists and Stalinists and professors and painters and bohemians and visionaries and idealists and grinning cynics." By the time Ginsberg stumbled to the stage, everyone present appeared well lubricated with wine, paid for with nickels and quarters that Kerouac had collected.[6]

Few knew what to expect from Ginsberg—least of all the poet himself. It was, after all, only his second public reading. Ginsberg was of average height, slim, with a thick crop of hair, complemented by his black-framed glasses. By all accounts, Ginsberg started reading slowly but in a clear voice. As the adrenaline kicked in and the booze haze receded, he became animated, "rather surprised by his own power," waving his arms, reciting the long strophes in extended, breathless fashion.[7]

As Ginsberg wailed, Kerouac grew boisterous. With eyes closed and head nodding, Kerouac sang out words of approval, repeating phrases as if at a revival meeting. After taking a slug from a gallon bottle of Burgundy, Kerouac started "beating tunes on empty bottles" in time with the lines of the poem. He chanted "Go! Go! Go!" as Ginsberg's recitation picked up speed and power.[8]

"I saw the best minds of my generation destroyed by madness, starving hysterical naked," Ginsberg intoned. With building confidence, he moved into the early part of the poem, each line beginning with "who." Gasps of shock and delight came from the audience when Ginsberg read: "Who let themselves be fucked in the ass by saintly motorcyclists, and screamed with joy." More than forty-five times in a row, he chanted the roll call of the "who"—all those who had suffered and frolicked on the hot rim of experience. The images hit hard, striking in their originality, confounding in their meaning: "hydrogen jukebox," "orange crates of theology," and "harlequin speech of suicide."[9]

The audience "gasped and laughed and swayed," according to one observer, like participants in an "orgiastic occasion."[10] The crowd was "standing in wonder, or cheering and wondering but knowing at the deepest level that a barrier had been broken."[11]

Never before, it seemed, had an audience heard a poem of such vigor, relentlessly detailing acts of sexual perversion, drug euphoria, divine and diseased madness, and sympathy for those forced to the periphery of society. Sweating and triumphant, Ginsberg concluded with a powerful nod toward fellow sufferers of American repression "with the absolute heart of the poem of life butchered out of their own bodies good to eat a thousand years."[12]

Rexroth was in tears, emotionally wrung by this poetic bomb blast. Gary Snyder felt that "we had finally broken through to a new freedom of expression," and come to the realization that "the imagination has a free and spontaneous life of its own, that it can be trusted that what flows from a spontaneous mind is poetry."[13] "The spiritual darkness" had lifted, at last.[14]

Later, in the indecent hours of the morning, Ginsberg and friends were eating dinner in Chinatown and then getting redrunk at a bar. Lawrence Ferlinghetti, the proprietor of City Lights Bookstore, reportedly sent a telegram that night to Ginsberg, echoing the words of Emerson to Whitman: "I greet you at the beginning of a great career—When do I get the manuscript of 'Howl'?"[15]

Ginsberg had no intention in early August 1955 to write a great poem. But the time was right.

In June 1954, after traveling for six months, Ginsberg landed in San Jose, California. The situation was steamy and complex. He was staying with his old pal Cassady and his wife, Carolyn, along with the couple's children. Things quickly became complicated—the same old "sexual drama" between Ginsberg and Cassady that dated back to 1947.[16] After catching the pair in flagrante delicto, Carolyn exiled Ginsberg from San Jose. He relocated to San Francisco, cleaning up his act and working various jobs, even finding a position with a marketing firm.

For some time prior, however, he had been depressed. His twenty-ninth birthday in June 1955 had signaled the end of his youth. He was, as he wrote to Kerouac, dragged down by life, feeling "very unsure of myself."[17] But life soon took some positive turns: he quit his job working for the marketing company and was living off unemployment compensation; his psychiatrist had given him sage advice: that he was a good person, that his homosexual urges were valid, and that he should pursue his desire to be a poet. And he was now in a relationship with Orlovsky, a strange man, at turns childlike and wise.[18]

In his shabby apartment, situated on a slope at the corner of Montgomery and Broadway, not far from the bohemian North Beach area, Ginsberg began composing *Howl*. Perhaps he listened to his favorite record, Bach's Mass in B Minor, or glanced at the Cezanne print on his wall; it had been a summer of delight in both Bach and Cezanne, one a master of form, the other a visionary of relations. In his journal he had announced a desire to emulate Cezanne: "To present to the mind's eye two equally strong images without editorial or rhetorical connection."[19]

"I sat down to blow" is how Ginsberg later described the initial moments of the poem to Kerouac. He planned to doodle around and see what emerged. He marveled at Kerouac, for whom such writing came with ease. A legend in beat circles, Kerouac had been trying unsuccessfully for years to get his novel *On the Road* into print. Other beats admired his improvisational and jaunty style, as well as his refusal to bow to tradition. Ginsberg had tacked to his wall Kerouac's admonitions for writers: "Blow as deep as you want to blow"; "Something that you feel will find its own form"; "Remove literary, grammatical and syntactical inhibition."[20]

Why not give it a try? Ginsberg thought. With the first sheet of "cheap scratch paper" in the typewriter, he began to type.[21] Seven pages of single-spaced poetry were pounded out in a single sitting—the first section of *Howl*. Later that day, he returned to the typewriter and wrote some of what would become the third section of the poem. Over the next few months, at first in San Francisco and then in a cottage in Berkeley, Ginsberg completed the poem. Although it had begun in spontaneity, Ginsberg carefully revised it over months, giving the poem a more certain rhythm and continuity. Yet he wanted the poem to flash with "eyeball kicks" for the reader, in the manner of a Cezanne canvas.[22]

Looking back on that initial day of work, Ginsberg stated, "I thought I [would]...just write what I wanted to without fear, let my imagination go, open secrecy and scribble some magic lines from my real Mind—sum up my life—something I wouldn't be able to show anybody, writ for my own soul's ear and a few other golden ears."[23]

Soon, however, Ginsberg knew that he was blowing something spectacular, with a "point of view," a "physiological" sense, and confessional, with "a secret that needed to be revealed.[24] It was a poem that captured varied aspects of a new sensibility. First, it was confessional; there was little doubt that Ginsberg had shared experiences detailed in the poem.[25] Months earlier he had hinted at this possibility in his journal: "I'll be my own subject matter, / all I know."[26] Second, it oozed excess, the words uncensored, the lines seemingly going on forever. And it dealt graphically with themes of madness, sex, and violence, both in the content and in its images. Much as the poem was about degradation and defeat, it was also about heroism and regeneration. Civil authorities, and some literary critics, would come to believe that Ginsberg had gone too far with this work.

Sometimes like a dark ghost, other times like a lofty angel, madness had long kept close company with Ginsberg. It threatened institutional confinement and shock therapy that would wipe clean his mental slate of creativity. Yet, as historian Jonah Raskin remarks, madness also "was the Beat badge of honor in a world gone insane with bombs and dictators, terror and tyranny."[27] Madness stalked nearly every line of *Howl*. "I'm with you in Rockland / where you scream in a straightjacket that you're losing the game of the actual pingpong of the abyss."[28] This was as it should be: no firm line between life and poetry. "Writing must come from your life"; it is about "really looking in the heart and writing."[29]

There was his mother, Naomi, once a girlish immigrant from Russia, astir with visions of Marxist revolution. Her first nervous breakdown occurred just before her wedding to Allen's father, Louis. Over time, she became a bloated and frightened figure, a peekaboo presence in his life. Once she locked herself in the bathroom, flirting with the idea of iodine overdose or razor blade slashes. Confinement to asylums and exile from the family became Naomi's normal routine. In 1947, Allen had signed the form authorizing Pilgrim State Hospital to have her electroshocked, injected with insulin, and lobotomized. As he phrased it later in his poem "Kaddish," "I saw her led away—she waved, tears in her eyes."[30] She would function, in the formulation of critic James Breslin, as "the psychotic mother" who became Ginsberg's "muse."[31]

As a young man at Columbia University, Ginsberg had grappled with madness, at least in the view of his advisors and university officials. He considered his displays of oddity and danger as simply experiments in living, pushing the envelope of liberation. During his initial year at college, he had fingered on the dirty glass of his dorm room window the words "Fuck the Jews." This earned him an official rebuke and expulsion. In 1948, he wrote to Kerouac, "I have decided that I am dead, given up, gone mad."[32]

Later, he cavorted with junkies and thieves. His off-campus apartment became a haven for stolen goods and illicit activities. Realizing that, in his words, "My pad is hot," Ginsberg decided to relocate his personal journals (full of incriminating information, both sexual and criminal) to his brother Eugene's place in Queens.[33] Driving him there in a stolen car were Little Jack Melody (he had done time for stealing a safe), junkie/writer Herbert Huncke, and Vicky Russell ("a naturally bitchy girl"). With Little Jack unsteady at the wheel, a turn was missed. The police were now in pursuit, and Little Jack headed the wrong way down a one-way street, pulling off to the side, careening and crashing. Chaos ensued. Ginsberg scrambled from the car, lost his glasses, and blindly scooped up scattered papers and journals. He escaped on the subway, trying to return home before the police arrived to arrest him. Thanks to a good lawyer, the intercession of bigwig Columbia professors, and his nervous, hangdog apologies Ginsberg avoided criminal charges.[34]

He was, however, sentenced to eight months at the New York State Psychiatric Hospital, starting late June 1949. His time was spent in intensive analysis and group meetings, playing ping-pong, writing, and becoming friends with another patient, Carl Solomon, to whom he would dedicate *Howl*. In the third section of the poem, Ginsberg recounted his experiences in the mental hospital with Solomon, who was presumably constrained in a straightjacket.[35] Ginsberg learned much from Solomon, especially about French culture. Together they struggled with the burden of genius and the demands of sexual gratification and identity. To Solomon, and all other bearers of the diagnosis of madness, Ginsberg proclaimed his solidarity again and again: "I'm with you in Rockland." To a degree, however, Ginsberg's period of confinement in a mental hospital, served as a sort of sabbatical, a time for reflection, for figuring out paths to pursue, and for finding some surcease from the harrowing situations with his mother and friends.[36]

The results proved mixed. Convinced that he must abandon his homosexuality, Ginsberg entered into a relationship with Helen Parker after getting discharged, losing his heterosexual virginity to her in 1950. He promised himself as well to tone down his rebellious instincts. Both these resolutions would be temporary.

Death and violence loomed large, alongside madness, in Ginsberg's life and in *Howl*—and in the lives and work of many creators of the New Sensibility. In the decade prior to Ginsberg's composition of the poem, his life had felt as if it had been littered with the dead bodies of close friends and family, not to mention the mountain of corpses produced in the Holocaust, Second World War, and Korean conflict. And ever present, in Ginsberg's mind, was the potential for atomic annihilation. All of this weighed on Ginsberg as he composed his poem and helped form the words "Who created great suicidal dramas on the apartment cliff-banks of the Hudson under the wartime blue floodlight of the moon & their heads shall be crowned with laurel in oblivion."[37]

As an undergraduate at Columbia, Ginsberg was part of an edgy coterie: the strikingly beautiful and habitually bored Lucien Carr; the handsome, athletic, and artistically talented Kerouac; and the drug-addled and slyly sinister William Burroughs. David Kammerer, an older homosexual acquaintance of Carr's from Saint Louis, arrived in the city one day in 1944 and became part of the group. Mainly, he was desperate to win Carr's affection. Kammerer failed miserably, and, according to some accounts, he tried to impose his drunken desire on Carr during a hot August night in Riverside Park. Carr stabbed Kammerer to death and dumped his body into the Hudson River. Kerouac helped dispose of the bloody blade.[38]

Death struck again and again in Ginsberg's circle. His friend Bill Cannastra perished on 12 October 1950. He was on a subway train with friends, apparently in good spirits. In one account, Cannastra suddenly decided to climb out the window of the train to get back to the station to go to some nearby bar. Carr offered a different view, stating that Cannastra had simply, and stupidly, stuck his head out the window in a daredevil manner and struck a pillar. An afternoon paper was headlined: "Loses Last Gamble for a Drink." Ginsberg concluded later that day: "It was not apparently a fully conscious suicide." The night before, at the San Remo bar in Greenwich Village, Cannastra had told

Ginsberg that he was "coming to an end." Cannastra had been dealing with his homosexual inclinations and his budding love for a woman, as well as with his depression and drinking. Perhaps Ginsberg saw in Cannastra—"head carnaged after sunset"—his own image and his own generation. He had certainly entertained his own thoughts of suicide, pushing them aside and curtly commenting: "Curiosity is the only thing that keeps me from suicide." A few years later, he acknowledged more maturely that the time had come to jettison the "chaotic element which is ultimately death-dealing."[39]

The "death-dealing" nature of "chaotic," drunken, and drug-infested lives hit home again a year later. Joan Vollmer, a mother figure of sorts to Ginsberg, was killed in Mexico in September 1951 by her husband, William Burroughs. It was a most absurd death. Accounts of what happened vary, but the most common one is that they were both inebriated as Burroughs fired his .38-caliber revolver to demonstrate his keen marksmanship by shooting a tumbler off Joan's head. He missed, and she was killed in an instant. Although indicted, Burroughs was able to flee Mexico and, in the end, receive a wrist-slap two-year suspended sentence for involuntary manslaughter.[40]

The trail of blood and violence in young Ginsberg's life was reflected in *Howl*, as was the violence of the society at large. John Clellon Holmes, a novelist, remarked that the beats were the first generation to come of age under the cloud of atomic annihilation—"the final answer to all questions" (see chapter 11).[41] Ginsberg's poetry prior to *Howl* was focused on images of apocalypse (influenced here by William Blake) but also composed after the Soviet Union had detonated its own atomic device in August 1949. Most notably, in the poem "Siesta in Xbalba" he combined imagery from the New Testament with more up-to-date political realities. Speaking of the United States, Ginsberg imagined "detonation of infernal bombs" which led to "the silent downtown... in watery dusk submersion."[42]

Nuclear-weapon metaphors energized *Howl*, most famously in the description of "angel-headed hipsters" who were "listening to the crack of doom on the hydrogen jukebox." This was one of many examples of Ginsberg's use of the surrealist technique of abrupt juxtaposition. But the image is haunting because it connects the liveliness of music with the destruction of the world. Later in the poem, he returns to the term "hydrogen," writing of the evil, "vast stone of war" that is Moloch, "whose fate is a cloud of sexless hydrogen." Moloch destroys not only through war but also through the voraciousness of capitalism, the repression of freedom, and the creation of fear.[43] Moloch, an evil God-king in the Old Testament, had reputedly demanded the sacrifice of children. In Milton's poem, *Paradise Lost*, Moloch was a fallen angel, waging war against God. In either case, he was a grim figure. While Ginsberg associated Moloch with evil, he also, in a manner, identified with him (if not explicitly in the poem) as revolting against the Father of staid, traditional poetry.[44]

Ginsberg's specific vision of Moloch was partly inspired by a nighttime view of the Sir Francis Drake Hotel in San Francisco, under the influence of peyote—"Moloch Moloch smoking in red glare downtown . . . with robust eyes and skullface, in smoke."[45] After this vision, Ginsberg "wandered down Powell Street muttering, 'Moloch, Moloch' all night," before settling into an all-night cafeteria to write the Moloch section of the poem "nearly intact . . . deep in the hellish vale."[46]

Moloch, embodied by the high tower with its pulsating lights, became a powerful, incantatory device in the poem, summoning forth all that Ginsberg disdained: materialism, conformity, numbing rationalism, love denied; it is the eruption of warfare, "whose fingers are ten armies!" It is cold death and living evil.[47]

Like Marlon Brando in the role of Johnny, Ginsberg in *Howl* was rebelling against much of what American culture and society "got" in the early 1950s, with bravado and excess. Ginsberg had seen *The Wild Ones* prior to composing his poem. Repression, in the service of conformity, had imprisoned him and his friends in jails and mental institutions and pushed them to suicide and depression. For Ginsberg Moloch was enforced conformity and death.

A year before Ginsberg composed *Howl*, the issue of conformity in America was being hotly debated among intellectuals, from both left and right-wing perspectives. Irving Howe wrote a piece, "This Age of Conformity," for the highbrow publication *Partisan Review*. His subtitle was "Notes on an Endless Theme, or, A Catalogue of Complaints."

Howe's particular bugaboo was mass culture. He claimed it lowered standards and promoted conformity. He feared that intellectuals had succumbed to its siren song and thus lost their critical edge. The natural stance of the intellectual, he argued, was to be alienated from society rather than from one's self. Too many of his fellow intellectuals, now that they had jettisoned the radical politics of the 1930s, had drifted into a lifeless conformity. The only hope, it seemed, was for a new, critical avant-garde to challenge the Moloch of conformity.[48]

From a more conservative perspective came a similar critique of conformity. Alan Valentine, who had once won Olympic gold as a rugby player and served as the youngest president of the University of Rochester in its history, weighed in with a book, *The Age of Conformity* (1954). Like Ginsberg, albeit without poetic vituperation, he condemned American conformity for its materialism, diminution of individualism, vulgarity, salaciousness, spiritual vacuity, fanatical tolerance, disdain for tradition, and the ignorance of the public.[49]

Ginsberg agreed with many of Howe's and Valentine's complaints about the numbing effects of materialism and conformity. To oppose conformity, to rail against the bourgeoisie, of course, had long been a staple, even a requirement for avant-garde, indeed for radical and conservative opponents of the status quo. For self-conscious avant-gardists like Ginsberg and his comrades, craving a new sensibility, they wanted to toss away bourgeois constraints and bring forth a "bop apocalypse."

Ginsberg went well beyond Howe's calm, traditionalist avant-garde stance through his allegiance to spontaneity in prose and embrace of excess. Against Valentine's clear dismissal of the salacious, Ginsberg embraced eroticism and sexual liberation as holy. He wrote of those "who let themselves be fucked in the ass by saintly motorcyclists and screamed with joy," and he announced further, "The bum's as holy as the seraphim! the madman is holy as you my soul are holy!"[50]

Howl was also a Whitmanesque ode to the joys of sexual activity, in its wild variety and uninhibited freedom. In the years prior to composition of the poem, Ginsberg had been an explorer—engaging in masochistic, occasional sex with Cassady, shadowy sex in subway bathrooms with strangers, and intercourse with a few women. In a sense, *Howl* is a confession and cataloging of the varieties of the sexual experience that hit prudish America right in the gut, or maybe a bit lower anatomically.

The poem was a roadmap of the homosexual underworld. In contrast with Cage and Rauschenberg, who kept their homosexuality under wraps or practiced silence in their works of art, effacing the personality, Ginsberg went the opposite route, big time. Masturbation, homosexuality, anal sex, pederasty, blow jobs, and more are mentioned and celebrated. Ginsberg takes his reader on a tour of sexual delights (which are all too readily repressed by conformist authorities): to "a Turkish Bath when the blond & naked angel came to pierce them with a sword;" "who blew and were blown by those human seraphim, the sailors, caresses of Atlantic and Caribbean love;" of those "with dreams, with drugs, with waking nightmares, alcohol and cock and endless balls."[51]

All of this, Ginsberg proclaimed in his "Footnote" to the poem, was "holy." Holy, Holy, Holy.

Howl was a revelation to those hankering to break from academic strictures about proper poetic form and content and for those yearning for a model of rebellion. Novelist and chronicler of the Greenwich Village scene Ronald Sukenick labeled *Howl* "a call to consciousness" against what he termed the "flat fifties." Poet Diane di Prima believed that the poem signaled that "a new era had begun" by veering sharply away from the erudite and constrained toward "the language of the streets." "My life changed overnight," recalled Ed Sanders, later to be part of the rock/radical group the Fugs, when reading *Howl* soon after its publication.[52]

Not all readers were enamored. John Hollander, an undergraduate acquaintance of Ginsberg at Columbia, now beginning his climb up the ladder of academic poetry and criticism, savaged *Howl*. In *Partisan Review* Hollander castigated Ginsberg's "utter lack of decorum of any kind in this dreadful little volume." The poem's confessional style—and its recounting of the horrible lives of his compatriots among the beats—dismayed Hollander. A "hopped up" and "improvised" method had led astray an otherwise talented young poet. Lionel Trilling, Ginsberg's former professor at Columbia and perhaps the leading man of letters in the United States in the mid-1950s, dismissed the poem as "all rhetoric without any music." Trilling indicted Ginsberg for striving self-consciously and dully "to be violent and shocking." Trilling, who had thrived in academe despite anti-Semitism, lived in a shell of restraint and refinement, hiding in his personal journal a desire to escape, to feel more and analyze less. Perhaps his vituperation against Ginsberg masked some of his own inner tensions, but he unkindly closed his criticisms of Ginsberg with the absurd proclamation that "there is no real voice here."[53]

Ginsberg responded to Hollander at great length, explaining patiently and pedantically about his methodology, long strophes, "surrealistic imagery," and more. He maintained that the poem was "built like a brick shit house." About their former professor, Ginsberg jibed that Trilling had a "tin ear" and was "absolutely lost in poetry." *Howl* was a broadside against constipated tradition, resting comfortably and confidently in both its excess and subject matter.[54]

In a sagacious letter to his lawyer brother, Eugene, while the manuscript of *Howl* was being printed in Europe before shipment to America, Ginsberg wrote, "I use cunts, cocks, balls, assholes, snatches, fucks, and comes liberally scattered around in the prosody." He asked, "Know a good lawyer?" He would soon need one.

On the evening of May 21, 1957, San Francisco undercover police inspectors Russell Woods and Thomas Pagee entered City Lights Bookstore. They purchased a copy of *Howl* and a copy of the avant-garde journal *The Miscellaneous Man*. The collector of customs for San Francisco had earlier that spring seized copies of *Howl*, explaining that it was a book "that you wouldn't want your children to come across." But when challenged by the American Civil Liberties Union and examined further by the United States attorney for San Francisco, the copies were released for distribution. A week later, however, after due consideration of the book by San Francisco's Juvenile Division, two undercover police officers arrested bookstore clerk Shigeyoshi Murao for selling the book. A warrant was issued for the arrest of Lawrence Ferlinghetti, the owner of City Lights Bookstore and publisher of *Howl*. No charges were filed against Ginsberg, who was at the time aboard that merchant marine ship somewhere near the Arctic Circle.[55]

Prior to leaving the continental United States, Ginsberg, along with poet Gregory Corso, had been at a party in Los Angeles. About seventy-five people were present, including Anaïs Nin, the bewitching memoirist. Someone began heckling Corso during his reading. A drunken Ginsberg, for unknown reasons, challenged the heckler to disrobe. Then, to his own "great surprise," Ginsberg opted to do so himself. He reveled in his liberating nakedness; the audience squirmed with embarrassment. He put his clothes back on and then read from *Howl*.

While this might appear as a silly, drunken eruption, it indicated the direction in which the emerging New Sensibility was headed. Part of what made Ginsberg central to the moment was his performative style. His content—confessional, confrontational, surging with eroticism—was controversial enough. But in his Six Gallery reading and subsequent ones, he delivered the poem with emotion, straining for effect and rhythm, transforming poetic diction and decorum. Certainly, his wanting to perform *Howl* naked was revolutionary, collapsing the presumed distance between poet and poem, performer and audience.[56]

Following service in the merchant marines and after trips to Mexico and then New York City, Ginsberg traveled to Tangier, where he was to reside while the obscenity trial played out. He tried to follow the proceedings closely and to serve as distant cheerleader: "I wish I were there; there could really, we could really have a ball and win out in the end inevitably." Always savvy as a publicist and promoter, Ginsberg, no less than Ferlinghetti, understood that the legal case would generate publicity for *Howl* and pump up sales, which it did.[57]

It was an auspicious time for the legal proceedings. In a major Supreme Court case, *Roth v. United States*, Justice William Brennan's majority opinion had laid out new rules for what might constitute obscenity. The "Brennan doctrine," delivered in April 1957, was a landmark decision for freedom of expression. According to Brennan, material could not be considered obscene simply because it contained dirty and upsetting words. Rather, these words must be understood in the context of the entire work. Moreover, the ruling dealt with intent: Were the offending words and the work overall aimed to excite prurient interests? If not, then the work was legal. Finally, if the work possessed literary merit, it was not obscene.[58]

The ruling, at least in theory, changed the playing field. Many of the classics of literature, James Joyce's *Ulysses*, D. H. Lawrence's *Lady Chatterley's Lover*, Edmund Wilson's *Memoirs of Hecate County*, as well as works by Henry Miller, had all earlier been judged obscene in court cases. Despite the Supreme Court ruling, resistance continued against some expression. Local police officials would continue to prosecute novelists, comedians such as Lenny Bruce, films such as Jack Smith's *Flaming Creatures*, and more. The New Sensibility, with its focus on erotic excess (at least in the view of moral custodians) remained well into the mid-1960s an affront to standards of decorum and moral values. But by then such works were being produced in seemingly unstoppable profusion.

The case against *Howl* was argued in the courtroom of Judge Clayton W. Horn. The defense waived the right to trial by jury, opting to let Horn decide the case. Horn was a conservative Republican who also taught Sunday school. But, as it turned out, he was fair and considerate.

With the help of a legal team gathered by the American Civil Liberties Union, led by criminal attorney Jake Ehrlich, the defense had a rather easy time of it. The argument was that while particular words might be obscene, their presence in the work was artistically necessary and valid. This was also the view of the United States Supreme Court, as Ehrlich lectured Horn: "Some people think that certain four-letter words in and of themselves destroy mankind from a moral standpoint. This, of course, is not the law." And, he added, "The court must construe the book as a whole."[59]

The defense trotted out some impressive witnesses. Each attested to the literary value of *Howl*. University of California literary critic Mark Schorer noted that some of the offensive words were common as "language of the street" and "absolutely essential to the esthetic purpose of the work." He also found a stirring critique of materialism, conformity, and militarism at the heart of the book, rendered in surrealist fashion. Also testifying on behalf of *Howl* was Walter Van Tilburg Clark, the Pulitzer Prize–winning novelist who wrote *The Ox-Bow Incident*. Kenneth Rexroth, the poet who had emceed the Six Gallery reading, further hailed the poem.[60]

Prosecutor Ralph McIntosh was outgunned from the start. He admitted to lacking a poetic sensibility, but he maintained repeatedly that the book was obscene simply because it contained dirty words and "lewd passages." He often asked witnesses for the defense to explain "obtuse" passages for him, content to rest his case on the poem having dirty words and being difficult for a layman to understand.[61]

McIntosh offered witnesses to condemn the work. The first admitted that the work had "literary value," albeit "negligible" literary value. Gail Potter, who identified herself as a teacher, was more assured: the work had "no literary merit" since it lacked "form, diction, fluidity, [and] clarity" of style. She was offended and upset that it had words that belonged in the gutter.[62]

On October 3, 1957, Judge Horn issued his ruling clearing Ferlinghetti (charges against his assistant Murao had already been dropped). Relying on the *Roth* decision, Horn had no choice but to find the book not obscene. For a work to be censored, the Judge announced, it had to do a lot of bad things— intend to "deprave or corrupt readers by exciting lascivious thoughts or arousing lustful desires" that would actually lead to "anti-social or immoral action." The offensive words in any book had to be considered in light of the work as a whole. And those words, "even if coarse and vulgar," must be allowed when the work in question had literary merit. Before dismissing the case against Ferlinghetti, Judge Horn quoted the French motto "Honi soit qui mal y pense" (Evil to him who evil thinks).[63]

The evil Moloch of censorship, at least in this case, had been vanquished. But new challenges to the status quo, in this case in the frenzied form of rock and roll, soon erupted.

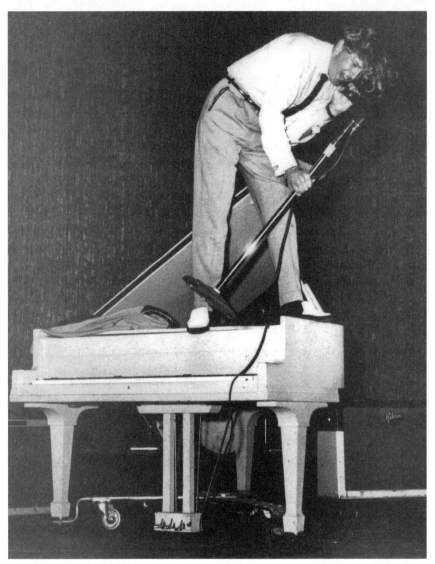

Jerry Lee Lewis (© Photofest)

"Great Balls of Fire"

JERRY LEE LEWIS

1957

It was getting awfully close to 9:00 p.m. on Sunday night, July 28, 1957, when *The Steve Allen Show* was scheduled to end. Viewers had already endured two sappy songs: Jodie Sands's "With All My Heart" and the Four Coins' "Shangri-La." Actors Shelley Winters and Tony Franciosa had done a comedy sketch about their recent marriage, and the show had involved the usual tomfoolery from Allen and his talented cast of regulars. Finally, after introducing an advertisement for Johnson Stride Wax, Allen reassured his audience: "Stay tuned for some rock and roll." The next performer, he said, "destroys the piano and everything."

After the messy floor in the advertisement had been miraculously cleaned and made brightly shining thanks to Stride Wax, Allen announced, "Here he is, jumpin' and joltin' Jerry Lee Lewis." The drummer and bass player wore sport coats, but Lewis had on a striped short-sleeved shirt that exposed his sinewy arms. His white shoes and white belt also stood out. He immediately attacked the piano and banged out his hit song "Whole Lotta Shakin' Goin' On." Careful listeners, if they could hear over the pounding piano, might have been able to discern lyrics, delivered in a lusty fashion: "Come on over baby well, we got the bull by the horn / We ain't fakin' / Whole lot of shakin' goin' on."[1]

The rhythm built and Lewis tossed his head back and forth, up and down. His pomaded blond hair started to flop wildly—first it came dangling down in the front, then some excited strands in the back began their own dance. He sat at a diagonal to the piano to keep better eye contact with the audience. His feet tapped with abandon. At one point in the song, he instructed a woman how to shake for him: "Easy now, shake, ah shake, you can shake one time for me." His voice grew lower and slower, and he shook his hand for emphasis: "All you gotta do, honey, stand in one spot." His confidence was that of a sexual veteran, a rockin' Casanova. "Shake one time for me." Then he glanced upward, in a state of religious or sexual ecstasy. He was greased lightning, unable to stay seated; he kicked the piano stool away, then he jumped and shaked all over. All of this from a twenty-one-year-old on national television for the first time.

Kids were delighted. The rock critic Robert Palmer, then a "pimply faced" twelve-year-old living in Little Rock, Arkansas, was dazzled, he recalled, "the first time I heard the pummeling beat, the casual sexiness, the leering invitation." He rushed to the local grocery store, where next to the meat department stood a rack holding the latest record releases. Without any money, Palmer shoplifted the record; he felt that he could not live without it.[2] Another fan remembered that "Lewis wasn't like any of the others....If they were wild, he was ferocious. If their music was sexy, his was promiscuous."[3] Kay Martin, a teen in Brooklyn, soon to become president of the Jerry Lee Lewis fan club, admitted that Lewis, unlike Elvis, "didn't want to cuddle you like a teddy bear, he wanted to show you his great balls of fire; he was telling the girls there'd be a whole lot of shakin' goin on."[4]

Adults, in contrast, were disgusted. One Texas radio station manager contacted Sam Phillips, whose Sun Records label featured Lewis, to inform him that he would not play "songs by niggers." After being told that Lewis was white, the manager maintained his disdain, telling Phillips that such lewd music was improper for his listeners.[5]

Jerry Lee Lewis was neither the most talented nor the most original of the singers in the early years of rock. But for a host of reasons, wrapped up in the ever present conundrum of race and sexuality, his music leered with more lust than that of most performers on the national stage. He refused, as rock historian Greil Marcus puts it, to accept limits, presenting himself as the embodiment of the southern redneck, a man who "seemed possessed" by demons both personal and social. Or, as another rock critic stated, "In a profession founded on excess, Lewis has made his name as one of the most excessive."[6]

Lewis's black contemporaries in rock and roll, Little Richard, Chuck Berry, and Fats Domino, carried greater burdens on their backs. They had to mask their sexuality behind smiles and innuendo. As writer Norman Mailer demonstrated in an essay in *Dissent* magazine, even presumably enlightened northerners embraced the myth of black males as sexually charged. In the South, segregation remained stubbornly rooted, and the myth of black lust for white women was widely employed to justify suppression of black rights. The strength of this myth was demonstrated tragically in 1955. Emmett Till, a fourteen-year-old black child from Chicago, was visiting relatives in Money, Mississippi. Till had been accused of the sin of whistling at a white woman. That woman's husband and her brother-in-law soon made Till pay with his life. They beat him brutally, gouged out one of his eyes, and then shot him. Tying heavy weights to his limp body, the brothers tossed him in the Tallahatchie River. His body was found three days later.[7]

By 1957, southern racism raged at fevered pitch. The 1954 Supreme Court decision in *Brown v. Board of Education* finally overturned doctrine that having separate black and white facilities was constitutional. Desegregation moved at a snail's pace. When it did occur, as in Little Rock, Arkansas, in 1957, trouble ensued. On a daily basis, a small number of black kids trudged from a bus to all-white Central High School, facing jeering, angry white mobs. Sometimes the pain came from beatings, or white students tossing the black kids' books to the ground. "Nigger go home" was written in lipstick on bathroom mirrors in the school.[8] These years also saw a renewal of Ku Klux Klan activity and White Citizens' Council assaults upon blacks.

Black performers walked a fine line when dealing with sexual issues, especially in front of white audiences. An uproar occurred on a television show, for example, in 1957 when an exuberant Frankie Lymon, the lead singer for the Teenagers, suddenly bounded onto the dance floor to take a turn or two with a white girl. As one show official remarked, "This could get us into trouble." And it did.[9] Traditional racial sensibilities were flouted also when blonde singer Dinah Shore gave black singer Nat King Cole a peck on the cheek after they had performed; many southern affiliates cancelled the show in angered reaction. But television was defying the constrained expectations of race and culture in the South. Growing up in the 1950s in Sardis, Mississippi, Horace Newcomb found that, for him and others, "television expanded our world and with that expansion challenged it in unexpected and doubtless, unplanned ways," opening up new views on race, pleasure, and even the nature of rebellion. It allowed a new sensibility to peer through.[10]

Despite such strained racial realities, African American singers continued to perform, including songs with sexual hints. After all, rhythm and blues and rock were to a degree about unleashed sexual energy. As historian David R. Shumway points out, in the 1950s kids did have sex on their minds, perhaps more than ever before. This did not mean, however, that depictions of it could be "sexually explicit." Quite the opposite. Violence and sexuality in comic books and television were controlled. For cultural conservatives, sexuality in rock and roll, then, had to be contained, or made nonthreatening, especially when the performer was a black male singing for a white female audience.[11]

No performer, with perhaps the exception of Jerry Lee Lewis, was more outrageous than Little Richard. His songs smoked with sexual innuendo and energy, and his onstage persona was highly sexualized, but to the point of nonthreatening camp. With his hair piled high and liberally pomaded, his eyeshadow, and his razor-thin mustache, Little Richard sang in a falsetto voice that trilled. His effeminacy seemed to mark him as sexually harmless to white women. But he faded quickly from the scene; by 1957, he had abandoned rock for the Church of God of the Ten Commandments.[12] The calling of the spiritual world conflicted with the secular world of sin while at the same time lending that conflict a tension that rocked the shoes off audiences.

Chuck Berry understood the essentials of rock and race brilliantly. He was a highly sexualized figure, with a lean profile and good looks—and hence was a threat, especially in live performances. But he also possessed a punning sophistication. While his hit song "Brown Eyed Handsome Man" might offend racial proprieties, it did so in a veiled, jocular manner. He changed the original lyrics, written in 1956, from "brown skinned handsome man" to "brown eyed handsome man." The song was still challenging, since the lyrics addressed well-to-do, presumably white women, telling them that they would be better served by going out with a brown eyed handsome man.[13] Despite his humor and talent, Berry paid the price for his "ambiguous" lyrics, overt sexuality, and disregard for customs and laws. In 1959 he was arrested for violating the Mann Act, which prohibited the transportation of minors across state lines for illicit acts. The girl in question was a fourteen-year-old Native American; Berry claimed that he was under the impression that she was "of African heritage" and twenty-one years old. After a drawn-out court case, Berry was forced to spend over a year in prison.[14]

Growing up in Saint Louis with middle-class parents, Berry had been exposed to gospel music, rhythm and blues, and plenty of country music—he could even yodel. Indeed, Berry's eclectic mixture sometimes confounded audiences. Appearing before a largely black crowd at Harlem's Apollo Theater in 1955, Berry received a lukewarm reception. "Don't nobody wanna hear that crap," yelled one disgruntled listener. Much to Berry's surprise, his reception by white audiences was more favorable.[15]

Berry had his finger on the pulse of teenagers. One rock historian referred to Berry as the "folk poet of the fifties" for his ability to express the "ordinary realities of the world."[16] He crossed class and racial lines to find common ground with teenagers in the mysteries of love, the boredom of high school, and the excitement of speedy cars. Even more importantly, he captured the ultimate power of rock and roll: its ability to allow one to imagine liberation from the forces of the past, from parental control, and from social etiquette.[17] "Roll Over Beethoven" (1956), as the title suggests, told youngsters to stop listening to the staid classical tradition and fly high with rock. Again, in "Rock 'n' Roll Music" (1957), Berry announced that all he wanted was "rock 'n' roll music, any old way you choose it."

Another manner of controlling the presumed dangers black sexuality posed for young white girls was to coopt and control the music. The recording industry was, after all, big business; they cared little if the records sold were by black or white singers. One solution was to slow down the beat and heat of black rhythm and blues by having it performed by white singers.[18] Pat Boone was perhaps the most successful of these crooners, singing covers but with an old sensibility. He was not a bad singer, really, especially on ballads. But he took the stuffing out of the rock songs, diminishing the beat and stilling the rhythm to make it less edgy and sexually charged. Perhaps his most outrageous appropriation was of Little Richard's "Long Tall Sally"—the original being a raucous veiled tribute to transvestites. Boone's version failed to become a big hit. *Billboard* remarked in response that "it certainly looks as tho the public is beginning to show a decided preference for the originals—regardless of their origins."[19]

Navigating sexuality was complicated but much less dangerous for white rockers. Elvis Presley did it successfully, at least early in his career. It was not for nothing that he was called "Elvis the Pelvis." His pelvic movements were seen as so sexually provocative that one time on television the lower half of his body was hidden from view. According to *Life* magazine: "He uses a bump and grind routine seen only in burlesque."[20] Presley did appropriate black musical style and movements that he had observed in Memphis clubs. Sam Phillips, head of Sun Records, the Memphis studio that produced many of the early rock hits, said, "If I could find a white man who had the Negro sound and the Negro feel, I could make a million dollars."[21] Elvis fit that bill to a tee.

Indeed, one problem early in Elvis's career was the perception—given his song choices and singing style—that he was a black man. His controlling and capable manager, Colonel Parker, remedied that situation, and with alacrity. He let it be known, when Elvis was first achieving airplay in Memphis, that he had graduated from Humes High School, which in that age of segregation meant that he had to be white.

Nonetheless, the path to success was marked by a constant tension between images of Elvis. On the one hand, with his black leather jacket, slicked hair, and black-style vocalizing and dancing, Elvis had an air of danger, fitting well into the juvenile delinquent corner of culture. In those years, parents and educators fretted mightily about delinquency, and movie companies made a mint producing such films as *Blackboard Jungle, The Wild One*, and *Rebel without a Cause* depicting teens in rebellion. Elvis tempered his rebelliousness with sterling southern manners and boyish sincerity. And he increasingly sprinkled his repertoire with sugary ballads such as "Love Me Tender" and gospel songs. Although in his second film, *Jailhouse Rock*, he played a young man who had served time in prison for manslaughter, the character he played emerged from jail with a mission to show himself to be a talented and good person. Military service and a series of inane films further diminished Elvis's status as a threat to morals.

Jerry Lee Lewis "made Elvis look like a boy scout," according to rock historian Reebee Garofalo.[22]

Lewis was a child of the poor (but not dirt poor) white south. The family lived in a shack, without electricity and indoor plumbing. The area around

Ferriday, in northeastern Louisiana, was sodden with humidity and blessed with bass-rich lakes. Then, as now, Ferriday had an African American majority population and plenty of churches—both black and white. His father, Elmo Lewis, was a large, angular, strong man with a gargantuan appetite for hard labor who relaxed by playing guitar. His income derived from farming (corn and cotton) and from carpentry, although he also helped run a still. For the latter activity, he was once imprisoned. Lewis's mother also labored long and hard, loved music, and was always supportive of Jerry Lee. She was devoted to the Pentecostal church. The family worked land owned by an uncle who was the richest man in town, highlighting how inequalities of wealth remained despite family connections.[23]

At an early age, Lewis proved himself to be a musical prodigy. He began with guitar, but after a visit to an aunt who owned a piano Lewis only wanted to boogie and slam the keys. By late 1943, thanks to building projects connected with the Second World War, Lewis's parents were working steadily, earning enough money to buy some land. And they also managed to purchase a used piano for their son. It was a generous move and wise choice. His sister reported that Jerry could "by his early teens...stop a train with his piano playing."[24] Lewis was certainly more adept at the piano than at school—his report card was strewn with Fs, thanks to his flagging attention and attendance. Lewis did not devote himself to piano study—he had only a couple of lessons. Along with friends and cousins, he explored the sleazy side of Ferriday, or at least what seemed sleazy to the perspective of congregants of the Pentecostal church.

Will Haney's Big House was a bar owned by an African American entrepreneur. Catering mostly to blacks, the bar offered music, drink, and gambling. Touring black rhythm and blues acts, Ray Charles, B. B. King, and others performed onstage in front of a handful of reserved tables. Victor Haney, Will's brother, served as security, his fist encased in brass knuckles. But daring and speedy young white children, such as Jerry Lee and his cousins, might sneak in sometimes to catch a glimpse of the performers and delight in the wild music.[25]

This sounds like a rehash of a familiar theme, the young southern white boy weaned on the blues. To a degree it rings true, but it is also inadequate. Influences are mingled and many, especially when it comes to music, and especially in the South. There is no reason to doubt the list of performers that Lewis acknowledged as his childhood heroes. When he was around twelve years old, Lewis heard a recording of Al Jolson singing "Down among the Shimmering Pines," and he was transfixed. He practiced that song over and over again, seeking to emote like Jolson. He adored country singers Jimmie Rodgers and Hank Williams. He would stand outside of the Ferriday movie theater and listen to Gene Autry, the singing cowboy, perform in his many popular films. Whenever near a radio, Lewis tuned in to country music, to *Barn Dance*, which later became *The*

Grand Ole Opry and another program, *Louisiana Hayride*.[26] He sopped it all up, with glee.

Popular music in general, and rock and roll in particular, was an amalgam of various styles and genres.[27] Sometimes they pushed against one another uneasily; sometimes they melded effortlessly; sometimes that combination created something original and exciting. In the process, what was "authentic" and "inauthentic" became confused.[28] Chuck Berry was known disparagingly by some blues purists as a "hillbilly rocker." African American Big Mama Thornton famously sang "Hound Dog," which Elvis later appropriated and made into a huge hit. This seems, at first glance, a clear case of white appropriation of a black song. However, the composers of the song were Jerry Leiber and Mike Stoller, a couple of Jewish guys from New York City. Then, again, they wanted to be "white negroes," effecting a black style and dating black women.[29] For all of the appropriation of black songs by Boone and others, Doo Wop singers regularly recorded songs that had been composed by whites in the 1930s and 1940s. The bloodlines of rock, then, especially in its early days, were perfectly fitted to an emerging New Sensibility that rejected strict separation of style, genres, and races. Of course, within a nexus of racism and cash, the terms of the exchanges were unequal, the benefits for whites more easily turned into serious money.

Lewis's musical sensibility grew out of his religious upbringing. Pentecostals, also known as "holy rollers," held theatrical and spontaneous church services. Singing was raucous and sermonizing inspired, the lines between sexual and spiritual ecstasy inexact. The Holy Spirit took hold of congregants—they would suddenly leap or faint with joy. Speaking in tongues was not uncommon, another sign that the Holy Spirit was suddenly dwelling within. Illnesses, it was believed, could be cured by a laying on of hands, with the sick falling backward as they were miraculously cured. In some congregations, with absolute belief in Biblical inerrancy, congregants proved the depth of their faith and presence of the Holy Spirit by handling poisonous snakes. Sometimes, in the heat of religious rapture, congregants danced or became wooden, twitched and screamed. The Pentecostal church, in sum, was a perfect spot for Lewis to perfect his own theatrical style. It also bequeathed to him a heightened, sometimes burdensome, tension between the sins of the flesh in the secular world and the necessity of redemption in the spiritual world.[30]

By the age of thirteen, Lewis was a professional performer, appearing in bars and juke joints, playing and singing in a boogie-woogie style. A gig at the Blue Cat Club in Natchez, Mississippi, earned him ten bucks. He performed often at his church, singing and playing piano. Given his repertoire at the Blue Cat Club, he was not living a conventionally holy life. Wracked by guilt, perhaps pressured by his mother, and also recently married and with a child, Jerry Lee embarked for the Southwestern Bible Institute of Waxahachie in Texas, a school associated with the Assemblies of God Church. With his talent for extemporaneous speech and his mesmerizing personality, he seemed a natural for the clergy. Students at Waxahachie were expected to demonstrate "clean conduct and conversation, modest apparel in dress, high standards of moral life."

It quickly became clear that a ministerial road was not to be traveled by Lewis. He skipped classes and escaped from the dormitory at night to hitchhike to Dallas, thirty miles away, to attend films, followed by making the rounds of nightclubs. After three months of at best desultory attendance at the school, as one story has it, Lewis was asked to perform "My God Is Real" at chapel service. Lewis obliged but played the hymn in fast-paced boogie-woogie style, doubling the tempo. Apparently, most in the audience began to feel the spirit— holy or otherwise. The authorities, however, failed to detect God's presence, and Lewis was expelled from the school. As he put it, "You can't get the Bible from all these silly books y'all got here."[31]

The rest of Lewis's story resembles the scenario captured in Chuck Berry's classic "Johnny B. Goode"—although the instrument of choice in this case was the piano rather than guitar. The song depicted a poor kid from the country who, thanks to talent and determination, became a rock star. After his failure at Bible school and the drudgery of various unskilled jobs, Lewis headed in 1956 to Memphis to court Sam Phillips, the owner of Sun Records. With immense brashness, not to mention talent, Lewis believed that he could be the next Elvis, Johnny Cash, Roy Orbison, or Carl Perkins. All he needed was a chance.

The folks at Sun Records were dazzled by Lewis's confidence and talent. In short order, they released his first recording, "Crazy Arms," which earlier that year had been recorded by Ray Price. It was a hit, and Lewis soon purchased a "red Cadillac convertible with white leather interior."[32] The song's themes were typical of country music: a lover who has been jilted but now longs for the woman because she "holds somebody new." Hints of Lewis's signature style were apparent. He opened with some fancy piano work, sliding his fingers across the keys a couple of times, and he took a long break in the middle of the song to play boogie-woogie style, before returning to country crooning. He repeated phrases for emphasis: "Not mine, not mine, not mine." It was Lewis's first hit, albeit on a small scale compared to what soon followed.[33]

With the huge popularity of his second recording, "Whole Lotta Shakin' Goin' On," the challenge was to find another song for Lewis to record. Sun Records let it be known that they were looking for material. Otis Blackwell, a prolific African American songwriter, born in Brooklyn, wrote songs infused with country and rhythm and blues styles. He had already scored hits with "Fever" (recorded first by Little Willie John for the R & B market, then by Peggy Lee for a huge national audience) and Elvis's "Don't Be Cruel."

"Great Balls of Fire," composed by Blackwell and sung by Lewis, came out as a record less than a month after the United States had been rattled by the Soviet Union's successful launch of a satellite into outer space. As the *New York Times* remarked, Sputnik "represented a step toward escape from man's imprisonment to earth and its thin envelope of atmosphere."[34] Sputnik's transmitters sent radio signals back to earth. While many youth were fascinated with Sputnik, they were beginning to exult in other possibilities for radio waves. Technology had developed transistor radios in 1954, although the initial models were expensive and bulky. But by December 1957, when "Great Balls of Fire" was a huge hit, teens could purchase a portable transistor radio for about $39.95, with prices dropping rapidly in 1958 thanks to imports from Japan. In a metaphorical sense, young people for the last couple of years had been going "out of this world" with the new beat of rock and roll. The task for Lewis's new song was to launch them for about two minutes, rather than the ninety-six required by Sputnik to orbit around the earth.

"Great Balls of Fire" reproduced much of the sound and sense of "Whole Lotta Shakin' Goin' On." The song was recorded at Sun Studio, probably in late August—and the first take was a keeper. "Great Balls of Fire," as Sam Phillips anticipated, got attention, given its sexually suggestive title and typical rhythmic explosions. It quickly became a hit single in November 1957. Concurrently, Lewis and his bandmates were filmed performing the new song in a studio, as part of an emerging genre, the rock and roll film. *Jamboree*, which hit national screens in December, was based on the flimsiest of conceits, but few viewers were there for the storyline. They wanted to see their rock heroes in action: Fats Domino, Buddy Knox, and Lewis (along with an odd medley of other acts, including for some reason the Count Basie Orchestra, featuring Joe Williams).

By this time, Lewis's ego had ballooned, although in this case it was tempered with critical acumen. Myra Lewis, his most recent bride, wanted to watch her husband's performance in the film at a private screening. Lewis refused to allow her to enter the theater until his one-minute-and-forty-second appearance on screen. "There ain't nothin' to it but my song, anyhow."[35]

Lewis's wild, leering performances while on tour brought home the sexual content to even the dullest of libidos. While working on the arrangement for "Great Balls" at Sun Studio, and after some serious drinking, Lewis and Sam Phillips "got into the damnedest religious argument."[36] Lewis referred to the song as the devil's music, which would lead straight to "H-E-L-L," as Lewis spelled out the word for emphasis or for fear of cursing. His vehemence was met with counterarguments. Sam Phillips saw no reason why a rock singer could not still do God's work in the secular world, perhaps even saving souls. "No! No! No! No!" shouted Lewis. "How can the Devil save souls? . . . Man, I got the *Devil* in me!" They argued until in the early hours of the morning. Finally, tired of the debate, Lewis, as he usually did, succumbed to the sinful side of his nature and recorded the song.[37]

> You shake my nerves and you rattle my brain
> Too much love drives a man insane
> You broke my will
> But what a thrill
> Goodness gracious great balls of fire.

So opened the song. Later, he sings, "Oooh, feels gooood.... I wants to love you like a lover should." It was a healthy dose of sin on vinyl. Lewis was enthralled, almost to the point of being out of control in love with this woman. With exuberance, he sings:

> You're fine, so kind
> Got to tell this world that you're mine mine mine mine.

Lewis was wild on the piano. He banged the keys and made the glissando central to his playing. His hair flopped with the music. He often paused between songs to neaten it, slowly extracting a comb from his pocket. The piano stool or chair was always kicked aside in the heat of passion, and he would also briefly play the piano with his feet. Sometimes he jumped atop the piano. This was showmanship, to be sure, but it evoked the Holy Spirit expressing itself in the salvation of rock and roll music. It was thrilling, edgy, even dangerous.

Although many parts of the story may be apocryphal, some maintain that at one performance Lewis set a piano on fire. At the Paramount Theater in New York City in March 1958, as part of a show organized by rock DJ Alan Freed, a dispute arose over which act would close the bill. There were plenty of high-quality performers: Chuck Berry, Jerry Lee, Buddy Holly, and Frankie Lymon. Lewis wanted to do it, but the honor fell to Berry. Lewis was relegated to the penultimate act. Always cocky, Lewis was pissed off. There seems agreement about the following. Lewis was singing, appropriately, "Great Balls of Fire," when he somehow managed to drip some lighter fluid onto the piano and set it on fire. With each telling of the story, of course, the fire has grown bigger. Lewis continued playing a bit while the fire burned. He strutted off the stage as the crowd went ballistic with excitement, and he passed Berry. According to Nick Tosches's account in his biography of Lewis, Lewis accosted Berry with the words: "Follow that, nigger." Lewis, who liked to embellish tales or lie outright, later said: "Burned that damn piana to the ground.... They forced me to do it, tellin' me I had to go on before Chuck."[38] Another account strikes a different note. Lewis had many bad traits, but he respected Berry's talent and that of other African American musicians. He was competitive. Once told that he would perform before Johnny Cash at a concert, Lewis went all out and, as he left the crowd swooning, said to Cash side-stage, "'Nobody follows the Killer.'" According to Rick Bragg, another Lewis biographer, in similar fashion that night, Lewis snarled at Berry, "I want to see you follow that, Chuck."[39]

Such shenanigans, real and imagined, have become part of rock folklore and inflamed parents, educators, and religious leaders around the country, especially in the Bible Belt southern states. Many cringed at the racial miscegenation at the heart of rock and roll, its affront to sexual propriety, its "primitivism," and its connection to an imagined spate of juvenile delinquency. Newspapers covered in sensational detail when fights and riots broke out at rock concerts.[40] In Birmingham, Alabama, in 1956, even such a smooth singer as Nat King Cole, who routinely played before segregated audiences in the South, was assaulted onstage by members of the White Citizens' Council screaming "Let's go get that coon." They hit Cole and threw him to the ground.[41] Record-burning rallies were organized by fundamentalist churches to save the souls of youngsters from the evils of rock music. Voices condemning rock were common in the North as well. John Carroll, a priest in Boston, stated: "Rock and roll inflames and excites youth like jungle tom-toms." In the Midwest, the "Crusade for Decent Disks" focused attention on the obscenity of rhythm and blues recordings. While much of the antagonism to rock was racially oriented, African Americans also found some songs too heated for their tastes. In 1954, the black group Hank Ballard and the Midnighters wanted to record a tune, "Sock It to Me, Annie" aimed at their usual black audience. But the title seemed too lascivious, so it was changed to "Work with Me Annie." Although it became a bona fide rhythm and blues hit, many black radio stations refused to air it.[42]

Tooting his own horn, Lewis claimed that many parents thought "Whole Lotta Shakin' Goin' On" was the "most *risqué* record that they had ever heard." *Look* magazine reported that he made "parents mourn for the comparative quiet of Presley."[43] Acts like Lewis threatened the stability of the white race. According to the Alabama White Citizens' Council, "The obscenity and vulgarity of the rock-and-roll music is obviously a means by which the white man and his children can be driven down to the level of the nigger."[44]

In the end, it was not the fanaticism of the cultural custodians, racists, or any musical letdown that caused Lewis to fade from public attention. He handed opponents of rock a challenge to propriety that even he could not weather.

In December 1957, Lewis went with a friend, Glenda Burgess, a large woman, twenty-two years of age, to obtain a marriage license. Burgess, however, was not his betrothed. Instead, he planned to marry a remote cousin, Myra Gale Brown, who was thirteen years of age. She was also the daughter of the band's bass player. Burgess filled out the form as if she were Brown. Armed with the marriage license, Lewis and Myra then drove down to a "real dive" in Mississippi, where Reverend M. C. Whitten married them under a banner reading "Where your sacred hour of today becomes tender memories of tomorrow."[45]

The marriage got off to a bumpy start. Learning about it, Myra's dad went for his pistol but then decided to talk to the district attorney. He calmed down, perhaps because a rift with Lewis would send him back to his old dangerous job working on electrical wiring high above the ground. Further complicating the marriage was its illegality—Lewis's divorce from his previous wife, Jane Mitchum, with whom he had a child, was not yet official. He had thus both married a minor and committed bigamy.[46]

In May 1958, while touring in Great Britain (and being paid the then immense sum of $100,000), the marriage made headlines. Not only was Myra thirteen, but she looked tiny, even when wearing pumps and fashionable clothing and with her hair done up. Great balls of editorial fire and indignation swirled. Lewis had come to represent all of the lasciviousness that critics associated with rock and roll. The uproar in England traveled quickly to the States. Radio stations refused to play the music of a moral degenerate. He had just finished making an appearance in another rock film, *High School Confidential*, with his song from the film poised for success. According to Lewis, the record "was pulled off the charts and off the radio in one day."[47] And Dick Clark would not book him anymore on *American Bandstand*.[48]

Lewis seemed surprised by the hubbub. In part, he was always protected by his armor of self-confidence. It was common in Lewis's home region for young men to take very young brides. As he later explained, "I was a twenty-one-year old kid, and I didn't know whether I was comin' or goin'." And, as he sometimes added, he loved Myra.[49]

He even printed a long letter in *Billboard* magazine, in June 1958, addressed to his fans. He confessed that his "life has been stormy." But he also felt he had done nothing knowingly illegal or immoral. He called press coverage of his marriage a case of "sensationalism...a scandal started to sell papers." Lewis continued, "I hope that if I am washed up as an entertainer it won't be because of this bad publicity."[50] By 1959, now with Myra and a newborn child, Lewis admitted that "he was about broke."[51]

He was also caught up in a host of calamities that plagued rock music. In February 1959, in stormy weather, a plane carrying rockers Buddy Holly and Ritchie Valens crashed, killing all aboard. Although overstated, it was a day when, as Don McLean later sang, "the music died." By 1960, the record industry was pummeled by bad publicity and from congressional investigations about a payola scandal. Disk jockeys had regularly accepted—indeed expected—cash from record companies in return for playing songs and making them hits. Many of the nation's leading disk jockeys came under scrutiny. Attention focused on Alan Freed, who was fired from his station and quickly faded from view a broken figure; Dick Clark, who denied everything—despite evidence to the contrary—survived the scandal.

The edge of rock became dulled. Instead of the energy of Lewis and other early rockers, the commercial apparatus of rock—record companies and advertisers—began pumping up "clean" acts, with less attention paid to talent than looks. Handsome, with a swirl of hair rigged to stay on his forehead, Fabian became a heartthrob for young girls with his hit "Tiger." He growled mildly, but he failed to rock. Other good-looking young men joined him in the limelight. Bobby Rydell, Frankie Avalon, Tommy Sands, and James Darren had hit recordings that are best forgotten. Rock had entered its brief dark period. It would last only a few years: a sensibility premised on energy, pleasure, sex, and transgression could not be kept long under wraps.

Robert Frank, New York City *(© Robert Frank, from* The Americans; *courtesy Pace/MacGill Gallery)*

{7}

"To Nullify Explanation"

ROBERT FRANK

1958

The editors of *Popular Photography*, a magazine of sparkling images, technical virtuosity, and plentiful advertisements, hated Robert Frank's *The Americans*, a collection of photographs that he had taken while touring the United States. His work was incompetent, they said, reeking with "contempt for any standards of quality or discipline in technique." It was full of "meaningless blur, muddy exposure, drunken horizons, and general sloppiness...out-of-focus pictures, intense and unnecessary grain, converging verticals, a total absence of normal composition." The content of the images, the message that they conveyed, further riled the editors to the point of hysteria: "His book is an attack on America"; "a wart-covered picture of America"; "marred by spite, bitterness, and narrow prejudices"; "a slashing and biting attack"; it revealed "the desire to shock and provide cheap thrills."[1]

Even Gilbert Millstein, who had helped to launch Jack Kerouac's career with a beaming review of *On the Road* in the *New York Times*, was turned off by Frank's vision. He damned the images for their harshness, distrust, and distaste toward their subjects. A reviewer for the *San Francisco Chronicle* agreed, finding Frank's images "merely neurotic, and to some degree dishonest," for all that they depicted was an "Ugly American."[2]

Some viewed his work with admiration, however. *U.S. Camera, 1958* featured a lengthy portfolio of his images. In addition to their own words of praise, they included the opinion of Walker Evans—a master of photography for decades—Frank's photographs: "Positive, large, and basically generous." A reviewer in the *New Yorker* lauded Frank's "brutal sensitivity," his awareness that behind the façade of middle class abundance and conformity lurked "latent violence."[3]

A statement from the artist accompanied the portfolio, which contained thirty images from his soon-to-be-published book. Frank acknowledged that his photographs represented his own point of view. As he later explained, "I always prefer the extreme."[4]

How could it be otherwise? What he wanted in his work, in addition to expressing his "extreme" vision, was to capture the "instantaneous reaction to oneself that produces a photograph." A good photograph, in his opinion—and in keeping with the aesthetics of the New Sensibility—was one that would "nullify explanation." Silence rather than deep interpretation, speed and spontaneity over compositional serenity.[5]

In April of 1958 Robert Frank took a car trip with Jack Kerouac to Florida. Kerouac's classic *On the Road* had been published in the fall of 1957, and he wanted to drive to Florida to pick up his mother, her cats, and some belongings (his typewriter, various manuscripts) and move her to a house he had purchased on Long Island. Kerouac, the presumed king of the open road, did not drive, so he slept a lot in the backseat, while Frank was at the wheel. They intended to publish text and images in *Life* magazine, a project which fell through but which furnished them with a couple of hundred dollars each, as well funds for "gas, oil, and chow." Kerouac observed and reported on Frank's method of taking photographs. "I was amazed," Kerouac recounted, "to see a guy, while steering at the wheel," take a photo through an "unwashed window." And, amazingly, the photograph worked. Their trip together was a tale of sudden stops whenever something caught Frank's eye. Unlike Evans, Frank did not linger, waiting for the lighting to be perfect. He caught what interested him at the moment, without undue anxiety. His subject matter was what would dominate the soon-to-be-published *The Americans*—cars, "the lonely look of a crossroad stoplight," African Americans, impoverished whites, and the iconography of America (advertising posters, flags).[6]

In contrast to the somewhat subdued tone in Kerouac's account of their Florida jaunt, his introduction to *The Americans* was a paean to Frank's beat-infused vision of America. It was an ode to spontaneity, to the freedom of the open road, to personal liberation, to the everyday. It related well to Kerouac's jazz-inflected prose, to Ginsberg's howling poetry, and to Cage's enlightened silences and clanging instruments: to that "crazy feeling in America when the sun is hot on the streets and music comes out of the jukebox or from a nearby funeral." Kerouac grooved to the rhythms that infused Frank's images. He thought they celebrated the best parts of the American spirit. But he dug a bit deeper to recognize that the photographs had a clear theme, sometimes clinging to the side of the eye, sometimes front and center, sometimes slightly hidden from view. There was, in the heart of the images, a sense of violence and death—the content that the New Sensibility engaged. The lingering on implicit violence—along with the theme of sadness—was excessive, and brilliantly so. But the New Sensibility also shared much with the beat vision: improvisation, spontaneity, and speed—a willingness to challenge traditional cultural hierarchies and to savor (and critique) the everyday vernacular.[7]

Frank wanted his photographs to be poetry: "When people look at my pictures I want them to feel the way they do when they want to read a line of a poem twice."[8] An interesting notion, but did it jibe with his other stated desire that his images "nullify explanation"? At another time, he stated as much, in words that were a Cagean (or Beckettian) minimalist mantra: "Best would be no writing at all." The photographs, in this view, would speak for themselves—combining content and style into a form of poetry. At once personal and public, the feeling and emotion of the image would suffice.[9] Kerouac grasped this perfectly. "Robert Frank, Swiss, unobtrusive, nice, with that little camera," he wrote, "sucked a sad poem right out of America onto film, taking rank among the tragic poets of the world."[10]

Frank had arrived in the United States in 1947, at the age of twenty-three. Small in stature, rock-hard in confidence, Frank had been an indifferent student in Switzerland, although he had been an avid reader of existentialist literature and an apprentice photographer. His German Jewish family had avoided the Holocaust by residing in physical comfort but mental anguish in Switzerland. Living in the midst of the Second World War, Frank "heard Hitler every day on the radio, the voice of terror."[11] This, he later stated, "made me less afraid and better able to cope with different situations because I had lived through that fear." In the United States, the fear that he captured on film was related to the specter of atomic annihilation and the tense state of racial relations in the United States.[12]

While Frank proved himself remarkably open to the American landscape, he carried his own baggage and personality to the United States. He was, as a Greenwich Village acquaintance put it, a blend of "European dourness and pessimistic wit."[13] Whether he was photographing in Wales, Peru, Spain, or Mississippi, those lenses of his personality informed each of his images.

His initial American sojourn in 1947 was short and largely unsatisfying. While he exulted in how America was "really a free country," unbeholden to traditions, he initially found that "everything goes so exceptionally fast and...the only thing that counts is MONEY."[14]

In New York City a year or so later, Frank began to carve out a niche as a commercial photographer. But he confronted that old bugaboo: "The only thing that mattered was to make more money."[15] And his restless energy demanded travel, so in 1948 he took his photographic equipment to South America, wandering around various nations, trying to see the new world with the Emersonian eyes of a child—with that sort of openness to experience, unhampered by social protocol. In typical Frank fashion, he sloughed off photographic expectations— "I didn't think of what would be the correct thing to do; I did what I felt like doing," creating a "diary" in images.[16]

One can wander only so long. In 1953 Frank was back in New York City, married to a beautiful artist, Mary Lockspeiser, with one child and another one about to enter the world. He had in the last few years, he said, "tried out things.... I learned about life. I learned about how to live in New York." He wanted desperately to leave the world of fashion and commercial photography, to jettison the making of images that he considered "lyrical" in order to put his particular imprint on his work.[17]

All roads by 1954 seemed to lead him to a new, ambitious project: "a visual study of a civilization," for which purposes the United States would serve quite nicely. In his 1955 application for a Guggenheim Fellowship, he acknowledged the hubris of his project: " 'The photographing of America' is a large order— read at all literally, the phrase would be an absurdity." All but declaring himself a modern-day Tocqueville, concerned less with politics and community and more with the rhythms and icons of American culture, he catalogued what he intended to capture on film: "a town at night, a parking lot, a supermarket, a highway, the man who owns three cars and the man who owns none." With glowing letters of support from diverse photographers of note, Frank got the Guggenheim funding and took off in a 1950 Ford sedan for the open road, often by himself, sometimes accompanied by his family.[18]

But Frank refused to follow in the footsteps of mentors such as Evans and Edward Steichen. Much as he respected them, and sometimes hewed closely to their subject matter, he was in determined revolt against their more tradi- tional, ordered sensibilities. Evans had made his reputation in the 1930s, working with the Works Progress Administration. James Agee handpicked him in 1936 to collaborate with him on a project, originally intended for *Fortune* magazine and later made into a book, *Let Us Now Praise Famous Men*, which brilliantly portrayed the poverty and dignity of tenant farmer families in the South. Like Frank, Evans was fascinated by advertising and signage, by rickety old build- ings—what one of his biographers called Evans's "politics of the vernacular." And he worked hard to ensure that the subjects of his images were respected, endowed with a quiet grace. But unlike Frank, Walker employed cumbersome equipment. He would carefully size up a shot, accounting for available light— and how much light might be around once shooting commenced. There was none of the spontaneity, the instantaneous reaction between photographer and subject that Frank desired.[19]

A devoted modernist and a fine portrait photographer, Steichen believed in the power of photography to improve humanity. In the late 1940s and early 1950s, many intellectuals and artists signed on to a cultural imaginary that stressed the commonality of the human condition. Thanks to a rising interest in cultural anthropology, mythology, and Freudianism, and a momentary de- cline of racialist thinking (a result of horror at the Holocaust), some came to view humanity as singular, devoid of essential differences, other than circum- stances (place of birth, cultural traditions, relative wealth, etc.).[20] But no matter where one resided, no matter one's skin color, one's religion, or ethnicity, all human beings felt pain, loved their children, and worked to feed and clothe themselves and their loved ones. This sentimental vision of united humanity was at the center of a 1955 widely traveled exhibition and then a photographic volume that graced many coffee tables in America, called *The Family of Man.* Although the works varied widely in quality—and many of them did capture hostility and suffering—they drove home vigorously the universality of the human condition. Seven early Frank images were included in the massive compendium. Taken in the United States, Peru, Spain, and Wales, they tended toward the dour and despairing (a Welsh coal miner with blackened face, a lonely beggar). But one image was enlivened, atypically for Frank. A bunch of women are having lunch at a hamburger joint. They sit at a counter, grinning because they are looking out the window at the photographer taking their picture. What especially stands out in the image, however, is the cacophony of signs—for pies, beans, and soup, all framed above by fluorescent lights and the word "HAMBURGERS" in bold lettering—precisely the sort of thing that would later appeal to Robert Venturi and Denise Scott Brown about Las Vegas signage (see chapter 20).[21]

Frank's style was predicated on his instantaneous response to a subject— feeling or emotion over conscious evaluation. Martialing such moments of emotion meant, as a first step, that the heavy equipment and large-format images favored by Evans and Steichen had to be abandoned. In their stead, Frank used a lightweight, 35 mm Leica camera that allowed him to shoot rapidly, from the hip.[22] He respected what was known among abstract expressionist painters as "the gesture," that moment of collision between canvas and artistic will. These artists, with whom he was chummy, he said, "reinforced my belief that you could really follow your intuition—no matter how crazy or far-off or how laughed at it would be. You could go out and make pictures that were not sentimental. You could photograph what you felt like."[23]

The road trip across the United States began in June 1955 and continued for another year, supported by the Guggenheim Foundation. Frank ventured to parts of the coastal South, then to Dearborn to photograph the Ford plant at River Rouge, and later deeper into the southern states. On the second leg, he headed west, even stopping at the 1956 Democratic Convention in Chicago. Back in New York City, settled in what would today be considered the East Village, Frank began the arduous task of examining thousands of negatives, making prints, and deciding on what belonged in the book project and in what order. He was confident that he had caught his subject in the manner he had intended: "I had a feeling of compassion for the people on the street.... That gave me the push—that made me work so hard until I knew I had something, but I didn't even know I had America."[24]

It was quite a tall order to encompass America, in its ocean-to-ocean mass and teeming plurality. He wanted to embrace a "cross-section of America," one that, of necessity, would reflect his "personal view."[25] On the first count, at least, as the reviews in *Popular Photography* and elsewhere indicated, many considered Frank neither compassionate nor extensive in his selection of images. And Frank, too, in certain moments admitted that he was always an angry outsider, distanced from American consensus and middle-class ideals: "I believe that it's good to be angry, if you're an artist.... The anger will make you work harder to produce things that will contain more conviction." Frank's own anger propelled *The Americans* beyond the realm of mere documentary or travelogue into a new style of critique and transcendence, always marked with what Allen Ginsberg called Frank's "quality of loneliness."[26]

Traveling around, often without the succor of the family circle and friends, does induce loneliness and feed alienation. Anger can surface easily when an individual confronts all sorts of hassles from law enforcement and others jittery about a Jewish guy with a foreign accent and a camera poking around their territory. Early in his journey, in July 1955 in Detroit, Frank wrote his wife that he had spent a night in jail, a result of having the wrong license plates on his car. He found the experience, he wrote, "depressing and I got scared." Five months later, in McGehee, Arkansas, Frank was arrested again. According to the police report, "He was shabbily dressed, needed a shave and a haircut, also bath. Subject talked with a foreign accent." Upon looking at the contents of the truck, the officer found lots of cameras and plenty of luggage, and the suspect seemed uncooperative—Might he be "in the employ of some unfriendly foreign power and the possibility of Communist affiliations"? The police interrogated Frank, finding it suspicious that he had been taking photographs of a major US auto plant. Listen to Frank describe one moment in the interrogation: "The lieutenant leaned back and inquired: 'Now we are going to ask you a question: Are you a commie?'" After nearly two days of hassle and degradation along these lines, Frank was freed and returned to his travels.[27]

His travails continued in Port Gibson, Mississippi. This time he captured the tense situation on film. A group of about seven teenagers, in front of a high school, saw that Frank was taking photographs nearby. "What are you doing here? Are you from New York?" one of the kids inquired. Frank responded: "I'm just taking pictures.... For myself—just to see." One of the kids then announced: "He must be a communist. He looks like one. Why don't you go to the other side of town and watch the niggers play."[28]

He was traversing America while the Red Scare lingered. As he surveyed "those faces, those people" in the United States, he came to discover a "kind of hidden violence. The country at that time—the McCarthy period—I felt it very strongly."[29]

We see the violence, fear, and death in many of his images. They are most powerfully conveyed by how he juxtaposed images. Although he later claimed that he was not placing or ordering the images (and Susan Sontag concurred, finding the presentation "deliberately random") into a logical progression—perhaps embracing the "random order" favored by Rauschenberg—there was a sequential logic to the images in *The Americans*.[30]

Consider a series of five images nestled side by side in the midsection of *The Americans*. In "U.S. 91, Leaving Blackfoot, Idaho," Frank depicted the interior of an automobile, with two intent, grimly serious young Native American males about to begin a journey. The next image was "St. Petersburg, Florida," an evocative study of elderly people sitting on two benches whose posts resemble the lanes of a highway. In the background of this image, counterposed to the rootedness of the old people in their waiting game of death, is a car—perhaps the one carrying the Idaho pair—streaking off to new horizons of possibility.

The next image similarly focuses attention on the death-in-life waiting of the old and the frenetic movement of the young. "Covered Car—Long Beach, California" shows the shadow of two palm trees. In front of them, in what might well be described as a Bauhaus crypt, is a tarp-shrouded car, immobile and dead. In this image, Frank examined the interplay of two symbols of the American dream, car culture and the liberation often associated with California. He presented both of them, however, as imbued with idle vanity and death. He dashed the expectation that the tarp might be lifted and the car reborn in the next photograph, an image of something else covered—this time a dead body, the victim of an accident, alongside the road of dreams and song, Route 66.

The final image in this montage returns us to the road and thus opens up a new set of possibilities. "U.S. 285, New Mexico" is an ode to the existential juxtaposition of life and death. In Frank's photograph, the road stretches forever into the night; the lanes of the highway suggesting escape, speed, and freedom. But they also evoke danger. Far ahead, in the passing lane, one can glimpse, ever so faintly, the outline of an oncoming vehicle, its headlights barely visible. Here, as in the other images, freedom shares the road with death, possibility with closure. The photographs expressed the road of life, especially those moments when we are in the passing lane, traveling fast. And yet, as we seek to avoid inertia and complacency, we must always remain cognizant of that other car, the car of death, immobility, old age, conformity, coming closer and closer.

Out of a total of about sixty images depicting faces in *The Americans*, only a handful revealed a smile or exuberance. And even then the smiling person was usually situated next to a sad individual, or the smile was patently false. In one compelling image, a young television performer, pretty in a mainstream manner, paraded her artificial smile, rendered even more unconvincing by her face being reproduced at that moment on the television monitor next to the stage set. Even happiness in Frank's world seemed falsified by a consumer-celebrity culture.

Frank presented images of self-important petty politicians. They are often shown suppressing a yawn or surrounded by tattered flags and banal political slogans on posters. When depicting workers, Frank caught them appearing alienated, burdened with a gut-wrenching sadness, gloomy and anonymous; he discovered them in all-night diners, elevators, buses, and bathrooms. In a photograph taken at the River Rouge factory, the workers' faces are indistinct, blurred, scary analogs to the speeding assembly line that enslaves them and turns them into machines.

Frank turned an ironic eye on the contrasts between the political and spiritual emptiness of Americans and the liveliness of material artifacts that surrounded them. "Bar—Las Vegas, Nevada" presented the naked loneliness at the heart of American life. A young man steps up to a jukebox; he appears to be languid, oblivious to the world surrounding him. The jukebox, however, is alive. One imagines it revving and pulsating with the strains of a lively beat. The man, rather than the jukebox, is the material object, the dead machine in the night. Frank admitted that he considered the jukebox an icon of America, and in photographing it more than once in *The Americans*, he hoped that it would grant an element of imagined sound to his images.[31]

The Americans, unlike most photographic collections, paid close attention to African Americans and the painful realities of segregation and racism. Yet he sometimes fell prey to a sort of misplaced envy for African Americans, shared by hipsters such as Kerouac, Ginsberg, and Norman Mailer (see chapter 9) that arose out of their alienation from middle-class American culture, their search for something spontaneous (which they discovered in jazz music). Kerouac's famous passage in *On the Road* captured this highly problematic sensibility: "At lilac evening I walked…in the Denver colored section, wishing I were a Negro, feeling that the best the white world had offered was not enough ecstasy for me, not enough life, joy, kicks, darkness, music, not enough night."[32]

In keeping with this sensibility, Frank depicted white Americans as the walking dead. The New Sensibility was devoted to creation that rejected much of the tradition and rhythms of white society in the atomic age. Conformity to such values equaled death, in both life and work. Frank made this apparent, for instance, in one photograph, "Charity-Ball—New York City." There we encounter a woman socialite, gaudy in jewels and bedecked in lifeless finery. Her grimace evinces severe ennui as she accepts on her cheek the kiss of a man whose long fingers wrap around her cold shoulders in a Dracula-like embrace. Even when America's upper crust were presented as smiling, as in "Cocktail Party—New York City," they appeared to be courting death: their wealth failed to free them but only seemed to weigh them down in the muck of despair. From Frank's photographs one might surmise that the blood of America had been sucked out by a materialistic, alienating, and absurd culture—a depiction in photographic form of the Moloch that had powered much of Ginsberg's *Howl*.

White Americans, in Frank's images, were burdened with dullness in spirit and life. This contrasts with the way that Frank depicted African Americans responding to life's trials. In "Funeral—St. Helena, South Carolina," a group of young black males lean against their freshly shined automobiles. There is less a sense of grief weighing them down than of boredom, an unwillingness to allow death to interfere with the enjoyment of the living. Another photograph of the same funeral juxtaposes the cold stiffness of the corpse in an open coffin with the movement of the living as they file by. Death is acknowledged—how can it be ignored?—but the need is to move beyond it, to get on with one's own engagement with life.

In contrast to the coldness of whites, Frank imagined African Americans as sexually vital and passionate. Of course, he was on shaky ground here, threatening to sink into the common racist symbolism of the emotional and sex-saturated Other that he deplored. In one marvelous image, "New York City," Frank showed three Puerto Rican women (perhaps transvestites), who are aware of Frank's presence; this is one of the rare noncandid shots. Instead of retreating from his lens, they strike a sexual pose. One caresses her own face, another thrusts out a hip. In the background, the third woman covers up, but not in a modest attempt to hide or to seek anonymity. The gesture is mocking and provocative, the fingers of her hand spread wide across her face.

Indeed, only African Americans regularly demonstrated emotion, deep feelings, or authenticity in *The Americans*. When he happens upon a group of African Americans from a motorcycle club, one looks at him warily, as if Frank is intruding on his private space. Consider, in this vein, the structure that Frank employed to organize one sequence of photographs. In "San Francisco," his own favorite image in the book, Frank had clearly disturbed the peace and quiet of a black couple who had been sitting on a hillside enjoying a beautiful view of the city below. The woman and man react to Frank's sudden intrusion—his vaunted invisibility again had failed him. They greet him with disdain and anger. Frank later referred to that look as saying, "You bastard, what are you doing!"[33] The next photograph, "Belle Isle—Detroit," shows white people in a setting that is as idyllic as the previous shot of the San Francisco hills. But these folks seem oblivious to the beauty of their surroundings and uninterested in Frank's presence. In another image, also titled "Belle Isle—Detroit," Frank depicted a moving convertible full of young black boys enjoying cool breezes on their bare chests, perhaps anticipating or still reveling in the joys of their beach outing. Their freedom arises from their relaxed relationship to nature. In contrast, Frank then offered an image of an elderly couple sitting in an enclosed hardtop automobile, stuck in heavy traffic. They seem less angry than numbed by the wait.

Other photographs return to the liveliness of African Americans. In one, Frank caught a black baby next to a jukebox; unlike the passive young man in Las Vegas, this child is joyful and kinetic—alive to the sounds of life. Even a shot of a large black woman sitting on a chair in an open field, an image that might suggest the ultimate loneliness, instead shows her striking a jaunty pose. Her smile positively illuminates the surrounding empty landscape. Though alone, she is not alienated; she lives in the moment.

Frank recognized the limits American racism placed upon black freedom. He had traveled the terrain of segregated America, finding it distasteful and unfair. As he put it in a letter to his parents in Switzerland, "America is an interesting country, but there is a lot here that I do not like and that I would never accept. I am trying to show this in my photographs."[34]

He captured one aspect of this disdain in the image that he chose for the cover of the American edition of *The Americans*. Here, African American freedom is constrained. In this particularly powerful image there is no celebration of black sexuality, spontaneity, and emotions. The image shows the faces of a number of people sitting by the open windows of a New Orleans trolley car. There is pain and despair, aching in its detail and depth, in the face of one black man that demands our attention. He is framed by the window, as he looks with perhaps fear outside. In the seats in front of him—capturing the reality that African Americans had to sit in the back of buses and trolleys—a white boy, dapper in a bow tie, is blessed by his wealth and color.

Another poignant expression of racial realities in *The Americans* is found in the image "Charleston, South Carolina." A richly black-skinned nurse, clothed in starched white uniform against a background of blurry white streets and institutional white walls, holds a very pale white baby. The immobile child stares, wide-eyed, straight ahead. It has a sagacious look well beyond its years, like the white child on the bus, anticipating the hidden benefits of whiteness. The attitude of the surrogate mother is uncertain. Though she holds the baby close, her look is not directed toward the child, whose reality seems alien to her. The woman appears to be lost in thought as well. Perhaps she too is contemplating her separateness from the child; perhaps she is thinking about the foreclosed futures of her own children as against the expansive possibilities of the privileged white child that she encloses in her arms.

The Americans nearly closed the book on Frank's photographic career. In his last photographic series for many years, begun in 1958, Frank traveled on buses in New York City, photographing scenes that resonated with his sense of immediacy. Although he was taking his photographs from the inside of a bus, he remained as always an outsider. The images, he remarked, have "to do with desperation and endurance," which he associated with living in New York.[35] Taking photographs from a moving bus meant that the images were often jerky and blurred, but that was not a problem for Frank's aesthetic.

As much as the images in *The Americans*, his bus photographs were about loneliness, about broken dreams—and about movement, in search if not of meaning, then at least motion for its own sake. In one photograph, a large, suited black man, with black fedora, head hanging down, passes a white woman, who is erect in her bearing and well-dressed, with a white hat. Neither has any sense of the existence of the other. A thin, nervous man, cigarette in hand, standing next to a building, has wind-up toys dancing on the street, for sale at fifty cents apiece. In a commercial vehicle, with its back doors swung open wide, leans a slim black man, hands in pockets, elegant in his simple outfit, staring into space.

By 1959 Frank had abandoned photography. He was now drawn to the speed and movement, as well as the community, involved in filmmaking.[36] Much that had been central to his photographic vision translated nicely into film. Along with painter Alfred Leslie, he made *Pull My Daisy*, originally titled *The Beat Generation*. A strange combination of madcap comedy and often over-the-top symbolism, the film concerned a bishop's visit to a couple (based on Neal and Carolyn Cassady). Over the course of the evening, however, their zany friends intrude on the solemnity of the event.

Kerouac narrated in his inimitable fashion:

Yes, it's early, late or middle Friday evening in the universe. Oh, the sounds of time are pouring through the window and the key. All ideardian windows and bedarvled bedarveled mad bedraggled robes that rolled in the caves of Amontillado and all the sherried heroes lost and caved up, and translyvanian heroes mixing themselves up with glazer vup and the hydrogen bomb of hope.[37]

The actors were Frank's pals, including poets Ginsberg and Gregory Corso and painters Larry Rivers and Alice Neel, with David Amram providing the score. As with his photography, the film had a choppy and jumpy editing style, which was in many ways anticipatory of the soon-to-emerge style of filmmaking known as cinéma-vérité. Reviewing the film for the *Village Voice*, Jonas Mekas exulted that *Pull My Daisy* offered "new ways out of the frozen officialdom and midcentury sterility of our arts, towards new themes, a new sensibility."[38]

Along with John Cassavetes's *Shadows*, with which it premiered in 1959, *Pull My Daisy* greatly influenced American filmmaking. Frank quickly found himself comfortable with the process of making a film. He was no longer an *isolato* with a Leica; he was now involved with a community, working out ideas and scenes with others, discussing cuts and edits, without diminishing the always strong stamp of his own spontaneous sensibility, accepting improvisation, and looking around various corners generally ignored by traditional culture.[39]

Gone was the time when he could exult, "As a still photographer I wouldn't have to talk with anyone. I could walk around and not say anything. You're just an observer; you just walk around, and there's no need to communicate."[40] Yet, in its manner, *The Americans* did communicate; its images resonated with an emerging generation that readily embraced the New Sensibility in the 1960s. And it did so without using any words, by nullifying any need of explanation on Frank's part—no small accomplishment.

Making a Connection

JUDITH MALINA AND JACK GELBER

1959

Rehearsals for the Living Theatre production of *The Connection*, scheduled to open in July 1959, were going badly. In late May, director Judith Malina had yet to cast the parts. The jazz musicians who would both act and play in the production were often incapacitated by drugs. In early June, after Jackie McLean, an immensely talented alto saxophonist, arrived late for rehearsals, Malina asked playwright Jack Gelber if he thought McLean was high on drugs. "That's heroin, baby," replied Gelber. McLean "faltered and fell, his eyes quivered, dilated, closed." When McLean finally shook it off, he apologized to Malina for being so "unfocussed and wandering." The apology itself was hardly reassuring: "I won't do it…often."[1]

As Gelber recalled, the musicians "were always high on heroin" and were so unreliable that they had to be replaced regularly. A few weeks later, one of the musicians was strung out, while another could not play unless he got some drugs quickly into his system. Each day seemed to sprout another crisis. In the midst of rehearsals, Gelber rushed to tell Malina that someone had "taken an overdose in [the] men's room." Sure enough, "slumped behind the toilet wall" was some fellow. When he finally came out of it, he explained, "I'm just tired." His sapped energy may have had something to do with the "size 24 hypodermic needle" on the floor of the restroom.[2] Another actor went berserk, "throwing things at the other actors and trying to kill people." Judith and her husband, Julian Beck, were forced to take him to Bellevue Psychiatric Hospital, an especially difficult task for them since they questioned the very notion of insanity.[3]

These events were, as Gelber realized, perfectly correlated to the play. Gelber intended *The Connection* to bring "drama and reality" closer together. It pivoted around a group of junkies, from varied backgrounds, waiting for their drug fixes to be delivered to an apartment. If such a scenario made up the entirety of the play, then it would have simply mimicked the existential angst of Samuel Beckett's *Waiting for Godot*, produced in New York only a few years earlier. Instead, *The Connection* was anchored deep within the New Sensibility: chaotic rather than ordered, almost a happening, on- and offstage, with a gritty realism punctuated by jazz improvisation.

But more was happening on the Living Theatre stage. One character, named Jaybird, has written a play about heroin addiction. Jim Dunn is presenting the play, serving as an emcee of sorts, sometimes as a director of a film of the event. He is accompanied by two photographers, who over the course of the play exchange clothing and identity with one another; at the end of the play, one of the photographers has decided that he wants a dose of heroin. Musicians, McLean included, are also on the stage, both as participants in the waiting game and in the dialogue, but also jamming, less an accompaniment to the action than as a central part of the play's ontology.[4] Sometimes they seem to be stoned. At various points in the drama, actors leave the stage to join the audience.

The actors addressed the audience from the stage. Viewers were told that they need not make a "connection" between "jazz and narcotics." Jim states that he is striving for "the authenticity of…improvised art." Leach, another junkie, remarks, "I mean this is a play, man. It's not really real" (44). Solly, an intellectual junkie, lectures: "Suicide is not uncommon among us. The overdose of heroin is where the frail line of life and death swings in a silent breeze of ecstatic summer."[5]

Jaybird's play had a script, but he preferred that the dialogue and music be improvisational and spontaneous. As the play progresses, Jaybird grows increasingly frustrated. He had wanted four heroes in the play, but none has emerged. Why, he asks Cowboy, the man who has procured the heroin, "can't you act like a hero? It's the basis of Western drama, you know. Can't you give an heroic speech?"[6]

Meanwhile, the effects of the drug-taking led to chaos onstage, with some actors nodding off, others falling, still others wandering off the stage. As one of the photographers is readied for his first dose of heroin, Jaybird protests: "It's not supposed to work this way. I've given you latitude. But this is too much." One of the addicts, Leach, calls Jaybird's bluff, telling him he's the playwright: "You're supposed to know all about it. I mean this is all a play, man. It's not really real." The more that the actors swear that they are not really using heroin, the more the plea rings hollow. "You don't think we'd use the real stuff? After all, narcotics are illegal."[7]

But as the characters tighten the tourniquets around their arms to make their veins pop out, they appear to be going beyond the playwright's expectations. Larry Rivers, who had considered being an actor for the play but ended up doing posters for it, reported that "there was real heroin in the capsules handed out to the anxious actors waiting onstage, some of whom shot up in front of the audience." The audience, according to Rivers, was titillated by this dose of realism. In her journals, however, the usually forthcoming Malina made no mention of onstage drug use.[8]

To further diminish distance between audience and actors and between "drama and reality," during the intermission performers mingled with the audience, hitting them up for a few bucks so that they might presumably be able to make a score later. Once the play resumes onstage, one character thanks "each and every kind, gentle and good contributor in the audience. You have helped a most noble cause...that flows in our veins."[9]

In its controlled chaos, the Living Theatre's production of *The Connection* anticipated what would soon be the newest expression of avant-garde rumbling: the happening. Just a few months later the painter and performance artist Allan Kaprow (yet another devotee of John Cage) staged what many consider the first happening, although obvious precursors can be found in Dada and in Cage's *Theater Piece no. 1*. Kaprow's piece, *18 Happenings in 6 Parts*, at the Reuben Gallery in New York City, featured carefully constructed sets. In a sense, there was nothing improvisational about the piece. But in the process of experiencing it, as gallery goers moved from room to room, changes in lights, sets, poetry, music, and speeches happened. In one room performers squeezed oranges. Actors and audience intermingled; the experience seemed singular and original—a veritable three-ring circus of sensory exhilaration. Kaprow maintained that the happening, building on the work of Jackson Pollock, demanded that "we must become preoccupied with and even dazzled by the space and objects of our everyday life, either our bodies, clothes, rooms, or, if need be, the vastness of Forty-second Street." The artist must now "utilize the specific substances of sight, sound, movements, people, odors, touch." And it was unique—resistant to repetition or purchase, thus challenging the monetary modus vivendi of the art world.[10] What Kaprow wanted in his happenings, as did Judith Malina in her theater, was a total work of art, unlimited in its range and materials, unafraid to err in excess.

For *The Connection*, the limitations of the stage, the melding of the music and dialogue, the self-reflexivity tied to realism signaled its status as a sort of happening. The play ended with playwright Jaybird pacing back and forth amid the chaos onstage, saying to the audience, "I wanted to do something far out. Yes, I'm guilty of trying to have a little shock value."[11] Both Malina and Beck had been enthused by reading Ginsberg's *Howl* in March 1958: "It is," Malina noted, "a scream of anguish and beatific love." Its focus on madness appealed to Beck: "I feel that it is my poem."[12] Meditating in the early 1960s about the creative value of madness, Beck announced: "Go into the madhouse and find out the truth." He proudly declared that the actors at the Living Theatre were "awkward" and "untutored." This allowed the Living Theatre to be more real and raw. "All niceness must then be exploded," Beck asserted.[13]

Imagine this potential scenario. Louis Calta, a second-string theater reviewer for the *New York Times*, has been unimpressed by the first half of the play. He stands in the lobby during the intermission, contemplating what he is going to write in his review. Perhaps he is chatting with someone. One of the

performers, with the befogged eyes of a real heroin addict, nudges toward
Calta and says, "Hey, man, dig this, I need some bread for a fix. You cool with
that? Spread a little jam on my hand, won't ya?" Wishing he was anywhere else
in the city but the theater lobby, Calta returns to his seat, fidgeting and glancing
at his wrist watch for the rest of the performance, waiting for the moment he
can exact recompense.

The Connection, Calta writes the next day in the New York Times, is "nothing
more than a farrago of dirt, small-time philosophy, empty talk and extended
runs of 'cool' music. There is a quality of sensationalism that undoubtedly will
offend the squares." Calta proudly considered himself one of their number, offended by contrivances intended to engage the audience in the action of the
play. Such "improvisations" struck Calta as "frustrating," like "looking through
a peephole into a darkened room." Calta probably wanted to grab his hat and
make for the nearest exit when during the play a character "rhetorically
screams at the audience and asks: 'Why are you here, stupid? You want to
watch people suffer?'" The Connection, Calta concluded, demonstrated how
heroin users fall into "a condition of listless weariness."[14] That was what Calta
claimed he felt as a member of the audience.

The review was devastating. The Living Theatre had just spent a huge
amount of money and put immense effort into constructing a new theater on
the corner of Fourteenth Street and Sixth Avenue. This theater had been the
dream of Julian Beck and Judith Malina for over a decade. Now, while the
paint on the walls had barely dried, it appeared to be in jeopardy, done in by a
play that has offended a reviewer for the most influential paper in the city.
Disaster loomed.

When we first encountered Judith Malina earlier in this volume, it was New
Year's Day 1952, and she was oscillating between despair and elation. She ached
with embarrassment over the debacle the night before when she had lost it onstage. Yet, after hearing Cage's Music of Changes, she was exhilarated by artistic
energy and a desire for change. As she puts it in a poem, "The change must
come now! / Even tomorrow will be too late." But how can she channel her
overflow of energy? "I desire to burn; but then I desire so many contradictory
things."[15]

The life of Judith Malina revolved around her desire to act and direct, to be an
avant-gardist of the highest order. She had remained married to Julian, and together they cared for their child, Garrick. Their relationship was intense; each
shared ambition for the Living Theatre. They were hardly lovers anymore; Julian's
inclinations, sometimes open, other times repressed, were homosexual in
nature. Judith was a lusty and active heterosexual, scooting through lovers, ranging from composers Lou Harrison and Alan Hovhaness to writer James Agee.
Hovhaness wrote of his love for Malina: "Your beauty, love for your talents, for
your brilliance, and most of all love for your passions."[16] Yet her passions

remained frustrated, and she sought guidance in therapy sessions with Paul Goodman (also a novelist, critic, and more), whose sexism sometimes sapped her confidence, while she also tried to prove herself Julian's equal as an artist. It was a rocky relationship.

During these years, Malina had become an antiwar, antinuclear activist. Along with Dorothy Day, leader of the Catholic Worker Movement, Malina refused to heed air raid warnings and drills, maintaining that they promoted a false sense of security. Arrested in 1955, Malina's spunk and her disdain for authority quickly came into play as she jousted with the judge. Her in-court screaming earned her a trip to Bellevue to determine whether she was psychologically sound. Thanks to a good lawyer, Malina did not linger long in the asylum.[17]

In 1957 she again challenged authority by refusing to take shelter during an air-raid drill. "We wanted to say no to the man in power...to say no to the cynics who fear that love won't work, and to the fools who think that hate will." Sent to the Women's House of Detention (Julian was also arrested and confined elsewhere), she came under Day's protection and guidance, spending much of her day mopping floors and finding her "mind disavowed." But she found relief in establishing close relationships with other prisoners, who were mostly incarcerated for prostitution and drug use, and the experience convinced her that community was not a utopian dream. If it was possible in prison, then why not in the theater, too?[18] Passionate about pacifism, Malina was, as always, heady with contradictions. As she put it in a haiku: "Hating violence / When I struck my beloved, / My hand hated me."[19]

When they were not in prison, Julian and Judith scurried to attend cultural events. They were regulars on the rounds of theater and art openings, and the parties that followed. It must have been exhausting. On a Saturday night in April 1958, Malina and Beck went to Hoboken for a party celebrating Goodman's novel *Empire City*. They then returned to the city for another party, at artist Rachel Rosenthal's, where they mingled with Cage, Cunningham, and Rauschenberg. Also present was experimental filmmaker Maya Deren, who "spurred on the bongo players." Such gatherings were, of course, a fun outlet: "Here one laughs and enjoys oneself thoroughly and then returns to the same tears that had been left midair."[20] But these parties also helped Julian and Judith make connections, raise funds, and gain sponsors so that the Living Theatre might live again.[21]

The Cherry Lane incarnation of the Living Theatre had ceased in the summer of 1952 when the New York City Fire Department declared the premises a fire hazard. Malina was so incensed that she reportedly ran after a fire department official while waving a bamboo spear that had been used in a production. Beck and Malina scoured the city for theater spaces, sometimes performing in makeshift circumstances. To support themselves, and to keep the dream of a theater alive, Julian got work at the New York Public Library, typing out entries for the card catalogue; later he worked as a shoe salesman.[22] They found a space for the Living Theatre, close to their Upper West Side apartment.

It was hardly perfect, since it lacked city approval, sufficient exits, and seating capacity. Nonetheless, Judith and Julian grabbed the opportunity in 1953 to have a home for their productions. After many run-ins with authorities, the theater was shut down in December 1955, for having sixty people in the audience for a theater that allowed seating for only fifteen.[23] The search began again.

Finally, in 1957, the Living Theatre, phoenix-like, reappeared. The new space had been a department store—its five stories offered plenty of room for the theater and offices. One floor would become rehearsal space for Cunningham's dance company. But the existing interior had to be gutted and redone. With the ardor of teens, Julian and Judith, along with supporters, set about the task.

They regularly put in twelve-hour shifts. First they had to gut much of the building; "six or seven of us, not even stopping to joke or to rest" tore down plaster walls and stripped away "dry old wood" into what looked like a funeral pyre. Then the process of rebuilding began, interrupted regularly by new problems (leaky roof, inadequate funds, failure to secure proper permits).

Throughout the summer of 1958 they labored. Stacks of lumber, over three thousand bricks, and other materials had to be moved into the structure, and reed-thin Julian staggered under the weight, while Judith was "bewildered utterly" by the challenge. But things slowly emerged; "The stage rose marvelous and mysterious out of the tile floor." Soon, Judith was upholstering the theater seats with "black and white striped awning material" and then "painting the seats in their subtle tri colors, a beige, a gray, a dull violet." She found the work arduous but "satisfying." They painted the theater ceiling black, the walls with "alternate stripes of black paint," all the while fending off creditors, battling unions, and beginning to cast for their initial production: William Carlos Williams's *Many Loves*. With the dawning of 1959, things looked up, as the finishing touches were applied to the theater, including "two copper enameled doors" that "recall[ed] the great doors of the Italian cathedrals."[24]

They desperately needed *Many Loves* to be a hit. It was a wise, somewhat safe production choice. Williams had composed the play in 1940, but it never had a major staging. Williams, who had helped Ginsberg along in his career, had also served as a mentor to Beck. The play had some nice experimental touches, offered slightly provocative sexual content, and was sophisticated in a Noel Coward sense, yet with rougher-edged figures and settings. One character proclaimed, "The theater is a trial, truly. It's not a play thing. But in the theater to kill you've got to kill! . . . Or they'll walk out on you."[25]

Audiences did not walk out on the play but the production did not kill either. It received a respectful review from Brooks Atkinson in the *New York Times*, although he struggled to understand the relationship between the three one-act plays, concluding them to be mere "character sketches." Malina's acting was solid (in three roles, "a strumpet," "a lesbian," and "a garrulous mother" with nary a maternal instinct) and Beck's stage sets imaginative.[26]

More than a middling success was needed. The next scheduled production, by Goodman, based on the story of Abraham and Isaac, showed no signs of blockbuster status. It was a "flop," Julian acknowledged, because it was moralistic and philosophical rather than imaginative and creative. It lasted for seven performances, and the financial situation of the Living Theatre daily grew more dire.[27]

They were determined to survive as a theater company and to live up to their principles. Malina and Beck insisted, "The theatre must be worthy of the life of each spectator." The "actor breathes" and the "spectator lives" and through some symbiosis, "life is intensified." The theater that they envisioned harkened back to its Greek origins, speaking in a universal language, engaging everyone in a common ritual. The goal, Malina and Beck proclaimed, was "catharsis," attained by the willingness of actor, director, producer to "expose themselves, body and spirit...at great risk." In turn, this would "produce catharsis and enlightenment for an anonymous audience." To reach this goal, "music, painting, sculpture, and dance" were "essential elements of the performance." Style, too, was of the essence. But it could not be derivative; it must be part of a process of discovery and experimentation.[28] Nothing less would suffice, but would such ideals attract audiences to the theater?

Little did they know that salvation was near to hand, thanks to Gelber's *The Connection*. It all began one evening in late March 1958, when Gelber, a young man with sandy-colored hair and an agreeable demeanor ("a hipster version of Huckleberry Finn"), showed up at the Malina/Beck apartment toting a manuscript of his play.[29] "The Becks were very nice," Gelber remembered. He was impressed and also taken aback by the bourgeois nature of their apartment, its book-lined walls. He was relieved to find out, after a brief discussion, that "they were very sincere and obviously knew something about drugs. They were asking me the right questions. They were not corny."[30]

Gelber had been born in Chicago, to a working-class Jewish family. After attending the University of Illinois at Urbana, he wandered around, working at jobs ranging from an apprentice steam fitter in a shipyard, to a rare-book dealer, to a "pressman and duplicating machine operator" at the headquarters of the United Nations. He had been writing short stories, but they had failed to find publishers because, as he put it, "My work falls between the academic and the slick."[31]

Gelber claimed that he had no special interest in the theater. But he was enmeshed in the jazz world, albeit in an odd manner. He enjoyed the music but was "attracted" to its "listeners." What he liked about them was that, he said, "They were either prostitutes whom I wanted to fuck, or people interested in literature." At the same time, living in San Francisco, he felt part of the beat scene and found it "stimulating," And he wanted to write, coming up with an idea for a play about addicts, connected in an "organic manner" through jazz music: "I had to write a play.... I had no choice." He was most proud of how the "play's structure follow[ed] the form of a jazz improvisation, with actors and musicians giving solos based on a common theme." Gelber wanted his work to be seen as sui generis. When asked if he had been influenced by the Nobel-winning playwright Luigi Pirandello, he replied that he had been influenced by many things, including his mother.[32]

Such cockiness was not in evidence the night he had presented his play to Malina and Beck. He was twenty-six years old, with a wife, and a child soon to arrive. His play about drug addicts had failed to find a producer, but he hoped that Malina and Beck, with their reputation for openness to something different, might give the manuscript a read. "I waited a long time for them to call," Gelber recalled. "I was like every nervous new author."[33]

They agreed to check it out, reportedly depositing it atop a stack of manuscripts, perhaps seventy in number, which they had gathered in their bathroom, where they tended to read submissions. The premise of the play—its improvisational jazz, its self-consciousness, and its gritty realism—immediately appealed to Julian. Fifty years later, Malina recalled that he ran into the bedroom announcing, "This is the play we want to do."[34]

Gelber later stated that it was Malina who had been immediately excited by the play, running out of the bathroom screaming to Julian, "It's terrific, it's great." However, Malina was at first skeptical.[35] Not about the content, certainly; she was familiar with drug addicts from her time at the Women's House of Detention. Rather, her hesitancy concerned the play's overly self-conscious avant-garde dimensions. By 1959, however, it was becoming less unusual for playwrights to break down barriers between audience and actors—this was something that Pirandello had done in *Tonight We Improvise*, a play that the Living Theatre would also stage.

Malina came around, and the play was on. Much to Gelber's surprise and delight, he was immediately summoned to help cast the play. He admired Beck and Malina's dedication to avant-garde ideals, such as rejecting divisions between life and work.[36] Malina loved interacting with Gelber: "He is shrewd, canny, enigmatic." He had connections with the world of junkies that lent bite to his play. Years earlier he had been renting a room on the Lower East Side, living with a young woman from the Middle East. All of a sudden one morning, while he was stirring cocoa over the stove, "police burst in with pistols." The young woman had recently served time for drug use, and the cops figured the apartment would be full of illicit drugs. The cops, he claimed, thought the cocoa might be heroin. They did manage to find a small amount of marijuana in the apartment, and Gelber decided to take the rap for it, even though it was the girl's, not his. He spent several weeks incarcerated in the Tombs before being released with a suspended sentence. Gelber put his familiarity with junkies into the play and brilliantly conjoined it with his appreciation for jazz improvisation.[37]

Malina's enthusiasm for the play coincided roughly with the period when she had been introduced to Antonin Artaud's revolutionary ideas about theater. As noted in chapter 1, M. C. Richards had preached about Artaud at Black Mountain College in 1952, and she had long been translating his key text, *The Theater and Its Double*. Malina was friends with Richards and probably began reading the translated work in the summer of 1958 while working on the theater. In March 1959, with the Living Theatre building imagined as a space not only for plays but for all sorts of performances (dance, poetry, discussion), Malina invited Richards to lecture on Artaud. The lecture by Richards, according to Malina, was "remarkably brave" for its dedication to the cause of a reformation in the status and function of the theater along Artaudian principles.[38]

While many of the plays presented in the past by the Living Theatre had an undercurrent of political content, they were generally allegorical in nature, rarely engaging with the contemporary moment. Gelber's *The Connection* was hip with a vengeance, full of existential themes and with challenging music, staging, and happenings, of a sort. This fit the prescription of Artaud's notion of the "theater of the cruelty," of an assault on the complacency of the audience that might result in a shift in perception that would in time destroy the authoritarian social state—no small order while the finances of the Living Theatre plummeted and unfavorable initial reviews proliferated.[39]

The negative review by Calta in the *New York Times* was quickly joined by one in the *New York Journal American*, a lowbrow newspaper, which stated, "To call last night's performance the work of amateurs would be an insult to amateurs." The reviewer disdained the play's four-letter-word usage and its criticisms of religion, morality, and patriotism. Judith Crist, reviewing *The Connection* in the *New York Herald Tribune*, was succinct in her condemnation: "The play deals with junk, and it is junk!"[40]

Malina had been pleased with the production. She had presented the play in a consciously crude fashion, demanding that the actors refrain from wearing makeup. And given the applause at the conclusion, she was certain that the audience appreciated what the Living Theatre had accomplished. It was even a victory in the Artaudian sense, because the audience, according to Malina, had "shook with terror and delight" at the content and staging of the play. She recalled a story from philosopher Martin Buber about a saint that had humbled himself by offering "his own excrement" to the Gods. Had she done this with her play? And had the gods, the critics, judged her sinful?[41]

What was to be done? Armed with a cause, Malina and Beck drew upon their connections with New York's avant-garde, seeking influential endorsements for *The Connection*. Malina was a fan of Allen Ginsberg, considering *Howl* "a poem of vast significance." In January 1959, she had cried during his reading of his poem "Kaddish." Noticing her runny mascara, Ginsberg was delighted: "That's always been my ambition—to make people cry by reading my poems."[42] In August, Ginsberg attended a performance of *The Connection*, and he promised Malina to write about the play for the *Village Voice*, which he did, finding the play "very *down* and accurate about people, played by great cats." The play was "a real turn-on to a native American theatre." Ginsberg concluded: "And therefore I declare that any drama critic who attacks this play is an out and out phony."[43] Other worthies were coaxed or cajoled by Malina to weigh in. Sometimes it proved easy; Malina had "boldly introduced" herself to Norman Mailer after he had seen the play, and got him to write something positive about it. He called *The Connection* "dangerous, true, artful, and alive."[44]

On August 24, 1959, a tall and strikingly handsome man arrived at the Living Theatre, in response to Allen Ginsberg's plea. This was Kenneth Tynan, the influential drama critic. During intermission, he proved to be enthusiastic about what he had seen. Every day following this, Malina wondered if a review would be forthcoming; after a week, she dropped him a reminder note. But no review. The theater's financial situation grew more horrendous. Con Edison had given them twenty-four hours to cough up $176 or have their electricity cut. The landlord was threatening eviction, and the telephone bill remained unpaid. In October, Tynan, accompanied by "two blondes," showed up again for the play to make sure that his initial impressions had not been in error. The next issue of the *New Yorker* proved that Malina's wait had been worth it.[45]

Tynan raved about the set, staging, acting, direction, and authenticity of the production. Tynan proclaimed *The Connection* "the first really interesting new play to appear off-Broadway in a good long time." While he went on at some length about how addiction was a tactical error in the battle against conformity, he remained impressed with how the addicts rang true to their own addictions. Gelber's lines, which might appear "flat, lifeless" in print, onstage were "vibrant with implication"—marking him as a leading voice in the beat movement. Malina, wrote Tynan, had done a wonderful job directing the play, managing to have a bunch of characters onstage—including musicians who both played and acted—without any of them getting lost or confused in the shuffle of the drama.[46] "The extravagant praise of the *New Yorker*'s review," Malina reported, "astonishes me as much as the initial insulting reviews stunned me." Alas, "our debts mount with our glory."[47]

The glory continued to mount in early fall of 1959 with an avalanche of positive reviews. In perhaps the most erudite review, Robert Brustein, in "Junkies and Jazz," acknowledged that the play was nontraditional and it "goes nowhere," nor at the end is there any sense of moral enlightenment. Luckily, Brustein found this refreshing. The drama was truthful—in an existential sense that Brustein in a book a few years later would refer to as part of "the theatre of revolt": revolt against artifice, pallid moralism, and the propriety of progress. The play itself was a hearty slap against inauthenticity and in favor of revolt. It spoke to the essentials of the human condition.[48]

Even the *New York Times* reconsidered *The Connection*. Its chief drama critic, Brooks Atkinson, understood how viewers of the play may have felt "mangled" by the sordidness of the play. And some might be dispirited by its refusal to condemn the use of narcotics, or by the "morbid languor" of its scenes, or by the fact that there was little "memorable" in the dialogue. Although the jazz music offered some "sizzling" numbers, its presence was tangential to the action taking place on the stage. After this recitation of demurrals, Atkinson admitted that *The Connection* was "an engrossing piece of theatre in an obsessive style." Present in the play were some of the insignia of a new sensibility—improvisation, spontaneity, and refusal to adhere to traditional genre definitions. The drama was an "experience," at once original and real. Malina's direction, he announced, had "purged the play of artificiality," ironically through artificial methods (the play within the play, the engagement of the actors with the audience, the self-consciousness by the actors about being in a play).[49]

The Living Theatre's next production, perhaps appropriately, was Pirandello's avant-garde classic *Tonight We Improvise*—another play designed to challenge the passive viewing habits of audiences. It was a middling success, running into the middle of 1960. But critical acclaim came to the Living Theatre when Gelber was awarded an Obie prize from the *Village Voice* for best play of the year. According to Living Theatre biographer John Tytell, Gelber and others in the company succumbed to what Beck called "Mammon's revenge," becoming prickly about profits.[50] In defense of Gelber, he had a wife and child to support, and he never disdained making a living from his theater work. "I was always fighting with the Becks about money," he recalled, but he found that he loved the fame and fortune (however fleeting it might be) and being part of the New York artistic scene.[51] By the end of 1959, Malina was a leading light of the stage, accepted by mainstream theater critics and playwrights. As praise for her direction of *The Connection* accumulated, she began to worry about "being trapped" into the mainstream theater, in the manner of the Groucho Marx line about not wanting to be a member of any club that would have him.[52]

The attention garnered by *The Connection* translated into new opportunities. Malina and the Living Theatre went to Paris in June 1961 to perform the play. Kenneth Tynan's sister-in-law, Shirley Clarke decided to make a film version of *The Connection* (leading to yet another court fight with authorities that wanted to censor the film for its depiction of drug culture).[53]

But the law was not finished yet with Malina and Beck. The Internal Revenue Service charged stiff interest fees on unpaid tax bills. In 1963, authorities seized the Living Theatre building for nonpayment of taxes. Malina and Beck, along with some of their actors, occupied their own building, refusing police orders to vacate. They even staged a performance, in the midst of this mania, of the play *The Brig*—a powerful play about the brutal treatment of marines imprisoned for various infractions of military rules.[54] The excitement ended when Malina, Beck, and cast members and supporters were arrested and charged with a medley of crimes. They used the proceedings to signal their anarchist disdain for the court—infuriating the judge and alienating the jurors. The courtroom had been transformed into an absurdist play of sorts, but one with real consequences. Malina proudly refused to allow the prosecutor to refer to them as guilty: "I can assert my innocence at any time in my life…and you cannot stop me! The only way to stop me is by cutting out my tongue." Beck announced that he cherished as a "moral obligation" his right "to demean the majesty of the court." The jury, unsurprisingly, found the rebellious Malina and Beck guilty, and the judge also held them in contempt of court.[55]

Since restrictions had not been placed on their travel, they embarked by ship to Europe for a period of exile and experimentation, only returning to the United States in 1968. Malina and Beck became ever more devoted to a radical theater based on Artaudian principles. They wanted to produce plays that reshaped the consciousness of audiences, which refused to bow to theatrical conventions, and to build a company that would be an alternative community. Malina, too, was moving now with more assurance into new directions, coming more and more to appreciate the value of spontaneity and improvisation rather than adherence to fixed scripts. By the mid-1960s, productions of the Living Theatre had become famous or infamous, according to one's tastes, for their barely controlled chaos, strong political content, and wild liberation. Malina wanted actors to engage in "exemplary actions" to banish barriers between them and the audience.[56]

In *Paradise Now* (1968), audience members were encouraged to come onstage to fondle (and to be fondled in turn) by seminude cast members. Certain phrases were repeated throughout the play: "I don't know how to stop the wars"; "I'm not allowed to smoke marijuana"; "I'm not allowed to take my clothes off." Political mantras, bedlam onstage, and sexually tinged interactions between actors and audience were intended by Beck and Malina to violate all Broadway taboos.

They certainly violated taboos in New Haven, Connecticut, on September 27, 1968. With Malina and Beck only recently returned from their four-year European exile, the performance of *Paradise Now* offended New Haven officials, who claimed that a sixteen-year-old had been participating in the onstage revelry, with only "a ribbon around his waist." Beck was arrested wearing "only a loin cloth" and charged along with others in the cast with indecent exposure.

Robert Brustein, who eight years earlier had praised *The Connection*, and who was now dean of the Yale School of Drama, defended the production on civil liberty rather than aesthetic grounds. He called the performance "a controlled happening" that was "remarkably harmless and even gentle." Yet, ever the critic, Brustein noted that he had "found the production tedious and without much theatrical value." Beck, in contrast, seconded by Malina, announced with pride, "We're breaking down the barriers that exist between art and life, barriers that keep most men outside the gates of paradise."[57]

Other former supporters such as Eric Bentley by 1968 had parted company with the Living Theatre. As he put it, "The LT has taken leave of its senses," not in an interesting, temporary sense but as a mode of being. He had grown tired of their political rhetoric and pose, their "various insults against the audience." Other critics chimed in, accusing the Living Theatre of practicing a form of left-wing fascism, of sloganeering, of bad acting. Being arrested and criticized for their excesses became for Malina and Beck a badge of courage, proof that at least on the stage they had entered into some place of paradise.[58]

Norman Mailer, cover image for Advertisements for Myself
(© Photofest)

All About Me

NORMAN MAILER

1960

A few hours into the morning of Sunday, November 19, 1960, novelist Norman Mailer stabbed his second wife, Adele, repeatedly in the chest and back with a penknife. They had been hosting a big bash in their spacious apartment on the Upper West Side of Manhattan. The party was supposed to celebrate the birthday of Mailer's friend Roger Donahue, a former boxer who had once played a bit part in *On the Waterfront*. It was also intended to kick off Mailer's quixotic campaign for mayor of New York City.[1]

The apartment was "packed wall to wall, mobbed with the wildest, most heterogeneous group imaginable," recalled stage director Frank Corsaro. At various points in the long evening, George Plimpton, society pianist Peter Duchin, sociologist C. Wright Mills, poet Allen Ginsberg, critic Norman Podhoretz, and actor Tony Franciosa mingled uncomfortably with street thugs and various oddballs. The booze flowed too freely, and Corsaro wondered "What the fuck am I doing here?" He and many others departed early from a party that stank of impending disaster.

Mailer had been in a dark, drunk, manic mood throughout the day. Around four in the morning, after most had fled the party, Mailer and Adele were in the kitchen. She, too, was drunk, and they had been raging at one another, with skill and anger, for months. It came to a head when Adele taunted him, as a bullfighter to a bull: "Come on you little faggot, where's your *cojones*, did your ugly whore of a mistress cut them off, you son of a bitch?" Perhaps it was then that Mailer pulled a penknife from his pocket. Bull-like, he charged at Adele, goring her repeatedly with his three-inch knife until she was bloody and he was spent.

Two days later, Mailer was arrested and confined to Bellevue Mental Hospital for seventeen days. One psychiatric report stated that he had experienced "an acute paranoid breakdown with delusional thinking"; he was diagnosed as "both homicidal and suicidal." Pictures of Mailer splashed in the daily newspapers, showing him at the time of his arrest neatly dressed but with a zombie-like look. Adele had been rushed to a hospital for emergency surgery the morning of the stabbing. She recovered from her severe injuries, but the nine-year relationship with Mailer died. Luckily for Mailer, she declined to press charges, and the imbroglio became yet another entry in the list of Mailer's outrageous acts over the previous five years.

The year 1960 should have been a very good one for Mailer. His new book, *Advertisements for Myself*, had been published in the late fall of 1959. Reviews were mixed but engaged. One reviewer reveled in its liveliness, humor, and versatility. Reviewing *Advertisements* in *The Nation*, fellow writer Gore Vidal found himself tired of Mailer's "forever shouting at us" with "swelling throbbing rhetoric." Yet he respected Mailer's reaching for a new style, finding "virtue in his failures." The book's sales, according to his editor William Minton, "proved to be pretty much of a bomb."[2]

Advertisements nonetheless perfectly displayed Mailer's monumental ego and talent. With typical bravado he announced at the outset of the volume, "I am imprisoned with a perception which will settle for nothing less than making a revolution in the consciousness of our time." In order to achieve this, Mailer searched for a new style and sensibility—at once revelatory and revolutionary but, above all else, hip.[3] This notion of hip, in Mailer's own calculation, would "introduce a new idea into America."[4]

The front and back covers of the book overflowed with self-regard. A photograph of Mailer, young and healthy looking with some sort of sailing cap atop his curly-haired dome, filled the front cover. The back cover featured four smaller pictures of the author—each one next to favorable snippets from reviews of his novels. Somehow Mailer had managed to be photographed wearing the same checkered shirt in 1955 and in 1958. In the latter picture, he sported a beatnik goatee. The checkered shirt served as a perfect metaphor for the last decade of his life—at once creative and destructive, daring and frustrating, but above all excessive and extreme.

His last two novels had been less than successful. *Barbary Shore* ("murky, bad and badly plotted") had not sold well, and *The Deer Park*, according to one reviewer, was "a thoroughly nasty book and a dull one."[5] Mailer's promise as novelist had once seemed unlimited. His first effort, *The Naked and Dead*, published in 1948, captured the absurdity of the Pacific campaign of World War II. Orville Prescott, reviewing for the *New York Times*, called it "overwhelming." Mailer was "as certain to become famous as any fledgling novelist can be."[6] The pressure, however, nailed Mailer to a cross of expectations. Drink, drugs, and failure had by 1960 turned him from the wunderkind of fiction into a laughingstock, more "an actor instead of a writer," Philip Roth remarked condescendingly.[7]

It is hard to say precisely when Mailer's downward spiral began. He had always craved escape from his cloistered, middle-class Jewish background.

Asserting his manhood became a pose and a necessity for him. No sooner had he graduated from Harvard (studying engineering but excelling in literature) than he signed up to fight in the Second World War. His patriotism and heroism probably played less of a role than his desire to experience the event of his era and to write about it at firsthand. Three years after his stint in the Pacific—where he saw a bit of action firing his rifle at phantoms in the jungle but mostly endured heat and boredom—Mailer had published his war novel. What lifted it from run-of-the-mill war novels then proliferating (although its employment of ethnic stereotypes in portraying soldiers was standard fare) was its ambition (modeled in many ways on *Moby-Dick*), its deeper intentions (to reveal the totalitarian nature of institutions, such as the US Army), and its existential intonations about the absurdity of life.

The novel catapulted Mailer to instant stardom, although by 1955 some of the burnish was gone. Mailer reeled from bad habits, which he cultivated enthusiastically. Like his sometime hero Hemingway, he drank to excess, bourbon being his drink of preference. For years he smoked two packs of cigarettes a day and popped Benzedrine and Seconal. According to a friend, Mailer "deliberately got wild with drugs—marijuana, then peyote and mescal[ine]." The drugs, along with the commercial failure of his novels, fueled his anger and violence—throwing him into some sort of "primitivism."[8] He befriended boxers, took boxing lessons, and boasted of his own pugilistic skills. He managed to find trouble. One night, walking his poodles in New York City, a passing sailor apparently made a remark about Mailer being queer for having such well-groomed, fancy dogs. Mailer jumped at the challenge. After the fight, one of Mailer's eyes was badly damaged.[9]

When not fighting, Mailer was on a quest to find himself, to open himself up to experience, not only by fisticuffs but with the aid of an orgone accumulator that he had set up in his apartment. The orgone accumulator was a large box, an invention of Wilhelm Reich, a onetime revolutionary Marxist psychologist, that was supposed to release positive energy; if so, the energy emanating from Mailer continued to flow in violent sprees and bouts of drinking. After "only four drinks" at a Provincetown bar, Mailer was walking with his wife Adele back to their summer home when he hailed a police car—later claiming that he had mistaken it for a taxi. At one point in what ensued, Mailer shoved one of the officers to the ground. The other police officer, William Sylvia, nicknamed "Cobra," retaliated with a baton blow to Mailer's skull. Mailer found himself in the local jail with a wound on the back of his head requiring about fifteen stitches. According to Sylvia, "Some of these guys," like Mailer, "you'd like to punch 'em in the mouth."[10] In this period, Mailer later admitted, "I had more than a bit of violence in me."[11]

Drink and violence riled his marriage, too. With a good sense for historic periodization, Mailer later called these years a time of "dull drifting" and "the Trouble."[12]

Mailer realized that the only way to overcome "the Trouble" was to sit at his desk and write, whether sober or not. He was often drunk, depressed, and raging, and his fiction suffered, growing stilted, disorganized, and mockingly ambitious. He worried in advance about "the nightmare of wondering what would happen if all the reviews were bad."[13] Such real and imagined adversity, however, pushed Mailer to explore new possibilities—writing that was self-analytic and confessional, raw and honest, pugnacious and portentous. He had always maintained that the personality of the writer was woven into the text and necessary for public attention, citing Hemingway as exemplary. Had a writer of American fiction ever attempted anything quite so audacious?

The content of *Advertisements for Myself* was varied in the extreme. In it were fictional pieces that dated back to Mailer's days as an undergraduate at Harvard, as well as selections from his published novels. One section was devoted to columns that he had contributed in the mid-1950s to help inaugurate the weekly newspaper the *Village Voice*, an association that soon foundered. Some pieces were works in progress. Indeed, Mailer offered a taste of what he proclaimed would be a massive novel. Included in *Advertisements* were poems of dubious distinction, articles attacking the cancer of conformity and mass culture, and a reprint of his most infamous piece, "The White Negro." There was something appealingly slapdash and engaging to it all. Nevertheless, as biographer Mary Dearborn notes, in *Advertisements* Mailer had imagined "a new sensibility on the horizon and wisely aligned himself with it by writing, in fact, its first polemic."[14]

This New Sensibility, as realized by Mailer, was performative—Mailer was a character in, as well as a commentator upon, his life and work. Mailer's personality stalked every page of the volume. It was a rant against middle-class conformity. Mailer was in pursuit of pleasures (often problematic ones) in violence, drugs, and sex. Spontaneity and freedom were opposed to the constraints of the old sensibility that had deranged American culture and politics. *Advertisements for Myself* featured what Mailer called "advertisements," italicized interludes of his opinions about himself and his work. Sometimes boastfully, often insightfully and honestly, Mailer commented on the pieces in the collection. He realized that such advertisements were often "more readable than the rest" of the book. In them he displayed his "personality as the armature of this book." It was a public performance, like a confession before an audience of priests, except in this case, rather than requesting forgiveness, what he wanted was attention. Mailer made his quest for "self-discovering" and "self-watching" into a public performance, to use critic Richard Poirier's term. For Mailer, this performance was many things: "an exercise in power," a form of narcissism, and a bid for publicity (whether good or bad mattered little) and sign of his need to be at the center of the historical moment.[15]

Mailer understood this explicitly—any publicity was better than no publicity. After *Deer Park* had been savaged by critics, Mailer took out an advertisement in the *Village Voice*, where he printed snippets from the harshest reviews, introducing them with blustery irony: "All over America 'The Deer Park' is getting nothing bur RAVES." Here are some of the "RAVES": "sordid," "crummy," "the year's worst snakepit in fiction." His columns in the *Voice* often drew spirited ripostes, and Mailer included them in *Advertisements* with the same glee, apparently happy that critics at least had spelled his name correctly. One reader wrote: "The very obvious trouble with you is you really suffer from illusion of grandeur." Another wrote, "This guy Mailer. He's a hostile, narcissistic pest. Lose him." Finally, reflecting on Mailer's use of the first-person in his columns, someone wrote: "You take up 98 per cent of your column talking about yourself. Very wrong.... Anyone who did not know what a swell guy you are might think that you were in love with yourself."[16]

Authors had long employed their personality—translated into celebrity status—to drive book sales. Mark Twain sold himself as much as he did his prose; ditto for Ernest Hemingway. In "The Crack Up," which F. Scott Fitzgerald published in *Esquire* in 1936, he confessed his excesses: "I suddenly was living hard" until "I suddenly realized I had prematurely cracked." But no one had been as forthright, almost to the point of boastfulness, about such maneuvers as Mailer: "The way to save your work and reach more readers is to advertise yourself." His advertisements and craving for celebrity status, at turns dark with despair and airy with ambition, were on full display in *Advertisements*.[17] It was a gutsy gamble.

He was frank and confessional about the "years of trouble." He had been "barren of new ideas," guilty of "dull drifting" in his life while admitting, "Self-pity is one of my vices." He wrote openly about how booze and drugs had been his closest companions; he looked back on the years from 1954 to 1959 as a time of pain, perhaps even witnessing a diminution of his powers: "There may have been too many fights...too much sex, liquor, marijuana, benzedrine and seconal, much too much ridiculous and brain-blasting rage at the miniscule frustrations of a most loathsome literary world, necrophilic to the core—they murder their writers, and then decorate their graves."[18]

Mailer seemed to be digging his own grave with advertisements that were excessive in their self-regard and bellyaching. In the opening advertisement, Mailer announced, "I have been running for President these last ten years in the privacy of my mind." His life was swirling about, and "anger has brought me to the edge of the brutal." To survive he must direct this "brutal" sensibility toward its proper targets. Thus, he warred against the "cancer" of his age—the conformity that was killing him and his fellow citizens. He summed up the politics and culture of the 1950s with brutal simplicity: "The shits are killing us."[19]

Mailer was a committed leftist. He supported Henry A. Wallace's doomed bid for the presidency in 1948, and he remained convinced that a bureaucratic totalitarianism was in the offing. The "air of our time," he reflected, was marked by "authority and nihilism stalking one another in the orgiastic hollow of this century."[20] That air was putrid with decay, a theme that he had tried to reflect through the claustrophobic atmosphere of a rooming house in his novel *Barbary Shore*. Increasingly, however, he came to believe that the threat came as much from the steady accumulation of middle-class comfort and complacency as it did from the government.

In 1952, as noted earlier, the *Partisan Review*, the journal of regard for intellectuals, polled various intellectuals and writers on the topic of "Our Country and Our Culture." The essential question was whether America's intellectuals had reconciled with their nation. In the 1930s and 1940s, they had opposed capitalism and been aghast at the national culture. Had the revival of capitalism, victory in the Second World War, the success of mass culture, and the entry of intellectuals into institutions of higher learning and national prominence effected a change in their attitudes about life in America?

Most of the respondents were overwhelmingly affirmative. Old antagonisms between intellectual and mainstream culture seemed to have dissipated in postwar America. Newton Arvin, a biographer of fine sensibility, echoing Emerson, announced that American intellectuals needed to distance themselves from Europe and embrace their native heritage. Lionel Trilling positively glowed about how the cultural situation in America was improving daily. This onetime parlor radical went so far as to proclaim, "Wealth shows a tendency to submit itself to the rule of mind and imagination, to refine itself, and to apologize for its existence by a show of taste and sensitivity." Intellect and power, Trilling observed, had begun to dance together enjoyably. Even the threat of mass culture, the particular bugaboo of intellectuals since the 1930s, might be tamed and directed into efficacious channels.[21]

None of the intellectuals polled responded with Mailer's vehement disdain. He chafed at the presumption that reconciliation between writer and nation was a positive thing. There is no need to repeat his thorny complaints here. He concluded with the simple view that "the great artists—certainly the moderns—are almost always in opposition to their society, and that integration, acceptance, non-alienation, etc. etc., have been more conducive to propaganda than to art."[22]

What was to be done? A new sensibility—which Mailer designated as the "philosophy of hip"—must battle the forces of conformity. Mailer craved hipness. Some, like James Baldwin, found him pathetic in this regard, an essentially square fellow striving with middle-class dedication to be cool. He struggled mightily to define and live hip, even compiling a list of qualities associated with it and juxtaposed with qualities attributed to square. The comparisons ranged from the pretentious to the silly, from the insightful to the absurd—a typical Mailer performance, probably jotted down while he skyed on marijuana. Under the heading "Hip," Mailer included "sex," "Negro," "Thelonious

Monk," existentialists such as Heidegger and Dostoevsky, and various terms: "wild" and "barbarians"—sort of like a dog marking the territory of the New Sensibility. He scorned, naturally, everything that he considered "square" or traditional, ranging from jazz musician Dave Brubeck, to "religion," to "Sartre." Mailer included Sartre in the square category only because he saw him as a rival for the honor of being the leading existentialist thinker.[23]

In 1957, Mailer issued his notorious manifesto of hip, "The White Negro: Superficial Reflections on the Hipster." He had first lit upon the idea in 1954, jotting down: "Wild thought. The atomic bomb may have kicked off hipsterism."[24] The notion of the hipster, however, was not original to Mailer. A fellow New York writer, Anatole Broyard, had as early as 1948 mused about the hipster as a coolly passionate connoisseur of "jive music" and marijuana. Affinities existed between this hipsterism and the beat sensibility of Kerouac and Ginsberg, although the latter rejected any association with violent behavior as unhip, part of the problem of their era rather than the solution to it.[25]

The essay appeared in the journal *Dissent*, a surprising venue. Edited by Irving Howe, *Dissent* was a social democratic periodical, devoted to reason as an agent of change. The only discernable explanation for Howe's accepting Mailer's torrential essay was its critique of conformity. As already noted, in 1954 Howe had penned "This Age of Conformity," complaining about the numbing effects of mass culture on the intellect, the ineffectiveness of alienation at producing political change, and the dangers in conformity and institutional power. In sum, "Every current of the *Zeitgeist*, every imprint of social power, every assumption of contemporary American life favors the safe and comforting patterns of middlebrow feeling."[26] Perhaps, then, Mailer's essay represented for Howe a powder-keg piece that would, if nothing else, stir up controversy.

It did.

Much of Mailer's essay was predictable—respouting criticisms of mass culture that had been common coin for intellectuals such as Clement Greenberg, Dwight Macdonald, and Howe. America was cringing under conformity, inching closer toward totalitarianism. Mediocrity reigned and courage to defy it seemed weak. If this diagnosis seemed insufficiently bleak, then Mailer upped the ante by returning to his 1954 postulate about a nuclear holocaust. "A stench of fear," Mailer opined, "has come out of every pore of American life, and we suffer from a collective failure of nerve."[27]

New possibilities, however, were emerging. In inner cities African Americans, in particular, were birthing a new character type marked by rebellion and violence. The hipster, or existential man, according to Mailer, recognized the contingency of existence in the Atomic Age. He was aghast at the cancer of conformity. Shrugging off both, the hipster courageously jived in a different key. He skated along the thin line of responsibility, digging the beat of his emotions and inner urgings (even, or perhaps especially, when they tilted in a psychopathic direction). Like a jazz musician, he improvised a tune of love,

danger, and freedom. Modern men (and men were clearly Mailer's main audience) must "set out on that unchartered journey into the rebellious imperatives of the self." If such a journey led to criminal behavior or an expression of
psychopathology, then so be it. Better to face the world with the "courage" of
the outlaw than with the dignity of the middle-class conformist.[28]

Much of this was the common jargon of existentialism. Between 1945 and
the early 1950s, and again in the early 1960s, existentialism was popular in
the United States. At first it was the excited property of intellectuals and writers. Glance at Ralph Ellison's *Invisible Man* (1952) and Richard Wright's *The
Outsider* (1953) on the fiction front, or the theology of Will Herberg, or in
the psychology of Rollo May, to get a sense of existentialism's sway. By 1960,
the leading works of existentialism—from Sartre's *Being and Nothingness* to
Heidegger's *Being and Time*—had been published in translation. Walter
Kaufmann's anthology of existentialism, however much it was biased toward
emphasizing a German fount for the tradition, was treasured by a generation
of college students. These same students devoured Camus's *The Stranger* in
French language classes or encountered *The Rebel* in introductory philosophy
and political science classes.[29]

Mailer was coy about the sources of his existentialism. He rarely addressed
Sartre, Camus, or Beauvoir. His knowledge of Heidegger was minimal, probably cadged from reading an essay in *Partisan Review* by Hannah Arendt, or by
skimming New York intellectual William Barrett's relatively breezy contribution, *Irrational Man*. The current crop of existentialists turned Mailer off because of their atheism; he preferred a religious perspective that found God
wounded but made stronger by our own courageous efforts against evil.[30] The
existentialist that he actually read and understood somewhat was Søren
Kierkegaard. Mailer liked Kierkegaard's edgy religious quality, his sense of the
absurd and tragic, and, perhaps most importantly, that he was dead—hence
Kierkegaard was no competitor with Mailer for being the king of the intellectuals, the consciousness of his time.

By the early 1960s, and already in "The White Negro," Mailer was feverishly
waving his existential flag. He appropriated existentialism as his own, skipping
over those parts that challenged his own perspective. It was a mania of sorts,
his favored adjective, as in "existential President" and "existential filmmaking."
It appeared as if every nonfiction sentence he wrote had some derivative of the
word existential in it. He titled a collection of essays *Existential Errands* (1972),
and he made an "existential film" called *Wild 90* in 1968. In sum, existentialism
was "a situation where we cannot foretell the end." But armed with such uncertain vision, we plunged ahead.[31]

Mailer suggested strongly that negroes (the designation of the period) were
especially open to hip existentialism because of racism. For generations they
had suffered from white violence. This made them acutely aware of the dangers of existence and opened them up to the rhythm of their own emotions.

When your entire existence depended upon the whim of racist power and privilege, then you developed existential sensibilities. Had Mailer stopped at this point, he would have mirrored the views of such distinguished black commentators on the blues and jazz sensibility as Ellison and Alfred Murray and agreed with the commentary implicit in Frank's images.

Such was not Mailer's style; he had to push things. He referred to the negro as a "wise primitive." Such primitivism was found in black sexuality, supposedly untainted by the dullness of middle-class proprieties. Without fretting about how his remarks on black sexual freedom complemented white racist views about black male sexuality, Mailer piled on the craziness, disguised as compliments. He failed to discern existentialism, as had Ellison and Murray, in the blues-gospel laments in black churches or in daily existence or in how black folks overcame indignities with quiet intensity. Instead, his roster of hipster heroes was populated by black pimps, or dope-injecting jazzmen. Indeed, he thrilled at the existential freedom of the murderer, who, when faced with a moment of choice, decided to plunge a knife into the heart of a victim. "Apocalyptic orgasm," he called it.[32]

He discussed such an "apocalyptic orgasm" in some detail, imagining the existential or psychopathic delights of murder: "The psychopath murders—if he has the courage—out of the necessity to purge his violence." And, then, dripping with controversial spleen, Mailer imagines "two strong eighteen-year old hoodlums," who "beat in the brains of a candy-store keeper," are still courageous. They are murdering not just a defenseless man, but "an institution as well." And by doing so, by trashing the value of "private property," these psychopathic hoodlums becomes "daring," and "the brutal the act, is not altogether cowardly."[33]

This drivel proved prescient for Mailer. Between 1955 and 1960, he tried, with schoolboy enthusiasm and discipline, to be a hipster. He hung out at jazz clubs, consumed huge quantities of liquor, marijuana, and other drugs. "The White Negro" was intended as a manifesto of hip, but Ginsberg pronounced it "very square."[34] Critic Alfred Kazin wrote Mailer, "You are the Rabbi of screwing, the writer who has managed to be so solemn about sex as to make it grim."[35]

Baldwin responded with a long piece in *Esquire*. He detailed his fraught friendship with Mailer—and their obvious differences of race and class. Mailer was simply incapable of dropping silly notions about male Negro sexual potency—it was a form of romantic longing on Mailer's part. He chided Mailer, telling him to grow up and take responsibility for the implications of his writing. This was the burden, and the responsibility, of the artist, hip or otherwise.[36]

In 1960 Mailer was a taut wire, ready to brawl and head-butt at the slightest provocation. He boasted about being able to withstand a hammer blow to the head without losing consciousness. Perhaps, then, on that foul early morning in the kitchen, Mailer had succumbed to the call of his inner hipster psycho-path. Good thing that Mailer was armed with a pocketknife rather than a switchblade.

"The White Negro" should not be dismissed out of hand for its excess, obses-siveness, inanity, racism, and violence. It sounded in an unkempt manner key themes that would emerge as central for the New Sensibility.[37] It exemplified a style that was based on an economy of emotional excess (though expressed in a cool way). The essay stressed that liberation was linked to a form of madness, orgasm, and the allure of violence, were paraded at least for readers with suffi-cient fortitude to stomach Mailer. Indeed, in its sensibility and concerns, the essay anticipated the 1960s and the fascination of white rebels with black revo-lutionary movements, celebrated violence as the means to liberation, swooned at the freedom presumed to inhere in excessive drug use, and paraded the ideal that the truly sane are those condemned as mad by mainstream society.

Some of the fights Mailer picked in *Advertisements* were personal and literary. In one piece, he pugnaciously evaluated his literary contemporaries. He pub-licly dismissed many writers (some of whom he claimed as friends) and praised a few. It was a sort of madly inspired piece, better left to the confines of the asylum that he had occupied for two weeks after his stabbing of Adele. But Mailer was in a macho phase, challenging everyone with his own prodigious and undirected talent, no matter how much it had failed him of late in fiction. He was, in effect, sizing up the room so that he could prove with his next novel that he had bested the competition.

He cut to the quick. "The only one of my contemporaries who I felt had more talent than myself was James Jones. And he has also been the one writer of my time for whom I felt any love." Alas, Jones suffered from too much drink; he had "imprisoned his anger, and dwindled without it."[38]

And this for a man and writer he loved and respected. Suffice it to say, the evaluation ended their friendship.

Mailer badly missed the mark when he pronounced that while his onetime pal William Styron had talent, he lacked courage to write a really important book. In Kerouac Mailer found "a large talent," but without "discipline, intelli-gence, honesty and a sense of the novel." Truman Capote was a "ballsy little guy, and he is the most perfect writer of my generation, he writes the best sentences word for word, rhythm upon rhythm"; unfortunately, he settled for surface rather than depth. Evaluations of Saul Bellow, Nelson Algren, J. D. Salinger, Paul Bowles, James Baldwin ("too charming a writer to be major"), Ralph Ellison ("a mistake to write prescriptions for a novelist as gifted as Ellison"), and a handful of other male competitors followed.[39]

At the end of the polemic, Mailer contemptuously addressed women writers of his generation. They were "always fey, old-hat, Quaintsy Goysy, tiny, too dykily psychotic, crippled, creepish, fashionable, frigid, outer-Baroque, *maquille* in mannequin's whimsy, or else bright and stillborn." He admitted reluctantly that he had enjoyed "the early work of Mary McCarthy, Jean Stafford, and Carson McCullers." There was, however, hope for a new dawn for women's writing, Mailer prophesied, when "the first whore becomes a call girl and tells her tale."[40]

Mailer's madness, overwrought confessionalism, and feverish feistiness spread across the pages of *Advertisements*, making it an original work with a different feel, a new voice, a stunning sensibility, no matter how many its miscues. He felt that he had been honest and brave in the volume. Those smarting under his lash found him boorish and narrow. He had, as he predicted, acquired "a dozen devoted enemies for life" with his evaluations. Styron wrote to Jim Jones that Mailer had "flipped his lid, or is gradually flipping it."[41]

Mailer had tossed down the gauntlet. It was time for him to put up or shut up. *Advertisements* in its style was brilliant and jaunty, a presentiment of the New Sensibility. But it was not a work of fiction—and that was the shelf upon which Mailer wanted his reputation to rest.

A month before Mailer assaulted Adele, his essay on John F. Kennedy and the Democratic National Convention splashed onto newsstands in the magazine *Esquire*. Clay Felker, one of its editors, had admired Mailer's *Advertisements* and commissioned him (paying him $3,500) to write about the convention.[42] He further promised to introduce Mailer to various politicos in the campaign. In addition, Mailer twice visited Kennedy's compound at Hyannis Port to interview the candidate.

"Superman Comes to the Marketplace" was vintage Mailer. It was also an early expression of the "New Journalism." In this mode, the writer presented himself forthrightly as a character in the reportage. In "Superman," this was done with some restraint, as Mailer referred to himself as he intruded into the story. Eight years later, in *The Armies of the Night*, his masterful narrative account of a demonstration against the Vietnam War at the Pentagon, Mailer would refer to himself in the text by his own name and various third-person pronouns. He had elevated himself to the role of an actor in history, thus jumping into the waters of the New Sensibility by making reportage into performance and by blurring the lines between history and fiction. Recognizing this fully, Mailer subtitled his book *History as a Novel / The Novel as History*.[43]

In the Kennedy piece, his prose cut cleanly. James J. Farley, onetime postmaster general and an eminence within the Democratic Party, was described this way: "Huge. Cold as a bishop. The hell he would consign you to was cold as ice." The Biltmore Hotel convention site appeared to Mailer as "one of the ugliest hotels in the world. Patterned after the flat roofs of an Italian Renaissance palace, it is eighty-eight times as large, and one-millionth as valuable to the continuation of man." Once inside, Mailer confronted a "hill of cigar smoke," finding the convention delegates dull, depressed, and driven.[44]

The essay offered minimal political analysis or context. Mailer steamed only when dwelling on his own pet peeves (shared by most adherents of the New Sensibility)—that mass culture, the mediocrity of the Eisenhower administration, and McCarthyism had sapped America of the collective strength displayed during the 1930s and early 1940s. The ship of the American state and society was adrift, threatening to run aground or sink in deep waters.

The solution, Mailer decided, was a new American hero. This hero would have movie star qualities and appeal. He would be expected to "fight well, kill well (if always with honor), love well and love many, be cool, be daring, be dashing, be wild, be wily, be resourceful, be a brave gun." He would be untamed by those representing the status quo, with its tepid sanity and perfervid and empty moralism.[45]

What America craved was a Mailerian hipster hero with "a patina of that other life, the second American life, the long electric night with the fires of neon leading down the highway to the murmur of jazz."[46]

Mailer anointed Kennedy for this mythical role. It was not so much Kennedy's positions on political issues that enthused him. Mailer, in fact, seemed relatively uninterested in Kennedy's views of domestic and foreign policy—something he would later come to regret. No, it was Kennedy's movie star, celebrity qualities, hitched to wartime heroism, that made Mailer (and other Americans) swoon. And make no mistake about it, Mailer fell hard for Kennedy.

In part, Kennedy learned that the quickest route to Mailer's heart was through his monumental ego. Kennedy's handlers knew that Mailer's article—due out just before the election—might receive big play, so they advised Kennedy about how to deal with Mailer. Upon being introduced to Mailer, the candidate Kennedy remarked that he had read Mailer's novels. Mailer expected Kennedy to cite *The Naked and the Dead*. It was a response that always sent Mailer into a tailspin of depression, dredging up as it did the relative failure and obscurity of his subsequent novels. But Kennedy stunned him when he praised *The Deer Park*. Mailer was charmed and thrilled, even to the point of rejecting the likely scenario that Kennedy had made the remark simply to seduce Mailer.[47]

Mailer gushed over Kennedy's vigor and good looks, his "excellent, even artful" manners. The candidate possessed "the eyes of a mountaineer," whatever that meant. Kennedy's ability to show a range of appearances without changing expression reminded Mailer of Brando (another apostle of the New Sensibility). Like Brando, Kennedy could not be easily contained, refusing reduction to a singular image. Mood, which Brando made into an icon of his acting, was something that Kennedy shared and allowed to express itself. Both seemed to comport themselves with the power and pleasure of the New Sensibility, the ability to defy convention. Noting that Kennedy's middle name was Fitzgerald, Mailer riffed on the F. Scott Fitzgerald connection. Kennedy's style evoked for Mailer images of Fitzgerald in the 1920s, a style that was elegant, youthful, and bursting with hope. Indeed, should Kennedy be elected, he might awaken the arts and open up a new "life of drama."[48]

Kennedy was a natural existential hero. In a section with the italic headings "*The Hipster as President Hero,*" Mailer beat the drum for Kennedy. Mailer even reported that a fellow writer at the convention had compared Kennedy with one of the hipsters in his novel *The Deer Park*—a comparison that Mailer found on the mark. The glow of Kennedy was enhanced, in Mailer's existential terminology, by his brushes with tragedy and death. He quoted from an account of how Kennedy, after his PT boat had been wrecked by the Japanese in the Second World War, had acted with endurance and heroism. Despite a badly injured back, Kennedy swam three miles to an island, towing along another sailor, via a life belt that Kennedy held between his teeth. Out of such experiences came an existential awareness that led to a tragic sensibility: he was "a man who has traversed some lonely terrain of experience, of loss and gain, of nearness to death, which leaves him isolated from the mass of others." This also opened the individual up to taking risks, to gambling, to clutching at greatness.[49]

Reflecting back on his paean to Kennedy after the election and various debacles in the administration, Mailer was more circumspect in his views. But he maintained, not without a soupçon of pride, that his essay "had more effect than any other single work of mine. . . . I was forcing a reality. . . . I took to myself some of the critical credit for his victory. Whether I was right or wrong in fact may not have been so important as its psychological reality in my own mind."[50]

Unfortunately, Mailer's own mind in the chilly days of November was overflowing with anger, sloppy with drink and drugs. But such a mind, in its own manner, proved strong enough to endure, maybe even to grow. Within the next few years, following divorce from Adele, Mailer married twice, with two children resulting. He worked on a new novel, *An American Dream*, published in 1965, his first in ten years. It featured a character named Rojack, a war hero who had served in Congress at one point with Jack Kennedy. The novel featured murder, a detailed anal rape scene, mysticism, and mania. Following along the path laid by Patricia Highsmith, Mailer allowed his hero to get away with murder.[51]

In its way, *An American Dream* was an exemplification of the New Sensibility, its excesses parading with a vengeance, bleeding from each and every page. It was daring, crossing boundaries of politeness, especially in its explicit depictions of sex.

Mailer was back from the edge of the abyss where he had stood in 1960. He had managed to channel his mania back into his fiction.

{ PART II }

Explosion, 1961–1968

Lenny Bruce and lawyer in court (© Photofest)

Say What?

LENNY BRUCE

1961

Looking like a carpet of cocaine, twenty inches of snow covered New York City on February 4, 1961. At midnight comedian Lenny Bruce bopped onto the stage at Carnegie Hall. Avid fans of the comedian had refused to allow inclement weather to prevent them from digging their idol at his moment of triumph—the joint was packed.[1] Carnegie Hall represented the highbrow, the epitome of class. Who hadn't at some time recited the old joke: "Excuse me, sir, how do I get to Carnegie Hall?" "Practice, kid, practice." Bruce was going big time tonight.

He had been practicing his shtick for years, in grim, slimy strip clubs, in cheap gin joints, and, in the last few years, in clubs that catered to sophisticated, hip audiences. For those too embarrassed or too poor to catch Bruce live at some venue, his comedy albums were hot sellers. On occasion, he had appeared on Steve Allen's network television show, offering a sanitized version of his regular act.

A little over a month before the concert, a fellow comedian had taken a public potshot at Bruce. Jack Carter, in the *New York Sunday Daily News*, complained that comedians such as Bruce were "embarrassing to the business." Carter continued: "He gets up there mouthing four-letter words of filth as if no one had ever heard them before.... His act is nothing more than unprofessional rambling."

Three days before Carnegie Hall, Bruce sarcastically responded: Do you "mean to tell me you've heard those words before?" If so, then Lenny Bruce worried that he might have overpaid a joke writer for curse words. Bruce closed by wondering if Jack Carter knew what was meant when he offered his fellow comic the words "Fuck you."[2]

At Carnegie Hall from midnight until 2:00 a.m., Bruce's audience was at once raucous and embarrassingly self-conscious; guilty pleasure mixed with satisfaction.[3] At any moment, much to the delight of the aficionados in the crowd, Bruce might cross the lines of common decency. This was why, in *Time* magazine's view, he was the reigning king of the sick comedians (Mort Sahl, Don Adams, and Shelley Berman were part of the fraternity), thanks to his full-throttled taking of comedy to its "extremes."[4] Or, according to *Billboard*, he was "a vulgar tasteless boor." Columnist Walter Winchell dubbed him "America's No. 1 Vomic."[5]

He was the Norman Mailer of comedy—outrageous, ballsy, combative, and bright. One commentator dubbed him the "sick white negro of comedy." Both of them connected with black culture; they were white hipsters that disdained conventionality. Bruce and Mailer were uninhibited in their use of drugs and booze, searching for rhythms that would evoke a new sensibility that would open up possibilities, both for themselves and for their audiences. If Mailer was a performance artist on the page (blurring the lines between the literary and the personal advertisement), then Bruce was active in bringing the language of the street and sex into the comedy club.[6]

Bruce, no less than Mailer, chafed at limits. Normally, there were some gags comedians shared among themselves, often when stoned or soused, away from audiences. One evening, Buddy Hackett tried to lift Bruce's sagging spirits at a club by telling him a joke too dirty to be bandied about onstage. Or at least it was for Hackett. But Lenny went onstage that night in 1958 and spit it out: "Kid looks up at father…and says, 'Daddy, what's a degenerate?'" The father answers: "Shut up, kid, and *keep sucking*!" The audience responded with shocked silence. Bruce gave them the finger, turned around, wiggled his ass, and then exited the stage.[7]

The Carnegie Hall material was edgy without being obscene. He opened with tame fare, a joke about the sagging fortunes of Miami Beach. Things had gotten so depressed there that elderly Jewish women were mugging Cuban exiles. Homosexual jokes almost always assured a good laugh. Mothers, he said, are "never hip" to their children being "faggots." When the son brings home sailors and marines to spend the night, the mother sighs lovingly, "Such a sweet kid to give them a place to stay for the night." Men, he announced, are "carnal creatures"; after fifteen years in prison, they'll "schtupp anything."

Bruce segued rapidly into more serious material. Morals were relative, a matter of power, he announced with mock-Nietzschean familiarity. He illustrated this "philosophical" position by noting that Christians had once been viewed as immoral, and hence were fed to the lions in ancient Rome—a fate, he remarked, far worse than being "schlubbed" from a lunch counter—as had happened the previous year to young African Americans protesting segregation in Greensboro, North Carolina. Next, he launched into a routine about a Ku Klux Klansman, touching on one of racists' central fears (and perhaps of his liberal auditors that evening as well): What would you do if your sister wanted to marry one of "them"? Presented in such general terms, of course, the Klansman would vehemently reply: "Never!" Ah, wondered Bruce, let's particularize the problem. What if you had the choice of marrying a white woman, say matronly singer Kate Smith, or a black woman, sultry Lena Horne. Would the answer be quite so resounding?

Lenny wowed that evening. He employed a combination of Yiddish and hipster patois, zany impressions, improvisation, and lewd riffs. He contemplated with horror the notion of former president Dwight D. Eisenhower kissing his wife, Mamie, on the mouth. He made clever comments as he struggled with a recalcitrant microphone.

The new year for Bruce had started with a bang. Alas, by the end of the year, his unbridled humor and choice of words would land him into a legal sinkhole from which he would never really emerge.

Two weeks prior to Bruce's Carnegie Hall triumph, America had celebrated the inauguration of a new president. For many Americans, John F. Kennedy entered office as a representative of a dynamic era dawning—a realization, in Mailer's view, of the emerging New Sensibility. He was young, the first president to have been born in the twentieth century. His wife, Jacqueline Bouvier Kennedy, was elegant and sophisticated. He was a war hero, famous for his exploits as skipper of PT 109 during the Second World War. He had published (even if he did not quite compose it) a bestselling book, *Profiles in Courage*, which caught politicians at critical moments, faced with difficult choices and acting with valor. His youth and possibility seemed boundless.

In comparison, the Eisenhower administration appeared crusty, boring to the point of narcolepsy—at least to liberals. Mailer proclaimed that Eisenhower represented "the needs of the timid, the petrified, the sanctimonious, and the sluggish."[8] The Eisenhower administration had been a meal ticket for satirist Mort Sahl, who poked fun at a president seemingly more energetic on the golf course than in the briefing room—"Eisenhower proved that we don't need a President."[9]

Kennedy seemed to be a breath of fresh air on cultural matters, promising to unleash pent-up energies. He was at least willing to sit through a Pablo Casals cello performance, invite Robert Frost to read an inaugural poem, and feign interest in novels such as Mailer's *The Deer Park*.[10]

Within a couple of years, the Kennedy luster would diminish. Even more than Eisenhower, Kennedy was a Cold Warrior, engaging the Soviets on all fronts, hot and cold. Fearful of appearing weak in the face of Communist threats, he built up America's already bulging nuclear arsenal, challenged the Soviets over Berlin, initiated a half-baked invasion of Cuba, and almost sleepwalked the world into a nuclear holocaust during the Cuban Missile Crisis. As the fight for civil rights began to spark, with African Americans in the South demanding equality and pushing hard against the indignities of Jim Crow segregation laws, his administration moved with a lethargy that seemed at odds with the course of history and its presumed liberal inclinations. With so much change in the air, comedians were blessed with increasingly provocative possibilities.

Bruce hit the big time when comedy was king. Top-flight comedians, head-lining in Vegas or at classy nightclubs, garnered big bucks and national expo-sure. While comedy had long been a feature of radio and vaudeville houses, it was now a staple of television. An appearance on the Sunday night Ed Sullivan Show epitomized success. But acts performing on that show had to labor within the strict confines of good taste, as Sullivan vigilantly scrutinized any potential violators of his taste code. Lenny Bruce never appeared on the pro-gram. The popularity of comic records helped lift comedy income higher. Albums such as Vaughn Meader's *The First Family* (1962) gently poked fun at the Kennedys, while Allen Sherman's *My Son, the Nut* (1963) featured the hit song "Hello Muddah, Hello Faddah," which humorously skewered children's summer camp experiences.

The most successful comics aimed jokes at the particular tastes of their au-diences. When on television, Bob Hope, Jack Carter, Joey Bishop, Totie Fields, and Henny Youngman performed one-liners or told crisp and clean stories, although they could get raunchy when performing in other outlets. Satire sneaked increasingly into the picture. In addition to Mort Sahl, the sophistication of Mike Nichols and Elaine May, Bob Newhart, and Shelley Berman appealed to more refined tastes. They were of the New Sensibility, to be sure, but without Bruce's rush to the extreme. Ditto cartoons that dealt with existential angst and the absurdity of life by Jules Feiffer and Walt Kelly. Youngsters—and their hip elders—gobbled up copies of *Mad* magazine, which shotgunned all aspects of American life.[11]

Lenny Bruce was born Leonard Alfred Schneider on October 13, 1925, and grew up on Long Island, the child of mismatched parents.[12] The mother vi-brated with personality, more of a pal than a caregiver. She wanted desperately to be in show biz but was "funniest offstage."[13] The father was a shoe salesman with larger ambitions and the discipline to achieve them. The parents divorced when Lenny was six, and he shuttled between them and a variety of aunts, uncles, and grandparents until his high school years. He was smart and talka-tive, the latter to the point of being disruptive in classes. Lenny later claimed that he was lonely and neglected as a child, although his biographer disputes this, finding him "spoiled rotten." For whatever reasons, at age fifteen he fled from home to live and work on a family-owned farm, forming what he felt was a close attachment with the hardworking family.

Less than a week after Bruce turned seventeen, all of 5'2" in height and a wisp at 120 pounds, he signed up for military service. A gunner's mate second class on the USS *Brooklyn*, he saw plenty of action off the coast of Italy. Bruce recalled glimpsing "pitiful, fresh dead bodies" floating on the water.[14] Two years of combat convinced him to leave the navy. He reasoned that since he had joined the service voluntarily, they should release him from duty without much rigmarole. Such was not the case, of course. His solution was to don woman's attire and opt for a Section Eight discharge. Under questioning by authorities, he denied being a homosexual. When next asked if he liked wearing women's clothes, Bruce responded, "When they fit."[15] He got his discharge, but it was a dishonorable one, later reversed, and he returned to the states not long before the war ended.

By 1947 Bruce had become a professional entertainer, sometimes working under the stage name Lenny Marseille. He started performing at burlesque houses, where he introduced the strippers and did a few impressions. It was frustrating, since he knew the audiences wanted strippers, not fledgling comedians. One night, early in his career, a couple of guys accompanied by two garishly made-up women heckled him, yelling, "Bring on the broads." He felt more naked onstage than the strippers. What was he going to do? The foursome, Bruce recalled, "shrieked with ecstasy," again, "Bring on the broads." Finally, he rose to the challenge: "I'd like to, but then you wouldn't have any company at the bar." It was his first laugh, and he was "hooked" on comedy, feeling the same "warm sensual blanket that comes" with an injection of morphine.[16]

Sex and drugs became Bruce's constant partners as he pursued his career in comedy. He traveled with a veritable drugstore of narcotics, and was especially enamored of heroin and Methedrine. When he was high, he imagined that he was "kissing God." Although he would never forsake casual sex, in 1951 he realized his fondest wet dream when he met and married Honey Harlow, a beautiful stripper who he described as "a composite of the Virgin Mary and a $500-a-night whore." She was an enthusiastic devotee of drugs and sex, and until their marriage unraveled in 1959 they delighted and tortured one another.[17]

As a "clean" comic, he had won on *Arthur Godfrey's Talent Scouts* on television. Bruce played anywhere he could get a booking—in small Brooklyn clubs (at one he earned twelve bucks a night, along with a spaghetti dinner), in the Catskills, in dingy burlesque parlors. He headlined the Strand Theatre in New York City in 1949 but bombed. Frustrated by his sagging career and tired of stale jokes, he evolved into a "dirty" comic. Initially, this simply meant that he told off-color jokes and used dirty words. One key to his success was an ability to connect with audiences. He was both a likable fellow and a con artist. But the comedy routine was serious. According to his biographer Albert Goldman, "The deeper Lenny sank into the schmutz, the higher he rose as an artist. The grosser and cruder the environment, the more ironic, imaginative, and brilliant became the art." He was cagey enough also to realize that "controversy makes money."[18] On his national television show, Steve Allen—who steadfastly supported Bruce's career—introduced him as "a comedian who will offend everybody...the most shocking comedian of our time."[19]

For many in the audience, "sick" humor was not kosher fare. A mountain slide of complaints arrived, which Allen dismissed by announcing on television his plan to have one controversial comedian like Bruce appear on his show each month. Although reporter Arthur Gelb liked Bruce's comedy, he warned readers: "He is not for your Aunt Lydia from Peoria or your Uncle Phil from Oshkosh—so leave them at home and take Tallulah Bankhead or Brendan Behan."[20]

No comic challenged American hypocrisy—the distance between ideals and reality, the contradictions of belief, the obscenity of politics, warfare, and racism—with more of an edge than Bruce.[21] The sensibility that he brought to the stage had aspects of the nihilism popularized by *Mad* magazine. In *Mad*, popular with adolescent rebels, the humor was sharp, but directed at everything—from politicians to teen idols, even to the prospect of atomic annihilation. Its typical refrain, uttered in each issue by its figurehead, Alfred E. Neuman, was "What, me worry?" In contrast, there was a moral edge to Bruce's jibes. His style, no less than the content, that was something quite new. He was once called "the earl of angst."[22]

Bruce was a hyperkinetic presence onstage—a quicksilver mind and speech with inspired pauses. In part, drugs contributed to his energy onstage—he regularly injected himself with speed, procuring prescriptions from a host of conned physicians. Yet he was naturally fidgety, with a mind "always in double time."[23] He long maintained a lean, agile build; he was typically dressed in black, hair bristled and greased, eyes darting and dragging at the same time. Cigarette in hand, no props (other than the microphone), Lenny was a serious comic. He had strong views about who was a comic and who wasn't. Anyone with acting talent could tell jokes effectively, he remarked. With good material and training, even the phlegmatic and wooden John Wayne might crack up an audience. But a true comic—and Bruce applied the designation to himself without hesitation—wrote the material himself *and* performed it onstage.

Hip phrases and Yiddish expressions dominated his act. The use of such language marked Bruce as an outsider, a marginal man. Dick Schaap, a sportswriter who was in Pittsburgh covering the 1960 World Series, heard that Bruce was performing in town. A native New Yorker and Jew, Schaap easily identified with Bruce's language, as did many others. But in Pittsburgh, it seemed, most of the audience snored in their beer. Even a critic in the *New York Times* admitted, "Most of his comments on jazz, modern art and other topics were in the tedious idiom of the chin-whisker crowd."[24]

Bruce drifted into a reverie about how being Jewish and hip was a conjoined cultural style, perhaps key ingredients of the New Sensibility. After all, in literature and the arts, Jews were emerging as key and controversial figures. Bruce was part of that same historical stream:

I neologize Jewish and *goyish*. Dig: I'm Jewish. Count Basie's Jewish. Ray Charles is Jewish. Eddie Cantor's *goyish*. B'nai Brith is *goyish*; Hadassah, Jewish. Marine corps—heavy *goyim*, dangerous. Koolaid is *goyish*,... Pumpernickel is Jewish, and, as you know, white bread is very goyish.

Instant potatoes—goyish. Black cherry soda's very Jewish.... Titties are
Jewish. Mouths are Jewish. All Italians are Jewish.[25]

Bruce's comedic style was improvisational and spontaneous—proudly beholden
to a jazz sensibility, akin to Kerouac and Ginsberg. He told an interviewer, "Jazz
musicians dig me."[26] He had a jazzman's soul, shared drugs with them, and
kept similar late-night hours. According to a eulogy in *Downbeat*, Bruce could
tackle a traditional subject and, by changing chords with his words, make it
into something cool.[27]

Ralph Gleason, a music critic and fan, in the album liner notes for *The Sick
Humor of Lenny Bruce* (1959), called Bruce a "jazz-oriented comic."[28] Jazz critic
and civil libertarian Nat Hentoff agreed, detecting a "beat" in Bruce's performances that was pure "bop." Gleason explained that "the accented kicked
in unexpectedly—but coherently;" Bruce "sometimes became a jazz combo—
each character's individual textures and ways of shaping time fused into
a whole."[29]

Bruce had certain themes in mind before he stepped onto the stage, bits of
ideas and musings. But he refused to be contained by them. If something happened—perhaps a chance to rib someone in the audience, a technical burp
from the sound system, or a miscue in the wings—he riffed on it. A microphone
screech led to a quick reference to vampire bats and a Bela Lugosi imitation.

Bruce charged forth with spontaneity and hyperbole, chuckling at the outrageousness of something that he had just uttered. It was, after all, improvised
and new to him.[30] He had, like any comedian, favored bits of material, but
he tweaked them constantly, refusing to let the bits, or himself, grow tired.
"I don't actually sit down and write out a routine," Bruce noted; "I'll ad-lib it on
the floor, but line by line, and eventually, it'll snowball into a bit. I'll never actually do the same routine twice. I'll do a routine awhile, then I'll get bored
with it."[31]

Like many artists in various media in this period and earlier, Bruce equated
spontaneity with authenticity—an unleashing of energy, depth of emotion,
and freedom of thought.[32] Paul Krassner, who worked with Bruce on his autobiography, described Bruce's style as "stream-of-consciousness." This meant
that he made leaps from one topic to another, sometimes weaving them together, sometimes leaving them scattered, sometimes pausing for a moment,
as if to enjoy his verbal foray. Material emerged unedited, unscrutinized by the
super-ego.[33]

Not all of Bruce's work was improvisational or stream of consciousness.
Indeed, one of his best bits was a collaborative routine with Eric Miller, an
African American friend and musician. Bruce played an offensive drunk at an
integrated party. Striking up a conversation with Miller, slurring his words
somewhat, he began to make the most inappropriate comments—capturing
the awkwardness of race relations at a tense historical moment. In a few minutes,

the drunk had brought up Aunt Jemima, fried chicken, watermelon, penis size, Mau Maus, almost every cliché associated with a racist mentality. But this cascade of offensive clichés was not presented in an off-putting manner. One sensed the drunk was trying to connect with this black stranger at the party. Touching on dangerous stereotypes was a tool in Bruce's trade, and his compatriot Miller played his character brilliantly—calm and wryly accepting. The drunk even invited the black man to his house, but warned him that he did not want "no coon doing it to my sister," just as Miller presumably would not want his own sister to make it with any heeb. The drunk punctuated the conversation by repeatedly telling the black man, "You're alright." And thereby he satirized white prejudice and humanized the black man (and his plight), all in a routine lasting a few minutes.[34]

Repetition of words and phrases served him well—and got him into trouble. Bruce would take a word considered to be obscene and then he would repeat it, scream it, and sometimes caress it in gentle parody. This shocked audiences, but it allowed him to segue into a familiar theme: that meaning was what we put onto things rather than inherent in them.

Bruce refused to define himself as a political comic. "I don't dig communism," he announced at Carnegie Hall. "It's one big phone company." To take a firm political stance was to foreclose possibilities and become predictable. But he could, on occasion, get preachy. Jumping off from his disdain for Communism, "since it upholds the philosophy of violence," Bruce touched on current political topics: American neo-Nazi leader George Lincoln Rockwell, bomb shelters, and Richard Nixon (a "megalomaniac"). He was, however, sympathetic to the civil rights movement. He said, "As a good American it would certainly feel hypocritical if, in my own country, sixth-generation Americans cannot sit at lunch counters or have trouble going to school. It is my country, I love it, I will fight for it, but when it is wrong, I will admit it."[35]

The "colored friend" skit succeeded in part because it depicted racism with a familiar face for his audiences. Instead of an easy-to-skewer southern cracker, Bruce took on liberal sanctimony. Moreover, he admitted, "I am part of everything I indict."[36] This allowed Bruce to satirize all sorts—from racists to liberals. He could get away, too, with bad-taste jokes about minorities in this fashion. In theory, at least, he promised to "never cram anything down anyone's throat."[37]

If there was a single theme resonant in Bruce's comedy, it was disdain for hypocrisy: "I want hypocrisy to stop, once and for all."[38] One pal said, "Lenny's problem was that he wanted to talk onstage with the same freedom he exercised in his living room."[39] Honesty, he claimed, was absent in America. Everywhere Bruce cast his sharp eye (in a fashion similar to Robert Frank) hypocrisy reigned, and he devoted himself to revealing it—in the end at great cost to himself and his career. As Ronald Sukenick, a self-professed bohemian writer, put it about Bruce: "If you play with shit, you get your hands dirty," and you "get hounded to death for saying 'fuck,' not for fucking."[40]

One day in 1961, Bruce overheard a story that shocked him. He was having breakfast with Paul Krassner, editor of the *Realist*, a magazine of humor and anarchist sensibilities. At another table, a fellow was saying that he had slapped his daughter because she had wanted to see Hitchcock's new film, *Psycho*. The father's objection to the film was that it depicted a partially clothed couple passionately kissing. For other Americans, however, the film was shocking because it successfully challenged Hollywood production codes with its famous shower scene when Tony Perkins stabs Janet Leigh repeatedly through the shower curtain, her blood running down the drain. That the father would protest a couple's kiss rather than the violence stunned Bruce. He incorporated this story into his performance that evening.[41]

Organized religion was a favorite Bruce target. In the early 1960s well over 95 percent of Americans believed in God. In the postwar years, just before the rise of evangelical Christianity, American religion had become comfortable and nonsectarian. In 1955 Will Herberg had demonstrated that Americans went to churches and synagogues more for a sense of community than for doctrinal truth; easy salvation had replaced strenuous self-examination and doubt. Ecumenicalism, it seemed, had triumphed with the election of the Catholic John F. Kennedy to the White House.

Religion had, at one point, been a Bruce scam. He was living with Honey in Miami and desperate for money. Bruce impersonated a priest from the Brother Mathias Foundation, of which he was the sole proprietor. He went around to wealthy neighborhoods raising money for the support of a leper colony in British Guiana. "Of course it was dishonest and corrupt." But he claimed that he had given some of the money to fight leprosy and rationalized that he had gainfully earned the rest by listening to the problems of donors for hours on end, acting as a priestly-analyst. Things got hot in Miami with the authorities, and although he beat the rap, he forever thought of organized religion as a con game, based in part on his own personal nefarious deeds.[42]

Bruce had no problem with faith as such, but he was aghast at the corruption that he espied at the center of organized religion. Its leaders were interested in power and profits; they scammed faith as a means to this end. "Every man who professes to be a 'Man of God' and owns more than one suit is a hustler," Bruce proclaimed, "so long as there are people in the world who don't have any."[43]

Rather than speaking in general terms about religious hypocrisy, Bruce named names. And he did so, in Hentoff's view, with "nakedly honest moral rage."[44] Although their names have faded from recognition, in the early 1960s Cardinal Spellman was more than a religious leader; he was a powerhouse, with deep political connections; and Fulton Sheen was a regular presence on television. In "Religions Inc." (1959), Bruce presented religious leaders as businessmen, concerned only with profits. Billy Graham, a well-known evangelical, tells his religious pals that membership in Catholicism is up nine points; Judaism is surging at fifteen points. A "religious novelty store in Chicago" was making a killing on combination crosses and stars of David; another good seller was a cocktail napkin that reads "Another Martini for Mother Cabrini." Oral Roberts, a Pentecostal minister, reported that he had found the "heavenly land," ripe for investment, in the vicinity of Chavez Ravine, new home of the Dodgers baseball team. Some of his fellow members in Religions, Inc., Roberts announces, might think him a dumb hick, but he retorts: "I got two Lincoln Continentals; that's how dumb I am." Their conference was interrupted by a collect call from the Vatican, from recently installed Pope John. He and Graham bemoan that too many folks are taking literally such Biblical admonitions as "Thou Shalt Not Kill" and universal brotherhood. Ending the conversation, Graham thanks Pope John for the pepperoni he recently sent and requests "a deal on one of those Dago sports cars." Such religious leaders, with grandiose visions of earthly profits, Bruce related in another routine, would certainly disdain the Second Coming. Word gets out that Jesus has reappeared in a Catholic church; Bishop Fulton Sheen and Cardinal Spellman wonder where he is seated: "The [pew] in the back.... The one that's glowing." In the spirit of Dostoevsky's Grand Inquisitor, they decide that Jesus is a problem, encroaching on their territory—both fiscal and spiritual.[45]

How do you define a Jew, Bruce asked his audience? The dictionary offered a precise definition of them as descendants of a tribe originating in Judea. But the real definition, which Bruce claimed that both he and his audience recognized, was more common: "A Jew is—*One Who Killed Our Lord.*" Bruce accepted collective responsibility for Jews killing Christ—no foisting it on the Romans. Nor had a Jewish party "got out of hand"—perhaps because of too much Manischewitz wine had been consumed. No, the truth of the matter was: "We killed him because he didn't want to become a doctor."[46]

After riffing on how civil rights leaders Martin Luther King and Bayard Rustin were "geniuses," he shouted to the audience: "By the way, are there any niggers here tonight?"

He continued: "I know one nigger who works here, I see him in the back. Oh, there's two niggers, customers, and, ah, *aha!* Between those two niggers sits one kike—man, thank God for the kike!" By the end of the routine, he has counted off "three kikes, one guinea, one greaseball...one hunky funky lace-curtain Irish mick."[47]

The audience, according to Hentoff, was stunned into silence and embarrassment. In a moment, he reeled them in, as he played with the power of words, on how we endow them with meaning. Words, like political power, must not paralyze us; they need to have their "covers off" so that we can get past them and deal with pressing issues. "The word's suppression gives it the power, the violence, the viciousness." The bit ended with him musing about President

Kennedy going on national television to introduce African American members of his cabinet with a yell of "niggerniggerniggerniggerniggerniggerniggernigger." Then, as if by magic, the word would lose its power to offend. But the word, certainly in the early 1960s, was double-edged, at least. Was it neutered by being uttered in such an extreme fashion?

Bruce went too far on Wednesday night, October 9, 1961, during a gig at the Jazz Workshop in the bohemian North Beach area of San Francisco. Not everyone, certainly not the San Francisco police, were prepared to let words be.

Bruce had experienced some tough times since his Carnegie Hall smash early in the year. He had fallen deathly ill, probably with some sort of staph infection caused by his manic use of narcotics. His temperature peaked at 107°. Bruce survived, and he seemed intent on no longer using drugs. But he adored his heroin high, and he thrived on the criminal swagger of the drug world. On September 29, he was busted in Philadelphia. Charging into Bruce's hotel room, cops confiscated a cornucopia of drugs and paraphernalia:

20 plastic and 5 glass syringes
4 hypodermic needles
36 ampules of Methedrine
11 tablets in a plastic vial
A glass bottle containing a clear liquid with a prescription number
    indicating that it was a narcotic
6 orange-colored capsules
13 white tablets, etc.[48]

A hearing was scheduled for October 9, which allowed Bruce to jet to the coast for his Jazz Workshop performance.

With unintended irony, the *San Francisco Chronicle* on the day after Bruce's gig had published an article with the title "A Handy Guide to Inoffensive Speech." Readers were lectured to avoid such phrases as "smart as a Jew" and "some of my best friends" and symbols such as watermelons in references to negroes, even if they were intended to be kindly. Camouflaged prejudice, the paper warned, was common. Another page featured a review of Bruce's act the previous night. He reportedly had candidly discussed his recent drug bust in Philadelphia and "talked about sex, bigotry, and America." According to the reporter, "The audience dug."[49]

Unfortunately, Officer James Ryan was in the audience for the show the following night—and he did not dig it. Bruce began his first set that night by reminiscing about one of his early gigs in North Beach at Ann's 440 Club. He had been unfamiliar with the venue and inquired about the joint. He was told that the place had offered a "damn fag show," frequented by "a bunch of *cocksuckers.*" But Ann's wanted to change its image, acts, and clientele, so Bruce took the booking.

A few minutes into his act, he switched to one of his familiar routines, "The Dirty Toilet," a riff about those afflicted with "dirty word" problems. There was, he proclaimed, no such thing as a dirty word—"Obscenity is a human manifestation." Another monologue that evening continued in this vein, a discourse about the words "to come." The words were nothing more, he lectured, than a preposition and a transitive verb. Then he offered some sentences. "Didja come *good?*"—repeated over and over, drawing out the sexual innuendo to the point of boredom and titillation. He closed the routine with the punchline: "*If you think I'm rank for saying it to you, you, the beholder, think it's rank for listening to it,* you probably can't come!"[50]

Following his first set, Bruce was informed of his pending arrest. "You're putting me on," he remarked in response to the jarring news.[51] The police sergeant told Bruce, "I took exception.... I'm offended because you broke the law. I mean it sincerely." The police wanted to "clean up" the area. Bruce, in all seriousness, tried to convince the officer that the best way to get rid of obscenity was to talk about it. He asked the officer: Is clap a dirty word? The officer responded, as if a straight man in a comedy routine: "Well, 'clap' is a better word than 'cocksucker.'" Of course, Bruce could not refrain from the obvious riposte: "Not if you get the clap from a cocksucker."

Hauled off to the police station for booking, Bruce was soon freed—thanks to the eager intercession of the club owner's lawyer and $357.60 in bail. They needed Bruce back onstage for his second set that evening. To add insult to injury, after reading about the arrest in the morning edition of the *San Francisco Chronicle*, the management of the hotel where he was staying banged on his door and woke Bruce up from his much-needed sleep. "We don't want people like you here." He managed to remain at the hotel and to finish his gig. The next night at the Jazz Workshop, however, Bruce kept it clean, even if he was as "miffed as a burned cat," according to a reporter. His routine was "so clean" that "people walked out in the middle." Bruce then flew back to Philadelphia to face the drug charges.[52]

Lenny Bruce eventually beat the raps, though not without tremendous emotional investment, legal fees, and court hearings. For the San Francisco trial, which began on November 17, 1961, he was charged with three violations of the penal code: for using the word "cocksuckers," for saying that "the man in the front booth is going to kiss it," and for the line "don't come in me, don't come in me." The judge at the municipal court level was clearly outraged by Bruce and his humor. Luckily for Bruce, he could appeal his conviction to a higher court, run by Judge Clayton Horn, who, as we have seen, had five years earlier dismissed similar obscenity charges against Ginsberg's *Howl*. But Bruce nearly undid his chances when he upset Judge Horn by sending him an "illiterate letter." "The monstrous rumor Judge Horn feels the defendant takes the matter lightly motivates this letter," Bruce wrote. "Odious is the matter, my arrest for obscenity has enfilmed my career with a leperous [*sic*] stigma that St. Francis could not kiss away at ethereal peak."[53]

Before the trial, Bruce's attorney had warned him: "You can't win a case based on 'cocksucker.'" Various witnesses attested to the relevant and artistic context of the words that Bruce had used at the Jazz Workshop. Victory seemed likely when Horn issued instructions to the jury. As he had with the Ginsberg trial, he showed himself perfectly attuned to the subtleties of the Brennan decision about the material having to be without redeeming social value and considered in its entirety, rather than being obscene by dint of particular offensive words. Given such a precedent, the jury had little choice but to acquit, no matter how unhappy they were with the verdict, as they later revealed. In addition to legal and other fees, Bruce had to face his contempt of court citation from the letter incident. Although he could have been sentenced to five days in jail, Horn fined him a hundred bucks, which a friend paid for him.[54]

Although the Ginsberg case should have established the precedent that the use of an "obscene" word must be considered within the context of the overall work, it was not applied forcefully or seriously to the work of a nightclub comedian such as Bruce, even if he had a reputation as a satirist. No doubt, too, his scathing criticism of religious leaders placed him high on the list of disliked comedians among police officers and prosecutors around the country. Although the Supreme Court had opened up free speech, it had left room for zealous prosecutors who considered certain comedy to lack redeeming social value. The freedom of the 1960s, the notion that anything goes, had yet to blossom fully.

Over the next few years, Bruce would be arrested repeatedly, for possession of narcotics and for obscenity in Chicago, New York, and Los Angeles. Richard H. Kuh, who prosecuted Bruce in New York City on obscenity charges, dismissed him as a mere pornographer. He claimed that while Bruce had once been an "effective panjandrum of social protest," he had become a spewing cyst of "obscenity and the evermore perverse shock of his club routines." Bruce's first arrest in New York City followed hard on the heels of the bust of Jonas Mekas, the avant-garde filmmaker, for showing Jack Smith's *Flaming Creatures*. That film was certainly odd—with nudity and sex, accompanied by a riot of a soundtrack. Today, the film would be considered naive; back then it was held by Kuh to be obscene.[55]

By 1965, after additional arrests for drugs and obscenity, Bruce was financially and spiritually bankrupt. Relief was granted courtesy of an excess of drugs injected on August 3, 1966.

The shockwaves that Bruce was producing in 1961 were being felt across the country. By 1962, in a host of different arenas, the New Sensibility, with its excess, openness to pleasure, and willingness to think about the unthinkable, was set to blossom. The main thing standing in the way of this new flowering, however, was an old problem, that of the threat of nuclear annihilation.

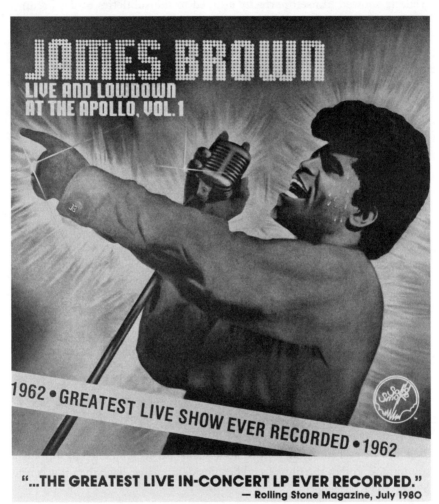

Album cover for James Brown, Live and Lowdown at the Apollo (© Photofest)

Pop Goes the Paradigm

1962

New York City, late October 1962. The overcast days are heavy with clouds and grim anticipation. The previously unthinkable now seemed all too real and raw. Soviet ballistic missiles, easily capable of hitting American targets, had been discovered in Cuba. President Kennedy has announced the establishment of a "quarantine" to prevent additional missiles from entering Cuban ports. Existing missiles in Cuba must be dismantled. *Life* considers the quarantine a "trip-wire for World War III."[1] Americans track the movement of Soviet freighters on the evening news or daily newspapers as the ships came closer and closer to the point of confrontation. It is the "most dangerous moment in human history," according to historian and presidential adviser Arthur M. Schlesinger Jr.[2]

Returning from school or work, New Yorkers cast lingering glances at the fallout shelter signs. Advisories are issued that citizens should maintain two weeks' worth of provisions. The deafening whir of air-raid sirens threatens to sound at any moment. Would Soviet premier Nikita Khrushchev be so foolhardy as to unleash a nuclear holocaust simply to have a military presence in Cuba and the Western Hemisphere? Might youthful President Kennedy, still smarting from the Bay of Pigs fiasco, be unwilling to back down or to compromise that he would let loose the dogs of nuclear war? Children around the country intone their bedtime prayers with particular devotion. "Time was deformed," recalled Todd Gitlin, "everyday life suddenly dwarfed and illuminated, as if by the glare of an explosion that had not yet taken place."[3]

Secretary of State Dean Rusk noted how the United States and the Soviet Union were "eyeball to eyeball," each side calculating, posturing, and waiting for the other's next move. At the United Nations, Ambassador Adlai E. Stevenson eloquently demanded that Soviet Ambassador Valerian Zorin confirm or deny whether his nation "has placed, and is placing medium and intermediate range missile sites in Cuba." Stevenson proclaimed boldly: "I am prepared to wait for my answer until hell freezes over." A nuclear hell on earth seemed at the moment a more likely possibility.

Twenty-one-year-old Bob Dylan is sitting late at night at Le Figaro Café in Greenwich Village, "waiting for the world to end." "The Russian ships were getting closer to Cuba," he wrote forlornly to his girlfriend, Suze Rotolo, who was in Perugia, Italy. Trying to put on a brave face, he admitted, "I honest to God thought it was all over—Not that I gave a shit any more then the next guy (that's a lie I guess)." It was "interesting" contemplating total destruction; he simply hoped that he might "die quick and not have to put up with radiation." He wisely concluded on a romantic note: "If the world did end that nite, all I wanted was to be with you."[4]

Legend has it, supported sometimes by Dylan himself, that he composed the song "A Hard Rain's a-Gonna Fall" in response to the Cuban Missile Crisis. But he had performed it at a hootenanny organized by Peter Seeger at Carnegie Hall a full month before the crisis, and again on October 5 at Town Hall. Truth be told, Dylan had been worrying about nuclear destruction over the past year, penning, for example, "Let Me Die in My Footsteps" about fallout shelters. He was hardly alone in his fears and in an openness to think in a livelier fashion about excess—in death and in music.

Thinking outside of the box, a willingness to entertain extreme scenarios, became the stock in trade of Herman Kahn and others in these years. He coined an apt term for this tendency, "thinking the unthinkable" (the title of a book he published in 1962). Forty years old, the tall and rotund Kahn was a combination of Lenny Bruce (he liked to joke, in rat-a-tat-tat fashion) and Bela Lugosi (feasting on "bloody hypotheticals"). *Life* magazine in 1959 had referred to his "valuable batch of brains."[5] Talking about the "war games" Kahn and his associates at the Hudson Institute were playing, a reporter stated: "The world of military analysis is bizarre and unsettling, where the unthinkable is thought about, sometimes with gusto."[6] Norman Podhoretz noted that Kahn "does seem to take a visible delight in thinking about the unthinkable."[7]

Those valuable brains fantasized about a relatively inexpensive "doomsday machine." It was a device that would be triggered after one country had attacked another with nuclear bombs. The result would be the destruction of the entire world. Kahn imagined that no nation would attack another armed with its own nuclear weapons knowing that such aggression would result in its mutual annihilation. An extreme solution, to be sure. But not absurd, so long as one presumed that nations act rationally. Nor was it removed from actual policy, in a sense. American and Soviet policy at the time was predicated on the doctrine of mutually assured destruction (MAD, a distasteful but perfect acronym). Both sides were restrained from using nuclear weapons against the other because it would result in an unleashing of massive arsenals of destruction that would signal the end of the world.

Kahn embraced catastrophe and apocalypse as an abstract *and* practical problem. Already the author of a massive work, *On Thermonuclear War* (1960), Kahn was paid to think about lots of stuff, such as: Was a nuclear war survivable, and what did it mean to win such a conflagration? At least he acknowledged that defeat would be an "unprecedented catastrophe."[8]

"In our time," wrote Kahn, "thermonuclear war may seem unthinkably immoral, insane, hideous or highly unlikely, but it is not impossible." Hence in *Thinking about the Unthinkable* he decided that it was possible to have a nuclear confrontation that flirted with, but did not go to the point of, total holocaust. Kahn laid out, in simple, direct language, how, despite perhaps sixty million dead Americans, proper planning might allow life to continue. With sufficient time, preparation, and ingenuity, survivors might come to thrive. Damned or blessed with a mordant sense of humor, Kahn became a poster child for mad logic and insane reason that seemed to sanction extremes of violence. Kahn became an obvious model for the deluded Dr. Strangelove in the 1964 Stanley Kubrick film.[9]

By 1962, a willingness to think in fresh ways was becoming common—in varied venues. Thomas S. Kuhn, like Kahn, was a forty-year-old genius with a background in physics. A professor at the University of California at Berkeley, with thinning hair and a face framed by black glasses, Kuhn possessed impeccable academic credentials. Unlike Kahn, his work was directed toward the past rather than the present. He published a new book in October called *The Structure of Scientific Revolutions*. Although he was restrained in his conclusions, many readers over the years took his essential concepts further than he had intended. His thesis was relatively simple. Under conditions of normal science, the community of scientists work under a shared paradigm, a way of seeing and interpreting the world. Problems to be investigated were considered minor kinks that needed to be fitted better into the ruling paradigm. Over time, however, anomalies may multiply—sometimes as a result of better technologies of investigation or failures of applied science—and lead to a crisis in the ruling paradigm. As if by magic, a counter paradigm emerges (sometimes it may have previously been shunted to the periphery of science as an absurd hypothesis) that better explained problems and which in turn becomes the new ruling paradigm. When this occurs, you have a scientific revolution.[10]

The "unthinkable" for Kuhn was that science might not function as a pure pursuit of truth. While Kuhn retained faith in scientific communities, his book suggested that scientists were straightjacketed by their ruling paradigm, unable to see other possibilities, narrowed by their presumptions, even blind to facts. Science was compromised. For example, the Ptolemaic-Aristotelian view was no different in its logic and function than the heliocentric one that followed.

As the philosopher Richard Rorty remarked years later, Kuhn's thesis was a "new map of culture."[11] Within a handful of years, the notion of a community working under a constraining paradigm had been extended in all directions—certainly far from the insular and theoretical worlds that Kuhn had focused upon, not on messy entities such as culture. Culture is best conceived in plural terms rather than as some absolute or Platonic ideal. True, at different moments, culture may lean more in one direction or another.

In 1962 culture seemed about to pop. The experimental and often extreme chipping away at conventions and expectations, as we have seen in previous chapters, was gathering momentum. Like a paradigm (loosely speaking), mounting cultural anomalies were moving culture into new directions. This was, in part, in the nature of accumulation. The music of Cage, the amoralism of Highsmith, the strutting of Mailer, and the lethal wit of Bruce were all contributing factors. Culture, to employ a sometimes overused phrase, had reached a tipping point. This is why in this chapter the focus widens, moving away from individual creators to a somewhat larger cast of characters and works that were, in a variety of ways, bringing the New Sensibility to a boiling point by focusing on madness, sexuality, and liberation.

The shift to a New Sensibility was fueled, too, by possibility and perplexity. Consumer culture and seemingly unstoppable economic growth (despite lingering inequalities of wealth distribution) blessed Americans with a sense of prosperity and promise. At the same time, the specter of nuclear annihilation cast a vast and terrifying shadow that suggested, in some ways, that sitting comfortably in cultural conformity made no sense at all.

The postwar period in the United States featured phenomenal economic growth. Between 1947 and 1960, the gross national product (GNP) had increased 56 percent, with occasional dips, the most recent occurring in 1960–1961. But in 1962, the economy was humming along. President Kennedy's "Economic Report to Congress," issued at the beginning of the year, proudly announced that the GNP was growing at a record rate, plant capacity had increased, unemployment had dropped, and prices were stable. American corporations, it should be noted, were making immense profits as well. Thanks to the Sputnik crisis of 1957, government money was pumped into universities, and by 1960, college enrollment figures had climbed 57 percent over what they were in 1950.[12]

Culture, too, seemed to be gaining in confidence. First Lady Jacqueline Kennedy brought to the White House a whiff of sophistication. Major figures in the arts performed there on a regular basis. As historian William Rorabaugh put it, a new "tone" of hope emerged.[13] The term "Camelot" was applied to that aura. Cellist Pablo Casals succumbed to its allure, giving up his boycott of the United States for its support of Franco's government in Spain to give a bravura performance at the White House in 1961. In April 1962 Kennedy dined with American Nobel Prize winners. In December, thanks to Jacqueline Kennedy's connection with Andre Malraux, the *Mona Lisa* voyaged to America, to be viewed by close to two million people. Another hopeful note was sounded in February 1962, when President Kennedy announced August Heckscher's appointment to a part-time position as coordinator of cultural affairs. Many read this as a sign of increasing attention to the role of the arts in American life.[14]

More Americans graduated from college than ever before. They may not have majored in the liberal arts, but they had been lectured about the importance of culture, or at the very least learned to feign an interest in the higher aspects of life. Wanting to be sophisticated and cosmopolitan, they flocked to art museums and gallery shows (which increasingly accommodated them with blockbuster shows and more accessible artworks), consumed cultural products (on- and off-Broadway shows boomed, ranging from Edward Albee's *Who's Afraid of Virginia Woolf?* to *A Funny Thing Happened on the Way to the Forum*), and discussion of film rose to greater heights. In 1962, for instance, critic Andrew Sarris added to this widening stream of sophistication with the essay "Notes on the Auteur Theory." It was a controversial argument that posited film directors must be evaluated in terms of their "signature" style, "technical competence," and "interior meaning." Films were the creative work of directors, expressing their unified vision on film. Sarris worked to establish—as was common with literature or music—a pantheon of important directors and their creations. This demanded a more serious group of critics and consumers, fully aware of the history of film. The year 1962 was a ripe time for such an argument. Foreign films and revivals of American classics were screened regularly in urban centers and on college campuses. Going to see a film, rather than a movie, was a sign of sophistication, of cultural renewal. Looking back on this period, Phillip Lopate called it "the heroic age of movie going."[15]

At this moment, madness and mental illness, central to the New Sensibility, gained ever greater and more controversial attention. "Is there such a thing as mental illness?" Thomas Szasz had asked in 1960. His shocking answer: "There was not." Szasz showed how mental illness was a grab-bag designation, a means of controlling the rebellious, and a dangerous fiction. The solution upheld by the medical establishment was part of the problem. Suddenly, the power of psychiatric institutions came under attack with increasing frequency. Renegade thinkers R. D. Laing in Britain and Michel Foucault in France, along with Szasz, Herbert Marcuse, and Norman O. Brown in the United States, led the charge. This diverse group, with fine credentials in the academic establishment, proposed that rationality was overrated, becoming itself an illness and a mechanism for social control. To his question "Who is mentally ill?" Szasz replied, "Those who are confined in mental hospitals or who consult psychiatrists in their private offices." In language not unlike Kuhn's, Szasz wrote about the need to "scrap" the dominant "conceptual model" of psychiatry. Some theorists went so far as to equate madness a sort of divine liberation. In this vein, Brown had proclaimed, of course, "What the great world needs, of course, is a little more Eros and less strife." To achieve this goal, repression ("The Disease Called Man") needed to be cast off in favor of Dionysian freedom (sexual and otherwise). "Dionysius does not observe the limit, but overflows," Brown announced, by way of William Blake; "for him the road of excess leads to the palace of wisdom."[16]

Joseph Heller's *Catch-22* (1961) and Ken Kesey's *One Flew Over the Cuckoo's Nest* (1962) joined in the engagement with repression and madness. Both novels railed against the logistics of power that stomped out life. Yossarian, a bombardier on a B-25, faces a bureaucracy which seems more insane than war itself. Military "logic" ensnares the individual in impossible paradoxes; even when you play by its rules, you find that the rules can change instantly. The only hope is to break free, and, if possible, to escape. A similar theme runs through Kesey's novel, which takes place in the seemingly therapeutic domain of an insane asylum. Maintaining order more than treating patients, however, is the essential function of the place. The main character, Randle McMurphy, rebels against the bureaucracy in the name of freedom. Slowly, the other residents, most of them afraid of liberation, come to live vicariously through him and his tales of "kid fun and drinking buddies and loving women and barroom battles over meager honors—for all of us to dream ourselves into."[17] But out of such dreams come real rebellions, with real costs. McMurphy leads an uprising, and he pays the terrible price of being lobotomized. Chief Bromden, a huge, mute Native American, also comprehends the reality of the hellhole; by staying silent, by faking madness, he maintains his sanity. And he escapes to tell his tale.

Poets, too, were exploring insanity—especially their own, in a confessional manner. Sylvia Plath began in 1961 to write a harrowing fictional account of a young woman, Esther Greenwood, who was consigned to a mental asylum. The novel follows many aspects of Plath's own life: in 1953, she had attempted suicide and spent a period in a mental asylum. As had occurred with Plath, shock therapy is administered to Esther—"Whee-ee-ee-ee-ee, it shrilled, through an air crackling with blue light.... A great jolt drubbed me till I thought my bones would break and the sap fly out of me like a split plant."[18]

In the fall of 1962, just after being deserted by her husband, the poet Ted Hughes, living in rural England, caring for two young children, and weakened from two serious bouts of flu over a period of a few months, Plath manically composed the bulk of her poetry collection *Ariel*. It was about treachery but also about madness, without hidden contrivances or references. In the face of pain, suicide becomes poetic and real, as in "Cut," finished on October 24, "Homunculus, I am ill / I have taken a pill to kill." Or, most painfully in "Lady Lazarus" (written between October 23 and 29): "Dying / Is an art, like everything else. / I do it exceptionally well."[19]

No poet in these years confronted her demons of madness and suicide with greater openness than Anne Sexton (chapter 15). Relatively speaking, the fall of 1962 was a good time for Sexton. She had just completed a year's fellowship at a newly inaugurated Radcliffe Institute seminar, and she had been featured in stories in both *Time* and *Newsweek* magazines. She had righted herself a bit after a relapse into anxiety and suicidal depression the previous June, which had landed her back in a mental hospital.[20]

One week before President Kennedy's address about missiles in Cuba, Sexton had consumed her usual three martinis before dinner and perhaps took some comfort in her newly minted book of poems, *All My Pretty Ones*. The collection featured confessional poetry taken to dizzying heights and brought back down to earth by artistic control. The poems chronicled the poet's life— and her crawl toward death. With a frankness both shocking and refreshing, the artist stripped herself bare—detailing an operation, depression, alienation, a suicide attempt, and a bone-crushing alienation from suburban, married life that she could not escape.

In the end, the artistry and honesty of the poetry triumphed, although readers feared that Sexton was spiraling downward. Even Sexton recognized this, telling a priest friend, Brother Farrell: "I am given to excess. That's all there is to it. I have found that I can control it best in a poem.... If a poem is good then it will have the excess under control."[21]

The American racial landscape was as rutted as ever. Only a few weeks before the Cuban Missile Crisis intruded on the national consciousness, a young man named James H. Meredith had planned on entering the University of Mississippi as its first black student. Governor Ross Barnett did everything he could to prevent this. Whites rioted on campus, leaving two dead. Federal intervention proved necessary to allow Meredith's admission. Court cases against segregation mounted and direct action increased, but there was still a sense of apathy among whites about the status of African Americans in both the South and North.

A white man from the South, John Howard Griffin, in the fall of 1961 went to extremes in order to challenge racial assumptions. He published a book that would receive widespread attention in 1962, and has ever since. Griffin had been terribly upset by racism. To make its harshness palpable to white readers, to evoke their empathy for the plight of African Americans, he decided to take extreme measures. In *Black Like Me*, Griffin recounted the weeks he had spent living as a black man traveling in the deep South. He had, via drugs (Oxsoralen), tanning machines, and cosmetics, transformed himself into a black version of his normal self. He reeled under constant threats. What made the experience so jarring for him and his readers was how Griffin's racial masquerade demonstrated the overwhelming absurdity of white racism. Readers knew that Griffin was a family man, a moral fellow, but he suffered for no reason other than his darkened skin. While such a premise might strike us as gimmicky, the book was really about the moral necessity of white empathy and support for the black freedom struggle. Malcolm X, one of the more radical black leaders on the scene, remarked that if "it was a frightening experience for him...a make-believe Negro," then imagine "what *real* Negroes in America have gone through for four hundred years."[22]

A willingness to talk frankly about sex entered the mainstream. Helen Gurley Brown's *Sex and the Single Girl* sold two million hardback copies three weeks after it was published at the end of May 1962. It was a retort of sorts to the masculine ideal and conventions of *Playboy*—an advice book, without a hint of feminist rhetoric. It was directed toward its stated audience—single, working women—complete with advice about money management, being independent, and working hard. Brown presented herself as an everywoman: "I am not beautiful, or even pretty....I am not bosomy or brilliant....I'm an introvert and I am sometimes mean and cranky."[23] Despite such deficiencies, she had married the "perfect man," and had secured financial stability and happiness without compromising her own desires.

Brown presented sex—within or without marriage—as healthy and natural Even when a single girl was involved in an adulterous relationship, or "indulging her libido," she could remain a "lady... [and] be highly respected and even envied if she is successful in her work." Brown spoke from experience.

Anyway, *Sex and the Single Girl* was giddy in its embrace of sexual ardor, of women gaining a sense of confidence (sexual and otherwise), of using sexual allure (through dress, makeup, and exercise) to secure a man and to help nurture a career. Women were counseled by Brown to give in to their urges, even to an affair where the sexual frisson might result in "unadulterated, cliff-hanging sex."[24]

In the view of the custodians of sexual conventionality, Brown had surrendered to the dangers of sexual excess and immorality. One reviewer called *Sex and the Single Girl* "about as tasteless a book as I have read this year." Norman Vincent Peale, an influential minister and author of bestselling advice books, condemned Brown's book as "one long flirtation of indiscriminate sex." Peale wondered, "Where do you draw the line?"

A good question: Where does one draw the line, especially in a culture that has been growing more rebellious over the last decade? What had once been thought scandalous was now readily available, though still under attack. In 1961, thirty-three years after it had first been published in Europe, Henry Miller's *Tropic of Cancer* was finally produced in an American edition. Yet he still complained in 1962 that "America is essentially against the artist, because he stands for individuality and creativeness."[25] In 1962, an American edition of *Naked Lunch*, William Burroughs's wild novel, was hauled out of warehouses and finally released to the public.[26] It made the once controversial *Howl* seem almost chaste in content and restrained in style. In language by turns clinical and fantastic, it narrated in non-

linear fashion the story of Bull Lee (essentially Burroughs). Lee's paranoid reveries, sexual shenanigans, and kaleidoscopic dreamscapes signaled a new, liberated sensibility at play in America. Here is a typical passage:

> Why so pale and wan, fair bugger? Smell of dead leeches in a rusty tin
> can latch onto that live wound, suck out the body and blood and bones
> of Jeeeeesus, leave him paralyzed from the waist down. Yield up thy
> forms, boy, to thy sugar daddy got the exam three years early and know
> all the answer books fix the World Series.[27]

But change rarely proceeds smoothly, nor is it absolute. Censorship, especially
at a local level, sometimes at the behest of citizen groups, newspaper editorials,
librarians, and others, continued. Aware of the spate of books that had previously been deemed unacceptable being published, an influential newspaper
columnist coined a term for such books: "paperback pornography." Reporting
in the *New York Times*, civil libertarian Anthony Lewis stated in January 1962,
"*Tropic of Cancer* has run into more massive opposition from censors across
the United States than any other serious publishing venture in memory.
Though 2,500,000 copies are in print, it is impossible to buy the book in most
parts of the country."[28] By 1964, the book finally escaped from the net of
censorship.

Fear lurked among the crowd of 1,500 people waiting to enter the Apollo
Theater on the frigid night of October 24, 1962, for a concert by James Brown
and His Fabulous Flames. Earlier that day, as Soviet vessels carrying arma-
ments neared the American blockade, the Joint Chiefs of Staff had ordered the
Strategic Air Command to go to level DEFCON 2 for the first time in history;
this meant a high level of preparedness for war.

Around midnight, Lucas "Fats" Gonder, emcee and organist, introduced
Brown in impeccable fashion. He recited rhythmically the names of Brown's
hit records, before calling Brown "Mr. Dynamite" and "the hardest working
man in show business."

Brown's singing and stage presence combined the spontaneous and the orchestrated, raw power and sentimental mush—but always in rhythm. Short
and muscular, angular in face, with the moves of boxer Sugar Ray Robinson,
Brown was a fantastic performer. He had fronted $5,700 of his own funds to
record his Apollo performances. That night he remembered a little old lady
who "must have been seventy-five years old," sitting right near one of the recording devices. She kept shouting: "Sing it mother.....r, sing it!" Brown worried about his investment being lost while he brought the crowd to a state of
ecstasy with his patented combination of upbeat and soulful numbers.[29] His
trademark was his scream, learned in black churches and honed by Brown to
secular perfection.[30] "There's only one thing I can say," and that was a scream

of pain: "Aaaaarggghhhh!" Then, to the audience, "I want to hear you scream."
A cathartic group of voices then joined with Brown.

In the midst of the song "Lost Someone," Brown remarked to the audience,
"It's getting' a little cold outside." This could have been a literal remark about
the weather, but it may also have been directed at the historical moment and
the potential of a nuclear holocaust. "I wonder if you know what I'm talkin'
about?" asked Brown. They knew. He then sang the perfect sentiment for this
charged moment: "Everybody needs someone," After another scream that was
less blood-curdling than ecstatic, Brown sang, "Feel so good, I wanna scream."
And with each scream, with every dance move, Brown and the audience
sweated through the potential of destruction by experiencing moments of
exhilarating liberation.[31]

Thankfully, the crisis resolved itself. As Rusk put it, Khrushchev blinked first,
deciding that a nuclear confrontation was too high a price to pay for having
missiles remain in Cuba. Some had pressured Kennedy to act decisively, to
either bomb the installations immediately or launch a massive invasion of the
island. A small number of advisers took the view that a deal could easily be
arranged to remove the missiles. Apparently, the president and his brother,
Attorney General Robert Kennedy, had read a recent bestselling book by historian Barbara Tuchman, *The Guns of August*. There she had detailed how
blunders and failure to consider complications brought about the horror of the
First World War. Perhaps such historical perspective helped to moderate the
warrior temperament of Kennedy. Although one could see the crisis as exemplary of the power of negotiation (the deal, kept secret, was for the United
States to remove some missiles from Turkey and to promise not to invade
Cuba, in return for the dismantling of the missiles in Cuba and the promise
not to reinstall them). Or the crisis could be seen as unnecessary, more a function of Cold War hysteria and macho extremism.

Whatever the case, only the cultural world exploded while James Brown
was onstage.

Flash forward exactly two years, to late October 1964 for the T.A.M.I. show
in Los Angeles. The British invasion has begun. The Beatles are making teenage
hearts throb; their records are the rage. Another English group, the Rolling
Stones, is rising in popularity. They are booked for the show, along with James
Brown. The old question arose—which act would close. The producers decided
to give that honor to Mick Jagger and the Stones—or that horror, because they
had to follow James Brown. The Stones, fresh and well-scrubbed, performed
well, singing five rhythm and blues tunes and one rockabilly number. Jagger
danced okay.

Brown danced with atomic explosiveness. Although his recollections are a
bit fuzzy, he stated that Jagger had been watching him perform from the side
of the stage, awed, transfixed, and anxious—going through an entire pack of

cigarettes while Brown gave what one rock commentator said was "universally regarded as the most astonishing performance in the history of rock and roll."[32]

"I hit the stage on fire," Brown recalled, and he "torched" his songs.[33] "I don't think I ever danced so hard in my life." With his hair pomaded to high altitude, wearing a double-breasted vest, Brown waltzed across the stage doing a seemingly impossible "shimmy on one leg."[34] During his classic "Please Don't Go," Brown repeated lines until they were drilled into the cement of everyone's soul. He built up, in the words of one analyst, "suspense and anticipation." Like a majestic lover, Brown was able to "manipulate, delay, renew, and finally shatter" the audience with his screams and repetitions.[35]

As was his practice, he then collapsed exhausted to his knees, so depleted by his songs about lovemaking or the need for love. One of the Flames helped him to his feet while Brown trembled; an aide rushed onstage to drape a plush white cape over his shoulders. Brown staggered off the stage, slowly and soulfully. But then, as if the Holy Ghost had entered him, he tossed off the cape and returned to sing anew. The routine was repeated three additional times. And he was still not finished, singing and dancing to his classic "Night Train." He was a man possessed and exhausted, yet still capable of doing full splits before finally blowing kisses to the crowd and letting the Rolling Stones, pale imitations of him, take the stage.[36]

Brown's music, with its finely toned perfectionism and elemental passion, was always in tension, stretched to the breaking point. His soulful embrace of excessive feelings was central to the New Sensibility. His music was at once a cry of grief and a scream of liberation. Onstage, he seemingly flirted with disaster—falling to his knees four times in a performance, slumping off the stage, but always returning triumphant, offering his audience a wonderful feast of excess.

Andy Warhol, Little Electric Chair *(1964–1965) (collection of the Andy Warhol Museum, Pittsburgh, and the Artists Rights Association)*

Picking His Nose at Tradition

ANDY WARHOL

1963

In the midst of the dark days of the Cuban Missile Crisis, Andy Warhol was scurrying around New York City. He cut quite a figure—blotchy skin, bulbous nose, fey mannerisms, and a blank stare. He had yet to adopt the persona ANDY WARHOL, the usually mute, bewigged impresario of mass produced pop art. But his desires were clear: "I want to be like Matisse," and "I want to be as famous as the Queen of England."[1] Warhol had been busy preparing for two exhibits, a pop-art group show at the Sidney Janis Gallery on October 31 and a solo show of paintings at the Stable Gallery on November 6. He hoped these shows would establish his reputation. They did. In the view of one art critic, they elevated Warhol to the status of "the defining artist of his era."[2]

A year later, Warhol was famous. He was the talk of the town, thanks in part to his depiction of Campbell's Soup cans one next to another, in four rows of eight each. He also made two films that tested the patience of audiences. He was creating repetitive, large silkscreens of celebrities ranging from Elizabeth Taylor to Elvis Presley. In November 1963, atop the art world, Warhol sat on his couch crying with his friend John Giorno as they watched coverage of the assassination of President Kennedy. He was working at the time on silkscreens for his Death and Disaster series, depicting car and plane crashes, suicides, and other gruesome events culled from the daily newspapers and pictorial archives.[3]

Since 1962, Warhol had been facing the wrath of many established artists and critics. For them, pop art, whether dealing with Campbell's Soup cans or airplane and automobile crashes, was inherently glib and demeaning. Such art, wrote critic Peter Selz in the summer of 1963, was nothing more than "banal and chauvinistic manifestations of our popular culture."[4] Another leading critic chimed in that pop art was "nostalgic eclecticism," capable at most of "a true billboard grandeur."[5] Traditionalist painter Fairfield Porter dismissed pop art as "an abortive attempt to show that painting today, especially that of the maturing avant-garde, is entirely in the hands of stuffed shirts."[6] In response to a Warhol exhibit, painters Mark Rothko, Robert Motherwell, Adolph Gottlieb, and others resigned in protest from the Janis Gallery. Warhol's revolt against the art establishment, according to critic Harold Rosenberg, "hit the New York art world with the force of an earthquake." Given the recently concluded Cuban Missile Crisis, a more apt metaphor would have been an atomic bomb blast.[7]

Not all critics cowered at the destructive force of the pop art movement, especially those that identified with the New Sensibility. Writing in *Art International*, Barbara Rose comprehended well the Dada roots of pop art and acknowledged its kinship with the subversive work of John Cage. All were in revolt against the "deadness" of established culture. Pop artists recognized the "glitter…vulgarity…and constantly changing face" of America. However, "by transforming the commonplace and the ordinary into the poetic or the arresting," pop artists, continued Rose, "force us to look freshly, to correct our corrupted vision."[8] A reviewer in the *New York Times* exulted in 1964 that Warhol had "destroyed Art with a capital A."[9]

Abstract expressionists took their art seriously, in a manner that was both touching and pretentious. They believed that the act of painting had evolved to the point where the artist confronted the canvas with either existential imperatives or analytic preciseness. Solutions to the problem of humanity or the challenge of a purely pictorial nature (resisting the desire for two dimensionality on the canvas) were of the essence. Each artwork was unique, endowed with an aura of world-historical import. They demanded purity, transcendence, and depth; they sneered at representational art and dismissed commercialism. For close to twenty years, abstract expressionism had flourished, aided by glowing reviews from the heavyweights of criticism Clement Greenberg and Harold Rosenberg. Sometimes the seriousness of the painters reached absurd levels of hyperbole. Artist Clyfford Still proclaimed that "a single stroke of paint, backed by work and a mind that understood its potency and implications, could restore the freedom lost in twenty centuries of apology and devices for subjugation."[10]

But in the last couple of years, the reign of abstract expressionism seemed to be ending. Gallery sales of their works had become stagnant, and their output had been diminished by alcoholism, madness, and suicides in their ranks, rendered palpable by the tragedies of Jackson Pollock and Arshile Gorky. Audiences and buyers yearned for something new. Warhol instinctively understood this—as well as the emerging zeitgeist of the era's New Sensibility.[11]

Warhol had long wanted to be taken seriously as an artist. His background in commercial art was a hindrance, as was his openly gay persona. While Jasper Johns and Robert Rauschenberg were also gay, that aspect of their lives was hidden, at least publicly. Nor did Warhol fit the image of the abstract expressionist as brooding intellect. Truman Capote (whom Warhol had bombarded in the late 1940s with fan letters) remarked that Warhol was a sphinx without a riddle.[12] Critic Hal Foster later characterized Warhol as "the great idiot savant of our time."[13] Reviewing an early exhibit, another critic chimed in that "Warhol was either a soft-headed fool or a hard-headed charlatan." In either case, the reviewer felt, the work stunk.[14] When interviewed about his art, Warhol lived up to his reputation of being either a blank slate or a brilliant provocateur. Asked in 1963 about the purpose behind his painting, Warhol replied, "The reason I'm painting this way is that I want to be a machine, and I feel that whatever I do and do machine-like is what I want to do." When his interviewer wondered why Warhol painted soup cans, his response was revealingly mundane: "Because I used to drink it. I used to have the same lunch every day, for twenty years" of Campbell's Tomato Soup and a sandwich.[15] Suffice it to say, Warhol had little truck with what he referred to as "the anguished, heavy intellects"—Franz Kline, Willem de Kooning, Mark Rothko, and Robert Motherwell, to name a few—of the abstract expressionists.[16] He found that world "very macho," too focused on producing "agonized, anguished art."[17]

Rather than torment his soul in search of transcendence, Warhol painted and silk-screened objects from everyday commercial culture. Commercial and popular cultural topics had been central to modernism, and they had cropped up in the 1950s in works such as Jasper Johns's American flags or in his bronzed renditions of two Ballantine Ale cans on a platform. Robert Rauschenberg mixed abstraction and popular culture artifacts in his combines. But the practitioners of pop, in comparison, weaved commercial and popular culture into the fabric of their work. In a desert of high modernism and seriousness, it was their artistic oasis. Roy Lichtenstein busily produced large-scale reproductions of comic book scenes and advertisements. The sculptor Claes Oldenburg was working to obliterate the lines between commerce and culture in his installation modeled on a Lower East Side variety store; his was overrun with art items for sale. They were at the forefront of the pop art movement, eschewing depth in favor of art that was both fun and of the moment.

Warhol was pop without apologies. He painted and reproduced images of products and stars that appealed to him. He painted thirty-two cans of Campbell's Soup because that was the number of different types the corporation produced. He was drawn to Coca-Cola for its ubiquity as an American product and for its democratic zest—after all, whether you were rich or poor, your bottle of coke tasted and cost the same. "A Coke is a Coke. . . . All the Cokes are the same and all the Cokes are good."[18] In 1962, following Marilyn Monroe's death, Warhol commemorated her with twenty-five silkscreen portraits. In 1963, he gave similar treatment to Elizabeth Taylor and Elvis Presley. He delighted in the silkscreen process, a mechanical form of reproduction; no two prints emerged precisely alike because of the vagaries in applying colors. The colors he used were glowing with life; the lips, in particular, of

Monroe and Taylor sparkled with sensual allure (and perhaps were designed as a critique of the scarified lips that de Kooning had incorporated in his Woman series). Sometimes, the face of Monroe was exiled from view and only lips were presented—on one print more than eighty-four lips and teeth were shown. "Marilyn's lips weren't kissable," Warhol reported, "but they were photographable."[19]

Warhol had by 1963 transformed the subject matter and mode of making art. Art became a "reproduction of a reproduction," according to critic Andreas Huyssen. The question that stymied Huyssen and other analysts of Warhol and pop art was simple and yet perplexing: Was Warhol celebrating commodity culture and celebrity, or was he subtly undermining it, perhaps taking it down a notch by poking fun at it? As Huyssen put it, "Affirmation or critique—that is the question."[20] Alas, there is no simple response. Certainly, as we shall see, Warhol's work was scooped up by rich collectors and embraced quickly, too, by major institutions of the art world, suggesting that his depictions of commodities and celebrities were not so devastating as to offend its beneficiaries. Yet the works can also be read as critiquing a culture that valorized commodities and celebrity, for the images bristled with the paint of anxiety and transiency. Looking at Warhol's work in 1963, critic Stuart Preston found pop artists like Warhol to be "genial jesters" of "often monstrous solemnities."[21] In a letter to the editor printed in *Art News*, R. Glaisek asked, "If the aim of Pop Art is not to satirize the heap of commercial dross custom-crafted for a consumer mentality and force fed to all of us, what is it?" Yet, for Glaisek, the art "has questionable value as a Thermo-fax duplicator of mediocrity."[22]

Inflation or deflation, mediocrity or brilliance—Warhol worried not a whit about such things.

Another pressing question was raised by the art critic Arthur C. Danto in 1964. Did Warhol's exhibit of Brillo cartons (constructed plywood replicas upon which he had silkscreened the familiar packaging) at the Stable Gallery end the practice of art as it had existed in Western culture? With his depictions of soup cans or Coca-Cola bottles the assault had been muted. After all, no viewer would take a bottle opener to a painting of Coca-Cola bottles, no matter how thirsty he or she might be. But with the Brillo boxes, Danto contended, Warhol had popped the artistic paradigm. In order to comprehend Warhol's boxes, the viewer had to come armed with knowledge and theory about the work. In sum, by "creating" and exhibiting boxes—as familiar to the eye as those which normally resided in a supermarket—Warhol had undermined the hierarchical status of the work of art once and for all. He had made plain what should have been obvious. For Danto, we come to art with our eyes and minds trained by a preexisting theory or paradigm. What made art art, then, were "theories" about what constituted art.[23]

The revolution that Warhol had effected was more than conceptual. His images of soup cans and Brillo boxes, his images of movie stars and the commonplace erased the line between high and low art—in terms of both style and subject matter. During the early 1960s, color television was being introduced into more homes; middle-class Americans delighted in Polaroid and Kodachrome color pictures.[24] This "culture of images" was Warhol's chosen terrain, but, unlike traditional artists who sought to create an aura of singularity around the particular work of art produced, Warhol delighted in creating works with repetitive images. If high art had concerned itself with the spiritual and technical (either in realism or in the relation of the paint to the picture plane or history of the medium), Warhol turned that around—art was now concerned with the mundane and accessible. Rather than putting in countless hours bringing the surface of the paint to perfection, Warhol churned out works in assembly-line fashion. Contrary to the vision of most artists as cultural originators of the highest order, Warhol quipped, "I think somebody should be able to do all my paintings for me."[25]

Whatever the veracity of Danto's views—after all, close examination of the boxes would have revealed that they were not cardboard; hence the distinction between the fake and real was appreciable[26]—a more pressing point for the evaluation might have been the recognition of the power of the critic (via reviews) and the curator (via the curatorial decision) to make an object into a work of art. Most viewers of Warhol did not trouble themselves with such epistemologically thorny questions about the nature of art. Instead, they enjoyed ogling Warhol's works, wondering about whether they should be taken seriously and appreciating their fun quality, their emphasis on surface over depth.

Warhol could not sit still as an artist. In 1963, even if he was no longer pushing his signature style in new directions, he was plunging into new waters of content, with a focus on violence—a topic central to the emerging New Sensibility. That same year he would pick up a movie camera and toss his celluloid hat into the ring of avant-garde filmmakers, once again, by excess either undermining or expanding the nature of the medium, according to one's tastes.

This focus on violence was hardly surprising; Warhol was not oblivious to the world around him. By the end of 1963, Kennedy had been felled by an assassin's bullet, the war in Vietnam had started to boil, and the dangers of the Cuban Missile Crisis lingered. And there was more—a fearful sense that the core of community in America had become corrupted by violence emerged with the killings in 1963 of black teens in a Birmingham church and with the murder, a year later, of a single white woman in Queens. Kitty Genovese had been bludgeoned repeatedly; her cries for help were presumed to have been ignored by neighbors out of apathy, coldness, or fear. In 1960 the attention of many had been riveted on the case of Caryl Chessman, a career criminal who had been sentenced to death for rape, kidnapping, and murder. Roughly handsome and articulate, Chessman proclaimed his innocence, writing of his plight in four books. Over the course of twelve years and eleven appeals, Chessman had evaded the gas chamber. His visage appeared on the cover of *Time* in March 1960, as his rendezvous with the executioner drew closer. Finally, in May, in San Quentin prison, Chessman was executed.[27]

By the early 1960s, a new fascination with, and graphic depiction of, violence had become common. Alfred Hitchcock's startling film *Psycho* haunted viewers. Here the violence of the famous shower-scene stabbing pushed aside cinematic restraint and the threat of censorship, helping to open the floodgates to a new era in the American cultural imagination.[28] Films such as *Dr. Strangelove* and *Fail Safe* (which came out the same month as the Cuban Missile Crisis) were, in Susan Sontag's view, sardonically marked by an "imagination of disaster." As historian Margot A. Henriksen put it, "A preoccupation with unnatural and early death was one of the strangest cultural phenomena of these years." Death, violence, and destruction had become, as the black radical H. Rap Brown would declare a few years later, as American as apple pie.[29]

The story of how Warhol lit upon the idea of a series of silkscreens dealing with violence is revealing. Warhol always admitted that he was open to suggestions from anyone about what might be a good subject for his art. At lunch with Warhol on June 4, 1962, Henry Geldzahler, a friend and curator, was carrying a copy of the *New York Mirror*, a tabloid whose front page that day was dominated by pictures of airplane debris from a midair collision over Brooklyn. A fan of Warhol and pop, Geldzahler wondered if pop needed a higher seriousness than depictions of Coca-Cola bottles, which he felt had been "glorifying American consumerism." "It's time to show," Geldzahler remarked, "that your work and your attitudes are serious." Shoving the newspaper in front of Warhol, Geldzahler told him he must depict "not just life, but death, too."[30]

Warhol responded enthusiastically: "It's enough affirmation of soup and Coke bottles."[31] The next day he handed Geldzahler a handprinted version of that very *Mirror* front page, titled *129 Die in Jet*. Throughout 1963 he extended the range and subtlety of the images. But the subject matter remained consistent—disaster and death.

According to some reports, Warhol was almost pathologically fearful of illness and death. He avoided sleep, often talking on the phone for hours to delay it. As a young child he had been painfully familiar with sickness and death. His parents, Andrej and Julia Warhola, were immigrants from Ruthenia, a region that seemed to nestle nowhere in particular (actually in the region on the southern slope of the Carpathian Mountains, straddling the borders of Poland, Slovakia, and Ukraine).[32] The youngest of three sons, Andy was a sickly child. At the age of four, he broke his arm. He was undoubtedly dyslexic. At six years of age he contracted scarlet fever, followed at eight by rheumatic fever, which developed into Sydenham's chorea. Otherwise known as Saint Vitus's dance, Sydenham's chorea is an illness of the central nervous system. Sometimes it can cause the sufferer to lose control of movement, resulting in what appears to be a mad dance of the limbs. Fearful of such outbursts, with almost albino-white skin, a bulbous nose, and red blotches on his face and upper body, Warhol entered his teenage years burdened with fears but artistically creative. And definitely gay.[33]

The health of his parents weighed on young Warhol. Andrej worked himself into an early grave. After surgery for gallbladder problems, he contracted jaundice. Yet he continued to do hard labor. At one job, after drinking contaminated water, he got hepatitis. Bedridden, he died a broken man in 1942. Within a few years, Julia took sick. She had suffered for years from bleeding hemorrhoids and then learned that she had colon cancer. A dangerous operation ensued, and Andy spent long periods of time sitting at her hospital bedside. Forced to live at home for weeks while his mother recovered, Andy prepared his own lunches, invariably dominated by a can of Campbell's Tomato Soup.

Despite illness, poverty, and shyness, Warhol had an iron will and stellar ambition. He managed to graduate the Carnegie Institute of Technology (today known as Carnegie Mellon University) in 1949. As one fellow student recalled, Andy "just drew like an angel." But he was an angel with a devilish side. He delighted in challenging the proprieties of his teachers. In his senior year, he did a painting for a Pittsburgh Associated Artists competition titled "The Broad Gave Me My Face, but I Can Pick My Own Nose." The title captured the content—a young man, clearly Warhol—with his finger assertively inserted into his left nostril. Suffice it to say, Warhol lost the competition.

Like so many, Warhol migrated to New York City, where he pursued a career in commercial art. He was energetic and agreeable to revision, always met deadlines, and was extremely talented. His initial commercial drawings appeared in 1949 in *Glamour*, accompanying an article titled "Success Is a Job in New York." By the mid-1950s, his line drawings of I. Miller shoes regularly appeared in the *New York Times*. In 1957 he was awarded the Art Directors Club Award for Distinctive Merit. In the view of master designer Milton Glaser, Warhol's shoe drawings had "an enormous sense of style.... When you gave him a shoe to draw, the shoe became more sophisticated. You got something extra."[34]

Despite success, Warhol never shook off fear of failure, anxiety about his looks, dread of falling back into poverty, or premonitions of death. The original idea for the Death and Disaster series, then, might have originated with Geldzahler's off-the-cuff suggestion at lunch one day, but the subject was hardwired into Warhol's imagination and life.

Warhol's attraction to celebrity was connected to his fascination with death. Warhol had begun working on images of Marilyn Monroe a few weeks after her suicide in August, 1962. He felt that his images of Monroe and other Hollywood stars were part of the Death and Disaster series. "I realized everything I was doing must have been Death," he reflected in 1963.[35] Likewise, his

Elizabeth Taylor portraits were initiated when she was seriously ill and maligned because of her illicit relationship with actor Richard Burton (both were married to others at the time). The repetition of the images and their size was something beyond mere glorification; it was a glimpse into the contingency of the moment, the heady shadow of death.[36] Yes, Warhol was attracted to the star quality of Marilyn, Liz, and many other celebrities. His *Gold Marilyn Monroe* paid homage on the highest level by enshrining the star in the same manner that religious figures from his boyhood church had been depicted, in flat, Byzantine style above the altar. But these images, like those of the saints, were depictions of death as much as life.

The star images evokes something transient and sad. *Gold Marilyn Monroe* is a large piece, with only her head depicted, against a background of unevenly applied gold paint. The image would have been snapshot-like if not for the touches ("violent colors") that Warhol added—his style in this period. The lips, as noted earlier, were resplendent, but so too was the golden hair, the arched eyebrows, and the blue-hued eyelids. The colors assaulted, but with a clarity of focus and representation that alerted viewers to Warhol's desire to preserve the allure of Marilyn, to fend off her physical demise through his artistic creation.[37]

Warhol would, of course, become known for his statement that someday everyone would experience their own fifteen minutes of fame. Among his earliest collectors were Robert and Ethel Scull. Their new money came from owning a fleet of taxi cabs. Not content to cultivate them as buyers of his work, Warhol made Ethel a subject for his work. Artists had historically done portraits of their sponsors, and Warhol continued the tradition, in his own peculiar manner. He had the stylish Ethel sit in a photo booth in the Times Square area as someone popped quarters into it for four shots at a time. Image after image of Ethel rolled out of the machine, sometimes wearing a bemused look, sometimes fussing with her hair, sometimes lost in thought, sometimes looking peevish, other times glamorous. *Ethel Scull 36 Times*, as the title suggested, offered up these photo-booth images, each then further individualized by the vagaries of the silkscreen process and the saturation and splash of colors. Although some might interpret the images as mocking—after all, the process is not quite the same as a patron sitting carefully for homage by an artist— Warhol insisted, "I always try to make the person look good." According to one account, the order of the images was determined by the Sculls, at Warhol's urging. Thus Warhol incorporated into the work a bit of the chance operations of John Cage while also capturing not his subject's character but her "look," her surface rather than her depth or character.[38]

Warhol was deeply cognizant that movie stars, and, indeed, all of us, exist under threat of imminent demise—in terms of both fame and life. In a commodity, celebrity culture, the image is everything, and it is often fickle and subservient to changing tastes. This was driven home especially in his homage to a star like Troy Donohue—boyishly attractive, seriously untalented, and soon to be forgotten.

Warhol also executed a series of large-scale silkscreens of Elvis, from *Flaming Star*, one of his many mediocre films. These were first shown at the Ferus Art Gallery in Los Angeles at the end of September 1963 (also in the exhibit were Warhol's Elizabeth Taylor images). Each image was over six feet tall. Gallery director Irving Blum remembered that they arrived at the gallery on a huge, uncut roll. What was he to do? Warhol said to go ahead and cut them as the director pleased and install them likewise. As Blum recalled, "Sometimes the images were superimposed one over the next. Sometimes they sat side-by-side." While this may seem a rather blasé attitude toward the installation, one historian argues that Warhol had "configured" the work sufficiently to absolve Blum of making big mistakes.[39]

A student reporter from the *Daily Bruin*, the UCLA newspaper, believed that the images were less homage than an extended contemplation of the nature of the commodity: "The effect is that of a sad and disgusted shudder. Toe to toe, repeated atop one another, poor Elvis becomes as thin and hazy as the idyllic illusion he publicly symbolizes; the assembly line produces the emptiness and sterility of soulless, over-managed property."[40] Warhol proudly announced of his production process (exemplified in the name that he gave to his studio: the Factory), "I did fifty Elvises in one day."[41]

Death and disaster dominated Warhol's art throughout 1963. From the first image of the wreckage of an airplane, Warhol moved toward ever more sensational and grizzly content. He barraged the public with death images, all rendered with Warhol's colorful industrial panache.

A Woman's Suicide (1963) was taken from a photograph of a woman tumbling from a balcony. Other works in the same vein from that year (drawn from newspaper morgues, often images deemed too graphic for public exposure) showed mangled bodies hanging out the doors of crashed automobiles. The images were gruesome, whether presented in black and white or in a purple or orange hues. Warhol experimented, as always, with a particular image in multiples, sometimes as many as twenty-five on a single panel. While the repetition might numb the viewer, it could also drive home the ubiquity of the disaster, how it not only filled the space of the venue where it was shown but intruded itself into the life of the victim, and perhaps by proxy into the life of the viewer.

Perhaps his most striking work depicted a lonely electric chair. Critic Norman Bryson referred to it as "the ultimate still life."[42] Silkscreened, repeated, and done in different colors; the image in *Lavender Disaster* and *Double Silver Disaster* was taken from a 1952 newswire photograph of the electric chair at Sing Sing Prison. The chair had presumably been the one that had been employed to execute Ethel and Julius Rosenberg. Although difficult to see in the color-splashed silkscreens, a door on the right side of the room displayed a sign with the word SILENCE. Had Warhol intended his electric chair silk-screens as a political statement? Warhol had been angered when Chessman was executed in California. While Warhol makes no reference to the particularity of the chair or to Chessman, the piece in its various styles was haunting—the most powerful of his Death and Disaster series, because it was, in effect, the most subtle, stark in its simplicity, shocking in its repetition.

Debate about Warhol's politics and whether there was any deep meaning to his work will never abate. He claimed to be only concerned with surfaces, eschewing depth or deep meaning. Was he offering a subtle critique of the death-dealing culture of the time? Warhol was not as apolitical as he let on, but he was also not overly engaged in politics, either. He was from a working-class background, a devout liberal Democrat, and someone worried about the fate of the world.[43] He was promiscuous, to be sure, in the images that he chose to print, but the Death and Disaster series testified to political concerns. Art historian Thomas Crow is correct in emphasizing how Warhol in 1963 carefully chose images that would expose "the open sores in American political life."[44] But he did so in a style that was at once cool and passionate, flirting with aestheticizing the violence.

Warhol focused on violence, too, in a series of images of race riots from Birmingham, Alabama. They retained his signature style but conveyed a sense of tension and immediacy—caught up in a dramatic narrative. The originals came from a *Life* magazine story headlined "The Dogs' Attack Is Negroes' Reward." German shepherd dogs, with teeth bared, lunge at demonstrators. One victim is a nattily turned-out African American with a stylish porkpie hat, but his pants have been ripped in several places by a police dog. This image has no words. Hence it could be viewed, as with other works by Warhol, as noncontextual, perhaps even overly aestheticized (one version was done in pinkish tones). But the race-riot images were anchored in such well-known contemporary events that they needed no explanation or context. Warhol was presenting in his manner the outrages that were then regularly occurring in the South.[45]

If we are looking for Warhol's willingness to complicate his presumed celebration of the commodity object, consider his images of tuna-fish cans. In 1963 a number of people had died from eating poisoned tuna fish from cans. In part, Warhol paid homage to some of these unknown celebrities, poor women that had become death statistics. In *Tunafish Disaster*, Warhol showed multiple images of the contaminated A&P tuna-fish cans. He included print from a *Newsweek* story: "Seized shipment: Did a leak kill..." repeated a number of times. Below pictures of two of the women, depicted as smiling, the caption reads "Mrs. McCarthy and Mrs. Brown (Tunafish Disaster)."[46] Commenting on the work, Warhol remarked, "I thought people should know about them sometimes.... It's not that I feel sorry for them, it's just that people go by and it doesn't really matter to them that someone unknown was killed so I thought it would be nice for these unknown people to be remembered by those who, ordinarily, wouldn't think of them."[47]

In 1963 Warhol started making films. He had begun going often to the Film-Makers' Cooperative on Park Avenue South. Under the benign and energetic direction of Jonas Mekas, the cooperative encouraged avant-garde filmmakers. Its aesthetic, at least as voiced by Mekas, was thoroughly avant-garde: in striving for "being new" in their work, artists realized "man's true vision" and undermined "bondage to Culture." The films that Mekas showcased and that Warhol watched bespoke a New Sensibility, exposing the "true feelings, the truths" of a new generation.[48] Anything seemed possible at that historical moment, as Warhol viewed explicit depictions of homosexuality, scribbles on film, rough cuts, and experiments in both style and form by filmmakers as varied as Kenneth Anger, Stan Brakhage, and Jack Smith.

In early summer 1963, along with his recently hired assistant, Gerard Malanga, and culture maven Charles Henri Ford, Warhol went to Peerless Camera in Midtown Manhattan. Warhol wanted to buy a film camera so that he could begin making movies. Malanga wisely suggested he purchase a Bolex 16 mm camera, since "Andy was not your technical expert." All he had to do with the camera was insert cartridges, "push the button and let it roll." According to Ford's recollection, "He just opened the lens and waved it around the room without even looking" once he had brought it home. "He had decided from the beginning that he was going to make 'bad' movies," which was in keeping with how he sometimes characterized pop as bad art.[49]

Warhol got to work immediately, unconcerned about technical limitations. After making some films of friends and traveling cross-country for his opening at the Ferus Gallery in Los Angeles, Warhol devoted considerable amounts of energy to becoming a filmmaker. His first films were, unsurprisingly, primitive, jumpy, poorly focused, and splotchy. No matter. Warhol worked simultaneously on two films, and neither one of them displayed any titles or credits on the screen; neither had any musical score. Yet they were conceptually rich and somehow visually lush. One was called *Kiss*, and the other was titled *Sleep*.

Kiss was shown serially, in three-and-a-half-minute batches, the amount of shooting that Warhol could capture on each film cartridge. The segments, later brought together into a fifty-four-minute film, were shot in different venues. As the title suggested, the film depicted kissing. It was a lip-locked film, sensual without being passionate—well in keeping with Warhol's appreciation for surfaces. One couple followed another on screen. It captured the varieties of the kissing experience—mostly heterosexual, but including two gay couples, and also an interracial couple (Rufus Collins, an African American, and Naomi Levine). This dance of lips (couples were shown from the neck up generally) included some ballet of the hands caressing the face, smoothing the hair, or touching the shoulder of partners. It was foreplay without intercourse. And even if in the final version it dragged on, challenging the attentiveness of even the most devoted connoisseurs of kissing, it managed nonetheless to be oddly liberating. Film critic Amy Taubin, who had seen it in 1963 in four parts, remembered how it flickered on the screen, "deep and impenetrable as archival nitrate." The film had been shot, as was Warhol's emerging habit, at twenty-four frames per second, but was screened at sixteen frames per second, making "its motion slower than life." "Never before in the history of the movies had the invitation to look but don't touch seemed quite so paradoxical." The film, Taubin concluded, was about the "play of light and shadow" more than "the oscillation of orifices."[50]

Sleep was about desire and death, playing with the liberating potential of boredom. Originally intending it to be eight hours in length, corresponding to the commonly recommended sleep cycle, Warhol ended up with a film that ran for six hours. The initial idea for the film arose from Warhol's voyeuristic and death-haunted personality. His friend John Giorno had once awakened in the middle of the night, after much drinking, to find Warhol wide awake (he was already addicted to amphetamines, sleeping only a few hours a night) and watching him.[51] That predawn morning, Warhol apparently decided to film Giorno asleep. He asked him if he would care to star in such a film; Giorno had immediately replied, "*I want to be like Marilyn Monroe!*"

Warhol shot Giorno sleeping over the course of various nights during a one-month period. Giorno disrobed and then imbibed his "usual vodka nightcap." Warhol then set up sufficient lighting and began using his Bolex, changing film every three or so minutes. Warhol moved the camera into different positions, set the lighting to catch shadows and light. He considered the finished result to be "*so beautiful.*"[52] Much of Warhol's work, as critic Wayne Koestenbaum put it, focuses on "the aroused or indifferent body."[53] Thus in *Kiss* there were aroused bodies, while in *Sleep* there was an indifferent body. But even when apparently indifferent, the body aroused Warhol. He could make love with his eyes (via the camera) without having to do anything—his preferred mode of sexual arousal and action, apparently.[54] Reflecting on Warhol's early films, John Yau offered the following, probably not intended as criticism: "Warhol raised the practice of Chinese water torture to the level of aesthetic experience, as well as taking us inside the mind-set of a self-loathing Peeping Tom."[55]

Was *Sleep* a joke? Could anyone manage to sit through a six-hour film of someone sleeping? In the fall of 1963, at the second screening of *Sleep*, Mekas, according to Stephen Koch, "greeted [Warhol] with a rope, led him to a seat in the second row from the back, and tied him down. Somewhere halfway through the film, Mekas decided to check that seat and see if the master had lingered with his disciples. 'I found the rope.' "[56] Alas, we have no record as to how long the notoriously attention-deficient Warhol was able to endure his own film.

The film obliquely saluted John Cage's aesthetic. Just as Cage used silence to allow ears to hear new things, so might six hours of a man sleeping give the mind opportunity to wander along new paths. Boredom became less an end than a means, a process of enlightenment in a Zen Buddhist sense. But repetition was never purely repetitious, since there were always subtle differences in the depiction of the object (as Rauschenberg understood) and in our perception of it (as one image builds upon another). And, of course, Warhol was a great admirer of Cage. He insisted to his crony Taylor Mead that Cage "really is great."[57]

Once Warhol had completed films such as *Kiss* and *Sleep*, the problem was what to do next. While many thought Warhol had gone as far as possible, he quickly proved them wrong. Within a year of making *Kiss*, Warhol filmed *Blow Job*, which, while not quite explicit, left no doubts in the minds of even the most naively virginal viewers of what was occurring. Within a year of making *Sleep*, on July 25, 1964, with Mekas's help, Warhol set up an immobile camera in an office some forty floors up in the Time-Life Building and trained the lens on the Empire State Building. Filming started around 8:00 p.m., just before sunset, and continued into the early morning hours. The result was a film eight hours long. The film caught the iconic character of the Empire State Building and further revealed that lack of movement did not equate with stillness. Viewers caught subtle changes in the lighting over time, the movement of clouds, flashes of lights from another building, even a quick glimpse of Warhol and another person reflected on the glass window. It would cost $354 to develop the gargantuan amount of film (654 feet), and Warhol, ever tight with his wallet, hesitated. He got funding from his mother by promising to include her in the credits. The film was, as one wag remarked, "an eight hour hard-on."[58] Excessive even for our Viagra age.

Susan Sontag, around the time of the publication of The New Sensibility. *(Getty Images)*

Naming the New

SUSAN SONTAG

1964

At the end of 1964, *Time* magazine extolled thirty-one-year-old Susan Sontag as "one of Manhattan's brightest young intellectuals." *Time* readers learned how Sontag had called camp a sensibility of "exaggeration" and adoration of the vulgar and the artificial. The article briefly mentioned that camp was often associated with homosexuals. Camp outlandishness, *Time* quoted Sontag as saying, was intended to "dethrone the serious" and ennoble the frivolous—to be a sort of "playful aestheticism."[1]

Less than six months after her splash in *Time*, Sontag was once again featured in a popular venue, in *Mademoiselle*, a magazine that aimed at "the smart young woman." Sandwiched between an advertisement for girdles and one touting a European vacation package, Sontag's article announced the stirring of something original, a new sensibility in American culture which

> reflects a new, more open way of looking at the world. It reflects new standards of beauty and style and taste. The new sensibility is definitely pluralistic; it is dedicated both to an excruciating seriousness and to fun and wit and nostalgia. It is also extremely history-conscious, voracious; and the velocity of its enthusiasms is very high speed and hectic. From the vantage point of this new sensibility, the beauty of a machine or the solution to a mathematical problem, of a painting by Jasper Johns, or a film by Jean-Luc Godard, and of the personalities and music of the Beatles are equally accessible.[2]

Susan Sontag was a phenomenon. Strikingly tall and slim, she hunched over as if embarrassed by her stature. Her saturnine visage was framed by luxuriant black hair, and she often wore a black turtleneck. She was edgy and kinetically charged, perhaps an effect of the amphetamines that allowed her to labor without cease, sometimes for days at a stretch. The avant-garde cinema gave her immense pleasure, as she gulped down the latest foreign films at the Beekman, New Yorker, and Embassy Theaters in New York City. Often, she sat through two or three films in a day. Her prose consisted of elongated sentences, along with feints, dead ends, piles of ideas, and, quite often, piercing aphorisms.[3]

By 1962 Sontag was wending her way through New York's cultural corridors. It had been a long time coming. An intellectual prodigy, she had been thrilled when her family moved from Tucson to Los Angeles in 1946, allowing her opportunity to read André Gide's journals in a local bookstore or grab the latest issue of *Partisan Review* at a newsstand. At age fifteen she was ready for college, longing for the high intellectual seriousness she associated with the University of Chicago. But her parents persuaded her to attend the University of California at Berkeley; after a year she could transfer. Perhaps her most notable experience at Berkeley was falling in love with Harriet Sohmers; they met over a shared passion for Djuna Barnes's novel *Nightwood*. Sontag now felt, she said, that "living is enormous."[4]

The start of the 1949 school year found her happily ensconced at the University of Chicago. Loving its Gothic buildings, neighborhood bookstores, and enshrinement of intellectual life, she felt "reborn."[5] In her second year at the university, Sontag suddenly got married. She had decided to audit Social Science II, taught by a twenty-eight-year-old PhD student named Philip Rieff. He was immediately smitten by the seventeen-year-old Sontag, who came late to his class, dressed in her usual outfit of blue jeans, plaid shirt, and her stepfather's army jacket. Against the shabbiness of the clothing, her beauty and intelligence shined. Rieff and Sontag were quickly engaged and married in December 1950. It is easy to imagine what Sontag saw in the young instructor. With a sharp, capacious mind, Rieff was writing a dissertation on Freud and moral theory. Most importantly, Sontag craved serious conversation about intellectual topics. Rieff supplied her fully with "the delirious amity of non-stop talking."[6]

Sontag finished her undergraduate degree in two years, thanks to her acing various placement exams. With degree in hand, she accompanied her husband to Brandeis University, outside Boston, where he was an assistant professor. The year of 1952 dawned for her with a new reality—pregnancy. Susan was open to having a child; it was an experience that she did not want to miss. She continued with a wide range of intellectual interests, writing poetry and short stories. One short story dealt with a couple about to have a child. The woman was concerned about the child's last name. The story reveals Susan's own anxiety about her new identity as Susan Rieff. The dark shadow of the story is in the conclusion. As the couple is walking, a car speeds toward them, about to kill the mother-to-be and, in a sense, resolve the problem of the child's name.[7]

The next five years found Sontag frustrated, hating her "feathered nest." She increasingly felt uncreative, stifled by Philip and child.[8] She had played a major role (researching, discussing, editing) in helping her husband publish his groundbreaking work, *Freud: The Mind of a Moralist*, published in 1959, which presented Freud as a necessary and conservative thinker. But she would receive no acknowledgment for her contributions.

Seeking escape, she won a fellowship to spend the 1957–58 academic year at St. Anne's College, Oxford.[9] Embarking by ocean liner for England on September 5, 1957, Sontag settled into life at Oxford. There she worked with such leading philosophers as A. J. Ayer and Iris Murdoch, the latter serving, no doubt, as the archetype of an intellectual that Sontag might emulate. Murdoch was both a novelist and an analytic philosopher. Sontag contemplated writing a dissertation on the "metaphysical presuppositions of ethics." She felt freedom such as she had not experienced since that first year at Chicago. She called herself Susan Sontag once again. A fellow student at Oxford later recalled the enigmatic and appealing presence of twenty-four-year-old Sontag as an object of desire on the part of some of the students—and out of their reach.[10]

Sontag soon abandoned Oxford for Paris, luxuriating in a simple room on the rue Jacob in the Latin Quarter, close to the Sorbonne. In Paris she wanted "to find a voice. To speak," and she would do so soon in fluent French. She read, as always, voraciously. She embraced the café life with gusto, meeting among others Allen Ginsberg and his partner, Peter Orlovsky; Alfred Chester, a sparkling writer and eminent character; and art critic Annette Michelson and her husband, Bernard Frechtman, who had translated into English some of Sartre's works. She also renewed an earlier relationship with Harriet Sohmers, ("games of sex, love, friendship. Banter, melancholy" but also marked by tension), with whom she would tour Europe.[11]

But first she wanted to end her marriage and reclaim her son. She worried that (in words that might have appeared in *Freud: The Mind of a Moralist*): "Price of freedom is unhappiness. I must distort my soul to write, to be free." Relationships with Harriett and Philip had compromised her own identity; loving involved "immolation of the self." She concluded, toward the end of her European sojourn, that "I think I can live without H[arriet] after all" and certainly without Philip.[12] She longed to be a novelist, out of "egotism" and because "there is something that I must say."[13]

Back in the United States, Sontag and her son settled in New York City. Editorial work and teaching at various schools paid the rent while she plugged away on her first novel, *The Benefactor* (1963)—a dreamy, difficult work that revealed more promise than polish. She gained the backing and friendship of many influential folks, and the prestigious firm of Farrar, Straus, and Giroux was committed to publishing her novel. Yet, having just broken up with Maria Irene Fornes, a talented playwright and a regal drama queen in private life, Sontag announced she had to break free of the inhibitions and neuroses that had hindered her in love and life. "I must become active." The agony of a volcanic romance gone sour haunted Sontag for the next two years.[14]

In August 1963 she asked herself, "How did everything go so wrong? How can I get myself out of this mess" (i.e., with Irene)? Her answer, jotted down three times was simple: "Do something." In effect, what she was doing in 1964 was realizing that her ability to feel and think had been damaged by her relationship; the end of their sex life meant "unbearable pain."[15] Ruminating about her own sensibility at this time of personal suffering, she translated her inner needs into cultural imperatives—"to recover our senses. We must learn to see more, to hear more, to feel more."[16] Attracted to transgression, she ate up everything that she found alive in the New Sensibility.

By the late 1960s, the notion that the personal is the political became increasingly prevalent. One reason for dwelling on the private agonies of Sontag's life is that they are connected with her public criticism. Feeling herself bereft of pleasure in her private world, she sought it in avant-garde culture. Castigating herself for a lack of emotion in her private life, she discovered it in the works of others. What she wanted, as she admitted in her journal, was "to go on pushing my sensibility further & further, honing my mind. Becoming more unique, more eccentric."[17]

By 1964, the New Sensibility was in full bloom in New York City. Avant-garde works, inspired by Dada and John Cage were performed, often under the auspices of Fluxus, an eclectic group of artists dedicated to exposing the surreal in everyday life.[18] Sculpture, dance, music, theater, and narration came together in happenings and performances. No longer would the artwork be entombed in museums. Art was to be an event, "concerts of everyday living," as composer and poet Dick Higgins stated.[19] A new notion of the body as a work of art was coming into view, the distance between audience and performer was lessening, sometimes to the point of obliteration. This is not to say that these works were no longer controversial. But they were becoming more common, and were soon to find expression in the culture at large.[20]

One piece *almost* made its mark. In a moment of madness or inspiration, Andy Warhol (along with nine other artists) was commissioned to do artwork for the façade of the New York State Pavilion at the upcoming world's fair. Warhol, as we saw in the previous chapter, was the king of the pop sensibility. His contribution, however, shocked officials, who had it removed from the façade. It was a mural titled *The 13 Most Wanted Men*, on which Warhol had reproduced headshots from wanted posters of thirteen criminals. As with much of his work from this period, interpretations of the piece varied. Was it simply a reproduction of a popular culture icon, such as his soup cans? Was it intended to alert visitors to New York City of criminals hiding in plain sight? Was it a camp gesture—with "Most Wanted" bearing more of a sexual rather than a legal significance?[21] Whatever it was, it fit in with the cool aesthetic that Sontag was beginning to explain to the public.

Yoko Ono, then a thirty-one-year-old artist associated with Fluxus, performed *Cut Piece* at Carnegie Hall in 1965. Dressed demurely in a black top (with buttons and long sleeves), black skirt, and fishnet stockings, Ono sat down onstage, Buddha-like. She generally stared ahead, placid, perhaps a bit wary at times. Like many in the New Sensibility, she wanted to undermine distance between artist and audience, so this piece depended as much on audience participation as on the artist. Audience members, one by one, ascended to the stage and picked up a pair of scissors lying next to Ono. One snip followed another, until Ono had been largely shorn of her clothing, although her white brassiere remained intact. Compared to later work by performance artists Marina Abramović or Chris Burden (see chapter 23), it was rather tame stuff. But in the early 1960s it dazzled. Like so much of the art of this moment, its meaning remained unclear. Was it about violence and objectification of women? Was it about Buddhist serenity in the face of violence (perhaps a nod in the direction of Vietnamese monks who had been self-immolating to protest against their government)? Was it about the audience as critics cutting away at the artist's work? All of the above? After all, as Sontag would remark, the new spirit in art was pluralistic, less concerned with interpretation than with pleasure and experiment.[22]

Robert Morris, who had already established a reputation for his minimalist sculpture, created *Site*—a "dance duet" that he performed with painter and performance artist Carolee Schneemann—at the Surplus Theater. It was both satire and homage to Manet's classic painting *Olympia*, where a nude model (who was also an artist of talent) reclines on a divan while the artist paints her. That work had shocked its nineteenth-century viewers by elevating a nude prostitute into a model of purity. Audiences saw Morris, wearing a mask of his own face (playing with his own identity), construction gloves, and a white outfit, with cut-off arms to flaunt his muscles. He then proceeded to remove a large plywood sheet, revealing Schneemann. For the remainder of the work, the audience's attention was riveted on Morris, who basically made himself and the plywood into a kinetic sculpture, moving around the stage, trying to balance a plywood sheet only to have it drop, then finally bringing the plywood back to its original position, thus reobscuring Schneemann. Morris then stepped back, folded his arm, and contemplated his handiwork.[23]

Schneemann staged a new piece of her own in November in New York City. It opened with four women in bikinis, doing a sort of Busby Berkeley number. They were soon joined by four men clad only in briefs. All cavorted about, sometimes hugging or tumbling, while a narrator read from a text composed by Schneemann; popular tunes ("My Boy Lollipop," for instance) played. A woman in a servant's outfit dropped raw chickens, fish, and sausages onto the performers, who employed the props in various ways—as aids to masturbatory fantasies, or as if fondling a baby. Schneemann described *Meat Joy*:

> Excessive, indulgent; a celebration of flesh as material: raw fish, chickens, sausages, wet paint, transparent plastic, rope, brushes, paper scraps. Its propulsion is toward the ecstatic, shifting and turning between tenderness,

wildness, precision, abandon—qualities that could at any moment be sensual, comic, joyous, repellent…in which the layered elements mesh and gain intensity by the energy complement of the audience….Our proximity heightened the sense of communality, transgressing the polarity between performer and audience.[24]

A total artwork, performed with delight—the audience, as per Schneemann's instructions, situated as close to the action as possible—the piece took joy in movement and pleasure in perversity.

So much was happening in the city. Cellist Charlotte Moorman organized the Festival of the Avant-Garde. She would later gain fame for playing her cello in the nude. One of her contributions was a collaboration with Cage. She played a piece of Cage's while he sat beside her; at one point he held a kazoo to her mouth for her to use. Schneemann, along with her husband, James Tenney, performed a piece for the festival with "bodies completely encased in metal debris." She also directed, with Nam June Paik, a piece by Allan Kaprow, *Push and Pull*. It resulted, said Schneemann, in the "utter destruction of the environment we built: old ladies, collared hairless businessmen astride cracked two by fours, beating each other and the remains of the environment with objects I had asked them to go into the streets close by and bring back soft materials, scraps, waste" to furnish the environment. But the audience, in her words, went "berserk."[25]

Pure pleasure and rebellion. It issued forth from earlier experimental work and happenings without impetus from the hubbub of the Beatles' arrival in New York in February 1964.[26] Indeed, one might wonder if the success of The Beatles and the freedom that became associated with them in general had been brewing since the earliest days of the New Sensibility.

Critics acknowledged the sea change in culture. Writing in 1962, the art critic Leo Steinberg remarked that the nature of avant-garde art was to "shock or discomfort," to cause "bewilderment," "anger," or "boredom" on the part of its audience. Years earlier, he had felt anxiety when encountering the work of Jasper Johns, whose work for example included a painting of a flag or a Ballantine Ale can rendered in bronze. Now he appreciated Johns and hypothesized about the process: avant-garde works were "outrageous for a season" before "undergoing rapid domestication."[27] Another art critic, Harold Rosenberg, worried about how art in the 1960s suddenly seemed less concerned with tradition and the art object (painting or sculpture) and more "self-conscious about being new and radical." What even constituted a work of art (and made it good or bad) seemed to be under siege. It made not only the art object but Rosenberg anxious.[28]

While art critic Barbara Rose wrote in 1965 that "a new sensibility in the arts had announced itself," she was unsure of what it was exactly. A new, minimalist style had emerged: cool, self-consciously boring, and daunting. Artists of the New Sensibility wanted to erase content from their work, in effect, to express emptiness and vacuum. The New Sensibility was "a negative art of denial and renunciation," of such "protracted asceticism" that it was "almost as hard to talk about as it is to have around" because of its "most ambivalent and...most elusive" nature.[29]

Two young script writers, David Newman and Robert Benton, took a stab at definition in the hip magazine *Esquire* in 1964. They were perfectly poised for the task. They were fiddling around with a script that would eventually become the film *Bonnie and Clyde* (1967)—an apotheosis of the violence, part of what they called the New Sentimentality (a term largely analogous with the New Sensibility). They agreed that self-indulgence—the artist as performer in public life—had become the in thing, a "virtue." The new poetry, encapsulated in the work of Robert Lowell, was about the "beauty of destruction, with the sanitarium as a favorite setting for a poem." Newman and Benton noted the "order of chaos" and the power of confession as central to the New Sentimentality. This vision brought together apparent opposites, cool and heat, excess and detachment: imagine Groucho Marx and Humphrey Bogart melded together.[30]

Tom Wolfe, the man in the white suit and fedora, recognized a new pizzazz in American culture. His focus, however, generally was outside of the world of avant-garde performance. Instead, he trumpeted the pleasures to be found in the lush colors used by automotive detailers, in the grit and grime of stock car racing tracks, and in the neon-lit avenues of Las Vegas. This came to a froth in his 1965 collection of essays, *The Kandy-Kolored Tangerine-Flake Streamline Baby*. As noted in the introduction, his "free-form" gaudy prose was designed to bury any notion of reportorial restraint or stylistic cramp. He named the phenomenon the "new sensibility," although that designation gets lost in the following paragraph:

America's first unconscious avant-garde! The hell with Mondrian, whoever the hell he is.... Artists for the new age, sculptors for the new style... The new sensibility—*Baby baby baby where did our love go*—the new world, submerged so long, invisible, and now arising, slippy, shiny, electric—Super Scuba-man!—out of the vinyl deeps.[31]

So many aspects of the pulsating New Sensibility had by 1964 become apparent that one critic pronounced it "the era of overkill." Prose became overheated; metaphors multiplied—words took on new colors and exuded energy. Confessional prose, too, became an expressive coin of this realm. Self-revelation replaced effacement as a mode of presentation, a way of being. Often, it was too much.[32]

Critic Richard Gilman emphasized "the confusion of realms" central to the New Sensibility. Purity of form had been replaced by manic mixing of styles.

With equal aplomb and seriousness, he ranged from analysis of Sontag and Marshal McLuhan (with his original and odd take on how technology fashions consciousness) to the minimalist fiction of Donald Barthelme, to the Living Theatre and the near pornographic prose of John Rechy—celebrating the new experiences in theater, art, happenings, and literature ushered in by the New Sensibility.[33]

Sontag was determined to wrap her mind around this New Sensibility. She found what was happening in American culture exciting and revolutionary.[34] In the end, the New Sensibility proved, perhaps appropriately in Sontag's view, to be largely "ineffable." Like any sensibility, she held, to define it was "to betray it."[35]

The New Sensibility for Sontag was mainly about pushing the boundaries of attention and dismissing content in favor of purity of images. This cultural turn departed from an earlier generation's adoration of a tragic sensibility and employment of Marxian or psychoanalytic interpretations. She was, in effect, lecturing an older generation of cultural critics (who worshipped the ideal of maturity and sanity) about a new culture, which was drawn toward madness and excess. "I'm attracted to demons," Sontag proclaimed; "maybe art *has* to be boring, now."[36]

She began to examine the New Sensibility via camp. While a sensibility was a predilection for a certain style, for a particular manner of organizing perceptions of the world, it remained somewhat mysterious, something without "system" or "proofs." Sontag's discussion of camp, then, took the odd but brilliant form of fifty-eight notes, overflowing with aperçu and insight speeding ahead in a hit-and-run manner. Such an approach, she claimed, had the advantage of being "tentative and nimble," a stylistic analogue of sorts to her subject matter, the "fugitive" but "powerful" presence of a sensibility.[37]

Sontag announced herself both drawn to and repelled by camp. Through "exaggeration" camp followers venerated objects which were commonly viewed as tasteless by the establishment.[38] Camp was, of necessity, over the top—joyously so. Although she failed to emphasize the centrality of camp to homosexual identity and culture, that subtext was clear in the article and highlighted in the piece that appeared in *Time* magazine. Sontag adored camp's vigor, vitality, style, experience, and aesthetic approach. "For Camp art is often decorative art, emphasizing texture, sensuous surface, and style at the expense of music." Camp was fun.[39]

With the appearance of an essay collection titled *Against Interpretation* in 1966, Sontag commenced her reign as queen of the New Sensibility. A reluctant monarch, she disdained categorization or limitation—preferring to be "promiscuous" and "pugnacious" in her tastes.[40] The essays, despite their daunting prose, were a sort of Baedeker guidebook of avant-garde literature, theater, and cinema (mostly European), with excursions into happenings and even science fiction films. Sontag's celebration of a New Sensibility made her

an immediate cultural superstar, an "evangelist of the new," as one early reviewer phrased it. A year after publication, *Against Interpretation* had sold over
ten thousand copies in hardback, with impressive numbers to follow paperback release in 1969. A Guggenheim Fellowship in 1966 attested further to
Sontag's presence.[41] Her photo appeared regularly in the popular press. She
had made it.

As the title emphasized, Sontag was against interpretation—a puzzling assertion for a volume of criticism. Sontag danced around the apparent contradiction by presenting herself as an enthusiast or connoisseur rather than critic
of the New Sensibility. Her antagonism to traditional interpretation was genuine, although it was more strategic than doctrinal. She bemoaned the modern
tendency to diminish the work of art by fitting it into rigid interpretive schema.
Such modes of criticism focused on content, context, and the intention of the
author. What did the book mean? How was it a reflection of the author's biography or time period? How might the language and form of the work be
brushed away to reveal a presumably more essential nugget of truth? Such
"incrustations of meaning" seemed "reactionary, impertinent, cowardly, [and]
stifling" ways of approaching works of art.[42]

She craved a more immediate and pleasurable relationship with text, painting,
film, or stage production. She discovered value not in the "deep" meaning of
the works—which were invariably hostile to summation, as in the befuddling
film *Last Year at Marienbad*—but in the "pure, untranslatable, sensuous immediacy of some of its images."[43] Film had come of age, with its directors now
demonstrating an awareness of its history tied to an ability to address by stylistic innovation problems peculiar to its own form. Such films were the "most
interesting works of art" because they were "not political or didactic"; instead,
they were "experimental, adventures in sensation, new sensory mixes."[44]

If this struck readers as a bit esoteric, Sontag offered other enticements. She
observed that the Maginot Line between works of high and low culture had
been transgressed—without ill effects. In contrast, throughout the 1950s and
into the 1960s, critics had railed against the pabulum of popular and middlebrow culture. While the former was rather harmless and easily ignored, the
latter was a venal specter threatening the purity of high art. Middlebrow, in the
common formulation proffered by critic Dwight Macdonald, diminished depths
and sentimentalized tragedy in great works of art by making them accessible
to an audience unwilling to grapple with complexity and difficulty. Middlebrow
dragged great art down to a level of insipidity.[45]

Openness to the plurality of possibility and pleasure in culture was now the
order of the day. "The purpose of art is always, ultimately, to give pleasure—
though our sensibilities may take time to catch up with the forms of pleasure
that art in any given time may offer," she stated.[46]

Sontag revealed a capacity for pleasure and camp in an essay on *Flaming
Creatures*. An independent film by Jack Smith, the film had achieved notoriety

and been banned, as already noted, when it was shown in 1963 at the Bleecker Street Cinema. Hazy, often out of focus, the film depicted various nude or semiclad individuals cavorting about, sometimes engaging in what looked to be orgies of pleasure and pathos. A penis appeared here, a drag queen appeared there. A New York court declared the work obscene.

Despite being amateurish and devoid of storyline, *Flaming Creatures* belonged for Sontag to the tradition of "the poetic cinema of shock." Its childish display of sexual shenanigans struck her as "witty." If pornography was designed to excite sexual desire, then *Flaming Creatures* was clearly in another genre. To a film aficionado, and a cosmopolite such as Sontag, the film was daring in its offbeat subject matter, inventive in its technique, and "a treat for the senses." Indeed, the film served as evidence in her battle against interpretation, since it proudly had "no ideas, no symbols, no commentary on or critique of anything." It simply was what it was, something to be enjoyed, like pop art. In sum, "a triumphant example of an aesthetic vision of the world" that opened up "the space of pleasure." In its celebration of excess and exaggeration, *Flaming Creatures* was an apotheosis, of sorts, of the New Sensibility; it had realized Sontag's goal of "an erotics of art."[47]

In an essay published in 1967, Sontag continued her examination of the key components of the New Sensibility. She was drawn to artists, mainly European, who shared her saturnine disposition—and who danced with madness.[48] More so, she believed that "the exemplary modern artist is a broker in madness." In her journals, she mused: "Madness as a defense against terror / Madness as a defense against grief." Freedom seemed to dwell in a mind that had become unhinged—"the 'value' in what is evil or lunatic." Finally, "art," she wrote in July 1964, is "a way of getting in touch with one's own insanity." One presumes that her "against interpretation" style offered a similar route.[49]

Theatrical expressions of madness Sontag found thrilling, as in the harrowing play *Marat/Sade* by the German playwright Peter Weiss. The play, which takes place in an insane asylum, was exemplary of "the desire to go beyond psychology," with mad characters almost rendering speech unnecessary. The use of its language as "incantation" linked it to the concern with ritual that was becoming central in the work of the Living Theatre.[50] The point of such art was to unhinge moral certitude and to overcome the passivity of expectations, to challenge the very ideal of sanity. Through a theater of shock, a culture of transgression, and an erotic aesthetic, the New Sensibility consumed Sontag.[51]

Sontag rarely wrote about the political situation blazing in 1964. It was as if she was so focused on cataloging and appreciating new effusions of culture (or ones that had been previously unknown to her) that she refused to board the train of politics. It was, however, the quiet before her storm. It was an extraordinary moment in American history, although in Tom Wolfe's view less for its events (war in Vietnam, student protests, civil rights struggles, and political assassinations) than for its revolution in manners or attitudes. Of particular import for Wolfe were " 'the generation gap,' 'the counter-culture,' 'black consciousness,' 'sexual permissiveness,' [and] 'the death of God' "[52]

Sontag agreed with Warhol's announcement: "Everything went young in '64." In cooler terms, Sontag noted, "Every age has its representative group—ours is youth."[53] However, the demographic explanation of a youth explosion as the motor of change confused the order of things. The development of a New Sensibility, experimental and transgressive, prone to push limits, as we have seen, had begun years earlier. It was only reaching fruition in 1964. Many of its youthful protagonists were jumping on a bandwagon that had already traveled some difficult roads. Sontag refused to weigh down her enthusiasm and prose with historical precursors or explanations of how this New Sensibility might be powered in part by an expansive, new sense of self, by a sense of potential atomic annihilation, or by an economy that was pumping out all sorts of goods for consumption. She just wanted to dance to its music.

In the article on the New Sensibility, Sontag had offered a laundry list of aesthetic forbearers: Nietzsche and Wittgenstein, Artaud, Breton, and Cage, among others. She failed, however, to examine the connection of the old with the new sensibility, or to historicize it as rooted in the 1950s. She felt herself caught up in a revolution of transgression—and it delighted her. "The only transformation that interests me is a total transformation," she declared in her journal in 1965.[54]

Such proclamations increasingly abounded in American culture. Critic Leslie Fiedler initially responded to them with dismay in the *Partisan Review* (the same issue included Sontag's "On Style"). The present generation, he argued, had lost its historical consciousness. "Drop-outs from history," he called them.[55] The "new irrationalists," or "new mutants," as Fiedler maintained, celebrated "prolonged adolescence to the grave" over reason and maturity. LSD had become "the radicalism of the young." Porno-politics (using a phrase from sociologist Lewis Feuer) and "porno-esthetics" (Fiedler's own coinage) were on parade, in film, theater, and music. Everything seemed reduced to sexual stimulation and immediate gratification, with confused gender roles (camp was making men effeminate) and celebration of insanity. The oft-anticipated atomic apocalypse had not happened, but Fiedler found that a new sensibility was creating "mutants." Fiedler considered these mutants of the radioactive New Sensibility to be barbarians at the gates, and in 1965 he was repelled by them. Ironically, Fiedler would soon drop his opposition and become a leading light of a new sensibility, writing about freaks and even getting busted for drug use.[56]

Fiedler's concern about the surrender of politics to esthetics, irrationalism, drugs, and self-indulgence was both right and wrong. Nothing in the New Sensibility militated against political commitment—as indicated by the work of Malina in the Living Theatre or Ginsberg or Mailer. But the New Sensibility, born of extremes, did fit well with a new style of politics emerging in the 1960s, one that could twine moral outrage with outrageous performance—a heady combination of Cage and Abbie Hoffman, as actualized by the Yippies.

Sontag was often a cheerleader for the New Sensibility. Yet, even in *Against Interpretation*, she expressed qualms. For example, she chafed at camp's failure (which, in fact, was part of its raison d'être) to confront political issues, reducing everything to style. As the violent pace of the war in Vietnam accelerated, Sontag became an avid protestor, convinced that the role of the avant-garde intellectual was to fight injustice. By 1966, while Sontag's taste in literature and art remained consistent with the New Sensibility, her tone harshened. She famously proclaimed: "America was founded on genocide," and "The white race *is* the cancer of human history." In 1968 she traveled to North Vietnam, working hard to establish her sympathy but also put off by their rather limited avant-garde sensibility.[57]

The flag of the New Sensibility waved by Sontag was marked by contradiction and paradox. This is unsurprising, since the New Sensibility was powerfully pluralistic, even promiscuous. But did that mean lack of coherence? The unity of the New Sensibility was wrought with tension, akin to how "a first-rate intelligence," according to F. Scott Fitzgerald, was "able to hold two opposed ideas in mind, at the same time and still retain the ability to function."[58] Indeed, this tension was what made the New Sensibility vibrant and exciting.

The core of the New Sensibility, to sum up, was excess, whether in the direction of minimalism or maximalism, captured equally by the musical bursts of Jerry Lee Lewis or the silences of John Cage. Apostles of the New Sensibility generally welcomed the sagging of the middle ground, which in politics meant the decline of postwar liberalism, predicated upon support for the Cold War. The content of the New Sensibility, as we'll see, delved deeper into violence, madness, and sexuality in the years to come. The lines that divided high and low culture or audience and performer would be dismissed as cultural creators reveled in a newfound freedom to wander in new directions, to explore without the fetters of censorship and good taste.

Like it or not, the New Sensibility had become by the mid-1960s the dominant cultural style in the United States.[59] In time, its excesses would grow and be codified, along with its content, allowing it to continue to be both outrageous and outstanding—as well as commonplace.

Looking back in 1996 on her days as a proponent of the New Sensibility, Sontag believed that she had gone overboard with her enthusiasm. During the 1960s, a time "filled with evangelical zeal," she had seen herself "as a newly minted warrior in a very old battle: against philistinism, against ethical and aesthetic shallowness and indifference." Then she had exulted as new, experimental works tumbled from presses and stages. Although she had championed popular culture, she refused to equate "the Doors and Dostoyevsky." Some authors that she had claimed to adore for their ability to stimulate through repetition had become boring. "I thought I *liked* William Burroughs and Nathalie Sarraute and Robbe-Grillet," she recalled, "but I didn't. I actually didn't."[60]

Although she remained convinced of the aesthetic power of this new sensibility, it had failed to dethrone capitalism; the transgressive nature of the New Sensibility had been a stylistic breakthrough injecting pleasure, excess, fantasy (often perverse), spontaneity, and choice into culture. All of this had been only quietly percolating in the 1950s (in part because of Cold War repression and nuclear anxiety). By the 1960s, these values had become predominant in American culture. None of these values, however, constituted an essential challenge to capitalism; indeed, as Thomas Frank has argued, a hip style or sensibility proved liberating to the advertising industry. Hip values, in some ways, mirrored the logic of capital expansion, albeit in new phantasmagoric worlds.[61] Sontag had recognized this as early as 1966: "I live in an unethical society that coarsens the sensibilities and thwarts the capacities for goodness of most people but makes available for minority consumption an astonishing array of intellectual and aesthetic pleasures."[62]

What might once have been limited for consumption by an elite minority would by the next century become available for mass consumption—thanks to the arrival of cable television and satellite dishes, not to mention the Internet. Now, almost anyone can partake of "an astonishing array of intellectual and aesthetic pleasures." There are worse sins.

John Coltrane (© Photofest)

Bob Dylan in 1965, from the film by D. A. Pennebaker
Don't Look Back (© *Photofest*)

"How Does It Feel?"

JOHN COLTRANE AND BOB DYLAN

1965

How does it feel to be booed while performing?

It happened to both Bob Dylan and John Coltrane in the summer of 1965. Dylan was onstage at the Newport Folk Festival in July and Coltrane at the Down Beat Jazz Festival in Chicago that August. Memories of both performances are foggy and often contradictory, but many attending recall rigorous booing: "You could hear it," Dylan remarked, "all over the place." Some in the audience, open to Dylan's electric turn, felt gypped by the brevity of his set. Al Kooper, playing keyboards, claimed that the "booing" arose because Dylan had "only played three songs."[1] Folk traditionalists were offended by Dylan's amped up music, with the help of the Paul Butterfield Blues Band, and by his refusal to perform protest songs. He seemed to have abandoned his friends for rock-and-roll bluster. "You couldn't understand a goddam word of what they were singing," Pete Seeger later complained (although he was upset about the poor sound system).[2] Some in the audience screamed "We want the old Bob Dylan," while others shouted "Traitor" or "Sell Out."[3] According to Dylan's pal Paul Nelson, the audience yelled, "Get rid of the electric guitar."[4] Another account, by singer Maria Muldaur, who was also there, found folk purists booing and chanting, "Are you with us?"[5] The answer to their question was obvious— Dylan was staking out new territory.

Dylan, by all accounts, was "shaken and disappointed" after the concert, yet determined to push his musical turn farther: "I know in my own mind what I'm doing."[6]

Harsh notes screamed from Coltrane's alto saxophone in Chicago. Bandmate Archie Shepp raved with lengthy explorations into the possibility of sounds on his own sax. Coltrane's liberation should have been anticipated by the audience at Soldier Field. His opening number that day, "Nature Boy," had been available on the album *The John Coltrane Quartet Plays*. While the initial batch of bars echoed the familiar tune (it had been recorded first in 1947 with Middle

Eastern inflections), Coltrane's version was from another galaxy.[7] When he was enthusiastic about a particular musical route, he kept going, without concern about length. "Well, if you like something for ten minutes," Coltrane stated, "why shouldn't you like it for 45 minutes?"[8]

To some ears, it sounded like noise, like musicians improvising madly, at impossible length. Interviewed a few weeks before the Chicago concert, after experiencing audience dissatisfaction during a performance in France, Coltrane acknowledged that his music tested the limits of his band—and audience. He was dedicated, however, to "playing it until you get it together."[9] Another time he remarked that chords were an "obsession" with him. Sometimes, in his pursuit of their potential, he seemed to be "approaching music by the wrong end of a telescope."[10] One youth present at Soldier Field did not boo, but recalled, "I was not able to understand what he was doing, other than it was ferocious and full out."[11] After sitting comfortably through hours of easy-listening jazz, the audience found Coltrane's music too dissonant and obsessive for their tastes; many walked out in disgust.[12]

Such complaints soon became commonplace. A year later, at Lincoln Center in New York City, Coltrane performed in a show billed as "Titans of the Tenor." The audience responded with some boos to his experimental, extreme jazz renditions. Traditionalist jazz critic Dan Morgenstern wondered, "Has he lost all musical judgment? Or is he putting on his audience? Whatever the answer, it was saddening to contemplate this spectacle, unworthy of a great musician."[13] That same year, McCoy Tyner, Coltrane's longtime pianist, left the band, finding the chaos onstage too much: "All I could hear was a lot of noise."[14]

Only those exiled to Siberia would have been surprised about the musical shifts of young Mr. Dylan and mature Mr. Coltrane. About half the numbers on Dylan's new album, *Bringing It All Back Home* (released in March), had been electric. He had already made clear in various interviews his disdain for "boring" protest songs—"finger-pointing" songs, he called them.[15] And by 1964 he had told a friend that rock was "where it's at for me."[16] He had always been chameleon-like, moving from a teenage rocker (idolizing Little Richard, briefly playing with Bobby Vee's band) to young folk musician. In 1964 he had been impressed with the energy of the Beatles' songs, then exploding on the American consciousness. He was determined to expand possibilities, not just with instrumentation but with content. Henceforth, he would incorporate poetic reflections, mysteriously confessional lyrics, and ramblings of visionary dreamscapes, into his music, as in the rollicking "Bob Dylan's 115th Dream" and "Subterranean Homesick Blues" and the beauty of "Love Minus Zero/No Limit."[17]

For many years, Coltrane, too, had been famous (or infamous, according to one's disposition) for musical style shifting. He had apprenticed in many bands, showing himself adaptable to the different styles demanded by Eddie "Cleanhead" Vinson, Thelonious Monk, and Miles Davis. He was always thinking about music, studying its theory and listening to all of its manifestations (Indian, Arabic, Brazilian). Now he was moving in the direction of "the New Thing," as it was called early on before becoming known as "free jazz." He would bound into it with abandon. As he admitted, "I am given to extremes."[18]

Born in part as a reaction to the commercialization of jazz and the rigidity of certain styles, "free jazz was wildly improvisational and experimental. Politically, it was presumed to reject European musical influence and to be rooted in the African American experience. The music, as developed by Cecil Taylor, Albert Ayler, and Ornette Coleman, was challenging, difficult to grasp. One jazz aficionado after hearing Coleman blow, admitted "He's out—real far-out...but I don't have any idea of what he is doing."[19] Shepp had once been a member of the heroin-fueled Living Theatre production *The Connection*. He played with Cecil Taylor around that time, too, but at first failed, he said, to "know what the cat was doing." Soon he "felt" the music and found himself. Shepp's playing was about rhythm, which he considered African in origin and was "liberated from thinking about chords." Shepp argued in 1965 that his music was "a reflection of the Negro people as a social and cultural phenomenon." Its "purpose ought to be to liberate America aesthetically and socially from its inhumanity."[20]

Both Dylan and Coltrane were rolling stones that gathered no moss. Yet they were in many ways disparate figures. Coltrane was thirty-eight and Dylan just twenty-four in the summer of 1965. From a poor but respectable black family in North Carolina, Coltrane had migrated north to Philadelphia and then, in 1945, entered the Navy, soon playing in the band the Melody Masters.[21] Deeply intelligent and well read, a bit self-contained, Coltrane was obsessed with mastering the saxophone, beginning with alto then moving to tenor. His playing initially was sketchy, but through practice, hour after hour, always aware of what others were doing on the instrument, he became something special.

Dylan, born to a middle-class Jewish family in Hibbing, Minnesota, was from an early age a maker of myths, imagining himself as a vagabond, a country rebel, and more. He was described, at the moment he was becoming famous, as an amalgam of possibilities, a combination of "Harpo Marx, Carol Burnett, and the young Beethoven"; in "appearance, the Ultimate Beatnik; cowboy boots, jeans, wrinkled work shirts and dark glasses, plus frizzy, unkempt hair and a lean, pale and haggard face." A fair description, but by the time the piece appeared in the *New York Times* in 1965, he had already dropped the beat look for the style of a rebel in motorcycle jacket.[22]

Details of biography matter little with Dylan and only a bit more with Coltrane. Both were sui generis. Dylan the weaver of tall tales, mask and myth maker; to track down the truth about Dylan, his wild claims and shuffling of facts, is a fool's errand. Coltrane, saintly in his dedication to sound, was a man who spoke his soul in his music, the rest of him was effaced.

Both of them, however, were sponges, absorbing influences aplenty. It has been widely suggested that each of them filched material or borrowed style too readily from others.[23] But part of their genius was their openness to new possibilities, their unwillingness to rest comfortably with what they had already mastered. When asked in the summer of 1965 about the next direction his music might take, Coltrane replied: "I don't know yet. I'm looking for new ground to explore." Realizing that change is of the essence, Coltrane stated, "We have to keep on cleaning the mirror."[24] Dylan wanted escape from the stranglehold of protest songs. It was second nature for Dylan to rebel against expectations. Critic Anthony DeCurtis wrote that Dylan had an "inherent discomfort with absolute positions," hence his rather cagey and confusing responses to generations of interviewers about his political, religious, and philosophical views. Dylan treasured few things more than his autonomy.[25]

It was creative necessity rather than opportunism that forced them down new, sometimes extreme paths. Ornette Coleman and Albert Ayler may have pioneered the Free Jazz style before Coltrane, but he made it his own form, expanding its borders—sometimes to ear-shattering extents. He pushed their ideas. Critic Ira Gitler once referred to Coltrane's music as constituting in and of itself "a sheet of sound." It "could have powered a spaceship."[26] Dylan borrowed melodies and styles of folksinging from Lead Belly, Woody Guthrie, Robert Johnson, Chuck Berry, and Dave Van Ronk, but he transformed material, thanks to his odd phrasing and emotional bite.

According to a distinguished historian, 1965 was "the inaugural year of the 1960s." A bold statement, certainly. It possesses a grain of truth, especially in terms of politics and race. In that busy year, hope wagged a happy tail. The economy was booming. In October the Dow Industrial Index peaked at the highest level in its eighty-year history, and gross national product shot upward. Unemployment at the close of 1965 was a scant 4.1 percent. For those caught in poverty, change seemed in the offing through President Johnson's Great Society programs. Having won a landslide election in 1964 over Republican Barry Goldwater, and with a hefty Democratic majority in both the Senate and Congress, Johnson was delighted to sign off on Medicare and Medicaid, the Office of Economic Opportunity, and much more. Anything seemed possible.

Even on the torturous terrain of race, progress appeared to be forthcoming. At Johnson's behest the Voting Rights Act passed—promising to guarantee the right to vote for African Americans in the South. But progress was opposed by reaction. White police in Selma, Alabama, on "Bloody Sunday" brutally beat civil rights marchers. A few weeks later, however, a march to Montgomery, Alabama, twenty-five thousand strong, was peaceful and attracted wide support. The government, with Johnson under pressure, was moving in the direction of greater racial equality, but it was a tough push.

The war in Vietnam, however, cast a foreboding shadow. With each passing month, its tentacles tightened around Johnson and his foreign policy advisors. By February, bombing of areas in North Vietnam had begun, soon morphing into the program called Operation Rolling Thunder. Agent Orange (a highly toxic defoliant) and napalm were authorized—and employed in copious amounts. American troop levels jumped upward: 40,000 more in April, another 21,000 in June, 50,000 more in late July, ballooning by the end of the year to a presence of 184,000. US casualties inched toward two thousand, with Vietnamese deaths staggering. The ideal of the Great Society, predicated on government spending, came into conflict with the costs of the war in Vietnam, and the deficit rose accordingly.

Protests against the Vietnam War quickened. By the fall of 1965, nationwide events had become common, and, beginning at the University of Michigan, teach-ins educated a generation of college students about the problematic history of the war and our ally South Vietnam (which had undergone a military coup in June).

More startling to many Americans was the mid-August explosion of violence in Watts, a black ghetto in Los Angeles. Years of discrimination, unemployment, and heavy-handed police tactics (almost all the police in the area were white) exploded out of a mundane arrest into a riot. Over the next five days, a total of thirty-four people were killed, thousands were arrested, and many businesses and homes burned to the ground. For white Americans, the road to racial progress became hazy in the smoke of Watts. For white Americans antagonistic to black rights and protest, the Watts riots made segregationist governor of Alabama George C. Wallace popular as a maintainer of law and order—taken by many to be a code term for clamping down on African Americans.[27]

In a pluralistic culture, hope and anxiety, sweetness and anger, received cultural expression in 1965. The film *The Sound of Music*, based on a Rodgers and Hammerstein Broadway hit musical from 1959, was a story of hope—about the triumph of love and music over evil. It featured seven adorable children. And the sound of music emanating from their mouths was sufficient (along with the allure of actress Julie Andrews) to unknit even the tightly furrowed brow of Captain Von Trapp. Critic Pauline Kael dismissed the film: "It's the big lie, the sugarcoated lie that people seem to want to eat," especially in America, where sentimentalism reigned supreme. American audiences were unfazed. The film grossed more than any other in the history of Hollywood (more than *Gone With the Wind*), and it won five Academy Awards. The soundtrack of the film was also an immense success.[28]

In a very different vein, the song "Eve of Destruction," a song beholden to Dylan in content and singing style, was a big hit in 1965. Sung with gruff sincerity by Barry McGuire, the tune was a *cri de cœur*. The song spoke to the historical moment—from the anxiety of the Cuban Missile Crisis to the paranoia

about madmen with an itchy trigger finger on atomic weapons. McGuire bemoaned the violence "flarin'" all around him: "Can't you feel the fear that I'm
feelin' today?" He even referenced the hatred in Selma, concluding: "And you
tell me over and over and over and over again, my friend / You don't believe
we're on the eve of destruction."

The Sound of Music and "Eve of Destruction" were symptomatic of the tensions and contradictions of the historical moment. But they were not the works
from 1965 that sung out with creative force. They were anchored in the past.
This was the moment for the New Sensibility, with its hard-driving experimentalism and sharpened poetry, to explode on the musical scene, thanks to Dylan
and Coltrane.

Both Dylan and Coltrane were concerned with civil rights and human destruction. Coltrane's "Alabama" commemorated the four black schoolchildren killed
by a bomb in Birmingham planted by members of the Ku Klux Klan in
September 1963. Coltrane's main melody was based on the rhythms that he
discerned in Martin Luther King Jr.'s speech about the murder. From auspicious silence to explosive tempo, over and over again, Coltrane and his band
made sound into musical oration. One critic remarked that Coltrane's music
expressed "all the emotions and expressions of the human being." Coltrane
"tells a story," as he "laughs, screams, whispers, cries, dances, groans, caresses
begs, demands."[29]

The Black Arts Movement, led by Amiri Baraka, Larry Neal, and Archie
Shepp, arose in tandem with the civil rights and black liberation movements.
They believed in something called a black aesthetic, a sort of consciousness
rooted in the shared heritage and experience of African Americans. Cultural
creation, done in this manner, would raise African Americans to a nationalist
and perhaps revolutionary consciousness. Problems arose, however, when black
artists depended upon white culture and a white audience. This led to inauthentic and polluted art. Music, according to some in the Black Arts Movement,
was the purest expression of a black aesthetic. Free jazz appeared to be the
newest manifestation of black identity, a music consisting of shouts and improvisational anarchy, pain and honesty that would lead to black liberation.
Just how this was to be accomplished by a sound that was perhaps unintelli-
gible to most listeners remained something of a mystery.[30]

Ralph Ellison and Albert Murray ridiculed the black aesthetic, claiming
that African American and white experiences were historically intertwined,
incapable of separation. Great art had to be receptive to the best and most vibrant in any cultural milieu, to practice a sort of amalgamation, shunning cultural exclusivity. The black aesthetic for them was merely a haughty term for a
nonexistent and dispiriting artistic ideal—the attempt of political radicals "to
impose ideology upon" the complexity of cultural creation.[31]

In 1965 Coltrane was performing in a free jazz style, often collaborating with its leading practitioners. But there is little indication that he bought into the ideology that surrounded it. Instead, as with so much of his work, his interest was musical more than political—it was a mode of playing that enthused him. Coltrane's music increasingly challenged traditional jazz categories, confounding his critics and audiences alike. All Coltrane wanted was to keep moving in unexplored dimensions of sound.[32]

Dylan had gained fame for his protest songs.[33] "Blowin' in the Wind" became a civil rights anthem of sorts, especially when he performed it at the March on Washington in 1963. Another song from that period, "The Lonesome Death of Hattie Carroll," told the story of a black hotel worker killed by a savage blow from the cane of William Zantzinger. The white murderer received a slap-on-the-wrist six-month jail sentence. This outraged Dylan, so he penned the haunting refrain:

> And you who philosophize disgrace
> And criticize all fears
> Take the rag away from your face
> Now ain't the time for your tears.

As Andrew Sarris observed, the song "is the only memorial Hattie Carroll is ever likely to have."[34] Other Dylan songs had targeted American militarism and fanaticism, as in "Masters of War," "Only a Pawn in Their Game," or "Talkin' John Birch Paranoid Blues."

And yet, in the midst of the social turmoil and change—perhaps because of it—Coltrane and Dylan embarked on inward musical journeys. Dylan, as biographer Ian Bell put it, entered his "apolitical phase."[35]

Coltrane, by 1965, was following an increasingly spiritual path, reaching out for transcendence, for acknowledgement of some sort of divinity. He had in the 1950s been a heroin addict and alcoholic, finally quitting heroin cold turkey in 1957. By the mid-1960s, he started using LSD, which impelled him more deeply into mysticism in music and philosophy. He wanted his music to possess "strong emotional content"—to reflect the times and his desire to be at one with the universe.

Dylan's songs became more personal and pointed, filled with poetic reverie and undiluted anger. Their lyrics were confessional but without easy markers for the audience to engage. He was now backed by rock musicians, making his music even more jarring and extreme. "You got a lotta nerve to say you are my friend," he sang harshly. He strove to be his own man. As his girlfriend from his early years in the Village put it, "Bob always did as he saw fit."[36] But he did so in a masked manner, so that the particulars of his confessional style were transformed into something more formidable, something more universal.

The year 1965 was a crucial and busy one for both artists as they moved in new directions. Coltrane's *A Love Supreme* (recorded in December 1964) was released. In that year alone, in addition to *The John Coltrane Quartet Plays*, released in June, he recorded three other works, *Kulu Sé Mama* (recorded in May and June), *Ascension* (recorded in late June), and *Meditations* (recorded in October). Dylan opened the year by recording *Bringing It All Back Home* (released in March), followed by *Highway 61 Revisited* (released in late August), with the hit single "Like A Rolling Stone." After a world tour, and taking time off from a US tour, Dylan recorded his haunting "Visions of Johanna," which would be part of his next work, *Blonde on Blonde* (released in 1966).

The idea for *A Love Supreme* came to Coltrane around four in the morning on a fall day after he had completed his daily meditation. He felt God's presence more fully than ever before and believed that God commanded him to compose a work of commemoration. According to his wife, Coltrane went into seclusion for four or five days, finally emerging "like Moses coming down from the mountain." He seemed beatific and enthusiastic: "This is the first time that I have received all the music for what I want to record, in a suite. This is the first time I have everything, everything ready."[37] Transposed onto paper, the score called for nine musicians, their instruments to sound out that "all paths lead to God." With the final notes, as he wrote on the score, the bass players were to "say Amen symbolically."[38]

A Love Supreme appeared in February 1965. Coltrane contributed the liner notes, which revealed his state of mind to be in perfect consonance with the music. He acknowledged that in 1957 he had "experienced, by the grace of God, a spiritual awakening" that had granted him "a richer, fuller, more productive life." As most jazz aficionados had grasped, for four years up until 1957, Coltrane's life seemed to be on a downward spiral because of his use of heroin. Redemption had put him on "Straight Street."[39] He intended *A Love Supreme* to be an offering of thanks to God.[40] Not only was he enjoying professional success (*Down Beat* magazine named him Jazzman of the Year for 1965), but he and his wife had greeted a second son in August. The recording, about a half an hour in length, consisted of four parts, "Acknowledgements," "Resolution," "Pursuance," and "Psalm"—in effect, Coltrane's version of a pilgrim's progress.[41]

The liner notes were accompanied by a poem that Coltrane had composed, appropriately titled "A Love Supreme." Coltrane's visions were ecumenical, suffused throughout nature and the self, in "thought waves—heat waves—all vibrations—all paths lead to God." And, most importantly for Coltrane, God in any guise—Christian, Jewish, Buddhist, or some other representation—was "gracious and merciful." Jazz music, with its pulse and vibrations—dropping down to a blues register or soaring as high as a note could climb—seemed to Coltrane the perfect vehicle to praise God and to express "ELATION—ELEGANCE—EXALTATION."[42]

Homage to God had certainly long been central to the African American experience, especially in gospel and, in some cases, the blues. It had only recently begun to assert itself in the jazz repertoire. In 1961 Grant Green had recorded a mellow album, *Sunday Morning,* and Duke Ellington had been composing for a few years in the early 1960s a series of works called Sacred Concerts, the first of which was finished in 1965. There was also Albert Ayler's *Spiritual Unity,* which was roughly contemporaneous with *A Love Supreme.*[43] Ayler, along with bassist Gary Peacock and percussionist Sunny Murray, offered an explosion of divine sound. Sections of the work were titled "The Wizard," "Spirits" and "Ghosts," with the latter two offered in different variations. What made the squeals of Ayler's sax and the band's unhinged rhythms holy were the brilliant pauses. It seemed as if, in the midst of chaos, God had breathed perfect calmness into the lifeblood of the music.

Coltrane knew exactly what he wanted from the score for *A Love Supreme.* It was to offer listeners a tale of his own journey to transcendence and belief, and, perhaps just as importantly, to suggest that "all paths lead to God," which he equated with "Ultimate Reality."[44] This Kierkegaardian and mystical perception was consistent with Coltrane's own spiritual inclination. Although he came from Baptist roots, his reading regimen was voracious and eclectic. He read about African religion and delved into the Kabbalah, as well as Buddhism. Astrology, scientology, Kahlil Gibran, and Edgar Cayce—he dug into all of them. At first, the diverse emanations of the Divine "screwed up" his head—could there, then, be but one God? After much soul searching, he concluded that all religions were essentially the same, however different their rituals and theology. Religion was simply about faith and redemption. In *A Love Supreme,* as Coltrane stated, "I just wanted to express something that I felt; I had to write it."[45]

The musical brilliance of *A Love Supreme* was in its ability to build a mood, a sense of security in the raucous banter of the various instruments, rollicking extremes of experimentation (pushing notes to their limits), and abrupt shifts in chords. Saxophonist Joshua Redman's characterization of jazz in general as being built around "tension and release" applies perfectly to the spiritual journey in *A Love Supreme.*[46] The tension that day in December, when all of the musicians were working on the album, must have been immense; perhaps because of this, and because of the need for release, they completed the work in a single, long session—a departure from Coltrane's common practice of recording sessions extending for days.[47]

The lights in the recording studio were turned down low to create the proper atmosphere for an album that chronicles movement from the darkness of a lost soul to the light of transcendence. Coltrane had written only a sketch of the score, and he offered the musicians little guidance, preferring to rely on their familiarity with one another's styles and "keeping the form in mind." Drummer Elvin Jones approached the music as he normally did—willing to "just follow" Coltrane's lead.[48]

Reminiscing almost four decades after the recording, Jones acknowledged that while "the quartet never really talked about the spiritual aspect," it lurked in the music and the camaraderie of the musicians. The result was an album Jones felt was "not even jazz. It broadened the concept of what music was. It's totally spiritual."[49]

The recording begins in unusual fashion, with Jones hitting a Chinese gong. As the tingle faded, Coltrane enters with tenor saxophone, playing the notes as if reciting a prayer. The opening passages are of great beauty and magnificent syncopation—as if he is taking listeners to church. As he intended in his score, the music riffs on the blues and features typical Coltrane touches. In the words of Ashley Kahn, Coltrane "starts to hang on phrases, playing long tones, nudging the music into a more meditative pocket."[50] There is the repetition of the piece. As Kahn further explains, "Coltrane blows the four-note pattern thirty-seven times in methodic succession." In the section "Acknowledgment," Coltrane does something striking. He begins to chant "A Love Supreme" away from the microphone. Luckily, producer Bob Van Gelder had changed the microphone level so that the words could be recorded in full. Nineteen times Coltrane utters the phrase, but on the fifteenth repetition, his "voice drops a whole step from F minor to E-flat minor."[51] He had achieved a work that blurred the lines between jazz improvisation and spiritual salvation, one that took notes to extremes as the only manner in which to pay homage to spiritual truth. It is a holy record.

Dylan was repeating phrases, but less transcendentally than Coltrane. He spit out "How does it feel?" with rage in his hit song "Like a Rolling Stone," which exploded on the radio airwaves in the summer of 1965.[52] It was unlike anything previously done in rock and roll. The voice was strident, raspy, and limited in range. No matter. Rock had often dealt with failed love or teen disappointment, but in formulaic and tender terms. This song bit into its subject matter, gnawing past tired adages to the beating heart of things. Rock, in Dylan's hands, had become a vehicle to express rage, to serve as a put-down. And the song tested the attention span of listeners, becoming one of the longest singles ever to play on Top 40 stations, going on for more than six minutes.[53]

The song had been a tough one to record. Dylan had to condense twenty-pages of lyrics—"this long piece of vomit," he called it.[54] He succeeded, but in the recording session problems arose. Dylan usually nailed most of his songs in one or two takes, but "Like a Rolling Stone" just didn't sound right. Two days in the middle of June had been wasted trying to refine the tune and try out different angles. Things came together, in part, by pure happenstance. The presence of a great guitarist Mike Bloomfield on the session rendered Al Kooper's guitar work superfluous. In the midst of increasing frustration in the studio, Kooper wandered over to the organ and began playing, hitting upon the opening for the song. Bloomfield joined in, the band cranked up, and Dylan then put down on vinyl a great song.[55]

From the introductory organ lines, the song drew listeners into its world. With Dylan's "Like a Rolling Stone," new vistas opened. He had managed to take the energy of some doo-wop (common to inane but energizing tunes like "Rama Lama Ding Dong") and wed it to something more real and poetic.

The initial words were sublime in being so out of place: "Once upon a time," sounding familiar to a generation reared on children's fables.[56] Dylan sings about a young woman, once haughty and regal, who is now adrift, reduced in stature, stripped of the power to beguile. She had been warned of a fall ("People call, say 'Beware, doll, you're bound to fall'"), but failed to take heed. She has fallen from grace thanks to her unchecked hubris, only to be left alone and friendless. The song offers no sense of lessons learned or hubris overcome, or redemption—only the haunting, mean-spirited bark of the chorus:

> How does it feel
> How does it feel
> To be on your own
> With no direction home
> Like a complete unknown
> Like a rolling stone?

"Like a Rolling Stone" hit a nerve with listeners, even if its particulars sometimes seemed mysterious to the point of obfuscation. One journalist remarked to Dylan at the end of 1965, "I don't understand *one* of your songs." Dylan's jaunty response was that if you don't get it, then the song was not meant for you. To a similar question, Dylan replied, "If I told you what our music is really about, we'd probably all get arrested."[57] Against those looking for deep meaning in his work, Dylan quipped that he was nothing more than an entertainer, "a song and dance man."[58] The song, and increasingly Dylan himself, resisted easy interpretation, perhaps exemplary of what Sontag had recently heralded as central to the New Sensibility, being "against interpretation."

Certainly many ignored this imperative to grasp deeper meaning, preferring to link the lyrics with the "facts" of Dylan's life. Most suspected that the song exacted revenge on a woman who had offended Dylan, scorning him when he was a scruffy nobody. Others wondered if it was about Edie Sedgwick, whose moneyed background and elfin beauty had failed to protect her from the seduction of drugs and the Warhol circle's narcissism. Some thought Dylan had been in love with her, or she with him; others that he had felt pity as a result of what was happening to her.[59] Might it be a riposte against the hedge of hypocrisy grown high in the 1950s and still obscuring the reality of a harsh, unfair world? Or might it be an existential lament, a recognition of our being thrown into the world, tossed about by contingency, and forced to navigate by dint of the courage to exist?[60]

Anger—laden with surrealistic imagery—became central for Dylan in this period. In "Ballad of a Thin Man," Dylan trained his sights on an eponymous figure, "Mr. Jones." As in "Like a Rolling Stone," the issues are illusion, ignorance, and fear of being alone:

> You hand in your ticket
> And you go watch the geek
> Who immediately walks up to you
> When he hears you speak
> And says, "How does it feel
> To be such a freak?"
> And you say, "Impossible"
> As he hands you a bone

The words are powerful and nicely confusing. What ticket is being handed in? In what manner is Mr. Jones a freak and why is he being given a bone? This song sounds like a critique of conformity, of stepping ever too gently out of one's normalcy, ever ready to retreat from the new and challenging. But the refrain of the song is what beckons, "Because something is happening here / But you don't know what it is / Do you, Mr. Jones?"

Some of the rage Dylan directed was against those who had dismissed and abandoned him when he took his electric turn away from folk music or those who seemed to cling to his fame. This became apparent in "Positively 4th Street," composed four days after the debacle at Newport.[61] It is a diatribe of hurt feelings and revenge against those who pricked his sensitive skin: "You got a lotta nerve to say you are my friend / When I was down, you just stood there grinning." The put-down concludes with Dylan explaining to this erstwhile friend that it is "a drag...to see you."

Thankfully, Dylan's prolific songwriting pen drifted beyond anger. He was experimenting with poetic dreamscapes, with stringing together images in a surrealistic fashion that would be beyond interpretation. This was common fare for serious poetry but rare in the idiom of rock music. He had gobbled up Rimbaud, Apollinaire, Blake, Ginsberg, and Eliot—drawn especially to their abrupt juxtapositions of images. That Dylan should identify with the outlaw poet Rimbaud is hardly surprising. Rimbaud, too, was an identity shifter, a wild palimpsest. Dylan recalled reading Rimbaud's words "I is someone else." As he put it, "When I read those words a bell went off. It made perfect sense." The persona of the Other dominated his poetry as he created an original dreamscape.[62] In one song, "Desolation Row," the lyrics create an atmosphere of mystery and the absurd: "They're painting the passports brown / The beauty parlor is filled with sailors / The circus is in town." A seemingly endless mix of fictional, historical, and biblical characters populate the over-eleven-minute song, from "Dr. Filth" and Einstein to Cain and Abel.[63]

Dylan in 1965 found a way to combine the raucous energy of rock with poetic rambles into the absurd. One magazine nominated Dylan "the American Yevtushenko," after the then-popular Soviet poet.[64] But Dylan rejected most labels, including poet. "I don't call myself a poet," he said in 1965, "because I don't like the word. I'm a trapeze artist."[65]

Dylan's images hit hard and fast. In "Subterranean Homesick Blues," memorable lines became part of the vocabulary of politics and sensibility in the 1960s. The radical wing of Students for a Democratic Society, which turned to violence in 1969, took their name from a line in the song, "You don't need a weatherman to know which way the wind blows." Others found a more peaceable anarchism in the line "Don't follow leaders / Watch the parkin' meters." Finally, in perhaps his strongest song of the year, along with "Like a Rolling Stone," Dylan devoted himself to the elusiveness of love and identity, trying to capture a love now vanished. "Visions of Johanna" (which would be released in 1966) is beautiful in its lyrics and wrenching in its content and floating surfaces of meaning. Charles Nicholl called it "an hour-of-the wolf song. It comes out of some back-room of the soul." The lyrics of the song would even be printed in *Glamour* magazine.[66] The song beckons with mysterious ruminations about Louise rather than Johanna, as Dylan takes us into the nightscape of New York City: from a beautifully mundane apartment where "the heat pipes just cough" to scenes of hookers riding the subway and night watchmen on patrol. Dylan is on familiar turf with his surrealist imagery: "Inside the museums, Infinity goes up on trial/ Voices echo this is what salvation must be like after a while." Yet, what remains and tugs at the memory of loves gone are the mentions of Johanna that conclude every stanza.

From the initial electricity of his guitar and backup band's reception at Newport in 1965 to the release of the double album *Blonde on Blonde* a year later—Dylan had brought a poetic energy into the realm of rock, a new sensibility that would soon force others (from Lou Reed to Patti Smith) to venture into the dangerous but fascinating seas of creativity.[67]

By the end of June, when he recorded *Ascension*, with seven musicians (including tenor saxophonists Pharoah Sanders and Archie Shepp and trumpeters Freddie Hubbard and Dewey Johnson) joining his regular quartet, Coltrane had convincingly embraced free jazz. Being a man given to extremes, Coltrane was establishing himself, according to jazz historian Ted Gioia, as "the most radical of this new school."[68] Some wondered if Coltrane had shifted anew, opting for chaos over the transcendental order of *A Love Supreme*.[69]

The album was forty minutes of music that traditionalist jazz fan and poet Philip Larkin would describe as "ugly on purpose."[70] Others in the jazz world, according to a *New York Times* columnist, would "squawk and shriek and bleat" about a work that was beyond their level of appreciation.[71] Certainly there was much that was shrill, circus-like cacophony of instruments blaring out their improvisations, a duel of sorts in which the logic of the piece shattered like a broken vase. At times, it sounded like modernity condensed into instrumental form, rushing about, blaring, and curdling the milk of serenity. The first seven minutes of the album were chaotic and edgy, somewhat like a Cage piece. It was nothing more, perhaps, than a group of musicians warming up, playing a wide array of scales, unaware of anyone else's presence or peace of mind. Suddenly, the first of the tenor sax solos lofts sweetly, nicely joined by steady drum beats from Elvin Jones, then beautiful piano from McCoy Tyner.

All of the solos—from the tenor saxophones, trumpets, drums, and piano—were testaments to the musicians' virtuosity, taking listeners to a higher plane of consciousness. There was a sort of organic wholeness to the work, a sensibility that was shared by eleven musicians for just about forty minutes of recording time. Soon, however, as the band members jump in, a trumpet solo of supreme beauty, its staccato notes ringing and lifting into a joyous scream, is tossed to the side, and we are back to group improvisation.[72] Coltrane was cognizant of the furor that he kicked up in *Ascension*, but with typical understatement, he reported that he enjoyed recording the album: "I enjoyed all of the individual contributions on that."[73] As always, time to move on.

Coltrane could move forward without abandoning familiar themes. The spirituality of *A Love Supreme* reappeared in *Meditations*, recorded in October. Again, he augmented his usual quartet with an extra drummer and pianist, and even added a percussionist from Africa. The opening number is called "The Father and the Son and the Holy Ghost." The feel in this number is apocalyptic, as if the Holy Trinity were engaged in a battle royal. The harsh tenor opening is quite different from the sweetly religious intonations that graced *A Love Supreme*. There is little chance that Coltrane intended to criticize Christianity in any fashion; he was quoted by Nat Hentoff on the album's liner notes as saying, "I believe in all religions." The other sections of the album continue with the religious theme, being titled "Compassion," "Love," "Consequences," and "Serenity."

While "Compassion" is toned down a bit, especially by a lovely piano solo, the reverie is interrupted by the entry of saxophone whirlwinds, about four minutes in. Only when the piano returns later is there anything that might feel like musical compassion. In "Love" the saxophones are often tender and exploring, and bassist Jimmy Garrison is magnificent with his plucking to evoke the depths of love. But love does not triumph as in the long section "Consequences." This is surprising, because Coltrane consistently argued in interviews for the power of love, as expressed in music, to uplift the individual. Perhaps in the aftermath of the Watts Riots and the escalation of the war in Vietnam, both of which weighed heavily on him, Coltrane decided that love was, to a degree, often misplaced, a function of trying to impose one's will upon another. This is speculation. We do find peace in the final section, "Serenity," as the saxophones repeat phrases in a meditative and soothing manner. Maybe, in a world of violence, the offer of moments of serenity was a significant achievement for Coltrane and his music.[74]

The times they were a-changing, especially for Coltrane. His longtime friends and associates in the quartet, Elvin Jones and McCoy Tyner, announced their departure from the band following *Meditations*. In part, they did not like playing with and against other drummers and pianists in the band. Nor did they agree with what Coltrane "wanted to do in music."[75] The new players that he added to the band presented him with new energy and spirit, and that was what he needed at the moment. As he explained in the fall, 1966, he had "to keep going all the way, as deep as you can. You keep trying to get right down to the crux."[76]

Disaster soon arrived for both Coltrane and Dylan. In 1967, before he turned forty-one, Coltrane died from a quickly developing cancer. Coltrane liked to say, "Life is change"—and that had defined his life and music.[77] At the end of July 1966, Dylan was injured in a motorcycle accident near his home in Woodstock, New York. Even if incapacitated, Dylan transformed necessity into opportunity, retreating and reinventing himself. He moved away from the raucous diversity of his double-album *Blonde on Blonde* to the more subdued acoustic sound of *John Wesley Harding* in 1967. The music was pared down, the content drifting between an ode to classic outlaws and to the harshness of the Old Testament.

Dylan and Coltrane, a pair of magical performers, shape-shifters. With their willingness to sup at the table of new possibilities already laid in the mid-1960s, they embraced the pluralism and possibility of the New Sensibility. It would never contain them—no cultural force could—but they would push its boundaries both in style and content.

Anne Sexton after winning the Pulitzer Prize for poetry (1966) (AP Images)

{ 15 }

Living and Dying

ANNE SEXTON

1966

The darkening of the house in November dusk was held in abeyance by the flicker of candlelight. It was Anne Sexton's thirty-eighth birthday, and it should have been a happy moment. Her book of poems, *Live or Die*, had been published in late September and would go on to win the Pulitzer Prize. Sexton was at the top of the staircase, probably holding a burning cigarette in one hand. If true to form, she grasped in the other hand a half-empty cocktail glass. Perhaps she had already taken some of her many prescription medications to dull the mania and control the depression. On the way down, one of her high heels caught on "the gold carpeted stairs."[1] Then, "sailing queerly like Icarus," she fell down the stairs, breaking her hip and spending ten days in the hospital.[2]

Icarus, who flew on waxen wings crafted by his father, Daedalus, ventured too close to the sun. The wax melted and Icarus plunged to his death. Sexton often turned to the figure of Icarus in her poetry. Like him, she wanted to escape, and she was drawn to the sun. Perhaps, too, she identified with his hubris, his desire to soar creatively. Alas, as with Icarus, the higher she lofted, the greater her fall back to earth.

In October, one of Sexton's many absurd, desperate love affairs had ended abruptly. Always craving affection, she had become involved with her psychiatrist—Dr. Frederick Duhl. On the couch in his office, they had sex, which was a therapy of sorts for her. Her husband, Alfred (known as Kayo from childhood) dutifully paid the bills, aware of, and frustrated by, what was transpiring. Once the affair had been discovered by Mrs. Duhl, it ended quickly.[3] Sexton was searching for a rock, something solid to hold onto. But she rarely found the proper object to satisfy her need for protection and love. Sexton chose to describe herself thusly: "I am watercolor. / I wash off."[4] But such affairs were both necessary and painful for her. Kayo realized this, writing to her: "I love you, want to make everything OK, but it's beyond my power." The wittiest commentary on this came from Sexton's friend poet Maxine Kumin, who wrote: "Imagine paying to get laid twice a week!"[5]

Sexton's poetry did not "wash off." It was indelible—a creative palimpsest of her torrid personal life. If Mailer was the king of unbound egotism, Ginsberg drenched with outrage and emotion, Sexton was the queen of relentless self-revelation. All shared an unhinged amount of "self-absorption," as poet Mona Van Duyn observed in 1970.[6] Sexton became famous as the "confessional" poet par excellence (she preferred the term "personal poetry" for her work). Against the dictum issued in 1927 by T. S. Eliot that poets should strive for "continual extinction of personality," Sexton stocked each page with the daily rhythms of her life and the deposits of her depressed mind. As one of her daughters put it, Sexton "made her illness into a career."[7]

This is not to suggest that she simply vented her personal feelings, letting her excess spill out onto the page. The honesty *and* artistry of the poetry triumphed. As Sexton told a correspondent, "I am given to excess. That's all there is to it. I have found that I can control it best in a poem.... If a poem is good then it will have the excess under control."[8]

Illness stalked nearly all of her poems, but she was not confined by it. She pushed the envelope of poetic content to include issues that had heretofore been hidden: menstruation, abortion, cancer, and childbirth. And, of course, the glory and failure of love. Sexton wrote with honesty, but as a creative artist she was fully capable of massaging and manufacturing facts to fit a mood, to capture an emotion, to render a poetic point. There had, of course, been many poets who trafficked in confession, from Donne to Whitman. And she had learned from her contemporaries W. D. Snodgrass and Robert Lowell. But as male poets their experiences were often confused with the universal, while Sexton's were better kept, in the mind of some critics, in the bathroom cabinet of her home. Lowell, her early mentor, who had assumed a confessional voice in *Life Studies*, judged that Sexton had taken the confessional form to extremes; she had become "meager and exaggerated," sometimes downright "embarrassing."[9] Another critic, comparing her to the mainstays of confessional poetry—Lowell, John Berryman, and Sylvia Plath—concluded that her work "carried to greater extremes" the imperative to confess, to display one's life upon the page.[10] Even Sexton's eldest daughter worried about her mom's "tendency to disrobe verbally in public."[11]

The New Sensibility focused on confession, madness, and rejecting a sharp distinction between the personal and the poetical. It was also about making art into performance. On the last issue, Sexton was an uncapped performative oil well; she was always acting out. Again, her daughter's remark is informative: she had an "inability to set limits for herself, to refrain from acting out nearly every impulse."[12] She demanded attention, thrived on it. "I am nothing," she recognized as early as 1958, "if not an actress off the stage."[13] There was, of course, a strong dose of narcissism in confessional poetry, especially in Sexton's. But her range was more broadly encompassing, more than a cataloguing of internal turmoil.[14] She was addressing, in many ways, the general plight of women in America. And she was forging an identity—that of poet—and juggling the reality of her madness with an attempt for some semblance of order in her work and life; she was, after all, married with two children when she came to national prominence as a poet.[15]

Sexton properly presented herself as the tormented poet. Her mania was neither self-induced nor caused by drink and drugs—she was mentally ill. The drink and drugs that she consumed in profound qualities only added to the tumult. For most of her adult life, she harbored with sad consistency a death wish. After her first suicide attempt in 1955, many others would follow or be roadblocked by sudden commitments to psychiatric hospitals.[16]

Death was her muse and her demon. Poetry may well have helped keep her alive. Again, Kumin on Sexton: "She lived her poetry, poetry was her life.... It had saved her life.... She was on loan to poetry, as it were. We always knew it would end. We just didn't know when or exactly how."[17]

Growing up as an indifferent student, unpampered by familial love, and in a house where liquor consumption was abundant, Sexton lacked direction and options. She later claimed to have been depressed as a teenager. She compensated for innate shyness by being flirtatious and witty—and she was strikingly attractive in a tall and willowy way. She had shown poetic promise in high school but laid aside her notebooks and became "boy crazy." Like so many young women growing up in the 1940s, marriage seemed laid out as her natural path. Although she was engaged to another boy, she fell hard for Alfred Sexton in May 1948. A few months later, after presumably missing a period and becoming convinced that she was pregnant, the youthful pair drove to North Carolina to marry. Her period arrived, but it failed to deter their love-struck plan to be married.[18]

Over the next eight years, their lives resembled that of many other young couples—military service for the man, occasional work for the woman, birth of girls in 1953 and 1955. But for Sexton depression was increasingly her constant companion. By 1956 depression had led to attempted suicide. In one of those remarkable moments, Sexton's psychiatrist Martin Orne, recognizing her need for a creative outlet and verbal talent, recommended that she begin writing poetry. She did, with enthusiasm, dedication, and self-exploration. The poetic turn constituted for her "rebirth at twenty-nine."[19]

Her talent and original voice were apparent from the outset, but she lacked much in the way of technique and a sense of the poetic canon. She started attending a poetry workshop at Boston University, where she became fast friends with Kumin. As each of them grew to fame as poets, they supported one another (although Sexton was generous as a critic and listener, she was the one that needed extra care, unable to deal with simple household chores, being alone, or navigating a trip to the supermarket). They often talked on the phone for an hour each day, reading lines of poetry to one another. Within a short time, Sexton was a dedicated presence in the lively field of Boston-area poetry— taking a graduate seminar with Lowell, hanging with fellow poets Sylvia Plath and George Starbuck. What she needed from these figures, she later acknowledged, was "taste"—the ability to separate the dreck from the diamonds. Her concern with proper form in these days was exacting and obsessive. Sometimes she would revise and redraft a piece hundreds of time, looking for the proper line, image, and rhythm.[20]

Poems flowed ceaselessly. Soon they were being published and fellowships were being awarded. By 1959, only a handful of years after taking up poetry, her first collection, *To Bedlam and Part Way Back*, was under contract with the prestigious publisher Houghton Mifflin.

Sexton's story—at least until she gained fame as a poet—could be viewed in the terms popularized in Betty Friedan's bestseller *The Feminine Mystique* (1963). The pace of liberation in all sectors of America was quickening. Examining "the problem without a name" through the lens of sociology and her own experiences, Friedan decried how women were denied liberation, shunted into suburban emptiness. It was a book that breathed with rage—at one point, she equated being a woman with the shocking metaphor of being in a Nazi concentration camp. The suburbs bred despair and loneliness. Women needed to liberate themselves, to find the "courage" to make hard choices and change their situation.[21] The book had an immediate impact. Activist Sheila Tobias recalled, "Almost every woman of my generation can remember where she was the day she first came upon" *The Feminine Mystique*. Her own "sense of life's possibilities changed" after reading the book.[22]

Turned on to the book by Kumin, Sexton read it enthusiastically, scribbling assents in her marginalia.[23] A year before Friedan's manifesto, Sexton had published her second collection of poetry, *All My Pretty Ones*, which dealt with her family history, loneliness, abortion, and various hospital rooms, all saturated with her pained death wish. The emptiness of suburban living was depicted in the poem "Housewife" ("The walls are permanent and pink").[24]

In many ways, Sexton had been a prisoner of domestic life, at least in the period before she engaged her poetic muse. Her poetry can be read as feminist, in its striving for a liberated voice and its recurrent themes, many of which were particular to women. According to poet Louise Brogan, Sexton "usually [wrote] from the center of feminine experience."[25] But to frame Sexton as a frustrated homemaker seeking creative outlet tells only part of the story. Although she often presented herself as a victim—of various forces, including her status as a woman dependent upon a man—she viewed herself, as critic Robert Boyers wisely observed, as both victim and tormentor.[26]

In the 1950s Sexton's mental illness roiled, and poetry failed to calm her. She exulted, however, in the fame and challenges that it brought. She continued to flirt with suicide and shuttle back and forth between staggering depression and manic excitement. She had many ruinous affairs—some carried out in correspondence, others in cheap motels. Her family life was combustible. When her husband was away on one of his many business trips, she trembled with loneliness and fear. Her mother-in-law and hired help managed the children and domestic chores while Sexton perched on her chair, engulfed in cigarette smoke and piles of books, in a trancelike state, and wrote poems. When Alfred was working locally, he would return home around five, and he and Anne began their lengthy ritual of cocktails, followed by banter that turned ugly—as Anne stuck her stiletto of criticism deep into her husband's hide. Unable to respond as an equal with verbal fisticuffs, Alfred would slap and punch Anne into silence. Her screams would sometimes bring the children rushing down from hiding upstairs to separate the combatants. Rather than being repulsed by her husband's physical punishment, she accepted it, especially when he was contrite, showering her with now guilt-ridden love. Her daughters, at tender ages, were forced to become caregivers for their mother, whose self-absorption was at once impressive and debilitating.[27]

The problem facing Sexton in 1966 was simple. She had a new book of poems under contract, which she intended to title *Live or Die*. As she glanced through the sheaf of poems ready for inclusion, it became apparent that nearly all of them dealt with her familiar subject of death. Where was the imperative to live? After all, as she noted in a New Year letter to the writer Tillie Olsen, "My work, at present, is [in] a dreadful slump," much like her marriage, which was "as fragile as a cracked egg." Such a "blue mood"[28] was evident in a poem she composed on February 1, called "The Addict."

Given Sexton's penchant for self-revelation in her poetry, it is difficult not to read the poem as largely autobiographical. For someone often fingering the sharply appealing edge of death but also connected with family, various lovers, and her creative world, Sexton's medications were her lifeline, coming out of "sweet pharmaceutical bottles." Her nightly dose of "eight chemical kisses" grants her existence but also serves as a "diet from death." Like everything else in her life, the medications are beloved and belabored, part of a "war" that promises no clear victory, other than a final dance with death.[29]

An answer of sorts to her "blue mood" and the dangerous drama of pill consumption arrived later in January. The family's Dalmatian, Penny, gave birth to eight puppies, as the Sexton family gathered round to celebrate the moment. The poem "Live" allowed a slant of bright light to lessen her generalized pain. It began, however, with typical Sexton lacerating honesty: "Well, death's been here / for a long time." Her suffering, couched in the imagery of religious desire, poured forth. She might clothe her body stylishly, but it failed to hide her desire to choke the life out of that very object. She realized that her own sickness troubled others, who often had to stand helplessly by as she wrestled with mental illness. But in the third stanza, a shift occurs away from the focus on gloom and death. First, she celebrates the sun. The dependable sun, giving warmth and life—"her yolk moving feverishly." Sexton was a lover of sunlight, but since 1964, when she had begun taking the drug Thorazine, she had become severely photosensitive.[30] But the metaphorical light of the sun had illumined—even if only temporarily—all that was worth cherishing: "a husband straight as a redwood," her daughters, and more. Instead of a powerless, heavily medicated victim, Sexton reframed the narrative, celebrating her role as an artist and homemaker: "an empress/I wear an apron/My typewriter writes...Even crazy, I'm as nice/ as a chocolate bar."[31]

Enter the Dalmatians as further affirmation of life. Each puppy emerges from their mother's womb to be held and nurtured. Sexton claims in the poem that she had been told by others that some of the puppies should be killed. "Pails of water" for drowning stood by but went unused. There was beauty in this birthing, and it warmed Sexton, making her think that she could push to the side her demons of death.

Ten days after completing "Live," Brice Howard and Richard Moore showed up at Sexton's house in Weston to film her for a National Education Television program, *USA: Poetry*. Sexton was spectacularly alluring and animated, seductive and playful. She performed brilliantly for the camera—although she maintained that "they could never get the real Anne Sexton with their camera eye and their sound box." How could they, since she was always theatrical on the page and stage, shifting her identity from romantic hijinks to dark shadows of depression and death?[32]

She began reading from "Menstruation at Forty," cigarette in hand, comfortable in the presence of the camera. The scene is interrupted by one of the Dalmatians; later Alfred is caught lurking in the background. Anne coaxes him into full view, despite his uneasiness—"Don't be camera shy," she says. At another point, she jokes with one of her daughters, hugging her manically, proclaiming, "We hate each other" while also shouting that they love each other dearly.

These domestic interruptions cannot blunt the piercing nature of the poem. As she continues with "Menstruation," she intones the line "I feel the November / of the body, as well as of the calendar," which records the coming of her birthday. At such times, Sexton is bewitched with suicidal thoughts, with a "hunt for death." However, the poem is revealing beyond its language of blood and death. It also captures a sense of loss, of the being that might have been which is washed away by the menstrual flow. It is about an unborn son whose presence would somehow redeem her. She reads it with her raspy voice, plaintive and powerful—a performance that somehow makes the blood seem both more and less real.

At one point during the filming, she sits listening in rapture to a piece of music. Her commentary is clearly pointed, a performance that proves daring and emotional. "This song is like making love," she states. If that were not a sufficiently shocking overture for a public television audience, she reveals to her interviewer, "I wouldn't want to have an orgasm in front of you." Her words, however, were edited out of the program.[33]

The fleeting nature of the orgasm, that spasm of raptured delight, segues into her reading of another poem, "Wanting to Die," which dwells on suicide and mortality. The poem makes clear that death's "sad bone...waits for me, year after year."[34]

The spring and summer of 1966 proved, as usual, both troubling and exhilarating for Sexton. She filled her lungs with love. She and the poet-novelist James Dickey were engaged in epistolary flirtation—she wanted a poetic soul to rely upon. He had been critical of her early works, finding *All My Pretty Ones* "a curious compound of self-deprecatory cynicism and sentimentality." Dickey also worried that the confessional mode had emerged as a "new orthodoxy"— "tedious" with success, little more than an "outspoken soap-opera," mostly of interest, he implied, to housewives. Such harsh comments, paradoxically, made him more alluring to Sexton. She felt that he recognized, and perhaps identified with, her "deep, painful" life.[35] They grew closer in 1966, and she was pulling off "her female con" on him.[36] As she contemplated a series of readings, which would take her near Dickey's domicile, she wondered if they should rendezvous: "I could meet you in the afternoon, perhaps early, or for dinner, cocktails yum yum and dinner." This was followed by a line, crossed out by Sexton, "And then go on from there." But she warned off Dickey, too. "I am more child than a woman. I am afraid of the dark. I am afraid of buildings."[37]

She was also afraid of traveling and being alone. Thirteen-year-old daughter Linda accompanied her on a reading tour to Pennsylvania, Maryland, and Virginia, with the heavy responsibility of acting as her mother's companion and caretaker. Despite feeling that her clothing was shabby and unsophisticated, Linda was at first exhilarated, staying in her first hotel and chatting with professors about Kafka. At the Baltimore airport, when her mother met with Dickey, Linda recalled being "an uncomfortable observer," as the poets drank plenty and left their food untouched. Her mother, she felt, flirted outrageously, without concern for her husband or for her daughter's presence. But this was only the start of the complicated journey.

As with most things, Sexton was ambivalent about reading her poetry. She needed the adulation of an audience, and she worked hard to achieve it. Yet she feared their rejection, so she needed to prime herself with plenty of booze prior to a reading. The key was for Sexton to have enough drink to lift her spirits and make her charming, but not so much as to incapacitate her—sometimes a difficult balancing act. Once onstage she shined, drawing on her emotions (some of her own poems, she admitted, caused "a lump in my throat"), casting a spell out of her pain and her glamour. During one reading she began sobbing; "embarrassed by the incident," she wondered about her relationship to audiences. Were they titillated by her emotion, or did they identify with her turmoil?[38]

Sexton gave a reading at Sweetbriar College in Virginia, where she met poet Philip Legler. At a reception, Sexton drank heavily and flirted outrageously, again seemingly unaware of, or unconcerned about, the near presence of her daughter. Linda Gray Sexton wrote, "Her obvious sexual invitation [to Legler] and her inebriation brought me great shame." Linda managed to convince Legler to take them back to their "seedy hotel," which he did. He carried Sexton from the car to the hotel bed. Linda fretted throughout the night that Sexton's strong combination of liquor and medications might be fatal, however, Linda wrote, "We made it through the long night."[39]

Back home in Weston, Sexton and Legler embarked upon a steamy correspondence. She gave him pointed comments both about his poetry and the dangers of madness. She warned him to keep their correspondence secret, at least from his wife. They shared a spiritual and creative kinship: "We're both mad mad mad." She recommended Thorazine, which "really calms me down and has more or less saved my life when it needed saving."[40]

By the end of spring, platonic affection for other men had turned into sexual affairs. These sexual relationships were important for Sexton, for they helped her to escape from a Thorazine-induced poetic silence (she had been pecking away at a novel which remained unpublished) and break forth in June, and again in October, with a bunch of poems about love and desire. Alas, by the end of the year a sense of betrayal and demise would bring forth different sorts of poems.

In June, however, she was happily encamped at a conference in East Hampton, on Long Island. Never wanting to travel alone or be uncared for, she had asked Bob Clawson, a teacher friend, to accompany her. As they were pulling away from her Weston home, Kayo and the kids implored Clawson: "Now, take care of Mom." The conference was exciting, attended by big-name poets such as Muriel Rukeyser, Denise Levertov, and John Hollander. But the real sparks came when Sexton and Clawson began a week-long tryst. On the last night of the conference, according to Diane Wood Middlebrook's account, Sexton professed her love for Clawson; she wanted a divorce from her husband so that she and Clawson could escape to Mexico, "marry, and live there, and write." She presented Clawson with drafts of love poems, presumably sparked by their romance. He read them and cried; "It was," he said, "the most romantic moment of my life."[41]

With good reason. The poems he read were "The Touch," "The Kiss," and "The Breast." Each tingled with fragility and romance, anger and salvation. She had felt "vulnerable" and sad. Even the dog, she claimed, considered her little more than "a case of dog food." She recounted how she had been "wronged all year" by "tedious nights," referring to her heavy menstrual bleeding, which she had feared signaled cancer. Her blood flow and cancer concern were quelled when she was prescribed birth control pills. Her body, she wrote in "The Kiss," was now "shot full of... electric bolts... Zing! / A resurrection." More than the pills, love had rejuvenated her.

Although Clawson may have delighted in the poems and believed himself to be the object of Sexton's affection, the poems had been composed with another person in mind. They captured her budding, and forbidden, romance with her psychiatrist, Frederick Duhl, as was evident in the poem "For My Lover, Returning to His Wife."[42]

It is ever so easy to dwell on the pain of Sexton's existence, her addiction to love, her mountain of fears, real and imagined. Suicide, even in budding moments of joy, always shadowed her. In July, she raided her "little nightly factory" of sleeping pills and overdosed, landing anew in a hospital to have her stomach pumped.[43] Writing to a friend soon after this brush with death, Sexton summoned forth the title of her book to express her frustrations. "Live or die, you fool, but don't mess with Mr. in-between."[44] She recovered quickly to face a new set of challenges that summer.[45]

Clouds of murder and madness shadowed the American landscape that summer. In Truman Capote's bestselling "non-fiction novel," *In Cold Blood*, he described with clinical detail how two ex-cons descended upon a farmhouse in western Kansas to rob a presumably rich family—and left no witnesses. It was a gruesome tale of murder: the lives of the four members of the Clutter family were brutally extinguished. When pushed for an explanation of the murders, Perry Smith recounted a life of being mistreated, tossed away as garbage. Although the Clutters had never done him any harm, he acknowledged, "Maybe it's just that the Clutters were the ones who had to pay for it."[46]

On July 14, twenty-four-year-old Richard Speck, a drifter with a long history of criminality and alcoholism, committed "one of the most savage multiple murders in the history of crime." He forced his way, with gun and knife, into a dormitory housing young nurses in Chicago. He corralled the women into a single room, then bound and gagged them. Methodically, he stabbed and strangled each nurse (raping some of them) in another room. One of the bound nurses managed to roll under a bed, finally freeing herself after the murder of her eight friends, to call for help: "They're all dead!... Oh, God, I'm the only one alive!"

She was able to give an accurate description of the assailant, but he eluded a massive dragnet for a time. In a cheap rooming house, knowing that his freedom was about to expire, he gulped down all that remained in a cheap bottle of wine. He then broke the bottle and with its shards slashed his wrists. The suicide attempt failed. After a trial, Speck was sentenced to death, but he escaped that fate on a legal technicality; he remained imprisoned until his death in 1991.[47]

Less than a month later, in Austin, Texas, a young man often described as "an all-American boy," a former Marine, now studying architectural engineering at the University of Texas, went berserk. He had long seemed tightly wound, taking on a heavy class schedule, working part time, and devotedly studying. Perhaps, too, amphetamine use had sparked paranoia in him. Unlike Speck, Whitman was from a middle-class background, married for a few years, and living near his mother. On a steamy hot Sunday, he decided that he wanted out from life—"Life is not worth living," he wrote. But for reasons that will never be clear, rather than simply killing himself, he decided that others, too, must be eliminated.

Although he claimed that he loved his wife and mother dearly, they were the first to perish at his hands on Sunday night and early Monday morning. He dispatched his mother with a bullet to the head, and he stabbed his wife to death. Then, on Monday morning, with meticulous care and planning, he prepared for more bloodshed. After shopping for another weapon—a shotgun that he then sawed off—he rented a lift for his Marine Corps footlocker and loaded it onto his black Chevrolet, heading to campus. In the footlocker were three rifles, a shotgun, two pistols, and provisions to last for days. He rolled his footlocker into the Administration and Library Building, finally making his way to the observation deck, with clear views of the campus, at a height of over 230 feet. After using the shotgun to kill some and wound others from a family that had been taking in the view, he barricaded himself and began sniping. He was, unfortunately, rated a "sharp shooter" by the Marine Corps. After two hours of violence, with a toll of sixteen dead and thirty-two wounded, a police officer managed to bring an end to it by killing Whitman. The horror lasted for ninety-six unendurable minutes.[48]

The mad summer violence did not end with the coming of fall. In November, an eighteen-year-old high school student in Mesa, Arizona, named Robert Benjamin Smith decided to use violence to gain fame. He had closely followed the blood orgies enacted by both Speck and Whitman. Benny Smith was described as an unimpressive kid, a young man without special qualities, a quintessential loner. He headed, armed, for a local beauty college, where he coldly gunned down five women. Upon arrest, Benny stated, "I wanted to kill about 40 people so I could make a name for myself." His admission was delivered with a chuckle and a grin on his face.[49]

Sexton, even in the midst of her own bloody dreams and depression, never imagined killing wantonly. But during this summer of blood, she composed an achingly powerful poem about killing. It offered no solution to the problems that haunted those with psychosis or mental illness, although perhaps it helped Sexton to tamp down her own demons by putting them on the page, by filtering them through the sieve of art.

She was committed to joining her husband on an African hunting safari. Soon after leaving the hospital after her overdose, they took off to London and Nairobi. It was difficult from the start, because Anne had no appetite for the killing of wild animals. And she knew that she was not cut out for Africa: "I'm scared of bugs, animals, blazing sun (having upped my Thorazine so I will really burn), voices in my head." She imagined the beauty of the "African skies," but her mental state was clear: "I am all fears."[50]

A "blood slaughter" was what she called the safari.[51] In her poem "Loving the Killer," she admitted her tortured love for her husband. She described him as armed with a gun and proud of his killing. The violence of the hunt and the mayhem of their marriage united them. She records how, upon returning home to Weston, the couple resumed the tedium of their arguments, each trying, according to Sexton, to prove "My loss is greater than yours! / My pain is more valuable!"

Yes, that summer in America the killer had "gotten out."

The answer to the contested question of whose "need is more desperate" was won by Sexton. Her excesses, her need for love and tenderness exhausted most around her. She and Kayo divorced in 1973, and her daughters struggled for many years to understand and to avoid replicating the tortured life of their mother.

In September 1974 Sexton had reflected in a letter about her poetic style and legacy. She accepted the appellation "confessional" poet. She admitted, "I do not know how I feel about such an old poem as 'Live.'" Such "poems stand for the moment they were written and make no promises to the future events and consciousness."[52] "So I say *Live, Live because of the sun, the dream, the excitable gift*."[53]

Certainly, the upbeat tone that she had achieved in "Live" had vanished from her own consciousness by Friday, October 4. On that day she achieved her dream, with a minimum of fuss and a maximum of efficiency. She showed no especial warnings of suicidal depression, having lunched with her pal Kumin earlier in the day and spending time going over the galley sheets for a new poetry collection, *The Awful Rowing Toward God*. That evening, she went into her garage and settled into the bucket seat of her red Ford Mustang. She sipped from a vodka martini, turned on the ignition, and listened to music. Then, as the exhaust fumes engulfed her, one hopes, she finally found the peace she had long desired.[54]

"Utmost Freedom of Imagination"

WILLIAM STYRON

1967

Day after day in the late afternoon, after listening to classical music, William Styron, intrepidly trudged up to his loft study. An alcoholic and depressive like Sexton, Styron desperately wanted to write the next great American novel. Pacing back and forth, he would ponder dialogue, scenery, and character motivation. Then he would pick up a no. 2 pencil and slowly write a sentence, perhaps a paragraph, crossing out and editing before getting back to thinking about what would come next. On a good day, he might have finished a couple of paragraphs on his yellow legal pad. As his daughter recalled, he strove for "extreme perfection."[1] What he had committed to paper by the end of the day, with few exceptions, went unrevised. Emerging from his cocoon by eight or nine o'clock, he would have a scotch or two, then join his wife and family for a late dinner and relaxation.[2]

For five years in the early 1960s, Styron had been composing *The Confessions of Nat Turner*. The book was "a meditation upon history," according to Styron, an attempt, he claimed, "to walk myself through a time and place" in order to imaginatively capture "what it must have been to have been a slave."[3] When completed, the book questioned the traditional lines drawn between history and fiction. As suggested by the title, the novel was "confessional," written in the first person, presumably reflecting the viewpoint of a slave. Styron recognized and relished the dangers of such an approach. The confessional form seemed contemporary, given the poetry of Sexton or the advertisements of Mailer; for Styron it was "a peculiarly 1960's form of address."[4]

The idea for a book on a bloody slave rebellion led by a mysterious figure named Nat Turner had long steeped in Styron's mind, at least since the late 1940s. He remarked, too, about having an abiding sort of "amateur interest in slavery."[5] He had begun working on the novel in 1952, while living in Paris and later in Rome, after his book *Lie Down in Darkness* had been published. That

novel, filled with existential dread and suicide, was beautifully written and garnered the types of reviews that for most first-time novelists exist only in their
dreams.[6] But a problem arose: How do you follow a successful first novel? Only
by upping the ante, only by dangling closer to the edge of the creative cliff.

A novel about a slave rebellion offered heady challenges for Styron. He was,
after all, a son of the white South, raised not far from the epicenter of the rebellion. His grandmother as a young girl, he recalled, had owned slaves.
Although he had been afflicted with racial bigotry—of a "foolish and fangless"
variety as a youngster—he felt he had outgrown it, thanks to his "groping for
enlightenment."[7] More importantly, he wanted to be recognized "as a writer
who is versatile enough to tackle everything."[8] His Nat Turner would be no
empty caricature, but instead a man exemplary of the "human condition"—
fitted with a desire for freedom.[9] There was a hint of impracticality to the project, because Styron was living in Europe. He pestered his correspondents in
the United States to procure research materials for him. "I don't know whether
I'm plunging into something over my depth," he confided to his father, "but
I'm fascinated anyway."[10]

The fascination never receded, but other projects dampened his enthusiasm
and distracted his attention. Progress was spotty as he struggled, he wrote, "to
regain my vision" for the book.[11] In the interim, he worked on a novella, *The
Long March* (1953). By early spring 1953, he finally admitted that the Nat Turner
novel "lies idle; Lord knows when I'll wrestle w/that; perhaps not for years."[12]
He found himself depressed, "dangerously suicidal," and in full-throttle crisis
of confidence. "I am as inspiration-less as a newt." He did not want to demean
himself by turning out "drivel"—he raised the stakes too high for that and suffered as a result.[13] If the first page was not "a real sockeroo," he wrote, "then I
tend to give up in anguish."[14]

By 1954 Styron had refocused. But not on the Nat Turner project. He was
now composing what would become his second full novel, *Set This House on
Fire*, which was finally published in 1960, to generally dismal reviews.

A year later, in 1961, he returned to the never-say-die Nat Turner book.
Styron wanted to write a book about "noble" themes, one that stretched his
talents as a writer and spoke to the present moment. He was actually pleased
by the paucity of primary material, feeling that it allowed him as a writer-cum-
historian to comprehend the motivations of the leader of a rebellion. In some
ways, he acknowledged, the novel was "historical" but also "psychological,"
even a story of "redemption."[15]

As the civil rights movement revved up in the South, a headier topic could
hardly be imagined. An additional factor in Styron's return to the subject may
have been his ego. While he often proclaimed distance from the New York literary scene, he craved recognition and respect from that writerly and intellectual community, especially after his former friend Mailer had "evaluated" him
as a novelist.[16] Did Styron, as Mailer wondered, have the "moral courage" to

"turn the consciousness of our time, an achievement which is the primary measure of a writer's size"?[17]

Months before this screed appeared, Styron noted that Mailer had "flipped his lid," because of excess drinking and drug-taking.[18] Once he and pal James Jones had read their evaluations, they were relieved to have been skewered less than most other novelists. But Mailer simply increased Styron's own worry that "the only way to become a major writer is to write books" so important that they catch "the consciousness of our time."[19]

Over the next five years, beginning at Martha's Vineyard in the summer of 1962, after the critical failure of *Set This House on Fire*, Styron spent "afternoons with Nat Turner."[20] He was impelled to prove to himself and Mailer that he could produce a novel with lofty qualities and popular appeal. At first, Styron moved with calm assuredness, piling up pages. Soon he complained: "I didn't know how to go on." Sometimes, casting about for an angle to take, he found inspiration in the oddest of places. Watching Orson Welles's classic film *Citizen Kane*, Styron realized that he had to take a "plunge" into memory, into the hidden, deep sources of what made Nat Turner tick.[21] The end was in sight by fall 1966, as Styron felt "a blind rush of creativity" and began composing the bloody passages dealing with the rebellion. By the end of January, the book was finished and the champagne uncorked.[22]

Before its official publication date of October 9, 1967, Styron was supremely confident that *The Confessions of Nat Turner* would be a success. An excerpt from the novel had appeared in *Harper's*, netting Styron a cool five thousand dollars. More impressively, the Book of the Month Club featured the novel and paid the author $150,000—"quite a chunk to earn off a slave's back," chirped Styron. In late November, Styron reported that the book was "approaching 100,000" copies sold. And his agent had just sold the film rights for $600,000, enough, Styron wrote, to "keep me in sour mash for the next couple of years."[23]

An avalanche of publicity and favorable reviews greeted the novel. Raymond A. Sokolov in *Newsweek* called it "the book of the year, and more than that...an act of revelation to a whole society."[24] Philip Rahv in the *New York Review of Books* praised Styron's ability to realize slaves as complex human beings. He found the work teeming with revolutionary possibility and meaning for the present. In a Sunday *New York Times* book review, Wilfred Sheed considered the novel "a kind of historical tone poem," although he had problems with the voices employed in the work. Eliot Fremont-Smith, also in the *New York Times*, remarked that *Confessions* was "one of those rare books that show us our American past, our present—ourselves—in a dazzling shaft of light."[25]

Perhaps the high point of renown arrived when Styron graced the cover of *Newsweek* magazine for October 16, 1967. In the foreground, at once surly and serene, of middling age, he looks boyishly pudgy and self-satisfied, clad in cardigan. In one hand he holds an ashy stogie; the other grasps a copy of his burnt-orange-covered novel, *The Confessions of Nat Turner*. Out of the book, mysteriously, rise two black-eyed Susans, perhaps a reference to their association with justice.

The background drawing, in black and white, depicted slaves in threadbare clothing, seething with righteous anger. In conspiratorial darkness, slaves huddle around Nat Turner as he unveils a plan for rebellion. His eyes burn with zeal, his left arm points in the direction of freedom road. A handful of slaves on that sultry evening in August 1831, in Southampton County, Virginia, had joined Turner in a bloody and doomed dash for retribution and freedom. The slaves murdered over fifty whites: "It was my object," Turner confided, "to carry terror and devastation wherever we went."[26] Finally, the slaveholding class regrouped and exacted its own gory toll. All the rebels, fifty-six in number, were executed. White bloodlust ran hot, and perhaps two hundred innocent slaves and free blacks were murdered. Draconian slave laws were passed, and whatever hopes might have been entertained for the freeing of slaves in the upper South were forgotten. Nat was captured and later tried and hanged, but not before he supplied lawyer Thomas Gray with a slim and incomplete account of his life and rebellion.[27]

Storms quickly threatened to rain on Styron's parade. The *Newsweek* article had predicted as much. One of the novel's greatest supporters was James Baldwin, then at the epicenter of the civil rights struggle. Growing up in Harlem, he had been burdened by poverty and domestic difficulties. He was odd in appearance—short and wiry, and his eyeballs seemed to enter the room before he did. After a brief stint as a fifteen-year-old Pentecostal preacher, Baldwin meandered his way toward a writing career. Disgusted with racism at home, in 1948 he emigrated to France, where he lived for close to a decade—an existence that granted liberation but at the cost of abysmal poverty. He published a moving, semiautobiographical novel in 1953, followed by *Giovanni's Room* in 1956, a novella of extreme beauty and sadness about a doomed homosexual relationship. He, along with Styron, maintained proudly: "Artists are here to disturb the peace."[28]

By the fall of 1962, Baldwin had laid it on the line about America's racial problem. In a letter composed to his fifteen-year-old namesake nephew, Baldwin with "brutal clarity" explained how whites viewed blacks as "worthless."[29] The subjection of the African American and the puffery of white notions of inherent superiority had defined race relations. The black past had been "rope, fire, torture, castration, infanticide, rape; death and humiliation; fear by day and night, fear as deep as the marrow of the bone." Hardly surprising, then, that members of the Nation of Islam (about whom Baldwin wrote at length) were not alone among blacks "to think of white people as devils."[30]

In the end, Baldwin knew only one possibility—liberation. It would be costly and difficult, occurring "before the law, and in the mind." But the time for justice was not in some distant future. Consciousness must be transformed in America. White America must "end the racial nightmare, and achieve our country, and change the history of the world." This was plain to see, so Baldwin famously concluded his book with biblical prophecy, as rendered in a slave song: "God gave Noah the rainbow sign, No more water, the fire next time!"[31]

Baldwin had lived in Styron's Connecticut homestead in the fall of 1960; the two often found themselves "drinking whiskey through the hours until the chill dawn." Recalling those days, Styron claimed to have been "reluctant to try to enter the mind of a slave." But Baldwin offered "encouragement" for the task, feeding Styron's own sense of "audacity" about the course he was taking. He may have included aspects of Baldwin in the character of Nat. "There's some of me in Nat Turner.... If I were an actor, I could play the part," maintained Baldwin.[32]

Baldwin, well-schooled in literary and racial politics, worried that many African Americans, in the midst of their own freedom struggle and in the process of defining their identities, would take umbrage at Styron's appropriation of a revolutionary black figure—with good reason. The New Sensibility, with its emphasis on breaking the bonds of bourgeois narrowness and traditions concerning art, identified with African Americans, alas, often in a simplistic manner, as with various beats and Mailer. For his own part, Styron generally avoided drawing explicit parallels between his version of Nat Turner and the current moment—a time he later referenced as one of deeply "chaotic racial politics."[33] But Baldwin knew that Styron was "going to catch it from black and white."[34] He had struck a tender nerve.

In Styron's telling, Nat Turner was a precocious and coddled house slave. He was educated at the behest of an enlightened slave master, who believed that slaves had intellectual potential and made of Nat an experiment to prove his point. Nat cherished the promise of freedom from bondage that his master had once promised for him. But cruel reality intervened, and Nat was sacrificed at the altar of economic necessity and the limits of benevolence. Nat's "most incredible, crucial psychological betrayal," this "manhood destroyed" moved Nat from normality to derangement, from religious belief to the religious zealotry of an "avenging Old Testament angel."[35] He imagines God's voice beckoning him to rebellion. Once the rebellion begins, Nat is at best a perturbed leader. Bloodthirsty Will threatens his leadership. When Nat's turn to kill comes twice, his sword proves as blunt as his will. Only when he confronts Margaret Whitehead, a young white girl whom Nat desires sexually, according to Styron, does he finally summon the terrible strength necessary to vanquish all that he had held dear. By murdering Margaret, he breaks his ties with his past and humanity—which he comes, apparently, to regret.

An immensely complex character—sexually, religiously, and psychologically, Styron's Nat Turner was brilliant and deluded, revolutionary and hesitant, chaste and in sexual turmoil. Nat was a hero of sorts, in Styron's opinion, but also "very definitely a psychopath, dangerously over the edge." Perhaps this was in part what attracted Styron to Nat in the first place.[36]

A slim volume, *William Styron's Nat Turner: Ten Black Writers Respond*, appearing in 1968, angrily rejected this presentation of Nat Turner as nothing more than a "Sambo" figure, a creation by a white southern writer. Lerone Bennett Jr. argued, "Nat Turner does not speak in William Styron's *Confessions*."

> The voice in this confession is the voice of William Styron.
> The images are the images of William Styron.
> The confession is the confession of William Styron.

The "real" Turner, according to Bennett, "was a virile, commanding, courageous figure."[37]

Styron, in contrast, had "emasculated" Nat, depicting him as unmarried and a virgin; he had even manufactured a homosexual frolic between Nat and another slave. Nor had he discussed the time that Nat ran away, a common form of slave rebellion.[38] Further, he had ignored many other "facts": that Nat had grandparents that encouraged him to read, that there was no evidence that Nat was in love with Margaret Whitehead or any white woman.

Although Styron admitted he had "no proof" of a relationship between Nat and Margaret, he posited "a very guarded sexual relationship."[39] In discussing the dynamic between Nat and his fellow rebels, Styron had "explained" what "I *smell* it to be true."[40] After reading the galleys of *William Styron's Nat Turner*, Styron was disgusted, finding it dishonest from the first to the last page and deeply upset by being called a racist.[41] He turned the table on his critics by denouncing them as the real racists for their inability to accept that "a writer, black or white, must be able to write about *any* human being of whatever color."[42]

The critics in general he called "brainwashed" and "black philistines."[43] After all, Styron claimed that Martin Luther King Jr., just prior to his assassination, had read the book "and admired it very much." Showing how tone-deaf Styron was to the black liberation movement and the tempo of his times, he predicted that the whole tumult would "blow over" soon.[44]

He was wrong, and he outrageously told a reporter, "For the last six months, I've felt like the only white man with Negroes on my back."[45] By the fall of 1968, a "stalker" seemed to be on Styron's trail. He realized this at the annual meeting of the Southern Historical Association in New Orleans. A panel titled "The Uses of History in Fiction" had been convened, featuring Styron along with fellow novelists Robert Penn Warren and Ralph Ellison. C. Vann Woodward, a distinguished historian of the South, served as the moderator.[46]

Ellison provocatively announced that novelists were simply born liars; that's what they do for a living; hence they "should leave history alone." Warren, who had chronicled in fiction the rise and fall of Louisiana politician Huey Long, maintained that good history combined imagination and fact. Woodward agreed, calling for historians to shed the armor of social scientific ideals (then in vogue) to see themselves as novelists narrating the past. Styron was clearly nervous, prattling on about Marxist theorist of literature George Lukacs and stating that the historical novelist should avoid having a "promiscuous blindness" to the facts.[47]

The proceedings heated up when the panel took questions from the audience. The first questioner challenged Styron for claiming that Turner was unmarried. Since the "original" confession made no mention of a wife, Styron felt he had no obligation to give him one in the novel. The questioner forced Styron to admit that Nat's obsession with the slaveholder's daughter Margaret Whitehead was "part of [his] fictional imagination." It was his novelistic choice to make her into something that might not have been a reality. It allowed Styron to offer redemption rather than senseless violence as the keynote for his novel.[48]

The second questioner was the "stalker." Styron recognized him as the dashiki-wearing protestor he had confronted earlier that year at Harvard University. Now he was in New Orleans to call Styron a liar once more.[49] He was incensed that Styron had reduced "the revolutionary black figure" Nat Turner to a man obsessively lusting after a white woman. Perhaps seeking to lessen the tension, Styron sadly referred to his African American antagonist as "my *bête noire*." They wrangled over Styron's intentions and implications in the book. Styron defended his "artistic needs"; the questioner condemned him for producing a work that "whites *wanted* to read." According to the critic, Turner was a revolutionary, pure and simple. In contrast, Styron drew Turner as "a ruthless and perhaps psychotic fanatic, a religious fanatic" with an unrealistic plan that led to further violence. This was a wrong-headed "white impression," in the words of his angry interlocutor.[50]

The battle lines on a host of issues had been drawn.

As the 1960s progressed, African Americans organized and pushed for equality. In 1960, direct action—beginning in Greensboro and followed by other sit-ins—brought the struggle to light. Many well-meaning whites, especially during the Freedom Summer drive of 1964, threw themselves into the battle for black equality. Stokely Carmichael, in the early 1960s, worked with the Southern Nonviolent Coordinating Committee in the South to integrate facilities and register blacks to vote. In 1967, with coauthor Charles V. Hamilton, he published *Black Power*, which, as its name suggested, and as Carmichael's increasingly incendiary prose hammered home, meant that the liberation of blacks must occur by their own actions, under their own leadership, and, if necessary, with recourse to violence (this was in strong contrast to Martin Luther King Jr.'s view of how to fight for freedom). The age of Black Power and identity politics had begun—and it did not take kindly to Styron's appropriation of a black hero and black voice rendered into a bundle of neuroses.

A sea change of controversy also rocked the study of slavery. For many years—with the exception of the work of African American scholars such as W. E. B. DuBois and Benjamin Quarles, joined by the white Marxist Herbert Aptheker—historians (such as U. B. Phillips) had presented slavery with a humane face, finding it a relatively benign institution that had brought discipline and religion to a race otherwise destined for savagery. This view was challenged for a mainstream audience in the preface to *A Peculiar Institution* (1956) by Berkeley historian Kenneth Stampp. He presumed that negroes and whites were cut from the same cloth, without significant racial distinctions other than patina of skin color.[51]

Historian Stanley Elkins published *Slavery* in 1959, a book Styron found "quite an eye-opener."[52] Influenced by literature on the Holocaust and concentration camps, particularly the work of Bruno Bettelheim, Elkins maintained that slavery was a total institution designed to demean any human, bringing them to "the level of an animal."[53] Bettelheim famously observed—he had been briefly placed in a concentration camp—that some inmates who had been broken in soul became passive and childlike, looking to the concentration camp guards as figures deserving authority and even admiration.

Elkins turned this perspective to the slave system in the United States, arguing that the cruelty of the institution had rendered many African Americans into Sambo figures, docile and loyal to their owners—just as concentration camp prisoners identified with their oppressors. Borrowing from this material, Styron wrote of slaves remaining loyal to their masters, rallying to fight against Turner and his rebels. But Styron also realized that these slaves had been wise to avoid a rebellion that had slim chance of success.[54]

So long as one presumed that the concentration camp experience was analogous to slavery, such a view had logic and historical value. But the connection and its implications came under attack by African American historian John Blassingame and white historian Eugene Genovese. Slavery was horrible but not a total institution. Differences existed from plantation to plantation (depending on their location, size, and crop). Slaves, blessed with the human spirit to persevere, in Blassingame's view, carved out spaces for communities that maintained dignity and acts of rebellion (disobedience, running away, and much more). In Genovese's rather complex interpretation in *Roll, Jordan, Roll*, slave owners upheld a paternalistic perception of themselves, which fed into an ideology that stressed the laziness and childlike qualities of the slaves. In return for not challenging the system by outright rebellion, slaves created clever ruses to win some rights, haggle for others, and gain humanity. In sum, slaves maintained their dignity in a system rife with inequity and contradictions.

Irony infused the debate between Styron and his critics about the "reality" of Nat Turner. Each relied, when it suited their purposes, on the *Confessions*, a twenty-page pamphlet Turner had dictated to Thomas Gray. Almost nothing is known about Gray, other than the comments he offered within the text of *Confessions*. Styron presents him as a ravaged, "pockmarked" man, familiar with drink, well-read, unsentimental, given to philosophical speculation.[55] Nor is it known whether Gray copied Turner's comments verbatim or used a loose hand in transcription.[56] Probably the latter. In some ways, Gray is the most interesting figure in the novel. A man of some education, conversant with religious issues and given to self-puffery, Gray took as his task to wring a confession *and* to show how Turner was an aberration among slaves. Otherwise, his actions could upset the presumption that slavery was a benign institution.

In the novel, Gray acknowledges Nat's intelligence and fanaticism. But he and Nat address one another across an unbridgeable divide. Peppered with questions by Gray, Nat barks, "Leave off studyin' about all this! We done what had to be done."[57] Gray cannot accept this; he must dig deeper into the meaning of the crime. If it is not a fluke, then it becomes a horrendous augury for the future. As he tells the court, "In the dark and privy stillness of our minds there are few of us who are not still haunted by worrisome doubts." How could "those very people under whose stewardship they had enjoyed a contentment and tranquility unequaled anywhere among the members of their race" have brought forth such undiluted horror, such an "awful toll in human ruin and heartbreak and bereavement" which presently "haunt us like the specter of a threatening black hand above the sweetly pillowed head of a slumbering babe"?[58]

Gray contents himself with a mask of contradiction and rationalization, the sort of self-deception necessary to sustain the ideology of the slaveholding class. The essential fact, in Gray's view, is that the rebellion failed. With the exception of his killing of Margaret Whitehead, Nat was "unable to carry out a *single feat of arms!*" Thus,

> qualities of irresolution, instability, spiritual backwardness, and plain habits of docility are so deeply embedded in the Negro nature that any insurgent action on the part of this race is doomed to failure; and for this reason it is my sincere plea that the good people of our Southland yield not, succumb not to the twin demons of terror and panic.[59]

Was this, as some of Styron's critics maintained, a sly commentary on the racial situation in 1967, an attempt on Styron's part to quell black revolutionary potential and to uphold the splintering liberal consensus of racial progress through accommodation? He was aware of the bloody rebellion in Africa led by Patrice Lumumba in the Congo in 1961 and of the revolutionary writings of Frantz Fanon, whom he found "very scary."[60] The furor in the black world, remarked Styron, demonstrated how "contemporaneous and universal" his story of Nat Turner was. But in the end, Styron supported evolution, not revolution, as the social and political solution while maintaining the necessity of experimentation and daring in the work of art.[61]

Was Styron's "meditation upon history" intended to be more than a consideration of racial issues? Might this rather odd novel be a meditation on the problematic nature of truth, about how the past resists the historian, not simply because the available facts are scanty, as in the case of Nat Turner, or because they are filtered through the amanuensis and mind of men like Gray? Was Styron, in effect, helping to launch the postmodern perspective?

Appearing around the time of *Confessions* were other major works that confounded the issue of truth and that blurred the line between fact and fiction. As noted, this had been done in Capote's *In Cold Blood* (1965) where the author's ample imagination and writerly skills were in evidence. But the question of where imagination began and fact ended haunted the work. The back flap of the book announced that *In Cold Blood* (which was subtitled *A True Account of a Multiple Murder and Its Consequences*) was "the culmination of [Capote's] long-standing desire to make a contribution toward the establishment of a serious new literary form: the Non-fiction Novel."[62] This new form would also be adopted by Norman Mailer in his *Armies of the Night*, which had begun appearing in excerpts in 1967. When published as a book in 1968, its subtitle revealed its method: *History as a Novel / The Novel as History.*[63]

In similar fashion, Styron sought to mess with existing perceptions of fact and fiction. He appended a brief "Author's Note" to *Confessions*. He had labored hard on this single page of text, although he later admitted that it had "buffaloed quite a few people," himself included: "I've never really been able to figure out just what I meant by it."[64]

Confessions, as a "meditation," would avoid the potholes of melodrama and romance associated with historical fiction. Styron considered himself a serious historian—studying the institution of slavery, southern customs, and more. He wanted to evoke a particular moment in history, "to walk myself through a time and place, in a manner of self-discovery." Such an act was a series of "tightropes" that demanded acute balance.[65] Styron wanted it both ways: to depict the facts of a real human being while making him into his own creation. He claimed allegiance to the facts that were available; he had "rarely departed from the *known* facts about Nat Turner and the revolt." Yet he acknowledged that he had employed "the utmost freedom of imagination" not just "in re-constructing events" but in delving into Turner's "early life, and the motivations for the revolt," which he had discovered in Nat's "psychology of suffering."[66]

Styron had been required to write history in a different key. The imagination of the novelist thus trespassed on the traditional territory of the historian. This resulted in a "work that is less an 'historical novel' in conventional terms than a meditation on history." In a late statement about this "meditation," Styron was more forthcoming. The novel he had written was, like other historical novels, an "actual flight from facts and the restrictions of pure data," so long as the task was undertaken without doing anything to "seriously compromise the historical record."[67] Yet listen once more as Styron twists and turns trying to figure things out. Nat was

> a projection of my own character of course, like any creation of a writer, but he had to differ from the historical figure as we know him. Otherwise I would have been forced to write a nonfiction biography.[68]

Does that clarify matters or simply land us in the swamp of blurred genres?

Another distinctive and controversial feature of the novel was its varied voices.[69] Styron presented Nat's consciousness in the first-person. While thinking hard about how to frame the narrative, Styron had read Camus's *The Stranger*. He was smitten with how Camus's main character, Meursault—who like Nat Turner has murdered, albeit for small reasons—narrates the story of his life through flashbacks. The "cosmic loneliness" of Meursault, alone in a jail cell, was what Styron wanted to achieve with Nat. Such an existential imperative fit well with the historical moment of the early 1960s and Styron's own philosophical proclivities.

It was also, in a way, part of the problem. The human condition was of necessity part of Nat's pedigree. But to transform Nat into such a singular brooding entity was, in effect, to remove him from the flow of a community, from a particular historical situation, as many of Styron's critics pointed out.[70]

Nor did Nat's voice mimic the cadences of a typical slave. Nat "was educated— not highly educated," stated Styron, "but a man, I think, of some genius—and therefore one has to allow him a mode of expression which will take in these complexities."[71] The tone was a sort of "fustian Victorianism" that allowed Styron to parade his powers of description and internal analysis. "The round iron stove sizzled and breathed in the quiet," Turner recalled, "filling the air with the scent of burning cedar."[72] The question that Styron consistently elided was how to grant Nat his own voice yet remain able to insinuate himself into Nat's reality. Slave dialect and personality were intertwined—and sufficiently complex to have challenged a novelist of Styron's ambitions.[73]

When Turner addressed other slaves, his voice was educated but simpler and more direct. Here Styron claimed familiarity with "recent backwoods" southern speech that allowed him to capture Turner's cadences from 130 years ago—a big presumption.[74] Finally, when Turner spoke with whites, his voice sometimes trembled with hesitancies or took on an Uncle Tom style: "Well, mastah, I tell you . . . it's always been my idea that a nigger should follow all the rules and regulations so far as he is able." Styron announced that he had wanted with this novel "to assume the person of a Negro and make it convincing."[75]

With no small amount of temerity, Styron boasted to a reporter that he had "absorbed by osmosis a knowledge of what it is to be a Negro." Indeed, Styron continued without apparent sensitivity to the anguished history of racial masquerades and appropriation, "I said to myself 'I'm going to be a Negro for this entire book.'"[76] After all, Styron must have imagined, if Flaubert could become

Emma Bovary ("C'est moi") then why couldn't he become Nat Turner? The book was an experiment in artistic creation, wasn't it?, Styron maintained.

Whereas Styron stood proud that he had managed to blur genres and speak in varied voices, one black scholar, Michael Thelwell, took him to task. Styron, Thelwell wrote, "straddles two genres" without transcending either. His work, then, served to "combine" the problems of both history and fiction, presenting to the public a work that suggests a certain sagacity and adherence to known facts. In the process, the fruits of Styron's imagination appear as facts, and the real facts, no matter how scanty, are transformed into fictions.

The very nature of truth, indeed of history, was slipping by 1967, partly as a result of increasing skepticism on the part of many about United States claims in the Vietnam War. Historians were still beholden to a search for truth, but from a new angle, attentive to the history of those excluded from power—an America from the bottom up, an America that was imperialist and racist. While such studies were predicated upon the belief that truth could be uncovered, they raised larger epistemological issues: To what degree is historical truth contingent on the viewpoint of the historian, the institutions within which the historian works, and the ideological constraints (and possibilities) of any historical moment?[77]

New ideals were slowly filtering into the academic mainstream. Hayden White, a young historian, published an influential paper, "The Burden of History," in 1966. The notion that history was somehow neutrally perched between social science and literature explained why the discipline was reeling with misdirection, frustrated attempts to nail down truth. The solution he sketched out was to take into account that historical writing consisted of "metaphoric constructions," no different than any other writing. Historians should be more open to creativity, to the Dionysian spirit. He cited Norman O. Brown's *Life against Death* as a serious "meditation" on history. A book of marked brilliance and peculiarities, it was largely ignored by historians. But its essential theme, couched in William Blake's view that excess is a royal road to wisdom, was part of the New Sensibility.[78] *Life against Death* was an "anti-history" book, which is precisely what made it live as a work of history. White linked the work to the New Sensibility: Brown had achieved "the same effects as those sought by a 'Pop artist' or by John Cage" or by a happening. One imagines that White would have been a staunch defender of Styron's novel.[79]

In other ways, too, the practice of history was under challenge, especially in terms of its claim to confront the facts and to be objective. At a conference held in Baltimore in October 1966, a young French philosopher mesmerized a crowd at the symposium "The Languages of Criticism and the Sciences of Man." Jacques Derrida, whose major book *Of Grammatology* was about to be issued in French, maneuvered the study of literature into an entirely new direction—one where texts were sites of uncertainty and play, and embedded and durable meaning was an illusion. When asked at the conference about what exactly he was hoping to achieve, Derrida replied, with no small degree of irony: "I was wondering myself where I was going.... I am trying, precisely, to put myself at a point so that I do not know any longer where I am going."[80] For one of the two conference organizers, truth as a transcendental ideal was dead; in its stead was only "radical discontinuity."[81]

Postmodernism had alighted upon American shores.

After the publication of *Confessions*, Styron was unsure what to do next. He worked on a novel about Japan and the warrior practice of bushido. He was nagged, however, by memories of an incident that happened soon after he had arrived in New York City. Living in a boarding house on a quiet street in Brooklyn, Styron had encountered some fascinating individuals with murky pasts. Styron opted to fill in the blanks. At least this time, he worried about the potential of controversy for the project. He intended to deal with the Holocaust through the persona of a non-Jewish victim—a beautiful Polish woman named Sophie, who was forced to make one of the most difficult choices imaginable. Included in the cast of characters would be Sophie's Jewish lover, a man of brilliance and madness. The novel became a monumental success, and it evoked little controversy and much praise. In part, the lack of furor had something to do with him assuming the voice of Stingo, a young man modeled on himself. By the time of its publication in 1979, doing outrageous things with the novel, assuming the voices of the mad and persecuted without presenting moral solvents, had become part and parcel of the New Sensibility.[82]

Cover for Gore Vidal's Myra Breckinridge *(1967) (© Photofest)*

"An Extreme Gesture"

GORE VIDAL

1968

Gore Vidal's father, Eugene, was no rube. Although he had been reared in South Dakota, he had been an Olympian, aviation pioneer, government administrator, and sexual adventurer. But he was appalled after reading his son's newest novel, *Myra Breckinridge*: "I never found rear ends sexually attractive." Eugene Vidal worried that Gore's novel had "gone too far."[1]

Some reviewers agreed with Eugene. In the *New York Times*, Eliot Fremont-Smith considered much in the novel "repulsive." *Myra* took the practices of the Marquis de Sade and repainted them in the colors of a "Mod and Pop" sensibility. While the novel was "brutally witty" at times, he stated that "the mind grows numb" against its onslaught of "Transvestitism, Bestiality, serious mutilation...pedophilia, necrophilia."[2]

Early winter 1967 found Vidal in his Rome apartment, situated by Largo di Torre Argentina, famous for its bus fumes and infestation of felines. He had recently returned from a trip to the United States promoting his latest novel, *Washington, D.C.*, in which he indulged his passion for politics and power. Now in Rome, before the heat set in, Vidal sat down one morning, as was his habit, to write a short piece for Kenneth Tynan's planned off-Broadway production *Oh! Calcutta!* Tynan hoped to gather other contributions from Samuel Beckett, Jules Feiffer, John Lennon, Edna O'Brien, and other artistic luminaries. When it finally debuted in 1969, the play was a smash, as much for its onstage nudity as for its dialogue.

Once Vidal had cast his first sentence—"I am Myra Breckinridge whom no man will ever possess"—he realized that he must write a full novel rather than a theatrical skit. And he knew it would be deliciously controversial: "I let *Myra* spring from my brow, armed to the teeth, eager to lose me ladies, book clubs, book-chat writers." But Myra would stand as "the only great 'woman' in American literature." With his usual discipline and fluidity, Vidal dashed off an initial draft in less than a month, although he would rework the piece, with five more drafts before the manuscript was completed.[3]

New York City during Vidal's recent visit had been abuzz with excitement and outrage over two new films, Andy Warhol's *Chelsea Girls* and Michelangelo Antonioni's *Blow-Up*. Andrew Sarris, film critic for the *Village Voice*, complained that "Warhol doesn't exploit depravity so much as he certifies it."[4] Over three hours long and with split-screen projection, the film paraded Warhol's "superstars"—the sultry Nico, various transvestites, and leather-clad boys chattered and exhibited themselves. After viewing the film, Vidal remarked to Warhol that he found it "kind of dull," a sentiment shared by many. Warhol replied in his deadpan manner, "Oh, yes, that's the point."[5]

Blow-Up, in contrast, was a far more intriguing cinematic specimen. At once a look into the ultrahip world of fashion photography and the London mod scene, it was an ingenious murder mystery. Above all, in director Antonioni's hands, it was an aesthetic triumph, many scenes vibrated with sensuous beauty. It was controversial, at least in the opinion of the MPAA, because it featured voyeurism (a scene where the photographer watches from his window as a couple make love) and displayed a brief snatch of pubic hair (when two nymphets engage in a wrestling match of sorts). Rather than a simple celebration of the mod sensibility, Sarris argued, Antonioni's film expressed "his divided sensibility, half-mod, half-Marxist," luxuriating in liberation and chafing at excess.[6]

Such a divided sensibility recalled Susan Sontag's discussion of camp in 1964. She admitted that she was "strongly drawn to Camp, and almost as strongly offended by it." Such ambivalence, she argued, gave her the necessary critical distance and appreciation to draw the outlines of the sensibility, without reducing it to a hard conceptualization. Also in the essay she famously downplayed the connection between homosexuality and camp. As with much of the New Sensibility, Sontag argued, camp was more about surface than depth. It was also ambivalent, in resting on "innocence" and at the same time corrupting it. Democracy and elitism, too, coexisted within camp, as active interpreters picked certain works of art (usually bad ones) and elevated them into a special realm—achingly bad or ugly enough to be good and beautiful. "It's good because it's awful," she observed. Camp nicely opposed the moral seriousness of traditional high culture with its sense of pleasure. Finally, she announced that "Camp and tragedy are antitheses," something that Vidal's *Myra Breckinridge* would prove mistaken.

The violence and suffering in *Myra* switched easily back and forth between gritty and camp modes of presentation. In keeping with the New Sensibility, *Myra* was about sexual liberation, about the varieties of the pleasurable experience. Everything was ladled on with excess. The novel was a skilled juggling act, keeping various balls in the air.[7]

Camp was resplendent in the United States by the mid-1960s. Nothing demonstrated this more than the wild success of *Batman* on commercial television in 1966. It was, as various reviewers pointed out, an extension of the Pop sensibility mastered by Warhol—all surface, no depth. The screen exploded with words, all caps, and with as many exclamation points, as in a sentence by Tom Wolfe: "WHAM!" "SPLAT!" "WOW!" Camp comedy was full of double entendre, in many ways winking self-consciously at its homosexually rooted sensibility, as the actors seemed stilted and deadpan. It was, as critic George Melly had it, "unconscious absurdity."[8] But it worked. Even disapproving art critic Hilton Kramer realized *Batman* "cuts across widely disparate levels of commercial, intellectual and esthetic activity." It was a "big put-on" that adults somehow got.[9]

By the time he was composing *Myra*, Vidal had read Sontag carefully. He had reviewed her experimental novel *Death Kit* in 1967. She possessed, he acknowledged, "great ambition" and deep knowledge of literature. But in attempting to catch the novelty of French experimental writers, she had proved disloyal to her roots, betraying natural propensities—which he rather condescendingly described as those of the "didactic, naturalistic, Jewish-American writer."[10]

In a lengthy essay, "French Letters: Theories of the New Novel," Vidal discussed Alain Robbe-Grillet and Nathalie Sarraute, writers that Susan Sontag, the doyenne of the New Sensibility, had embraced. They were experimental, working toward ridding the novel of elements of transcendence and omnipotent narration; they favored close, almost empirical observation, especially at the surface level.[11] Thus, Robbe-Grillet played with meaning, titling one of his novels *La Jalousie*, which in French referred to both window blinds which keep out voyeurs and to the jealousy that is often associated with voyeurs. He filled pages with dense clinical description of an insect splattered against a wall. These novels, as Sontag argued, opposed both the "style and structure" of traditional literature. She approved of it without hesitation (although many years later she would reveal that her "evangelical zeal" for the "fresh winds" from France had been mistakenly arduous).[12]

Vidal, ever aloof—beholden to traditional narrative structures—found all of this too much. He respected Sontag, referring to her mind as "interesting and interested." But he demurred at her experimental zeal in the novel, pop art, or the music of John Cage. Experimentalism and pure surface seemed pallid compared to the moral fervor and exciting display of style and narration in the traditional novel—like those he composed with stunning alacrity.[13]

Vidal had thus been thinking about Sontag, the French novelists, camp, and the New Sensibility while he worked on *Myra*. Here is the opening for the second chapter of *Myra*, written as one of her journal entries: "The novel being dead, there is no point to writing made-up stories. Look at the French who will not and the Americans who cannot."[14] A clear reference to the challenge that Vidal had addressed in "French Letters."

Myra Breckinridge would be, moreover, like Antonioni's *Blow-Up*, both an enthusiastic examination of the sexual revolution then erupting and a critique of experimental excess in the New Sensibility. The style of the novel—with camp sensibility front and center, with overwrought nostalgia for 1930s and 1940s films, dipping into pure pleasure and outrageous happenings, its mania and madness, violence and sexuality, and its pastiche—demonstrated Vidal's dynamic brilliance, as he resided both within and outside the New Sensibility.

Myra Breckinridge hit the public like a bombshell upon publication in February 1968, with a publicity campaign that was nonexistent. Advance copies of the book had not been sent to reviewers, and little about the content of the work had leaked. As if by magic, the book appeared and became a bestseller. Booksellers, impressed with Vidal's reputation and by the mystery of the marketing process, stocked it, hoping the book would prove potentially "winning" with the public. The volume was, perhaps fittingly, officially scheduled to debut on a leap-year February 29.[15]

The dust jacket for the book was dominated by a freaky image of a plaster statue of a woman that had revolved outside of the Chateau Marmont Hotel on Sunset Boulevard in Los Angeles. Vidal had stayed at the hotel in the 1950s while busy working on scripts for Hollywood films. The woman has a carnival-dummy face atop a body that is, by any standards, voluptuous. Her arms are sheathed with long gloves, one holding a wide-brimmed hat masquerading as a discus; her breasts appear to be covered with protective armor. The inside-cover flap offered scant information: "A new and very different novel by the author of *Julian* and *Washington, D.C.*" The back flap was blank, while the back cover featured death-mask images of the author.

Myra Breckinridge's story is a roller-coaster ride along tracks of sexuality and power, transformation and reclamation. It is easy to see the cover image as Myra, since she is described early on by Vidal in the over-the-top, lush meta-phors—often referring to Hollywood films—that recur throughout the book:

> To possess superbly shaped breasts reminiscent of those sported by Jean Harlow in *Hell's Angels* and seen at their best four minutes after the start of the second reel. What it is like to possess perfect thighs with hips re-sembling the archetypal mandolin from which the male principle draws forth music with prick of flesh so akin—in this metaphor—to pick of cel-luloid, *blessed* celluloid upon which have been imprinted in our century all the dreams and shadows that have haunted the human race....Myra Breckinridge is a dish, and never forget it, you motherfuckers, as the chil-dren say nowadays.[16]

Oh, Myra, with her conflicted past, complicated present, and absurd future. Where to begin?

Myra had been born Myron. He was a film historian, sweet but meek, working on a scholarly study of real-life film critic Parker Tyler. A homosexual, Myron was attracted to nonhomosexual men, to rough trade. He took the submissive position in sexual encounters; his tricks often beat him. A sex-change operation has transformed Myron into the mighty Myra. She has many missions to accomplish—to claim his/her share of money from the land upon which rests the highly financially successful (but artistically challenged) Hollywood Academy of Drama and Modeling of Uncle Buck Loner (a former Cowboy movie star); to destroy male dominance ("to change the sexes, to re-create Man"), thereby revenging the indignities that Myron has suffered—"Is there a man alive who is a match for Myra Breckinridge?"; to push polymorphous sexuality; to gain power; to end the population explosion; and also to finish that book on Parker Tyler.[17]

The rough center of the novel is Myra's rape of one of her students, Rusty Godowsky. Myra describes him as "tall, with a great deal of sand-colored curly hair and sideburns; he has pale blue eyes with long black lashes and a curving mouth.... It is safe to assume that he is marvelously hung." In sum, a hunk, the myth of the macho male incarnate. Alas, he is smitten with Mary-Ann, who is "an extremely pretty girl with long straight blonde hair (dyed), beautiful legs and breasts, reminiscent of Lupe Velez."[18]

Myra is determined to demolish Rusty's macho manhood (ironically, Rusty is actually a sensitive and gentle lover) and free up Mary-Ann for herself. She tries to undercut Rusty's confidence, hectoring him about his poor posture, which will prevent him from becoming a movie star. Under pretense of being required to give Rusty a physical examination, she begins to work her evil magic in the school infirmary. Rusty is largely clueless, despite the exam being scheduled for 10:00 p.m., when no one else will be around campus. Vidal gives Myra camp dialogue ("I am certain, for if there is a god in the human scale, I am she"). When Rusty protests against intrusions on his dignity, Myra responds, "Do that again, Rusty, and I will punish you." She finally strips Rusty of his underpants and evaluates his penis. It is "not a success," although "both base and head are uncommonly thick."[19]

Let's cut to the violent chase, when the "true terror" commences. Totally cowed into passivity by Myra, Rusty lies on the examination table, "ready for the final rite." Myra then lifts her skirt to reveal a strapped-on dildo of immense proportions. "Rusty cried out with alarm.... 'Jesus, you'll split me!'" But Myra ignores him; she has work to do: "I spread him wide and put my battering ram to the gate." Rusty eventually becomes a homosexual.[20]

After being struck by a car (perhaps on purpose), now imprisoned in a plaster body cast, Myra reverts back to Myron. The accident has caused her breasts to lose their stuffing ("Where are my breasts? *Where are my breasts?*"). Her hair has been shorn, and lack of female hormones means that "strange patches of beard" have appeared.[21]

Three years later, Myra, now Myron, resides in a modern home in the San Fernando Valley, "with every modern convenience," including "an outdoor barbecue pit which is much admired by the neighbors." Myron occupies this suburban paradise with his wife, Mary-Ann. They are, of course, childless (which fits Myra's disdain for excess population), "raising dogs and working for Planned Parenthood," practicing Christian Scientists living "a happy and normal life" cultivating their own garden.[22]

Who would have thought it possible?

Vidal's *Myra Breckinridge* was perfectly suited for the moment in America known as the sexual revolution. Practices once taboo or confined to darkened bedrooms burst into the light of culture and practice.

There was no single cause for the sexual revolution. Certainly, Federal Drug Administration approval in 1960 for birth control pills helped. "Welcome to the post-pill paradise," exclaim two characters in John Updike's novel *Couples* (1968).[23] The raging hormones of the baby boom generation, coming of age sexually in a society that valorized freedom, played a role, too. Sex sold, of course, as *Playboy* and *Cosmopolitan* magazines recognized. The New York League for Sexual Freedom had been lobbying to remove censorship of various words and prohibition of certain sexual acts. Court victories against censorship continued to pile up, allowing publication in Grove paperback editions of long suppressed classics such as John Cleland's *Fanny Hill* and D. H. Lawrence's *Lady Chatterley's Lover*. Newer works, such as the then anonymously authored tale of bondage *The Story of O* and William Burroughs's *Naked Lunch*, were freed for examination—in the case of the latter begrudgingly. The court found it "grossly offensive" but concluded that it was not pornographic.[24]

By 1967, little seemed off-limits anymore. The Fugs, a radical rock group in the Lower East Side of New York, recorded songs using most outrageous lyrics, such as this line by poet Ted Berrigan: "And I'm getting almost as much pussy as the spades."[25] Jim Morrison, of the rock group the Doors, emoted sexually onstage before thousands. In the endless stream of underground newspapers could be found language once unprintable and cartoons that were brilliantly explicit and gross, such as those by Robert Crumb. Lest one imagine the sexual revolution existing mainly below ground, Philip Roth in 1967 published in the highbrow journal *Partisan Review* a story titled "Whacking Off." Its final line: "Enough being a nice Jewish boy, publicly pleasing my parents while privately pulling my putz. Enough!"[26]

"Enough!" agreed those heading to San Francisco in 1967 for the "Summer of Love" celebration. The hippies had arrived, promising to "make love, not war" and to free themselves from bourgeois repression (thus in practice trying to realize the dreams of philosophers Norman O. Brown and Herbert Marcuse). At Golden Gate Park, perhaps a hundred thousand hippies and hippie wannabes listened to former Harvard professor and guru of LSD Timothy Leary enjoin them to "turn on, tune in, drop out." Even *Newsweek* magazine swooned:

> For the hippies sex is not a matter of great debate, because as far as they are concerned the sexual revolution is accomplished.... Physical love is a delight—to be chewed upon as often and as freely as a handful of sesame seeds.[27]

Such chewing upon sexual freedom was hardly confined to rural hippie communes. Robert H. Rimmer scored a bestseller in 1966 with his ode to sexual freedom in the novel *The Harrad Experiment*. One of his female characters stated: "Sometimes I wake up in the night and for a sleepy moment I may forget whether I am with Stanley, Jack or Harry, and then I feel warm and bubbly."[28] Sexual freedom was not always depicted as quite so bubbly, as in the soon-to-be released film *Bob and Carol, Ted and Alice*, where sexual freedom flexed its muscles rather weakly.

In Hollywood and on Broadway, the sexual revolution reared its many heads. In 1968 *The Graduate* dealt with an illicit affair between a young man and an older woman (complicated by his growing enchantment with her daughter); *Midnight Cowboy* focused on a male prostitute and his lowlife pal. Within a few years, hardcore films would be shown in neighborhood theaters. The comic titillation in *Barbarella* (1968) was camp, but the sexual energy flowing out of a tight-suited space traveler, played by Jane Fonda, was not. She learns that taking a pill for sexual satisfaction is no substitute for the real thing. *Hair*, with its valorization of hippie ideals, began off-Broadway in 1967 but proved such a smash hit that it relocated to the Great White Way in 1968, retaining its songs, ideas, and display of full frontal nudity.

Homosexuality made it to Broadway, thanks to Mart Crowley's play *The Boys in the Band*, which debuted at the same time as *Myra Breckinridge*. The play revolved around the painful lives of gay friends cornered together at a birthday party. It exposed many raw feelings that some in the gay community found denigrating; for others it demonstrated, the suffering caused by being forced to live inside the closet. Critic Rex Reed—who would later play Myron Breckinridge in the horrendous film version of the novel—wrote that, unlike most other plays, which avoided homosexuality or kept it in shadows, *Boys* presented the diversity of the homosexual experience and heroic attempts by characters wanting to get on with life—no small accomplishment.[29]

The sexual revolution, it soon became clear, was not always as "bubbly" as billed. For all of its talk about sexual freedom, the vision was mainly that of the heterosexual male. Radical feminism, beginning to emerge in these years, decried how the ideal of sexual revolution was a male construct fostering a "rape culture" in the United States.[30] Even the hippie heaven of Haight-Ashbury in San Francisco proved to be no sexual utopia. Joan Didion in *Slouching towards*

Bethlehem (1968) caught the dark undercurrents that diminished the dream in the Haight. Walking the same streets, cartoonist Robert Crumb faced reality clearly: "Guys were running around...saying, 'I'm you and you are me and everything is beautiful so let's get down and suck my dick.'"[31]

Vidal's relation to his fictional character Myra was complex, like that of any author to one of their creations. He told an interviewer for *Playboy* magazine in 1969, "I exalted neither Myra nor her views."[32] In another interview, nearly twenty years later, he stated: "I have nothing in common with Myra Breckinridge except total admiration. She is magnificent, she is mad as a hatter, and yet that is one of my voices."[33] At the same time, Vidal labeled his portrayal an "impersonation," although who he was impersonating was unclear—there had been a transvestite, John Breckinridge, known as Bunny, "a famous queen," familiar to his mother's circle of friends. But this association did not occur to Vidal as he was unfurling his creation.[34] Rather, Vidal was proud that he could create new and different voices in his prose—and he was pleased by the camp sensibility that he had achieved with Myra.

In contrast to the sexual puritanism of Myra, Vidal appeared to be a libertine. On sexual matters, as on many other topics, Vidal was resoundingly matter-of-fact and pluralistic. He announced in 1966, without blinking an eye, "Homosexuality is now taken entirely for granted by pornographers because we take it for granted." Quite a statement, one imagines, for most closeted gays, three years before the Stonewall riots and the birth of a widespread gay liberation movement.[35]

Vidal consistently maintained that what people did in the privacy of their bedroom was beyond government concern. Along with Sontag, adhering to one principle of the New Sensibility in art and life, Vidal upheld the expansion of experience and pleasure as a life goal—so long as certain standards were observed. Human beings were naturally bisexual and polymorphously perverse—and this was nothing to be troubled by. Vidal claimed that he had been "setting records for encounters with anonymous" young men (he hated the term "homosexual" for various reasons), and he also had sex, on occasion, with women. There is "nothing innate in us," he wrote, "that can be called masculine or femme."[36] He claimed, "I never had the slightest guilt or anxiety about what I took to be a normal human appetite."[37]

Vidal, however, separated sex from love. Sex was about power, love was about commitment. And in this aspect he resembled Myra. She had exercised power over men but, in the end, after reverting back to Myron, entered into a monogamous and sexually tame but caring relationship with his beloved Mary-Ann.[38] Vidal's enormous sexual promiscuity was, he once claimed, helpful to his writing: "The more active I am the better I write."[39] But he established a long-term relationship with Howard Auster (who worked in advertising and was an accomplished singer). After an initial sexual encounter, the two settled into a chaste relationship that was, by all accounts, devoted and deep.[40]

Sexual intercourse, however, was about domination—as much for Vidal as for Breckinridge. He was staggeringly blunt, for instance, about his sexual preferences.[41] Vidal stated that he was not homosexual because he "never sucked cock or got fucked." In any case, Vidal disapproved of sexual activities being "ghettoized" or "categorized," in large part because then outside powers, such as the state, seek "to assert control of them."[42] Undoubtedly, Vidal preferred, in keeping with ancient Greek custom and working-class culture, to be in the dominant position sexually.[43] In sum, to be in control.

To what degree Myra's rape of Rusty touched nerves (or evoked harsh memories) for Vidal is unclear. In his memoir *Palimpsest,* Vidal revealed his most unnerving sexual experience. Lean of build and nineteen years of age, Vidal had picked up an older and heavier man. In a room, this fellow pushed Vidal onto his back and put him in "an expert half nelson" hold. Vidal stated, "I bucked like a horse from the pain" of being penetrated from the rear, until he finally broke free. "We rolled across the floor, slugging at each other. Then, exhausted, we separated. He cursed; dressed; left. That was my first and last experience of being nearly fucked."[44]

In contrast, Vidal enjoyed telling the story of how he and a drunken Jack Kerouac had checked into the Chelsea Hotel one evening. After showering, they had sex—with Vidal certain that he was in the sexually dominant position. Kerouac, stinking drunk, simply accepted the situation.[45]

For both Vidal and Myra, then, sex was about power, about a will to dominate, and about how to derive pleasure from both. "Sex is politics," Vidal stated, and he wanted victory.[46] With his usual aloofness and blasé attitude toward things, unsurprisingly, Vidal was not overly impressed by the sexual revolution. Like Myra, he was in but not of the sexual revolution. Both of them ("Holy Myra Malthus") had a phobia about overpopulation: "In an overpopulated world I do not think that people should be allowed to breed incontinently."[47] Vidal looked at the sexual revolution with a sigh of having been there and done that. He preferred to dwell in nostalgia, recalling when the screen sizzled with romance and stars were somehow regal in their sexuality. He also longed for the days of his youth when, presumably, homosexual encounters with mainly straight men appeared easier to achieve. In his view, "The quality of the trade has fallen off. When I was young there was a floating population of hetero males who wanted money or kicks or what have you and would sell their ass for a period of their lives."[48]

Passivity, sexual or otherwise, seemed to be the least apt word to describe the thunderstorm of political violence that overtook America in 1968. By the summer, Vidal would be wrapped up in it, as a participant of sorts, on national television.

Violence opened the year thanks to the Tet Offensive in Vietnam. Huge numbers of Viet Cong, at the end of January, launched a near-suicidal attack against various targets in South Vietnam. More than one thousand US forces were killed, along with more than 2,300 men from the Army of the Republic of Vietnam. The attacks, from a statistical point of view, were a total failure—forty thousand Viet Cong perished. Many Americans had presumed that the United States was winning the war and that the cities of South Vietnam were immune from attack, and in dispelling this the massive offensive was a huge public relations victory. Walter Cronkite, a newscaster often seen as a sort of a conscience for America, shocked many when he stated, "We are mired in a stalemate." The violence in Vietnam would grow, more troops would be committed, and the American economy would be sapped.[49]

Violence exploded on the streets of urban America following the assassination of Martin Luther King Jr. in Memphis on the evening of April 4. Increasingly frustrated by the war in Vietnam, divisions within the civil rights movement, FBI harassment, and much more, King was growing increasingly unsure whether nonviolent protest could turn America around. He wondered, "Maybe we just have to admit that the day of violence is here … and let violence take its course" as a necessary first step to heal "a sick nation." The violence that followed his assassination took a toll—forty-six dead (forty-one of them black), 21,000 arrested, 3,000 injured—but it did not heal the nation.[50]

A real-world Myra existed in the streets of New York City. Valerie Solanas had been on the periphery of Warhol's Factory scene, with walk-on roles in a couple of his films. She had left him a manuscript for a play, *Up Your Ass*, which he had not returned. She was daily growing more paranoid. She had penned something called *The SCUM Manifesto*, in which she attacked males as biologically inferior and "emotionally limited." *The SCUM Manifesto*, perhaps reflecting on Warhol's *Death and Disaster* series, noted that "the males like death—it excites him sexually, and, already dead inside, he wants to die." Solanas decided to grant Warhol this presumed hidden wish, firing bullets into him at close range. He barely survived. She was arrested, found to have "paranoid schizophrenia," and sentenced to a mental hospital.[51]

The rock group Buffalo Springfield at the end of 1966 had caught this sense of anxiety in a lyric: "Paranoia strikes deep / Into your life it will creep." Every day witnessed antiwar protestors increasingly agitated and frustrated with the continuation of a war that they considered impossible to win and morally reprehensible. Demonstrations mounted against the war; males burned their draft cards. A few weeks after the King assassination, students at Columbia University, upset by the war and angered at the decision of the university to expand facilities into Harlem, took over Hamilton Hall and other campus buildings. One of the student leaders, Mark Rudd, wrote a letter to Columbia president Grayson Kirk, perfectly encapsulating the new, violent turn of 1968:

There is only one thing left to say. It may sound nihilistic to you, since it is the opening shot in a war of liberation. I'll use the words of LeRoi Jones, whom I sure you don't like a whole lot: "Up against the wall, motherfucker, this is a stick-up."[52]

The takeover succeeded in stymying Columbia's building plans, but it ended with New York City police marching onto campus to forcibly remove the students. In the account of Marvin Harris, a professor of anthropology, "Many students bled profusely from head wounds opened by handcuffs, wielded as weapons. Dozens of moaning people lay about the grass unattended." The war had come home.[53]

Sontag spent part of spring in Hanoi. Her report documented in painful detail the effects of American bombing on civilians; she praised the resiliency and struggle of North Vietnam. Little of the ambivalence that she had brought to her cultural essays appeared in this piece, although she did find her North Vietnamese hosts a bit wooden and the state undemocratic. The trip to Hanoi did not radicalize Sontag; it only supported her earlier contention, noted earlier, that "the white race *is* the cancer of human history." And that the entrenched Cold War leadership of the United States was the leading agent spreading that cancer.[54]

Vidal seconded such views, by and large. He was a long-time opponent of American imperial designs, and the situation in Vietnam was simply another in a long line of mistakes. His overall political position was a bit conflicted, perhaps. On the one hand, he was an elitist, distrustful of democracy for its many wrong turns and narrow perspective. On the other hand, he was a fighting liberal (becoming increasingly radical) who supported progressive causes, such as civil rights. He had been closely associated with the Kennedy clan and ran unsuccessfully for a congressional seat in New York.

Vidal and others continued to hope that change could come via political means, at least through early spring. President Lyndon B. Johnson had decided not to seek reelection after being surprised by a strong challenge from antiwar senator Eugene McCarthy in the New Hampshire Democratic presidential primary. Johnson anointed his loyal vice president Hubert H. Humphrey as his successor. Robert F. Kennedy, senator from New York, joined the race but was assassinated just after winning the California presidential primary on June 6.

This heatwave of violence and frustration showed no signs of abating as summer arrived. The Republicans, at their convention in Miami, nominated Richard M. Nixon as their candidate, hardly a man to inspire hope among the disaffected. All eyes focused now on Chicago, where antiwar activists sought to nominate someone other than Humphrey, and where radical activists (led by the anarchic Yippies) looked to score media attention and protest the war.

In Chicago protestors massed, staying in two of the city's major parks. The police decided to enforce an 11:00 p.m. curfew at Lincoln Park. Should the students in the park exit peacefully? Some of them ached for a confrontation. Abbie Hoffman, a leader of the Yippies, reportedly said that if police closed the park, then protestors would "loot and pillage" the city. Saner minds, such as Allen Ginsberg, viewed such remarks as incendiary: "The park isn't worth dying for." When not making threats, Hoffman and his comrade Jerry Rubin captured media attention by outrageous stunts, such as nominating a pig, "Pigasus," as their presidential candidate. It was an act at once disrespectful of the office of president and of the police (who were regularly denigrated as "pigs").

On the night of August 28, all hell broke loose. Heavily armed police, behind a massive barrage of tear gas, moved in to exact vengeance and rid the streets of protestors. Mailer captured it succinctly: "Police cars rolled up, prisoners were beaten.... The rain of police, maddened by the uncoiling of their own storm," had their way with the demonstrators.[55] The violence was intense and nationally televised. Protestors chanted for what seemed an eternity: "The whole world is watching, the whole world is watching."[56]

Vidal was among those watching and being watched. Along with archconservative William F. Buckley Jr., Vidal had been hired to provide spirited commentary and debate on the Miami and Chicago conventions. Fireworks were eagerly anticipated by ABC television, since it was well known that Buckley and Vidal despised one another. Vidal found Buckley given to "reckless ad hominem attacks." According to Louis Auchincloss, Buckley considered Vidal "not the devil's emissary but the devil himself."[57] But one reviewer, after their performance at the Republican Convention in Miami, dismissed them as "major bores."[58] At Chicago, they would be the opposite of boring; their spoken violence would escalate into a perfect complement for what was occurring in the streets.

On the night of August 27, Vidal and Buckley vigorously debated the war in Vietnam while discussing the Democratic platform and the policies of the Johnson administration. Vidal called Buckley a "warmonger," pointing out that he favored use of nuclear weapons against missile facilities in the People's Republic of China. Then, after moderator Howard K. Smith requested that they "not talk at the same time," Vidal went on the offensive, citing Buckley's support for an invasion of Cuba based on what he viewed as the bogus and antiquated grounds of the Monroe Doctrine. Vidal called Buckley "the most war-minded person in the United States," deluded by visions of American empire, mistaken in believing we could achieve victory in Vietnam, and simply pushing the nation toward "total disaster." At one point, Vidal told Buckley to stop pointing his tongue—a well-known Buckley affectation. Buckley, for his part, sneered that there was certainly no "encyclopedia of morality" to be found in Vidal's published work.

Things exploded between Buckley and Vidal around 9:30 p.m. on August 28, as the police were doing their dirty work in the streets of Chicago. Buckley viewed the police as upholding law and order; Vidal differed completely. After telling Buckley to "shut up a minute," Buckley attacked Vidal for giving comfort to the enemy, which resulted in the death of American soldiers. Vidal responded by saying, "The only pro-crypto-Nazi I can think of is yourself" (although he claimed to have mistakenly, in the heat of the moment, inserted Nazi rather than his intended term, fascist).

Buckley seethed, spitting out his retort, "Now listen, you queer, stop calling me a crypto-Nazi or I'll sock you in your goddam face and you'll stay plastered." Administering what he imagined might be a coup de grace, he called Vidal a pornographer, a viewpoint no doubt encouraged by Buckley's reading (or more probable skimming) of *Myra Breckinridge* prior to Chicago. Vidal maintained his patrician composure.

Their battle continued into 1969 when Buckley published an essay in *Esquire*, "On Experiencing Gore Vidal." Apparently, expanding one's realm of experience, a tenet of the New Sensibility, was alien to Buckley's tastes. He mocked the notion that *Myra* was "not pornographic," as Vidal had claimed on the *Merv Griffin Show* on television. Further upsetting Buckley were Vidal's assertions that bisexuality and homosexuality were natural. *Myra* offered "gratification only to sadist-homosexuals, and challenges only the taxonomists of perversion." Finally, Vidal mimicked de Sade, except that he was "more intellectual than bawdy." At the end of this vituperation, Buckley apologized for having called Vidal a "faggot." In the next issue of the magazine, Vidal responded with views about bisexuality and homosexuality. He finally unsheathed his sword, stating that Buckley had been "hysterical" in Chicago, "looking and sounding not unlike Hitler, but without the charm." Lawsuits were duly filed.[59]

The violence that the New Sensibility had made a focus for its style and subject matter, perfectly captured in the films *Bonnie and Clyde* in 1967 and *The Wild Bunch* in 1969, was now ripping apart not only the nation but the consciousness of its artists. Vidal had addressed it with his characteristic distance. Others would jump into the roiling waters, perhaps no one as much as LeRoi Jones, who transformed from Greenwich Village bohemian/hipster into Amiri Baraka, black nationalist and dreamer of violent revolution.

PART III

Cultural Commonplace, 1969–1974

"Terribleness"

AMIRI BARAKA

1969

In late 1969, LeRoi Jones, now preferring to be called Amiri Baraka, was on a popular television show hosted by David Frost. Under the hot studio lights and glare of a mostly white audience, Baraka announced that present-day America resembled the nation long ago when the "Ku Klux Klan rode." A clearly agitated Frost responded, "There is nothing like that! Come on, nothing like that at all." Baraka was actually in a moderate mood that evening, for instead of calling white people evil, he acknowledged that "not all white people are necessarily magnetized toward evil." Nevertheless, in a "white nation," "evil things" seemed to come naturally. "But do you ever feel, LeRoi," asked Frost, "it makes matters more difficult when you go to extremes?"[1]

Going to extremes was Baraka's modus operandi. "If I write as an angry black man, that's the way it is."[2] Looking back at this period, he admitted that his reputation as "a snarling, white-hating madman" had been valid. "I was struggling to be born, to break out from the shell" in a "dash for freedom."[3] This frenzied dash brought much attention to Baraka. In the *New York Times* in November 1969, he mocked the paper's readers for ignorance of "the difference between John Coltrane and Lawrence Welk." Welk smelled of a rotten cultural carcass, while Coltrane blew freedom with every saxophone note. Jones rejected the hippie counter cultural revolution: "The great deluge of nakedness and homosexuality…within the Euro-Am meaning world" was simply a continuation of a "beast value system." He also blasted the "Pimp Art" of the Black Panthers for kowtowing to white revolutionary ideologies. Against such degeneration and stupidity, Jones upheld the "raised consciousness" of the true black artist, representing himself and his community. Such artists were creating a new sensibility, a black sensibility. It brooked no compromise with established racism; its rhetoric seethed with violence and ideals of liberation. In the talented, fevered hands of Baraka, it was a weapon, but it was also in its stylistic and rhetorical excesses part of the New Sensibility.[4]

The piece appeared in the *Times* days before his play *Slave Ship* opened at the Brooklyn Academy of Music. Although the play had been composed in the mid-1960s, this was its first full-throttled production. With darkness dominating the stage, interrupted by strobe lights, the play presented aspects of the black experience—the pain of middle passage, the humiliations of slavery, and the uncashed check for freedom. In the view of *Times* theater critic Clive Barnes, *Slave Ship* was "a propaganda play…a black militant play…a 'get whitey' play." It caused him to feel "shame, compassion," and a kind of "pointless guilt." He presumed that blacks in attendance experienced "shame" but also "a certain self-righteousness in the discomfiture of whitey."[5]

Whatever feelings the play provoked, Jones's article created controversy. In letters to the editor, some condemned Baraka roundly. One reader, A. S. Doc Young, castigated the newspaper for printing such blatant babble. Taylor Mead, who had been part of Warhol's circle and had appeared in Jones's early play *Baptism*, was disgusted by his "new maniacally egotistic catechism and the usual learning by rote how to hate."[6]

Readers of the *New York Times* should have been familiar with Baraka's militancy. An article earlier in 1969 had offered a detailed and cutting account of his separatist views. It discussed Baraka's demands that whites not meet his plane nor share the stage with him at a public reading at the University of Pennsylvania. Black students staked out the entrance to the theater and told fellow blacks that they should self-segregate themselves in the balcony for the speech. Baraka read poems excoriating white racism, making whites in the audience squirm. His speech was a "black speech" aimed at raising black consciousness—nation-forming, as Baraka would have it. According to the reporter, by mid-speech, Baraka focused only on those in the balcony. The upshot of the speech was simple: "be black, be black, be black."[7]

The Penn program included a performance of *Jello*, a brief play that spoofed the Jack Benny television program. Benny's complaining but complacent black servant Rochester is transformed in the drama. Now Rochester is gruff and tough, telling Benny that he wants all of his money; at one point he also sexually molests Benny's wife. Baraka remarked that the play was intended to "commit us collectively to revolution, i.e. NATIONALIST LIBERATION. Theater that does not do this," he said, "is bullshit."[8]

Baraka courted controversy while managing to be productive. In 1969 alone, a collection of earlier poems appeared as *Black Magic*. A lengthy anthology that he edited with Larry Neal, *Black Fire*, was ushered into a paperback edition in January. Along with *Jello*, Baraka wrote a new play, *The Death of Malcolm X*, and he was working on a short nationalist manifesto, *It's Nation Time*. In this year, too, he collaborated with a black photographer on the book *In Our Terribleness*, which appeared in 1970. All these projects were designed as bullets aimed at the white beast and to open space for a black sensibility to emerge. His poetry and prose were dipped in violence, paranoia, and invective.

Yet Baraka was a complicated, talented, and confused artist. "Why are the beautiful sick and divided like myself?" he asked in a poem.[9]

Baraka has often been viewed as a changeling, jumping from one position to another. For critic Darryl Pinckney, "Baraka's writing is defined by vehement repudiations, littered with discarded identities. Much is swept under the carpet, and the frayed edges are then nailed down with a sledge hammer."[10] This is true, to a degree, but Baraka was always consistent in his contempt for bourgeois normalcy and racism, and in favoring experimental literary and theatrical techniques.[11] After a brief sojourn at Howard University and being dishonorably discharged from the United States Air Force for possessing left-wing literature, Jones moved to Greenwich Village. He married a white, Jewish woman and fathered two children with her. He also had a long-term affair with white poet Diane di Prima, having one child with her (he had pushed her to have their first pregnancy aborted).[12] During these years, up until 1965, he was influenced by projectivist poetry, especially as practiced by Charles Olson and Robert Creeley, and shared many poetic associations with Allen Ginsberg and the beats.

His political radicalization picked up pace after a trip to Cuba in 1960. During the early 1960s, when African Americans struggled and died for voting rights and desegregation, Jones increasingly turned his attention to racial issues, producing some of his finest but also most controversial work. In *Black Dada Nihilismus*, he wrote of the

> ugly silent death of jews under
> the surgeon's knife. (To awake on
>
> 69th street with money and a hip
> nose. Black dada nihilismus, for
>
> the umbrella'd jesus.

Soon the poem's invective grew:

> Come up, black dada
>
> nihilismus. Rape the white girls. Rape
> their fathers. Cut their mother's throats.
>
> Black dada nihilismus, choke my friends
> in their bedrooms

and so on. It poetically "murdered his old friends," wrote ex-wife Hettie Jones.[13]

Jones's play *Dutchman*, first staged in 1964, was explosively powerful. Set on a subway car, the play begins with Clay, a young African American male, minding his own business. Soon, he is successively hectored, seduced, and murdered by a white vamp named Lula. At one point Clay sheds his bourgeois serenity and rants at length, splaying "hip white boys" and calling for "crazy niggers turning their backs on sanity." States Clay, "And I sit here, in this buttoned-up suit, to keep myself from cutting all of your throats." After Lula dispatches Clay with her sharp tongue and knife, other passengers help her throw the body out of the train. Another sort of Clay negro gets on board, no doubt to be subjected to the same treatment. A Stepin Fetchit–like conductor suddenly appears, doing a soft shoe, greeting the new victim and then tipping his hat at Lula. In one deft, deadly stroke, Jones has condemned black complacency and integrationism, as well as whites' murderous intentions. It was, he wrote, "about the difficulty of becoming a man in America," and Lula captured "the insanity of this hideous place."[14] One imagines that he would have been pleased by a review that stated *Dutchman* was "designed to shock.... Its basic idea, its language and its murderous rage" signified an "extended metaphor of bitterness and fury."[15]

In another shocking play from this period, *The Slave*, Jones confronted a nightmare scenario. A rebel army of blacks is laying siege to a city. The leader of the rebels, Walker Vessels, crosses into the white section and breaks into the home of his white ex-wife, Grace, and her husband, Easley (his former professor of literature). Armed and threatening, tongue loosened by drink, Vessels confronts and kills (literally and figuratively) the weak-kneed liberalism of Easley and claims that his wife had betrayed him. She is incredulous about how he can fault her for not loving him when his hatred for whites is so vehement and extreme. It soon becomes apparent that he is in the house not only to rehash old complaints but also to regain custody of their children: "Those two lovely little girls upstairs are niggers. You know, circa 1800, one drop makes you whole." Suddenly, bombs hit the house and Grace is killed. Before she expires, Vessels tells her the girls are dead. "They're dead," are the final words of the play. The suggestion here is that Vessels has murdered them, although in some interpretations he may mean that they are dead as interracial children, now reborn as black.[16]

All of this work was obviously linked to Jones's own personal life and political shifts. Blacks, in his worldview, needed to break from the white world, in order to find their own identities—and to link with a black community and sensibility. Clay was an appropriate name for his dramatic character—a black man, to be sure, but also capable of being molded into various possible sculptures. Jones may have felt like clay in his early years, being shaped by his associations with white people in the Village. And he experienced the guilt associated with a break from the white world, from family and friends. As he had phrased it in the poem "An Agony. As Now": "I am inside someone / who hates me."[17]

By 1965 Jones was a force in theater and poetry. This brought the contradictions of his private life into public view. In a cutting piece, "LeRoi Jones and the Tradition of the Fake," critic Stanley Kauffmann called out Jones for preaching racial separatism and revolution while living a secure, middle-class life, supported in large part by white audiences. He was either a living contradiction or a hypocrite.[18]

Jones was increasingly sensitive about this without Kauffmann's scolding. If whites were, as he increasingly put it, a "cancer," how could he cohabit with one? He later claimed his split with Hettie Jones (who was a poet herself) occurred because she was having an affair. If so, then the hardly monogamous Jones was, at best, a chauvinist. In reality, his position as a firebrand railing against black moderation and white liberal racists was untenable so long as he remained with Hettie. He first moved to another apartment a few blocks away before making his break with the white world in 1965 and moving to Harlem, where he dedicated himself to building a cultural apparatus to stage plays, perform music, and develop a new black sensibility. As he had indicated in an early work, *Blues People* (1963), the black experience in America was singular, itself a "real" culture. "Real" black culture was "*always* radical" compared to the formalities of traditional American culture.[19]

In Harlem, Jones set up the Black Arts Theater and School. He continued to write revolutionary poetry, prose, and plays intended to harness and create a black consciousness.[20] In his essay collection *Home* (1965), he proclaimed that "the Black Artist's role in America is to aid in the destruction of America as he knows it."[21] In 1967 he emphasized again, "What's needed now for the 'arts' is to get them away from white people." In 1969 the choice was either with the revolution or against it: "The Negro artist who is not a nationalist…is a white artist.…He is creating death snacks, for and out of dead stuff."[22] In the poem "Black Art," he craved revolutionary poetry: "Poems are bullshit unless they are / teeth or trees or lemon piled / on a step." Poetry must deal with reality.

By 1967 Jones was largely living in a black world, although he continued working with mainstream, white-owned publishing houses. After his brief stint in Harlem, he headed for Newark, his hometown, to build a cultural center and to agitate for black nationalism. In 1966 he married a black woman, Sylvia Robinson (Amina Baraka), with whom he would father five children. The Newark riot/rebellion hurtled him into the national news. It was an exciting moment, Jones recalled, when "time [was] speeded up" and "all that was pent up and tied [was] wild and loose, seen in sudden flames and red smoke."[23] Another black radical, Hoyt W. Fuller, remarked after the riots: "The Black Revolt is as palpable in letters as in the streets."[24]

Along with some pals, Jones was soaking up the street action, delighting in the revolutionary hubbub. Suddenly, he was surrounded by "a riot of red lights blinking. Like Devils or pieces of hell." Accounts of what happened next differ. Jones claimed that he had been singled out by local cops as one of "the bastards who have been shooting at us." According to Jones, the cops began beating him with guns and nightsticks until he was "removed from conscious life." He said, "I was being murdered and I knew it."[25] The intervention of a crowd, angered by the police brutality, saved his life. Police reported that Jones had been in-jured by a bottle thrown by a rioter. They also stated that he had in his posses-sion two .32-caliber handguns. He was arrested and tried.

Released on steep twenty-five-thousand-dollar bail, Jones was able to partici-pate in a Black Power conference in Newark. The beating and its aftermath con-tributed, Jones wrote, to major changes in his life. He shook off the last vestiges of bohemianism—"My individualism and randomness, my Western white ad-dictions [a pack a day of Gauloises], my Negro intellectualism." Jones was reborn as Amiri Baraka, and he began wearing "a bright-colored dashiki and fila (hat)."[26]

The trial of Jones/Baraka was a circus. While the jury was being chosen, Jones objected to the prospect of an all-white jury of his "oppressors." Judge Kapp took offense and ordered Jones held in contempt of court. He screamed out in protest, "Take me into custody for what? Because I won't be judged by this kangaroo court?"[27]

On November 7, 1967, a jury of ten white men and two white women found him guilty on the weapons charge, punishable by up to three years in prison and a fine of one thousand dollars. Judge Kapp sentenced Jones immediately to thirty days in jail for his earlier contempt of court. During the month in jail, Jones wrote a searing play, *Great Goodness of Life*, taking out his frustrations against "Uncle Tom" blacks.

Following conviction, Jones appeared before Judge Kapp for sentencing. In discussing Jones's fate, the judge read from a recently published poem of Jones's, "Black People!" Some of the words offended the judge so deeply that he replaced them with the word "blank." The poem was incendiary. "Up against the wall mother fucker this is a stick up!" If this were insufficient to raise Kapp's ire, the poem imagined a new world, where "the white man is dead."[28]

There then occurred a remarkable contretemps between the judge and Jones. Jones asked if the judge was offering the poem as "evidence" against him. In any case, Jones demanded that he be allowed to read it aloud in full. The judge dismissed the poem as a "diabolical prescription to commit murder and to steal and plunder." Jones countered: "I'm being sentenced for the poem. Is that what you are saying?" The judge then claimed that such a poem (and a talk that Jones had delivered at Muhlenberg College) "causes one to suspect that you were a participant in formulating a plot to ignite the spark on the night of July 13, 1967 to burn the city of Newark." Jones sarcastically inter-rupted the judge: "You mean you don't like the poem, in other words."

The judge was not amused. "It is my considered opinion," he lectured Jones, "that you are sick and require medical attention." To which Jones replied, "Not as sick as you." This verbal battle proved counterproductive. Judge Kapp sen-tenced him severely "to serve a term of not less than 2 years and 6 months . . . [and to] pay a fine of $1,000." Jones appealed the verdict while out on bail; eventu-ally victory came when a court ruled that there had been insufficient evidence to convict Jones.[29]

By 1969, rage, violence, and paranoia had come to dominate the social and cultural scene. Baraka was hardly alone in thinking that "revolution would be immediate."[30] About eighty members of the Cornell University Afro-American Association in April occupied the Willard Straight Student Union on campus. They were protesting the burning of a cross on the lawn of an African American sorority. Black students also demanded immediate institution of an Afro-American studies program. What made the scene more outsized than the bloody occupation at Columbia in 1968 was that the African American students were heavily armed. One young warrior was captured famously in a photograph with rifle in hand, his torso girded by a bandolier. All ended peacefully, but Professor Allan Bloom condemned what he considered professorial surrender to extremism. Humanities professors, he claimed, "ran like lemmings into the sea, thinking they would refresh and revitalize themselves in it. They drowned."[31]

Meanwhile, the war in Vietnam dragged on despite Richard M. Nixon having been elected on a platform of "peace with honor." In the wake of the trial of the Chicago Seven (radicals who had been indicted for conspiracy and other acts committed during the days of the Democratic National Convention in 1968), members of the Weatherman faction of SDS (Students for a Democratic Society) staged a "days of rage" protest in October 1969, designed to "bring the war home." Only a couple of hundred participated, but they gained maximum publicity with war whoops and combat regalia. They streamed onto the Gold Coast area of Chicago where they overturned cars, broke windows, and grappled with police. It was futile and silly—nothing more than outbursts of a failed revolution.[32]

A more meaningful revolt also occurred that summer in Greenwich Village at the Stonewall Inn, a seedy, mob-owned place where gays gathered. But on one night in late June, after a typical episode of police harassment, bar patrons fought back. As one person recalled, "I had got to the point where I did not want to be bothered anymore." Others agreed, pushing back against the cops, who were shoving gays into paddy wagons. A group of queens, according to one account, started rocking the wagons; the cops were assaulted with words; and someone yelled out, "Gay power!" No longer, gays announced after the riot, would they have their rights denied.[33] Gay and straight women, too, were expressing their anger in more extreme fashion. Women in the Redstockings Manifesto, released in July 1969, declared, "In fighting for our liberation we will always take the side of women against their oppressors.... The time for individual skirmishes has passed. This time we are going all the way."[34]

Utopian ideals reigned briefly after the August Woodstock concert. Around four hundred thousand young people there grooved to music, anarchistic living, abundant nudity and drug intake, and lived to rave about it. But by December such sweet memories were shattered by the dark throb of a Rolling Stones concert at Altamont Speedway in California. Hells Angels, hired to provide security and insure peace, bludgeoned one person to death and terrified others. Joni Mitchell's song "Woodstock" imagined war planes "turning into butterflies across our nation" while the theme for Altamont was summed up best by a line from "Gimme Shelter," "War, children, it's just a shot away."

Extreme violence proliferated on movie screens across the country, nowhere more so than in Sam Peckinpah's film *The Wild Bunch*. Viewers gasped at the extended gun battle that concluded the film. In bloody detail bodies were pierced and blasted to and fro in an operatic orgy of killing. What Peckinpah caught on screen became a national sensation of horror in August when Charles Manson, a drifter and charlatan, and his gang slaughtered pregnant actress Sharon Tate and four others at her posh home in the Hollywood Hills.

Baraka glowed red hot with this new identity and revolutionary zeal at his point. "Will the machinegunners please step forward?" he wrote in "A Poem Some People Will Have to Understand."[35] Black Power was being turned into reality, in the view of Baraka and others. A new "attitude, an inward affirmation of the essential worth of blackness," was arising, according to theologian James H. Cone.[36] The armed and romantically menacing Black Panthers were becoming cultural heroes for many whites and blacks, but their days were numbered due to internal squabbling and a concerted effort on the part of the FBI to eradicate them. A Harvard sociologist found that between 5 and 20 percent of the black population felt "estrangement" and "bitterness" about their lives and situation in the United States. Black radicals, sociologist Gary T. Marx concluded, were a small minority, but they pushed more moderate blacks to take harder stands.[37] A review of the cultural situation found that "politics and passion" in black drama pointed toward separatism and hatred for whites. While Baraka's plays displayed "passionate irony hidden almost to the last in a white velvet glove," the playwright was increasingly discarding such gloves in favor of brass knuckles.[38]

Baraka's paranoia soared in his play *The Death of Malcolm X*. Along with most black militants, Baraka had greatly respected Malcolm's black nationalism and well-channeled anger. By 1965, Malcolm was challenging the supremacy of Elijah Muhammad within the Nation of Islam and moving slowly toward a more open vision of interracial cooperation. According to most accounts, Malcolm was gunned down at the Audubon Ballroom in New York City in 1965 at the behest of Elijah Muhammad and his cronies, who feared his popularity and moderating tone.[39]

Baraka considered the assassination of Malcolm X to be a conspiracy launched at the upper echelons of the United States government, in cooperation with the Ku Klux Klan and carried out by African Americans. Like so much of his work from this period, as critic Werner Sollors notes, the play was agitprop designed to highlight white evil.[40] The play opens with blacks having their brains taken out and white brains put in; other blacks are being brainwashed to serve their white masters. An instructor tells them, "Now repeat after me… White is right."

It is an absurdist play, although it is hard to tell if Baraka intended it as such. Men prance about in Uncle Sam suits, wearing "long hats." In New York City, a "Negro integrationist" is awarded "a life sized watermelon made of precious stones and gold." In another part of the city, Malcolm X has begun a lecture, warning the audience about the evil of whites and calling for revolution and land for blacks. In a "prearranged manner," the assassins act. With Malcolm dead, a Klansman laughs while he fingers a "girl's snatch," and "ofays together at a party in USam suits" are dancing and chanting: "White! White! White!"[41]

In addition to penning racially provocative plays, Baraka worked hard to develop a black aesthetic or a new *black* sensibility. The ideal was defined variously, but it boiled down to the view that blacks had a different cultural consciousness than whites, one that was purer and better. But, as Baraka later acknowledged, the notion was somewhat inchoate and confused, relying more on an attitude or style than a fully articulated aesthetic. And it was based on the premise that there was a singular, correct black perspective. The style, Baraka demanded, was to be "as Black as Bessie Smith or Billie Holiday or Duke Ellington or John Coltrane.... We wanted it to express our lives and history, our needs and desires. Our will and our passion. Our self determination, self respect and self defense."[42]

Consciousness arose from interplay between African heritage and American oppression. The imperative for black artists such as Baraka, playwright Ed Bullins, poet Sonia Sanchez, and many others was to develop this consciousness. Stephen Henderson, a theorist for the black aesthetic movement, maintained that black poetry was written by an identifiably black person and was "somehow *structurally* black," an admittedly vague definition. Its rhythms were to be found in jazz, blues, black speech, and the soul shouts of James Brown.[43] According to Larry Neal, black poetry—when it was true to black consciousness—was more than an aesthetic taste; it served the goal of "a cultural revolution in art and ideas."[44] Like the New Sensibility, it aspired to liberation.

To foment a black aesthetic, Baraka and Neal brought out a bulky anthology of essays and poems, along with short fiction in a volume appropriately titled *Black Fire*. His introduction read like an incantation or pep talk. He introduced the writers as follows: "These are the founding Fathers and Mothers, of our nation. We rise, as we rise (agin). By the power of our beliefs, by the purity and strength of our actions."[45] In his own collection of poetry, *Black Magic*, also published in 1969, Baraka spoke autobiographically. His early poetry and plays had been saturated with "death, suicide...caught up in the deathurge of this twisted society. The work a cloud of abstraction and disjointedness, that was just whiteness" or the "European influence" marked by "hopelessness and despair." Now he had been freed from such shackles. Thanks to black art, "a beginning, a rebeginning, a coming in contact with the most beautiful part of myself, with ourselves," his work took on a prophetic flavor, "self-consciously spiritual, and stronger."[46]

Baraka was at this time under the charismatic influence of Maulana Karenga, a UCLA graduate student and community activist. According to Karenga, blacks must sharpen their "cultural expression" and sense of community. A black nationalist, Karenga claimed, "should be a man who saves his brother from a sinking boat. But he should also teach them how to save themselves by being a good swimmer."[47] In 1966, as part of his program to raise black consciousness and build community, Karenga began popularizing his notion of Kwanzaa, which he based on African rituals and which he hoped would serve to replace Christmas for African Americans. He also wanted blacks to celebrate holidays such as the birthday of Malcolm X. Although he generally eschewed violence and believed that building a black nationalism would be a long-term struggle, members of his organization (US, short for US Black People) were often in conflict with the Black Panther Party. In jockeying for dominance on the UCLA campus in 1969, two Black Panthers were murdered, presumably by followers of Karenga's organization. In its more peaceful moments, the organization sponsored a dance troupe and produced albums devoted to African rhythms. Baraka bought into nationalist principles and Karenga in a big way, although he rejected Karenga's view that the blues were "reactionary."[48]

Writing in *The Black Scholar* in November 1969, Baraka outlined Karenga's principles under the title "A Black Value System." The seven principles were, sans their Swahili appellations: unity, self-determination, collective work and responsibility, cooperative economics, purpose, creativity, and faith. Although a bit like the Ten Commandments, Baraka admitted, they had a "more profound" meaning for black people. They were the antidote to the "mind control" of blacks that he had outlined in his play about Malcolm X. The principles were valuable, Baraka wrote, because "Black creativity, *Kuumba*... is what will save us—not just 'artists' but all of us—after all is said and done—nothing else."[49]

Baraka was slowly moving away from the venomous antiwhite, anti-negro rhetoric that had dominated his work. Why bother hitting the same tired note? "Draw away from the diseased body," he decided. He tried focusing on a positive message: "Embrace the blackness." In 1969 Baraka wanted to celebrate black life, its everyday hum, rhythm, and spontaneity. He did this most creatively—and erratically—with the book *In Our Terribleness*. Its subtitle read *Some Elements and Meaning in Black Style.*[50]

In the massive corpus of writings about Baraka, critics generally ignore *In Our Terribleness*, finding it disjointed and a bit precious in design. Baraka acknowledged as much, referring to it as "spontaneous, an utterance of desire and need." But it was also, as intended, "definitely from black to black and was meant to express, define and clarify us to ourselves" by paying attention to "how the black man looks and sounds and why he does what he does." In sum, an example of "functional black art."[51] *Terribleness* was a collaboration between Baraka and a photographer, Fundi (Billy Abernathy). Fundi lived in Chicago and was a street photographer, seeking to document the pride of the black community. He was much less given to irony than Robert Frank. Baraka got to know Fundi during frequent trips in the late 1960s to Chicago for Black Power meetings. The volume bears a dedication encouraging the adherents to spread the message of Kawaida, a synthesis of sorts of the philosophy and customs of African culture advocated by Karenga. Upon turning the dedication page, readers encountered a reflective silver sheet, with the title of the book embossed upon it. It allowed readers to view their faces, as if in a mirror. This was intended, presumably, to force them to acknowledge their blackness, to examine themselves for signs of blackness. If few were found (in visage and consciousness), then a self-transformation might be effected by reading the volume.

In Our Terribleness was a celebration of black life. As such, it follows in the tradition of *The Sweet Flypaper of Life* (1955), a collaboration between black photographer Roy DeCarava and black poet Langston Hughes. That book, however, tells a fictional story through Hughes's captions to DeCarava's photographs of people living in Harlem. It was largely upbeat despite its honesty in showing poverty and displacement.[52]

Baraka was attempting in *Terribleness* an "inversion" of language and values.[53] Street jive and barbershop chatter were the rhythms of the book. Baraka was particularly taken with how blacks changed the meaning of words, especially those weighted with ethical judgments. For instance, in black argot, bad had been transformed from a negative word into a word that, when verbally drawn out, implied something cool or hip. Baraka exulted in "bad, bad, bad ass niggers." Hence, too, with the title for his book, "terribleness" was transformed into a favorable attribute, connected with "living force."

As in some of his earliest poetry, Baraka had his ear not only to the ground of popular culture but also to spontaneity and orthographic experimentation.[54] He was seeking to do what Coltrane did in music—to achieve "freedom from restraint," to touch "ecstasy."[55] He played with type, line breaks, and more. And the content was harsh: "Roy Wilkins is a dumb slave. The future rulers are black." Here Baraka took a swipe at a moderate black activist while upholding his ideal of a new black sensibility becoming revolutionary consciousness.

Much of the book was cheerleading for the ideals of Black Pride and Black Is Beautiful. He called black people "THE MAGIC PEOPLE…Prophets of the Planet."

However uncritical of black life and the problems of urban ghettoes, *In Our Terribleness* was a welcome relief from the hurricane of hate that had been raging for years in Jones/Baraka's prose and poetry. He believed that he had caught the rhyme and reason of the black sensibility—and he embraced it with gusto. "Our hipness is anything we touch." The book—after all of the paranoia, violence, and hatred of his earlier work—was alive with laughter. And, Baraka wrote, "The laughter powered me."

"I Just Love Freaks"

DIANE ARBUS

1970

Click, click, click goes her camera. Later she will develop image after image, all troubling and singular: a Mexican dwarf sitting atop a bed; a Jewish giant in the Bronx towering over his parents; two men dancing together; a transvestite at a drag ball; a woman sitting in a wheelchair, face covered with a scary mask; a hermaphrodite with pet dog; mentally disabled persons in a field; a dominatrix standing over a kneeling client; and an albino sword swallower working at a carnival.

Welcome to the world of Diane Arbus in 1970. She was delighted to wander amongst those shunted to the back alleys, mental hospitals, circuses, and freak shows. While she categorized many of her subjects as freaks, she also called them "aristocrats," because "they've already passed their test in life."[1]

Arbus had become nationally known in 1967 when she was one of three photographers (along with Garry Winogrand and Lee Friedlander) featured in the show *New Documents* at the Museum of Modern Art in New York, curated by John Szarkowski. Arbus's thirty images for the show included her usual selection of straight-on shots of human oddities, oddballs, and outsiders. Her work was displayed in a separate room, cordoned off in a manner so that viewers that might be offended by her images of "the grotesque in life" could avoid seeing them. The *New York Times* reviewer was conflicted about her work, finding it "relatively static and haunting." Arbus was able to transform the beautiful into the bizarre. While discovering empathy and even a bit of humor in her work, the reviewer concluded that some of the work "borders close to bad taste."[2] Arbus often returned to the museum to eavesdrop on conversations in the gallery. The ceaseless flow of negative comments depressed her—"ugly," "hateful," and "repulsive."[3] Forty years after the show, her curator Szarkowski admitted that he continued to find her images "shocking."

Custodians each night reportedly removed the spittle of angry visitors from the work.[4]

While the *New Documents* show made her famous, she had not profited financially. Her images proved to be the kind that few collectors wanted to grace their walls. Museums regularly requested prints, but sometimes without remuneration or mere token payments. Her most pressing concern, then, was to earn money, which she made by doing freelance photo shoots, mostly for magazines. Although she had grown up in a wealthy family on Central Park West in New York City, the family fortune did not support her during adulthood. She had, with her husband Allan, made a good living doing commercial photography; but his heart was in acting and hers in creative photography. By 1969 they had divorced, and he was in California pursuing an acting career (he eventually landed a regular role as the psychiatrist Sidney on the hit show *M*A*S*H*).[5]

Arbus worked commercial gigs on a fairly regular basis to keep herself financially afloat. In 1969, for *Harper's Magazine*, she photographed bestselling author Jacqueline Susann long-leggedly splayed across the lap of her husband, who is sitting on a chair; he was, for all we can tell, naked. She had done work, too, for the *London Sunday Times* and *Nova Magazine*. As with all of her commercial photography, it was often quite intriguing in conception and realization. One series consisted of portraits of eight individuals "who think they look like other people." Decked out in appropriate regalia, they do bear uncanny resemblances to Queen Elizabeth, Winston Churchill, Elizabeth Taylor, and others of renown. In 1970, she was promised the cover for a special section on children's fashions for the *New York Times*; her image was of two four-year-olds, a black girl and a white boy, holding hands.[6] Although Arbus considered the image "minor," she had the temerity to envision it as "a major civil rights breakthrough" by showing "miscegenation, junior style." The newspaper chose not to use it.[7]

Nevertheless, 1970 opened on a hopeful note. Arbus had moved into a wonderful, inexpensive apartment in Westbeth. Once the industrial headquarters for Bell Laboratories, the structure in the West Village designed by architect Richard Meier was intended as housing for creative artists. Her apartment featured a sleeping alcove—her bed was covered with a bedspread that she had stitched together, a strange amalgamation of pieces of fur from many different animals (otter, badger, mink, seal, and more). Above the bed was a large blackboard listing varied projects. "Best place I ever had," she announced.[8]

One of her current projects was "A Box of Ten Photographs." The plastic box holding 16" x 20" images was "white like a frame," looking "almost like ice." Arbus intended an edition of fifty, each one priced at one thousand dollars. Alas, she sold only four of the boxes in her lifetime (one to painter Jasper Johns), but she was determined to make it a commercial success: "I had better peddle them in real earnest."[9] The box included two images from 1963 as well as recent photographs of the Mexican dwarf and Jewish giant. The collection was representative of Arbus's oeuvre, for instance, *Boy with Straw Hat Waiting to March in a Pro-War Parade* (1967). The boy in the photo wears a straw hat; he is in a dark suit jacket and sweater. On his lapels are a miniature American-flag bow tie pin (mimicking his own bow tie), a small "Bomb Hanoi" button, and a much larger button reading "God Bless America; Support Our Boys in Vietnam." The young man's ears stick out; his look is grim, his smile as flat as a dead man's EKG. Illuminated by Arbus's flash, the image was disconcerting—a piece of Americana that has somehow taken a wrong turn.

Included in the collection was her 1970 image of Eddie Carmel, the Jewish giant from the Bronx. She had first photographed Carmel in 1960 at the Barnumesque Hubert's Museum in Times Square. Arbus was a frequent visitor (as was Lenny Bruce) to that seedy palace of the eerie since the 1950s. For twenty-five cents you encountered Estelline, an African American sword swallower; Jack Dracula, an immense man whose body was covered with over three-hundred tattoos; fire dancers; magicians; midgets; exotics from other lands; contortionists; and, for a small extra fee, a room downstairs where fleas performed. Carmel was billed as "The World's Biggest Cowboy." At close to eight feet in height and more than three hundred pounds this was certainly not deceptive, at least, where size was concerned.[10] Size did not convey power, however. Arbus always felt that he was "on the point of dying."[11]

Carmel was a bright, sensitive young man living with his parents in a lower-middle-class section of the Bronx. He knew that he was a "freak" in the eyes of nearly everyone. He wanted independence and needed money (sometimes asking Arbus for shooting fees). His orthodox Jewish parents had immigrated to the Bronx from Israel. He once joked, "My luck, I have midget parents."[12] In one of her early photographs of the family, taken in 1960 in the Carmel's living room, Eddie stands erect and proud, a skyscraper. Both he and his father wear dark slacks and white shirts, while the mother is in a simple dress, looking up at her son. Her look is hard to read—it could be disbelief or disgust, pride or amazement. The photograph failed to enthuse Arbus, because it caught the trio in a "normal pose." She wanted something more unsettling.[13]

Ten years later, Arbus returned to the Bronx to nail down what she considered a proper portrait of Carmel and his family. She believed that the parents and son could not stand one another—and that enmity was what she should try to capture.[14] The image that she chose to print was from a contact sheet with eleven other shots. Since Carmel's initial engagement with Arbus, he had begun to sag physically and had to use a pair of canes. The parents have visibly aged; the father is more formally dressed, this time in a dark suit. The mother wears a simple, patterned dress. All but two of the images on the proof sheet are empathetic, as Eddie plants his huge hands on the shoulders of his parents, for both support and love. Another image has Carmel with his canes, flanked by his parents, neither of whom are quite looking up at him; their glance is directed elsewhere.

Arbus printed and exhibited one image of Carmel—now famous. He stands a few feet away from his parents. His mother looks up at him, with her hands behind her back, as if trying to take in the immensity (physical and emotional) of her hulking son. The father is stately, with one hand in his coat pocket, and he seems to be staring at his son's midsection.[15] It is a scene of utter pathos, disconnection, and remoteness—exactly what Arbus wanted.

Arbus's work might be called "confessional photography," an apt but odd designation for someone who was, in essence, taking portraits of others. But in each shot—and in the choice of which image to print—Arbus was writing herself into the images. Her work was a road map of her desires, frustrations, and fantasies. This did not mean, however, that she reduced her subjects to a whim of her imagination. When it worked best, her photography was a form of tense dialogue that blurred lines between creator and creation. As critic A. D. Coleman argued, her work "demanded her own self-revelation as the price for the self-revelation of her subject. This process is by necessity intuitive, for it cannot be systematized, dependent as it is on the constantly fluctuating state of one's finally secret soul."[16] True enough, but, as indicated by her choice of which image of Eddie Carmel to print and display, there was a central moment in the process when the photographer chose a reality. The photographer makes an ethical choice as much as an aesthetic one. For Arbus to succeed she could not exploit her subject; she had to allow them to project their own visions of themselves onto the picture plane along with her own, hence the ultimately dialogic nature of the portraiture process.

In keeping with the New Sensibility, Arbus wanted experience, delighted in edging closer to the mad, to the mentally incapacitated, to the freaks who comported themselves with a strange yet affecting dignity, to the hope of sexual liberation, to the blurry boundaries of gender. She sought to render outsiders visible, to present their flaws as singular yet also universal in the sense that we are all, in some way, operating in that "gap between intention and effect." "Everybody has that thing where they need to look one way but they come out looking another way and that's what people observe," Arbus noted. It was part of what was "ironic in the world."[17] She was crossing lines, exalting in notions of liberation through sexuality and madness. In Arbus's subject matter, intermingling of life and art, and hunger for sensation, she was part of the New Sensibility.

Arbus's sensibility resembled Robert Frank's in *The Americans*. Both were intense individuals yet capable of identifying with those perceived as outside of the complacent middle class (African Americans on Frank's part). Arbus once remarked, "I hate the idea of composition....I work from awkwardness."[18] This suggests an affinity with Frank, especially in terms of an unwillingness to worry about photographic mishaps, such as blurriness or aspects of the image being off kilter. But each had a different relation to their subjects. Frank was a phantom, on the periphery of the action, using a lightweight camera, barely focusing. He had nothing more than a momentary connection with his photographic subject, and the subject was often unaware of being photographed. Arbus, in contrast, with her strange amalgam of shyness and fellow feeling, especially in the presence of freaks, established relationships with her subjects, some of which lasted for years. She managed to make people who were viewed as freaks, presumably by themselves and certainly by the public, willingly sit for image after image.

Consider another image from 1970, *Mexican Dwarf in His Hotel Room in N.Y.C.* The sitter was Lauro Morales, nicknamed Cha Cha. A jaunty, confident Morales is perched atop a bed, one arm resting on the bedrail. A blanket covers most of his lower body, except for his protruding stubby toes; he is naked, save for a porkpie hat. A bottle of whiskey rests behind him on the nightstand. Morales looks straight at Arbus, his smile framed by his pencil-thin moustache. He seems comfortable with himself and the world, with his lapping chest flab and diminutive size. The image has a postcoital feel to it. In Arbus's view, "Taking a portrait is like seducing someone."[19]

Had Arbus and Morales just had sex? Her sitters, she remarked, "tend to like me. I'm extremely likeable with them." Yet, she acknowledged, "I think I'm kind of two-faced. I'm very ingratiating. It really kind of annoys me."[20] She had first photographed Morales in 1957, when he worked at the circus, and she reconnected often with him until she caught him in that hotel room thirteen years later. What might have begun as mere curiosity had become something more. It was, as one critic argued, a case of Arbus "undercutting stable notions of identity" in order to "challenge essential categories" and "fixed meanings." The multiplicity of possibilities in her images, argues critic Maggie Nelson, is the source of her power and the fascination of her images.[21]

Arbus was known to have sex sometimes with her subjects, as if capturing their image alone was insufficiently transgressive.[22] She also liked to "go into people's houses—exploring," she said, "doing daring things I've not done before—things I'd fantasized about as a child....I'm not vicarious—I really am involved."[23] Arbus was working on various series of photographs with sexual themes, ranging from depictions of group sex to transgendered individuals (shades of Myra Breckinridge). On one proof sheet were twelve images of a couple sitting together on a couch. The woman, white or Hispanic, is usually nude, although sometimes she wears a see-through negligee. Her partner, a black man, has his shirt off but is wearing pants. Most images show them kissing and caressing. But one image jars: a different woman enters into the picture—a naked Arbus lying upon the man's lap. He smiles broadly and has one hand on her naked thigh. She has a wan smile on her face, registering little emotion, mostly looking exhausted.[24] Arbus, then, like so many others in the New Sensibility, jumped into the sexual revolution with ardor, both as a lifestyle and as a subject matter.

In any perusal of the expanse of Arbus's photographs, it is apparent that she had an uncanny ability to insinuate herself into the lives of others—whether it be a working-class family with children, eccentrics of all varieties, transvestites, or couples strolling in a park. As noted, she strove to ingratiate. But she also viewed herself as "like a vulture."[25] Being attractive and rail-thin made her less intimidating. One of her earliest subjects, the tattooed Jack Dracula, stated, "She had no personality whatsoever."[26]

Not all warmed to Arbus, and vice versa. Perhaps the equation runs roughly as follows: the more famous or mainstream the sitter, the less enthusiastic and intimate Arbus's encounter with them. One of Arbus's photographs of Mailer showed him dressed in a three-piece suit, filling up a chair, hand gesturing with cigarette to make a point. Mailer's look is wary, nearing the edge of impatience. What stands out from the photograph is how Mailer seems to be leading in an aggressive manner with his crotch.[27] She got him right. "Giving a camera to Diane Arbus," Mailer stated, was "like giving a hand grenade to a baby."[28]

Commissioned to photograph and write about Mae West, the queen of camp, then seventy-one years old, Arbus traveled to Hollywood in 1964. The text was favorable: "Imperious, adorable, magnanimous, genteel and girlish, almost simultaneously." These words, as with the photographs, could be applied with equal fervor to Arbus. But the candidness of Arbus's camera and aesthetic was to reveal the obvious: time has taken a toll on the goddess of sex. In one image, West lounges in her opulent bed, folds of rich drapery behind, an ornate lamp beside the bed. With platinum-blond hair perched high, squinting perhaps under the weight of eyelashes elongated beyond belief, West snuggles with one of her pet monkeys. When the piece appeared in *Show* magazine, West's lawyers threatened to sue, finding the pictures "unflattering, cruel, not at all glamorous." Arbus was stunned by the reaction.[29]

One final example. Jump ahead to 1971. Arbus has been hired to photograph Australian feminist Germaine Greer, author of the bestselling *Female Eunuch*. Greer had recently debated Mailer about feminism at Town Hall in New York City. The views of both were well-known and opposed, so folks got the fireworks they desired. Mailer's newest book, *The Prisoner of Sex*, flayed feminism. Mailer claimed that Valerie Solanas's *SCUM Manifesto*—a radical feminist screed published less than a year before its author shot Andy Warhol—was "extreme, even the extreme of the extreme," but he proclaimed it "nonetheless a magnetic north for Women's Lib," proof that the movement was puritanical about sex, frustrated by failure, and hollow in feeling.[30] At the sold-out Town Hall event, Mailer was onstage along with Greer; Jacqueline Ceballos, head of the New York chapter of the National Organization for Women; lesbian dance critic Jill Johnston ("All women are lesbians, except those who don't know it naturally," and "all men are homosexuals"); and literary critic Diana Trilling. In the audience were Susan Sontag, Betty Friedan, beat poet Gregory Corso, and Arthur M. Schlesinger Jr., among other New York glitterati. At one point in the proceedings, Johnston began embracing and making out with two other women onstage. "Come on, Jill . . . be a lady," Mailer admonished.[31] But the debate was mostly a performance piece, full of well-whittled vituperation. At a party later, Mailer introduced his parents to Greer—and there was even some talk of Greer and Mailer debating feminism again on a television show.[32]

Not long after this fiasco, Arbus entered Greer's room at the Chelsea Hotel for a photo session. Greer's initial impression of Arbus was favorable: "She charmed me in her safari jacket and short-cropped hair." Almost immediately, Arbus told Greer to lie down on the bed; then Arbus, too, leaped onto the bed: "[She] hung over me with this wide-angle lens staring me in the face . . . click-clicking away." Greer tried to resist, not wanting such intense close-ups. If Arbus had been a man, Greer related to Arbus biographer Patricia Bosworth, "I'd have kicked her in the balls."

The images were never used, although one can be found in the volume *Diane Arbus: Magazine Work.* It is a close-up, traditional and flattering, despite facial lines and minor blemishes. Greer is not lying on the bed; instead she is staring into the camera, composed and calm. Her eyes are wide, her lower lip full, with a ringed finger crossing her jaw, as if to emphasize her concentration.

What drove Arbus's obsession to photograph those she referred to as freaks and to climb onto couches and into beds with her subjects? What explains her roaming around the city at all hours of the night seeking someone to photograph, someone to bed for the night? Why this craving for experience, this need to be on the wild side, to seek solace with the most unusual sort of folks? Was it from lack of parental love, a sense of being cossetted as a rich child, having a split identity? William Todd Schultz, in a psychological examination of Arbus's inner life, admits that it remains a mystery. Her famous line about photographs being "a secret about a secret" obtains. She was that secret within a secret.[33]

With the mysterious Ms. Arbus, perhaps, it is best to adopt a stance of anti-interpretation, to avoid trying to drain the deep waters of her self-evidently troubled psyche for explanations. Arbus was obviously driven to be among the odd and to record them, usually empathetically. In her life and images she demonstrated, whenever opportunity allowed, a will to transgress. For all of her identification with her subjects, she did not shirk from capturing their otherness, which made viewers uncomfortable. As photographer Sylvia Plachy recalled, "Arbus's pictures frightened me when I met them."[34]

There is a passage in Carson McCullers's novel *The Member of the Wedding* (1943) where the deeply confused adolescent character Frankie goes to a circus sideshow and sees a "morphidite," a "Half-Man Half-Woman." Although she is struck by the person "divided completely in half," one side clothed in "leopard skin," the other in "brassiere and spangled skirt," it is the eyes of the person that haunt Frankie, who was "afraid of the long Freak eyes."[35] Frankie's response, a mixture of fascination and horror, was no doubt a common response to freaks. But Arbus, with her close-ups and flash, managed to look straight into and behind the eyes, perhaps not only to capture their soul but to reveal her own.

Arbus, like Warhol and Vidal, was fascinated with the idea that "genders are in flux." She took many powerful images of transvestites and drag queens over the years.[36] Sometimes the images were tame, almost dainty. At other times, they were harsh and depressing. In *Transvestite at a Drag Ball* (1970), a fellow wears a sagging negligee, revealing drooping chest flab. He is bedecked with cheap pearls and costume jewelry, with a wig and feather hat atop his head. His pancaked face, with outsized features, reveals a person seemingly deflated with life.[37]

A Naked Man Being a Woman (1968) offers a different man, his face made up, posing provocatively with his penis tucked between his legs.[38] Behind him is the ubiquitous bed, sheets messy, the floor littered with refuse and a beer can. But he is regal in his pride. In a third image, taken in 1967, a young man lounges on a leather chair, wearing a bra, panties, and women's dress shoes. He too hides his penis by crossing one leg over the other. He stares, almost blankly, at the camera, his face neatly composed and attractive—again, a young man comfortable with the shedding or mixing of identity. These are three images of similar subjects, but each is endowed with different emotional registers. Arbus was drawn to the otherness of transvestites, but she recognized the plurality of their experiences. Neither a cheerleader nor a critic, she accepted their essential humanity, which society clearly rejected—and that was a breakthrough.

On a trip to Maryland in 1970, Arbus took various shots of circus performers. One presents an overweight young woman in a sort of bikini. The aesthetic allure of the image comes mainly from how the wind billows in contrasting ways the woman's white cape and the dark circus tent behind her. The woman looks supremely comfortable; this is her world and Arbus respects that.[39] Another shot from that trip, *Albino Sword Swallower with Her*

Sister, captures the similarity of their coloring and hair (Arbus took many images over the years of twins). The wind pushes one sister's hair while the other's remains in place. One wears normal regalia, the other some sort of costume. Sameness within difference.[40] *Hermaphrodite and a Dog in Carnival Trailer* evokes both the mundane and the strange. The dog's head rests on the hermaphrodite's hairy "male" leg. This person, like the other circus performers and transvestites, bears an obviously divided identity but without apparent apprehension. The look on the poser's face can only be described as serene.[41]

The sexual revolution engaged Arbus as both voyeur and participant. She was also willing to follow the subject matter into places hitherto kept from plain sight—into the world of sadomasochism and bondage. As with all of her work, it reveals much ambiguity, neither a simple celebration nor a condemnation, but a coming to terms with the experience, no more, no less. *Dominatrix with a Kneeling Client, N.Y.C.* (1970) shows the dominatrix standing erect, exuding power, a muscular torso contained in an outfit of bustier, black fish-net stockings, and knee-length black leather boots. She looks straight at the camera and seems to be holding a riding crop pushed flush against her client's naked butt. He wears nothing other than long socks; while his head is indistinct, it appears that he is kissing one of her boots. It is all about power and submission. But in another image, *Dominatrix Embracing Her Client* (1970), we have a different emotional tone. The middle-aged client, still naked but for his socks, is now upright. But he and the dominatrix are hugging, more out of affection or recognition of one another than sexual heat. Tender without a hint of sentimentality.[42]

By 1968 Arbus was scattered and a mess. She had been hospitalized that summer for hepatitis—her "romance with death," in her words. While recuperation proved slow, she was flush with ideas for new photographic series: returned runaways, criminals, people who have had plastic surgery, beauty queens, elderly twins, families, singles going to the Catskills to meet other singles, and much more. At times she felt scared, depressed, and "paranoid and besieged."[43]

Out of this wealth of pictorial possibilities one emerged. In June 1968, she wrote, "Someone is getting me permission they swear, from someone at the head of the New Jersey prisons and mental hospitals to photograph in them, just for me."[44] The bureaucratic wheels turned slowly, but Arbus was busy with commercial assignments. Yet, she acknowledged, "I would like to photograph mentally retarded people, idiots, imbeciles (morons are the smartest of the three). Especially the cheerful ones." Today, Arbus's words seem joltingly insensitive. She began at this time to look into literature on madness, reading psychiatrist R. D. Laing, with his disdain for divisions between the sane and the insane. Laing, she wrote, "seems so extraordinary in his empathy for madness that it

suddenly seemed like he would be the most terrific guide." She wanted to examine a world that had been, in a sense, closed off from public view, and to do
so with sympathy rather than exploitation of difference.[45]

Permission to photograph at the Vineland mental health facility in New
Jersey finally came in the summer of 1969. Writing to her daughter Amy, Arbus
was exultant and voluble, as she described her subjects at the mental institution: "Some of them are perfectly rational, but simple and tend to repeat things.
One lady said, 'Oh God,' every time she saw me. 'You're cute,' she'd say.... Could
say more but those are the things she kept wanting to say over and over. And
many of them just love to hug."[46]

Early in the project, which would continue into 1971, Arbus was enraptured: "I took the most terrific pictures." Arbus regularly quoted the odd
and cute statements made by residents at the institution. A new book, she
imagined, might emerge: "I could do it in a year.... It's the first time Ive [sic]
encountered a subject where the multiplicity is the thing. I mean I am not
just looking for the best picture of them." And she was excited about writing
the text for the volume—"I ought to be able to write it because I really
adore them."[47]

Some analysts have suggested that the series frustrated Arbus. In this view,
she was stymied in her attempt to connect with her subjects; they were "absorbed" in their own worlds—largely oblivious to Arbus and the camera.
Furthermore, she could not identify with these subjects by participating in
their world.[48] This is balderdash. Many of her subjects were extremely engaged
with Arbus, and she with them. They were no more "absorbed" in their world
than Jack Dracula with his torrent of tattoos. The connection between her and
her subjects at Vineland was intense and often delightful. But, as with all of her
work, she was transgressive, working to capture "things which nobody would
see unless I photographed them."[49]

The series shared many of the signature aspects of Arbus's earlier work. She
had again entered another world, one that had been shuttered to most in society. Some of the individuals were photographed in their beds—"Barbara is
sweet and bright and modest. When I did her in bed in her flowered night-
gown she lowered her eyes before raising them."[50] But many of the best
images—at once revealing and disquieting—were shot outdoors. And, in typical fashion, Arbus liked to pair individuals.

In one image (all were untitled) we see two young people with Down
syndrome in a field, a wooded area in the background. Both are chubby and
happy—taking in the breeze, smiling. Another has three women playing in
the grass; one is doing some sort of acrobatic move, hiding her face. The two
behind her are contrasts: one studies the acrobat while the other looks at
the sky, a huge smile visible. They are just plain having fun. Other images
were taken during a Halloween celebration—the perfect bewildering moment

for Arbus. These images, however, are not scary; they are, as Arbus noted, "so lyric and tender and pretty."[51] A young woman in one image looks straight at the camera; in one hand she has a Styrofoam cup; her other hand holds onto her party hat. There is the same wooded background as in the earlier image, although a wandering piece of trash undermines the utopian potential for the image. In another photograph from the series, a single individual stands in that open field; their gender is indeterminate; they are covered with a white sheet and wearing a mask—and they are aligned with a nicely cast shadow.

Still another image depicts four individuals with Halloween outfits and various masks. They could be anyone's kids decked out for the holiday. A central goal of Arbus's work, especially with her celebrity photographs, was to strip away masks. With freaks and the mentally impaired, in contrast, she appreciated the masks, both literally and figuratively.[52] Wearing masks made the people at Vineland normal. In this picture, despite their scary masks, they seem less disoriented than the subjects of many of her images of so-called normal individuals, ranging from girls at fat camp, to a demented-looking kid with a toy grenade, to a pro–Vietnam War demonstrator.

Sontag hated Arbus's images of freaks. Writing about Arbus in the early 1970s, Sontag unleashed an attack that was impassioned and over the edge—not to mention surprising. After all, both had celebrated experience, opening themselves to a pluralistic aesthetic and sensibility. Sontag had shown familiarity with the world of transvestites and oddness in her essay on *Flaming Creatures* and in her discussion of camp. Arbus's world, then, was hardly alien territory, at least in its subject matter, for Sontag.

But Sontag and the world had changed by 1970. The war in Vietnam had not ended; in fact, it had expanded into Cambodia and Laos. Protests at home had engulfed college campuses, leading to the slaughter of students at Kent State and Jackson State Universities. The social fabric of liberalism was tearing. The liberation potential of rock culture, too, was spinning into disarray. By the end of the year both Janis Joplin and Jimi Hendrix would be dead from drug overdoses. The 1960s, Sontag wrote, was "the decade in which freaks went public and became a safe, approved subject in art," albeit one with troubling ethical implications for viewers. She no longer had patience for artists such as Warhol, whose "twin poles of boringness and freakishness" now seemed only to contribute to the decadence and disaster of the late 1960s and early 1970s.[53]

In fierce prose, Sontag condemned Arbus's "venturing into the world *to collect* images that are painful." Arbus had only two stylistic approaches to her subjects—presenting them either in "deadpan" fashion or with "relish." Neither approach allowed viewers to feel empathy for freaks.[54] Her images transformed difference into sameness: "Anybody Arbus photographed was a freak" (34–35). Arbus was guilty of "lowering the threshold of what is terrible." At the core of her overall argument, Sontag dismissed Arbus for making "history and politics irrelevant . . . by atomizing it into horror" (32–33).

The attack was personal at times: Arbus was revolting against her privileged background by entering a world of freaks; she turned to them in order to "vent her frustration at being safe" (43). Arbus was also fitted into Sontag's general diatribe against photography and the power of the camera: "Like guns and cars, cameras are fantasy-machines whose use is addictive. . . . There is still something predatory in the act of taking a picture . . . a sublimated murder, a soft murder, appropriate to a sad, frightened time" (14). Finally, why didn't Arbus have the guts to confront particular horrors of the historical moment: "Thalidomide babies or napalm victims" (42)?

By the time Sontag's diatribe against Arbus and photography had appeared, Arbus had committed suicide. Unlike Sexton's, it was a suicide unforetold, but it too was unsurprising. Too much interpretive license is required to argue that Arbus's long association with freaks pushed her into the abyss. One might just as validly claim that her experience with and passion for freaks kept her going as long as she did.

Was Arbus guilty of the sins Sontag accused her of? In bringing freaks into the public view she could claim that, rather than weakening the spectator's empathy and understanding, she had made them more attuned to difference. In the end, as with all artists, Arbus had written her personal vision on freaks as much as she had done on the straight world. She certainly demonstrated more empathy with freaks than with her commercial subjects or middle-class sitters. In the images of those in a mental institution, she revealed their shared sense of community as they engaged in play, affection, and life together.[55]

Thirty years later, Sontag returned to the issue, although not specifically to her judgments concerning Arbus's work. She admitted that she had a "quarrel" with her earlier views. Images of pain, or of freaks, might not "shrivel sympathy." While we lived in a world where reality had become a spectacle, the value of "atrocious images" was that they might "haunt" us, pushing us—as political theorist Hannah Arendt had once demanded—to think, to reflect, and "to pay attention." A powerful and necessary imperative, one that Arbus's images had done much to encourage.[56]

In 1972 there was a large retrospective of Arbus's work (125 pieces) at the Museum of Modern Art in New York City. It brought awareness of many images long shunted to the periphery. As always, some shuddered in the glare of Arbus's subjects. Others viewed her subjects with new insight and greater appreciation. Art critic Hilton Kramer remarked at the time that Arbus had been central to the development of a "new aesthetic attitude"—marked by "radical candor and an extraordinary sympathy." Kramer may have overstated the prevalence of sympathy in her work—at least in terms of how she depicted "normals." But such antagonism to bourgeois culture, to the sanctity of middle-class values, and her openness to difference and experience placed her in the ranks of those establishing the New Sensibility. After a stint at MOMA, her show traveled around the United States and other nations, eventually attracting seven million viewers.[57]

Hunter S. Thompson (© Photofest)

Denise Scott Brown (photo by Robert Venturi, Las Vegas, NV, 1966, *courtesy of Venturi, Scott Brown and Associates)*

Vegas, Baby!

ROBERT VENTURI, DENISE SCOTT BROWN, HUNTER S. THOMPSON

1971

You were hooked by the first line: "We were somewhere around Barstow on the edge of the desert when the drugs began to take hold." The November 11 issue of *Rolling Stone* announced that the author of these lines in the long piece "Fear and Loathing in Las Vegas" was one Raoul Duke, described as "a weapons consultant to our Sports Editor, Hunter S. Thompson." This was clearly a joke, since readers of the magazine knew that Thompson was simply adopting a persona for his wild journey into the soul of America, as seen from Las Vegas. The cover, by artist Ralph Steadman, showed Mr. Duke, with blood-red goggles, looking like an alien atop a motorcycle, racing toward nothing but trouble. The only disappointment with the piece was that its length necessitated a two-week wait until its conclusion in the next issue. Readers were left hanging with the line "I was going back to Vegas. I had no choice."[1] After the second installment had run, a prisoner from San Quentin wrote: "Raoul Duke, whew," with a postscript: "And to think I may hafta parole to Las Vegas."[2]

That fall, at the Whitney Museum in New York City, architects Robert Venturi and Denise Scott Brown were honored with a major exhibition. Reviewers spoke of them as practicing "Pop" or "protest" architecture. They were fascinated with neon signs and billboards, with the "dumb and ordinary." Ada Louise Huxtable, the eminent art critic, remarked that they should have constructed a billboard bearing the revolutionary motto "To the Barricades."[3] The Whitney Museum was simply a warm-up for the battle, which would be waged, unsurprisingly, in a book published a few months later which detailed their sensibility as realized in the signs and streets of Las Vegas.

Tom Wolfe, with his ear always attuned to new murmurs in the American sensibility, had preceded Thompson, Venturi, and Scott Brown to Vegas. And they learned from him. When Wolfe first began stalking the New Sensibility in 1964, he naturally lit upon Las Vegas. His essay "Las Vegas (What?) Las Vegas

(Can't Hear You! Too Noisy) Las Vegas!!!!" opened the collection *The Kandy-Kolored Tangerine-Flake Streamline Baby*. The essay began in typical Wolfe style—"Hernia, hernia, hernia" in various forms, repeated well over forty times. Then the question, from some guy named Raymond, who was hopped up on drugs and the sensory beat of a Vegas casino at 3:45 a.m. on a Sunday morning: "What is all this *hernia, hernia* stuff?" Turns out that the hum of hernia is nothing more than the "accumulated sound" of craps dealers' "running sing-song" and the "baroque stimuli" that co-existed along with the cling and clang of an army of slot machines stationed in the casino. Raymond's echoing of this drone while at the craps table gets him politely but firmly escorted from the casino.[4]

Wolfe relates how the noise of Vegas recalls "one of those random-sound radio symphonies by John Cage." Noise and stimulation are pervasive, nonstop. Even where quiet might be obtained, near a hotel swimming pool or in an elevator, Muzak is ever-present. The assault on the ears is equaled by a constant all-you-can-handle buffet for the eyes and mind. "Las Vegas has succeeded in writing an entire city," Wolfe remarks, with "electronic stimulation, day and night." In his rented car "the radio could not be turned off," so he must endure Dion's "Donna the Prima Donna." Here is pure Wolfe prose, which, as Denise Scott Brown noted, captures the jingle-jangle of Vegas: "The wheeps, beeps, freeps, electronic lulus, Boomerang Modern and Flash Gordon sunbursts soar on through the night over the billowing hernia-hernia sounds."[5] Oh, yeah.

The town was a gigantic gaggle of signs. You noticed neither buildings nor trees, he announced; your attention fixed on the ubiquity of signs, glowing neon at night and yet hardy by day. "They…oscillate, soaring into shapes before which the existing vocabulary of art history is helpless." The larger, gaudier, more enticing the sign, the better. In the midst of what seemed to be chaos, however, the effect of the signs and architecture in Las Vegas were strangely cohesive, and the "style was Late American Rich."[6]

Wolfe was a pygmy amid a forest of signs, which called out a tune of liberation and fantasy—and sex. In the cocktail lounge of one of the hotels, he watched waitresses "bobbing on their high heels, bare legs and décolletage-bare backsides set off by pelvis-length lingerie of an uncertain denomination." The same type of uniform was found on the streets—women with "their bouffant hair high above," perhaps mimicking the height of Las Vegas's signs.[7]

Ever distanced, what Wolfe giveth as praise he taketh away as madness. Excess, at the craps table or slot machines, staying up all night, absorbing the sheer narcotic energy, exacted its toll. People felt cheated, venereal disease ran rampant, a tidal wave of drugs rushed in, and the mental wards were as busy as the casinos. Wolfe had seen the future, lit up in the dark desert.[8]

In the spring of 1971, Hunter S. Thompson made two trips to Vegas.[9] In March he covered the Mint 400 race for *Sports Illustrated*. In April, the guru of drugs arrived for an even more brilliantly absurd assignment, to report on the National District Attorneys Association's Conference on Narcotics and Dangerous Drugs. Sending Thompson on either assignment was a recipe for disaster. He was "loose and crazy with a good credit card in a time when it was *possible* to run totally wild in Las Vegas...and then get paid for writing a book about it."[10] Somehow, things insanely fell into place for Thompson.

The Mint 400 was a race for off-road vehicles and motorcycles in the desert, sponsored by a local Vegas casino for the last four years. Early in the morning of the event Thompson is drinking at a hotel bar. Later, the motorcycles take off in an "incredible dustcloud" so intense that Thompson realizes that he cannot see the race. He follows in a "press Bronco" into the heart and heat of the desert, but this bravado proves futile. Dropping any pretense of covering the race, he retreats "to drink heavily, think heavily, and make many heavy notes."[11] *Sports Illustrated*, unsurprisingly, rejected his submission. But the piece was soon transformed into something quite different, first for *Rolling Stone* magazine and then published as a book in 1972.

In a red Cadillac convertible ("the Great Red Shark") Thompson, along with his "attorney," a wild three-hundred-pound "Samoan" (actually a radical Chicano lawyer named Oscar Acosta) armed with a .357 magnum, is speeding to Vegas—literally and figuratively.[12] They have packed well for the trip, at least when it came to drugs, which included marijuana, mescaline, acid, amphetamines, and alcohol, among several others.[13]

Thompson had a well-earned reputation for breaking rules and dancing with danger. Standing six foot three, with an athlete's graceful body, he had a menacing glare and often acted eccentrically. A troublemaker as a young man, hardly fodder for conformity or college, Thompson went into the military, working as a journalist and causing so much trouble that he was mercifully given an honorable discharge.[14] By dint of incessant reading and natural talent, he slowly established himself as a reporter. Fame came to him when he insinuated himself into a Hell's Angels chapter in Oakland. A single article in *The Nation* blossomed into a highly successful book.

Hell's Angels: A Strange and Terrible Saga is a shocking book. It opens by carefully critiquing mainstream press coverage of the Angels, finding that the press had often convicted the group of crimes for which they were innocent. Thompson was no apologist, however. His portrait of the Angels was tough in its own manner—detailing their extreme sense of community (an attack on one of them is met with a response by all), their aura of violence and alcoholism and the reality behind it, and their love affairs with their Harleys. He narrated the work in the voice of an insider while indicating that his status was unstable and insecure. By the end of the book, he has made his distance from the gang clear by absences taken to write his account. At a party he gets into an argument with one Angel, and he is cold-cocked and severely stomped by members of the gang. He was lucky to survive.[15]

The book also deals graphically with other distasteful aspects of the gang (rapes, initiation rituals, sheer meanness, and violence) while managing to depict various Angels as individuals. Ralph "Sonny" Barger comes across as a cool customer, capable of dealing with authorities without ever surrendering his air of dangerous allure. While Thompson clearly admires Barger and feels a camaraderie with some of the other Angels, he refers to them as "losers," men who were essentially peripheral to society, underemployed, undereducated, undersocialized. He calls them, perhaps picking up on Leslie Fiedler's term, "mutants," because they were "urban outlaws with a rural ethic and a new, im-provised style of self-preservation."[16]

Hell's Angels lifted Thompson out of poverty and brought him many re-porting jobs. But for years Thompson had been noodling around with an idea for a book about the American dream. He had a hard time defining the precise nature of the dream. Sometimes he associated it with the Horatio Alger ideal that anyone by dint of hard work and luck could rise in society—but at what cost?—or he connected it with the ideal of Jay Gatsby, F. Scott Fitzgerald's character who was able to reinvent himself.[17] At other times he seemed to define the dream as the hassle-free consumption of drugs and the liberation of sexuality. In his own mind, his book on the American dream was linked with another project on American violence; he was, in his prose and life, splashing around in the New Sensibility.

By 1969 Thompson was fretful. Nixon had been elected president and, along with his anticrime cronies, wanted to wage a virulent campaign against drugs. The war in Vietnam continued to take a toll on the American psyche, beyond the violence that it unleashed. Covering the Chicago Democratic National Convention's bedlam in the streets, Thompson had a Chicago cop's baton jabbed in his stomach. The scene in Chicago depressed Thompson deeply, but it fitted perfectly with his book project "The Death of the American Dream."[18]

He had accumulated many pages of notes, and sometimes the book was imagined as an ironic elegy to the 1960s. Although he tried to keep that project separate from *Fear and Loathing*, the two became intertwined, as indicated by the published book's subtitle, *A Savage Journey to the Heart of America*. "I've decided to write the first Fictional Documentary Novel," he joked to newsman Hughes Rudd in the fall of 1968, with a title of "Hey Rube! The Memoirs of Raoul Duke." At the very least, this was premature exuberance, but Mr. Duke would become the alter ego that Thompson employed in *Fear and Loathing*. Yet that book remained dim in the future; his project on the American dream, as he assessed it in December 1969, was "about 400 pages...and it's all bullshit."[19]

Finally, everything came together with the trips to Vegas in the spring of 1969. What better venue, after all, for analysis of the American dream? A place to imagine escape from the mundane, a fantasy world, bubbling with contin-gency—with most pilgrims losing money. And, of course, located close to the atomic test sites—in essence, on the sharp edge of apocalypse.[20]

Thompson traveled there with plenty of drugs and a perfect partner in Acosta, who was perhaps even more of a maniac than Thompson himself. The topics that Thompson was purportedly to write about—the Mint 400 and the district attorney's drug conference—proved to be insubstantial or peripheral to his hunt after the great American dream. But in Las Vegas the fiction and the reality were able to create a sort of parallel universe for Thompson's adrenaline prose and allowed him to stick a fork into the rump of the American dream. It was done.

Following in the footsteps of Wolfe, Capote, and Mailer, Thompson raised the pace to frenetic levels. He was proud to have been included in Wolfe's anthology *The New Journalism*, but his book on Vegas did not strive for documentary or objective precision. His editor for the book was uncertain whether it should appear on the fiction or nonfiction list. Genre distinctions were of little interest to Thompson. Years later he was willing to label his book "a fantasy." Yet he also claimed, "I didn't really *make up* anything."[21] Perhaps Douglas Brinkley, who edited Thompson's letters, expressed it best: Thompson had the "gift of making his exaggeration seem more realistic than cold truth." And more interesting. Does it matter that no human being could survive the amount of drugs Thompson reported taking in Vegas? Exaggeration of his normal drug intake helped to create scenes that felt right and that mimicked the neon-lit head-trip that was Las Vegas. And such shenanigans, perhaps, appealed to the dangerous belief of his readers that drug excess need not prove fatal. The style of the book was pure gonzo, a term that had been used to characterize the first-person, drug-clouded, hypercomedic, and jolting prose style. It was also, as James E. Caron has pointed out, in the American tradition of the yarn, of spinning an outrageous tale.[22] Thompson had hit the jackpot in Vegas, precisely because it offered him a large canvas: "Free Enterprise. The American Dream. Horatio Alger gone mad on drugs in Las Vegas. Do it *now*: pure Gonzo journalism."[23]

The story was about Thompson's wanting to be high but needing to assuage the concomitant paranoia, all while reporting on two events and searching for the American dream: a perfect set of conditions for a comedic and tragic storm. People ventured to Vegas for escape, for the chance of winning big, for the opportunity to sin without being judged.[24] Thompson reported that Vegas was "a town full of bedrock crazies," a place where "nobody even notices an acid freak." But distinctions must be made. Las Vegas "is not a good town for" some types of drugs, such as psychedelics. "Reality is too twisted."[25]

Everything about Thompson's Vegas sojourn screamed excess. But with Thompson, presumably addled by drugs much of the time that he is in Vegas, it is hard to know what was fact and what fantasy. He reportedly had wanted to take notes while things happened, but that was obviously impossible, since he often seemed unable to stand up. Two days after rocking around Vegas, he spent a day and a half locked in a room at the Mint Hotel in Vegas writing copious notes.[26] A true account was, of course, impossible, but capturing a feel for the place and his adventures was doable. He claimed that an underage girl that Acosta has picked up and had sex with is now crazed by drugs. Ensconced and paranoid in their room, she has with her forty to fifty portraits, which she has created à la Warhol, of Barbra Streisand, who she wants to meet. Nothing is too strange. Neon signs are so "gigantic"—"millions of colored balls running around a very complicated track"—that they block his view of the mountains. Nothing in Vegas, not even the crime, is understated. Charles Manson would thrive in this city, Thompson opines, so long as he was a good tipper.[27]

The narrator imagines at one point that he has discovered the "vortex," or the "main nerve," of the American dream in the casino Circus Circus. Built in 1968, at a cost of fifteen million dollars, the hotel/casino was topped by what looked to be a circus-tent crown, in pink and white. Something always seemed to be happening at the place, jugglers, high wire performers, and more. It attracted both gamblers and families with children, making it even more surreal.[28] Thompson or Raoul Duke—it is impossible to distinguish between the author and his fictional persona—experiences the place the first time high on ether, which makes him appear stumbling drunk. He concludes, "The Circus-Circus is what the whole hep world would be doing on a Saturday night if the Nazis had won the war. This is the Sixth Reich." It is pure spectacle, like the Nazi Olympics of 1936.[29]

Thompson's drug-induced madness is demeaning and delightful, by turns, never more so than when he manages to haul his mescaline-sodden body to the meeting of district attorneys and does not get busted. He goes beyond solipsism by looking at the bigger picture—the alluring madness that is Vegas is the American reality of the present moment. After all, what could be more insane than district attorneys who know nothing about drugs scheming to control them? Or an America where paranoid Richard Nixon occupies the White House? Or a nation where Lieutenant William Calley has become a hero despite (or for some fanatics because of) his mass murdering of unarmed civilians in Vietnam? Or the naiveté of the young who "thought they could buy Peace and Understanding for three bucks a hit"? This is Thompson at his most cynical and jarring, linking his account with what is happening in America in the early 1970s. His conclusion is especially sobering: "Their loss and failure is ours, too."[30] It is a collective failure; indeed, it is the failure of the American dream.

Writing *Fear and Loathing in Las Vegas* proved difficult for Thompson. The first part came easily (six or seven days of intense work, he claimed, relying on the notes that he had jotted down heatedly at the Mint Hotel), but the second part proved resistant to his desire for a "speed-writing project." Thompson wrote the book under a relatively benign drink-and-drug regime of Wild Turkey and speed to keep going. His problem with the material was simple—and typical for him—"I need some framework for this thing." The American dream, in all of its gaudy illusiveness and contradictions, became the theme that unified the book's excesses to a degree. Locked in a hotel room with an editor, under a strict deadline, Thompson finished the book, although the ending appears a bit arbitrary, as if the pages had been plucked from the typewriter for express delivery to the printer.[31] Just as the book was about to be published, Thompson accepted a commission from *Rolling Stone* to cover the upcoming presidential primaries. Spending time with Richard M. Nixon, Hubert Horatio Humphrey, Edmund Muskie, and other pols would furnish Thompson with a hyperreality equal to Vegas while also permitting him to continue his examination of the vanished American dream.[32]

Architects Robert Venturi and Denise Scott Brown also journeyed to Las Vegas, if not precisely in search of the American dream, then to examine how that city—with its stylistic eclecticism and bounty of signs—might be a tonic for architects lost in their own desert of modernist thinking.

The first edition of their book *Learning from Las Vegas* was controversial in form and content. It was outsized—fourteen by eleven inches—like its subject. It had two covers. The hardcover was sufficiently enticing: very dark (blue/green), with the title in upper-case gold letters. Above the striking title was a rectangular image of iconographic bluster—a billboard featuring a woman in a bikini advertising suntan oil; it stands to the side of a roadway with a taxi heading away from the image's frame. In the background looms the Vegas Strip, dominated by signs and buildings. But this is sheathed by a transparent dust jacket. On this is printed the chapter titles, in black print, which obscures but does not hide the hardback-cover image and print. The cover, like the subject itself, is nearly overwhelming. The authors of the book disdained the crazy yet effective juxtaposition of the cover. Nor did they like the "white page aesthetic" inside, which presumably jumbled their illustrations and undermined their analysis. When the book was reissued in 1972, the dust jacket was gone: less proved to be more.[33]

Venturi and Scott Brown's response to the book's design was surprising. The cover had none of the sleek design common to modernist style, but that should not have been a problem. Venturi had ruffled the purist feathers of his modernist architectural brethren with an earlier book, *Complexity and Contradiction in Architecture* (1966), with claims that "less is a bore," and "more is not less."[34] On both these counts, the cover succeeded royally. Nor were the architects against outrageousness, in statement or design. Venturi and Scott Brown maintained that "Las Vegas is to the Strip what Rome is to the Piazza," and "Amiens [Cathedral] is a billboard with a beautiful building behind it."[35] One of Venturi's most famous works, the Guild House, a facility for the elderly in Philadelphia, was a simple-looking building, although its proportions and windows were a bit odd. The building, in pop art style, sported its name in large letters on the façade. Atop the roof was a very large gilded television antenna that served no function other than a symbolic one. Venturi said the structure was "like the big, distorted Campbell Soup can in Andy Warhol's painting."[36] For a competition to design the National Collegiate Hall of Fame in New Jersey (1967), Venturi included, as David B. Brownlee describes it, "a stupendous signboard, proportioned like a football field, with 200,000 programmable lights that could re-create the great moments of historic games."[37] If anything, the cover was understated in comparison.

Brown and Venturi exemplified in their writing and architecture many of the tenets of the New Sensibility as Susan Sontag had explained them only a handful of years earlier. They were self-professed pluralists and populists. While much of their criticism was aimed at high modernism, also known as the International Style, they did not reject it out of hand. Rather, they felt that it had grown predictable and moribund. And they never hesitated to praise the energy of early modernism. Vitality in thought and architecture was central to their vision, a form of liberation. Rather than viewing the architect as hero or the building as a monument for the ages, they preferred the architect to be a jester figure and the building to wink with irony. The modernist structure would be better off if, horror of horrors, it boasted atop the sign, "I AM A MONUMENT." If the International Style strove for purity, Venturi and Scott Brown celebrated exaggeration, ugliness (albeit of a certain sort), and the goofiness of a pop sensibility. Buildings should bridge the divide between high and low culture, "Viva Ordinary rather than Extraordinary."[38] Chaos, complexity, contradiction—these were the ideals that Scott Brown and Venturi proclaimed, while also claiming that a new sort of order might emerge from such an inclusive framework.[39]

As with Sontag and camp, Venturi and Scott Brown admitted to ambivalence. In part, this was the logical outcome of a pluralistic, open perspective. On what epistemological basis could one achieve objective perspective sufficient to condemn anything without putting it to the pragmatic test—did it work, and for what reasons? The starting point for them was to understand, to be open to possibility, to come at it with a "non-chip-on-the-shoulder" approach. The architect must be anchored in the history of architecture and open to new possibilities.[40]

"We have always said we didn't know whether we hated or loved what we saw."[41] As Venturi put it in 2007, Las Vegas "horrified and fascinated us." Venturi made a religion out of wanting things both ways—"closed yet open."[42] He loved "ambiguous manifestations of both-and," which resulted in paradox and complexity. The aim of *Learning from Las Vegas* was to think about that city, its signs and symbolism, as a case study of how chaos can slide into a different type of order. If forced to render a "judgment," which meant foreclosing another option or possibility, Scott Brown preferred to do it with a sigh of regret.[43]

Scott Brown recalled that she had felt an "aesthetic shiver" the first time she laid eyes on Vegas in April 1965. Nearly fifty years later, she still thrilled to "the Strip against a very clear blue sky." The space "shrieked of chaos." During her first visit, she had stayed at the Dunes Hotel, for "eight dollars a night." She was then driving west, heading to a teaching position at UCLA. In November 1966, she took Venturi to Las Vegas, and they began collaborating on an essay about A&P grocery store parking lots. A couple of years later, Scott Brown and Venturi, now married and teaching at Yale, decided to organize a seminar with Vegas as the "object of study." Along with their students, they went to Las Vegas for "ten intense days" in October 1968—making films, taking pictures, recording sounds, mapping, gathering all sorts of information. "We visited the Young Electric Sign Co. plant, interviewed people there, and got from the Aladdin a detailed description of [Venturi's] design philosophy."[44] Students enjoyed free room and board at the Stardust Hotel, and the entire crew attended the opening of Circus Circus—later, as we have seen, it served as the nightmare vortex for Thompson's American dream. At the end of the seminar, they exhibited their work. It was a chaos of images and meanings, a sort of pop epic, presented in "deadpan" style, according to Venturi. Tom Wolfe even attended.[45]

The revolution being led by Venturi and Scott Brown was apparent in *Learning from Las Vegas.* They wanted to show how the "extreme" and "exaggerated" visual landscape of the city was nonetheless oddly unified and full of vitality.[46] Signs dotted the landscape and communicated meaning. "Symbol dominates space," they wrote, and exists along with a pervasive sense of movement, of speed. The signs were also exemplary of the "commercial vernacular" common to Main Streets across the United States, albeit in more monumental proportions in Vegas. They approvingly quoted Tom Wolfe on the signs: "They soar in shapes before which the existing vocabulary of art history is helpless."[47]

For many architects and urban planners this was precisely the nature of the problem—they found such signage gross, kitschy, and disordered. Venturi had upset many planning commissions seeking to regulate signage along America's boulevards by asking in 1966, "Is not Main Street almost all right?"[48] The Vegas Strip, too, was "almost all right." But the phrasing, as with Sontag, revealed ambivalence. When attacked for such statements, Scott Brown coolly replied on his behalf, well, he did say "almost."[49]

When Venturi and Scott Brown turned to signs, they were struck by their communicative zest and power. But they did little analysis of this form of communication. There was no attempt, for example, to consider Las Vegas signs in terms of Marshall McLuhan's theories about how media technology creates new environments, nor did they employ semiotics. Las Vegas was, in a sense, an "electric" speeded-up environment, with instantaneous reaction times (the toss of the dice, the jangle and flash of a slot-machine jackpot). It could, in McLuhan's terms, be seen as a form in and of itself and a "cool" medium, in his idiosyncratic terminology.[50]

They were also, of course, interested in the architecture of Vegas. First, however, they needed to discuss two types of buildings. One they called duck buildings. A famous photograph in a book by architect and critic Peter Blake showed a Long Island building from 1931 which was shaped like a duck, which signaled to all its function as a store selling ducks and eggs. A similar example would be a hamburger joint shaped like the object that it sold. They found such structures banal and boring. Second, they dismissed the huge, often glass-façaded modernist structures that were elegant, without a fault. These buildings were nothing more than "silly." Modern architects "have been designing dead ducks," in one way or another.[51]

Instead, Venturi and Scott Brown appreciated what they called "decorated sheds." Buildings of this type were common in Las Vegas. The decorated shed, they averred, employed "systems of space and structure" in "the service of program, and ornament [which] is applied independently of them."[52] This was what Venturi had done with the Guild House. Keep in mind that the Vegas that they were examining in the late 1960s had yet to sprout the monumental structures and Disneyland features that dominate the Strip today.

They admired the gargantuan, pulsating neon signs, revolving sculptures, and kitschy oddments. Unlike Thompson, they took them in without the deleterious effects of drugs on their consciousness. The signs themselves were sufficiently psychedelic. They beckoned drivers from the highway, and they were visible from miles away. They promised visitors pleasure and possibility, among other things. In their chaotic manner, they worked. The signs exhibited "vitality," showing the "value of symbolism and illusion in an architecture of vast space." And, perhaps most important of all, they were "fun."[53]

Venturi and Scott Brown examined some of the hotels, such as Caesars Palace. They delighted in its eclectic nature. It made the "ugly and ordinary" into something spectacular, with its various architectural styles mixed with humor and impunity. Many viewed the statues of Venus and David as pure kitsch—in bad taste. No, claimed Scott Brown and Venturi; the sculptures "grace the area around the porte cochere." Even the Palace's sign was "enriched" by the presence of sculptures of "Roman Centurions" at its base, "lacquered like Oldenburg hamburgers, who peer over the acres of cars and across their desert empire to the mountains beyond." Everything about Caesars was merrily "off-center" or teeming with a "combination of styles." Indeed, they concluded, "the agglomeration of Caesars Palace and of the Strip as a whole approaches the spirit if not the style of the late Roman Forum with its eclectic accumulations."[54]

The Vegas Strip captured the "messy vitality" that Venturi had celebrated in *Complexity and Contradiction*. The "iconography and mixed media of the roadside commercial architecture," Venturi and Scott Brown contended, "will point the way, if we look." The Flamingo Hotel sign was striking—the casino's name stretched out horizontally in neon, cursive script, above a colonnade (lighted, of course) that connected with the Strip. The Flamingo Hotel was essentially a silo structure with letters spelling out its name at its upper reaches. This architectural creation, for Venturi and Scott Brown, served as a "model to shock our sensibilities towards a new architecture."[55]

Scott Brown and Venturi appreciated the role of pop art in opening up new ways of seeing and thinking. They had read Wolfe on Vegas, appreciating not only his focus but his means of expression, his ability to employ "a prose style suitable to the description of Las Vegas."[56] In *Complexity and Contradiction*, Venturi wrote of the "vivid lessons" offered by pop art. Pop rejected false dreams of "pure order" in favor of appreciation for the chaos of the everyday and "contradictions of scale and context." He ended the main text of the volume with an invocation of the power of pop and its subject matter and style: "And it is perhaps from the everyday landscape, vulgar and disdained, that we can draw the complex and contradictory order that is valid and vital for our architecture as an urbanistic whole."[57] Pop further offered "new meaning to the immediate objects of our daily lives, often by changing their contexts."[58]

In her essay on the pop sensibility, published in 1969, Scott Brown praised pop's nonjudgmental approach and openness to plurality.[59] The work of such artists as Robert Rauschenberg and Roy Lichtenstein, as well as the Beatles and Dylan, was now established and taken seriously. In *Learning from Las Vegas*, the authors celebrated "Pop artists," such as Warhol, who "have shown the value of the old cliché used in a new context to achieve a new meaning—the soup can in the art gallery—to make the common uncommon."

This was liberating, to be sure, but Venturi and Scott Brown were sufficiently well-versed in literary history to know that such juxtapositions and shifts were also part of the living legacy of modernism. Borrowing a term from literary critic Richard Poirier, which they had come upon in an issue of the *New Republic*, they celebrated the "decreative impulse" in T. S. Eliot and in the "multitudinous styles" and openness to the sound and sense of everyday life that defined the genius of James Joyce's *Ulysses*.[60] This was the lively legacy of modernism before it had become ossified. In *Learning from Las Vegas*, Venturi and Scott Brown saw pop art as revivifying that older imperative—and they were thrilled.[61] As noted earlier, in many ways the New Sensibility was a new wave of modernism but also a wave of the postmodern—depending on how one chose to view it. In either case, it was surely part of the New Sensibility then regnant.

The insights and style drawn from pop and early modernism—mixed media, vitality, rejection of the staid, and more—could infuse architecture with new relevance and energy. Indeed, such innovations were already apparent in the "billboard aesthetic" that was the focus of *Learning from Las Vegas*. Scott Brown and Venturi were especially impressed with the work of artist Ed Ruscha. Along with their students, they visited his Los Angeles studio as part of their Las Vegas trip. Ruscha had a Robert Frank sort of aesthetic, an unwillingness to dwell on a scene, preferring to capture it quickly on his camera. With deadpan humor, Ruscha became in the early 1960s a chronicler of Los Angeles signage, architecture, and automobile culture. Using a small camera, he collected images of gas stations (always adorned with signage) and apartments.

He also photographed every building on the Sunset Strip (*Every Building on the Sunset Strip*, 1966), this time using a 35 mm camera mounted atop an automobile that cruised the street at a slow speed. It was a type of Andy Warhol project; whereas Warhol filmed someone sleeping, Ruscha made a long sheet of photographs of one building next to another. This technique would be featured in *Learning from Las Vegas*, as the students tried to document, in Ruscha style, every structure that lined the fabled Strip.[62]

"In the fine arts a new horror-giving energy source has been discovered: the popular," announced Scott Brown, much to the consternation of some architects. Critic Kenneth Frampton responded to this pop mania with incredulity, well before publication of *Learning from Las Vegas*.[63] The vision that Scott Brown and Venturi celebrated, in his view, was of "instant institutionalized vandalism," represented by kitsch objects and stupid parking lots. They seemed unable to realize that they were supporting "an industrially brutalized folk culture" that was ersatz; it was devastating the visual and physical environment rather than simply glittering benignly. Like pop artists (writers for the *New York Times* labeled Venturi and Scott Brown as "Pop Architects"), they refused value judgments; nor did they acknowledge the wealth and power behind the facades and signs.[64] They had surrendered, without a real fight, to an "urban society…organized towards self-defeating ends, on a sociopolitical basis that is totally invalid." Rather than transcending the numbing nature of kitsch, Scott Brown had offered a "perverse exultation" of it.[65] And, in comments that many would echo over the years, they showed a singular disregard for power, for the purpose of the signs—to create consumers, market commodity objects, and secure profits for business. On this score, Scott Brown protested meekly that she and Venturi were "analyzing Las Vegas for its physical form and not for its social or economic values." They were focused on "one variable" in their research—the "physical form" of the city, as expressed in its signage.[66]

One thing that drew them to Ruscha, and to pop in general, was his "deadpan style." According to Venturi, "We just wanted to look at Las Vegas in a dead-pan way which is a more poetic way of long standing."[67] In fact, in her reply to Frampton, Scott Brown argued strangely that Ruscha's work, like their own, was "not nonjudgmental." It was simply "deadpan."[68] Such a style, with its ironic distance, furnished Venturi and Scott Brown with ammunition to attack high modernism and to use language that was increasingly coming to be associated with postmodernism. But without burning bridges, in keeping with their celebration of plurality and openness.

Were Scott Brown and Venturi, then, connoisseurs of pop chaos, cheerleaders for the energy of early modernism, and exemplars of an emerging postmodernism? The architect Charles Jencks, who chronicled the decimation of the dream of modernism (pure in style and conception, rational, and orderly), also enumerated the streams of what he called "Post-Modern Architecture." The new architecture dealt with fragments (what better way to undermine imposed and lifeless order?), "ambiguity and jokes," mixing of style and meta-phor, and suspension of "normal categories of time and space, social and ra-tional categories...to become 'irrational' or quite literally impossible to figure out." The famous example employed later to illustrate this phenomenon ap-peared in Fredric Jameson's analysis of the Bonaventure Hotel in downtown Los Angeles, a structure that had no apparent central point, so that one was constantly disordered. The aim of all this was to "develop a stronger more rad-ical variety" of building.[69]

Such desires jibed well with imperatives of the New Sensibility and the views of Scott Brown and Venturi. Nevertheless, perhaps because of their "deadpan" propensities, they distanced themselves from the postmodernist designation. They identified more with the "revolutionary zeal" of early modernism than with the "classicism" that they oddly associated with postmodernism.[70] In 1978 Venturi stated, "I shall talk as an architect, not as a theoretician, but a Modern architect—not a Postmodern or neo-Beaux-Arts architect."[71] "Stylish post-modernism has picked up the image but not the substance of our quest."[72] In a 1997 interview, Scott Brown was more precise. Their historical sensitivity and desire for social planning distanced them from much of postmodernism. But perhaps she stated this in a deadpan manner, thus rendering the statement at once revelatory and concealing.[73]

A coda. The destruction of modernist notions of social planning and architec-ture became apparent, for some, a few months after publication of *Learning from Las Vegas*. On March 18, 1972, the first buildings of the Pruitt-Igoe public housing development in Saint Louis were razed. Only twenty-years old, once an ideal of perfection in urban planning, the project had become, in the words of a Saint Louis housing official, a "blot on the city," an incubator for crime and desolation. Thirty grim orange buildings, each eleven story tall, covering fifty-seven acres, displayed facades of broken windows and graffiti. The first blasts sounded from close to the ground. In a moment, explosives in two adjacent buildings ignited, and all three structures collapsing into themselves, clouded by a miasma of smoke. What remained, after the smoke had dissipated, was "the haunting eeri-ness of a bombed city...as if the holocaust had occurred the night before."[74]

What some saw as destruction of an old, false dream of order, others her-alded as the birth of new possibilities. In a famous analysis, Jencks, with no small amount of hyperbole, announced that destruction of the Pruitt-Igoe projects marked "the death of modern architecture." Jencks refused to shed a tear. Instead, he pronounced a new development—postmodern architecture, which for him flirted with the " 'irrational' or quite literally impossible to figure out." It paraded an eclecticism without bounds, fragmentation, "non-recurrent motifs, ambiguities and jokes," always moving in the direction of "the myste-rious, ambiguous and sensual." In many ways this was the type of ideals that Sontag had praised in the New Sensibility, and that would be central to the fiction of Thomas Pynchon and Samuel R. Delany.[75]

Scene from Deep Throat *(1972) (© Photofest)*

Divine in Pink Flamingos *(1972) (© Photofest)*

Erectile Destruction

SAMUEL R. DELANY AND THOMAS PYNCHON

1972

By the early 1970s, the United States appeared headed for a collective nervous breakdown. Bestselling books detailed the nation's "unraveling," marred by "dislocation," "disorientation," and "frustration." Many reasons were proffered for this descent into "misery, neurosis, and physical illness." The usual culprits were trotted out—the war in Vietnam, urban unrest, shifting gender relations, materialism, and the wobbly conclusion of the 1960s—all this before the Watergate scandal had squelched any naïve faith in American political leadership. Social critic Alvin Toffler worried about the jarring reality of life in a time of intense acceleration. Technologies of varied sorts produced overstimulation and excess that the population was ill-prepared to handle. It seemed no one was immune. Recall that amid the neon glow and the clatter of slot machines in Vegas (along with a pharmacopeia of drugs), our erstwhile friend Raoul Duke appeared "to have broken down completely."[1]

Nervous breakdown, a sense of "bewilderment," fed into existing veins of paranoia and madness. For those suffering from the malady, drugs offered a double-edged razor of escape. Religion (homegrown fundamentalisms and mystical imports) promised answers for all problems. The appeal of conspiracy theories was intense: everything could be explained, all contradictions resolved, all facts connected, simply by assertion and shards of evidence. Rather than a solution for the wearying effect of excess on the psyche, conspiratorial visions and mystical reveries became manifestations of it.

Nowhere was this more apparent than in two great works of fiction that were coming to life in 1972. These books caught the historical moment and pushed fiction into new territory.[2] Both realized the New Sensibility with exceptional brilliance. Genre distinctions in each book were dismissed. Ambiguity was enshrined. A passive reader was doomed. Sex saturated their pages. Ideals of liberation strutted alongside realities of control and destruction; cause and effect become confused. These huge novels—*Gravity's Rainbow* was over 750 pages, while *Dhalgren* pushed past 800 pages—refused easy categorization or summary. Around four hundred named characters populated *Gravity's Rainbow*; the novel was abuzz with references to films and popular culture; lyrics from perhaps forty songs dotted the pages. It included learned discussions of technology, of the history of the colonial destruction of the Herero tribe in southern Africa, Puritan theology, and too much to mention even in passing. Both books overflow and overwhelm with shifting narrative voices, more plots than a large cemetery, and prose that raced breathlessly or slowed to an aching crawl. The books were labyrinths of excess designed to entrap the reader in uncertainties.[3]

Here is science fiction writer William Gibson on *Dhalgren*: "I have never understood it.... That has never caused me the least discomfort, or interfered in any way with my pleasure in the text.... *Dhalgren* is not there to be finally understood. I believe its 'riddle' was never meant to be 'solved.'" The work was "experimental," "*something else*, something unprecedented."[4] Edward Mendelson famously referred to *Gravity's Rainbow* as an "encyclopedic narrative"— nothing seemed to escape its ken. Added critic David Leverenz, "The book was an act of calculated hostility against my own need to find out what it was about. In fact, *that* was what it was about."[5]

Thomas Pynchon delivered his manuscript to his publishers in January 1972. Then titled *Mindless Pleasures*, it would be published at the end of February 1973 as *Gravity's Rainbow*.[6] Although still not thirty-five years of age when he completed the manuscript, he was already famous for two novels, *V.* (1963) and *The Crying of Lot 49* (1966). Pynchon had spent five years working on the new novel, living mostly in Manhattan Beach, California—always far from the New York publishing scene. His paranoia and desire for privacy were singularly intense. Hardly any pictures of him exist. We know that he is tall and slim. His undergraduate pal from Cornell University Richard Fariña may have had him in mind in describing a character as having "huge teeth jutting forward like a beaver's."[7] Pynchon sometimes hung towels over windows for added privacy and quiet. Sometimes he remained in the apartment for weeks, working on his manuscript. But he was not a hermit. He ambled over to a café, the Fractured Cow, once reportedly bringing a steak with him to be cooked in their kitchen. While eating his dinner, he often wrote with intense concentration. He dated some women, including the daughter of Phyllis Coates, who had briefly portrayed Lois Lane on the *Superman* television show in the early 1950s and who lived across the street from him. Sometimes he had drinks with friends at the neighborhood bar. He never talked about his work, although most of his neighbors knew he was an author. All agreed that his knowledge was vast and his intelligence superior.[8]

Samuel R. Delany at this time was busy writing two novels simultaneously, *Dhalgren* (1974) and *Hogg* (not published until 1995); he also had a pornographic novel in the finished bin called *The Tides of Lust* (reissued as *Equinox*), which would come out in 1973. In contrast to Pynchon's manic anonymity, Delany unveiled his life for examination. Born to a middle-class black family in Harlem (his father owned a mortuary), he revealed his genius early, and he attended the Bronx High School of Science. He dropped out of college, married his girlfriend, the poet Marilyn Hacker, and together they lived as bohemians on the Lower East Side. For about six months in the late 1960s, Delany was part of a communal living situation. He took full advantage of the local avant-garde scene; indeed, in the summer of 1960 he had attended Allan Kaprow's *Eighteen Happenings in Six Parts*.[9]

Before he had turned twenty, Delany published his first work of science fiction, *The Jewels of Aptor* (1962). Over the next decade, he pumped out nine more volumes in that mode, including the Nebula Award–winning, *Babel-17* (1966). Delany reeled under various strains—overwork led to a nervous breakdown, with a three-week stay in a mental hospital. Although he had married Hacker, he knew that he was homosexual. Nonetheless the two maintained their relationship for many years and would in 1974 have a child together. But Delany was regularly on the prowl for homosexual "instant sex" during evening scurries to the rough dock area on the west side of the city. On one of his romps, around 1964, his partner turned out to be Jack Smith, the director of the avant-garde classic *Flaming Creatures*. Delany was impressed, since he had read Sontag's piece on it in when it had first appeared.[10] He also traveled frequently, composing *Dhalgren* in twelve different cities from its inception in January 1969 to its completion in September 1973. It was, he admitted, a "strange, mysterious, highly sexual, and experimental novel."[11]

Both novels featured befuddled protagonists in the midst of urban destruction. In *Dhalgren*, "the Kid" is in his late twenties but earned his nickname thanks to his baby face. He cannot remember his own name, although parts of his past are clear to him, and he knows that he is half Native American.[12] He recalls with especial clarity a childhood memory, appropriately, of being lost for hours until his parents found him wandering the streets. For unknown reasons, the Kid has come to the ravaged city of Bellona (although it is possible that he has been there the entire time). Bellona was once a thriving midwestern metropolis, its population now reduced from two million to a mere one thousand souls. Shrouded in a permanent haze, parts of it ablaze, the city is cut off from the rest of the nation. Why all of this is the case remains unclarified. "It is a city of inner discordances and retinal distortions," we are told. How this came about is left "opaque," although hints are proffered.[13]

Delany was writing, of course, at the time of the urban race riots of the 1960s and in the midst of urban decline. The riots were a response to police harassment, lack of political power, a dearth of employment opportunities, poor housing, and more. All of this was exacerbated by a tanking economy in the early 1970s. Inflation was rising; the price of a gallon of milk had become disgraceful. An oil embargo in 1973 and 1974 made gasoline expensive and scarce (creating rationing and long lines waiting for the few pumps with gas available). By the mid-1970s a new phenomenon known as stagflation (inflation without economic growth) had bloomed ugly. Major cities by the mid-1970s were unable to keep up services; crime increased; job opportunities plummeted (by 40 percent in Detroit); whites fled to the suburbs and Sun Belt. The fiscal plight of New York City became untenable. Mayor Abraham Beame headed to Washington to plead for financial help. The *New York Daily News* summed up the president's response as: "FORD TO CITY: DROP DEAD."

The majority of those who continue to live in Bellona are blacks—and it is regularly remarked how the white population seems to have forgotten about their existence. Perhaps there has been a race war, or some type of natural disaster, given later oddities that appear in the novel. People manage to survive in Bellona, mostly by living off the canned food stuffs remaining in abandoned houses and stores. It is, as one character puts it, a "saprophytic" existence—living off dead matter.[14] For all we know, the city may be nothing more than a fiction of desolation in the unstable mind of its main character. It is all very confusing. Some people—a poet (who may be a figment of the Kid's imagination) and a former astronaut—visit Bellona. And some people leave.

The jolting opening line of *Gravity's Rainbow* tosses readers into the London blitz: "A screaming comes across the sky."[15] In the midst of this terror, we are introduced to Lt. Tyrone Slothrop, a schlub with one peculiar attribute—he apparently has sexual intercourse in areas that are soon to be devastated by incoming V-2 rockets. Slothrop has a "talent for phallic rocket-dowsing," as one critic phrased it.[16] What makes this perplexing, and problematic, is that there is no easy explanation for this phenomenon, except for an amazing fact—a mad Pavlovian scientist had trained Slothrop's penis, when he was an infant, to become erect when rather mysterious stimuli are present. But if this is the cause, then the nature of cause and effect is undermined, since Slothrop's erections are predictive but often without any apparent stimulus. To further complicate matters, Pynchon's characters are fascinated with the antireality of the rockets—they travel at the speed of sound, so that you can be killed by a rocket before hearing its scream of impending doom. "Them fucking rockets. You couldn't adjust to the bastards."[17]

Edward Pointsman, a behaviorist scientist, demands, at any cost, to understand the connection between Slothrop's erections and the landing of V-2 rockets. Others from murky organizations are drawn to Slothrop as well, which leads to encounters both painful and comic. In his sallies around Europe, in the months around the end of the Second World War, Slothrop tries to elude his pursuers and learn more about a strange substance, Imipolex G, and about a potential rocket primed for mass destruction. He is also a man with a malleable identity. His roots reach deep into the soil of Puritan New

England, with its repression, anxiety, and fevered distinctions between the elect and the damned. But in the course of the novel, he appears at various times as a zoot-suiter, the comic book figure Rocketman, a reporter named Ian Scuffling, a Russian soldier, and, during a celebration taking place in a small German village, Plechazunga, a pig hero. Spontoon and Muffage (S&M) are medical officers aiming to castrate Slothrop, under orders from Pointsman. With especially poor timing, Major Duane Marvy, another of Slothrop's pursuers, puts on a pig costume, convinced that no MP will bother any "innocent funseeking pig." He is mistaken for Slothrop and gets castrated.[18]

In a novel pulsating with paranoia, there are a few moments of transcendence—through the eventual disintegration of Slothrop. It is reminiscent of Emerson's famous epiphany: "All mean egotism vanishes. I become a transparent eye-ball; I am nothing; I see all; the currents of the Universal Being circulate through me; I am part or particle of God." Slothrop's disintegration mirrors the increased fragmentation of the novel.[19]

The paranoia and conspiracy at the heart of *Gravity's Rainbow* fit perfectly with the Watergate Scandal.

On February 16, 1971, presidential aide Alexander Butterfield explained to Nixon the functioning of a hidden taping system in the Oval Office. Even Nixon's closest advisors were unaware of the system, which was the way Nixon wanted it. The tapes revealed Nixon intensely involved in foreign affairs (sometimes in a brilliantly insightful, albeit amoral manner) and as a foul-mouthed, anti-Semitic, racist, and paranoid figure. He trusted no one, a feeling which increased when Daniel Ellsberg, after photocopying seven thousand pages of text, leaked the Pentagon Papers to the *New York Times*. Publication revealed chicanery and deceit about the war in Vietnam at the highest levels of government, its role in the overthrow of the Diem regime, its initial justification for massively scaling up the war effort (an imagined or mistaken attack upon US warships in the Gulf of Tonkin in 1964), and much else.

In short order after publication of the papers, Nixon's team of operatives, known as "the plumbers," broke into the offices of Ellsberg's psychiatrist in search of incriminating evidence to destroy Ellsberg's credibility. They came up empty-handed, but within a year's time some members of the group would break into the offices of the Democratic National Committee in the Watergate complex.[20] Despite the efforts of Democrats, the Watergate fiasco played no role in the election of 1972, which saw Nixon romp over his opponent, Senator George McGovern from South Dakota. But Watergate refused to go away, thanks in large part to the investigative efforts of two reporters from the *Washington Post*. By 1974 it was clear that Nixon and his team were guilty of various crimes. The president was likely to be impeached by the House of Representatives, and with a certainty of conviction by the Senate, he resigned his office. Vice President Gerald R. Ford (Spiro T. Agnew had resigned the position for bribery, tax evasion, and other charges) became the new president, but only after he had agreed to grant Nixon a full pardon for his obstruction of justice.

The universe of *Gravity's Rainbow* stinks with the heavy scent of conspiracy and paranoia.[21] The excess central to the New Sensibility easily adjusted to this historical moment, bringing paranoia into its embrace. London is "the City Paranoiac."[22] And not just because of the V-weapons landing with a swish of deadly contingency; in London and Berlin, and other major urban centers, a "million bureaucrats are diligently plotting death" in various acronymic organizations and with industrial firms, such as I. G. Farben, General Electric, and other international cartels, together controlling everything from plastics to rockets.[23] As Pynchon surmised, truth is stranger than even his fiction. Nixon's reelection committee, which ended up knee-deep in the muck of Watergate, was named the Committee for the Re-Election of the President: CREEP.

In perhaps his best line in the novel, Pynchon quips: "What happens when paranoid meets paranoid? A crossing of solipsisms."[24] Late in the novel, one of the characters supplies a brief taxonomy of paranoiacs. According to Prentice, the humanist Roger Mexico is "a novice paranoid." Such a person can only go so far by believing in "a well-developed They-system." Alas, there's another half to the story, as understood by those suffering from "creative paranoia," which requires "developing at least as thorough a We-system as a They-System." This only further confuses Mexico, as well it should.[25] Nevertheless, along with Pig Bodine, in the name of anarchy and freedom, they crash a cartel dinner party. Their weapon is crude, alliterative language, which is all they have got: Mexico says, "I can't seem to find any *snot soup* on the menu." In response, Bodine jokes, "Yeah, I could've done with some of that *pus pudding*...with a side of— *menstrual marmalade*."[26] No victory is achieved, but they do manage to disappear from the novel—perhaps liberation in and of itself.

Despite the obsession with paranoia (and high number of deaths), Pynchon has enough humor and irony to leaven somewhat the density and despair of such themes. Consider the hilarious and disturbing section "The Story of Byron the Bulb." Byron is an "immortal" light bulb, which upsets Phoebus (the international light bulb cartel headquartered in Switzerland). They fear Byron since he (it?) never burns out (thus upsetting the principle of planned obsolescence) nor does it use electricity (thus depriving the power companies of income). As usual, Pynchon displays his vast research about how these companies were historically in cahoots to control power and light. Byron is a revolutionary of sorts, another reason why he must be unplugged. What if "a few Bulbs, say a million, a mere 5% of our number" flamed out in a "Guerilla Strike"? Like Slothrop, Byron manages to escape, sometimes in the most awkward manner. In Hamburg, with the bulb snatchers on his trail, Byron is placed by a male prostitute up the ass of one of his johns. The man, "a cost-accountant who likes to have light bulbs *screwed into his asshole*," who is also high on hashish, forgets the bulb up his anus. Later, Byron is plopped down in the toilet, floating for days "over the North Sea" before ending up in use at a hotel, with further adventures in the offing. Byron will, Pynchon informs us, "be screwed into mother (*Mutter*) after mother, as the female threads of German light-bulb sockets are known, for some reasons that escapes everybody."[27]

The world occupied by the Kid in *Dhalgren*, in contrast, is marked by the decline of technology (electricity in Bellona is at best erratic), the absence of bureaucracy and its enforcing minions, and the demise of the traditional family unit. It is, in many ways, an arbitrary place—the newspaper is issued sporadically, with dates that have no logic. At the same time, or perhaps because of the freedom of contingency, Bellona is a vision of an anarchist paradise, marred, however, by the knowledge that there is no such place as paradise.

While Delany was working on *Dhalgren*, the crumbling ideal of the patriarchal American family was being displayed on network television. In January 1971, a new television show, *All in the Family*, debuted with wild success. It captured the divisions that rent American families, with Archie Bunker an exemplar of the "silent majority" (although he was rarely silent when it came to cracking wise about his dislikes) while managing to present him as more than simply a narrow bigot. His morals were rigid and contradictory, constantly challenged by the New Sensibility and liberation that he neither understood nor embraced.[28] In 1971 the Public Broadcasting System spent weeks filming an American family living in Santa Barbara. Two years later, *An American Family* shocked audiences with its cinéma-vérité format, a peephole into the secret lives of the well-to-do but disintegrating Loud family. Before the show ended, Pat Loud had demanded a divorce from her husband, and Lance Loud, one of their children, had announced he was homosexual and determined to become a rock star.

In Bellona the traditional family became an illusion mirroring the apparent disintegration of family across the United States in the late 1960s and early 1970s. The Kid is hired by Mary Richards, a housewife madly striving to maintain an ideal family, to remove debris from an apartment in her building in preparation for the family relocating to presumably quieter confines. She is upset that the realty company in charge of the building has not responded to her complaints nor to her desire to move to the other apartment. Of course, as nearly everyone realizes, in Bellona the realty company is no more functional than everything else.

Mrs. Richards gallantly—and with a touch of madness—works to maintain order in a world run amok. She prepares dinner, sloshing together odds and ends from canned goods. Dinner is a formal occasion; the family awaits the return of Arthur Richards from work (but that, too, is a fiction, since he no longer has any employment). Daughter June, presumed to be the quintessence of virginal innocence, had, during the initial hours of the calamitous transformation of Bellona, engaged in violent sex in the streets with George Harrison, an especially well-endowed African American who she knew only by the heat of their mutual sexual desire. Since then he has become something of a superstar in the city, appearing naked in various poses on posters and even having a new moon that has mysteriously appeared named in his honor. In the midst of moving to the new apartment, June—perhaps by accident, perhaps not—pushes her younger brother Bobby to his death down an open elevator shaft. He had been threatening to tell their mom that June had secreted away a poster of Harrison. Another son lives in the city, under a new identity. The mother lives in severe denial, enabled by the rest of the family.

Alternative modes of community emerge to replace the traditional family. Anarchy, in Delany's vision, fosters benign order rather than violent disorder. Certainly his relationship with his wife was unconventional, even according to the loosened standards of the 1960s. During the winter of 1967 and early spring of 1968, Delany had been a member of a band and a commune both named Heavenly Breakfast. Most of the money supporting the commune came from drug dealing. The place, as Delany makes clear, was neither a democracy nor a utopia. But it was a space where sexual freedom reigned: "Sex, for all practical purposes, was perpetual, seldom private and polymorphous if not perverse."[29]

Upon arrival in Bellona, the Kid is greeted warmly by members of a hippie-like commune. Another early acquaintance is Tak, a former engineer who had spent time in prison for having sex with a minor. But Tak (who has a copy of Hunter S. Thompson's *Hell's Angels* in his bookcase) proves a generous host, sharing his provisions, offering the Kid a place for the night, and dispensing wisdom aplenty. He and the Kid will have consensual sex and become friends.

Much of the danger that presumably lurks in Bellona is attributed to a gang known as the Scorpions. Early in the novel, the Kid has a painful run-in with them. In time, however, he becomes a leader of the Scorpions, who live communally, look after one another, and prove to be rather tame in their outbursts. One of their main enjoyments is going on "runs," entering abandoned buildings and causing damage. Scorpions are Hell's Angel–like in that they have group solidarity and adorn themselves with chains. But they are also malleable in identity, sporting animal holograms.

At the outset of the novel, the Kid finds a loose-leaf notebook full of jottings. He keeps it and adds to it, creating a poetry that may or may not constitute revisions of what was already in the notebook—and which may have been in the possession of the Kid from the beginning, with all of the marks therein his own. (Delany had once lost a notebook with parts of *Dhalgren* in it.) Although the name Dhalgren appears among a list of names in the notebook, we also learn that there are at least four distinct handwritings gracing its pages. This could indicate multiple writers or the fragmented identity of its author.[30] The fog of mystery only deepens—it will not lift.

The first line in the notebook is mysterious: "*To wound the autumnal city. / So howled out for the world to give him a name.*" The Kid admits that such stuff is "pretty weird." He is soon preoccupied with the book, writing poetry, revising material already inscribed in it, almost always "puzzled at what he had done."[31] The Kid worries grievously, as many writers do, about whether or not a comma belongs in a certain spot—sometimes it seems to appear or disappear of its own will. When misplaced, like Kid's memory, it causes him tremendous unease, a sort of "quaking" with anxiety. Delany had experienced a nervous breakdown under the pressure of writing for a living, and the Kid admits that he may not touch pen to paper again, because, he says, "It's too hard.... I think it would kill me."[32]

Like memory, writing and authorship are confused. On the page in the notebook before the one containing the list of names is written: "In an age glutted with information, this 'storage method' is, necessarily, popular. But these primitive..." The remainder of the thought is missing.[33] "Glutted with information" is a good way of describing *Gravity's Rainbow*—and indeed one arm of the New Sensibility. Consider only the initial twenty pages of the book. We are introduced to well over ten characters by full name. And what names they are: Teddy Bloat, Osbie Feel, Maurice "Saxophone" Reed, Lord Blatherard Osmo, Bartleby Gobbitch, Corydon Throsp, and Joaquin Stick. In addition to the wonderfully funny and inventive names, Pynchon slips in puns and jokes. "Pirate" Prentice is driven to a destination "by his batman, a Corporal Wayne." (For those unfamiliar with the original comic strip or television and film versions, Bruce Wayne is the superhero Batman.) A goodly part of these pages is given over to Prentice's preparing an intricate banana breakfast (recipe included).

In the space of these initial pages, with his usual aplomb, Pynchon mixes high and mostly low cultural references, adopting the refusal of the New Sensibility to respect such divisions. Osbie Feel, in a masturbatory sort of moment, sings "Tell Miss Grable you're not able, / Not till V-E Day, oh." From pin up girl Betty Grable, she of the impossibly long legs, to W. C. Fields, Cary Grant, and Fuzzy-Wuzzies, the pop culture references fly. We are treated to a quote from physicist P. M. S. Blackett, perhaps mainly chosen for his initials: "You can't run a war on gusts of emotion."[34] Mention is made of the Crystal Palace (a spectacle of architecture from the Victorian period), of "second sheep" (a reference to Puritan theology), of "the mark of Youthful Folly" (a reference to the *I Ching*), and much more. French and German words appear, as well as words that are onomatopoeic: "whoomp." There is also a glorious reference to "bureaucratic smegma."[35] In Greek, smegma refers to soap, but in English it means "the secretion of a sebaceous gland; *specifically*: the cheesy sebaceous matter that collects between the glans penis and the foreskin or around the clitoris and labia minora"[36]—an apt conjoining of meanings, since the relationship between individuals in the novel is often mediated by shadowy bureaucracies and through sexual emissions—dirty meanings that soap cannot clean up.

Every page of *Gravity's Rainbow* teems with excess and absurdity. What about the "giant Adenoid," perhaps "as big as St. Paul's" cathedral, that threatens London? "This lymphatic monster" is met with fear, "cheap perfume," dancing chorus girls, and "observer balloons." The Adenoid is reported by the balloonists to be sloshing about in Hampstead Heath at the moment, acting "like a stupendous *nose* sucking in snot." The army comes to fight "the fiendish Adenoid," which is described as having "a master plan." But they fail:

> The Adenoid is blasted, electric-shocked, poisoned, changes shape here and there....A hideous green pseudopod crawls toward the cordon of troops and suddenly *sshhlop!* wipes out an entire observation post with a deluge of some disgusting orange mucus in which the unfortunate men are *digested*—not screaming but actually laughing, *enjoying* themselves.[37]

And this in only the first twenty pages of the novel.

Pornography, or at least works dealing explicitly with sex, had by 1972 gone mainstream. Modernist and experimental books once banned for explicit sexual content were now readily available in paperback editions. Enfolded within the plentiful pages of *Gravity's Rainbow* and *Dhalgren*, and even more in Delany's two other novels from these years, is plenty of hardcore sex and coprophilia. By this time the New Sensibility, with all of its excesses, faced relatively little censorship, although this is not to suggest that Nixon's silent majority was pleased with its cultural blossoming.

Underground newspapers regularly printed comics and dialogue that were sexually graphic, to the extreme. Although a few years earlier, some films, usually Swedish or Italian imports, had depicted sex in a graphic manner, these films had been challenged in court and forced to show in limited venues and only during late-night hours. *Deep Throat* (1972), all sixty-two X-rated minutes of it, helped to change all of this. In the view of cultural critic Ellen Willis, it was "the first porn movie to become a cultural event." It was also "a huge moneymaker." Its allure, some tried to argue, was in its quasi-feminist agenda— unlike traditional porn, the film concerned a woman achieving orgasm after orgasm. But this premise was thinner than an ultra-thin condom. The star, named Linda Lovelace, is sexually hobbled by an anatomical oddity; her clitoris is located deep down in her throat. The only way she can achieve orgasm— well, you get the point. The film was, Willis concluded appropriately, "about as erotic as a tonsillectomy."[38] Middle-class couples, however, lined up to watch this film about a young woman enamored of, and exceedingly skillful in, fellatio. That same year, *Behind the Green Door* opened, with its all-American, beautiful star Marilyn Chambers cavorting around. For those desiring a wee bit of acting talent in a porn star, Georgina Spelvin sizzled in *The Devil in Miss Jones* (1973).[39]

Limits on grossness seemed to have evaporated overnight. Graced with a wonderful sense of humor and irony, which allowed him to get away with lots of excess, John Waters premiered his film *Pink Flamingos* in 1972. Its star was an overweight drag queen named Divine. Along with her mother, Divine lives in a pink trailer with, of course, pink flamingos in front. The storyline is unimportant, other than to note that there is spouting blood in the film when a bunch of cops get hacked to death and then consumed. The film concludes with Divine, accompanied by two pals, walking down a street. A dog shits nearby, and Divine greedily picks up the poop in her hands and puts it in her mouth, gagging a bit and then smiling.

There is plenty of hardcore sex in *Dhalgren*, including a ménage à trois between the Kid, Lorna, and Denny, an underage boy. Delany had pushed it when describing the controversial sexual encounter between George Harrison and young June Richards. The heat burns as hotly as the fires of the riot that surrounds the pair—although whether it was a rape or consensual remains (as do most things in *Dhalgren*) up for grabs.

But in novels *The Tides of Lust* and *Hogg*, Delany refused to sugarcoat or hide anything. This was in keeping with his own personal penchant for revelatory memoir—he details his own particular sexual tastes, ranging from men with stubby, unkempt fingers to various sadomasochistic practices. For Delany, the transgressive nature of sexual experience is its own reward, casting off bourgeois repression, and perhaps opening a royal road to liberation. But in the novels, the path is made difficult by unbalanced power relations and pure horribleness.

In a 2004 interview, Delany quoted William Blake's familiar line "The road of excess leads to the palace of wisdom" in support of his pornographic compositions. The wisdom to be gained from *Hogg*, at best, appears to be that jealousy is an unnecessary emotion and contrary to liberation. An "active sexual life," according to Delany, undermines jealousy. Certainly the sexual life of Mr. Hogg and his pals is fully activated. But is such violent transgression morally valid when it leads to suffering, according to the novel?[40]

Hogg is gross. He is drenched in his own urine and feces. He needs sex on an almost hourly basis. The narrator of the tale, a teen called the Cocksucker, joins him in various "adventures." Hogg picks up money by engaging in professional "cunt bustin'." Hogg, along with Cocksucker and cronies Nigg and the Wop, is employed by men who have been humiliated by women to return the favor—a thousand times over. These "rape artists" assault one woman in the most vicious manner imaginable, while also having sex with one another during the romp. These sex scenes are offensive in their description and in their misogyny. They are joined by examples of horrific self-abuse, as when one character decides to drive a thick nail through his penis and then, using pliers, twists it around into a ring. He manages to survive, only to become a serial killer whose main refrain is "It's All Right."[41]

Hogg and *The Tides of Lust* seem to accept child sexual slavery, without any concern. At one point the Cocksucker is sold to a black fisherman named Big Sambo, who lives on a boat with his young daughter, Honey-Pie. She regularly services her father's sexual appetite. In *The Tides of Lust* the protagonist, the Captain (his ship is named *The Scorpion*, a clear reference to the gang in *Dhalgren*), has bought siblings in Bombay; they travel with him as crew and sexual objects for his lust. As the novel opens, Kristen is fifteen and Gunner is thirteen; they are sexually omnivorous. While the story is dotted with occasional reflections on art, the story of Faust, and recondite references to sixteenth-century necromancy, it is really an explosion of pornography—with anal sex galore, gang rape, and drinking of urine.[42]

Let's deal first with scatology. Slothrop, under the influence of sodium amyl (one of the euphoria-inducing drugs Hunter S. Thompson had packed for Vegas), relates a dream of sorts about the time he was at the Roseland State Ballroom, in an African American section of Boston. Appropriately, much of the account is a jazz riff, with references to a young Malcolm X (who actually worked at the joint) and to Charlie Parker. At some point, his harmonica goes "PLOP" into the "loathsome *toilet!*" Slothrop reaches into the toilet, inching deeper into its depths, "his virgin ass" exposed but unpenetrated. Shit surrounds him and he becomes "shit-sensitized," able to "identify certain traces of shit as belonging to this or that Harvard fellow of his acquaintances."[43] Memories of this episode occur twice more in the novel, and eventually Slothrop and his harp will be reunited.[44]

Sadomasochism figures centrally in two episodes, although it is not presented as necessarily liberating.[45] Nor is titillation the goal; it is more about the interplay between submission and freedom, weakness and domination. Brigadier General Ernest Pudding, who lost 70 percent of his men at the Battle of Ypres in the First World War, now atones for the death of those men by being dominated by the beautiful and mysterious Domina Nocturna. She tells Pudding, "You shall have your pain tonight...pain. The clearest poetry, the endearment of greatest worth." And she humiliates him royally, pissing into his mouth, then defecating and making Pudding consume her turds, "bread that would have only floated in porcelain waters somewhere" (a reference back to Slothrop's foray in the toilet).[46]

Katje is a sexually active young woman, to put it mildly. She is a sexual slave (of sorts), along with a young man named Gottfried, to the whims of Weissmann. Also known as Blicero ("White Death"), Weissmann looms as a figure of daunting evil and fanaticism that brings to mind Captain Ahab. Yet he has a poetic soul and is enamored of Rilke's poetry.[47] Humiliation of various sorts is the order of the day in Weissmann's world. Sometimes Blicero tries to push his "weary, often impotent penis" into Gottfried's meek mouth.[48] Unlike Katje, who is free to escape this sexual triangle, Gottfried is utterly in thrall to Blicero's sexual needs and to his larger plans. Critic Paul Fussell refers to the scene with this trio as "fantastic, ennobling, and touching, all at once."[49]

Much of the sex, with its sadomasochism and erections, is related to power and domination and, of course, connected with the penis-shaped V-2 rockets that open the novel and with the strange substance Imipolex, which figures in the construction of a new, earth-shattering rocket. In one scene, a fellow named Drohne, "a plastics connoisseur," is having an erection. A bit later he explains that Imipolex is "the material of the future." Perhaps the substance is connected with Slothrop's "hardon reflex."[50] Perhaps not. We do learn, however that Imipolex proves capable of causing intense sexual arousal and "is the first plastic that is actually *erectile*." This must be the stuff that dreams and rockets are made of.[51]

How to end a dystopic novel like *Dhalgren*? With the same mystery that rumbles throughout the book. A new disaster—a crashing plane, something that "looks like lightning," darkness invading the city, dust swirling, who the heck knows— but explosions may be happening. Under "slowly moiling clouds, the side came off a twenty-story building." Almost all the characters highlighted in the novel are part of a chaotic mass exodus heading out of the city. Someone says to George Harrison, "Them white men gonna kill us all 'cause of what you done today to that poor little white girl." Today? Wasn't that supposed to have occurred before the novel's timeline began? Is this a case of eternal recurrence? A glimpse of one character, Reverend Amy, seems to indicate her "rage," but closer examination suggests that "the expression struggling with her features was nearer ecstasy."[52]

"The burning city," writes Delany, "squatted on weak, inverted images of its fires." Those fleeing are met by a young woman who is heading to Bellona, just as the Kid had once done. Or is she a further figment of his own imagination, a sort of double for him? The girl is given an orchid, returning to the starting point of the novel. We learn that she writes with her left hand, furthering the connection between the destructive orchid and the power of writing. The Kid, we presume, is "too weak to write much." The final words of the novel break off in midsentence: "I have come to"[53]

Gravity's Rainbow concludes with poor Gottfried and the fate of our nation in the era of Richard M. Nixon. Gottfried is comfortably tight in the tail section of Rocket 00000, in an "Imipolex shroud," or what could be viewed as a condom.[54] He is something like a virgin ready to be sacrificed. The smell of the Imipolex that is "wrapping him absolutely" like a swathed baby brings back joyous childhood memories—no doubt sexual. Perhaps Gottfried, like Slothrop, has been conditioned as a baby to respond to certain stimuli.

The rocket—its "ascent will be betrayed by Gravity"—is headed for the Los Angeles area, specifically the Orpheus Theatre on Melrose Avenue.[55] The night manager of the theater is one Richard M. Zhlubb, whose nasal condition earns him the moniker "the Adenoid." Yes, we have returned to the early pages of the novel when a giant Adenoid threatened London. But it is now somewhat clear that this fellow Zhlubb is actually a stand-in for another adenoidally challenged figure, Richard M. Nixon!

Does all of this paranoia and absurdity in Pynchon's tale now hit close to home?

Erica Jong, around the time of the publication of Fear of Flying *(© Photofest)*

Zipless Abandon

ERICA JONG

1973

Early in the novel *Fear of Flying*, the fantasy of the "zipless fuck" is unveiled. It is the ultimate fuck, "a platonic ideal," or at least a prelude to masturbatory satisfaction. Yet, under certain circumstances, it's a fantasy that can be realized. Consider this. You are riding on a train, and you and a certain fellow lock eyes with swelling desire. Names and nationalities are unspoken. All that transpires is pure sexual congress, without any filibustering about room temperature, long-term commitment, or implications for unmentioned spouses or lovers. Anonymity and brevity are the hallmarks of a good zipless fuck. How, then, is it platonic in nature? Because despite the potential exchange of bodily fluids, the humping of sweaty bodies, and the intermingling of salty tongues, "the zipless fuck is absolutely pure...free of ulterior motives" other than, well, sexual pleasure.

The "zipless fuck" episode, as recounted by a delightful and sometimes distraught narrator named Isadora Wing, is a fantasy—one that she has personally never experienced. But as the pages of the novel unfold, she will experience in vivid detail a good deal of fucking, a threesome, and even a "zipless fuck" scenario.

Jong regaled readers with Isadora's anxieties and hopes, her wretchedness and allure, not to mention descriptions of her menstrual flow, forays in masturbation, expertise in the use of a diaphragm, and boredom with her marriage. Wing condemns her husband for, in her words, "never buying me flowers. And not talking to me. And never grabbing my ass anymore. And never going down on me, ever."[1]

One reviewer considered the book "a diatribe against marriage, against the dread dullness of habitual, connubial sex, against the paucity of means of reconciling the desire for freedom and the need for closeness, against childbearing." Writer William Brashler (who published a baseball novel this year), was so disgusted with this "thoroughly obnoxious book" that after reading about sixty pages he "threw it against the wall."[2]

No wonder that Jong later remarked that some of her critics imagined that *Fear of Flying* "represented the decline of Western Civilization."[3]

By the end of 1973, when first-time novelist Erica Jong published *Fear of Flying*, depictions of sex were startling but no longer readily considered by the public as pornographic. Ginsberg, Mailer, Bruce, and Sexton had pushed the envelope. Philip Roth's bestselling novel *Portnoy's Complaint* (1969) had thrilled, and disgusted, readers with its graphic sexual scenes, narcissistic, masturbating narrator, and obsessive confessional tone, and, let's not forget, Mr. Portnoy's rather imaginatively strained relationship with his ultra-Jewish mother. All the dirty linen of upwardly striving Jews had been displayed for the goyim to observe. In the section "Whacking Off" (which had appeared first within the highbrow pages of *Partisan Review*), Roth wrote, "Then came adolescence— half my waking life spent locked behind the bathroom door, firing my wad down the toilet bowl, or into the soiled clothes in the laundry hamper, or *splat* up against the medicine-chest mirror, before which I stood in my dropped drawers so I could see how it looked coming out." Just wait until thirteen-year-old Alexander Portnoy has real sex as an adult![4] Not surprisingly, reviewers may have occasionally wondered if the book was thinly disguised memoir, but all recognized that its salacious content and ribald humor had made it a monumental success.[5] Erica Jong stated, "I loved that book....I reread *Portnoy's Complaint* many times."[6]

Pornography, or at least works dealing explicitly with sex, as seen in the previous chapter, had gone mainstream.[7] The 1960s were, as noted, the time of the sexual revolution. Gone were the older taboos against sex before marriage, concerns about unwanted pregnancy (use of the birth control pill had become widespread in the early 1960s), and fear of being considered a slut for enjoying sex with more than one partner. While it is nice to indulge in nostalgia for the Elysium of the sexual revolution, for many women it was stillborn. Males, freed of concerns about getting their sexual partners pregnant (at least as part of *their* responsibility), reveled in the possibility of sex without commitment and continued to objectify women, now castigating them as prudes if they were closed to sex. Many politically committed, idealistic young women worked in the civil rights and antiwar movements. Sometimes they put their bodies on the line by going into Ku Klux Klan–infested regions of the South to register African Americans as voters and to support civil rights. Violet Liuzzo's temerity in working on behalf of civil rights cost her her life. Yet women in radical organizations continued to be relegated to secretarial work, cranking the mimeograph machines or typing press releases. And they were expected to put their bodies on the ground for sex with alpha-male leaders, which they were told served both the movement and the sexual revolution. As the charismatic Black Power leader Stokely Carmichael was reported to have put it, "The only position for women in the movement is prone."[8]

Such dissatisfaction with the missed potential of left-wing politics as a royal road to liberation for women fed into the second wave of feminism in the 1960s and 1970s. Using organizing and office skills learned in various movements, radical women began to agitate for social and legal equality, for reproductive freedom, and much more. The women's movement was never really a single entity; some women found common ground with the National Organization for Women (founded in 1966), with its middle-class ideology; other women preferred consciousness-raising and direct-action approaches. Some women, including radical feminists Roxanne Dunbar and Ti-Grace Atkinson, floated the idea that celibacy might best allow women to break free from the yoke of males. Others increasingly argued that women loving women was the key to both personal and political liberation. This was the position of a group in the early 1970s called Radicalesbians in New York City. For feminist critic and activist Jill Johnston, writing in 1973, the split between straight and gay women was immense. To be a lesbian meant that one was not sleeping with the enemy but was also in the vanguard against patriarchy, combining the personal and political, as all revolutionaries must do. This sentiment, of course, was hardly restricted to feminists; it was a key point for followers of the New Sensibility.[9]

Despite schisms in feminism, victories were achieved in the early 1970s, most importantly on January 22, 1973, when the United States Supreme Court ruled in the case of *Roe v. Wade*. At issue was whether the Fourteenth Amendment, protecting privacy, applied to a woman's right to have an abortion. The case had been brought before the court by Norma McCorvey, who was impoverished and pregnant with her third child. In the case, originally filed in 1970 when she was six months pregnant, she had been referred to as Jane Roe. Although legal rigmarole prevented her from having an abortion (she gave the child up for adoption), the decision was a tremendous victory for women's liberation—enshrining their right to control their own bodies. As McCorvey put it in her memoir, "Prior to *Roe v. Wade*, approximately one million women had illegal abortions each year. Approximately 5,000 of these women were killed."[10] She was proud to have been the Joan of Arc of reproductive rights.

Everywhere one turned in 1973, the fight for women's rights raged, often in unlikely places. "The Battle of the Sexes" was perhaps the most egregious and fascinating example. It was a much ballyhooed tennis match between Billie Jean King and Bobby Riggs. The match was televised nationally on September 21, watched by an audience of forty million; an additional 30,492 were present at the Houston Astrodome for the occasion. The winner-take-all purse was a sweet one hundred grand, but both winner and loser realized that ancillary earnings would top that figure. ABC planned to make a killing, too, with commercials for the two-hour special bringing in over $1.2 million.[11]

Some referred to it as a "circus"—with good reason. Riggs was wheeled to the tennis court on a rickshaw, led by Bobby's bosomy beauties; King arrived on some sort of Egyptian-themed litter and carried by scantily clad young

men. Once the athletes were free from their conveyances, the hoopla continued apace. Riggs presented King with a two-foot-long Sugar Daddy candy
bar. Perhaps it was a joke about him being a monetary sugar daddy for King,
or implied that he was a sucker for taking her on. Not to be outdone, King offered Riggs "a little male chauvinist piglet," in recompense for the many sexist
statements that Riggs had spewed during the buildup to the confrontation.[12]

Aside from the hustle and hype, something more was happening in this
match. Four months earlier, Riggs had suckered Margaret Court, a leading
woman's tennis star, to play him for $10,000. With goofy shots, and sheer
chutzpah, the fifty-five-year-old has-been had managed to defeat Court easily.
Court's humiliation struck King as a setback for women's tennis. A strong feminist, King had organized the National Women's Tennis Federation and fought
for equity in purses for tennis championships for men and women. She had
furthered the cause by hooking up with Virginia Slims, a cigarette brand mar-
keted to women, to sponsor a tournament that paid women handsomely. Not
only did she have to take up Riggs's challenge, she had to beat him, or else her
accomplishments for women's tennis "might go right out the window." One
leading male tennis player, Gene Scott, stated: "You see, women are brought up
from the time they're six years old to read books, eat candy, and go to dancing
class.... They can't compete against men.... Maybe it'll change some day. But
not now."[13]

King demolished Riggs in straight sets, 6–4, 6–3, 6–3. She was hailed as the
"Joan of Arc of athletics."[14] King made no claim for her ability to beat a quality
male player in his prime. She simply wanted to put to rest the view that women
could not compete, that women's tennis was less interesting than the men's
game and hence less deserving of recompense. In the process, she was happy
to walk away with more money that anyone had ever won in a tennis match.
And what was wrong, after all, with scoring a small victory in the proverbial
battle of the sexes?

Into the ferment of this moment in sex and gender controversy came Erica
Jong's *Fear of Flying*. She was only thirty-two years of age at the time of publication, but she had already issued two books of poetry, *Fruits and Vegetables*
(1971) and *Half-Lives* (1973). The latter volume, as Jong remarked, contained
"poems about obsessive sexuality." Her own reading of confessional poets
Sylvia Plath and Anne Sexton (who became a friend) had broadened horizons
for what poetry—and her novel—could accomplish. It contained thinly veiled
allusions to the vicissitudes of her life, including sexual ones: of her husband:
"Cooking or fucking, you live in your skin." And one poem captured in a
handful of words the imperative that defined *Fear of Flying*: "She stands on the
edge / still hoping / she can fly."[15]

Jong had been working on a novel for many years. But she later realized that
she was writing against herself, against her inclinations. The novel, with the

working title *God on West End Avenue*, was Nabokovian in style—"because I loved Nabokov and had read and reread everything of his." The novel, written in a first-person male voice, was "about a young madman who thought he was God." She abandoned the project, she later claimed, because it was "difficult to sustain the madman's viewpoint and also show the things that were happening in the outside, 'sane' world." Inhabiting the mind of a madman, she said, "finally overwhelmed me." As well it should have, for the additional reason that her first husband had gone mad, experiencing delusions of divinity. Another abortive novel followed, until "with great trepidation" she turned her considerable enthusiasm and talent to *Fear of Flying*.[16]

Within a few years, the manuscript was ready. The book's cover was as busy as the novel's heated prose. It depicted a colorful Cupid, with a red sash hiding his private parts. The part of the sash in Cupid's hands looks to be in the shape of a penis, but this could be an overinterpretation. Androgynous, this Cupid looks a bit like Jong, with curly blond hair. Adam and Eve frolic in Cupid's wake, hardly ill at ease at being forced out of the Garden of Eden. The main locales for the novel, Austria and New York City, are also depicted, the former through architecture, the latter via a small map of Manhattan. A plane is aloft at the top of the cover, and at the bottom is a train—conveyances of escape and freedom. The plane, like freedom, as we learn early in the novel, also brings the potential for fear of crashing. A train, in contrast, is identified as a perfect place for a "zipless fuck," in reality or as a place to dream about it.

On the inside back cover, readers encountered a picture of the author. Jong is striking, her blonde locks flowing and her smile glistening. Normally, an author's photograph would not merit any attention. But it does on occasion, as it once had with Truman Capote's rather louche portrait on the back cover of *Other Voices, Other Rooms*. There is really nothing inherently vixen-like in the photograph of Jong. But, thanks to the content of the novel and its erasure of lines between fiction and experience, the picture became an object of discussion—or, perhaps, more of desire.

Initial reviews of the book were mixed, until novelist John Updike weighed in with "Jong Love" in the *New Yorker*. Updike was the perfect reviewer—impeccable literary credentials and a long list of novels that explored with brashness the sexual mores of middle-class Americans, especially from a male point of view. His adoration was boundless. He called *Fear of Flying* "this lovable delicious novel." And so, too, was its author. "On the back jacket flap," Updike noted, "Mrs. Jong, with perfect teeth and cascading hair, is magnificently laughing." Since the line between the author and the content of the book was blurred, Updike also noted that Jong/Isadora was "admiring…even of the impotence, madness, and defective hygiene of her many awful lovers." What more could a sagging middle-aged reviewer want than a beautiful author, with sterling feminist credentials, who could not only endure such problems but admire them?

The novel, in Updike's paean, was better than *Catcher in the Rye* ("a smart kid's lament" and "innocence as an ideal") and *Portnoy's Complaint* ("the New York voice on the couch" and "cruel"). She shared those work's humor and idealism, while staying in the real world. The novel was well-acquainted with the raging war between the sexes, but it managed not to dig a trench between them. It offered hope of reconciliation—and sexual release.[17]

Soon after, the aged king of sexual license, Henry Miller, compared *Fear of Flying* with his own, long-banned but now available, classic, *Tropic of Cancer*. He wrote a fan letter to Jong in April 1974; "I don't know when I've read a book by a woman which has made such an impact on me." *Fear of Flying* was "gay, witty, thoroughly uninhibited" in its writing and, he perceptively remarked, with a "serious side," full of suffering. "It is a text book as well as a novel or autobiography."[18] Biographer Nancy Milford was impressed and insightful, writing to Jong: "For all its wit and sexual daring it is a sad book."[19]

The same conflation between author and character was in evidence among reviewers less smitten with Jong and her book. A reviewer for *The Nation* consigned the novel to the unfulfilling, narcissistic, politically irrelevant genre of "dear diary" complaining.[20] Critic Patricia Meyer Spacks agreed: the novel was burdened with "self-pity and self-display." Its characters, most damningly, "directly articulate the author's beliefs or sensibility."[21]

If Updike was seduced by Jong's attractiveness, literary critic Alfred Kazin was repelled by it. He titled his piece "The Writer as Sexual Show-Off." "Erica's sweet, confiding blond prettiness" was on display in "interview after interview," where she admitted, no doubt with a certain coyness, that *Fear of Flying* was "autobiographical" and that Isadora's "lovable weaknesses could be hers." The book was not a novel but a confessional, coming from "a regular girl who confides to her reader that she is always looking for love but determined not to be dominated." She is the face of feminism as a "nice, pretty Jewish girl."[22]

Women reviewers also examined the confluence between author and character—and the author's photograph. Film critic Molly Haskell reviewed the book favorably in New York's *Village Voice*: "'Fear of Flying' is definitely a vehicle for exceeding the limits on the open road." As to the dust-jacket image of Jong, Haskell noted "her blond hair billowing across her sensually grinning face, ripe, juicy."[23]

Jong was dismissed by some as a "sexual show-off." It was a heady time for her—she was a bestselling novelist, interviewed everywhere, solicited for her opinion, especially on sexual matters, and often paid quite nicely. Thus, the May 1975 issue of *Esquire* featured a story by Jong titled "Notes on Five Men." Therein she discussed the "woman's sensibility" with respect to Paul Newman, Al Pacino, Robert Redford, Steve McQueen, and Charles Bronson.

There is truth, of course, to the charge leveled by academic Charlotte Templin that Jong's reception focused on her more as "a woman rather than as a writer." But in an emerging age of celebrity this was the fate of many serious writers. Some opted for it consciously—Sexton comes readily to mind. Others, such as Sontag, had a more ambivalent relationship to it. Jong, in addition to relating her views about male movie stars, readily dispensed sexual advice in *Playboy* magazine, appeared regularly on television and radio shows, and worked tirelessly to promote both herself *and* her novel.[24] The *Playboy* interview was particularly gutsy, as Jong—often with tongue in cheek—talked about sexual preferences (intimacy above all, but in the act a large cock and sure stroke were best), pornographic movies (ten minutes watching one made her want to spring home for the real thing, but longer viewing was a turnoff) and openness to the varieties of the sexual experience ("I think it's nice to do it in all different positions, different ways, including hanging from the chandelier"). Jong was in command of her performance for *Playboy*, a publication aimed at heterosexual males.[25]

Whatever her heady relationship to celebrity, Jong was keenly aware that her persona was embedded in the novel. She related a conversation that she had with her friend Anne Sexton. She asked Sexton, "What do I do when men come up to me...and start saying, 'Hey, baby, I want a zipless fuck'? And Anne replied, 'Thank them. Thank them and say, "Zip up your fuck until I ask for it."[26]

Ah, there it is again, the equation of the novel with an autobiography. Two questions arise: Was it true, and, if so, was it a problem or just an indicator of how the New Sensibility was tied into the feminist ideal of the personal and the political being intertwined?

Jong was inconsistent about how much of her own life was reflected in the saga of Isadora Wing. One interviewer prefaced her first question to Jong as follows: "This is the question everybody's asking, so let's get it over with: How much of *Fear of Flying*'s Isadora Wing is really Erica Jong?" Jong's reply: "Sure, there's a lot of me in Isadora, but a lot of characters and events in the book are totally invented. I didn't set out to write autobiography." At best, the book could be called a "mock memoir" in the same manner *as Portnoy's Complaint* or *Tropic of Cancer*. She admitted in the *Playboy* interview that while "Isadora is an alter ego," she "is 100, 000 times more audacious, more outrageous."[27] "I hate the confusion between myself and the character," she told a reporter, "because the book is hyperbole. I don't think I'm as sexy as Isadora." Nonetheless, the reporter emphasized, no doubt to Jong's chagrin, "Everything that happens to Isadora happened first to her creator."[28] Novelist Cynthia Ozick wrote Jong that *Fear of Flying* was a memoir "fully fictionalized." In reply, Jong admitted that her book "has the *feel* of a memoir—but there's more fiction in it than I can remember."[29] Finally, in another interview, Jong lamented, "But as long as I'm young and pretty, things will not be easy. People confuse me with my writings."[30]

With good reason, beyond both Isadora and Jong being "young and pretty." For example, both characters had been married and divorced from a bearded young man who had gone insane; both were married to a Chinese American psychiatrist; both were from the Upper West Side, grew up wealthy, and were educated at Barnard and Columbia; both had been in psychoanalysis for years; both had lived in Germany; both had mothers with artistic leanings. But this does not mean that the novel was a simple transcription of life onto the page. No less than with Sexton, it was experience rendered into art, by dint of voice, narrative techniques, and vision.

But, then, what is the problem? Some critics refused to see the art in the telling. The criticism lodged by Kazin against Jong was similar to that thrown against confessional poets or Roth in *Portnoy's Complaint*, that the self must be distanced from the words on the page, lest it be insufficient as art. But the presumption is mistaken. First, no writer can capture with absolute veracity him- or herself and translate it onto the page. The very act of writing is selective, and hence marked by the intercession of an editing, even censoring mind (even with Kerouac's attempts at spontaneous prose). Nor is there anything inherently problematic about using one's experiences and inserting them into the story. In biography or memoir the material must be reined in by a regime of truth, of fact-checking. In a novel, such constraints do not apply.

Another potential concern with too close an identification between author and character is lack of perspective, or a perspective that erases nuance, coming as it does presumably unfiltered from the writer. The same criticism, it would seem, applies to memoir or autobiography. The essential key, then, is whether the writer—in whatever mode of presentation—writes with self-examination, with openness to complexity, and without resorting to stereotyping. And it is also necessary for the fiction writer to prove, in confessional or "mock memoir" writing, that they are part of an historical moment, transforming themselves from a self-recording, narcissistic unit into something more.

Jong succeeded admirably on these fronts. She caught and rode the waves of the feminist and sexual revolutions to shore.

Fear of Flying is a spirited and lusty Bildungsroman. It traces Isadora Wing's coming to terms with her own anxieties and limitations. At the outset of the novel she is afraid of flying, in a literal sense, but also in the sense of being afraid of experiencing life, undertaking a journey, committing to her artistry.[31] Yes, many of her fantasies revolve around uninhibited sex, but it is more complicated than that. She takes pains to make clear that her husband is an accomplished, insatiable lover. But his silences and stony demeanor make her feel alienated from him. Yes, in the spiral of the novel, Isadora does attempt to break free sexually. But the results are mixed—and ironic—at best. And that is as it should be. Fantasy is a vehicle of both escape and avoidance; it is also a means to coming to terms with limits and to discovering new possibilities in art and life. As Jong later put it, "In *Fear of Flying*, I wanted to slice open my protagonist's head and reveal the fantasies within.... Most of the sexual escapades were disappointing compared to the lavishness of Isadora's fantasy life. Perhaps that's the case with most people."[32]

Early in the novel, while at a psychiatric conference, Isadora eyeballs the ultimate partner for a "zipless fuck"—a blond, handsome, hippyish Laingian psychiatrist with a perfect name Adrian Goodlove. He claims to live for the moment, open to all pleasures, most assuredly including sexual ones. Alas, the outwardly virile Adrian is, much of the time, impotent. Beyond the sexual element, Adrian represents—at least in Isadora's still developing consciousness—an ideal of freedom. She opts to flee with Adrian on a road trip, but the journey is mostly frustrating and sometimes harrowing.

Finally, arriving in Paris, Isadora is determined that she will return to her husband, if he allows. Liberation certainly has its limits and betrayals, as Isadora learns the hard way. "I'd like to *kill* you," she screams at Adrian, after finding out that his claims to be unencumbered in relationships is a sham. His mocking response: "'I only wanted to give you something to write about,' he laughed."[33]

All of the male characters in the novel, no less than the female lead, are presented with warts intact, but also with their good sides gleaming. Isadora's first husband may start out as an odd genius that develops into a raving paranoid, but he is exciting, and she recognizes how she benefits from her relationship with him, in both healthy and problematic ways. And such, too, is the case with herself.

The novel is about coming to self-consciousness and liberation. Isadora Wing succeeds in the former admirably, albeit with difficulty. The latter, she comes to recognize, is the result of a difficult process, a long journey. Isadora, alone in a Paris flea-bag hotel, awakens to find herself with "blood welling up between [her] legs." She continues: "If I parted my thighs even a little, the blood would gush down and stain through to the mattress." The bloodletting is, of course, symbolic—indicating that she is not pregnant and that her twenty-eight-day ordeal may be coming to a conclusion: "Menstruation was always a little sad—but it was also a new beginning." She will not confuse liberation with license, or give in to absurd romantic longings. "I knew I wouldn't screw up my life for the sake of a great self-destructive passion."[34]

She leaves Paris by train. A "young train attendant in a blue uniform" helps her with her heavy luggage. He reappears later, asking if Isadora might prefer to have a compartment of her own—what a kind gesture, she thinks. He even begins "pushing the armrests up to make a bed for [her]. Then," she goes on, "he ran his hand along the seats to indicate that it was a place to lie down." In a few moments, "His hand was between my legs and he was trying to hold me down forcibly." Isadora calls him a "pig" and escapes to another compartment, filled with people, finding comfort and protection in their midst. And then she comes to her realization:

It dawned on me how funny that episode had been. My zipless fuck! My stranger on a train! Here I'd been offered my very own fantasy. The fantasy that had riveted me to the vibrating seat of the train for three years in Heidelberg and instead of turning me on, it had revolted me![35]

The novel ends with Isadora installed in husband Bennett's London hotel room, waiting for his return. She is determined, it seems, to continue the relationship, but also to survive, aware at last that her fear of being herself, of flying into new realms of experience and art, has finally dissipated. She becomes the existentialist that Adrian claimed to be: "Surviving meant being born over and over. It wasn't easy, and it was always painful. But there wasn't any other choice except death."[36]

Fear of Flying was an immense success. Within a few years, thanks to a paperbound edition in 1975 with a sexy cover of a partially naked woman, the book had sold six million copies. As Jong liked to relate, the book had clearly touched a nerve among readers. Certainly, many were attracted to the book for its sexual content. But, in fact, by the 1970s much steamier content was readily available, both on the screen and in romance literature and magazines. In 1973 *Playgirl* magazine debuted, with its centerfolds of male nudes. A year earlier, actor Burt Reynolds was shown bare-assed in a centerfold for *Cosmopolitan* magazine. Clearly, if women wanted to find lusty writing and sexual scenes, they could turn elsewhere. Certainly, despite Kazin's criticisms, Jong was a serious writer, which did grant legitimacy to her work. She had, after all, previously published two collections of poetry, won writing awards, taught part-time at Columbia, and had her novel offered by a mainstream publishing house.

The book resonated because it was of its time and place—a salvo in the war of the sexes. Its appeal was in part that it was written by a woman, with ribald humor and matter-of-fact dealing with sex—often in minute detail. This was a time when second wave feminists were dissecting the canon of literature, finding sexism and patriarchy in its very sinews. This was a mission of the highest order. Feminist critic and activist Kate Millett, in her influential *Sexual Politics* (1970), opened her attack with a diatribe against Henry Miller, who would soon champion Jong. Miller's protagonist "is always some version of the author himself, is sexually irresistible and potent to an almost mystical degree," wrote Millett. But sex and literature serve the purposes of patriarchy, the "male assertion of dominance over a weak, compliant, and rather unintelligent female."[37]

Jong maintained that one could be a strong feminist and a devotee of Miller. Her novel was a reversal of the Henry Miller ideal of the male as sexual predator. Isadora's husband is potent but passive; Adrian is impotent but active. Isadora walks a tightrope between being a loony dame falling head-over-heels in love with an attractive idiot and being a strong female figure. After all, as one reviewer pointed out, one of the problems with Isadora Wing as narrator is that she is so smart, capable, and biting in her observations. Perhaps in this ambivalence, in presenting a character of some complexities as unresolved, Jong created in Isadora Wing some version of everywoman, or at least, a fantasy of everywoman.[38]

Many women readers found the novel spoke to their own frustrations—with marriage, career, sex, and the feeling that they were unable to liberate themselves. And they reveled in its self-revelation and honesty.[39]

One reader from England announced, "It's my story. If you had lived next to me or even inside my skin all of my life, you could not have created a more vivid or real portrait of my doings, my feelings, my fantasies, my (mis)adventures, in short, my history." In her first fan letter, Scena Lee Brooks, from West Palm Beach, wrote, "I just had to let you know 'Fear of Flying' hit the nail on the head. A 'zipless fuck'—how many girls have just wanted that," and then she proceeded, in great detail, to relate her own personal story. In the same vein, Gene Steinman, from Lula, Georgia, shared intimate aspects of her life in six single-spaced, typed pages. "To me, the novel is pure allegory. Allegory for the reason that I have traveled the same road." Even some men wrote to Jong to celebrate her achievement: "I don't think I've ever read a book so filled with love and humor and poetry," one male reader wrote. And, like Updike, he was smitten. "I'll just say that I've fallen in love with you from this great distance.... I hope that you will keep on writing forever." And, by the by, he would be happy to buy her a beer anytime she happened to be in Greensboro.[40]

With her characteristic bravado (perhaps consciously mimicking Mailer's ambition to "create a revolution in the consciousness of our time"), Jong stated that *Fear of Flying* "signaled a switch in the female consciousness and encouraged women to change their lives." As the letters quoted above attest, she succeeded in that goal. Equally important, and connected with that desire, was how the novel captured sexual *jouissance*, the notion that women had roiling and unfulfilled (and valid) sexual wants and fantasies. As Jong put it, "You can have pleasure; sex is not so serious." Hence, the "zipless fuck" became "a catch phrase that was needed at that moment in history."[41]

But freedom is never absolute, never unanchored in social, class, gender, and economic webs of significance. The sexual revolution in the minds of some had confused license with liberation. For others, it had not gone far enough in challenging patriarchal and other presumptions. Jong was well aware of this, as she continued to chart Isadora's life journey in other novels.[42]

Chris Burden, Trans-fixed *(1974) (© Chris Burden; courtesy Gagosian Gallery)*

Crucified and Shot

CHRIS BURDEN

1974

The morning mist lingered around the seaside town of Venice, California, on April 28, 1974. On the quiet, sleepy street inaptly named Speedway Avenue, strange doings were afoot. Twenty-eight-year-old artist Chris Burden was already infamous for his piece *Shoot*. In it he had had himself shot in the arm—for art, for experience, for who knows what reason. Since then he had been buzzing with ideas and carrying them out in performances, ranging from nearly being electrocuted, to locking himself in a small locker for five days, to writhing across a floor strewn with broken glass, to name only a few. Today he had something else in mind.

Burden was joined by only a handful of others, including his lawyer, in the shabby, peeling-paint garage. At the appointed moment, Burden, clad in dark jeans, white T-shirt, and sneakers, backed up to a blue Volkswagen Beetle, brought himself up on the bumper, and leaned against the sloping backside of the car. He then lifted his hands up so that his attorney could drive two nails through the palms of his hands and into the car roof. The VW engine revved up—a sound that Burden later described as a loud whistle. His pals then rolled the car into the middle of the street. The engine had whirred loudly for two minutes, as if screaming in lieu of Burden's silence. The performance piece ended when the car was pushed back into the garage and the nails removed, freeing him from the Volkswagen. The audience for the piece was confined to his co-conspirators and a handful of local residents gawking from their windows. Artifacts from the performance were a photograph of Burden stoically impaled upon the car and the two nails, which would later be exhibited with a plaque. "Physically, it was no big deal," he later stated; all that remained was "a little scar, a little black thing" on each of his palms, the stigmata of Burden's excess. The hardest part, he admitted, had been the anticipation.

The piece was laden with religious symbolism. Despite such heaviness, the performance managed to resist interpretive closure. Although Burden was not

Catholic, he had lived in Italy and been surrounded by images of Jesus on the Cross. "I've thought," Burden later revealed, "about being crucified lots of times." Certainly the piece could be read as a mea culpa from Burden, ironically atoning for earlier outrages against his body and establishment art. Maybe it was a wry commentary, too, on postwar America's willingness to forget the intimate connection between the "people's car" (Volkswagen) and the atrocities of Nazi Germany (during the Second World War, the car was partly built by slave labor). Was it, art historians asked, a sort of shamanistic performance, or simply an act of male power and ego?[1] Or perhaps it was just another opportunity for young Mr. Burden to offend the sensibilities of almost everyone by abusing his body and living up to his reputation as the bad boy of the art world.[2] In an understatement, one art historian remarked, "Burden has made an entire career of defining the edge." And, no doubt, of transgressing it. The pleasure, to his mind, came from "redefining art."[3]

Whatever his motivations, Chris Burden's performances in the early 1970s were exemplary of the New Sensibility. The distance from Cage's $4'33''$ to Burden's performance pieces is minimal, of degree more than kind. If Cage wanted to open the audience up to sounds heretofore unheard, Burden tried to open them up to the pain of everyday life. Cage and Sontag were fascinated with the power of boredom to create new possibilities. So, too, was Burden, as he slept in a bed for twenty-two days without rising, or as he hunched in a locker for five days. His projects, too, might be read as demolishing the lines— ethical and otherwise—between performer and audience, an enterprise that harkened back to the Living Theatre. He was, in effect, restructuring the public sphere for both artist and audience.[4]

Like Mailer, Burden's outrageousness was played out in macho fashion on the public stage. Parts of Burden's "body text" could have been borrowed verbatim from Sontag's musings on performance and the potential payoff of boredom, while he shared Wolfe's fascination with media and car culture. No less than Warhol, Burden was about the presentation of self, sometimes on a cross, sometimes masked, but always with an eye toward maximum shock. Indeed, Burden purchased time on television to run advertisements. One of them flashed his name and the title of the artwork, then showed a few seconds of him from the piece as he moved snail-like in agony across a glass-strewn gallery floor. In another, he pronounced the names of great artists, Leonardo Da Vinci, Michelangelo, and Vincent Van Gogh, among others. The piece concluded with the utterance of the name Chris Burden—and the information that the spot had been paid for by Chris Burden.

Burden was the New Sensibility in extremis. He was a harbinger of the orchestrated violence and outrageousness of the punk sensibility that was beginning to emerge during these years. On occasion, Burden referred to himself as the "Lou Reed of the art world."[5] But all of his shenanigans, even the most outrageous, were done for the oldest of reasons, a desire to respond to a set of artistic and personal imperatives. As he admitted, "I wanted to be taken seriously as an artist."[6] *Shoot*, he reiterated, was not designed to "get publicity" but to be a "real important" work of art.[7]

Born in Cambridge, Massachusetts, Burden led a peripatetic early existence, his family following his engineer father to live in France and Italy. Coming back to the United States, Burden attended Pomona College and later received an MFA from the University of California, Irvine. He shared his father's scientific bent; in many ways he was a tinkerer in the Cage mode. He was also early on a fan of Duchamp's ironic art. Drawn to art, architecture, and literature, Burden at one point wanted to be a sculptor: "I really liked making things."[8]

He began his career in the minimalist mode, associated with Donald Judd, Robert Irwin, and Robert Morris. This movement was in part designed to challenge the angst surrounding abstract expressionist process, with its heroic gestures. Instead, minimalism dealt with bare essences, surface beauty in sculpture, with no importance attached to the process of production (often much of the work was farmed out to freelance fabricators). There would always be a minimalist aspect to Burden's work, except in his case the object of the art was his own body: "I am the sculpture."[9] He always maintained that he followed the injunction of Judd to make his work "interesting." He wanted to "pare it down to something essential," to make his work about the purity—and limits—of experience.[10]

As with Cage, an element of chance, of the unexpected, was always present. "I do things to find out what'll happen," he announced.[11] The element of risk, the potential of dying for one's art, added a titillation of danger and an air of absurdity to Burden's work. As one gallery director put it, "We hoped he would show up and do something dreadful to himself."[12]

The advantages of working with the body were varied. In terms of the more recent history of body art in the 1960s, as historian Sally Banes and others have demonstrated, it defied the power of the art business and high-blown notions of the art object. After all, like a happening, what occurred to the body of the artist during the performance could not easily be assigned a cash value; it could not be owned and sold. It was also, generally, a one-time event, experienced directly (although it could be documented to varying degrees). And it was, in effect, a final blow against the reign of the traditional art object, the ideal of a permanent piece of work, forever fixed in reality. Body art or performance art gave truth to the concerns of many about "the anxiety of the object" or the dematerialization of the artwork. Performance art demanded a new language of analysis and a different sensibility on the part of both artist and audience. Burden was aware of this, hence his desire to push his work—and his body—to extremes.[13]

Performance art boomed in the 1970s. Most of the pieces offered strong political commentary. Feminists employed performance art to undermine the male gaze and objectification of women's bodies and to support abortion rights. In one particularly controversial piece from 1974, Lynda Benglis paid three thousand dollars to have an ad placed in the avant-garde magazine *Artforum*. The image provoked outrage and delight, as it pictured a nude Benglis (although she did wear sunglasses) holding a massive dildo that reached out from her pubic region. It probably was about women's subordinate position in the arts and the macho flavor of some artwork (Burden's perhaps included).[14]

Burden was part of this flowering, but his work avoided direct political commentary. For his MFA project at UC Irvine, Burden devised a fascinating piece. A row of lockers, stacked three high, lined a hallway wall at the university. Locker number five was to be Burden's home for five days. What he liked about the locker space was that it existed prior to the piece; there was nothing to be built. "I didn't know what it was going to feel like," Burden stated; "that's why I did it." The top locker—"home"—was fitted with "five gallons of bottled water" that Burden could access. The locker below had a five-gallon bottle for his urine; Burden had fasted for a number of days before beginning the piece. At the appointed hour, he scrunched himself into the tiny middle locker (two feet high, two feet wide, and three feet deep). Folks passed by the locker, sometimes talking with Burden (as if to a confessor figure, he imagined) through the air holes. The only "relic" from the performance (besides a picture of the locker) was the lock that had secured Burden in the space.[15]

Other pieces worked in a similar manner. His *Bed Piece*, from 1972, found him spending twenty-two days in bed. In contrast to John Lennon and Yoko Ono, who had stayed in bed comfortably while entertaining guests, making love, and sipping champagne, Burden did nothing other than exist. The bed was set up in a Venice Beach gallery. Burden disrobed and climbed into the Spartan bed, with white sheets and pillow case. He remained silent for the entirety of the performance. Visitors to the gallery approached the bed warily, rarely coming closer than fifteen feet. Burden felt their presence, claiming, "In their minds I had become an object…a repulsive magnet."[16] The challenge was that Burden was a live object. Gallery director Josh Young had been surprised when Burden's wife told him that complete responsibility for Burden's survival now rested with the director and gallery. Burden planned nothing more than to stay in bed.[17]

In his performance pieces Burden liked to make demands on himself *and* upon the audience. *Shoot* (1971) was less about endurance than about immediacy and presence of experience. But, as with almost all of his pieces, it was also about passivity—on the part of both the artist and the audience. He called the event an "action," an homage of sorts to the work that Otto Mühl and others in the hard-core actionist movement of the early 1960s. They had created orgies of blood art. Nor was the notion of gunplay absent from performance art prior to Burden. In 1970, at the Museum of Conceptual Art in San Francisco, Mel Henderson had paced the floor with a .30-caliber rifle in hand, before finally firing one shot at an image of a tiger projected onto a wooden sawhorse covered in paper.[18]

"I will be shot with a rifle at 7:45 p.m." read the announcement.[19] The event was to take place in F-Space, a gallery founded by Burden and other art students in an industrial building in Santa Ana. *Arts Magazine* in 1978 would call it "the single most notorious piece."[20] Although estimates vary, there were probably between eight and twelve friends of Burden's present for the event. Also included was a tall, thin, long-haired young man entrusted with the task of shooting Burden with a bullet from a .22-caliber rifle, at a range of about fifteen feet. The young man had practiced with the rifle and apparently shown himself to be both a good marksman and willing to take the risk. Burden later claimed, "I was trying to get him just to graze my arm, to actually nick it."

At the appointed moment, Burden took his place in front of a white wall. He was wearing his signature white T-shirt, arms down, looking relatively relaxed. He later claimed to be thinking, "I hope this guy doesn't miss." He did not—but he did more than nick the flesh. The bullet hit Burden's upper left arm and exited. Burden related that the impact of the bullet "felt like a truck hit my arm at 80 m.p.h."[21] Images of Burden after the impact show him bewildered and dreamy eyed, on the verge of shock. A medic friend put some dressing on the wound before hurrying Burden to the hospital. A police report kindly listed the shooting as an accident. No one was prosecuted. Burden later said that the performance was, like all art, "an *inquiry*," the asking of questions. Stated Burden, "I don't think I am trying to commit suicide."[22] He later referred to the piece as "instant sculpture."[23]

Let's look at a few additional pieces of orchestrated violence from this period to get the full flavor of Burden's sensibility. In March 1972 Burden performed *Match Piece* at the Pomona College Museum. What made it singular in Burden's corpus was that the violence in this case was directed not at himself but at someone else. Within the confines of an all-white gallery space, Burden sat on the floor, in an all-white outfit, feet bare. He had set up a television monitor in front of him, along with another by which the audience could view the performance. About twelve feet away from him, lying prone, was his wife, Barbara. She was totally nude. Every few minutes, while watching a television with the sound turned up high, Burden prepared a match missile, basically wrapping aluminum foil around a match and lighting it. The preparation of each match missile took about one minute. The matches were attached to paper clips, and with a flick of his fingers, Burden sent them darting in various directions. Match after match was set off in this manner, with about fifteen of them ending up upon the body of Barbara Burden. When they did, she flinched and flicked them away.[24]

Many in the audience were uncomfortable with both the sadism and sexism of the piece. Burden showed no awareness of the audience, as the piece continued for nearly three hours. Finally, with most of the audience having exited the gallery, Burden got up and went to fetch his wife's clothes, and the piece concluded.[25]

In 1974 Burden continued visiting violence upon his body.[26] Some acts were relatively benign. In one piece, an audience sat facing a freight elevator. Inside the elevator was Burden wearing only a pair of blue jeans. A volunteer was requested from the audience. He then was taken to the elevator, entered it, and then found himself traveling to the basement. The audience was told there was a sign in the elevator that read "Please push pins into my body." Faced with this request, the volunteer obliged, thankfully meekly, by sticking four pins into Burden's stomach and one into his foot. The elevator returned to the floor where the audience was, and the volunteer emerged from it. The piece concluded with Burden being transported back to the basement, one assumes to have the pins removed. The relic: the push pins and the stainless steel bowl in which they had been kept.[27]

In *Velvet Water* at the School of the Art Institute of Chicago in May, Burden essentially undertook to drown himself, with audience members watching it happen via television monitors. He addressed the audience through one camera, stating, "Today I am going to breathe water which is the opposite of drowning, because when you breathe water you believe water to be a richer, thicker oxygen capable of sustaining life." He then put his face into the sink full of water, for about five minutes. He then "collapsed choking." End of performance.[28]

A month later at the prestigious Art Basel fair in Switzerland, Burden opted again for the outrageous. The performance opened the art fair. Burden lay down at the top of a stairwell and had a friend, Charles Hill, kick him repeatedly. The force of the kicks drove Burden to tumble down the stairs, usually a few at a time. The kicking continued until he had descended the two flights of stairs. The ritual of violence, of falling in pain, was restaged in July in Graz, Austria, no doubt just after the bumps and bruises from the first performance had healed.[29]

What is one to make of this burst of orchestrated violence undertaken in the name of art? *Esquire* magazine, always seeking to take the pulse of American culture, reported that Burden's willingness "to lay his life on the line" fit well with "the sensibility of the Seventies." But that sensibility was hardly worth dying for: that "the artist [was] now ready to lay down his life over a silly pun" seemed absurd to the magazine writer.[30] Burden came of age—intellectually and artistically—in the late 1960s and early 1970s. It was, as we have seen, an extremely violent, tumultuous period.[31] How could art confront the momentous events of this period without simplistic didacticism or plaintive protest?

Burden felt that his works reflected back upon American society the violence that was its own beating heart. The dangerous line that he walked (or slithered) with each performance—not always successfully—was that his works had to critique the sensationalism of the era without exemplifying it.

Burden was deeply opposed to the war in Vietnam (in 1991 he designed a war memorial to acknowledge the millions of Asians killed in the conflict).[32] The *Shoot* piece could be seen as rendering the distant violence palpably up-close and personal by having it occur within the confines of an art space and in front of an audience of friends. In a similar manner, the piece *Trans-fixed* (where he is nailed to a VW) could be viewed as a protest against war, with Burden symbolically assuming the role of Christ suffering for the sins of Americans. Perhaps, too, he was making a prescient comment about how over time enemies are transformed by circumstance and capitalism into allies. His general political stance was mainstream radical for the period: he believed that capitalism was voracious and that television polluted the minds of viewers and seduced them into the false world of consumption. Mechanization, at factories like the GM plant in Lordstown, Ohio, saw workers being reduced as much as possible to mere automatons on the assembly line—Burden's work could be read as reanimating the body—in all of its contusions and constraints. At the moment when pornography was going mainstream, Burden's performance art might be read as critiques of the reduction of the body (especially the female body) to the lowest levels of objectification (if one chooses to read *Match Piece* in such a manner). Almost all commentators agree on a connection between Burden's personal politics and his performances in these years. But hyperbole sometimes clouds the issue. According to one analyst, Burden "questioned the American dream, the military industrial complex, and all forms of authority and power."[33]

Burden invariably explained the drive behind his performances as a desire to test limits, of endurance, pain, and experience. There is almost a sense of "Oh, gosh, did I really do that?" associated with him in these years. Innocence, however, coexisted with a firm knowledge on Burden's part of the history of performance art and the difficulties of establishing an artistic reputation by sticking to the mundane.

He repeated similar sentiments in interviews. "I mainly do these things," he stated, "to see what will happen."[34] Why, he was asked, did he decide to have himself shot? "Well, it's something to experience. How can you know what it feels like to be shot if you don't get shot? It seems interesting enough to be worth doing it."[35] Rather than his pieces being simply sensationalist, "masochistic" and violent, they were about "vulnerability," about the artist seeking and recording experiences. Burden maintained that he was a sort of Walter Mitty, thinking about situations and then throwing himself into them. Everything he did, he claimed, was well thought out, carefully planned: "I'm not a masochist at all. I mean I wear my seat belt, I don't drive a motorcycle any more."[36]

The "majority of the stuff I've done," Burden claimed, "was not about violence."[37] Instead, he wanted to communicate a sense of isolation and passivity, a feeling that the artist was being effaced by the commercially oriented art establishment.

As with a prisoner up against a wall, facing a firing squad, the existential loneliness and dread—and the contingency of the shooter's aim—figured as central elements in *Shoot*. Being shuttered for five days within the tiny space of a locker was also about being shut off from humanity; ditto spending twenty-two days in bed. In other pieces from the early 1970s, Burden disappeared for three days without informing anyone (he had checked into a hotel room and did not eat, read, or watch television), or took a small boat to a deserted island, essentially distancing himself from civilization. In *You'll Never See My Face in Kansas City* (1971), Burden spent three days in the city; the entire time he wore a ski mask. The ski mask constituted the relic for that performance. Burden's face remained unrevealed.[38] In *Jaizu* (1972), dressed in white, Burden sat on a chair in a gallery; he wore sunglasses. In front of him were two cushions, beside them "a small box of marijuana cigarettes." One at a time, viewers were allowed into the space—to light up, to talk with the artist. Burden, for his part, maintained absolute silence. Unbeknownst to his audience members, the interior of his sunglass lenses were painted black, so that he was "virtually blind." The piece, performed over two days, five hours each day, included Burden being assaulted by one viewer; another person "left sobbing hysterically."[39]

Burden also upended the notion of detachment between artist and artwork when it served performance purposes. The New Sensibility in part pivoted on the confessional mode. Burden caught this aspect in a rather remarkable art piece called *The Confession* (1974). Burden spent four days before the official performance in Cincinnati, Ohio, interacting with folks—at the hotel and restaurants, in the normal course of events connected with the show. He then contacted twenty-five of these individuals (none of whom knew him well) and asked them to come to the Contemporary Art Center on a Thursday evening at 8:30 p.m. Those who attended were seated around a television monitor. Burden appeared on screen and unburdened himself with intimate details about his love life and exposed every raw nerve, it seemed, in his life. "I felt," he commented, "that I had lost control of my life." The audience, who came to the event not knowing what to expect, sat uncomfortably as this veritable stranger on a screen babbled on intimately. Finally, exhausted from his self-revelation, Burden "was unable to continue." Those present "left quickly without discussion among themselves."[40]

Burden's pieces were often as much about the audience as about himself. It was, as with the Living Theatre and all performance artists following in the footsteps of Antonin Artaud, trying to reduce the distance (literal and otherwise) between performer and audience. In Burden's best pieces, the work was about audience passivity, to be sure, but also about the ethics of the audience in the midst of a performance. It was about audience responsibility—an issue long current, as in Yoko Ono's *Cut-Piece*.[41]

Issues of responsibility, of passively avoiding ethical action, were central to this period. Hannah Arendt's notion of the "banality of evil," however wrongly applied to Adolf Eichmann's Holocaust criminality, seemed a fitting concept for the willingness of many Americans to participate in the apparatus of the war in Vietnam, by manufacturing napalm, by working on bombs, and by simply accepting the status quo. In the early 1970s, Stanley Milgram's famous experiment, highlighted in an article, "The Perils of Obedience," in *Harper's Magazine*, showed normal people being rigidly obedient to authority. When ordered to give potentially fatal shocks (or so they imagined) to subjects, over 60 percent carried out the task. The phrase "If you are not part of the solution, then you are part of the problem" echoed in the ears of many opposed to the war and racism.

Consider how in *Shoot* Burden had willingly put himself in danger, with the audience implicit in this act. None of them stood up to question the event, to worry about the marksmanship of the young man about to shoot Burden. They chose, in effect, to accept Burden's premises and not to show overt concern for the dangers inherent in the action. Their passivity became part of the piece—a willingness on their part to allow something outrageous to happen. Burden saw the audience present as "witness" to his act, but in a passive manner.[42]

Two other pieces confronted the responsibility of the audience. *Prelude to 220, or 110*, which took place at the F-Space Gallery in Santa Ana in 1971, began with Burden anchored to the floor with copper bands. A pair of buckets filled with water flanked him. In the buckets were live electrical wires. Over the course of three nights, audiences entered the gallery, wandered around, and observed Burden. Had any of the audience stumbled and knocked over a bucket, Burden would have been electrocuted. He later remarked that he was not worried about that happening—"I had absolute faith that they wouldn't.... After all," Burden confided, "I'm not suicidal."[43]

Burden challenged his audience anew in a 1975 piece called *Doomed*. It was similar to other pieces from that time: *White Light/White Heat* and *Oracle*. In all of them, Burden went for extended periods without eating or communicating. With *Doomed*, he gauged the audience's willingness to allow him to suffer, perhaps to the point of death. The event attracted close to a thousand spectators.[44]

The setup for the piece was simple: a clock on the wall and the artist lying on the floor between a sheet of plate glass and the gallery wall. Burden planned to stay put, without moving, eating, drinking, or having access to a bathroom. Roger Ebert, then a reporter for the *Chicago Sun-Times*, covered the performance. It was a difficult assignment, since the piece was of indeterminate length. He reported that some in the audience came close to Burden, trying to get his attention and failing. One member of the audience said, "He can hear us, and he doesn't answer, but he can't help listening.... It's like God." Like God or not, most in the audience were as perplexed by the nonaction as Ebert. Many of them left after ten minutes of waiting for something to transpire. Every few hours, Ebert called in to find out what was happening and asked how many remained in the audience. What had started out with a "circus" atmosphere had become "like a shrine…very mysterious and beautiful." Hour after hour passed, with the gallery staff unaware (like those in attendance) that "responsibility for ending the piece" rested with them. For forty-five hours and ten minutes, nothing happened. Finally, someone "placed a container of water inside the space between the wall and the glass." Burden then arose, smashed the clock face with a hammer, and exited.[45]

Burden claimed that he had never felt close to death. Yes, thirst and hunger haunted him, and he did pee in his pants. He had not expected the piece to last so long. "I thought perhaps the piece would last several hours," he told Ebert. Once he realized that the piece was going to continue despite shrinking audience and overtime pay for guards, "I was pleased and impressed that [the museum curators] had placed the integrity of the piece ahead of the institutional requirements of the museum." But as the hours turned into a second day, Burden began to wonder, "My God, don't they care anything at all about me? Are they going to leave me here to die?"[46]

Conclusion

THE SHOCK OF THE OLD—AND NEW

By 1974, the New Sensibility, no less than Burden, was alive and prospering, a position that it continues to hold in American culture. The New Sensibility still causes controversy even as it has become ubiquitous. In its best emanations it remains both outrageous and outstanding.

John Cage, who was there at the beginning, was still up to his old tricks in 1974. Now in his early sixties, he decided to return, in a sense, to the silence of 4'33"—but with a change, of course. He would include spoken words, more or less, in his new piece, *Empty Words*, presented at the Naropa Institute in Boulder in August. Cage averred that there were twenty-seven different things you could do with/to a sentence. He chose as his base text Thoreau's *Journals* (mainly sentences dealing with music and sound). He parsed, splayed, split, and did all sorts of other things to the sentences, using the method he derived from the *I Ching*. The results were then transcribed into four "lectures," with each subsequent lecture more disjointed than the last. In a radio interview prior to the performance, Cage suggested that potential concertgoers without tickets need not worry if the concert was sold out. Just wait outside for a short time, he advised. Plenty of seats would soon become available.

With good reason. The concert was, in effect, an A-bomb dropped on syntax. Silences of inordinate length were punctuated by what seemed to be an occasional bird call. Cage read, with his glorious basso voice, such things as the following: "Bou-a the dherlyth gth db tgn-phl ng." This "nonsyntactical writing" was meaninglessness—in all languages, he proudly declared.

The lecture had been scheduled for two hours. The audience grew restive toward the hour-and-a-half mark, some began to laugh, some to yell, while others tossed objects onto the stage, engaging in their own forms of entertainment to fill the silence. Allen Ginsberg feared for Cage's safety, so along with some pals he formed a protective cordon around the artist. Cage confronted the audience with an apt summation of his career and of the logic of the New

Sensibility: "I know what limb I'm out on, I've known it all my life." He further urged the audience to open itself up to boredom and meaninglessness. This had long constituted Cage's royal road to creativity and freedom—it could change the world by opening minds and thereby dethroning militarism and totalitarianism. In Boulder, Cage had failed to open many minds. But his audience had become part of the performance, a key element in the aesthetic of the New Sensibility.[1]

A year later, Lou Reed shocked audiences with his latest album. He had been a member of the Velvet Underground, which began as a sort of house band for Andy Warhol. They would play while Warhol films were projected behind them. A rock poet of considerable talent, with an effectively monotone voice and prickly demeanor, Reed had sung of heroin highs, copping drugs, transvestites, and the grit of despondency. In the process, miraculously, listeners felt liberated. But in his album *Metal Machine Music* (two discs!), he took a new turn. Reed offered an explosion of feedback from two guitars, each tuned in an unusual manner. The music sounded like a massive traffic jam, horns blaring, brakes screeching. In its own manner, the "music" was as much a drone as Cage's earlier music had been, but without the mesmerizing effects. Some wondered if the album was a sick joke or prank, perhaps Reed's angry settlement of a contractual obligation with a record company. Maybe Reed was following in the footsteps of the avant-garde, taking Cage's excessive minimalism into the realm of excessive maximalism. Reed claimed that *Metal Machine Music* "would clear the room" and that he had not even fully listened to it himself.

The result, opined music critic James Wolcott in *Rolling Stone*, was "a jab of contempt," a "droning, shapeless provocation." The New Sensibility, after all, had been enshrined for years now; could this sort of excess ("like the tubular-groaning of a galactic refrigerator") be expected to upset anyone? To Walcott it seemed, then, a bit "old-fashioned."[2]

Wolcott raised a significant question, applicable to the New Sensibility or to any avant-garde. At what point might they become repetitive and exhausted? And there are other questions, first raised in the introduction, to be answered: Does excess have its limits? Is the New Sensibility anything more than a mere product to be consumed? On the one hand, it could easily be argued that the excess today—in confessionalism, violence, sexual explicitness, blurred genres—that had its origins in the New Sensibility has grown stale, trite, and commodified. On the other hand, and this is my own view, the New Sensibility, ushered in with Cage's excess in minimalism and maximalism back in 1952, remains vibrant today and is essential to creative growth, despite obvious misfires. The excess of the New Sensibility is to be celebrated, not as a simple end, but as a process, an experimental imperative for finding new truths, new critiques, and going in new creative directions. Although this book has concluded with 1974, the New Sensibility lives on, with ever new emanations.

Punk music, which exploded on the scene in the early 1970s and continued throughout the decade, was certainly an ode to excess. Or at least to energy and noise—and to rebellion, decadence, and liberation. In its highest moments—with groups such as The Ramones, Television, and The Stooges—it could be excitedly anarchic: an apocalyptic, Dionysian ritual made flesh. The surging energy of punk often swerved in dangerous directions. Thanks to excessive intake of drugs, on the part of both the performers and the audience, shows were often calamitous. Performers challenged the audience—and vice versa—with vehemence and violence. Fights broke out regularly. Iggy Pop vomited onstage, staggered in a drug- and drink-infused haze, and sometimes fell into the audience. Occasionally, he was covered with blood yet still pumping out his songs. For all of its obvious excess, in some ways, punk was also a return to roots, to the early days of rock, when the lyrics were simple and the musicianship rudimentary—a sort of eternal return.[3] Punk also offered a sense of community and liberation, a refusal to bow to constraints and expectations.

Punk, with its elementary excess followed a path already traveled by Cage, Ginsberg, the Living Theatre crew, and Jerry Lee Lewis. Would these exemplars of the New Sensibility have welcomed punk into the tradition? Who knows, who cares? Norman Mailer praised the expressive power of graffiti in 1974, and John Cage was adored by many in punk music, ranging from Patti Smith to Richard Hell, David Byrne, and Debbie Harry. Other initiators of the New Sensibility refused to go with the cultural flow. Yet Iggy Pop delighted in Allen Ginsberg, and Ginsberg delightedly returned the favor by photographing Iggy.[4]

The essential excess and subject matter of the New Sensibility thrived during the economic downturn of the 1970s and was buoyed by capitalism run amok during the 1980s. In that period of greed, captured so strikingly in Tom Wolfe's novel *The Bonfire of the Vanities* (1987), excess in art fit snugly—in terms of scale, dismissal of traditional boundaries between high and low, and in profitability. In some cases, as historian David Steigerwald and others argue, where there is a "proliferation of products," fashion trumps originality or channels it into the mainstream.[5] This may be true in some cases, but not in all.

The artist Jeff Koons may be exemplary of the troubled connection between art and commerce, in the New Sensibility being packaged for ready consumption. Before he became a full-time artist, he was a commodities broker. He followed Warhol in terms of literally opening a factory, with scores of employees, to produce art of vast scale, favoring a camp or kitsch sort of style. By the 1980s, he was ubiquitous on the art scene, with works that featured, for example, basketballs floating on distilled and salted water, inflatable toys, and strange sculptures. Perhaps his most infamous work, *Michael Jackson and Bubbles* (1988), was a set of three pieces, depicting the reigning rock star with his pet chimpanzee. One of the pieces sold at auction for $5.8 million—a feast of excess, at least for the artist. Koons also worked with various media for a series that explored, as explicitly as possible, the sexual pleasure he enjoyed with his wife, Ilona Staller, who was a porn star. That work was shown in a major show at the Whitney Museum in New York City in 1991. But, then again, he does sometimes hit the mark with his over the top art, as in his large-scale paintings of tulips.[6]

In all areas of American culture, from the 1970s to the present, a sense of excess has continued unabated.[7] Take the confessional turn. In 1978, historian and critic Christopher Lasch coined the term "the culture of narcissism" as a critique of what he viewed as the increasingly hedonistic and empty culture of the "me" generation with its members' need to talk self-centeredly about themselves and their "issues." Confessionalism became a cultural commonplace, with *Oprah* in the 1980s and then with the nastiness of *The Jerry Springer Show* in the 1990s. Reality television programs such as *The Real World* in the 1990s and *Jersey Shore* more recently, and the bare-all emotional revealing in books by Elizabeth Wurtzel and Emily Gould, have raised gossip and confession to levels of excess heretofore unimaginable. The precursor confessionalism of Sexton and Mailer, once so radical, now appears dainty and subdued. As the decades have unfolded, the confessional imperative (often unedited and spontaneous) has become ubiquitous, thanks also to new technological options—blogs and tweets. Indeed, in 2008 the word "overshare" (to reveal too much in public) had entered into Webster's New World Dictionary.[8]

So too had excess in performance (with a violent edge) moved well beyond the confines of Chris Burden's pieces. Johnny Knoxville and his *Jackass* cohort (appearing on television and films) demonstrate either how stupid they are for attempting dangerous stunts or how an army of viewers is prepped for the potential vicarious thrill of someone else getting seriously injured. For example, in an early stunt, Knoxville donned an inexpensive bulletproof vest and shot himself in the chest with a .38-caliber handgun. The distance from the violence of Chris Burden to that of Johnny Knoxville may not be that large, but it is significant. At least in Burden's work, as pondered by critic and poet Maggie Nelson, the audience was implicated in the violence—if in no other fashion than by their refusal to intervene and put a stop to it.[9] The passive reception of violence in film (as well as in video games) has reached epic proportions. Consider the popularity of such films as *Saw* (2004) and *Hostel* (2005). In the latter, directed by Eli Roth, people are tortured, body parts severed, and gore served up as the raison d'être for entertainment. A recent television program, *Fargo*, features excellent acting and spirited dialogue. But must each scene of violence go on for a moment or two longer, so that the blood oozes, the pain pulsates with such abandon?

Despite, or perhaps because of, its ubiquity, the New Sensibility has retained the power to outrage. Beginning in the late 1980s, as the so-called culture wars began to rage and the conservative and Christian revolution took center stage, there was an angry reaction. On the Senate floor Alfonse D'Amato of New York damned Andres Serrano's *Piss Christ*, which was a plastic crucifix submerged in Serrano's urine. The fact that it had been displayed in a museum that had received some funding from the National Endowment for the Arts provoked his anger. The case of the "NEA four" spurred further controversy in 1990. Four edgy performance artists—Karen Finley, Tim Miller, John Fleck, and Holly Hughes—had been cleared to receive grants, until a newspaper column revealed the sorts of things that they did in their art. Finley, who had long explored in her performance pieces the status of women in a rape culture, the suicide of her father, and more, became tarred as the "chocolate lady" because she had on occasion covered herself with chocolate during performances. "Art as transgression, or any transgressive act," wrote Finley, "becomes a Rorschach test for the culture."[10] Such has always been the case with the New Sensibility.

These artists were sometimes outrageous and excessive, willing to push the boundaries of audience expectations and comfort levels. My wife and I were among the first to arrive for a Tim Miller performance in Santa Barbara, and she suggested that we take seats in the front row. I demurred, preferring the relative anonymity and protection of the middle of the small auditorium. Was I right! At one point in the performance, Miller grabbed the leg of a fellow sitting in the front row and proceeded to masturbate himself against it.

There seemed no end to the controversies of the 1990s. Robert Mapplethorpe's images of sadomasochism further inflamed the culture wars, finally resulting in the cutting off of funding for NEA grants to individual artists. The government exited itself from supporting such edgy art. Liberals (such as Tipper Gore) and conservatives united in their distaste for the excessive violence and misogyny (not to mention crude language) of rap music. Despite occasional lawsuits and public eruptions against specific shows, the art of excess shows no signs of abating.

Excess, as exemplified by the New Sensibility, is not, of course, to everyone's tastes. When its form is uncontrolled and its performers mostly interested in growing rich and famous, then its cultural presence can be troubling, even degrading. One could also argue that the excess that had once been relevant for shock and artistic progress in the 1960s quickly became numbing, necessitating an upping of the voltage. Given the acceleration in violence (in Vietnam and urban crime) and in pornography (readily available in neighborhood theaters), had Carolee Schneemann's 1964 celebration of a communal sense of liberation (bodily and spiritually) in *Meat Joy* (chapter 13) become tame and irrelevant? Paul McCarthy's critique of it, *Sailor's Meat* (1975), was about detachment, denigration, and desperation. Transgressive sex and food consumption were linked like sausages in McCarthy's work. Aware of the problem of liberation through transgression (cooptation of pleasure by a commodity culture and the postmodern dilemma of finding an outside point for criticism and more), McCarthy critiqued Schneemann's seemingly naive optimism of freedom through excess. She worked within the folds of the New Sensibility as developed, for example, by Samuel R. Delany. For a tradition to thrive, it must be open to the point of almost breaking.[11]

There is much in the recent years of the New Sensibility (now, of course, not so new, but ever developing) that should be applauded. The drive for excess and the subject matter of the New Sensibility remain essential for continued cultural openness and creativity. It is at its best, in my view, when vision and execution jibe with an acute appreciation for what historian Roger Shattuck once referred to as the tension between "liberation and limits." Such balancing upon the high wire of the New Sensibility has made possible television series such as *The Sopranos* and *Breaking Bad*. So, too, the experimental and bounding work of such diverse artists as poets Franz Wright and Anne Carson (whose work defies genres), novelists Ben Lerner and Kate Zambreno, filmmaker Quentin Tarantino, photographer Nan Goldin, comedian Sarah Silverman, and rapper Kanye West, to name but a few.

Consider an especially monumental work of excess, as growing out of the tradition of the New Sensibility: Kara Walker's sculptural piece *A Subtlety*. The work overflows with meaning and is over the top in scale. A "subtlety" was once a term for sculptural sugary confections made for wealthy folks to admire and then devour. And, with delicious irony, Walker nods toward the reality that the sugar used for much of the sweet things in life, at least into the nineteenth century, came from the backbreaking work of slaves in the Caribbean who produced it for export. Walker's piece acknowledges this but goes beyond it. The temporary work, which debuted in spring 2014, was exhibited in the soon-to-be demolished Domino Sugar Factory in Brooklyn, a familiar site for New Yorkers. In that building, often under harsh working conditions, workers (mainly African American) had processed the sugar that became a dangerous staple of the American diet. Walker's sculpture, contained within the immense factory building, was outsized. Using huge pieces of polystyrene as the skeleton, Walker then applied a "skin" made out of sugar (mixed with water for adhesion). The sculpture weighed thirty-five tons and was thirty-five feet high and seventy-five feet long. Although white because of the sugar, the sculpture clearly depicted a mammy figure, full breasted and thick-lipped, sphinx-like, wearing a bandana. The figure's butt and vulva are fully in evidence. In addition to the monumental mammy sphinx, there are smaller figures of young boys, five feet high, carrying trays. The melting of their sugar bodies is suggestive of bleeding, of centuries of suffering.

The ironies of the piece are obvious. Begin with its title: *A Subtlety, or the Marvelous Sugar Baby, an Homage to the unpaid and overworked Artisans who have refined our Sweet tastes from the cane fields to the Kitchens of the New World on the Occasion of the demolition of the Domino Sugar Refining Plant*. So much for subtlety. This is about representations of gender, about the realities of race, labor, and oppression—about the "blood sugar" appearing on American tables. But the piece is linked to the New Sensibility by its nerve, edge, temporality, bulk, and in-your-face attitude.

Excess tempered by the limitations of history, pain, and an artist's sensibility in this case made for great art—a feast of excess, if you will.[12]

{ NOTES }

Introduction

1. Kyle Gann, *No Such Thing as Silence: John Cage's 4'33"* (New Haven, CT: Yale University Press, 2010), 191; John Cage, in conversation with Daniel Charles, *For the Birds* (Boston: Marion Boyars, 1981), 104.

2. On the event, see Martin Duberman, *Black Mountain: An Exploration in Community* (New York: W. W. Norton, 1993), 372–77.

3. Kristine Stiles, "Burden of Light," in *Chris Burden*, ed. Fred Hoffman (Newcastle upon Tyne, UK: Locus+, 2007), 30–31.

4. Tom Wolfe, *The Kandy-Kolored Tangerine-Flake Streamline Baby* (New York: Farrar, Straus & Giroux, 1965), xvii.

5. Susan Sontag, "One Culture and the New Sensibility," in *Against Interpretation and Other Essays* (New York: Picador, 1990), 303.

6. Richard Poirier, "The Aesthetics of Radicalism," *Partisan Review* 41, no. 2 (1974), 193–94. Also Poirier, *The Performing Self: Compositions and Decompositions in the Languages of Contemporary Life* (New Brunswick, NJ: Rutgers University Press, 1992). This period saw the famous definition of fame from historian Daniel J. Boorstin, "The celebrity is a person who is known for his well-knownness," a definition that Warhol certainly understood in relation to his "superstars." Boorstin, *The Image: A Guide to Pseudo-Events in America* (1961; repr., New York: Vintage, 1992), 57.

7. Douglas Barzelay and Robert Sussman, "Interview with William Styron," in *Conversations with William Styron*, ed. James L. W. West III (Jackson: University Press of Mississippi, 1985), 103.

8. Lucy R. Lippard, *Pop Art* (New York: Oxford University Press, 1966), 99.

9. On the escapades of the Living Theatre, see Aldo Rostagno with Julian Beck and Judith Malina, *We, The Living Theatre* (New York: Ballantine, 1970).

10. For the quotes on happenings, see Allan Kaprow, *The Blurring of Art and Life*, ed. Jeff Kelley (Berkeley: University of California Press, 1993), 62, 8. Such a blurring did not sit well with all critics, for example, Michael Fried, who disdained theatricality in the arts. See his famous essay "Art and Objecthood," *Artforum* 5 (Autumn 1967), 12–23. On happenings as critique, see Judith F. Rodenbeck, *Radical Prototypes: Allan Kaprow and the Invention of Happenings* (Cambridge, MA: MIT Press, 2011), xiii. On the genre, and some of its earliest expressions, see Michael Kirby, *Happenings: An Illustrated Anthology* (New York: E. P. Dutton, 1965). Also indispensable is the lavishly illustrated volume by Mildred L. Glimcher, *Happenings: New York, 1958–1963* (New York: Monacelli, 2012).

11. Marshall Berman, *All that Is Solid Melts into Air: The Experience of Modernity* (New York: Simon & Schuster, 1982), 319.

12. Richard Gilman, *The Confusion of Realms* (New York: Random House, 1969).

13. Benjamin DeMott, "The Age of Overkill," *New York Times Sunday Magazine* (19 May 1968), 77; Norman O. Brown, *Love's Body* (New York: Random House, 1966), 187.

14. John Gruen, *The New Bohemia* (New York: A Capella, 1990), 14.

15. Walter Kerr, *The Decline of Pleasure* (New York: Simon & Schuster, 1962), 41; Claes Oldenburg, quoted in Max Kozloff, "The New American Painting" in *The New American Arts*, ed. Richard Kostelanetz (New York: Horizon, 1965), 111; Sontag, *Against Interpretation*, 14; Robert Motherwell, *The Collected Writings*, ed. Stephanie Terenzio (New York: Oxford University Press, 1992), 150.

16. Michael S. Sherry, *Gay Artists in Modern American Culture: An Imaginary Conspiracy* (Chapel Hill: University of North Carolina Press, 2007); Christopher Bram emphasizes how writing was a key vehicle for gays in *Eminent Outlaws: The Gay Writers Who Changed America* (New York: Twelve, 2012). On the contested nature of masculinity in this period, see James Gilbert, *Men in the Middle: Searching for Masculinity in the 1950s* (Chicago: University of Chicago Press, 2005). Gore Vidal, *Myra Breckinridge* (Boston and Toronto: Little, Brown, 1969), n.p. Perhaps Myra's desire became reality for rioting transvestites at the Stonewall Inn in 1969. For a smart discussion of the value and vicissitudes of camp, see Daniel Harris, *The Rise and Fall of Gay Culture* (New York: Hyperion, 1997), 8–39.

17. R. D. Laing, *The Politics of Experience* (1967), excerpted in *The Sixties: The Art, Attitudes, Politics, and Media of Our Most Explosive Decade*, ed. Gerald Howard (New York: Marlowe, 1995), 199.

18. David Ehrenstein, "King of Hearts," available online at http://www.criterion.com/current/posts/956-king-of-hearts.

19. Sexton to Brother Dennis Farrell, 16 July 1962, in *Anne Sexton: A Self-Portrait in Letters*, ed. Linda Gray Sexton and Lois Ames (Boston: Houghton Mifflin, 1977), 144

20. Sontag, *Against Interpretation*, 276.

21. Andreas Huyssen, *After the Great Divide: Modernism, Mass Culture, Postmodernism* (Bloomington: Indiana University Press, 1986), vii. The chasm was often traversed, see Kirk Varnedoe and Adam Gopnik, *High and Low: Modern Art, Popular Culture* (New York: Museum of Modern Art, 1991).

22. Liesl Olson, *Modernism and the Ordinary* (Oxford: Oxford University Press, 2009), esp. 5, 33–57.

23. Quoted in Hugh Kenner, *The Pound Era* (Berkeley: University of California Press, 1973), 550–51.

24. Quoted in Janet Malcolm, *Two Lives: Gertrude and Alice* (New Haven, CT: Yale University Press, 2007), 12.

25. Greenberg, "Surrealist Painting," (1944) in *The Collected Essays and Criticism: Perceptions and Judgments, 1939–1944*, ed. John O'Brian (Chicago: University of Chicago Press, 1986), 225. Of course, Greenberg was writing during World War II. At that historical moment perhaps the relevance of Dada should have been apparent.

26. Michael North, *Novelty: A History of the New* (Chicago: University of Chicago Press, 2013), 10, 172ff.

27. Edmund Wilson, *Axel's Castle: A Study of the Imaginative Literature of 1870 to 1930* (New York: Scribner's, 1931), 2. On the birth of the postmodern in the 1960s, see Marianne DeKoven, *Utopia Unlimited: The Sixties and the Birth of the Postmodern* (Durham, NC: Duke University Press, 2004). Was the New Sensibility solely an American phenomenon? Certainly similar things were happening in Great Britain during the same time frame. See Richard Weight, *Mod: A Very British Style* (London: Bodley Head, 2013); Bernard Levin, *Run It Down the Flagpole: Britain in the Sixties* (New York: Atheneum, 1971); Francis Wheen,

Strange Days Indeed: The 1970s; The Golden Age of Paranoia (New York: Public Affairs, 2009); Robert Hewison, *Too Much: Art and Society in the Sixties, 1960–1975* (London: Methuen, 1986). In England, especially in the 1950s, issues were related to class. A further question: Was the New Sensibility articulated because of capitalist development? No doubt rising standards of living especially helped the development of a youth culture, in both nations. However, a reaction against aspects of the modernist ethic, creating a new style, with a specific subject matter, strikes me as more compelling as an explanation.

28. Irving Howe, "The Culture of Modernism," in *The Decline of the New* (New York: Harcourt, Brace & World, 1970), 3–33; Harry Levin, "What Was Modern?" (1960) in *Refractions: Essays in Contemporary Literature* (New York: Oxford University Press, 1966), 271–95; Susan Stanford Friedman, "Definitional Excursions: The Meanings of Modern/Modernity/Modernism," *Modernism/Modernity* 8, no. 3 (2001), 493–513; Suzi Gablik, *Has Modernism Failed?* (New York: Thames & Hudson, 1984); Peter Bürger, "The Decline of Modernism," in *The Decline of Modernism*, trans. Nicholas Walker (University Park: Pennsylvania State University Press, 1992), 33–44. The issue of modernism is connected with that of the rise of the avant-garde, yet another area of contention. Did the avant-garde die because it became commonplace, corrupted, or coopted? Helpful on this issue are Peter Bürger, *The Theory of the Avant-Garde*, trans. Michael Shaw (Minneapolis: University of Minnesota Press, 1984); Renato Poggioli, *The Theory of the Avant-Garde*, trans. Gerald Fitzgerald (Cambridge, MA: Harvard University Press, 1968); John Weighton, *The Concept of the Avant-Garde: Explorations in Modernism* (LaSalle, IL: Open Court, 1973); Rosalind Krauss, *The Originality of the Avant-Garde and Other Modernist Myths* (Cambridge, MA: MIT Press, 1986), and the highly challenging Paul Mann, *The Theory-Death of the Avant-Garde* (Bloomington: Indiana University Press, 1991). Finally, for an excellent review of modernism(s), see Douglas Mao and Rebecca L. Walkowitz, "The New Modernist Studies," *PMLA* 123, no. 3 (2008), 737–48. It deals with modernism as a transnational phenomenon and explores the circulation of its texts and the role of dissemination and mass media technologies.

29. Particularly valuable, in part for extending the notion of the 1960s back to the 1950s, is Robert Genter, *Late Modernism: Art, Culture, and Politics in Cold War America* (Philadelphia: University of Pennsylvania Press, 2010), especially for his appreciation for modernism as a living entity and the difficulties of pinning it down. He covers quite a different group of figures than do I. Also invaluable are Stuart D. Hobbs, *The End of the American Avant Garde* (New York: New York University Press, 1997); W. T. Lhamon Jr., *Deliberate Speed: The Origins of a Cultural Style in the American 1950s* (Washington: Smithsonian Institution Press, 1990); Daniel Belgrad, *The Culture of Spontaneity: Improvisation and the Arts in Postwar America* (Chicago: University of Chicago Press, 1998); Howard Brick, *Age of Contradiction: American Thought and Culture in the 1960s* (New York: Twayne, 1998); and Fred Kaplan, *1959: The Year That Changed Everything* (Hoboken, NJ: John Wiley, 2009). On the postmodern, see Huyssen, *After the Great Divide*; Thomas Crow, *The Rise of the Sixties* (New Haven, CT: Yale University Press, 1996); Fredric Jameson, *Postmodernism, or The Cultural Logic of Late Capitalism* (Durham, NC: Duke University Press, 1991). Of late, some analysts have begun to look at postwar modernism as an international phenomenon, and for a nice attempt at defining a modernist sensibility see Richard Pells, *Modernist America: Art, Music, Movies, and the Globalization of American Culture* (New Haven, CT: Yale University Press, 2011), x. See also Michael Denning, *Culture in the Age of Three Worlds* (London: Verso, 2004); David Steigerwald, *Culture's Vanities: The*

Paradox of Cultural Diversity in a Globalized World (Lanham, MD: Rowman & Littlefield, 2004). For the quote on "Free-Style Classicism," see Charles Jencks, *Post-Modernism: The New Classicism in Art and Architecture* (New York: Rizzoli, 1987), 7.

30. Antin quoted in Henry M. Sayre, *The Object of Performance: The American Avant-Garde since 1970* (Chicago, 1989), xi. See also Antin, "Modernism and Postmodernism: Approaching the Present in American Poetry," *Boundary 2* (1972), 98–133; Ihab Hassan, *The Dismemberment of Orpheus: Toward a Postmodern Literature* (1971; Madison: University of Wisconsin Press, 1982), 263.

31. Harold Rosenberg, *The Tradition of the New* (Chicago: University of Chicago Press, 1982), 9.

32. Of course, some protested the value of the term and its definitions. Arthur O. Lovejoy famously counted thirteen different, contradictory meanings).

33. Daniel Wickberg, "What is the History of Sensibilities?: On Cultural Histories, Old and New," *American Historical Review* 112 (June 2007): 663. Raymond Williams, *The Long Revolution* (New York: Columbia University Press, 1961), 46–50; Michael Baxandall, *Painting and Experience in Fifteenth-Century Italy* (London: Oxford University Press, 1972), 30–32; Clifford Geertz, *The Interpretation of Cultures* (New York: Basic Books, 1973), 5.

34. Lionel Trilling, "Reality in America," in *The Liberal Imagination* (Garden City, NY: Anchor, 1953), 7.

35. Howard, "Introduction," *The Sixties*, 16.

36. George Lipsitz, "Who'll Stop the Rain?: Youth Culture, Rock 'n' Roll, and Social Crises," in *The Sixties: From Memory to History*, ed. David Farber (Chapel Hill: University of North Carolina Press, 1994), 209; David Farber, *The Age of Great Dreams: America in the 1960s* (New York: Hill & Wang, 1994), 52. In his discussion of the militarization of the United States, Michael S. Sherry notes examples of culture following that line but remarks that the "diversity" of culture made it unusual to march in lock-step with such a trend. Sherry, *In the Shadow of War: The United States since the 1930s* (New Haven: Yale University Press, 1995), 158.

37. Susan Sontag, "The Imagination of Disaster," in *Against Interpretation* (New York: Picador, 1990), 213, 224, 13–14.

38. The phrase comes from Jeff Nuttall, *Bomb Culture* (New York: Delacorte, 1968). William Faulkner recognized how the atomic bomb had altered the cultural field. In his Nobel Prize address of 1950, he stated: "There is only one question: When will I be blown up? Because of this, the young man or woman writing today has forgotten the problem of the human heart in conflict with itself which alone can make good writing." Quoted in Paul S. Boyer, *By the Bomb's Early Light: American Thought and Culture at the Dawn of the Atomic Age* (New York: Pantheon, 1985), 251.

39. Norman Mailer, "The White Negro," in *Advertisements for Myself* (New York: G. P. Putnam's Sons, 1959), 339; Allen Ginsberg, *Howl* (New York: Harper Perennial, 2006), 4.

40. Kenneth Rexroth, "San Francisco Letter," *Evergreen Review* 1, no. 2 (1957): 11.

41. John Cassidy, "Forces of Divergence: Is Surging Inequality Endemic to Capitalism?," *The New Yorker*, 31 March 2014, 70.

42. Sontag quoted in Liam Kennedy, "Susan Sontag: The Intellectual and Cultural Criticism," in *American Cultural Critics*, ed. David Murray (Exeter, UK: Exeter University Press, 1995), 80. Lhamon posits a connection between the employment of "a deliberatively speedy style" and "consumer economics" occurring in 1955. This is not unreasonable, but such close connections sometimes seem strained. Lhamon, *Deliberate Speed*, 7.

43. Fitzgerald quoted in Ann Douglas, *Terrible Honesty: Mongrel Manhattan in the 1920s* (New York: Farrar, Straus & Giroux, 1995), 4; Thomas Frank, *The Conquest of Cool: Business Culture, Counterculture, and the Rise of Hip Consumerism* (Chicago: University of Chicago Press, 1998). For the claim that "the only satisfactory semantic meaning of modernity lies in its association with capitalism," see Frederic Jameson, *A Singular Modernity: Essay on the Ontology of the Present* (London: Verso, 2002), 13.

44. Quoted in Morton Feldman, *Give My Regards to Eighth Street: Collected Writings of Morton Feldman*, ed. B. H. Friedman (Cambridge, MA: Exact Change, 2000), 32.

45. Gunn quoted in George Melly, *Revolt into Style: The Pop Arts* (New York: Anchor, 1971), 41.

46. Tarantino quoted in Anthony Julius, *Transgressions: The Offences of Art* (Chicago: University of Chicago Press, 2003), 41.

47. Stuart Hall, "Notes on Deconstructing 'The Popular,'" in *People's History and Socialist Theory*, ed. Raphael Samuel (London: Routledge & Kegan Paul, 1981), 228. See also Denning, *Age of Three Worlds*, 98; Herbert J. Gans, *Popular Culture and High Culture: An Analysis and Evaluation of Taste* (New York: Basic Books, 1974), esp. 75–93. For the view that high culture has been reduced to ruins, see James B. Twitchell, *Carnival Culture: The Trashing of Taste in America* (New York: Columbia University Press, 1992), 253–74.

48. Kael quoted in Craig Seligman, *Sontag and Kael: Opposites Attract Me* (New York: Counterpoint, 2004), 56.

49. Sontag, "Thirty Years Later...," in Sontag, *Against Interpretation*, 307–12.

50. Karen Finley, "Politics," in *A Different Kind of Intimacy: The Collected Writings of Karen Finley* (New York: Thunder's Mouth, 2000), 99ff.; John Frohnmayer, *Leaving Town Alive: Confessions of an Arts Warrior* (New York: Houghton Mifflin, 1993).

51. Roxane Gay, "The Audacity of Voice," *Time*, 6 October 2014, 50.

52. Roger Shattuck, *Forbidden Knowledge: From Prometheus to Pornography* (San Diego: Harcourt Brace, 1996), 6.

53. Rauschenberg quoted in Barbara Rose, "Artful Dodger," *Artforum* 36 (Summer 1998), 31.

54. As I scan the roster of figures discussed in this book, it is obvious that males predominate and that African American women are absent, as are Latina/o cultural creators. As noted earlier, there are a good number of homosexuals. And, for the same reason, quite a large number of Jews—hardly surprising, since in the 1950s and 1960s a Jewish cultural flowering was afoot in the United States. Saul Bellow and Bernard Malamud in writing, along with Mark Rothko in painting, were dominant figures. But a slightly younger generation of Jewish artists—influenced perhaps more by assimilation than exile, more by potential atomic destruction than the Holocaust—came to the fore. They were both in and out of mainstream society, which gave them both the license and the imperative, perhaps, to push their art to extremes, to go too far. In contrast, for those individuals from communities still shackled by racial and economic injustice, the clarion call of excess was both more politically and artistically problematic.

55. Quoted in Damion Searls, "Book of Wander: W. G. Sebald's Unsystematic Search," *Artforum* 21 (April/May 2014), 42.

56. Thomas Buckley, "100 Fight Arrest of Lenny Bruce," *New York Times*, 14 June 1964. Among those signing were Mailer, Vidal, Styron, and Baldwin. The support was widespread, however, with theologian Reinhold Niebuhr, critic Lionel Trilling, and poet Robert Lowell.

57. Morris Dickstein, *Gates of Eden: American Culture in the Sixties* (New York: Basic Books, 1977), 51–88, and Dickstein, *Leopards in the Temple: The Transformation of American Fiction, 1945–1970* (Cambridge, MA: Harvard University Press, 1999); Daniel Bell, "The Sensibility of the Sixties," in *The Cultural Contradictions of Capitalism* (New York: Basic Books, 1976), 120–45; Irving Howe, "The New York Intellectuals," in *The Decline of the New* (New York: Harcourt, Brace & World, 1970), 260; Roger Kimball, *The Long March: How the Cultural Revolution of the 1960s Changed America* (San Francisco: Encounter, 2011), 81–100. For a positive view of the New Sensibility as a form of praxis, see Herbert Marcuse, "The New Sensibility," in *An Essay on Liberation* (Boston: Beacon, 1969), 23–48. For a witty attack on excess, viewed in terms of vulgarity, see Twitchell, *Carnival Culture*.

Prelude

1. Judith Malina, *The Diaries of Judith Malina, 1947–1957* (New York: Grove, 1984), 201–3, 72. Unless otherwise noted, all Malina quotes are from this volume. A slightly different account of her embarrassment on the stage that evening is in Harold Norse, *Memoirs of a Bastard Angel: A Fifty-Year Literary and Erotic Odyssey* (New York: Thunder Mouth, 1989), 223–25. For a fine history of the group, see John Tytell, *The Living Theatre: Art, Exile, and Outrage* (New York: Grove, 1995). Helpful for their essential tenets and later work is Julian Beck, *The Life of the Theatre* (1972, New York: Limelight, 1986); Aldo Rostagno, with Julian Beck and Judith Malina, *We, the Living Theatre* (New York: Ballantine, 1970). On Malina as a "taste bender," see John Bernard Myers, *Tracking the Marvelous: A Life in the New York Art World* (New York: Random House, 1983), 24, 194.

2. Kenneth Rexroth, *Beyond the Mountains* (San Francisco: City Light, 1951), 31–33.

3. Judith Malina, "Excerpts from a Patient's Journals" (ca. 1952), box 68, Living Theatre Papers, Beinecke Library, Yale University.

4. Malina, *Diaries*, 178, 6.

5. Judith Malina, *The Piscator Notebook* (New York: Routledge, 2012), 5, 31, 17.

6. Malina, *Diaries*, 144.

7. Malina, *Diaries*, 170.

8. On the Malina/Beck relationship, see Tytell, *Living Theatre*, 92–99.

9. Malina, *Diaries*, 102.

10. Malina, *Diaries*, 150.

11. Malina, *Diaries*, 97–101.

12. Malina, "Excerpts from a Patient's Journals," 37.

13. Kenneth Silverman, *Begin Again: Biography of John Cage* (New York: Alfred A. Knopf, 2010), 65.

14. Malina, *Diaries*, 189, 252.

15. Cage, *Silence: Lectures and Writings by John Cage* (Middletown, CT: Wesleyan University Press, 1979), xii.

16. Malina, *Diaries*, 202.

17. Tytell, *Living Theatre*, 94–95; 98–104.

18. Tytell, *Living Theatre*, 225–42.

19. Malina, "MS. of Journal" (1952), box 7, Living Theatre Papers, Beinecke Library, Yale University, 594.

Chapter 1

1. John Gruen, *The Party's Over Now* (Wainscott, NY: Pushcart, 1989), 158.

2. R. P., "Tudor Tries Hand at Experimenting," *New York Times*, 2 January 1952, 20. A good analysis of *Music of Changes* is Grant Chu Covell, "1951 and Cage's *Music of Changes*" *La Folia: On Line Music Review*, April 2006, http://www.lafolia.com/archive/covell/covell200604cage1951.html.

3. Kay Larson, *Where the Heart Beats: John Cage, Zen Buddhism, and the Inner Life of Artists* (New York: Penguin, 2012). For an interpretation of *4'33"* less inclined to emphasize Cage's Buddhism and general philosophy, see Liz Kotz, *Words to Be Looked At: Language in 1960s Art* (Cambridge, MA.: MIT Press, 2007), 13–26. For a delightful overview of Cage, and others connected with the New Sensibility (although the author does not use the term), see Calvin Tomkins, *The Bride and the Bachelors: Five Masters of the Avant-Garde* (New York: Viking, 1965).

4. Quoted in Gruen, *Party's Over*, 158.

5. John Cage, *Silence: Lectures and Writings by John Cage* (Middletown, CT: Wesleyan University Press, 1979), 110. The layout of the sentence in the printed version is rather intricate.

6. Irving Sandler, in Amy Newman, *Challenging Art: Artforum, 1962–1974* (New York: Soho, 2000), 167.

7. Cage, *Silence*, 94.

8. Larson, *Where the Heart Beats*, 174–82.

9. Cage, *Silence*, 57–58. James Pritchett, *The Music of John Cage* (Cambridge, UK: Cambridge University Press, 1994), is excellent on Cage's process of composition and musical imperatives.

10. Jean-Jacques Nattiez, ed., *The Boulez-Cage Correspondence*, trans. Robert Samuels (Cambridge, UK: Cambridge University Press, 1993), 106–7.

11. Virgil Thomson, *An Autobiography* (New York: E. P. Dutton, 1966), 353.

12. Quoted in Richard Kostelanetz, *John Cage (ex)plain(ed)* (New York: Schirmer, 1996), 49, 74.

13. John Cage, in conversation with Daniel Charles, *For the Birds* (Boston: Marion Boyars, 1981), 57.

14. Quoted in David Revill, *The Roaring Silence: John Cage: A Life* (New York: Arcade, 1992), 110.

15. For some skepticism about the Cage and Schoenberg anecdote, see Brent Reidy, "Our Memory of What Happened Is Not What Happened: Cage, Metaphor, and Myth," *American Music* 28 (Summer 2010): 211–27.

16. On some aspects of his life, especially his homosexual relationships in Los Angeles before marriage, see Jill Johnston, *Jasper Johns: Privileged Information* (New York: Thames & Hudson, 1996), 115–20.

17. Revill, *Roaring Silence*, 61–86.

18. Liesl Olson, *Modernism and the Ordinary* (Oxford : Oxford University Press, 2009).

19. "Music: Percussionist," *Time*, 22 February, 1943, available online at http://content.www.time.com/time/subscriber/article/0,33009,774357,00.html.

20. "Percussion Concert: Band Bangs Things to Make Music," *Life*, 15 March 1943, 46, 48.

21. R. P., "Prepared Pianos Give Odd Program," *New York Times*, 11 December, 1946, 40.

22. "Sonata for Bolt and Screw," *Time*, 24 January 1949, available online at http://www.time.com/time/subscriber/printout/0,8816,799692.00.html.

23. Cage to Boulez, in Nattiez, *Boulez-Cage*, 78.

24. Revill, *Roaring*, 162–63; Cage, *Silence*, 8. This story is central to the Cage mythos, but it is improbable that Cage heard either his nervous or circulatory systems.

25. Cage, *Silence*, 58, 59.

26. Morton Feldman, *Give My Regards to Eighth Street: Collected Writings of Morton Feldman*, ed. B. H. Friedman (Cambridge, MA: Exact Change, 2000), 115.

27. Kenneth Silverman, *Begin Again: A Biography of John Cage* (New York: Alfred A. Knopf, 2010), 102–3. Harold Norse, *Memoirs of a Bastard Angel* (New York: William Morrow, 1989), 207–8.

28. Lionel Trilling, "Our Country and Our Culture," *Partisan Review* 19, no. 3 (May-June, 1952): 319.

29. Stephen Spender, "The Modernist Movement Is Dead," *New York Times Book Review*, 3 August 1952, 1, 16.

30. "All Eyes on Doris Day," *Colliers*, 9 August 1952, 10–12.

31. On Kitt see "Midnight Purrs and Shouts," *Life*, 4 August 1952, 48; on Hemingway, see Robert Gorham Davis, "Review of *The Old Man and the Sea*," in *New York Times Book Review*, 7 September 1952, 1, 20. Harry Smith was in search of authenticity, turning to the past to find it. In 1952 his three-volume anthology of roots music was issued. He "was looking for exotic records…in relation to what was considered to be the world culture of high class music." Harry Smith, quoted in Rani Singh, "Harry Smith, an Ethnographic Modernist in America," in *Harry Smith: The Avant-Garde in the American Vernacular*, ed. Andrew Perchuk and Rani Singh (Los Angeles: Getty Institute, 2010), 30.

32. Calvin Tompkins, *Off the Wall: Robert Rauschenberg and the Art World of Our Time* (New York: Penguin, 1980), 52–53.

33. For an evocative account of the music scene, see Christian Wolff, "Experimental Music around 1950 and Some Consequences and Causes (Social-Political and Music)," *American Music* 27 (Winter 2009): 424–40.

34. Gruen, *Party's Over*, 175.

35. Revill, *Roaring*, 102–3; Feldman, *Give My Regards*, 97.

36. On the Artists' Club and the excitement in New York City at this time, see Jed Perl, *New Art City: Manhattan At Mid-Century* (New York: Alfred A. Knopf, 2005); Irving Sandler, *A Sweeper-Up after Artists: A Memoir* (London: Thames & Hudson, 2004), 26–42; William B. Scott and Peter M. Rutkoff, *New York Modern: The Arts and the City* (Baltimore: Johns Hopkins University Press, 1999), 310–19. Sandler does not recall Cage as a regular at either the Cedar Tavern or the Club, in contrast to Feldman. For an account more critical of the politics of the American avant-garde, see Serge Guilbaut, *How New York Stole the Idea of Modern Art: Abstract Expressionism, Freedom, and the Cold War*, trans. Arthur Goldhammer (Chicago: University of Chicago Press, 1983).

37. Dan Wakefield, *New York in the Fifties* (Boston: Houghton Mifflin, 1992), 19.

38. Material on this concert is drawn from Carolyn Brown, *Chance and Circumstance* (New York: Alfred A. Knopf, 2007), 25–26; Gann, *No Such Thing*, 1–3, passim; Revill, *Roaring*, 165ff.; Nyman, *Experimental Music*, 3–30.

39. Revill, *Roaring Silence*, 165.

40. Gann, *No Such Thing* 14, 15, 20.

41. Jill Johnston, *Marmalade Me* (Hanover, NH: University Press of New England, 1998), 63.

42. Cage, *Silence*, 93.

43. Feldman, *Give My Regards*, 151.

44. Cage to Boulez, 22 May 1951, in Nattiez, *Boulez-Cage*, 96. Reading Artaud, he wrote, "gave me the idea for a theater without literature. Words and poetry may, of course, enter into it. But the rest, everything that is in general *non-verbal*, may enter into it as well." A perfect vehicle, then, for Cage's pluralist vision of art which was designed simply to have art "introduce us to life." See Brown, *Chance*, 21; Cage, *For the Birds*, 52.

45. Material on Black Mountain and the piece is drawn from Martin Duberman, *Black Mountain: An Exploration in Community* (New York: W. W. Norton, 1993), 370–75; Revill, *Roaring Silence*, 161ff.; Silverman, *Begin Again*, 113–20; Brown, *Chance*, 6–21; Vincent Katz, ed., *Black Mountain College: Experiment in Art* (Cambridge, MA: MIT Press, 2002), 133–39; Calvin Tompkins, *Off the Wall*, 66–75.

46. On Cage's wide influence, see Sally Banes, *Greenwich Village 1963: Avant-Garde Performance and the Effervescent Body* (Durham, NC: Duke University Press, 1993), 28. For a piece highly critical of Cage's work, see Richard Taruskin, "No Ear for Music: The Scary Purity of John Cage," *New Republic*, 15 March 1993.

47. Richard Gilman, *The Confusion of Realms* (New York: Random House, 1969).

48. Caroline A. Jones, "John Cage and the Abstract Expressionist Ego," *Critical Inquiry* 19 (Summer 1993): 628–65. See also Michael S. Sherry, *Gay Artists in Modern American Culture: An Imagined Conspiracy* (Chapel Hill: University of North Carolina Press, 2007), 196–97. Of course, Cage's outrageous excess in music might be seen as having affinities with a camp sensibility as outlined by Susan Sontag. See Sontag, "Notes on Camp," in *Against Interpretation, and Other Essays* (New York: Farrar, Straus & Giroux, 1966), 275–92.

49. Quoted in Stuart D. Hobbs, *The End of the American Avant Garde* (New York: New York University Press, 1997), 59.

Chapter 2

1. Sylvia Plath, *The Bell Jar* (1963; repr., New York: Alfred A. Knopf, 1998), 5.

2. Sam Hunter, *Robert Rauschenberg: Works, Writings and Interviews* (Barcelona: Edicions Poligrafa, 2006), 63; Walter Hopps, *Early Rauschenberg: The Early 1950s* (Houston: Houston Fine Art Press, 1991) 150–53; Carolyn Brown, *Chance and Circumstance: Twenty Years with Cage and Cunningham* (New York: Alfred A. Knopf, 2007), 84–85.

3. Clement Greenberg, *The Collected Essays and Criticism: Affirmations and Refusals, 1950–1956*, ed. John O'Brian (Chicago: University of Chicago Press, 1993), 122. Greenberg was a formalist, seeing Jackson Pollock as leading the charge in painting. Rosenberg, in contrast, was more interested in the existential relationship between the artist and canvas.

4. Brown, *Chance and Circumstance*, 85.

5. Leo Steinberg, *Encounters with Rauschenberg* (Chicago: University of Chicago Press, 2000), 16–19.

6. Mary Lynn Kotz, *Rauschenberg/Art and Life* (1990, repr., New York: Harry N. Abrams, 2004), 82; Brian O'Doherty, *American Masters: The Voice and the Myth* (New York: Random House, [1973]), 191; Barbara Rose, *Rauschenberg: An Interview* (New York: Vintage, 1987), 51;

Irving Sandler, *A Sweeper Up after Artists: A Memoir* (London: Thames & Hudson, 203), 251; Andrew Forge, *Rauschenberg,* (New York: Harry N. Abrams, 1969), n.p.; Brendan W. Joseph, *Random Order: Robert Rauschenberg and the Neo-Avant-Garde* (Cambridge, MA: MIT Press, 2003), 91; Calvin Tomkins, *Off the Wall: Robert Rauschenberg and the Art World of Our Time* (New York: Penguin, 1980), 96–97; "Robert Rauschenberg—Erased De Kooning," YouTube, uploaded 15 May 2007, https://www.youtube.com/watch?v=tpCWh3IFtDQ.

    7. Hopps, *Early Rauschenberg,* 161.

    8. Rose, *Interview,* 51.

    9. Steinberg, *Encounters,* 20–21.

    10. "Robert Rauschenberg—Erased De Kooning," YouTube.

    11. Kotz, *Rauschenberg,* 89.

    12. Joseph, *Random Order,* 89; Rosalind E. Krauss, "Notes on the Index: Part 1," in *The Originality of the Avant-Garde and Other Modernist Myths* (Cambridge, MA: MIT Press, 1986), 8–199; Robert S. Mattison, *Robert Rauschenberg: Breaking Boundaries* (New Haven, CT: Yale University Press, 2003), 56–57; Roni Feinstein, "Random Order: The First Fifteen Years of Robert Rauschenberg" (PhD diss., New York University, 1990), 85–139.

    13. John Cage, "On Robert Rauschenberg," in *Silence* (Middletown, CT: Wesleyan University Press, 1979), 98.

    14. Feinstein, "Random Order," 4–5.

    15. Kotz, *Rauschenberg,* 76.

    16. James Fitzsimmons, "Art," *Arts and Architecture* 70 (October 1953): 34.

    17. Hubert Crehan, "Raw Duck," *Art Digest* 27 (September 1953): 25; in the same issue was a more favorable notice of the work, Dore Ashton, "Bob Rauschenberg," 21, 21; Tomkins, *Off the Wall,* 85.

    18. Sandler, *Sweeper Up,* 250.

    19. Rauschenberg, "Interview with Richard Kostelanetz," (1968) in Hunter, *Rauschenberg,* 134.

    20. Hunter, *Rauschenberg,* 55.

    21. Cage, "On Robert Rauschenberg," 102; Tomkins, *Off the Wall,* 71.

    22. Cage, "On Robert Rauschenberg," 107.

    23. Forge, *Rauschenberg,* n.p.; Joseph, *Random Order,* 57.

    24. Joseph, *Random Order,* 67–68.

    25. On Duchamp see Calvin Tomkins, *Duchamp: A Biography* (New York: Henry Holt, 1996), and Jerrold Seigel, *The Private Worlds of Marcel Duchamp: Desire, Liberation, and the Self in Modern Culture* (Berkeley: University of California Press, 1995). Carlos Basualdo and Erica F. Battle, eds., *Dancing around the Bride: Cage, Cunningham, Johns, Rauschenberg, and Duchamp* (New Haven, CT: Yale University Press, 2012), deals fully with the presence of Duchamp and his influence on Cage, Cunningham, Johns, and Rauschenberg.

    26. Basualdo and Battle, *Dancing around the Bride,* 310.

    27. O'Doherty, *American Masters,* 201; Rose, *Interview,* 56.

    28. Joseph, *Random Order,* 89; Feinstein, "Random Order," 116. The Duchamp piece was *Object with Hidden Notes* (1916).

    29. Eliot, "Tradition and the Individual Talent," in *Selected Essays, 1917–1932* (New York: Harcourt, Brace, 1932), 3–11.

    30. Kotz, *Rauschenberg,* 89; Rauschenberg, "Statement," in *Sixteen Americans,* ed. Dorothy Miller (New York: Museum of Modern Art, 1959), 58.

31. Cage, "On Robert Rauschenberg," 99.

32. Hopps, *Early Rauschenberg*, 162.

33. Joseph, *Random Order*, 60.

34. Hopps, *Early Rauschenberg*, 114–15.

35. Feinstein, "Random Order," 105.

36. Brown, *Chance and Circumstance*, 35; Kotz, *Rauschenberg*, 76; Joseph, *Random Order*, 81–82. According to Feinstein, "Random Order," Rauschenberg's intent "was to provoke the spectator to see" (104, 105).

37. Helen Molesworth, "Before Bed," *October* 63 (Winter 1993): 71–72. In contrast, see Jonathan Katz, " 'Committing the Perfect Crime': Sexuality, Assemblage, and the Postmodern Turn in American Art," *Art Journal* 67, no. 1 (Spring 2008): 38–53. See also Marjorie Perloff, "Watchman, Spy and Dead Man: Jasper Johns, Frank O'Hara, John Cage and the 'Aesthetic of Indifference,' " *Modernism/Modernity* 8, no. 2 (2001): 197–223.

38. Mattison, *Robert Rauschenberg*, 32.

39. Robert Rauschenberg, "Interview with Kostelanetz," in Hunter, *Rauschenberg*, 144.

40. Basualdo and Battle, *Dancing around the Bride*, 215; Cage quoted in Benjamin H. D. Buchloh, "Conceptual Art, 1962–1969: From the Aesthetic of Administration to the Critique of Institutions," *October* 55 (Winter 1990): 112.

41. Roth, "Aesthetic of Indifference," in *Dancing* Around, 209–13. She does view Johns's flag paintings from 1954 as more engaged with the patriotism of the historical moment. Joseph argues that Cage, from his earliest days, had a "recognition of the capitalist totalization of the globe." Joseph, *Random Order*, 19. On how a Kierkegaardian "No" applied to artists, see Harold Rosenberg, "The American Action Painters," in *The Tradition of the New*, 32.

42. Jonathan Katz, " 'Committing the Perfect Crime': Sexuality, Assemblage, and the Postmodern Turn in American Art," *Art Journal* 67, no. 1 (Spring 2008): 45, 51.

43. Exemplary of this thesis are: Serge Guilbaut, *How New York Stole the Idea of Modern Art: Abstract Expressionism, Freedom, and the Cold War*, trans. Arthur Goldhammer (Chicago: University of Chicago Press, 1983), and Eve Cockcroft, "Abstract Expressionism, Weapon of the Cold War," *Artforum* 12 (June 1974): 39–41.

44. Hunter, *Rauschenberg*, 46.

45. William Seitz, *The Art of Assemblage* (New York: Doubleday, 1961), 116.

46. Joseph, *Random Order*, 17.

47. Rose, *Interview*, 72.

48. Michael Sherry, *Gay Artists in Modern American Culture: An Imagined Conspiracy* (Chapel Hill: University of North Carolina Press, 2007), 101.

49. Kotz, *Rauschenberg*, 71; Cage, "On Robert Rauschenberg," 101.

Chapter 3

1. The significance of a jacket in *On the Waterfront* is also apparent. For an analysis of it, and of the film in general, see Leo Braudy, *On the Waterfront* (London: BFI, 2005), 38ff.

2. J. Hoberman, *An Army of Phantoms: American Movies and the Making of the Cold War* (New York: New Press, 2011), 253–54.

3. The origins of this line lie in a conversation between director Stanley Kramer and a biker. Peter Manso, *Brando: The Biography* (New York: Hyperion, 1994), 339.

4. Susan L. Mizruchi is especially good on Brando as a minimalist actor, influenced by reading and his passion for modern jazz. Mizruchi, *Brando's Smile: His Life, Thought, and Work* (New York: W. W. Norton, 2014), xxii, xxxvii.

5. Susan Sontag, *Against Interpretation* (New York: Farrar, Straus & Giroux, 1966), 3–14. On the centrality of spontaneity in this period, although it omits Brando, see Daniel Belgrad, *The Culture of Spontaneity: Improvisation and the Arts in Postwar America* (Chicago: University of Chicago Press, 1988).

6. Angela Carter, *Notes for a Theory of Sixties Style* (London: Chatto & Windus, 1997), 105. And teens consumed leather jackets as visible signs of rebellion, albeit coopted ones. Grace Palladino, *Teenagers: An American History* (New York: Basic Books, 1996), 96ff.

7. Elia Kazan, *A Life* (New York: Alfred A. Knopf, 1988), 525; David Downing, *Marlon Brando* (New York: Stein & Day, 1984), 46, 53. See also the essays on the film in Joanna E. Rapf, ed., *On the Waterfront* (Cambridge, UK: Cambridge University Press, 2003).

8. A. W., "Astor Offers 'On the Waterfront,'" *New York Times*, 29 July 1954, 18.

9. *The Wild Ones* was actually first released on 30 December 30 1953. "Cinema: A Tiger in the Reeds," *Time*, 11 October 1954.

10. Louis Berg, "Streetcar to Hollywood," *Los Angeles Times*, 16 July 1950, 116.

11. Marlon Brando, *Brando: Songs My Mother Taught Me* (New York: Random House, 1994), 121.

12. Manso, *Brando*, 257.

13. Brando, *Songs*, 223.

14. Hedda Hopper, "Actor Defies Usual Movie Customs: Hollywood Shaken by Nonconformity of Marlon Brando," *Los Angeles Times*, 7 May 1950.

15. Stefan Kanter, *Somebody: The Reckless Life and Remarkable Career of Marlon Brando* (New York: Alfred A. Knopf, 2008), 94; Darwin Porter, *Brando Unzipped* (New York: Blood Moon, 2005), 295.

16. Manso, *Brando*, 286–87; Carlo Fiore, *Bud: The Brando I Knew* (New York: Delacorte, 1974), 106–7; Ty Burr, *Gods Like Us: On Movie Stardom and Modern Fame* (New York: Pantheon, 2012); Berg, "Streetcar to Hollywood,"116.

17. Manso, *Brando*, 430.

18. Truman Capote, "Profiles: The Duke in His Domain," *New Yorker*, 19 November 1957, 56.

19. Rita Moreno, *Rita Moreno: A Memoir* (New York: Celebra, 2013), 155, 160; Manso, *Brando*, 284–85.

20. Graham McCann, *Rebel Males: Clift, Brando and Dean* (New Brunswick, NJ: Rutgers University Press, 1991); David K. Johnson, *The Lavender Scare: The Cold War Persecution of Gays and Lesbians in the Federal Government* (Chicago: University of Chicago Press, 2004); Robert J. Corber, *In the Name of National Security: Hitchcock, Homophobia, and the Political Construction of Gender in Postwar America* (Durham, NC: Duke University Press, 1993); David Savran, *Taking it Like a Man: White Masculinity, Masochism, and Contemporary American Culture* (Princeton, NJ: Princeton University Press, 1998). On Brando's bisexuality see Manso, *Brando*, 89–91, 161–65. See also the rather sensationalistic Darwin Porter and Danforth Prince, *Pink Triangle: The Feuds and Private Lives of Tennessee Williams, Gore Vidal, Truman Capote and Famous Members of Their Entourage* ([New York]: Blood Moon, 2014), 32, passim.

21. Trilling, "The Kinsey Report," in *The Liberal Imagination* (New York: Viking, 1950), 216–35; Bart Beaty, *Fredric Wertham and the Critique of Mass Culture* (Oxford: University of Mississippi Press, 2005). On the report and American society, see Miriam G. Reumann,

American Sexual Character: Sex, Gender, and National Identity in the Kinsey Reports (Berkeley: University of California Press, 2005).

22. Joanne Meyerowitz, *How Sex Changed: A History of Transsexuality in the United States* (Cambridge, MA: Harvard University Press, 2004), 51–97. See also Elizabeth Fraterrigo, *Playboy and the Making of the Good Life in Modern America* (New York: Oxford University Press, 2009), esp. 48–79.

23. James T. Patterson, *Grand Expectations: The United States, 1945–1974* (New York: Oxford University Press, 1996), 314; on the rise of television, see Douglas T. Miller and Marion Nowak, *The Fifties: The Way We Really Were* (Garden City, NY: Doubleday, 1977), 338–67.

24. On the centrality of this metaphor for the period, see W. T. Lhamon Jr., *Deliberate Speed: The Origins of a Cultural Style in the American 1950s* (Washington, DC: Smithsonian Institution, 1990).

25. Patterson, *Grand Expectations*, 348–69, 269–94.

26. Jeff Young, ed., *Kazan: The Master Director Discusses His Films* (New York: Newmarket, 1990), 150.

27. On Brando and his makeup practices, see Mizruchi, *Brando Smiles*, 54–56.

28. John Bak, "'sneakin' and spyin'" from Broadway to the Beltway: Cold War Masculinity, Brick, and Homosexual Existentialism," *Theatre Journal* 56 (May 2004): 225–49.

29. McCann, *Rebel Males*, 2.

30. Michael T. Schuyler, "He 'coulda been a contender' for Miss America: Feminizing Brando in *On the Waterfront*," *Canadian Review of American Studies* 41, no. 1 (2011): 100–103.

31. Richard Schickel, *Brando* (New York: Thunder's Mouth, 1991), 90. On the politics of the film, see Braudy, *On the Waterfront*, and Peter Biskind, "The Politics of Power in 'On the Waterfront,'" *Film Quarterly* 29 (Autumn 1975): 25–38.

32. Leo Braudy, "'No Body's Perfect': Method Acting and 50s Culture," *Michigan Quarterly Review* 35 (Winter 1996): 194–98; James Naremore, *Acting in the Cinema* (Berkeley: University of California Press, 1988), 200–202.

33. Whereas Stanislavski also preached the value of improvisation. See Naremore, *Acting*, 201.

34. Kanfer, *Somebody*, 37; McCann, *Rebel*, 84–85.

35. Stella Adler, *The Art of Acting*, comp. and ed. Howard Kissel (New York: Applause, 2000), 22, 165; Eduard J. Erslovas, "On the Waterfront and the Method" (MA thesis, California State University, Long Beach, 1993), 26–42.

36. Brando, *Songs*, 80–81.

37. McCann, *Rebel*, 89.

38. Foster Hirsch, *A Method to Their Madness: The History of the Actor's Studio* (New York: W. W. Norton, 1984), sees Brando as beholden to Strasberg, a reading that Brando would reject. Brando, *Songs*, 122.

39. Brando, *Songs*, 175ff.; Manso, *Brando*, 339–42.

40. Stanley Kramer, *A Mad, Mad, Mad, Mad World: A Life in Hollywood* (New York: Harcourt Brace, 1997), 55–57.

41. Kanfer, *Somebody*, 116; Martin Rubin, "'Make Love Make War': Cultural Confusion and the Biker Film Cycle," *Film History* 6 (Autumn 1994): 360ff.; Jerold Simmons, "Violent Youth: The Censoring and Public Reception of the Wild One and the Blackboard Jungle," *Film History* 20, no. 3 (2008): 381–83.

42. Brando, *Songs*, 202.

43. Brando, *Songs*, 64, 71.

44. Kazan, *A Life*, 255.

45. Brando, *Songs*, 178–79.

46. Kanfer, *Somebody*, 130; Brando, *Songs*, 198.

47. Budd Schulberg, *On the Waterfront: A Screenplay* (Carbondale: Southern Illinois University Press, 1983), 104. The dialogue quoted in the text is as it appears in the script.

48. Brando, *Songs*, 199.

49. Brando, *Songs*, 418.

50. Brando, *Songs*, 126.

51. "A Tiger in the Reeds," *Time*, 11 October 1954.

52. Brando, *Songs*, 5–7. On his problematic childhood see Kanfer, *Somebody*, 4–8.

53. Brando, *Songs*, 125; Joe Morello and Edward Z. Epstein, *Brando: An Unauthorized Biography* (New York: Crown, 1973), 45. For more on these psychological stresses, see Manso, *Brando*, 244–46.

54. Harold Clurman, *All People Are Famous* (New York: Harcourt, Brace, Jovanovich, 1974), 260.

55. Robert Brustein, "The New Hollywood: Myth and Anti-Myth," *Film Quarterly* 12 (Spring 1959): 23–26.

56. Pauline Kael, "The Glamour of Delinquency," in *I Lost it at the Movies: The Essential Kael Collection, '54 to '65* (New York: Marion Boyars, 2002), 51.

57. Brando, *Songs*, 176.

58. Robert Tanitch, *Brando* (London: Studio Vista, 1994), 54.

Chapter 4

1. On this connection see Michael Trask, "Patricia Highsmith's Method," *American Literary History* 22, no. 3 (2010): 584–614. David Riesman, in collaboration with Reuel Denney and Nathan Glazer, *The Lonely Crowd: A Study of the Changing American Character* (New Haven, CT: Yale University Press, 1950), 9, 20–3. On the shift in identity and character more generally, see Wilfred M. McClay, *The Masterless: Self and Society in Modern America* (Chapel Hill: University of North Carolina Press, 1994), esp. 226–68.

2. See Patricia Highsmith, afterword to *The Price of Salt*, in *Selected Novels and Short Stories*, ed. Joan Schenkar (New York: W. W. Norton, 2011), 577–80.

3. Joan Schenkar, *The Talented Miss Highsmith: The Secret Life and Serious Art of Patricia Highsmith* (New York: St. Martin's, 2009), 269.

4. Andrew Wilson, *Beautiful Shadow: A Life of Patricia Highsmith* (London: Bloomsbury, 2003), 152.

5. Schenkar, *Talented*, 282. Highsmith recorded this observation on July 1, 1950, a day after she had stalked Senn's home in New Jersey.

6. On Kathleen Senn see Schenkar, *Talented*, 50–51, 267–68, 270–73.

7. Schenkar, *Talented*, xviii.

8. Wilson, *Beautiful Shadow*, 167; Schenkar, *Talented*, 273.

9. Schenkar, *Talented*, xviii.

10. Wilson, *Beautiful Shadow*, 21.

11. Schenkar, *Talented*, 87.

12. Schenkar, *Talented*, 27, 157–70.

13. Schenkar, *Talented*, 130–37.

14. Schenkar, *Talented*, 293. On Koestler and his relations for women, see Noel Malcolm, review of *Koestler: The Indispensable Intellectual*, by Michael Scammell, *Telegraph*, 14 February 2010, http://www.telegraph.co.uk/culture/books/7205860/Koestler-The-Indispensable-Intellectual-by-Michael-Scammell-review.html.

15. James Sallis, review of *The Selected Stories of Patricia Highsmith*, *Boston Review*, 1 October 2001, http://bostonreview.net/fiction-books-ideas/james-sallis-review-selected-stories-patricia-highsmith.

16. Hillis Millis, "Bruno Takes Over," *New York Times Book Review*, 21 May 1950, 15.

17. Schenkar, *Talented*, 282.

18. Highsmith, *Selected Novels*, 25. The themes of murdered wives, confused identities, and guilt also figure in Highsmith's next novel, *The Blunderer*, published in 1954.

19. Wilson, *Beautiful Shadow*, 123.

20. Highsmith, *Selected Novels*, 66.

21. Highsmith, *Selected Novels*, 173. On Guy and Bruno's merging identities see Noel Mawer, *A Critical Study of the Fiction of Patricia Highsmith: From the Psychological to the Political* (Lewiston, NY: Edwin Mellen, 2004), 64–100.

22. Odette L'Henry Evans, "A Feminist Approach to Patricia Highsmith's Fiction," in *American Horror Fiction: From Brockden Brown to Stephen King*, ed. Brian Doherty (New York: St. Martin's, 1990), 107.

23. Highsmith, *Selected Novels*, 232, 235.

24. Highsmith, *Selected Novels*, 239.

25. Wilson, *Beautiful Shadow*, 153; Schenkar, *Talented*, 263–65.

26. Schenkar, *Talented*, 287–88.

27. Schenkar, *Talented*, 287–89; Wilson, *Beautiful Shadow*, 156–60.

28. Wilson, *Beautiful Shadow*, 168.

29. Jaye Zimet, *Strange Sisters: The Art of Lesbian Pulp Fiction, 1949–1969* (New York: Viking Studio, 1999), 27; Schenkar, *Talented*, 279.

30. David K. Johnson, *The Lavender Scare: The Cold War Persecution of Gays and Lesbians in the Federal Government* (Chicago: University of Chicago Press, 2006); Elaine Tyler May, *Homeward Bound: American Families in the Cold War Era* (New York: Basic Books, 1988); Joanne Meyerowitz, "Beyond the Feminine Mystique: A Reassessment of Postwar Mass Culture, 1946–1956," *Journal of American History* 79 (March 1993): 1455–82.

31. Miriam G. Reumann, *American Sexual Character: Sex, Gender, and National Identity in the Kinsey Reports* (Berkeley: University of California Press, 2005).

32. Russell Harrison, *Patricia Highsmith* (New York: Twayne, 1997), 101; Highsmith, *Selected Novels*, 579. Especially insightful, and entertaining, on the novel is Terry Castle, "Pulp Valentine: Patricia Highsmith's Erotic Lesbian Thriller," *Slate*, 23 May 2006, http://www.slate.com/articles/news_and_politics/pulp_fiction/2006/05/pulp_valentine_4.html.

33. Highsmith, *The Price of Salt*, 341, 375.

34. Highsmith, *Selected Novels*, 393.

35. This anticipates the famous road trip undertaken by Humbert Humbert in Nabokov's *Lolita*.

36. Highsmith, *Selected Novels*, 522, 536.

37. Highsmith, *Selected Novels*, 546.

38. Highsmith, *Selected Novels*, 567–68.

39. Highsmith, *Selected Novels*, 575.

40. Wilson, *Beautiful Shadow*, 187.

41. George Cotkin, *Existential America* (Baltimore: Johns Hopkins University Press, 2003).

42. Fiona Peters, *Anxiety and Evil in the Writings of Patricia Highsmith* (Farnham, UK: Ashgate, 2011), 171.

43. Schenkar, *Talented*, 117.

44. On Chambers see the excellent biography by Sam Tanenhaus, *Whittaker Chambers* (New York: Random House, 1997).

45. Schenkar, *Talented*, 29.

46. Schenkar, *Talented*, 430–32.

47. Schenkar, *Talented*, 89, 323–25.

48. Wilson, *Beautiful Shadow*, 179.

49. Wilson, *Beautiful Shadow*, 187.

50. Peters, *Anxiety*, 30.

51. Anthony Channell Hilfer, "'Not Really Such a Monster': Highsmith's Ripley as Thriller Protagonist and Protean Man," *Midwest Quarterly* 25 (Summer 1984): 361–74; Patricia Highsmith, *The Talented Mr. Ripley*, in Highsmith, *Selected Novels*, 34, 38.

52. Highsmith, *Talented*, 53. On Ripley as a perversion of the Horatio Alger success-story ideal, see Alex Tuss, "Masculine Identity and Success: A Critical Analysis of Patricia Highsmith's *The Talented Mr. Ripley* and Chuck Palahniuk's *Fight Club*," *Journal of Men's Studies* 12 (Winter 2004): 97; Highsmith, *Talented*, 53.

53. Highsmith, *Talented*, 100. On Ripley's gestures see Erlene Hubly, "A Portrait of the Artist: The Novels of Patricia Highsmith," *Clues* 5, no. 1 (1984): 128.

54. Highsmith, *Talented*, 104. For an intriguing take on Ripley as a "male lesbian," see Slavoj Žižek, "Not a Desire to Have Him, But to Be Like Him," *London Review of Books*, 21 August 2003, 13–14.

55. Highsmith, *Talented*, 192. For a reading of the murder as mimicking Christ's crucifixion, see Leonard Cassuto, *Hard-Boiled Sentimentality: The Secret History of American Crime Stories* (New York: Columbia University Press, 2008), 142.

56. Highsmith, *Plotting and Writing Suspense Fiction* (Boston: The Writer, 1966), 51; Highsmith, *Talented*, 289.

Chapter 5

1. Ginsberg to Robert LaVigne, 3 August 1956 and Rebecca Ginsberg, 11 August 1956, in *The Letters of Allen Ginsberg*, ed. Bill Morgan (New York: Da Capo, 2008), 139–41; Bill Morgan, *I Celebrate Myself: The Somewhat Private Life of Allen Ginsberg* (New York: Penguin, 2006), 220–22.

2. Barry Miles, *Ginsberg: A Biography* (New York: Simon & Schuster, 1989), 188–220.

3. Quoted in Jane Kramer, *Allen Ginsberg in America* (New York: Random House, 1969), 48.

4. Jack Kerouac, *The Dharma Bums* (New York: Viking, 1958), quoted in Allen Ginsberg, *Howl: 50th Anniversary Edition* (New York: Harper Perennial, 2006), appendix 2, 166. The

best account of the Six reading, and of *Howl,* is Jonah Raskin, *American Scream: Allen Ginsberg's* Howl *and the Making of the Beat Generation* (Berkeley: University of California Press, 2004), 13–19. See also Steven Watson, *The Birth of the Beat Generation: Visionaries, Rebels, and Hipsters, 1944–60* (New York: Pantheon, 1995), 180–87; and Miles, *Ginsberg,* 188–213. On Ginsberg's poem within the context of the San Francisco poetry renaissance, see Michael Davidson, *The San Francisco Renaissance: Poetics and Community at Mid-Century* (Cambridge, UK: Cambridge University Press, 1989), 76–85.

5. Quoted in Ginsberg, *Howl,* appendix 2, 167.

6. Quoted in Ginsberg, *Howl,* 168.

7. Ann Charters, *Beat Down to Your Soul,* (New York: Penguin Books, 2001), 375; Gregory Corso, with Allen Ginsberg, "Literary Technique and the Beat Generation," in *Deliberate Prose: Selected Essays, 1952–95,* ed. Bill Morgan (New York: HarperCollins, 2000), 241.

8. Corso, "Literary Technique," 241; Charters, *Beat Down to Your Soul,* 518.

9. Ginsberg, *Howl,* 3–6.

10. Jack Goodman, quoted in Rebecca Solnit, *Secret Exhibition: Six California Artists of the Cold War* (San Francisco: City Lights, 1990), 48.

11. Michael McClure, *Scratching the Beat Surface* (San Francisco: North Point, 1982), 15.

12. Ginsberg, *Howl,* 6.

13. Snyder, "Notes on the Beat Generation," in Charters, *Beat Down to Your Soul,* 518.

14. McClure, *Scratching,* 13.

15. Bill Morgan, *I Celebrate Myself,* 209.

16. Allen Ginsberg, *The Book of Martyrdom and Artifice: First Journals and Poems, 1937–1952,* ed. Juanita Liebermann-Plimpton and Bill Morgan (New York: DaCapo Press, 2006), 169.

17. Ginsberg to Kerouac, 5 June 1955, in Bill Morgan and David Stanford, eds., *Jack Kerouac and Allen Ginsberg: The Letters* (New York: Viking, 2010), 298; Kramer, *Allen Ginsberg in America,* 42.

18. Michael Schumacher, *Dharma Lion: A Biography of Allen Ginsberg* (New York: St. Martin's, 1992), 192.

19. Allen Ginsberg, *Journals: Mid-Fifties, 1954–1958,* ed. Gordon Ball (New York: HarperCollins, 1995), 139–40.

20. Ginsberg to Kerouac, 25 August 1955, in Morgan and Stanford, *Jack Kerouac and Allen Ginsberg,* 319.

21. Schumacher, *Dharma Lion,* 200.

22. Quoted in Schumacher, *Dharma Lion,* 197.

23. Quoted in Miles, *Ginsberg,* 187.

24. Allen Ginsberg, "First Thought, Best Thought," in Ginsberg, *Composed on the Tongue,* ed. Donald Allen (Bolinas, CA: Grey Fox, 1976), 106.

25. On the confessional aspects of the poem, especially in relation to other confessional poets of the period, see Anne Hartman, "Confessional Counterpublics in Frank O'Hara and Allen Ginsberg," *Journal of Modern Literature* 28, no. 4 (Summer 2005): 50–53.

26. Ginsberg, *Journals,* 115.

27. Raskin, *American Scream,* 81; Schumacher, *Dharma Lion,* 196.

28. Ginsberg, *Howl,* 7.

29. Allen Ginsberg, "Interview with Tom Clark" (1965) and "Interview with Barry Farrell" (1966), both in Ginsberg, *Spontaneous Mind: Selected Interviews, 1958–1996,* ed. David Carter (New York: HarperCollins, 2001), 24, 55.

30. Allen Ginsberg, "Kaddish," in *Collected Poems, 1947–1997* (New York: HarperPerennial, 2006), 230.

31. James Breslin, "Allen Ginsberg: The Origins of 'Howl' and 'Kaddish'" *Iowa Review* 8 no. 2 (Spring 1977): 94.

32. Ginsberg to Kerouac, ca. 16 December 1948, in Morgan and Stanford, *Jack Kerouac and Allen Ginsberg,* 53.

33. Ginsberg, *Letters of Allen Ginsberg,* 33.

34. Watson, *Birth of the Beat Generation,* 110–12.

35. Ginsberg, *Howl,* 7.

36. On his hospitalization see the revisionist piece by Janet Hadda, "Ginsberg in Hospital," *American Imago* 65 no. 2 (Summer 2008): 229–59. Although Ginsberg dedicated *Howl* to Solomon, he actually later claimed to have had his mother in mind. See Schumacher, *Dharma Lion,* 208. Ginsberg was not confined to Rockland; he was at the New York State Psychiatric Institute. Raskin, *American Scream,* 90.

37. Ginsberg, *Howl,* 5.

38. Graham Caveney, *Screaming with Joy: The Life of Allen Ginsberg* (New York: Broadway, 1999), 33–37.

39. Ginsberg, *Book of Martyrdom,* 503, 123; Ginsberg to Helen Parker, 12 October 1950, in Ginsberg, *Letters of Allen Ginsberg,* 62.

40. Ginsberg to Neal Cassady, 7 September 1951, in Ginsberg, *Letters of Allen Ginsberg,* 74–75.

41. John Clellon Holmes, "The Philosophy of the Beat Generation" in Charters, *Beat Down to Your Soul,* 231.

42. Ginsberg, *Collected Poems,* 118.

43. Ginsberg, *Howl,* 3, 6, 7. After the Cuban Missile Crisis of 1962, Ginsberg became fixated on nuclear apocalypse.

44. I thank my editor, Brendan O'Neill, for this suggestion.

45. Ginsberg to Kerouac, 25 August 1955, in Morgan and Stanford, *Jack Kerouac and Allen Ginsberg,* 319.

46. Allen Ginsberg, "Literary Technique and the Beat Generation," in Ginsberg, *Deliberate Prose,* 230.

47. On Moloch as capturing some of Ginsberg's feelings toward his father, see Breslin, "Origins of 'Howl' and 'Kaddish,'" 92–93.

48. Howe, "This Age of Conformity," *Partisan Review* 21 (January–February, 1954): 7–33.

49. Alan Valentine, *The Age of Conformity* (Chicago: Henry Regnery, 1954).

50. Ginsberg, *Howl,* 4, 8.

51. Ginsberg, *Howl,* 4.

52. Quoted in Ronald Sukenick, *Down and In: Life in the Underground* (New York: Beech Tree, 1987), 95, 116. See also Diane di Prima, *Recollections of My Life as a Woman: The New York Years* (New York: Viking, 2001), 163.

53. All of these quotes are in Ginsberg, *Howl,* 156, 161. One of Trilling's most engaging fictional pieces, "Of This Time, of That Place" deals with a mentally unhinged but immensely talented and rebellious student. Some have speculated that it was based on Ginsberg, but Trilling stated in a letter that Ginsberg was not the model but that Ginsberg identified with the main character. Moreover, Trilling stated that he never doubted Ginsberg's rationality. Trilling to Leslie Fiedler, 17 May 1964, box 1, Lionel Trilling Papers, Rare Book and Manuscript Library, Columbia University.

54. Quoted in Ginsberg, *Howl: 50th Anniversary Edition*, 162–64.

55. Court transcripts, letters, newspaper clippings, and almost all information regarding the case against *Howl* can be found in Bill Morgan and Nancy J. Peters, eds., *Howl on Trial: The Battle for Free Expression*, (San Francisco: City Lights, 2006), 2–3. J. W. Ehrlich, ed., *Howl of the Censor: The Four Letter Word on Trial* (San Carlos, CA: Nourse, 1956), has a fuller copy of the transcript.

56. Ginsberg to Robert Creeley, 11 December 1956, in Ginsberg, *Letters of Allen Ginsberg*, 147.

57. Ginsberg to Ferlinghetti, 10 June 1957 in Ginsberg, *Letters of Allen Ginsberg*, 155.

58. See the discussion of *Roth* in Edward De Grazia, *Girls Lean Back Everywhere: The Law of Obscenity and the Assault on Genius* (New York: Random House, 1992), 273–326.

59. Morgan and Peters, *Howl on Trial*, 130. See also De Grazia, *Girls*, 327–42.

60. Morgan and Peters, *Howl on Trial*, 136.

61. Morgan and Peters, *Howl on Trial*, 131.

62. Morgan and Peters, *Howl on Trial*, 181.

63. Morgan and Peters, *Howl on Trial*, 198.

Chapter 6

1. The lyrics for the song had been revised somewhat. Gone was: "You wear them dresses, the sun comes shining through / I can't believe all that mess belongs to you." Colin Escott, *Good Rockin' Tonight: Sun Records and the Birth of Rock 'n' Roll*, with Martin Hawkins (New York: St. Martin's, 1991), 195. On the history of the song, first recorded in 1955 by Big Maybelle and produced by Quincy Jones for OKeh records label, see Nick Tosches, *Country: The Twisted Roots of Rock 'n' Roll* (New York: Da Capo, 1996), 70. On Lewis, see the first-rate biography by Rick Bragg, *Jerry Lee Lewis: His Own Story* (New York: HarperCollins, 2014).

2. Robert Palmer, *Jerry Lee Lewis Rocks!* (New York: Delilah, 1981), 7.

3. Quoted in Paul Friedlander, *Rock and Roll: A Social History* (Boulder, CO: Westview, 1996), 49.

4. Palmer, *Lewis Rocks!*, 22.

5. Linda Martin and Kerry Segrave, *Anti-Rock: The Opposition to Rock 'n' Roll* (Hamden, CT: Archon, 1988), 75.

6. Greil Marcus, *Mystery Train: Images of America in Rock 'n' Roll Music*, 5th ed. (New York: Plume, 2008), 169; Escott, *Good Rockin'*, 189.

7. Stephen J. Whitfield, *A Death in the Delta: The Story of Emmett Till* (New York: Free Press, 1988), places the murder within the context of southern lynchings.

8. Pete Daniel, *Lost Revolutions: The South in the 1950s* (Chapel Hill: University of North Carolina Press, 2000), 193.

9. John A. Jackson, *American Bandstand: Dick Clark and the Making of a Rock 'n' Roll Empire* (New York: Oxford University Press, 1997), 55–58.

10. Horace Newcomb, "The Opening of America: Meaningful Difference in 1950s Television," in *The Other Fifties: Interrogating Midcentury American Icons*, ed. Joel Foreman (Urbana: University of Illinois Press, 1997), 104. Newcomb also discusses how the television show *Have Gun, Will Travel*, about Paladin, a sophisticated gunman, challenged traditional sensibilities for the Western genre, 119.

11. David R. Shumway, "Watching Elvis: The Male Rock Star as Object of the Gaze," in Foreman, *The Other Fifties*, 125–27.

12. Glenn C. Altschuler, *All Shook Up: How Rock 'n' Roll Changed America* (Oxford: Oxford University Press, 1963), 162–63.

13. Bruce Pegg, *Brown Eyed Handsome Man: The Life and Hard Times of Chuck Berry* (New York: Routledge, 2002), 67–68; Howard A. DeWitt, *Chuck Berry: Rock 'n' Roll Music* (Fremont, CA: Horizon, 1981), 77–82. On Berry's ability to code protest, see George Lipsitz, *Time Passages: Collective Memory and American Popular Culture* (Minneapolis: University of Minnesota Press, 1990), 115.

14. Chuck Berry, *The Autobiography* (New York: Harmony, 1987), 202–3.

15. Berry, *Autobiography*, 116–17.

16. Carl Belz, *The Story of Rock* (New York: Oxford University Press, 1969), 61–62.

17. Imagine because the distance between listening to music and being liberated was often immense. See, Martha Bayles, *Hole in Our Soul: The Loss of Beauty and Meaning in American Popular Music* (New York: The Free Press, 1994), 108. On Berry's brilliance, see Robert Christgau, *Any Old Way You Choose It: Rock and Other Pop Music, 1967–1973* (New York: Cooper Square Press, 2000), 140–8.

18. Richard Aquila, *That Old Time Rock & Roll: A Chronicle of an Era, 1954–1963* (New York: Schirmer, 1989), 27ff.

19. Brian Ward, *Just My Soul Responding: Rhythm and Blues, Black Consciousness, and Race Relations* (Berkeley: University of California Press, 1998), 50; Altschuler, *All Shook Up*, 78–80.

20. Quoted in Grace Palladino, *Teenagers: An American History* (New York: Basic Books, 1996), 129.

21. Robert J. Cain, *Whole Lotta Shakin' Goin' On: Jerry Lee Lewis* (New York: Dial, 1981), 42. On Phillips and race see Peter Guralnick, *Last Train to Memphis: The Rise of Elvis Presley* (Boston: Little, Brown, 1994), 96, 134–35.

22. Reebee Garofalo, *Rockin' Out: Popular Music in the USA* (Boston: Allyn & Bacon, 1997), 139; Cain, *Whole Lotta Shakin'*, 18.

23. Although he sometimes gets carried away with his prose and his claims, Nick Tosches captures Jerry Lee Lewis in brilliant fashion in *Hellfire* (New York: Grove, 1982). On Lewis's youth see the book by his sister, Linda Gail Lewis, *The Devil, Me, and Jerry Lee*, with Les Pendleton (Atlanta: Longstreet, 1998), 13–22.

24. Bragg, *His Own Story*, 65–66. L. G. Lewis, *The Devil*, 14.

25. Garofalo, *Rockin' Out*, 134; Palmer, *Lewis Rocks!*, 29.

26. Palmer, *Lewis Rocks!*, 26; L. G. Lewis, *The Devil*, 23.

27. Craig Morrison, *Go Cat Go!: Rockabilly Music and Its Makers* (Urbana: University of Illinois Press, 1996), 31ff.

28. For the "authenticity" of black rhythm and blues tradition, see Nelson George, *The Death of Rhythm & Blues* (New York: Pantheon, 1988); for sophisticated ripostes to this notion, see Ward, *Just My Soul*, and George Lipsitz, "'Ain't Nobody Here but Us Chickens': The Class Origins of Rock and Roll," in Lipsitz, *Rainbow at Midnight: Labor and Culture in the 1940s* (Urbana: University of Illinois Press, 1994), 303–34, and Steve Perry, "'Ain't No Mountain High Enough': The Politics of Crossover," in *Facing the Music*, ed. Simon Frith (New York: Pantheon, 1989), 51–87.

29. George, *Death*, 62–65.

30. And white gospel music as well. See Jim Curtis, *Rock Eras: Interpretations of Music and Society, 1954–1984* (Bowling Green, OH: Bowling Green State University Press, 1987), 29–32.

31. Tosches, *Hellfire*, 72–74.

32. Bragg, *His Own Story*, 171.

33. Joe Bonomo, *Jerry Lee Lewis: Lost and Found* (New York: Continuum, 2009), 20.

34. "Round the World in 96 Minutes," *New York Times*, 6 October 1957, 193.

35. Myra Lewis, *Great Balls of Fire: The Uncensored Story of Jerry Lee Lewis*, with Murray Silver (New York: William Morrow, 1982), 111–12.

36. Kevin Crouch and Tanja Crouch, *Sun King: The Life and Times of Sam Phillips, the Man Behind Sun Records* (London: Piatkus, 2008), 153.

37. The conversation was recorded. See Tosches, *Hellfire*, 129–33.

38. Quoted in Tosches, *Hellfire*, 145–46.

39. Bragg, *His Own Story*, 189, 254.

40. Martin and Segrave, *Anti-Rock*, 13, 27.

41. Ward, *Just My Soul*, 95.

42. Altschuler, *All Shook Up*, 74; Ward, *Just My Soul*, 107, 91.

43. Quoted in Cain, *Whole Lotta Shakin'*, 12, 18.

44. Jimmy Gutterman, *Rockin' My Life Away: Listening to Jerry Lee Lewis* (Nashville: Rutledge Hill, 1991, 71.

45. Tosches, *Country*, 73.

46. Lewis, *Great Balls*, 118–22.

47. Palmer, *Lewis Rocks!*, 62.

48. Tosches, *Hellfire*, 166.

49. Bonomo, *Jerry Lee Lewis*, 18.

50. Cain, *Whole Lotta Shakin'*, 25–31. Nabokov's novel *Lolita*, with its story of a pedophiliac, was issued in the United States in August 1958 to great acclaim and shock. On the book, and its reception, see Brian Boyd, *Vladimir Nabokov: The American Years* (Princeton, NJ: Princeton University Press, 1991), 356–83. On the connection between *Lolita* and Norman Mailer's *An American Dream* (chapter 9), see John Whalen-Bridge, "Murderous Desire in *Lolita* (with Related Thoughts on Mailer's *An American Dream*)," *Nabokov Studies* 7 (2002–3), 75–88.

51. Cain, *Whole Lotta Shakin'*, 32.

Chapter 7

1. The reviews are collected in Anne Wilkes Tucker, ed., *Robert Frank: New York to Nova Scotia* (Houston: Museum of Fine Arts, Houston, 1986), 36–37. Parts of this chapter originally appeared in my article "The Photographer in the Beat-Hipster Idiom: Robert Frank's *The Americans*," *American Studies* 26 (Spring 1985): 19–33.

2. Gilbert Millstein, "In Each a Portrait," *New York Times*, 17 January 1960, 7; William Hogan, "Photo Coverage of the Ugly American," *San Francisco Chronicle*, 27 January 1960, 25.

3. "Review," *New Yorker*, 14 May 1960, 203–4.

4. William S. Johnson, ed., *The Pictures Are a Necessity: Robert Frank in Rochester, NY, November 1988*, (Rochester, NY: International Museum of Photography George Eastman House, 1989), 116.

5. Quotes in Tom Maloney, ed., *U.S. Camera 1958* (New York: U.S. Camera, 1957), 90, 115. *The Americans* was first published in a French edition in 1958, with an American edition appearing in 1959.

6. The article, "On the Road to Florida," only appeared in print in the *Evergreen Review* in 1970. Reprinted in Tucker, *New York to Nova Scotia*, 38–41. I have been unable to find an explanation for the rejection. Kerouac did write that Frank blamed Kerouac's text for its being turned down. Kerouac to Joyce Glassman, 4 June 1958, in Jack Kerouac and Joyce Johnson, *Door Wide Open: A Beat Love Affair in Letters, 1957–1958* (New York: Viking, 2000), 148.

7. W. T. Lhamon Jr., *Deliberate Speed: The Origins of a Cultural Style in the American 1950s* (Washington, DC: Smithsonian Institution Press, 1990), 125–35; Daniel Belgrad, *The Culture of Spontaneity: Improvisation and the Arts in Postwar America* (Chicago: University of Chicago Press, 1998), 196–221.

8. Robert Frank, *Moving Out*, ed. Sarah Greenough and Philip Brookman (Washington, DC: National Gallery of Art, 1994), 98.

9. Robert Frank, *The Lines of My Hand* (New York: Pantheon, 1989), n.p. Frank did, however, like words on signs to appear in his images. The French edition of *The Americans*, to his chagrin, was accompanied by words: those of writers offering observations about the United States.

10. Jack Kerouac, "Introduction," in Robert Frank, *The Americans: Photographs* (New York: Aperture, 1959), i–vi.

11. Robert Frank, "Statement," in Robert Frank and Francois-Marie Banier, eds., *Henry Frank: Father, Photographer, 1890–1976* (Göttingen, Germany: Steidel, 2009), n.p.

12. Johnson, *Pictures Are a Necessity*, 26–27. See also Dennis Wheeler, "Robert Frank Interviewed," *Criteria* 3 (June 1977): 4–7.

13. Joyce Johnson, *Minor Characters* (New York: Washington Square, 1984), 254.

14. Quoted in Martin Gasser, "Zurich to New York: 'Robert Frank, Swiss, unobtrusive, nice…,'" in Frank, *Moving Out*, 47.

15. Quoted in Gasser, "Zurich to New York," 100.

16. Quoted in Gasser, "Zurich to New York," 104.

17. Quoted in Gasser, "Zurich to New York," 106–8.

18. Tucker, *New York to Nova Scotia*, 20–21.

19. On Evans's method, see Belinda Rathbone, *Walker Evans: A Biography* (New York: Houghton Mifflin, 1995), 123–24; for the "politics of the vernacular," see James R. Mellow, *Walker Evans* (New York: Basic Books, 1999), 213ff. For the view that Frank lacked Evans's humanity, see William Stott, "Walker Evans, Robert Frank, and the Landscape of Dissociation," *Artscanada* 31 (December 1974): 83–89.

20. Michael Leja, *Reframing Abstract Expressionism: Subjectivity and Painting in the 1940s* (New Haven, CT: Yale University Press, 1993), 77–79.

21. Eric J. Sandeen, *Picturing an Exhibition: The Family of Man and 1950s America* (Albuquerque: University of New Mexico Press, 1995), 155–80; Edward Steichen, comp., *The Family of Man: The Greatest Photographic Exhibition of All Time* (New York: Museum of Modern Art, 1955), 91.

22. Tod Papageorge, *Walker Evans and Robert Frank: An Essay on Influence* (New Haven, CT: Yale University Art Gallery, 1981), 3–4.

23. Quoted in Johnson, *Pictures Are a Necessity*, 36.

24. Tucker, *New York to Nova Scotia*, 10.

25. Maloney, *U.S. Camera 1958*, 115.

26. Frank quoted in Johnson, *Pictures Are a Necessity*, 37; Allen Ginsberg, "Robert Frank to 1985—A Man," in Tucker, *New York to Nova Scotia*, 74.

27. All quotes from Tucker, *New York to Nova Scotia*, 22, 24–26.

28. Frank, *Lines of My Hand*, n.p.

29. Johnson, *Pictures Are a Necessity*, 41.

30. Susan Sontag, *On Photography* (New York: Farrar, Straus & Giroux, 1978), 61.

31. Such was also the case in the image "Political Rally—Chicago," where a tuba can be imagined making music. On this photograph see Gene Markowski, *The Art of Photography: Image and Illusion* (Englewood Cliffs, NJ: Prentice Hall, 1984), 38–39.

32. Kerouac, *On the Road* (New York: Signet, n.d.), 148.

33. Johnson, *Pictures Are a Necessity*, 173.

34. Tucker, *New York to Nova Scotia*, 28.

35. Frank, *Moving Out*, 204.

36. Frank was hardly alone among adherents of the New Sensibility in turning to film in some manner—consider Andy Warhol, Susan Sontag, Norman Mailer, Bob Dylan, and Gore Vidal.

37. Frank, *Moving Out*, 220.

38. Quoted in Calvin Tomkins, *The Scene: Reports on Post-Modern Art* (New York: Viking, 1976), 173.

39. Amy Taubin, "Circling: Beginnings, Congratulations, Renewals: Robert Frank's Personal New American Cinema," in *Frank Films: The Film and Video Work of Robert Frank*, ed. Brigitta Burger-Utzer and Stefan Grissemann (Zurich: Scalo, 2003), 90.

40. Quoted in Eugenia Parry Janis and Wendy MacNeil, eds., *Photography within the Humanities* (Danbury, NH.: Addison House, 1977), 53.

Chapter 8

1. Malina Journal, Violet Copy, 3 June 1959, Living Theatre Records, Beinecke Library, Yale University (hereafter Living Theatre Records). Excellent on many areas of their life and work is John Tytell, *The Living Theatre: Art, Exile, and Outrage* (New York: Grove, 1995). See also Charles L. Mee Jr., "The Beck's Living Theatre," *Tulane Drama Review* 7, no. 2 (Winter 1962): 194–205. Although he does not mention the Living Theatre, Fred Kaplan's book is fascinating and wide-ranging in its coverage of what was going on during this crucial year. Kaplan, *1959: The Year Everything Changed* (New York: John Wiley, 2009).

2. All quotes in paragraph from Malina Journal, Violet Copy, 27 June, 1959, Living Theatre Records.

3. John Gruen, *The Party's Over Now: Reminiscences of the Fifties—New York's Artists, Writers, Musicians, and Their Friends* (New York: Pushcart, 1989), 100.

4. Gelber, *The Connection* (London: Faber & Faber, 1960), 14–15.

5. Gelber, *Connection*, 44, 27.

6. Gelber, *Connection*, 55.

7. Gelber, *Connection*, 15.

8. Larry Rivers, *What Did I Do?: The Unauthorized Autobiography*, with Arnold Weinstein (New York: HarperCollins, 1992), 354.

9. Gelber, *Connection*, 41.

10. Allan Kaprow, "The Legacy of Jackson Pollock" (1958), in Kaprow, *The Blurring of Art and Life*, ed. Jeff Kelley (Berkeley: University of California Press, 1993), 7, 9; Mildred L. Glimcher, *Happenings: New York, 1958–1963* (New York: Monacelli, 2012), 36–37; Philip

Ursprung, *Allan Kaprow, Robert Smithson, and the Limits to Art*, trans. Fiona Elliott (Berkeley: University of California Press, 2013), 30–34. Beck and Malina were aware of Kaprow's work. According to one historian, Beck had actors from *The Connection* participate in *18 Happenings*. But they did not do so before the play opened, as Judith Rodenbeck argues in "Madness and Method: Before Theatricality," *Grey Room* 13 (Autumn 2003): 67.

11. Gelber, *Connection*, 61.

12. Malina Journal, 25 March 1958, box 6, Living Theatre Records.

13. Julian Beck, *The Life of the Theatre* (1972; repr., New York: Limelight, 1986), 13, 7–8. On the overall ideology of the Living Theatre, part R. D. Laing, part anarchism, part Artaud, see R. L. Montgomery, "The Idea(l) of the 'Group' in Radical Theatre: A Dramaturgical Analysis of Three American Theatre Groups of the 1960s" (PhD diss., University of Canterbury, 2002), 14–15.

14. Calta, "Theatre: World of Narcotics Addicts," *New York Times*, 16 July 1959, 30.

15. Malina Journal, 1952, box 7, Living Theatre Records.

16. Hovhaness to Malina, 18 January 1954, Living Theatre Records. On her love affairs, see Malina, *Journal*, 152, 293; Tytell, *Living Theatre*, 98.

17. Tytell, *Living Theatre*, 133–35. On the arrests, see "31 Flouting Test Seized by Police," *New York Times*, 16 June 1955, 19.

18. Malina and Beck, "Response to Arrest," box 68, Living Theatre Records. On her incarceration, see Judith Malina, *The Diaries of Judith Malina, 1947–1957* (New York: Grove, 1984), 441–62.

19. Malina, haiku, no date, ca. mid-1950s, box 125, Living Theatre Records.

20. Malina, "Journal," 28 April 1958, box 6, Living Theatre Records.

21. Malina, "Transcript of Diaries," 28 April 1958, First Computer Printout, box 13, Living Theatre Records.

22. Tytell, *Living Theatre*, 85, 92–98.

23. "Living Theatre Quits Premises," *New York Times*, 12 December 1955, 38.

24. All quotes on building project come from Malina Journal, various entries, May 1957–January 1959, box 6, Living Theatre Records.

25. William Carlos Williams, *Many Loves, and Other Plays* (New York: New Directions, 1961), 90.

26. Brooks Atkinson, "Avant-Garde 'Many Loves,'" *New York Times*, 14 January 1959, 28.

27. Tytell, *Living Theatre*, 153–54.

28. "Membership Application for The Living Theatre," box 16, Gelber Papers, Fales Library, New York University.

29. Description of Gelber is in David Newman, "Four Make a Wave," *Esquire*, April 1960, 46.

30. Gruen, *Party's Over*, 97–98.

31. Charley Johnson, "A Local Connection," *Richmond Independent*, 30 September 1959, in biographical clippings, Jack Gelber Papers, Fales Library, New York University.

32. Quoted in Gruen, *Party's Over*, 95. See also Newman, "Four Make a Wave," 46; Johnson, "Local Connection."

33. "The Living Theatre at Cooper Union: A Symposium with William Coco, Jack Gelber, Karen Malpede, Richard Schechner and Michael Smith," *Drama Review* 31, no. 3 (Autumn 1987), 107.

34. Jerry Tallmer, "Judith Malina Resurrects a Living Classic," *Villager*, 21–27 January 2009, 1.

35. Gruen, *Party's Over*, 98.

36. "Living Theatre at Cooper Square," 108.

37. Malina, "Journals," 22 May 1959; 16 April 1958, box 6, Living Theatre Records.

38. Malina, "Journals," 26 May 1959, box 6, Living Theatre Records.

39. Malina, "Journals," 24 July 1958; 6 March 1959, box 6, v. 3, Living Theatre Records; Antonin Artaud, *The Theatre and Its Double*, trans. M. C. Richards (New York: Grove, 1958), 42, 81.

40. Jim O'Connor, "The Connection is Junk," *New York Journal American*, 16 July 1959; Judith Crist, "Review," *New York Herald Tribune*, 16 July 1959, in "Scrapbooks," box 17, folder 903, Jack Gelber Collection, Fales Library, New York University.

41. Malina, "Journals," 23 July 1959, box 6, Living Theatre Records.

42. Malina, "Journals," 25 March 1958; 26 January 1959, box 6, Living Theatre Records.

43. Malina, "Journals," 13 August 1959, box 6, Living Theatre Records; Allen Ginsberg, "Letter to the Editor," *Village Voice*, 2 September 1959, box 15, Jack Gelber Papers, Fales Library, New York University.

44. Malina, "Journals," 4 August 1959, box 6, Living Theatre Records; Mailer quoted in Tytell, *Living Theatre*, 158.

45. Malina, "Journals," 24 August 1959; 4 September 1959; 15 September 1959; 8, 9 October 1959, box 6, Living Theatre Records.

46. Kenneth Tynan, "Off-Broadway: Drug on the Market," *New Yorker*, 6 October 1959, 126–29.

47. Malina, "Journals," 9 October 1959, box 6, Living Theatre Records.

48. Robert Brustein, "Junkies and Jazz," *Theater*, 28 September 1959, 29; Brustein, *The Theatre of Revolt: Studies in Modern Drama from Ibsen to Genet* (1964; repr., Chicago: Ivan R. Dee, 1991), 4, 8, 27, 30.

49. Atkinson, "The Connection," *New York Times*, 7 February 1960, X1.

50. Tytell, *Living Theatre*, 164.

51. Gruen, *Party's Over*, 101; Jack Gelber, "Julian Beck, Businessman," *Drama Review* 30, no. 2 (Summer 1986): 6–29.

52. Malina, "Journals," 24 November 1959, box 6, Living Theatre Records.

53. Respondent's brief for the Court of Appeals, State of New York, box 16, folder 891, Gelber Papers, Fales Library, New York University.

54. The play is discussed in Tytell, *Living Theatre*, 179–90.

55. Tytell, *Living Theatre*, 187–200.

56. Patrick McDermott, "Portrait of an Actor, Watching: Antiphonal Feedback to the Living Theatre," *Drama Review* 13, no. 3 (Spring 1969): 78.

57. William Borders, "Indecent Exposure Charged to Becks," *New York Times*, 28 September 1968, 27.

58. Aldo Rostagno, *We, The Living Theatre*, with Julian Beck and Judith Malina (New York: Ballantine, 1970), 225–27. This book is a good compendium for the radical phase of the troupe.

Chapter 9

1. Accounts of the party and the stabbing, by Corsaro and others, are in Peter Manso, *Mailer: His Life and Times* (New York: Simon & Schuster, 1985), 311–27; Adele Mailer, *The Last Party: Scenes from My Life with Norman Mailer* (New York: Barricade, 1997), 347–50;

Carl Rollyson, *The Lives of Norman Mailer: A Biography* (New York: Paragon House, 1991), 135–41; J. Michael Lennon, *Norman Mailer: A Double Life* (New York: Simon & Schuster, 2013), 280–83.

2. Harry T. Moore, "The Targets Are Square," *New York Times*, 1 November 1959, BR 4; Gore Vidal, "The Norman Mailer Syndrome," *The Nation*, 2 January 1960, available online at https://lareviewofbooks.org/review/the-norman-mailer-syndrome-by-gore-vidal; Manso, *Mailer*, 273.

3. Norman Mailer, *Advertisements for Myself* (New York: G. P. Putnam's Sons, 1959), 17–22. Critic Norman Podhoretz maintained that Mailer actually had the capacity to achieve his goal of capturing the historical moment. See Podhoretz, "Norman Mailer: The Embattled Vision," in *Doings and Undoings: The Fifties and After in American Writing* (New York: Farrar, Straus, & Giroux, 1964), 178.

4. Norman Mailer, *The Presidential Papers* (New York: G. P. Putnam's Sons, 1963), 9.

5. Charles Poore, "Books of the Times," *New York Times*, 24 May 1951, 33; Orville Prescott, "Books of the Times," *New York Times*, 14 October 1955, 25.

6. Orville Prescott, "Books of the Times," *New York Times*, 7 May 1948, 21. Prescott did take Mailer to task, however, for his use of "explicitly vile speech."

7. Robert Guttwillig, "Dim Views through Fog," *New York Times*, 13 November 1960, BR 68. Although Roth admired much in Mailer, his remarks on this day were intended to be critical, no doubt referring to Mailer's dangerous public persona.

8. Manso, *Mailer*, 231.

9. Lennon, *Double Life*, 211–12.

10. Manso, *Mailer*, 291.

11. Mailer, *Advertisements*, 267.

12. Mailer, *Advertisements*, 229.

13. Mailer, *Advertisements*, 241.

14. Mary V. Dearborn, *Mailer: A Biography* (Boston: Houghton Mifflin, 1999), 156–58, 106, 132 for quote. Mailer was convicted of public drunkenness but acquitted of the more serious offense of disorderly conduct.

15. Mailer, *Advertisements*, 7, 219; Richard Poirier, *The Performing Self: Compositions and Decompositions in the Languages of Contemporary Life* (New Brunswick, NJ: Rutgers University Press, 1992), xxi, 87.

16. Mailer, *Advertisements*, 249, 281, 288, 313.

17. Mailer, *Advertisements*, 21. For an account of the problematic nature of writers and celebrity, focusing on Mailer, see Christopher Lasch, *The New Radicalism in America, 1889–1963: The Intellectual as a Social Type* (New York: Alfred A. Knopf, 1966), 336–38. Fitzgerald, "The Crack-Up," in *The Crack-Up* (New York: New Directions, 1964), 70.

18. Mailer, *Advertisements*, 22.

19. Mailer, *Advertisements*, 17, 19.

20. Mailer, *Advertisements*, 94.

21. See the contributions by Arvin, Trilling, and Mailer in "Our Country and Our Culture," special issue, *Partisan Review* 19 (May–June 1952): 288, 319–26.

22. Mailer, *Advertisements*, 190.

23. On Mailer's rivalry with Sartre see George Cotkin, *Existential America* (Baltimore: Johns Hopkins University Press, 2003), 184–85. Quotes are from Mailer, *Advertisements*, 424–25.

24. Mailer's journal for various novel projects, quoted in Lennon, *Double Life*, 189.

25. Anatole Broyard, "A Portrait of the Hipster," *Partisan Review* 15 (June 1948): 721–27.

26. Irving Howe, "This Age of Conformity," *Partisan Review* 21 (January–February 1954): 31. Howe continued to admire the piece, although he regretted not excising the passage where Mailer thrills at the murder of an innocent man. Manso, *Mailer*, 254.

27. Mailer, *Advertisements*, 338.

28. Mailer, *Advertisements*, 339.

29. Cotkin, *Existential America*, 184–209.

30. On Mailer's rather singular theology see Robert Solotaroff, "The Formulation Expanded: Mailer's Existentialism," in *Down Mailer's Way* (Urbana: University of Illinois Press, 1974), 82–123.

31. "Existential Aesthetics," interview with Laura Adams (1975), in *Conversations with Norman Mailer*, ed. J. Michael Lennon (Jackson: University Press of Mississippi, 1988), 213; Mailer, "Some Dirt in the Talk: A Candid History of an Existential Movie Called Wild 90," *Esquire*, 19 December 1967, 194; Mailer, *The Presidential Papers* (New York: G. P. Putnam's Sons, 1963), 9, 26. In many ways, Mailer was trying to make the hipster into a new sort of indigenous American mythical hero. See Stanley T. Gutman, *Mankind in Barbary: The Individual and Society in the Novels of Norman Mailer* (Hanover, NH: University Press of New England, 1975), 93ff.

32. Mailer, *Advertisements*, 349.

33. Mailer, *Advertisements*, 347.

34. Manso, 258.

35. Lennon, *Double Life*, 253.

36. Baldwin, "The Black Boy Looks at the White Boy" (1961), in *The Price of the Ticket: Collected Nonfiction, 1948–1985* (New York: St. Martin's/Marek, 1985), 290–303.

37. Morris Dickstein rightly places Mailer at the center of a shift toward a new sensibility. He further sees Mailer as upholding a moral imperative but displacing earlier moral ideals held by the bulk of the New York intellectuals. See Dickstein's *Gates of Eden: American Culture in the Sixties* (New York: Basic Books, 1977), 51ff. On Mailer's adherence to a strict moralism, see Diana Trilling, "The Radical Moralism of Norman Mailer," in *The Creative Present: Notes on Contemporary American Fiction*, ed. Nona Balakian and Charles Simmons (Garden City, NY: Doubleday, 1963), 149–71.

38. Mailer, *Advertisements*, 463.

39. Mailer, *Advertisements*, 464–73.

40. Mailer, *Advertisements*, 472.

41. Styron to Jim and Gloria Jones, 24 March 1959, in *Selected Letters of William Styron*, ed. Rose Styron (New York: Random House, 2012), 263. Mailer quote, *Advertisements*, 472.

42. Dearborn, *Mailer*, 249.

43. Norman Mailer, *The Armies of the Night* (New York: New American Library, 1968). On this issue, see J. Michael Lennon, "Norman Mailer: Novelist, Journalist, or Historian?," *Journal of Modern Literature* 30 (Fall 2006): 91–103.

44. Norman Mailer, "Superman Comes to the Supermarket," in *The Presidential Papers* (New York: G. P. Putnam's Sons, 1963), 36, 33, 35.

45. Mailer, *Presidential Papers*, 39–40.

46. Mailer, *Presidential Papers*, 31.

47. Dearborn, *Mailer*, 150–51; Norman Mailer, *Existential Errands* (Boston: Little, Brown), 46–47.

48. Mailer, *Presidential Papers*, 54, 59.

49. Mailer, *Presidential Papers*, 48. Mailer's account of Kennedy's heroism came from Joe McCarthy, *The Remarkable Kennedys* (New York: Dial, 1960).

50. Mailer, *Presidential Papers*, 60.

51. Norman Mailer, *An American Dream* (New York: Dial, 1965).

Chapter 10

1. Dick Schaap, *Flashing before My Eyes* (New York: William Morrow, 2001), 69.

2. Lenny Bruce, "A Letter to Jack Carter," 1 February 1961, in *The Almost Unpublished Lenny Bruce: From the Private Collection of Kitty Bruce* (Philadelphia: Running Press, 1984), 86. It is unclear if the letter was ever sent.

3. Paul Krassner, *Confessions of a Raving Unconfined Nut: Misadventures in the Counter-Culture* (New York: Simon & Schuster, 1993), 64.

4. "The Sickniks," *Time*, 13 July 1959, http://content.time.com/time/magazine/article/0,9171,869153,00.html.

5. Gerald Nachman, *Seriously Funny: The Rebel Comedians of the 1950s and 1960s* (New York: Pantheon, 2003), 391; Stephen E. Kercher, *Revel with a Cause: Liberal Satire in Postwar America* (Chicago: University of Chicago Press, 2006), 413.

6. Hardly surprising that an article on Bruce by Jonathan Miller was titled "The Sick White Negro," *Partisan Review* 30 (Spring 1963): 149–55; for a less enthusiastic take on Bruce as a "white negro," see Andrew Ross, *No Respect: Intellectuals and Popular Culture* (London: Routledge, 1989), 89–92.

7. Albert Goldman, *Ladies and Gentleman—Lenny Bruce!!*, with Lawrence Schiller (New York: Penguin, 1974), 219.

8. Norman Mailer, "Superman Comes to the Supermarket," in *The Presidential Papers* (New York: G. P. Putnam's Sons, 1963), 43.

9. Kercher, *Revel*, esp., 202–13.

10. Arthur and Barbara Gelb, "Culture Makes a Hit at the White House," *New York Times*, 28 January 1962, 165; Mailer, "Superman," 48.

11. On comedy in this period, see Kercher, *Revel*, and Nachman, *Seriously Funny*.

12. A quick biographical sketch is in Nachman, *Seriously Funny*, 397–401.

13. Honey Bruce, *Honey: The Life and Loves of Lenny's Shady Lady*, with Dana Benenson, ed. Bob McKendrick (Chicago: Playboy, 1976), 154.

14. Lenny Bruce, *How to Talk Dirty and Influence People: An Autobiography* (Chicago: Playboy, 1965), 16.

15. L. Bruce, *How to Talk Dirty*, 23; Goldman, *Ladies*, 102, 86–117.

16. L. Bruce, *How to Talk Dirty*, 30.

17. L. Bruce, *How to Talk Dirty*, 38; Krassner, *Confessions*, 64.

18. Goldman, *Ladies and Gentlemen*, 158, 323.

19. "lenny bruce," YouTube, uploaded 11 November 2012, https://www.youtube.com/watch?v=oCplnUgaohU.

20. Gilbert Millstein, "Man, It's Like Satire," *New York Times Sunday Magazine*, 3 May 1959, 29; Arthur Gelb, "Comic Gives Socks with Moral," *New York Times*, 8 May 1960, 44.

21. Frank Kofsky, *Lenny Bruce: The Comedian as Social Critic and Secular Moralist* (New York: Monad, 1974), 73; John Limon, *Stand-Up Comedy in Theory, or Abjection in America* (Durham, NC: Duke University Press, 2000), 22.

22. Nachman, *Seriously Funny*, 393.

23. H. Bruce, *Honey*, 154.

24. John P. Shanley, "Lenny Bruce, 'Beatnik,' on 'One Night Stand,'" *New York Times*, 13 May 1959, 75.

25. John Cohen, comp. and ed., *The Essential Lenny Bruce* (New York: Ballantine, [1967]), 31; Ioan Davies, "Lenny Bruce: Hyperrealism and the Death of Jewish Tragic Humor," *Social Text* no. 22 (Spring 1989): 92–114; Maria Damon, "The Jewish Entertainer as Cultural Lightning Rod: The Case of Lenny Bruce," *Postmodern Culture* 7, no. 2 (1997).

26. Arthur Steuer, "How to Talk Dirty and Influence People," *Esquire*, November 1961, 155.

27. Orrin Keepnews, "The Existential Jazz Aura of Lenny Bruce," *Downbeat*, 3 November 1966, 20.

28. L. Bruce, *Almost Unpublished*, 19.

29. Nat Hentoff, *Free Speech for Me—But Not for Thee: How the American Left and Right Relentlessly Censor Each Other* (New York: HarperCollins, 1992), 327. On "jazz modernism," see Alfred Appel Jr., *Jazz Modernism: From Ellington and Armstrong to Matisse and Joyce* (New York: Alfred A. Knopf, 2002).

30. Neil Schaeffer, "Lenny Bruce without Tears," *College English* 37 (February 1976): 564.

31. L. Bruce, *Almost Unpublished*, 19; Miller, "Sick White Negro," 150.

32. Daniel Belgrad, *The Culture of Spontaneity: Improvisation and the Arts in Postwar America* (Chicago: University of Chicago Press, 2008).

33. Krassner, *Confessions*, 62.

34. Cohen, *Essential*, 15–19.

35. L. Bruce, *Almost Unpublished*, 13.

36. Krassner, *Confessions*, 69.

37. L. Bruce, *Almost Unpublished*, 18.

38. L. Bruce, *Almost Unpublished*, 29.

39. Lenny Bruce, "On the Great Debate," *The Realist*, March/April 1961, 30; Krassner, *Confessions*, 71.

40. Ronald Sukenick, *Down and In: Life in the Underground* (New York: Beech Tree, 1987), 83.

41. Krassner, *Confessions*, 61. On the shock of *Psycho* and its revolutionary presence in American culture, see David Thomson, *The Moment of Psycho: How Alfred Hitchcock Taught America to Love Murder* (New York: Basic Books, 2009).

42. L. Bruce, *How to Talk Dirty*, 52–72.

43. Steuer, "How to Talk Dirty," 155.

44. Nat Hentoff, "Satire, Schmatire," *Commonweal*, 7 July 1961, 377.

45. L. Bruce, *How to Talk Dirty*, 96; William Karl Thomas, *Lenny Bruce: The Making of a Prophet* (Hamden, CT: Archon, 1989), 38–39. The routine appears on his 1959 album.

46. Cohen, *Essential*, 30.

47. Cohen, *Essential*, 11–12. Bruce was one of the few comedians, white or black, until Richard Pryor that employed the word in routines. See Randall Kennedy, *Nigger: The Strange Career of a Troublesome Word* (New York: Pantheon, 2002), 38–39.

48. Goldman, *Ladies and Gentlemen*, 351, 375.

49. Articles in *San Francisco Chronicle*, 4 October 1961, 8, 9.

50. Ronald K. L. Collins and David M. Skover, *The Trials of Lenny Bruce: The Fall and Rise of an American Icon* (Naperville, IL: Sourcebooks, 2002), 47ff.; Goldman, *Ladies and Gentlemen*, 380–81.

51. Ralph J. Gleason, "Lenny Bruce's Obscene Language Pinch in Frisco after Philly Rap," *Variety*, 11 October, 1961, 64.

52. Goldman, *Ladies and Gentlemen*, 382–84; Gleason, "Bruce's Obscene Language," 61; "Cops Seize Lenny Bruce—'Dirty Talk,'" San Francisco Chronicle, 5 October 1961, 1; "Hotel Heave-Ho Caps Lenny Bruce's Day," ibid., 1.

53. Goldman, *Ladies and Gentlemen*, 403–404. For information on the Ginsberg trial, see chapter 5.

54. Collins and Skover, *Trials*, 67–75.

55. Richard H. Kuh, *Foolish Figleaves?: Pornography in—and Out of—Court* (New York: Macmillan, 1967), 175 ff.; see chapter 13 for more on *Flaming Creatures*.

Chapter 11

1. "The Blockade: The U.S. Puts It on the Line," *Life*, 2 November 1962, 35.

2. Michael Dobbs, *One Minute to Midnight: Kennedy, Khrushchev, and Castro on the Brink of Nuclear War* (New York: Alfred A. Knopf, 2008), xii. Other quotes on the crisis come from this text. Also useful are: Tom Engelhardt, *The End of Victory Culture: Cold War America and the Disillusioning of a Generation* (New York: Basic Books, 1995); Margot A. Henriksen, *Dr. Strangelove's America: Society and Culture in the Atomic Age* (Berkeley: University of California Press, 1997).

3. Todd Gitlin, *The Sixties: Years of Hope, Days of Rage* (New York: Bantam, 1993), 98.

4. Letter quoted in Suze Rotolo, *A Freewheelin' Time: A Memoir of Greenwich Village in the Sixties* (New York: Broadway, 2008), 194–95.

5. Sharon Ghamari-Tabrizi, *The Worlds of Herman Kahn: The Intuitive Science of Thermonuclear War* (Cambridge, MA: Harvard University Press, 2005), 56.

6. Arthur Herzog, "Report on a 'Think Factory,'" *New York Times*, 10 November 1963, 46.

7. Norman Podhoretz, "Herman Kahn and the Unthinkable," in *Doings and Undoings: The Fifties and After in American Writing* (New York: Farrar, Straus & Giroux, 1964), 315.

8. Herman Kahn, *On Thermonuclear War* (Princeton, NJ: Princeton University Press, 1960), 101.

9. Herman Kahn, *Thinking about the Unthinkable* (New York: Horizon, 1962), 21; Ghamari-Tabrizi, *Worlds of Herman Kahn*, 41–45. By the end of the month, another book on nuclear war would appear, Eugene Burdick and Harvey Wheeler's *Fail-Safe* (New York: McGraw-Hill, 1962).

10. Excellent on Kuhn is Paul Hoynigen-Huene, *Reconstructing Scientific Revolutions: Thomas S. Kuhn's Philosophy of Science*, trans. Alexander T. Levine (Chicago: University of Chicago Press, 2003). For Kuhn's explanation of the limits of his theory, see various essays by him in his book *The Road since Structure: Philosophical Essays, 1970–1993, with an Autobiographical Interview*, ed. James Conant and John Haugeland (Chicago: University of Chicago Press, 2000). For one example of how art critics employed Kuhn, see Caroline A. Jones, "The Modernist Paradigm: The Artworld and Thomas Kuhn," *Critical Inquiry* 26 (Spring 2000): 488–528.

11. Richard Rorty, "Thomas Kuhn, Rocks, and the Laws of Physics," *Common Knowledge* 6 (Spring 1997): 8.

12. John F. Kennedy, *Economic Report of the President to the Congress* (Washington, DC: United States Government Printing Office, 1962), 5; George Cotkin, "The Commerce of Culture and Criticism," in Mark C. Carnes, ed., *The Columbia History of Post–World War II America* (New York: Columbia University Press, 2007), 182.

13. W. J. Rorabaugh, *Kennedy and the Promise of the Sixties* (Cambridge, UK: Cambridge University Press, 2002), xviii. The period, especially around 1962, was marked by increased criticism of various institutions and practices, in Rachel Carson's work on the chemical abuse of the environment, Michael Harrington's exposure of the extent of poverty, Jane Jacobs on how developers undermined neighborhoods, to name but a few. And, a new organization, Students for a Democratic Society, began that year.

14. "Arts and Culture in the Kennedy White House," JFK Library website, http://www .jfklibrary.org/JFK/JFK-in-History/Arts-and-Culture-in-the-Kennedy-White-House.aspx; "Heckscher Gets Post," *New York Times*, 23 February 1962, 37.

15. Quoted in Ray J. Haberski Jr., *"It's Only a Movie": Films and Critics in American Culture* (Lexington: University Press of Kentucky, 2001), ix.

16. Thomas Szasz, *The Myth of Mental Illness: Foundations of a Theory of Personal Conduct* (New York: Paul B. Hoeber, 1961), ix–x. Szasz's new concept for psychiatry was a sort of game-theory model linked with medicine, therapy, and "ethical, political, religious, and social considerations." Norman O. Brown, *Life against Death: The Psychoanalytic Meaning of History* (New York: Vintage, 1959), 322, xii–xiv, 174.

17. Ken Kesey, *One Flew Over the Cuckoo's Nest* (New York: Viking, 2012), 218. Also fitting into this fascination with madness could be Vladimir Nabokov's novel *Pale Fire* (1962).

18. Sylvia Plath, *The Bell Jar* (New York: Knopf, 1998), 136. For another poet in this mode, see chapter 15 on Anne Sexton.

19. Sylvia Plath, *The Collected Poems*, ed. Ted Hughes (New York: HarperPerennial, 2008), 235, 245.

20. On Sexton see Diane Wood Middlebrook, *Anne Sexton: A Biography* (Boston: Houghton Mifflin, 1991); Sexton to Tillie Olsen (Spring 1962), in *Anne Sexton: A Self-Portrait in Letters* (Boston: Houghton Mifflin, 1991), 139. The poem is in *The Complete Poems of Anne Sexton* (New York: Mariner, 1999), 108.

21. Sexton to Farrell (16 July 1962), in Sexton, *Self-Portrait*, 144.

22. George Cotkin, "The Hate Stare," in *Morality's Muddy Waters: Ethical Quandaries in Modern America* (Philadelphia: University of Pennsylvania Press, 2010), quote on 119.

23. Helen Gurley Brown, *Sex and the Single Girl* (New York: Barnes & Noble, 2003), 3; Jennifer Scanlon, *Bad Girls Go Everywhere: The Life of Helen Gurley Brown* (New York: Oxford University Press, 2009), 58, 86.

24. Brown, *Sex*, 226.

25. Henry Miller, "The Art of Fiction no. 28," interviewed by George Wickes, *Paris Review*, Summer-Fall 1962, available online at http://www.theparisreview.org/interviews/ 4597/the-art-of-fiction-no-28-henry-miller.

26. Edward de Grazia, *Girls Lean Back Everywhere: The Law of Obscenity and the Assault on Genius* (New York: Random House, 1992), 391.

27. William Burroughs, *Naked Lunch: The Restored Text*, ed. James Grauerholz and Barry Miller (New York: Grove, 2001), 105.

28. E. R. Hutchinson, *Tropic of Cancer on Trial: A Case History of Censorship* (New York: Grove, 1968), 97–98, 83.

29. James Brown, *James Brown: The Godfather of Soul*, with Bruce Tucker (New York: Macmillan, 1986), 135.

30. R. J. Smith, *The One: The Life and Music of James Brown* (New York: Gotham, 2012), 113.

31. Doug Wolk, *Live at the Apollo* (New York: Continuum, 2011); James Brown, "Live at the Apollo," Polydor 2482 184, 2004, compact disk.

32. Marc Eliot, "Introduction," in James Brown, *I Feel Good: A Memoir of a Life of Soul* (New York: New American Library, 2005), 29.

33. Brown, *I Feel Good*, 126–27.

34. Brown, *Godfather*, 153.

35. Martin Munro, *Different Drummers: Rhythm and Race in the Americas* (Berkeley: University of California Press, 2010), 189.

36. Steve Binder, dir., *T.A.M.I. Show*, (Los Angeles: Dick Clark Productions, 2009), DVD.

Chapter 12

1. Matisse quote in Kenneth Goldsmith, *I'll Be Your Mirror: The Selected Andy Warhol Interviews* (New York: Carroll & Graf, 2004), xvii.

2. Arthur C. Danto, "Soup to Butts," *Artforum* 41, no. 1 (September 2002): 51. See also Louis Menand, "Top of the Pops: Did Andy Warhol Change Everything?," *New Yorker*, 11 January 2010, 57–65;

3. Like so much associated with Warhol, it is difficult to discern the authenticity of his reactions and accounts of it. For him being deeply affected by the Kennedy assassination, see Tony Scherman and David Dalton, *POP: The Genius of Andy Warhol* (New York: HarperCollins, 2009), 185 and Victor Bockris, *The Life and Death of Andy Warhol* (New York: Bantam, 1989), 140. According to Warhol, while he liked Kennedy, his reaction was restrained; mostly he claimed to have been upset that everyone was being made by television and radio to feel sad. Andy Warhol and Pat Hackett, *POPism: The Warhol '60s* (New York: Harcourt Brace Jovanovich, 1980), 60.

4. Peter Selz, "Pop Goes the Artist," *Partisan Review* 20 (Summer 1963): 314.

5. Thomas B. Hess, "The Phony Crisis in American Art," *Art News* 62, no. 4 (Summer 1963): 27.

6. Fairfield Porter, "The Education of Jasper Johns," *Art News* 62, no. 10 (February 1964): 62.

7. Rosenberg quoted in Melissa Mayer, *Night Studio: A Memoir of Philip Guston* (New York: Penguin, 1988), 150.

8. Barbara Rose, "Dada: Then and Now," *Art International* 2, no. 1 (25 January 1963): 27–28.

9. Stuart Preston, "Old and New Ways of Seeing Things," *New York Times*, 26 April 1964, X21.

10. Quoted in Caroline A. Jones, *Machine in the Studio: Constructing the Postwar American Artist* (Chicago: University of Chicago Press, 1996), 22.

11. Henry Geldzahler, quoted in Calvin Tomkins, "Moving with the Flow," *New Yorker*, 6 November 1971, 87.

12. Bockris, *Life and Death*, 60.

13. Hal Foster, "Death in America," *October* 75 (Winter 1996): 37.

14. Henry J. Seldis, "In the Galleries," *Los Angeles Times*, 13 July 1962, section 4, 6.

15. Goldsmith, *I'll Be Your Mirror*, 18. On his Campbell's Soup cans, see Gary Indiana, *Andy Warhol and the Can That Sold the World* (New York: Perseus, 2010).

16. Warhol and Hackett, *POPism*, 44.

17. Warhol and Hackett, *POPism*, 13, 15.

18. Warhol, *The Philosophy of Andy Warhol (From A to B and Back Again)* (San Diego: Harcourt Brace, 1975), 101.

19. *Andy Warhol "Giant" Size* (London: Phaidon, 2006), 186.

20. Andreas Huyssen, "The Cultural Politics of Pop," in *After the Great Divide: Modernism, Mass Culture, Postmodernism* (Bloomington: Indiana University Press, 1986), 146.

21. Cecile Whiting, *A Taste for Pop: Pop Art, Gender, and Consumer Culture* (Cambridge, UK: Cambridge University Press, 1997); Alice Goldfarb Marquis, *The POP! Revolution* (Boston: Museum of Fine Arts, 2010); Benjamin H. D. Buchloh, "Andy Warhol's One-Dimensional Art: 1956–1965," in *Andy Warhol*, ed. Annette Michelson (Cambridge, MA: MIT Press, 2001), 1–48; Christin J. Mamiya, *Pop Art and Consumer Culture: American Super Market* (Austin: University of Texas Press, 1992); John Canaday, "Pop Art Sells On and On—Why?," *New York Times*, 31 May 1964, SM7, 48, 52–53; Stuart Preston, "On Display: All-Out Series of Pop Art," *New York Times*, 21 March, 1963, 8.

22. R. Glaisek, "Letter to the Editor," *Art News* 62, no. 7 (November 1963): 6.

23. Arthur C. Danto, "The Artworld," *Journal of Philosophy* 61 (October 1964): 571–84; Danto, "The Art World Revisited: Comedies of Similarity," in *Beyond the Brillo Box: The Visual Arts in Post-Historical Perspective* (Berkeley: University of California Press, 1992), 33–53; *Andy Warhol* (New Haven, CT: Yale University Press, 2009).

24. David Lubin, *Shooting Kennedy: JFK and the Culture of Images* (Berkeley: University of California Press, 2003), 33–37, 256. Lubin does reference Warhol, with a comparison between his films and the Zapruder recording of the assassination.

25. Andy Warhol, "What is Pop Art?," interview with G. R. Swenson, *Art News*, November 1962, 26.

26. Paul Mattick, "The Andy Warhol of Philosophy and the Philosophy of Andy Warhol," *Critical Inquiry* 24 (Summer 1998): 966–67.

27. Kevin Cook, *Kitty Genovese: The Murder, the Bystanders, the Crime that Changed America* (New York: W. W. Norton, 2014); Theodore Hamm, *Rebel and a Cause: Caryl Chessman and the Politics of the Death Penalty in Postwar California, 1948–1974* (Berkeley: University of California Press, 2001).

28. David Thomson, *The Moment of Psycho: How Alfred Hitchcock Taught America to Love Murder* (New York: Basic Books, 2009).

29. Margot A. Henriksen, *Dr. Strangelove's America: Society and Culture in the Atomic Age* (Berkeley: University of California Press, 1997), 197; Susan Sontag, "The Imagination of Disaster" (1965), in *Against Interpretation* (New York: Picador, 1990), 209–25.

30. Henry Geldzahler, *Making It New: Essays, Interviews, and Talks* (New York: Turtle Point, 1994), 359–60.

31. John Wilcock, *The Autobiography and Sex Life of Andy Warhol* ed. Christopher Trela (New York: Trela, 2010), 67.

32. Raymond M. Herbenick, *Andy Warhol's Religious and Ethnic Roots: The Carpatho-Rusyn Influence on His Art* (Lewiston, NY: Edwin Mellen, 1997), 89ff.

33. Biographical material is drawn from Bockris, *Life and Death*, 6–50; Scherman and Dalton, *Pop*, 1–15; Bob Colacello, *Holy Terror: Andy Warhol Close Up; An Insider's Portrait* (New York: HarperCollins, 1990), 10–20; David Bourdon, *Warhol* (New York: Harry N. Abrams, 1989).

34. *New York Times*, 18 April 1956, 34; Bourdon, *Warhol*, 42; Glaser quoted in Scherman and Dalton, *Pop*, 15.

35. Goldsmith, *I'll Be Your Mirror*, 19, 88.

36. Jennifer Dyer, "The Metaphysics of the Mundane: Understanding Andy Warhol's Serial Imagery," *Artibus et Historiae* 25, no. 49 (2004): 41.

37. *Warhol "Giant,"* 184.

38. Scherman and Dalton, *Pop*, 162–64; *Warhol "Giant,"* 254–55.

39. David McCarthy, "Andy Warhol's Silver Elvises: Meaning through Context at the Ferus Gallery in 1963," *Art Bulletin* 88, no. 2 (June 2006): 355–56.

40. McCarthy, "Andy Warhol's Silver Elvises," 357.

41. *Warhol "Giant,"* 190–91, 197.

42. Quoted in Bennett Capers, "On Andy Warhol's *Electric Chair*," *California Law Review* 94, no. 1 (January 2006): 249.

43. In 1964 Warhol supported Robert F. Kennedy's successful campaign for senator in New York. "We're for Robert Kennedy," *New York Times*, 27 October 1964, 25.

44. Thomas Crow, "Saturday Disasters: Trace and Reference in Early Warhol," in *Modern Art in the Common Culture* (New Haven, CT: Yale University Press, 1996), 62–63. On Warhol as humanist see Gregory Battock, "Humanism and Reality: Thek and Warhol," (1965) in *The New Art: A Critical Anthology*, ed. Gregory Battock, (New York: Dutton, 1973), 15.

45. *Warhol "Giant,"* 236–37; Anne M. Wagner, "Warhol Paints History, or Race in America" *Representations* 55 (Summer 1966): 98–119.

46. *Warhol "Giant,"* 232–33.

47. Goldsmith, *I'll Be Your Mirror*, 94.

48. Jonas Mekas, "Notes on the New American Cinema," (1962) in *Film Culture Reader*, ed. P. Adams Sitney (New York: Cooper Square, 2000), 104, 107.

49. Steven Watson, *Factory Made: Warhol and the Sixties* (New York: Pantheon, 2003), 97; John Wilcock, *The Autobiography and Sex Life of Andy Warhol*, ed. Christopher Trela (New York: Trela, 2010), 54.

50. Watson, *Factory Made*, 117–19; Amy Taubin, "****," in *Who Is Andy Warhol?*, ed. Colin McCabe (London: British Film Institute, 1997), 24–25.

51. Bockris, *Life and Death*, 131–32.

52. Watson, *Factory Made*, 104–5.

53. Wayne Koestenbaum, *Andy Warhol* (New York: Viking, 2001), 13.

54. See comments by Charles Henri Ford in Wilcock, *Autobiography*, 57, 62.

55. John Yau, *In the Realm of Appearances: The Art of Andy Warhol* (Hopewell, NJ: Ecco, 1993), 77.

56. Stephen Koch, *Stargazer: The Life, World and Films of Andy Warhol* (New York: Marion Boyars, 2002), 35–36. On Warhol's films, also see Douglas Crimp, *"Our Kind of Movie": The Films of Andy Warhol* (Cambridge, MA: MIT Press, 2012); J. J. Murphy, *The Black Hole of the Camera: The Films of Andy Warhol* (Berkeley: University of California Press, 2012).

57. Wilcock, *Autobiography*, 246; Mead quoted in Branden W. Joseph, "The Play of Repetition: Andy Warhol's *Sleep*," *Grey Room* 19 (Spring 2005): 23.

58. Watson, *Factory Made*, 160–61; Warhol and Hackett, *POPism*, 42.

Chapter 13

1. "Taste," *Time*, 11 December 1964, 75.

2. Susan Sontag, "Opinion Please from New York," *Mademoiselle*, April 1965, 58–60.

3. On Sontag, see Liam Kennedy, *Susan Sontag: Mind as Passion* (Manchester, UK: Manchester University Press, 1995); Phillip Lopate, *Notes on Sontag* (Princeton, NJ: Princeton University Press, 2009); Carl Rollyson and Lisa Paddock, *Susan Sontag: The Making of an Icon* (New York: W. W. Norton, 2000).

4. Susan Sontag, *Reborn: Journals and Notebooks, 1947–1963*, ed. David Rieff (New York: Farrar, Straus & Giroux, 2008), 30.

5. Sontag, *Reborn*, 18.

6. Sontag, "The Letter Scene," *New Yorker*, 18 August 1986, 28.

7. Susan Rieff, "Dialogue" (August 1952), coll. 612, box 146, folder 1, Susan Sontag Papers, Charles Young Research Library, UCLA (hereafter Sontag Papers).

8. Sontag, *Reborn*, 128.

9. Sontag, *Reborn*, 140, 98–99, 135, 193.

10. Judith Grossman, *Her Own Terms* (New York: Soho, 1988), 222.

11. Sontag, *Reborn*, 157, 166, 177. On Sontag's life in Paris, see Alice Kaplan, *Dreaming in French: The Paris Years of Jacqueline Bouvier Kennedy, Susan Sontag, and Angela Davis* (Chicago: University of Chicago Press, 2012) 81–141.

12. Sontag, *Reborn*, 175, 187, 205.

13. Sontag, *Reborn*, 157, 166, 177. On Sontag's life in Paris, see Kaplan, *Dreaming in French*, 81–141.

14. Susan Sontag, *As Consciousness Is Harnessed to Flesh: Journals and Notebooks, 1964–1980*, ed. David Rieff (New York: Farrar, Straus & Giroux 2012), 25; on her torturous love life, see Edward Field, *The Man Who Would Marry Susan Sontag* (Madison: University of Wisconsin Press, 2005), 161ff.

15. Sontag, *Consciousness*, 25, 30; Sontag, "Journals," (8 September 1964), box 125, folder 1, Sontag Papers.

16. Sontag, "Against Interpretation," in *Against Interpretation* (New York: Farrar, Straus & Giroux, 1990), 14.

17. Sontag, "Journal" (4 January 1966), box 125, folder 4, Sontag Papers.

18. Henry M. Sayre, *The Object of Performance: The American Avant-Garde since 1970* (Chicago: University of Chicago Press, 1989); Sally Banes, *Greenwich Village 1963: Avant-Garde, Performance, and the Effervescent Body* (Durham, NC: Duke University Press, 1993).

19. Sayre, *Object*, 109.

20. Cage's influence cannot be overstated. See, for example, Liz Kotz, *Words to Be Looked At: Language in 1960s Art* (Cambridge, MA: MIT Press, 2007), 59ff.

21. Holland Cotter, "Most Wanted, Most Haunted," *New York Times*, 25 April 2014, 21, 25. On one venue for much of the experimental work occurring in New York City, see Sally Banes, *Democracy's Body: Judson Dance Theater, 1962–1964* (Durham NC: Duke University Press, 1993).

22. Julia Bryan-Wilson, "Remembering Yoko Ono's *Cut Piece*," *Oxford Art Journal* 26, no. 1 (2003): 99–123. Video of one performance is available online, "Yoko Ono—Cut Piece (1965)," YouTube, uploaded 28 February 2013, https://www.youtube.com/watch?v=lYJ3dPwa2tI. Sontag, "Against Interpretation," 10–14.

23. Maurice Berger, *Labyrinths: Robert Morris, Minimalism, and the 1960s* (New York: Harper & Row, 1989), 82–83; Yvonne Rainer, *Feelings Are Facts: A Life* (Cambridge, MA: MIT Press, 2006), 244. The piece can be seen online at http://artforum.com/video/mode=large&id=31196. This was the period when minimalism became central, with its

challenge to abstract expressionist ideals of the meaning of the artwork and the artist. For a key statement of this movement, see Donald Judd, "Specific Artists" (1965), in *American Artists on Art: From 1940 to 1980*, ed. Ellen H. Johnson (New York: Icon, 1982), 105–11.

24. Carolee Schneemann, *Imagining Her Erotics: Essays, Interviews, Projects* (Cambridge, MA: MIT Press, 2003), 60–74; Schneemann to James Tenney (30 May 1964), in *Correspondence Course: An Epistolary History of Carolee Schneemann and Her Circle*, ed. Kristine Styles (Durham, NC: Duke University Press, 2010), 83–84. One version of the piece can be seen online at http://artforum.com/video/mode=large&id=31196; Schneemann to Jean-Jacques Lebel (7 February 1966), in Styles, *Correspondence Course*, 100. *Meat Joy* was first performed in Paris.

25. Schneemann to Moorman (26 September 1980), in Styles, *Correspondence Course*, 323.

26. Mikal Gilmore, "How the Beatles Took America," *Rolling Stone*, 16 January 2014, 41–47, 69.

27. Leo Steinberg, "Contemporary Art and the Plight of its Public," in *Other Criteria* (New York: Oxford University Press, 1972), 5.

28. Harold Rosenberg, *The Anxious Object: Art Today and Its Audience* (New York: Horizon, 1964), 53, 61–75.

29. Barbara Rose, "ABC ART," *Art in America* 53, no. 9 (October 1965): 58–69. On some similar themes, see the essay by Ivan C. Karp, "Anti-Sensibility Painting" (1963), in *Pop Art: A Critical History*, ed. Steven Henry Madoff (Berkeley: University of California Press, 1997), 89.

30. David Newman and Robert Benton, "The New Sentimentality," *Esquire*, July, 1964, 25–28.

31. Tom Wolfe, *The Kandy-Kolored Tangerine-Flake Streamline Baby* (New York: Farrar, Straus & Giroux, 1965), xvii.

32. Benjamin DeMott, "The Age of Overkill," *New York Times Magazine*, 19 May 1968, 104. See also DeMott, *Supergrow: Essays and Reports on Imagination in America* (New York: Dell, 1969).

33. Richard Gilman, *The Confusion of Realms* (New York: Random House, 1969).

34. Not being historians, neither of them realized that the essentials of this New Sensibility had been stirring in American Culture since at least 1952.

35. Susan Sontag, "Notes on Camp," in *Against Interpretation*, 276.

36. On Trilling, see Leland Poague, "Introduction," in *Susan Sontag: An Annotated Bibliography, 1948–1992*, ed. Leland Poague and Kathy A. Parsons (New York: Garland, 2000), lxi. In a sense, she was also aligning herself with aspects of Clement Greenberg's views about the artist exploring the nature of the medium rather than focusing on content. Thus, she remarks: "I recall that when I wrote 'Notes on Camp,' I had in the back of my mind as both a role model and anti-model Clement Greenberg's very influential "Avant-Garde and Kitsch." Sontag to Michael Kammen (4 Sept. 1992), box 164, folder 2, Sontag Papers. On this connection, see Kennedy, *Mind as Passion*, 23–29. See also James Penner, "Gendering Susan Sontag's Criticism in the 1960s: The New York Intellectuals, the Counter Culture, and the *Kulturkampf* over 'The New Sensibility,'" *Women's Studies* 37 (2008): 921–41. Sontag, "Journals" (3 January 1966), box 125, folder 4; (circa 1965), box 125, folder 2, Sontag Papers. In fact, Trilling could sometimes sound like Sontag in his opposition to earlier left criticism. The theme is resplendent in Trilling, who upholds against the moral predictability of the old left, moral tragedy, complexity, variousness, and irony. See Lionel Trilling, *The Liberal Tradition* (New York: Viking, 1950), xiv.

37. Sontag, "Notes on Camp," in *Against Interpretation*, 276.

38. The problem with camp was that it any ethical aspects. For more on this, see Kennedy, *Mind as Passion*, 33–35. Also, Daniel Schreiber, *Susan Sontag: A Biography* trans. David Dollenmayer (Evanston, IL: Northwestern University Press, 2014), 78–83.

39. Sontag, "Notes on Camp," in *Against Interpretation*, 278.

40. Barbara Ching and Jennifer A. Wagner-Lawlor, "Introduction," in *The Scandal of Susan Sontag* ed. Barbara Ching and Jennifer A. Wagner-Lawlor (New York: Columbia University Press, 2009), 3. Sontag, "Afterword: Thirty Years Later," in *Against Interpretation*, 309.

41. On Sontag as evangelist see Burton Feldman, "Evangelist of the New," *Denver Quarterly* 1 (Spring 1966): 152–56; on her success see Rollyson and Paddock, *Sontag*, 102; Sohnya Sayres, *Susan Sontag: The Elegiac Modernist* (New York: Routledge, 1990), 34. For reviews see Benjamin DeMott, "Lady on the Scene," *New York Times*, 23 January 1966, 239; Eliot Fremont-Smith, "After the Ticker Tape Parade," *New York Times*, 31 January 1966, 28; Robert Mazzocco, "Swingtime," *New York Review of Books*, 9 June 1966, available online at http://nybooks.com/articles/archives/1966/jun/09/swingtime. It should be noted that the titles and content of these reviews focus on the hip, swinger image of Sontag in the arts.

42. Sontag, "Against Interpretation," 7.

43. Sontag, "Against Interpretation," 9.

44. Sontag, "One Culture and the New Sensibility," in *Against Interpretation*, 300.

45. Andrew Ross, *No Respect: Intellectuals and Popular Culture* (New York: Routledge, 1989); Paul R. Gorman, *Left Intellectuals and Popular Culture in Twentieth-Century America* (Chapel Hill: University of North Carolina Press, 1996).

46. Sontag, "One Culture and the New Sensibility," 303.

47. Susan Sontag, "Jack Smith's *Flaming Creatures*," in *Against Interpretation*, 227, 230–31.

48. As Phillip Lopate notes, "She romanticized male depression as an aristocratic retreat." Lopate, *Notes on Sontag*, 114.

49. Sontag. "Journals" (notes, 1965), box 125, folder 6, Sontag Papers; Sontag, *Consciousness*, 42. Last quote is in Schreiber, *Susan Sontag*, 75.

50. Sontag, "Marat/Sade/Artaud," in *Against Interpretation*, 168–69.

51. Sontag, "The Pornographic Imagination," in *Styles of Radical Will* (1969; repr., New York: Farrar, Straus & Giroux, 2002), 43–48.

52. Tom Wolfe, "The New Journalism," in *The New Journalism* (New York: Harper and Row, 1973), 29.

53. Andy Warhol and Pat Hackett, *POPism: The Warhol '60s* (New York: Harcourt Brace Jovanovich, 1980), 70; Sontag, *As Consciousness Is Harnessed*, 78.

54. Lopate, *Notes on Sontag*, 32; Sontag, *As Consciousness Is Harnessed*, 83, 73.

55. Leslie Fiedler, "The New Mutants," *Partisan Review* 32 (Fall 1965): 509.

56. Fiedler, "New Mutants," 511, 523, 524; Mark Royden, *Too Good to Be True: The Life and Work of Leslie Fiedler* (Columbia: University of Missouri Press, 2002).

57. Susan Sontag, "What's Happening in America" (1966), in *Styles of Radical Will*, 195, 203.

58. F. Scott Fitzgerald, "The Crack-Up," in *The Crack-Up* (New York: New Directions, 1964), 69.

59. Not all critics, of course, registered appreciation for the experimentalism of the New Sensibility. In a far-ranging piece titled "The New York Intellectuals," Irving Howe blasted it for anti-institutionalism, refusal to compromise, violence, anti-intellectualism, and more. It "makes nihilism," he concluded, "seem casual, good natured, even innocent." From his

perspective; it was modernism run amok. Howe, "The New York Intellectuals," in *The Decline of the New* (New York: Harcourt, Brace & World, 1970), 248ff. In this same vein, see Daniel Bell, "The Sensibility of the Sixties," in *The Cultural Contradictions of Capitalism* (New York: Basic Books, 1976). The New Sensibility, he writes, is the name for the ideology of the counterculture, with its "attack on reason itself." And, he further relates, "What the new sensibility did was to carry the premises of modernism through to their logical conclusions" (143). For a more ambivalent take see Fiedler, "New Mutants." Excellent on all of this is Robert Boyers, "On Susan Sontag and the New Sensibility," *Salmagundi* 1 (1966): 27–38.

60. Sontag, "Afterword," 308–12. On the potential of the New Sensibility, at least in its sexual openness, see Herbert Marcuse, "The New Sensibility," in *An Essay on Liberation* (Boston: Beacon, 1969), 23–48. For her revised views on reading, see the excellent essay by Joan Acocella, "The Hunger Artist," in *Twenty-Eight Artists and Two Saints: Essays* (New York: Vintage, 2008), 450.

61. Thomas Frank, *The Conquest of Cool: Business Culture, Counterculture, and the Rise of Hip Consumerism* (Chicago: University of Chicago Press, 1997). This is related to questions about the power, persistence, and cooptation of the avant-garde, an issue that is highly complex and contentious. For an excellent summary of these concerns, see Mike Sell, *Avant-Garde Performance and the Limits of Criticism: Approaching the Living Theatre, Happenings/Fluxus, and the Black Arts Movement* (Ann Arbor: University of Michigan Press, 2008).

62. Susan Sontag, "Trip to Hanoi," in *Radical Will*, 224.

Chapter 14

1. Quoted in Clinton Heylin, *Bob Dylan: Behind the Shades* (New York: Summit, 1991), 143–45.

2. Quoted in Mike Marqusee, *Wicked Messenger: Bob Dylan and the 1960s* (New York: Seven Stories, 2005), 151.

3. Howard Sounes, *Down the Highway: The Life of Bob Dylan* (New York: Grove, 2011), 180–85; Robert Shelton, *No Direction Home: The Life and Music of Bob Dylan* (New York: William Morrow, 1986), 306. See also Jim Miller, "Bob Dylan," in *The Dylan Companion*, ed. Elizabeth Thompson and David Gutman (New York: Da Capo, 2001), 18; Marqusee, *Wicked Messenger*, 149–55; Ian Bell, *Once Upon a Time: The Lives of Bob Dylan* (New York: Pegasus, 2012), 359–72. For a skeptical account of the booing, see David Hajdu, *Positively 4th Street: The Lives and Times of Joan Baez, Bob Dylan, Mimi Baez Fariña, and Richard Fariña* (New York: Farrar, Straus & Giroux, 2001), 210–12.

4. Quoted in Greil Marcus, *Like a Rolling Stone: Bob Dylan at the Crossroads* (New York: Public Affairs, 2005), 154.

5. Muldaur quote in Nigel Williamson, *The Rough Guide to Bob Dylan* (London: Metro, 2006), 48.

6. Shelton, *No Direction Home*, 303, 306.

7. Frank Kofsky, *John Coltrane and the Jazz Revolution of the 1960s* (New York: Pathfinder, 1970), 232–33.

8. Louise Davis Stone, "The Jazz Bit: A Chat with John Coltrane," in *Coltrane on Coltrane: The John Coltrane Interviews*, ed. Chris DeVito (Chicago: Chicago Review, 2010), 222.

9. Michael Hennessey, "Dropping the Ball and Chain from Jazz," in DeVito, *Coltrane on Coltrane*, 239; Ben Ratliff, *Coltrane: The Story of a Sound* (New York: Farrar, Straus & Giroux. 2007), 96–97.

10. Lewis Porter, *John Coltrane: His Life and Music* (Ann Arbor: University of Michigan Press, 1999), 229–30.

11. Howard Mandel, comment to Alex W. Rodriguez, "Share Your John Coltrane Stories," *Lubricity* (blog), 7 May 2009, http://lubricity.wordpress.com/2011/05/01/share-your-john-coltrane-stories/.

12. For Dylan at Newport, see Marcus, *Like a Rolling Stone*, 254–59. See also Alan Light, "Bob Dylan as Performer," in *The Cambridge Companion to Bob Dylan*, ed. Kevin J. H. Dettmer (Cambridge, UK: Cambridge University Press, 2009), 59–60.

13. Dan Morgenstern quoted in *The John Coltrane Companion: Five Decades of Commentary*, ed. Carl Woideck (New York: Schirmer, 1999), 222.

14. Porter, *Coltrane*, 266.

15. Interview with Nat Hentoff, *New Yorker*, 24 October 1964, in *Bob Dylan: The Essential Interviews*, ed. Jonathan Cott (New York: Wenner, 2006), 22.

16. Williamson, *Rough Guide*, 44.

17. Bob Spitz, "The Mad Years," in *Dylan: A Biography* (New York: W. W. Norton, 1989), 267–368.

18. As recalled by Harold Lovette in J. C. Thomas, *Chasin' The Train: The Music and Mystique of John Coltrane* (Garden City, NY: Doubleday, 1975), 104.

19. Iain Anderson, *This is Our Music: Free Jazz, the Sixties, and American Culture* (Philadelphia: University of Pennsylvania Press, 2007), 63.

20. LeRoi Jones, "New Tenor Archie Shepp Talking," in *Black Music* (New York: William Morrow, 1967), 151–52, 154.

21. Porter, *Coltrane*, 38.

22. Thomas Meehan, "Public Writer no. 1?," *New York Times Magazine*, 12 December 1965, 45.

23. Coltrane was deeply influenced by Ornette Coleman; see Porter, *Coltrane*, 202–5.

24. Coltrane interviewed by Michel Delorme and Claude Lenissois, "Coltrane: Star of Antibes: 'I Can't Go Farther,'" Nat Hentoff, "Meditations Liner Notes," both in DeVito, *Coltrane on Coltrane*, 246, 264.

25. Anthony DeCurtis, "Bob Dylan as Songwriter," in Dettmer, *Cambridge Companion*, 48; Bell, *Once Upon a Time*, 342.

26. On the question of influence, arguing for Coltrane's effect on Ayler, see Kofsky, *Jazz Revolution*, 293–321. On Coltrane's sound see Thomas, *Chasin'*, 106. Around this time, Phil Spector was developing his signature "wall of sound" in pop recordings.

27. James T. Patterson, *The Eve of Destruction: How 1965 Transformed America* (New York: Basic Books, 2012).

28. Kael quoted in Brian Kellow, *Pauline Kael: A Life in the Dark* (New York: Viking, 2011), 95. The stridency of her review contributed to Kael's being dismissed as movie critic for *McCall's* magazine.

29. Bill Cole, *John Coltrane* (New York: Schirmer, 1976), 150.

30. Scott Saul, *Freedom Is, Freedom Ain't: Jazz and the Making of the Sixties* (Cambridge, MA: Harvard University Press, 1973), 224–43. For a strong statement of the new aesthetic see Larry Neal, "The Black Arts Movement," in *The Black Aesthetic*, ed. Addison Gayle Jr. (Garden City, NY: Doubleday, 1971), 272–90.

31. Ralph Ellison, "Review of *Blues People*," in *The Collected Essays of Ralph Ellison*, ed. John F. Callahan (New York: Modern Library, 1995), 286.

32. On expectations regarding Coltrane see Saul, *Freedom Is*, 224–25.

33. On the complexities of identity with Dylan in this period, see Barry Shank, " 'That Wild Mercury Sound': Bob Dylan and the Illusion of American Culture," *Boundary 2* 29, no. 1 (2002): 97–123.

34. Andrew Sarris, "Don't Look Back," in Thompson and Gutman, *Dylan Companion*, 88. On the song and Zantzinger see Marqusee, *Wicked Messenger*, 89; historian Peter Bacon Hales remarked that "atomic anxiety pervaded" Dylan's early work. Hales, *Outside the Gates of Eden: The Dream of America from Hiroshima to Now* (Chicago: University of Chicago Press, 2014), 259.

35. Bell, *Once Upon a Time*, 377.

36. Suze Rotolo, *A Freewheelin' Time: A Memoir of Greenwich Village in the Sixties* (New York: Broadway, 2008), 243.

37. Quoted in Tony Whyton, *Beyond A Love Supreme: John Coltrane and the Legacy of an Album* (Oxford: Oxford University Press, 2013), 22.

38. Thomas, *Chasin'*, 183–84; the score can be viewed online at: http://cdn8.openculture .com/wp-content/uploads/2013/09/love-supreme-manuscripts.jpg.

39. Ratliff, *Story of a Sound*, 51.

40. The liner notes and poem for the album are available in DeVito, *Coltrane on Coltrane*, 225–28.

41. Porter, *Coltrane*, 232.

42. "Liner Notes," in DeVito, *Coltrane on Coltrane*, 227–28.

43. Jimm Cushing, personal communication, 8 November 2013.

44. Thomas, *Chasin'*, 171–72.

45. Thomas, *Chasin'*, 118; Porter, *Coltrane*, 258. Coltrane was also well read in musical theory; he was once referred to as "theory mad." Ratliff, *Story of a Sound*, 51; Michel Delorme and Claude Lenissois, "Coltrane, Star of Antibes: 'I Can't Go Farther,'" in DeVito, *Coltrane on Coltrane*, 244.

46. Quoted in Ashley Kahn, *A Love Supreme: The Story of John Coltrane's Signature Album* (New York: Viking, 2002), 77. Kahn is excellent on the album. The most technical analysis of *A Love Supreme* is in Porter, *Coltrane*, 231–49.

47. Kahn, *A Love Supreme*, 84.

48. Kahn, *A Love Supreme*, 86, 92–93.

49. Jones quoted in Kahn, *A Love Supreme*, x.

50. Kahn, *A Love Supreme*, 102.

51. Kahn, *A Love Supreme*, 104.

52. Cole, *Coltrane*, 160.

53. Marcus, *Like a Rolling Stone*, 87–151; Bell, *Once Upon a Time*, 18–20, 401–10. Bell finds the song "bitter and vengeful" but somehow "joyous."

54. Williamson, *Rough Guide*, 298.

55. For a discussion of the recording sessions, take by take, see Marcus, *Rolling Stone*, 203–25.

56. Lyrics for all of Dylan's songs are available at the official Bob Dylan website, http:// www.bobdylan.com/us/songs.

57. Williamson, *Rough Guide*, 297.

58. Shelton, *No Direction Home*, 285.

59. Heylin, *Behind the Shades*, 153–54; Michael Gray, *The Bob Dylan Encyclopedia* (New York: Continuum, 2006), 603–4.

60. On Dylan as existentialist see Shelton, *No Direction Home*, 269–70.

61. Williamson, *Rough Guide*, 49.

62. Bob Dylan, *Chronicles* (New York: Simon & Schuster, 2004), 288.

63. For Dylan as a poet of talent see Christopher Ricks, *Dylan's Visions of Sin* (New York: Ecco, 2005) and Frank Kermode and Stephen Spender, "The Metaphor at the End of the Funnel" (1972), in Thompson and Gutman, *Dylan Companion*, 155–62.

64. Shelton, *No Direction Home*, 227.

65. Interview with Nora Ephron and Susan Edmiston (August 1965), in Cott, *Essential Interviews*, 49.

66. Nicholl, "Just Like the Night," in Thompson and Gutman, *Dylan Companion*, 123; the song, originally titled "Freeze Out," was recorded in October 1965, with his new backup group, "The Hawks," and appeared on the double-album *Blonde on Blonde*. See Sean Wilentz, *Bob Dylan in America* (New York: Doubleday, 2010), 111–12. On his writing it and the session recording it, see Heylin, *Behind the Shades*, 144–45. On *Glamour* (June 1966) see Greil Marcus, *Bob Dylan: Writings, 1968–2010* (New York: Public Affairs, 2010), 377.

67. On the complexities of deciphering Dylan in a work such as "Visions of Johanna," see Bell, *Once Upon a Time*, 432–33. By 1966, Dylan had become awed by Allen Ginsberg's poetry and person. See the interview with Robert Shelton (March 1966), in Cott, *Essential Interviews*, 86–87.

68. Ted Gioia, *The History of Jazz* (New York: Oxford University Press, 1997), 351.

69. Cole, *Coltrane*, 169.

70. Quoted in John Gennari, *Blowin' Hot and Cold: Jazz and Its Critics* (Chicago: University of Chicago Press, 2006), 254. The same designation might, of course, be applied to Dylan's voice.

71. John S. Wilson, "Jazz and the Anarchy of the Avant-Garde," *New York Times*, 24 April 1966, X23.

72. Eric Nisenson, *Ascension: John Coltrane and His Quest* (New York: DaCapo, 1995), is excellent. Tommy L. Lott, "When Bar Walkers Preach: John Coltrane and the Crisis of the Black Intellectual," in *John Coltrane & Black America's Quest for Freedom*, ed. Leonard L. Brown (Oxford and London: Oxford University Press, 2010), 107–8. For a brief musical analysis of the different versions of *Ascension*, see Porter, *Coltrane*, 262–63.

73. Frank Kofsky, "Interview with John Coltrane" (18 August 1966), in DeVito, *Coltrane on Coltrane*, 285. On the complexities of understanding both *Ascension* and *Meditation* in their various recordings, see Anthony Brown, "John Coltrane as the Personification of Spirituality in Black Music," in Brown, *Black America's Quest for Freedom*, 55–71.

74. Hentoff, "*Meditations* Liner Notes," in DeVito, *Coltrane on Coltrane*, 263–64.

75. Kofsky, "Interview," 295.

76. Nat Hentoff, "*Live at the Village Vanguard Again!*: Liner Notes," in DeVito, *Coltrane on Coltrane*, 321.

77. "Interviews with John Coltrane," in DeVito, *Coltrane on Coltrane*, 272; on the final stage of Coltrane's musical journey, *Expressions*, see Nisenson, *Ascension*, 266–68.

Chapter 15

1. Sexton to Lois Ames, 19 November 1966, in Anne Sexton, *Anne Sexton: A Self-Portrait in Letters*, ed. Linda Gray Sexton and Lois Ames (Boston: Houghton Mifflin, 2004), 305.

2. Anne Sexton, "The Break," in *The Complete Poems of Anne Sexton* (New York: Mariner, 1999), 190; Diane Wood Middlebrook, *Anne Sexton: A Biography* (Boston: Houghton Mifflin, 1991), 266.

3. Middlebrook discusses the affair but uses a pseudonym for Duhl. See Middlebrook, *Sexton*, 258–66; Linda Gray Sexton, *Searching for Mercy Street: My Journey Back to My Mother, Anne Sexton* (Berkeley, CA: Counterpoint, 2011), 142.

4. Sexton, "For My Lover Returning to His Wife," in Sexton, *Complete Poems*, 189, 190.

5. Quoted in Middlebrook, *Sexton*, 259, 261.

6. Mona Van Duyn, "Review of *Love Poems*," in *Anne Sexton: The Artist and Her Critics*, ed. J. D. McClatchy (Bloomington: Indiana University Press, 1978), 141.

7. Linda Gray Sexton, *Half in Love: Surviving the Legacy of Suicide; A Memoir* (Berkeley: Counterpoint, 2011), 47. Eliot, "Tradition and the Individual Talent," in *Selected Essays, 1917–1932* (New York: Harcourt, Brace and Company, 1932), 7.

8. Sexton to Farrell (16 July 1962). in Sexton, *Self-Portrait*, 144.

9. Robert Lowell, *Life Studies and For the Union Dead* (New York: Farrar, Straus & Giroux, 1990), 82; Lowell, "Anne Sexton," in McClatchy, *The Artist and Her Critics*, 71.

10. Ben Howard, "Reviews," in McClatchy, *The Artist and Her Critics*, 177.

11. Jo Gill, *Anne Sexton's Confessional Poetics* (Gainesville: University Press of Florida, 2007), 4, 10–17; J. D. McClatchy, "Anne Sexton: Somehow to Endure," in McClatchy, *The Artist and Her Critics*, 247; L. G. Sexton, *Mercy Street*, 35.

12. L. G. Sexton, *Mercy Street*, 112.

13. Middlebrook, *Sexton*, 62. For negative assessments of the celebrity status achieved by Sexton and others via their confessional poetry, see David Haven Blake, "Public Dreams: Berryman, Celebrity, and the Culture of Confession," *American Literary History* 13 (Winter 2001): 716–36, esp. 719; Charles Molesworth, " 'With Your Own Face On': The Origins and Consequences of Confessional Poetry," *Twentieth-Century Literature* 22 (May 1976): 163–78.

14. Karen Alkalay-Gut, "The Dream Life of Ms. Dog: Anne Sexton's Revolutionary Use of Pop Culture," *College Literature* 32 (Fall 2005): 50–73.

15. Claire Pollard, "Her Kind: Anne Sexton, the Cold War and the Idea of the Housewife," *Critical Quarterly* 48 (Autumn 2006): 1–24.

16. L. G. Sexton, *Mercy Street*, 55–64.

17. Maxine Kumin, "A Friendship Remembered," in Kumin, *To Make a Prairie: Essays on Poets, Poetry, and Country Living* (Ann Arbor: University of Michigan Press, 1979), 92.

18. Anne Sexton, "Typewritten Biography," reproduced in Arthur Furst, *Anne Sexton: The Last Summer* (New York: St. Martin's, 2000), 4. For details on her early years, turn to Middlebrook, *Sexton*, 1–30.

19. Sexton, "Interview with Patricia Marx," in *No Evil Star: Selected Essays, Interviews, and Prose*, ed. Steven E. Colburn (Ann Arbor: University of Michigan Press, 1985), 70.

20. Sexton, "Interview with Patricia Marx," 80–81.

21. Betty Friedan, *The Feminine Mystique* (1963; repr., New York: W. W. Norton, 1997), 15, 317, 314.

22. Sheila Tobias, "Betty Friedan and the Feminine Mystique," in *Faces of Feminism: An Activist's Reflections on the Women's Movement* (Boulder, CO: Westview, 1997), 58–59.

23. L. G. Sexton, *Mercy Street*, 112.

24. Anne Sexton, "Housewife," in Sexton, *Complete Poems*, 77.

25. On Sexton and feminism, see Jane McCabe, " 'A Woman Who Writes': A Feminist Approach to the Early Poetry of Anne Sexton," in McClatchy, *The Artist and Her*

Critics, 216–17; Diana Hume George, *Oedipus Anne: The Poetry of Anne Sexton* (Urbana: University of Illinois Press, 1987). Brogan, "Review," in McClatchy, *The Artist and Her Critics*, 126.

26. Robert Boyers, "*Live or Die*: The Achievement of Anne Sexton," in McClatchy, *The Artist and Her Critics*, 207. For a view of Sexton as preening victim, see Geoffrey Thurley, *The American Moment: American Poetry in the Mid-Century* (New York: St. Martin's, 1978), 90.

27. On the affairs and various forms of family turmoil, see Middlebrook, *Sexton*, 245–67; L. G. Sexton, *Mercy Street*, 83–92.

28. Sexton to Tillie Olsen, circa New Year's Day, 1966, in Sexton, *Self-Portrait*, 278.

29. Anne Sexton, "The Addict," in Sexton, *Complete Poems*, 165–66. On her drug and alcohol consumption, see Middlebrook, *Sexton*, 139–40; 210–11.

30. L. G. Sexton note, in Sexton, *Self-Portrait*, 246–47.

31. Anne Sexton, "Live," in Sexton, *Complete Poems*, 167–70.

32. Sexton to Claire S. Degener (29 March 1966), in Sexton, *Self-Portrait*, 286. On Sexton and performance anxiety see "The Freak Show," in Sexton, *No Evil Star*, 33–38.

33. Middlebrook, *Sexton*, 247–48.

34. Anne Sexton, "Wanting to Die," in Sexton, *Complete Poems*, 142–43. Parts of the film are available online: https://vimeo.com/31859432.

35. Dickey, "Dialogues with Themselves," *New York Times* (28 April 1963), 294. Dickey, "Review of To Bedlam," in McClatchy, *The Artist and Her Critics*, 118.

36. Middlebrook, *Sexton*, 250.

37. Sexton to James Dickey (24 March 1966), in Sexton, *Self-Portrait*, 282–83.

38. Sexton, "Comment on 'Some Foreign Letters,'" and "The Freak Show," in Sexton, *No Evil Star*, 17, 33–34.

39. L. G. Sexton, *Mercy Street*, 125–26.

40. Sexton to Legler (28 April 1966, 2 May 1966), in Sexton, *Self-Portrait*, 288–92.

41. Middlebrook, *Sexton*, 255–57.

42. Anne Sexton, "For My Lover Returning to His Wife," in Sexton, *Complete Poems*, 188.

43. Sexton to Philip Legler (2 May 1966), in Sexton, *Self-Portrait*, 292.

44. Sexton to Lois Ames (2 August 1966), in Sexton, *Self-Portrait*, 298.

45. Sexton to Lois Ames (2 August 1966), in Sexton, *Self-Portrait*, 297, 298.

46. Truman Capote, *In Cold Blood* (New York: Random House, 1965), 302.

47. Alfred Friendly Jr., "Richard Speck's Chicago," *New York Times*, 18 July 1966, 16; Austin C. Wehrwein, "8 Student Nurses Slain in Chicago Dormitory," *New York Times*, 15 July 1966, 1, 14.

48. Albin Krebs, "The Texas Killer: Former Florida Neighbors Recall a Nice Boy Who Liked Guns," *New York Times*, 2 August 1966, 15; "Nation: The Madman in the Tower," *Time*, 12 August 1966.

49. "Crime: Slaughter in the College of Beauty," *Time*, 18 November 1966; Mara Bovsun, "Beauty Salon Massacre," *New York Daily News*, 25 March 2008, http://www.nydailynews.com/news/crime/beauty-salon-massacre-article-1.273663.

50. Sexton to Lois Ames (2 August 1966), in Sexton, *Self-Portrait*, 298.

51. Sexton to Lois Ames (7 September 1966), in Sexton, *Self-Portrait*, 299.

52. Sexton to Rise and Steven Axelrod (10 September 1974), in Sexton, *Self-Portrait*, 421.

53. Anne Sexton, "Live," in Sexton, *Collected Poems*, 170.

54. L. G. Sexton, *Half in Love*, 26.

Chapter 16

1. Alexandra Styron, *Reading My Father: A Memoir* (New York: Scribner, 2011, 154.

2. James L. W. West III, *William Styron: A Life* (New York: Random House, 2008), 276; West, "A Bibliographer's Interview with William Styron," in *Conversations with William Styron*, ed. James L. W. West III (Jackson: University Press of Mississippi, 1985), 204–5.

3. C. Vann Woodward and R. W. B. Lewis, "The Confessions of William Styron," in West, *Conversations*, 87.

4. Douglas Barzelay and Robert Sussman, "William Styron on *The Confessions of Nat Turner*," in West, *Conversations*, 103.

5. Robert Canzoneri and Page Stegner, "An Interview with William Styron," in West, *Conversations*, 67.

6. On connections between *Confessions* and Styron's earlier work, see Marc L. Ratner, "Styron's Rebel," *American Quarterly* 21 (Autumn 1969): 595–608.

7. William Styron, "A Voice from the South" (1989), in Styron, *This Quiet Dust, and Other Writings* (New York: Vintage, 1993), 57–58.

8. Styron to Elizabeth McKee (14 May 1952), in *Selected Letters of William Styron*, ed. Rose Styron (New York: Random House, 2012), 127.

9. Styron to William Styron Sr. (20 May 1952), in Styron, *Letters*, 130.

10. Styron to William Styron Sr. (1 May 1952), in Styron, *Letters*, 123; in "This Quiet Dust" (1965) he recalled first hearing about the rebellion in the 1930. Styron, *Quiet Dust*, 12.

11. Styron to Robert Loomis (27 May 1952), in Styron, *Letters*, 134.

12. Styron to William Styron Sr. (3 March 1953), in Styron, *Letters*, 168–69.

13. Styron to Norman Mailer (1 June 1953); Styron to Mac Hyman (15 August 1953); Styron to Maxwell Geismer (24 March 1953), in Styron, *Letters*, 184, 186, 175.

14. Styron to Norman Mailer (1 June 1953), in Styron, *Letters*, 184.

15. Canzoneri and Stegner, "An Interview," 70–73.

16. Styron to Norman Mailer (17 March 1958), and notes, in Styron, *Letters*, 250–51.

17. Mailer, *Advertisements for Myself* (New York: G. P. Putnam's Sons, 1959), 465.

18. Styron to James and Gloria Jones (24 March 1959), in Styron, *Letters*, 263.

19. Styron to James Jones (7 December 1959, 15 September 1959), in Styron, *Letters*, 274, 269.

20. Styron to Robert Loomis (3 April 1962), in Styron, *Letters*, 324.

21. The reference to "columbine" in the novel by Nat serves as a device to recall his youth; it is akin to Hearst's "Rosebud," the name of a sled that he had as a child. Styron had originally thought of "dogwood" as the connection but decided it was too similar to "Rosebud." Ben Forkner and Gilbert Schricke, "An Interview with William Styron," and Michael West, "An Interview with William Styron," in West, *Conversations*, 196, 225.

22. On its composition see West, *A Life*, 335–71.

23. Styron to Robert Penn Warren (21 February 1967); Styron to William Blackburn (29 November 1967), in Styron, *Letters*, 412, 429–30.

24. Raymond A. Sokolov, "Into the Mind of Nat Turner," *Newsweek*, 16 October 1967, 69.

25. Philip Rahv, "Through the Midst of Jerusalem," *New York Review of Books*, 26 October 1967; Wilfred Sheed, "The Slave Who Became a Man," *New York Times Book Review*, 8 October 1967, 1–2; Eliot Fremont-Smith, "A Sword is Sharpened," *New York Times*, 3 October 1967, 45. Fremont-Smith reconsidered the book more critically another time, in two articles in, *New York Times* (1 August 1968, 29; 4 October 1967).

26. Nat Turner, "The Confessions of Nat Turner," in *The Nat Turner Rebellion: The Historical Event and Modern Controversy*, ed. John B. Duff and Peter M. Mitchell (New York: Harper & Row, 1971), 22.

27. On the rebellion see Stephen B. Oates, *The Fires of Jubilee: Nat Turner's Fierce Rebellion* (New York: Harper & Row, 1975); the essays in Kenneth S. Greenberg, ed., *Nat Turner: A Slave Rebellion in History and Memory* (New York: Oxford University Press, 1973); Scot French, *The Rebellious Slave: Nat Turner in American Memory* (Boston: Houghton, Mifflin, 2004).

28. James Baldwin, "Interview with Studs Terkel" (1961), in *Conversations with James Baldwin*, ed. Fred L. Standley and Louis H. Pratt (Jackson: University of Mississippi Press, 1989), 12, 21.

29. James Baldwin, *The Fire Next Time* (New York: Dial, 1963), 21.

30. Baldwin, *Fire Next Time*, 112.

31. Baldwin, *Fire Next Time*, 119–20.

32. William Styron, *Havanas in Camelot: Personal Essays* (New York: Random House, 2008), 96, 99, 101–2; Sokolov, "Into the Mind," 67. On Baldwin as model for Nat see Charles Joyner, "Styron's Choice: A Meditation on History, Literature, and Moral Imperatives," in Greenberg, *Nat Turner: A Slave Rebellion*, 204.

33. William Styron, "Introduction," Styron, *Quiet Dust*, 4.

34. Sokolov, "Into the Mind," 67; Stanley Kauffmann, "Styron's Unwritten Novel," *Hudson Review* 20 (Winter 1967–1968): 675–80.

35. Canzoneri and Stegner, "An Interview," 73, 88.

36. Styron to Louis D. Rubin (8 July 1974), in Styron, *Letters*, 511.

37. John Henrik Clarke, ed., *William Styron's Nat Turner: Ten Black Writers Respond* (Boston: Beacon, 1968), 4–5.

38. His pal the historian Arthur M. Schlesinger Jr. had wondered about this omission, although he otherwise supported Styron's history with enthusiasm against his critics. Schlesinger to Styron (27 July 1967), in *The Letters of Arthur Schlesinger, Jr.*, ed. Andrew Schlesinger and Stephen Schlesinger (New York: Random House, 2013), 337.

39. Canzoneri and Stegner, "An Interview," 75.

40. Canzoneri and Stegner, "An Interview," 77.

41. Styron to William Blackburn (19 April 1968), in Styron, *Letters*, 435. Styron was, at least in casual conversation and letters, capable of offhand racist remarks. See Styron to Blackburn (14 November 1968), in Styron, *Letters*, 444–45.

42. Styron to Donald Gallagher (10 February 1971), in Styron, *Letters*, 457.

43. Barzelay and Sussman, "William Styron on *The Confessions*," and Rust Hills, "Conversation: Arthur Miller and William Styron," in West, *Conversations*, 107, 173.

44. Styron to Hope Leresche (18 April 1968), in Styron, *Letters*, 434.

45. Joyce Haber, "A Frank Discussion of 'Nat Turner,'" *Los Angeles Times*, 29 May 1968, C7.

46. Ralph Ellison, William Styron, Robert Penn Warren, and C. Vann Woodward, "A Discussion on the Uses of History on Fiction," *Southern Literary Journal* 1, no. 2 (Spring 1969): 57–90.

47. Ellison et al., "Uses of History," 62, 73, 60–61, 58–59, 75.

48. Ellison et al., "Uses of History," 78–79; Donald W. Markos, "Margaret Whitehead in *The Confessions of Nat Turner*," *Studies in the Novel* 4 (Spring 1972): 52–59.

49. Ellison et al., "Uses of History," 79–80; West, *A Life*, 392.

50. Ellison et al., "Uses of History," 80, 81–83.

51. On Styron's reading of the historical literature on slavery see Styron, *Dust*, 35–38; West, *Conversations*, 112. He also had the support of many leading historians. See, in particular, Eugene Genovese, "The Nat Turner Case," *New York Review of Books*, 12 September 1968, 34–37. Subsequent issues found the debate still stirring. On the debate and its varied meanings see Okon E. Uya, "Race, Ideology and Scholarship in the United States: William Styron's Nat Turner and its Critics," *American Quarterly* 15 (Winter 1976): 63–81; Ernest P. Williams, "William Styron and His Ten Black Critics," *Phylon* 37, no. 2 (1976): 189–95; Herbert Shapiro, "The Confessions of Nat Turner: William Styron and his Critics," *Negro American Literature Forum* 9 (Winter 1975): 99–104; D. Michael Sink, "A Response to Critics: The Confessions of Nat Turner," *Clearing House* 48 (October 1973): 125–26.

52. Styron to Donald Harrington (15 January 1964), *Letters*, 157; *Quiet Dust*, 15.

53. Woodward and Lewis, "Confessions of William Styron," 91.

54. Canzoneri and Stegner, "An Interview," 78.

55. William Styron, *The Confessions of Nat Turner: A Novel* (New York: Random House, 1967), 27.

56. A vexing problem in many slave narratives.

57. Styron, *Confessions*, 39.

58. Styron, *Confessions*, 83.

59. Styron, *Confessions*, 88.

60. Styron to Schlesinger (29 July 1967), in Styron, *Letters*, 427.

61. Styron to William Styron Sr., (24 February 1961), in Styron, *Letters*, 309.

62. Truman Capote, *In Cold Blood* (New York: Random House, 1965).

63. Jack Behar, "History and Fiction," *Novel* 3 (Spring 1970): 260–65. He focused on Styron's problems with language.

64. Barzelay and Sussman, "William Styron on *The Confessions*," 94.

65. Woodward and Lewis, "Confessions of William Styron," 87.

66. William Styron, "Hell Reconsidered" (1968), in Styron, *Quiet Dust*, 107.

67. William Styron, "Introduction," in Styron, *Quiet Dust*, 7.

68. Forkner and Schricke, "Interview with William Styron," 193.

69. George Core, "*The Confessions of Nat Turner* and *The Burden of the Past*," *Southern Literary Journal* 2 (Spring 1970): 117–34.

70. William Styron, *Darkness Visible: A Memoir of Madness* (New York: Random House, 1990), 21.

71. Canzoneri and Stegner, "An Interview," 71.

72. Styron, *Confessions*, 77.

73. Richard Gilman, "Nat Turner Revisited" (1968), in Duff and Mitchell, *Nat Turner Rebellion*, 234–35.

74. Canzoneri and Stegner, "An Interview," 69–71.

75. George Plimpton, "William Styron: A Shared Ordeal," *New York Times*, 8 October 1967, BR2; Styron, *Confessions*, 72–73.

76. Alden Whitman, "William Styron Examines the Negro Upheaval," *New York Times*, 5 August 1957, 13.

77. William E. Akin, "Toward an Impressionistic History: Pitfalls and Possibilities in William Styron's Meditation on History," *American Quarterly* 21 (Winter 1969): 805–12.

78. Norman O. Brown, *Life against Death: The Psychoanalytic Meaning of History* (New York: Vintage, 1959), 175.

79. Hayden White, "The Burden of History," *History and Theory* 5, no. 2 (1966): 112, 128–29.

80. Bret McCabe, "Structuralism's Samson," *Johns Hopkins Magazine*, Fall 2012, available online at http://hub.jhu.edu/magazine/2012/fall/structuralisms-samson.

81. Richard Macksey, "Anniversary Reflections," in *The Structuralist Controversy: The Languages of Criticism and the Sciences of Man*, ed. Richard Macksey and Eugenio Donato, rev. ed. (Baltimore: Johns Hopkins University Press, 2007), xviii.

82. Styron to Prince Sadruddin Aga Khan (5 July 1979), in Styron, *Letters*, 536.

Chapter 17

1. Gore Vidal, "Interview," *Playboy*, June 1969, 93; Robert Hofler, *Sexplosion: From Andy Warhol to A Clockwork Orange—How a Generation of Pop Rebels Broke All the Taboos* (New York: It Books, 2014), 19.

2. Fremont-Smith, "Like Fay Wray if the Light is Right," *New York Times*, 3 February 1968, 27.

3. Gore Vidal, *Myra Breckinridge* (Boston: Little, Brown, 1968), 3. On the book see Fred Kaplan, *Gore Vidal: A Biography* (New York: Random House, 1999), 577–602; Bernard F. Dick, *The Apostate Angel: A Critical Study of Gore Vidal* (New York: Random House, 1974);141–70; Robert F. Kiernan, *Gore Vidal* (New York: Frederick Ungar, 1982), 94–109. For his drafts, see series I, compositions, folders 65–71, Gore Vidal Papers, Harvard University. A guide to the papers is available online at http://oasis.lib.harvard.edu/oasis/deliver/deepLink?_collection=oasis&uniqueId=hou01943. On Vidal's upsetting expectations see Gerald Clarke, "The Art of Fiction L: Gore Vidal" (1974), in *Conversations with Gore Vidal*, ed. Richard Peabody and Lucinda Ebersole (Jackson: University of Mississippi Press, 2005), 42.

4. Andrew Sarris, *Confessions of a Cultist: On the Cinema, 1955/1969* (New York: Simon & Schuster, 1970), 274.

5. Gore Vidal, "Interview with Hollis Alpert and Janos Kadar" (1977), in Peabody and Ebersole, *Conversations*, 80.

6. Sarris, *Confessions*, 284. See also Paul Monaco, *History of the American Cinema: The Sixties* (Berkeley: University of California Press, 2001), 62.

7. Susan Sontag, "Notes on Camp," in *Against Interpretation* (New York: Farrar, Straus & Giroux, 1966), 278, 281, 283, 287, 292. On how camp was both oppositional and contained see Andrew Ross, "Uses of Camp," in *No Respect: Intellectuals and Popular Culture* (New York: Routledge, 1989), 169. Helpful on tragedy and parody in *Myra* are Dick, *Apostate Angel*, 159–60; Purvis E. Boyette, "*Myra Breckinridge* and Imitative Form," *Modern Fiction Studies* 17 (Summer 1971): 229–38.

8. George Melly, *Revolt into Style: The Pop Arts* (London: Oxford University Press, 1989), 192.

9. Hilton Kramer, "Look! All Over! It's Esthetic…It's Business…It's Supersuccess!," *New York Times*, 29 March 1966, 33; Jack Gould, "Too Good to Be Camp," *New York Times*, 23 January 1966, 109. See also Andy Medhurst, "Batman, Deviance and Camp," in *The Many Lives of Batman: Critical Approaches to a Superhero and His Media* (London: Routledge, 1991), 149–63.

10. Gore Vidal, "Miss Sontag's New Novel" (1967), in *United States: Essays, 1952–1992* (New York: Random House, 1993), 377. On the Sontag-Vidal connection see Dennis Altman, *Gore Vidal's America* (London: Polity, 2005), 131.

11. Gore Vidal, "French Letters: Theories of the New Novel," in Vidal, *United States*, 89–110; Susan Sontag, "Nathalie Sarraute and the Novel," in Sontag, *Against Interpretation*, 100–11. On Vidal and the New Novelists, see Dick, *Apostate Angel*, 151–53.

12. Susan Sontag, "Thirty Years Later..." (1995), in *Where the Stress Falls* (New York: Farrar, Straus & Giroux, 2001), 268–73.

13. Vidal, "French Letters," 91. Jay Parini remembers conversations with Vidal about Sontag's work. Parini, personal communication, 24 March 2014.

14. Vidal, *Myra*, 4.

15. Lewis Nichols, "Underground," *New York Times*, 28 January 1968, BR32.

16. Vidal, *Myra*, 5.

17. Vidal, *Myra*, 26, 148. Parker Tyler was, in fact, an influential gay historian of film.

18. Vidal, *Myra*, 30.

19. Vidal, *Myra*, 234, 161, 177.

20. Vidal, *Myra*, 182, 184.

21. Vidal, *Myra*, 259–60.

22. Vidal, *Myra*, 263.

23. John Updike, *Couples: A Novel* (New York: Random House, 1996), 63, 111.

24. David Allyn, *Make Love, Not War: The Sexual Revolution; An Unfettered History* (Boston: Little, Brown, 2000), 55, 66.

25. Ed Sanders, *Fug You: An Informal History of the Peace Eye Bookstore, the Fuck You Press, the Fugs, and Counterculture in the Lower East Side* (New York: Da Capo, 2011), 180.

26. Philip Roth, "Whacking Off (A Story)," *Partisan Review* 34 (Summer 1967): 399.

27. Quoted in John D'Emilio and Estelle B. Freedman, *Intimate Matters: A History of Sexuality in America* (New York: Harper & Row, 1988), 307.

28. Quoted in Douglas Martin, "Robert H. Rimmer Obituary," *New York Times*, 11 August 2001, A13.

29. Rex Reed, "Breakthrough by 'The Boys in the Band,'" *New York Times*, 12 May 1968, D1.

30. Allyn, *Make Love*, 106. On radical feminists in relation to sexual liberation see Alice Echols, *Daring to Be Bad: Radical Feminism in America, 1967–1975* (Minneapolis: University of Minnesota Press, 1989), esp. 139–201.

31. Quoted in Allyn, *Make Love*, 103.

32. Vidal, "Interview," 92.

33. Charles Russ, "Interview with Gore Vidal" (1998), in Peabody and Ebersole, *Conversations*, 98

34. Kaplan, *Biography*, 579.

35. Gore Vidal, "Pornography" (1966), in *Gore Vidal: Sexually Speaking: Collected Sex Writings*, ed. Donald Weise (San Francisco, Cleis, 1999), 39.

36. Gore Vidal, "Women's Liberation and Its Discontents" (1971), in Vidal, *United States*, 585.

37. Gore Vidal, *Palimpsest: A Memoir* (New York: Penguin, 1995), 102; Vidal, "Some Memories of the Glorious Bird and an Earlier Self" (1976), in Vidal, *United States*, 1139–40. For Vidal's views on homosexual activity see his "Doc Reuben" (1970), in Vidal, *Sexually Speaking*, 51–56.

38. Things get complicated, however, in the sequel, *Myron: A Novel* (New York: Random House, 1974).

39. Gore Vidal, "The *Fag Rag* Interview" (1974), in Peabody and Ebersole, *Conversations*, 18.

40. Gore Vidal, *Snapshots in History's Glare* (New York: Abrams, 2009), 77.

41. On Vidal and homosexuality, in politics and literature, see Altman, *Gore Vidal's America*, 127–54.

42. Larry Kramer, "The Sadness of Gore Vidal" (1992), in Vidal, *Sexually Speaking*, 254.

43. George Chauncey, *Gay New York: Gender, Urban Culture, and the Making of the Gay Male World, 1890–1940* (New York: Basic Books, 1994), 33ff.

44. Vidal, *Palimpsest*, 95.

45. Kaplan, *Biography*, 369; Gore Vidal, *Two Sisters: A Memoir in the Form of a Novel* (Boston: Little, Brown, 1970), 213. There is a story, lurid and perhaps apocryphal, that Kerouac wanted revenge for this outrage, so he had his pal Neal Cassady pick up Vidal, take him to the Chelsea Hotel, and then rape him. "Vidal kicked and screamed," according to Cassady's account, which goes in great detail. For this alleged event see Darwin Porter and Danforth Prince, *Pink Triangle: The Feuds and Private Lives of Tennessee Williams, Gore Vidal, Truman Capote, and Famous Members of Their Entourages* (New York: BloodMoon, 2014), 301–2.

46. Vidal, *Sexually Speaking*, 97. For a smart and funny analysis of these themes, see Catharine R. Stimpson, "My O My O Myra," in *Gore Vidal: Writer against the Grain*, ed. Jay Parini (New York: Columbia University Press, 1992), 191–93.

47. Jon Wiener, "The Scholar Squirrels and the National Security Scare: An Interview with Gore Vidal" (1988), in Peabody and Ebersole, *Conversations*, 112; Robert J. Stanton and Gore Vidal, eds., *Views from a Window: Conversations with Gore Vidal* (Secaucus, NJ: Lyle Stuart, 1980), 236; Vidal, *Sexually Speaking*, 228.

48. Stanton and Vidal, *Views from a Window*, 147; "The Gay Sunshine Interview" (1974), in Vidal, *Sexually Speaking*, 225–26.

49. On the events of 1968, see Mark Kurlansky, *1968: The Year that Rocked the World* (New York: Random House, 2005); Cronkite quote on 61. See also Terry H. Anderson, *The Movement and the Sixties: Protest in America from Greensboro to Wounded Knee* (New York: Oxford University Press, 1995); David Farber, *The Age of Great Dreams: America in the 1960s* (New York: Hill & Wang, 1994); Maurice Isserman and Michael Kazin, *America Divided: The Civil War of the 1960s* (Oxford: Oxford University Press, 2000). On the period from an international perspective, see Gerard J. DeGroot, *The Sixties Unplugged: A Kaleidoscopic History of a Disorderly Decade* (Cambridge, MA: Harvard University Press, 2008); Arthur Marwick, *The Sixties* (Oxford: Oxford University Press, 1998); Paul Berman, *A Tale of Two Utopias: The Political Journey of the Generation of 1968* (New York: W. W. Norton, 1996).

50. Kurlansky, *1968*, 115; Anderson, *The Movement*, 192.

51. Valerie Solanas, *The SCUM Manifesto*, available online at http://www.ccs.neu.edu/home/shivers/rants/scum.html; Jennifer Pan, "Trasher Feminism: Valerie Solanas and Her Enemies," *Dissent* (Spring 2014): 83–86.

52. Kurlansky, *1968*, 197.

53. Kurlansky, *1968*, 207.

54. Susan Sontag, "Trip to Hanoi" (2008), and "What's Happening in America" (1966), in *Styles of Radical Will* (New York: Picador, 2002), 237, 203.

55. Norman Mailer, *Miami and the Siege of Chicago* (1968; repr., New York: New York Review Books, 2008), 169.

56. On Chicago see David Farber, *Chicago '68* (Chicago: University of Chicago Press, 1988).

57. Vidal, *Snapshots*, 166; Kaplan, *Biography*, 594.

58. Jack Gould, "TV: Politics Fails to Lure Viewers from Adventure," *New York Times*, 7 August 1968, 87.

59. On the exchange see Christopher Bram, *Eminent Outlaws: The Gay Writers Who Changed America* (New York: Twelve, 2012), 122–27; William F. Buckley Jr., "On Experiencing Gore Vidal," *Esquire*, August, 1969; Vidal, "A Distasteful Encounter with William F. Buckley, Jr.," *Esquire*, September 1969. See also "Feuds: Wasted Talent," *Time*, 22 August 1969. The courts eventually threw out Vidal's suit. Buckley dropped the suit against Vidal but collected over $100,000 in damages from the magazine. "Buckley Drops Vidal Suit, Settles with Esquire," *New York Times*, 26 September, 1972, 40.

Chapter 18

1. "David Frost Interviews LeRoi Jones," in Amiri Baraka, *Conversations with Amiri Baraka*, ed. Charlie Reilly (Jackson: University of Mississippi Press, 1994), 62, 66, 69.

2. Stewart Smith and Peter Thorn, "An Interview with LeRoi Jones" (1966), in Baraka, *Conversations*, 13. In 1967 Jones began using the name Amiri Baraka. He did so inconsistently, well into 1969. When speaking of him and his work prior to 1967, I will employ LeRoi Jones, switching to Amiri Baraka for later works.

3. Amiri Baraka, *The Autobiography of LeRoi Jones/Amiri Baraka* (New York: Freundlich, 1984), 194.

4. LeRoi Jones, "To Survive 'The Reign of the Beasts,'" *New York Times*, 16 November 1969, D1, 2. In a review, Jack Richardson considered works by Baraka, Harold Cruse, Eldridge Cleaver, and James Baldwin—all pointing toward a "black sensibility." He complained, however, "Exactly what that sensibility is, of course, no one seems to know." See Richardson, "The Black Arts," *New York Review of Books*, 19 December 1968, available online at http://www.nyb.com/articles/archives/1968/dec/19/the-black-arts-2. Similar demands for no interaction with whites had happened before. See Peter Greenberg, "LeRoi Jones Asks Black Privileges for WSA Talk," *University of Wisconsin Cardinal*, 7 February 1969, 1.

5. Clive Barnes, "The Theater: New LeRoi Jones Play," *New York Times*, 22 November 1969, 46. On the play see Mike Sell, *Avant-Garde Performance and the Limits of Criticism: Approaching the Living Theatre, Happenings/Fluxus, and the Black Arts Movement* (Ann Arbor: University of Michigan Press, 2008), 223, 248–50.

6. A. S. Doc Young, "Letter to the Editor," *New York Times*, 30 November 1969, 38; Taylor Mead, "Letter to the Editor," *New York Times*, 14 December 1969, D15.

7. Gerald Weales, "What Were the Blacks Doing in the Balcony: The Day LeRoi Jones Spoke on Penn Campus," *New York Times*, 4 May 1969, SM 38–41, 44, 48, 52–56.

8. Amiri Baraka, *Jello* (Chicago: Third World, 1970), 8.

9. Martin Duberman claimed that Jones was after "private catharsis" more than serious communication. Duberman, "James Meredith and LeRoi Jones" (1966), in *The Uncompleted Past* (New York: Random House, 1969), 135. Ross Posnock usefully highlights the ambivalence and ambiguity of Jones and other black artists in white America. Posnock, *Color and Culture: Black Writers and the Making of the Modern Intellectual* (Cambridge, MA: Harvard University Press, 1998), 245. The poem is "Cold Term," in Jones, "Black Art," in *Black Magic: Collected Poetry, 1961–1967* (Indianapolis: Bobbs-Merrill, 1969), 91.

10. Pinckney, "The Changes of Amiri Baraka," *New York Times*, 16 December 1979, BR3.

11. See two excellent works, Werner Sollors, *Amiri Baraka/LeRoi Jones: The Quest for a "Populist Modernism"* (New York: Columbia University Press, 1978), 185, and Jerry Gafio Watts, *Amiri Baraka: The Politics and Art of a Black Intellectual* (New York: New York University Press, 2001); see also Kimberly W. Benston, *Baraka: The Renegade and the Mask* (New Haven, CT: Yale University Press, 1976). Also helpful is Lloyd W. Brown, *Amiri Baraka* (Boston: Twayne, 1980). On his artistic development see William J. Harris, *The Poetry and Poetics of Amiri Baraka: The Jazz Aesthetic* (Columbia: University of Missouri Press, 1985), and Theodore R. Hudson, *From LeRoi Jones to Amiri Baraka: The Literary Works* (Durham, NC: Duke University Press, 1973).

12. On these years see Hettie Jones, *How I Became Hettie Jones* (New York: E. P. Dutton, 1990); Diane di Prima, *Recollections of My Life as a Woman: The New York Years* (New York: Viking, 2001).

13. LeRoi Jones, "Black Dada Nihilismus," in *The Dead Lecturer* (New York: Grove, 1964), 61–64; H. Jones, *How I Became*, 237.

14. Jones, "LeRoi Jones Talking," in *Home: Social Essays* (New York: William Morrow, 1965), 188.

15. William Taubman, "The Theater: 'Dutchman,'" *New York Times*, 25 March 1964, 46.

16. LeRoi Jones, *The Slave*, in *Dutchman and The Slave: Two Plays* (New York: Morrow, 1964), 55, 88

17. Jones, *Dead Lecturer*, 15.

18. Stanley Kauffmann, "LeRoi Jones and the Tradition of the Fake," *Dissent* 12, no. 2 (Spring 1965): 207–12.

19. Baraka, *Autobiography*, 168; LeRoi Jones, *Blues People* (New York: William Morrow, 1963), 235.

20. For a smart critique of Jones's work in Harlem, from a nationalist perspective, see Harold Cruse, *The Crisis of the Negro Intellectual* (New York: William Morrow, 1967), 362–68.

21. LeRoi Jones, "state/meant," in *Home: Social Essays* (New York: William Morrow, 1965), 251–52.

22. Amiri Baraka, *Raise, Race, Rays, Raze: Essays since 1965* (New York: Random House, 1971), 33, 98.

23. Jones/Baraka, *Autobiography*, 259–60.

24. Hoyt W. Fuller, "Towards a Black Aesthetic," in *Black Expression*, comp. Addison Gayle Jr. (New York: Weybright & Talley, [1969]), 263.

25. Jones/Baraka, *Autobiography*, 261–62. See also Peniel E. Joseph, *Waiting 'til The Midnight Hour: A Narrative History of Black Power in America* (New York: Henry Holt, 2006), 183–88.

26. Jones/Baraka, *Autobiography*, 266.

27. Walter H. Waggoner, "LeRoi Jones Jailed in Manacles after Outburst in Jersey Court," *New York Times*, 25 October 1967, 30.

28. LeRoi Jones, "Black People!," in Jones, *Black Magic*, 225.

29. Walter H. Waggoner, "LeRoi Jones Guilty in Weapons Case," *New York Times*, 7 November 1967, 24; "LeRoi Jones Wins Retrial in Jersey," *New York Times*, 24 December 1968, 24; and "Court in Jersey Clears LeRoi Jones," *New York Times*, 17 January 1970, 16. Material on the trial is in Hudson, *From LeRoi Jones*, 28–31. Jones had been arrested for assault on Shepard Sherbell, the editor of a literary magazine. The charge was dismissed in

1967. See "Assault Charge Dismissed against Negro Playwright," *New York Times*, 20 January 1967, 72. He would return to court in 1969. See "LeRoi Jones Is Accused of Receiving Stolen Goods," *New York Times*, 18 March 1969, 49.

30. D. B. Melhem, "Revolution: The Constancy of Change" in Baraka, *Conversations*, 194.

31. Alexander Downs, *Cornell '69: Liberalism and the Crisis of the American University* (Ithaca, NY: Cornell University Press, 1999); Allan Bloom, *The Closing of the American Mind: How Higher Education Has Failed Democracy and Impoverished the Souls of Today's Students* (New York: Simon & Schuster, 1987), 353.

32. Todd Gitlin, *The Sixties: Years of Hope, Days of Rage* (Toronto: Bantam, 1987), 392–94.

33. Martin Duberman, *Stonewall* (New York: Dutton, 1993), 193, 195.

34. For a copy of the manifesto, see the Redstockings website, http://www.redstockings .org/index.php?option=com_content&view=article&id=76&Itemid=59. On the Redstockings, see Alice Echols, *Daring to Be Bad: Radical Feminism in America, 1967–1975* (Minneapolis: University of Minnesota Press, 1989), 151–54.

35. Amiri Baraka/LeRoi Jones, "A Poem Some People Will Have to Understand," in *Selected Poetry of Amiri Baraka/LeRoi Jones* (New York: William Morrow, 1979), 55.

36. James H. Cone, *Black Theology and Black Power* (New York: Seabury, 1969), 8.

37. Peter Kihiss, "Negro Attitudes Found Hardening," *New York Times*, 26 October 1969, 53.

38. Clive Barnes, "Black Theater: Of Politics and Passion," *New York Times*, 22 September 1969, 36.

39. See Manning Marable, *Malcolm X: A Life of Revolution* (New York: Viking, 2011).

40. Sollors, *Amiri Baraka*, 206–10.

41. Amiri Baraka, *The Death of Malcolm X*, in *New Plays from the Black Theatre*, ed. Ed Bullins (New York: Bantam, 1969), 2–20.

42. Amiri Baraka, "The Black Arts Movement," in *The LeRoi Jones/Amiri Baraka Reader*, ed. William J. Harris (New York: Thunder's Mouth, 1999), 502.

43. Stephen Henderson, *Understanding the New Black Poetry: Black Speech and Black Music as Poetic References* (New York: William Morrow, 1973), 7, 21, 30ff.

44. Larry Neal, "The Black Arts Movement" (1968), in *The Black Aesthetic*, ed. Addison Gayle Jr. (Garden City, NY: Doubleday, 1971), 273; James Edward Smethurst, *The Black Arts Movement: Literary Nationalism in the 1960s and 1970s* (Chapel Hill: University of North Carolina Press, 2005); David Lionel Smith, "The Black Arts Movement and Its Critics," *American Literary History* 3 (Spring 1991): 93–110. Also, for a look back on the movement and its idealism, see Houston A. Baker Jr., "The Black Spokesman as Critic: Reflections on the Black Aesthetic," in *The Journey Back: Issues in Black Literature and Criticism* (Chicago: University of Chicago Press, 1980), 133.

45. Amiri Baraka and Larry Neal, eds., *Black Fire: An Anthology of Afro-American Writing* (1969; repr., Baltimore: Black Classic, 2007), xxiii.

46. Amiri Baraka, "An Explanation of the Work," in Baraka, *Black Magic*, n.p.

47. Maulana Karenga, *The Quotable Karenga*, ed. Clyde Halisi (Los Angeles: US Org., 1967), 9.

48. On Karenga see the excellent Scot Brown, *Fighting for US: Maulana Karenga, the US Organization, and Black Cultural Nationalism* (New York: New York University Press, 2003), 12 and passim. See also Komzoi Woodard, *A Nation within a Nation: Amiri Baraka (LeRoi Jones) and Black Power Politics* (Chapel Hill: University of North Carolina Press, 1999), esp. 159ff. On Baraka and Karenga, see Joseph, *Waiting*, 216–19; Henry C. Lacey, *To*

Raise, Destroy, and Create: The Poetry Drama, and Fiction of Imamu Amiri Baraka (Troy, NY: Whitson, 1981), 126–27. For Baraka's take, see Baraka, *Autobiography*, 252ff.

49. Amiri Baraka, "A Black Value System," *The Black Scholar* 1 (November 1969): 58.

50. Amiri Baraka and Fundi (Billy Abernathy), *In Our Terribleness: (Some Elements and Meaning in Black Style)* (Indianapolis: Bobbs-Merrill, 1970). Unfortunately, the book is unpaginated. For a brief discussion of Fundi see Margo Natalie Crawford, "Black Light and the Wall of Respect: The Chicago Black Arts Movement," in *New Thoughts on the Black Arts Movement* (New Brunswick, NJ: Rutgers University Press, 2006), 24. In his otherwise superlative work on Jones/Baraka, Werner Sollors neglects to mention *In Our Terribleness*. More attention is paid to the work in Clyde Taylor, "Baraka as Poet," in *Imamu Amiri Baraka (LeRoi Jones): A Collection of Critical Essays* ed. Kimberly W. Benston (Englewood Cliffs, NJ: Prentice-Hall, 1978), 117–18. Critical of Baraka for his sentimentalism and romanticism of black life is Jennifer Jordan, "Cultural Nationalism in the 1960s: Politics and Poetry," in *Race, Politics, and Poetry: Critical Essays on the Radicalism of the 1960s*, ed. Adolph Reed Jr. (Westport, CT.: Greenwood, 1986), 44–45.

51. Amiri Baraka, "Talk with Mel Watkins" (1971), in Baraka, *Conversations*, 91. Baraka reportedly tried to get his publisher to pay for a book launch party to be catered by his sister. Bobbs-Merrill refused. Hudson, *From LeRoi Jones*, 141–42.

52. Roy DeCarava and Langston Hughes, *The Sweet Flypaper of Life* (New York: Hill & Wang, 1967).

53. Harris, *Poetry and Poetics*, 23. Clyde Taylor, "Baraka," in Benston, *Imamu Amiri Baraka*, 117. *In Our Terribleness* did not receive much attention in the mainstream press, but it got a boffo review by Ron Welburn, "In Our Terribleness," *New York Times Book Review*, 14 February 1971, 10, 12.

54. For popular radio culture in his work, see LeRoi Jones, *Preface to a Twenty Volume Suicide Note* (New York: Totem, 1961), 10–14.

55. Charlie Reilly, "An Interview with Amiri Baraka" (1991), in Baraka, *Conversations*, 243.

Chapter 19

1. Diane Arbus, *Diane Arbus* (Millerton, NY: Aperture, 1972), 3. Only the introduction is paginated. Quote for title comes from a conversation between Arbus and the feminist Susan Brownmiller; see Patricia Bosworth, *Diane Arbus: A Biography* (New York: Alfred A. Knopf, 1994), 239.

2. Jacob Deschin, "People Seen as Curiosity," *New York Times*, 5 March 1967, 129.

3. Bosworth, *Arbus*, 247–49.

4. Quoted in Leo Rubinfein, "Where Diane Arbus Went," *Art in America* 9 (October 2005): 67.

5. For biographical information on Arbus, see selections from Arbus's writings in Diane Arbus, *Revelations* (New York: Random House, 2003); see 183–89 for the year 1967.

6. Arbus, *Revelations*, 198–202. This book is an immense compilation of images, parts of letters, journal entries, and more.

7. Arbus, *Revelations*, 206, 207.

8. Arbus, *Revelations*, 206, 218.

9. Arbus, *Revelations*, 214.

10. Gregory Gibson, *Hubert's Freaks: The Rare-Book Dealer, The Times Square Talker, and the Lost Photos of Diane Arbus* (Orlando, FL: Harcourt, 2008), esp. 53ff. On freaks, in myth and reality, see Leslie Fiedler, *Freaks: Myths and Images of the Secret Self* (New York: Simon & Schuster, 1978). Fiedler has little to offer on Arbus.

11. Arthur Lubow, "The Woman and the Giant (No Fable)," *New York Times*, 13 April 2014, AL, 24.

12. Amy Waldman, "Revisiting a Life," *New York Times*, 23 September 1999, E5.

13. Arbus, *Revelations*, 153.

14. See her comments in Elisabeth Sussman and Doon Arbus, *Diane Arbus: A Chronology, 1927–1971* (New York: Aperture, 2011), 68.

15. Arbus, *Revelations*, 209. On the image, see Carol Armstrong, "Biology, Destiny, Photography: Difference According to Diane Arbus," *October* 66 (Fall 1993): 43.

16. A. D. Coleman, "Diana Arbus: Her Portraits Are Self-Portraits," *New York Times*, 5 November 1972, D33.

17. Diane Arbus, *Diane Arbus*, 2.

18. Diane Arbus, *Diane Arbus*, 9–10. Janet Malcolm considered her "an old-fashioned photographer" because she took portraits. Malcolm, "Diana and Nikon," *New Yorker*, 26 April 1976, 117. For more on her photographic style, see Hilton Kramer, "Arbus Photos, at Venice, Show Power," *New York Times*, 17 June 1972, 25.

19. Arbus, *Revelations*, 66; Bosworth, *Arbus*, 193.

20. Diane Arbus, *Diane Arbus*, 1.

21. Lubow, "The Woman," 24; Christoph Ribbat, "Queer and Straight Photography," *Amerikastudien* 46, no. 1 (2001): 32; Maggie Nelson, *The Art of Cruelty: A Reckoning* (New York and London: W. W. Norton, 2011), 142. On her desire to disrupt expectations, see Frederick Gross, *Diane Arbus's 1960s: Auguries of Experience* (Minneapolis: University of Minnesota Press, 2012), 105.

22. Bosworth, *Arbus*, 291.

23. Bosworth, *Arbus*, 178–79. On the fantasy aspects of Arbus's work, see Lisa A. Baird, "Susan Sontag and Diane Arbus: The Siamese Twins of Photographic Art," *Women's Studies* 37 (2008): 982.

24. Arbus, *Revelations*, 180.

25. Bosworth, *Arbus*, 224.

26. William Todd Schultz, *An Emergency in Slow Motion* (New York: Bloomsbury, 2011), 76.

27. Doon Arbus and Marvin Israel, eds., *Diane Arbus: Magazine Work* (Millerton, NY: Aperture, 1984), 31.

28. Mailer quoted in Bosworth, *Arbus*, 227.

29. Arbus and Israel, *Magazine Work*, 58–61; Bosworth, *Arbus*, 197.

30. Norman Mailer, *The Prisoner of Sex* (Boston: Little, Brown, 1971), 49–51. The key parts of the book had appeared earlier in an article in *Harper's Magazine*. Mailer's animus was directed at criticisms of him and other male writers, such as Henry Miller, in Kate Millett, *Sexual Politics* (Garden City, NY: Doubleday, 1970). One of her cutting insights was that Mailer made the male protagonist's penis a character in his novels.

31. Israel Shenker, "Norman Mailer vs. Women's Lib," *New York Times*, 1 May 1971, 19.

32. According to writer Dotson Rader, Greer had been "tracking Norman like a bounty hunter," eager to flee with him to her room at the Chelsea Hotel to get it on. That meeting of the minds and bodies, alas, fizzled out during an argument in the cab. See J. Michael

Lennon, *Norman Mailer: A Double Life* (New York: Simon & Schuster, 2013), 441–43. For a milder view of the amity between Mailer and Greer, see Mary V. Dearborn, *Mailer: A Biography* (Boston: Houghton Mifflin, 1999), 295.

33. Schultz, *Emergency*, 4.

34. Sylvia Plachy, "Get the Picture?" *Village Voice*, 24 September 1985, 54.

35. Carson McCullers, *The Member of the Wedding* (New York: Mariner, 2004), 20.

36. Gross, *Arbus's 1960s*, 130, 46.

37. Diane Arbus, *Diane Arbus*, n.p.

38. Arbus, *Revelations*, 98.

39. Arbus, *Revelations*, 243.

40. Arbus, *Revelations*, 212. Another shot shows the circus performer swallowing a sword, which looks like a cross.

41. Diane Arbus, *Diane Arbus*, n.p.

42. Arbus, *Revelations*, 66.

43. Arbus, *Revelations*, 190, 196, 200.

44. Arbus, *Revelations*, 191.

45. Arbus, *Revelations*, 196–97, 201.

46. Arbus, *Revelations*, 202.

47. Arbus, *Revelations*, 203.

48. Schultz, *Emergency*, 178; Louis A. Sass, "'Hyped on Clarity': Diane Arbus and the Postmodern Condition," *Raritan* 25 (Summer 2005): 35–36. For a different view, see Rubinfein, "Where Diane Arbus Went," 66–67.

49. Diane Arbus, *Diane Arbus*, 15.

50. Arbus, *Revelations*, 204.

51. Sussman and Arbus, *Chronology*, 85.

52. The images discussed are bundled at the end of the unpaginated *Aperture* volume. For a less positive view of the images, see Robert Bogdan, *Picturing Disability: Beggar, Freak, Citizen, and Other Photographic Rhetoric* (Syracuse, NY: Syracuse University Press, 2012), 132–35. On Arbus and masks see Geoff Dyer, *The Ongoing Moment* (New York: Pantheon, 2005), 42.

53. Susan Sontag, *On Photography* (New York: Farrar, Straus & Giroux, 1977), 43, 44. Subsequent citations of this work appear as page references in the text. See also Sass, "Hyped on Clarity," 10. Arbus's work, according to writer and photographer Eudora Welty, "totally violates human privacy, and by intention." See Dyer, *Ongoing Moment*, 42. On the Sontag and Arbus dispute see Baird, "Susan Sontag and Diane Arbus," 971–86.

54. Rubinfein, "Where Diane Arbus Went," asserts that Sontag was upset less by the freakishness of Arbus's subjects than by their "fatedness," their lack of options. 75.

55. Arbus was, unsurprisingly, a fan of the 1932 cult film *Freaks* directed by Tod Browning popular during the late 1960s and early 1970s,.

56. Susan Sontag, *Regarding the Pain of Others* (New York: Farrar, Straus & Giroux, 2003), 104, 114, 117.

57. Hilton Kramer, "125 Photos by Arbus on Display," *New York Times*, 8 November 1972, 52.

Chapter 20

1. Hunter S. Thompson, "Fear and Loathing in Las Vegas: A Savage Journey to the Heart of the American Dream," *Rolling Stone*, 11 November 1971, 38, 48.

2. Roger Fong to Editor, *Rolling Stone*, 9 December 1971, 3.

3. Ada Louise Huxtable, "Celebrating 'Dumb, Ordinary' Architecture," *New York Times*, 1 October 1971, 43.

4. Tom Wolfe, "Las Vegas (What?) Las Vegas (Can't Hear You! Too Noisy) Las Vegas!!!!," in *The Kandy-Kolored Tangerine-Flake Streamline Baby* (New York: Farrar, Straus & Giroux, 1965), 3–5.

5. Wolfe, "Las Vegas," 7, 14; Denise Scott Brown, "On Pop Art, Permissiveness and Planning," in *Having Words* (London: AA, 2010), 56.

6. Wolfe, "Las Vegas," 12.

7. Wolfe, "Las Vegas," 8, 10.

8. On Vegas, see Hal Rothman, *Neon Metropolis: How Las Vegas Started the Twenty-First Century* (New York: Routledge, 2002), which chronicles the fantasy aspects of the city. See also Marc Cooper, *The Last Honest Place in America: Paradise and Perdition in the New Las Vegas* (New York: Nation Books, 2004). Novelists, too, have been drawn to Vegas. For a contemporary of Thompson's see John Gregory Dunne, *Vegas: A Memoir of a Dark Season* (New York: Random House, 1974), and the great work by his wife, Joan Didion, *Play It As It Lays: A Novel* (1970; repr., New York: Noonday, 1991).

9. On Thompson's influences see William Stephenson, *Gonzo Republic: Hunter S. Thompson's America* (London: Continuum, 2012); on Thompson as both "modest and self-depreciating at the same time he was being a mad-dog journalist," see William McKeen, *Hunter S. Thompson* (Boston: Twayne, 1991), 50.

10. "Unpublished Jacket Copy for Fear and Loathing in Las Vegas," in Hunter S. Thompson, *The Great Shark Hunt: Gonzo Papers, Strange Tales from a Strange Time* (New York: Simon & Schuster, 2003), 104.

11. Hunter S. Thompson, *Fear and Loathing in Las Vegas: A Savage Journey to the Heart of the American Dream* (New York: Vintage, 1998), 37–40.

12. On Acosta, who sometimes referred to himself as Samoan, see Oscar Zeta Acosta, *The Autobiography of a Brown Buffalo* (1972; repr., New York: Vintage, 1989), 5–7, 48. For more on Acosta as madman, see Jann S. Wenner and Corey Seymour, *Gonzo: The Life of Hunter S. Thompson, An Oral Biography* (New York: Little, Brown, 2007), 143–44.

13. Thompson, *Fear and Loathing*, 3–4.

14. Paul Perry, *Fear and Loathing: The Strange Saga of Hunter S. Thompson* (New York: Thunder's Mouth, 2004), 27–29.

15. Hunter S. Thompson, *Hell's Angels: A Strange and Terrible Saga* (New York: Ballantine, 1994), 272–73.

16. Thompson, *Hell's Angels*, 260.

17. On Thompson and Gatsby see Peter O. Whitmer, *When the Going Gets Weird: The Twisted Life and Times of Hunter S. Thompson* (New York: Hyperion, 1993), 176ff.

18. Thompson to Selma Shapiro (10 September 1968), Thompson to Hughes Rudd (18 October 1968), in *Fear and Loathing in America: The Brutal Honesty of an Outlaw Journalist, 1968–1976*, ed., Douglas Brinkley (New York: Simon & Schuster, 2000), 123, 140. On Thompson and the American Dream see Perry, *Strange Saga*, 123–68.

19. Thompson to Bernard Shir-Cliff (12 December 1969), in Thompson, *Fear and Loathing in America*, 229.

20. Ken Cooper, " 'Zero Pays the House': The Las Vegas Novel and Atomic Roulette," *Contemporary Literature* 33 (Autumn 1992): 528–44.

21. Thompson to Jim Silberman (15 June 1971), in Thompson, *Fear and Loathing in America*, 406.

22. Douglas Brinkley, "Interview with Thompson" (2000), quoted in Jeff Kass, "Still Gonzo After All These Years" (2000), in *Conversations with Hunter S. Thompson*, ed. Beef Torrey and Kevin Simonson (Jackson: University Press of Mississippi, 2008), 159, 162; James E. Caron, "Hunter S. Thompson's 'Gonzo' Journalism and the Tall Tale in America," *Studies in Popular Culture* 8, no. 1 (1985): 1–16.

23. Thompson, *Fear and Loathing*, 12.

24. Cooper, "Zero Pays the House," 528–44.

25. Thompson, *Fear and Loathing*, 24, 47.

26. Perry, *Strange and Terrible Saga*, 158.

27. Thompson, *Fear and Loathing*, 27, 106.

28. Allen Hess, *Viva Las Vegas: After Hours Entertainment* (San Francisco: Chronicle, 1993), 88–89.

29. Thompson, *Fear and Loathing*, 46.

30. Thompson, *Fear and Loathing*, 178.

31. Thompson to Jim Silberman (9 May 1971), in Thompson, *Fear and Loathing in America*, 384.

32. Hunter S. Thompson, *Fear and Loathing on the Campaign Trail '72* (New York: Simon & Schuster, 2012); Thompson to Silberman (20 February 1973), in Thompson, *Fear and Loathing in America*, 510. Thompson's hopes were buoyed by the campaign and nomination of George McGovern, but his defeat was overwhelming.

33. Robert Venturi, Denise Scott Brown, and Steven Izenour, *Learning from Las Vegas* (Cambridge, MA: MIT Press, 1972). There have been questions about who deserves credit for writing the book. Discussions have often been sexist, supposing Venturi to be the central figure. The book was a collaboration between Venturi and Scott Brown. Izenour's role has always seemed less clear, hence he is omitted from discussion in this chapter. See Denise Scott Brown, "Sexism and the Star System" (1989), in Scott Brown, *Having Words*, 79–89. See also Joan Kron, "The Almost Perfect Life of Denise Scott Brown," *Savvy* 1 (December 1980): 28–35. On the cover see Kester Rattenbury and Samantha Hardingham, *Robert Venturi and Denise Scott Brown: Learning from Las Vegas* (London: Routledge, 2007), 30–32; Martino Stierli, *Las Vegas in the Rearview Mirror: The City in Theory, Photography, and Film*, trans. Elizabeth Tucker (Los Angeles: Getty Research Institute, 2013), 28–47; Aron Vinegar, *I Am a Monument: On Learning from Las Vegas* (Cambridge, MA: MIT Press, 2008), 36–39, 111ff. For excellent discussion on Thompson, as well as Venturi and Scott Brown's discovery of Vegas as "the key location, both literally and symbolically of postmodern American culture," see Marianne DeKoven, *Utopia Limited: The Sixties and the Emergence of the Postmodern* (Durham, NC: Duke University Press, 2004), 73ff. A nice overview of the book is Louis Hellman, "Learning from Las Vegas," *Built Environment* 8, no. 4 (1982), 267–71.

34. Robert Venturi, *Complexity and Contradiction in Architecture* (New York: Museum of Modern Art, 1977), 17.

35. Venturi, Scott Brown, and Izenour, *Learning from Las Vegas*, 14, 24.

36. Venturi, Scott Brown, and Izenour, *Learning from Las Vegas*, 66–68, 86; David B. Brownlee, "Form and Content," in *Out of the Ordinary: Venturi, Scott Brown and Associates; Architecture, Urbanism, Design*, ed. David B. Brownlee, David G. DeLong, and Kathryn B.

Hiesinger (New Haven, CT: Yale University Press, 2001), 22–23; Grace Glueck, "Don't Knock Sprawl," *New York Times*, 10 October 1971, D16.

37. Venturi, Scott Brown, and Izenour, *Learning from Las Vegas*, 116; Brownlee, DeLong, and Hiesinger, *Out of the Ordinary*, 41. See also Vincent Scully, "Robert Venturi's Gentle Architecture," in *The Architecture of Robert Venturi*, ed. Christopher Mead (Albuquerque: University of New Mexico Press, 1989), 25–26; Robert Venturi and Denise Scott Brown, *A View from the Campidoglio, Selected Essays, 1953–1984*, ed. Peter Arnell, Ted Bickford, and Catherine Bergart (New York: Harper & Row, 1984), 14–15. For a takedown of the Guild House, see Tom Wolfe, *From Our House to Bauhaus* (New York: Farrar, Straus & Giroux, 1981), 111.

38. Robert Venturi and Denise Scott Brown, *Architecture as Signs and Systems: For a Modernist Time* (Cambridge, MA: Belknap Press of Harvard University, 2004), 39.

39. Venturi, Scott Brown, and Izenour, *Learning from Las Vegas*, 100; Gary Wolf, review of *Learning from Las Vegas*, by Robert Venturi, Denise Scott Brown, and Steven Izenour, *Journal of the Society of Architectural Historians* 32 (October 1973): 258–60.

40. Venturi, Scott Brown, and Izenour, *Learning from Las Vegas*, xviii.

41. Rattenbury and Hardingham, *Robert Venturi*, 89, 97.

42. Venturi quoted in Rattenbury and Hardingham, *Robert Venturi*, 69; Venturi, *Complexity and Contradiction*, 23.

43. Quoted in Vinegar, *I Am a Monument*, 81. Yet Venturi and Scott Brown could, along with Izenour, write an introduction to a book on Vegas and exclaim, "Long live the big symbol and little building! Long live the building that is a sign! Long live Las Vegas!" In Hess, *Viva Las Vegas*, 7.

44. Scott Brown, *Having Words*, 14, 74.

45. Martino Stierli, ed., *Las Vegas Studio: Images from the Archives of Robert Venturi and Denise Scott Brown* (Zurich: Scheidegger & Spiess, 2008), 15.

46. Venturi, Scott Brown, and Izenour, *Learning from Las Vegas*, 58; Scott Brown, *Having Words*, 15; Rattenbury and Hardingham, *Robert Venturi*, 81.

47. Venturi, Scott Brown, and Izenour, *Learning from Las Vegas*, 10, 53.

48. Venturi, *Complexity and Contradiction*, 104.

49. Vladimir Paperny, "An Interview with Denise Scott Brown and Robert Venturi" (2005), http:/www.paperny.com/venturi.html.

50. Marshall McLuhan, *Understanding Media: The Extensions of Man* (New York: McGraw-Hill, 1965), 7–23.

51. Venturi, Scott Brown, and Izenour, *Learning from Las Vegas*, 109.

52. Venturi, Scott Brown, and Izenour, *Learning from Las Vegas*, 64.

53. Venturi, Scott Brown, and Izenour, *Learning from Las Vegas*, 58.

54. Venturi, Scott Brown, and Izenour, *Learning from Las Vegas*, 50–51, 110.

55. Venturi, Scott Brown, and Izenour, *Learning from Las Vegas*, 87, 107; Hess, *Viva Las Vegas*, 53.

56. Scott Brown, *Having Words*, 56.

57. Venturi, *Complexity and Contradiction*, 104.

58. Venturi and Scott Brown, *Architecture as Signs*, 177.

59. Virginia Wexman, "Pop: The New Architecture," *Soundings* 54 (Summer 1971): 191–201.

60. Venturi, *Complexity and Contradiction*, 20, 22.

61. Venturi, Scott Brown, and Izenour, *Learning from Las Vegas*, 58.

62. Stierli, *Rearview Mirror*, 132–37.

63. Kenneth Frampton, "America 1960–1970: Notes on Urban Images and Theory," *Casabella* 359–60 (December 1971): 33, 36.

64. Tician Papachristou and James Stewart Polshek, "Venturi: Style, Not Substance?" *New York Times*, 14 November 1971, D24.

65. Frampton, "America 1960–1970," 36.

66. Denise Scott Brown, "Pop Off: Reply to Kenneth Frampton," in Venturi and Scott Brown, *View from the Campidoglio*, 34–37. A later, more measured view is in Martin Filler, "The Spirit of '76," *New Republic*, 16 July 2001, 32, 35. On the relation between the work of Venturi and urban critic Jane Jacobs, see Peter L. Laurence, "Contradictions and Complexities: Jane Jacobs's and Robert Venturi's Complexity Theories," *Journal of Architectural Education* 59 (February 2006): 49–60.

67. Stierli, *Las Vegas Studio*, 15.

68. Scott Brown, "Pop Off," 35.

69. Charles Jencks, *The Language of Post-Modern Architecture* (New York: Rizzoli, 1977), 9–10, 127–28; Frederic Jameson, *Postmodernism, or The Cultural Logic of Late Capitalism* (Durham, NC: Duke University Press, 1991), 39–44. For a devastating critique of Jameson's failure to acknowledge the politics of the structure, see Mike Davis, "Urban Renaissance and the Spirit of Postmodernism," *New Left Review* 151 (May–June 1985): 106–31. Davis was responding to an earlier piece of Jameson's, about signifiers run wild, "Postmodernism, or The Cultural Logic of Late Capitalism," *New Left Review* 146 (July–August 1984), esp. 80–84.

70. Scott Brown, "Pop Off," 115.

71. Quoted in Brownlee, DeLong, and Hiesinger, *Out of the Ordinary*, 178.

72. Scott Brown, *Having Words*, 18.

73. Philippe Barrière and Sylvia Lavin, "Interview with Denise Scott Brown and Robert Venturi," *Perspecta* 28 (1997): 133.

74. Many videos of the demolition are available, such as "Pruitt-Igoe Sequence—'Trouble in Utopia'—Narrated by Robert Hughes [1981]," YouTube, uploaded 12 October 2008, https://www.youtube.com/watch?v=cd7VOz_Wstg. See two special reports, "St. Louis Is Revising Housing Complex," *New York Times*, 19 March 1973, 32; "City Life: St. Louis Project Razing Points Up Public Housing Woes: At First It Was Perfect," *New York Times*, 16 December 1973, 72

75. Ada Louise Huxtable, "A Prescription for Disaster," *New York Times*, 5 November 1972, D23; Jencks, *Language of Post-Modern Architecture*, 9, 126–28.

Chapter 21

1. Philip Slater, *The Pursuit of Loneliness: American Culture at the Breaking Point* (1970; repr., Boston: Beacon, 1990), xxi, 3; Alvin Toffler, *Future Shock* (1970; repr., New York: Bantam, 1990), 4, 10–12; 18, 39–41, 55; Hunter S. Thompson, *Fear and Loathing in Las Vegas: A Savage Journey to the Heart of the American Dream* (1971; repr., New York: Vintage, 1998), 161. On the period, see the excellent work by Andreas Killen, *1973: Nervous Breakdown: Watergate, Warhol, and the Birth of Post-Sixties America* (New York: Bloomsbury, 2006); Philip Jenkins, *Decade of Nightmares: The End of the Sixties and the Making of Eighties America* (Oxford: Oxford University Press, 2006); and Bruce J. Schulman, *The Seventies: The Great Shift in*

American Culture, Society, and Politics (New York: Free Press, 2001). For the nervous breakdown at its peak, see Jonathan Mahler, *The Bronx Is Burning: 1977, Baseball, Politics, and the Battle for the Soul of a City* (New York: Picador, 2005). The Nixon quote is from a first-rate account of American society and politics in this period, Rick Perlstein, *Nixonland: The Rise of a President and the Fracturing of America* (New York: Scribner, 2008), 559.

2. On the works as part of the postmodernist moment, see Brian McHale, "Modernist Reading, Postmodernist Text: The Case of *Gravity's Rainbow*," *Poetics Today* 1 (Autumn 1979): 85–110; Marc W. Redfield, "Pynchon's Postmodern Sublime," *PMLA* 104 (March 1984): 152–62. For Delany, see Robert Elliot Fox, *Conscientious Sorcerers: The Black Postmodernist Fiction of LeRoi Jones/Amiri Baraka, Ishmael Reed, and Samuel R. Delany* (New York: Greenwood, 1987), 93–119. Delany rejected the term postmodern. Samuel R. Delany, interview with *Matrix Magazine* (2001), in *Conversations with Samuel R. Delany*, ed. Carl Freedman (Jackson: University of Mississippi Press, 2009), 72.

3. Good overviews of *Gravity's Rainbow* and its bewildering diversity are Robert D. Newman, *Understanding Thomas Pynchon* (Columbia: University of South Carolina Press, 1986); Thomas Moore, *The Style of Connectedness: Gravity's Rainbow and Thomas Pynchon* (Columbia: University of Missouri Press, 1987); William M. Plater, *The Grim Phoenix: Reconstructing Thomas Pynchon* (Bloomington: Indiana University Press, 1978); Thomas H. Schaub, *Pynchon: The Voice of Ambiguity* (Urbana: University of Illinois Press, 1981); Mark Richard Siegel, *Creative Paranoia in Gravity's Rainbow* (Port Washington, NY: Kennikat, 1978). On Pynchon, along with other practitioners of black humor of the sixties, see Morris Dickstein, *Gates of Eden: American Culture in the Sixties* (New York: Basic Books, 1977), 13–14, passim. Excellent essays are in the following collections: George Levine and David Leverenz, eds., *Mindful Pleasures: Essays on Thomas Pynchon* (Boston: Little, Brown, 1976); Harold Bloom, ed., *Thomas Pynchon's Gravity's Rainbow* (New York: Chelsea House, 1986); Charles Clerc, ed., *Approaches to Gravity's Rainbow* (Columbus: Ohio State University Press, 1983); and Richard Pearce, ed., *Critical Essays on Thomas Pynchon* (Boston: G. K. Hall, 1981). On Pynchon's earlier big novel see W. T. Lhamon Jr., "Pentecost, Promiscuity, and Pynchon's *V.*: From the Scaffold to the Impulsive," in Levine and Leverenz, *Mindful Pleasures*, 69–86, and his early remarks on *Gravity's Rainbow*, "The Most Irresponsible Bastard," in *New Republic*, 14 April 1973, 24–28. All readers of the book can profit from Steven C. Weisenberger, *A Gravity's Rainbow Companion*, 2nd ed. (Athens, GA: University of Georgia Press, 2006), and Douglas Fowler, *A Reader's Guide to Gravity's Rainbow* (Ann Arbor, MI: Ardis, 1980). On epistemology in Pynchon see James W. Earl, "Freedom and Knowledge in the Zone," in Clerc, *Approaches*, 229–30; Robert L. Nadeau, "Readings from the New Book of Nature: Physics and Pynchon's *Gravity's Rainbow*," *Studies in the Novel* 11 (Winter 1979): 454–71; Thomas Melley, "Bodies Incorporated: Scenes of Agency in *Gravity's Rainbow*," *Contemporary Literature* 35 (Winter 1994): 709–38. A good place to start for Delany is his memoir of early years, *The Motion of Light in Water: Sex and Science in the East Village* (Minneapolis: University of Minnesota Press, 2004), and Delany, *About Writing: Seven Essays, Four Letters, and Five Interviews* (Middletown, CT: Wesleyan University Press, 2005), esp. 274–75. See also Mary Kay Bray, "Rites of Reversal: Double Consciousness in Delany's *Dhalgren*," *Black American Literature Forum* 18 (Summer 1984): 57–61; Todd A. Comer, "Playing at Birth: Samuel R. Delany's Dhalgren," *Journal of Narrative Theory* 35 (Summer 2005): 172–95; K. Leslie Steiner, "Samuel R. Delany," Pseudopodium, http://www .pseudopodium.org/repress/KLeslieSteiner-SamuelRDelany.html.

4. William Gibson, "The Recombinant City," in Samuel R. Delany, *Dhalgren* (New York: Vintage, 2001), xi.

5. Edward Mendelson, "Gravity's Encyclopedia," and David Leverenz, "On Trying to Read *Gravity's Rainbow*," both in Levine and Leverenz, *Mindful Pleasures*, 161, 230–31.

6. On the publishing history of the novel see Gerald Howard, "Rocket Redux," *Bookforum* 121 (June–September 2005): 32, 36–40.

7. Richard Fariña, *Been Down So Long It Looks Like Up to Me* (1966; repr., New York: Penguin, 1996), 17.

8. Garrison Frost, "Thomas Pynchon and the South Bay," *The Aesthetic*, http://www.theaesthetic.com/NewFiles/pynchon.html.

9. Samuel R. Delany, *The Motion of Light in Water*, 202–3.

10. Delany, *Motion*, 145, 215f.

11. Samuel R. Delany, interview with Lance Olson (1989), in Freedman, *Conversations*, 22–23.

12. Peter S. Alterman, "The Surreal Translations of Samuel R. Delany," *Science Fiction Studies* 4 (March 1977): 25–34.

13. Delany, *Dhalgren*, 35, 14.

14. Delany, *Dhalgren*, 352.

15. Thomas Pynchon, *Gravity's Rainbow* (New York: Penguin, 2000), 3.

16. Louis Mackey, "Paranoia, Pynchon, and Preterition," in Bloom, *Pynchon's Gravity's Rainbow*, 61.

17. Pynchon, *Gravity's Rainbow*, 21.

18. Pynchon, *Gravity's Rainbow*, 617.

19. On the Emersonian aspects of the novel see Joseph W. Slade, "Religion, Psychology, Sex, and Love in *Gravity's Rainbow*," in Clerc, *Approaches*, 153, and Joel D. Black, "Probing a Post-Romantic Paleontology: Thomas Pynchon's *Gravity's Rainbow*," *boundary2* 8 (Winter 1980): 229–54. On the disassembling of Slothrop, see Tony Tanner, "*Gravity's Rainbow*: An Experience in Modern Reading," in Bloom, *Pynchon's Gravity's Rainbow*, 77; Tanner, "Paranoia, Energy and Displacement," *Wilson Quarterly* 2 (Winter 1978): 143–50; Schaub, *Pynchon*, 135; Mackey, "Paranoia, Pynchon, and Preterition," 61; Philip E. Simmons, *Deep Surfaces: Mass Culture & History in Postmodern American Fiction* (Athens, GA: University of Georgia Press, 1997), 157–58.

20. Douglas Brinkley and Luke A. Nichter, eds., *The Nixon Tapes* (Boston: Houghton Mifflin Harcourt, 2014); on the installation see 3–5. On use of the Internal Revenue Service to undermine Nixon's political opponents see 170, 262.

21. Christopher Lehmann-Haupt, "The Adventures of Rocketman," *New York Times*, 9 March 1973.

22. Pynchon, *Gravity's Rainbow*, 174.

23. Manfred Putz, "The Art of the Acronym in Thomas Pynchon," *Studies in the Novel* 23 (Fall 1991): 371–82.

24. Pynchon, *Gravity's Rainbow*, 402.

25. Pynchon, *Gravity's Rainbow*, 650–51.

26. Pynchon, *Gravity's Rainbow*, 729.

27. Pynchon, *Gravity's Rainbow*, 660–68.

28. Emily Nussbaum, "The Great Divide: Norman Lear, Archie Bunker, and the Rise of the Bad Fan," *New Yorker*, 7 April 2014, 64, 66, 68.

29. Samuel R. Delany, *Heavenly Breakfast: An Essay on the Winter of Love* (New York: Bantam, 1979), 9.

30. Delany, *Dhalgren*, 349.

31. Delany, *Dhalgren*, 32, 79.

32. Delany, *Dhalgren*, 357–58.

33. Delany, *Dhalgren*, 531.

34. Pynchon, *Gravity's Rainbow*, 9, 13.

35. Pynchon, *Gravity's Rainbow*, 8, 18.

36. *Merriam-Webster.com*, s.v. "smegma," http://www.merriam-webster.com/dictionary/smegma.

37. Pynchon, *Gravity's Rainbow*, 15–16.

38. Ellen Willis, "Hard to Swallow," *New York Review of Books*, 25 January 1973, http://www.nybooks.com/articles/archives/1973/jan/25/hard-to-swallow/.

39. On these films and the sexual revolution, see David Allyn, *Make Love, Not War: The Sexual Revolution; An Unfettered History* (Boston: Little, Brown, 2000), 234ff.

40. "TK Enright Interviews Samuel Delany about *Hogg*," (2004), in Freedman, *Conversations*, 126, 133.

41. Samuel R. Delany, *Hogg* (Normal, IL: Black Ice, 1994); for one of the gang rapes see 53–64, 186–89; Harold Bloom, "Introduction," and Richard Poirier, "Rocket Power," in Bloom, *Pynchon's Gravity's Rainbow*, 1–2, 20.

42. Samuel R. Delany, *The Tides of Lust* (Manchester, UK: Savoy, 1980), most readily available as an e-book. For a nuanced view of the ethics of sexual excess in Delany, see Lewis Call, *BDSM in American Science Fiction and Fantasy* (New York: Palgrave Macmillan, 2013), esp. 70–71; Mary Catherine Foltz, "The Excremental Ethics of Samuel R. Delany," *SubStance* 37, no. 2 (2008): 41–55.

43. Pynchon, *Gravity's Rainbow*, 64–66.

44. Lawrence Wolfey, "Repression's Rainbow: The Presence of Norman O. Brown in Pynchon's Big Novel," *PMLA* 92 (October 1977): 873–99; Newman, *Understanding Thomas Pynchon*, 125.

45. Although the word "fuck" is used regularly in the novel, it never refers to sexual intercourse. See Christopher Ames, "Power and the Obscene Word: Discourses of Extremity in Thomas Pynchon's *Gravity's Rainbow*," *Contemporary Literature* 31, no. 2 (Summer 1991): 198.

46. Pynchon, *Gravity's Rainbow*, 237–39.

47. Richard Locke, "One of the Longest, Most Difficult, Most Ambitious Novels in Years," *New York Review of Books*, 11 March 1973. On the mystical aspects of sadomasochism see John Hamill, "Confronting the Monolith: Authority and the Cold War in *Gravity's Rainbow*," *Journal of American Studies* 33 (December 1999): 417–36.

48. Pynchon, *Gravity's Rainbow*, 105.

49. Paul Fussell, *The Great War and Modern Memory* (1975; repr., New York: Oxford University Press, 1989), 333. He also notes that Pynchon's treatment of Pudding is suggestive of how the Great War figures in our "insane contemporary scene," 329.

50. Pynchon, *Gravity's Rainbow*, 496, 87.

51. Of course, many have noted the connection between rockets and penises. See Alfred Kazin, "We See From the Periphery, Not the Center: Reflections in an Age of Crisis," *World Literature Today* 51 (Spring, 1977), 193. For a more nuanced view, see Leo Bersani, "Pynchon,

Paranoia, and Literature," *Representations* n25 (Winter, 1989), 111. Also, on the assembly of the rocket, Raymond M. Olderman, "The New Consciousness and the Old System," in Clerc, *Approaches*, 199–228. On the connection between life and death through the rocket, see Plater, *Grim Phoenix*, 157.

52. Delany, *Dhalgren*, 792–94.

53. Delany, *Dhalgren*, 799–801.

54. Pynchon, *Gravity's Rainbow*, 769.

55. Pynchon, *Gravity's Rainbow*, 774.

Chapter 22

1. Erica Jong, *Fear of Flying: A Novel* (New York: Holt, Rinehart & Winston, 1973), 26.

2. Quoted in Gretchen McNeese, "*Playboy* Interview" (1975), in *Conversations with Erica Jong*, ed. Charlotte Templin (Jackson: University of Mississippi Press, 2002), 36.

3. Benjamin DeMott, "Couple Trouble: Mod & Trad," *Atlantic*, December, 1973, 125; McNeese, "*Playboy* Interview," 37; "Book TV 2013 Book Expo America: Erica Jong, 'Fear of Flying,'" YouTube, uploaded 2 July 2013, https://www.youtube.com/watch?v=4z6P3e4V6uY.

4. Philip Roth, *Portnoy's Complaint* (New York: Library of America, 2005), 289.

5. Bernard Avishai, *Promiscuous: Portnoy's Complaint and Our Doomed Pursuit of Happiness* (New Haven, CT: Yale University Press, 2012).

6. Elaine Showalter and Carol Smith, "An Interview with Erica Jong," (1974) in Templin, *Conversations with Erica Jong*, 29.

7. On these films and the sexual revolution, see David Allyn, *Make Love, Not War: The Sexual Revolution: An Unfettered History* (Boston: Little, Brown, 2000), 234ff.

8. For a history of women and the struggle see Sara Evans, *Personal Politics: The Roots of Women's Liberation in the Civil Rights Movement and the New Left* (New York: Vintage, 1979).

9. Ruth Rosen, *The World Split Open: How the Modern Women's Movement Changed America* (New York: Viking, 2000), 172–75; Alice Echols, *Daring to Be Bad: Radical Feminism in America, 1967–1975* (Minneapolis: University of Minnesota Press, 1989).

10. Norma McCorvey, *I Am Roe: My Life, Roe v. Wade and Freedom of Choice*, with Andy Meisler (New York: HarperCollins, 1994), 208.

11. Gail Collins, *When Everything Changed: The Amazing Journey of American Women from 1960 to the Present* (New York: Little, Brown, 2009), 245–48; Billie Jean King, *Billie Jean*, with Kim Chapin (New York: Harper & Row, 1974), 164–87.

12. King, *Billie Jean*, 180: "It's a Ms.-Match—Riggs (Oink) Slaughtered," *Los Angeles Times*, 21 September 1973, D1.

13. King, *Billie Jean*, 180; Gerald Eskenazi, "$100,000 Tennis Match: Bobby Riggs vs. Mrs. King," *New York Times*, 12 July 1973, 52.

14. Neil Amdur, "'She Played Too Well,' Says Riggs of Mrs. King," *New York Times*, 22 September 1973, 21.

15. On Plath and Sexton see Jong to Pat Barr, 20 October 1973, correspondence, Erica Jong Papers, Rare Book and Manuscript Library Collection, Columbia University (hereafter Jong Papers); Erica Jong, *Half-Lives* (New York: Holt, Rinehart & Winston, 1973), 93, 39.

16. Erica Jong, "Writing a First Novel," *Twentieth Century Literature* 20, no. 4 (October 1974): 264–66.

17. All quotes from John Updike, "Jong Love," *New Yorker*, 17 December 1973, 149–51.

18. Reprinted in Erica Jong, *The Devil at Large: Erica Jong on Henry Miller* (New York: Grove, 1993), 11.

19. Milford to Jong, 28 August 1973, Jong Papers.

20. Ellen Hope Meyer, "The Aesthetics of Dear Diary," *The Nation*, 12 January 1974, 55–56.

21. Patricia Meyer Spacks, "Fiction Chronicle," *Hudson Review* 27, no. 2 (Summer 1974): 285, 291.

22. Alfred Kazin, "The Writer as Sexual Show-Off; or, Making Press Agents Unnecessary," *New York*, 9 June 1975, 40–41.

23. Molly Haskell, "Review of *Fear of Flying*," *Village Voice Literary Supplement*, 22 November 1973, 27.

24. Charlotte Templin, *Feminism and the Politics of Literary Reputation: The Example of Erica Jong* (Lawrence: University Press of Kansas, 1995), 1.

25. McNeese, "*Playboy* Interview," 52, 47.

26. McNeese, "*Playboy* Interview," 40.

27. Barbara A. Bannon, "Erica Jong" (1977), in Templin, *Conversations with Erica Jong*, 71.

28. Jane Wilson, "Erica Jong: Her Life is an Open Book," *Los Angeles Times*, 24 November 1974, D1, D9.

29. Ozick to Jong, 26 July 1973; Jong to Ozick, 13 August 1973, Jong Papers.

30. Robert Louit, "Erica Jong: Writing about Sex Is Harder for a Woman" (1978), in Templin, *Conversations with Erica Jong*, 85.

31. Robert J. Butler, "The Woman Writer as American Picaro: Open Journeying in Erica Jong's *Fear of Flying*," *Centennial Review* 31, no. 3 (Summer 1987): 308–29; Joan Reardon, "*Fear of Flying*: Developing the Feminist Novel," *International Journal of Women's Studies* 1 (1978): 306–20.

32. Erica Jong, *Seducing the Demon: Writing for My Life* (New York: Tarcher/Penguin, 2006), 70.

33. Jong, *Fear of Flying*, 293–94.

34. Jong, *Fear of Flying*, 328–29.

35. Jong, *Fear of Flying*, 331.

36. Jong, *Fear of Flying*, 339.

37. Kate Millett, *Sexual Politics* (Garden City, NY: Doubleday, 1970), 5–7.

38. Haskell, "Review," 27.

39. For a lesbian version of Isadora, but one with more confidence about her sexuality and place in the world, see Rita Mae Brown, *Rubyfruit Jungle* (1973; repr., New York: Bantam, 1988).

40. Judith Willhite Will to Jong, 8 January 1975; Seena Lee Brooks to Jong, 8 November 1974; Gene Steinmann to Jong, 13 November 1975; Charles Young to Jong, 7 January 1975, all in Jong Papers.

41. John Kern, "Erica: Being the True History of the Adventures of Isadora Wing, Fanny Hackabout-Jones, and Erica Jong" (1981), in Templin, *Conversations with Erica Jong*, 125; Charlotte Templin, "Interview with Erica Jong" (1990), in Templin, *Conversations*, 166 *with Erica Jong*.

42. Barbara Ehrenreich, Elizabeth Hess, and Gloria Jacobs, *Re-Making Love: The Feminization of Sex* (Garden City, NY: Anchor Press/Doubleday, 1986), 176–78.

Chapter 23

1. Thomas McEvilley, "Art in the Dark," *Artforum* 21 (Summer 1983): 62–71; Henry M. Sayre, *The Object of Performance: The American Avant-Garde since 1970* (Chicago: University of Chicago Press, 1998), 102. On his fascination with crucifixion see Donald Kuspit, "Chris Burden: The Feel of Power," in *Chris Burden: A Twenty-Year Survey* (Newport Harbor, CA: Newport Harbor Art Museum, 1988), 37.

2. Chris Burden interview, *High Performance* 2, no. 1 (March 1979): 7, 9.

3. Matthew Day Jackson, "TV AD," in Lisa Phillips, ed., *Chris Burden: Extreme Measures* (New York: Skira Rizzoli, 2013), 170; Larry Grobel, "Chris Burden: Picasso Used Canvas. Michelangelo Used Marble. Chris Burden Uses His Body," *Playgirl*, April 1978, 64.

4. Frazer Ward, *No Innocent Bystanders: Performance and Audience* (Hanover, NH: Dartmouth College Press, 2012), 7–11. On Burden see 81–108.

5. Sydney Smith, "Chris Burden Talks about Performance, Is Confused about iPods at the New Museum," *NYU Local*, 15 November 2013, http://nyulocal.com/entertainment/2013/11/15/chris-burden-talks-about-sculpture-performance-and-those-sticks-with-the-music-on-them-at-the-new-museum/. See the measured comments on Burden in Maggie Nelson, *The Art of Cruelty: A Reckoning* (New York: W. W. Norton, 2011), 111.

6. Peter Schjeldahl, "Performance: Chris Burden and the Limits of Art," *New Yorker* 14 May 2007.

7. Chris Burden, "In Conversation with Jon Bewley," in Adrian Searle, *Talking Art 1: Chris Burden, Sophie Calle, Leon Golub, Dan Graham, Richard Hamilton, Susan Hiller, Mary Kelly, Andres Serrano, Nancy Spero* (London: Institute of Contemporary Arts, 1993), 26. Jump ahead a few decades to 2004. In a performance art class at UCLA, students were doing their final projects in front of the class and the professor, Ron Athey. In the 1990s, Athey had been famous for doing violence to his body. In one piece, he "inserted a series of hyperdermic [*sic*] needles into his arm from wrist to shoulder and then jabbed a 15-cm [6 in] long needle through his scalp." According to Athey, the performance depicted his HIV-positive status, his depression, and his long history of suffering, as well as being an exploration into the pleasure of pain.

Joseph Deutch was the last student to perform. Looking dapper in coat and tie, instead of his usual sloppy attire, Deutch in front of the class pulled out a handgun from a paper bag and proceeded to load a single bullet into the gun's chamber. He then spun the cylinder, aimed the pistol at his head, and pulled the trigger. The gun did not fire, and Deutch left the room. A moment later, the sound of the gun discharging was heard.

He returned to find the classroom in "pandemonium." Deutch explained that the gun was a fake (supposedly a hand-carved replica of a .357 magnum) and the explosion in the hall nothing more than a "big firecracker" going off in a can. His intention, he related, was "to test whether, in this seen-it-all-age, an audience still could have an indelibly shocking experience and be left wondering whether what it had witnessed was make-believe or real." One student complained to university officials and an investigation ensued, but no disciplinary action was taken against the student.

At the time of this performance, Burden was a superstar professor in the art department. When he learned of the performance, he was angry and stunned, calling it an act of "domestic terrorism." He wanted the student expelled from the university. When the school declined to punish Deutch, Burden and his wife, fellow artist Nancy Rubins, retired in protest. When Deutch learned of their displeasure, he stated, "The thing I hadn't counted on was Chris and Nancy's freaking out to the extent they did."

Burden claimed that the audiences for his artwork knew what to expect. This was true to an extent, but the violence that he absorbed surely had an emotional effect upon those present. By 2004, when violence was hardly unexpected or out of place on college campuses and society at large, perhaps Burden's disgust was that such a performance could shock precisely because gun violence had become so common. If so, then the violence of the New Sensibility, once aesthetic and presumably a palliative experience, had become ingrained in the crust of reality. It is unknown what grade Deutch received for his work. Tracey Warr, eds., *The Artist's Body* (London: Phaidon, 2000), 110; Jenny Hontz, "Gunplay as Art, Sets Off a Debate," *Los Angeles Times*, 5 February 2005, B7, 13; Mike Boehm, "The Shot 'Heard' 'round UCLA," *Los Angeles Times*, 9 July 2009; "UCLA Student Who Staged Russian-Roulette Says It Was a Test," *Blouin ArtInfo*, 23 January 2007, http://www.blouinartinfo .com/news/story/699/ucla-student-who-staged-russian-roulette-suicide-says-it-was-a-test.

8. Glenn Phillips, "Interview with Chris Burden" (18 May 2010), in Rebecca McGrew and Glenn Phillips, eds., *It Happened at Pomona: Art at the Edge of Los Angeles, 1969–1973* (Claremont, CA: Pomona College Museum of Art, 2011), 272.

9. Grobel, "Chris Burden," 51.

10. Fred Hoffman, "Chris Burden: Some Reflections," in *Chris Burden* (Newcastle upon Tyne, UK: Locus +, 2007), 356; George Melrod, "Interview: Chris Burden," *Art Ltd.*, August, 2012, http://www.artltdmag.com/index.php?subaction=showfull&id=1346451183&archive= &start_from=&ucat=28&; Ward, *No Innocent Bystanders*, 86–87.

11. Grace Glueck, "Winning the West," *New York Times*, 16 April 1962, D19.

12. Paul Schimmel, quoted in Jan Herman, "Burden Takes Art from Crucifixion to Re-Creation," *Los Angeles Times* (26 April 1988), D9.

13. Sally Banes, *Greenwich Village 1963: Avant-Garde Performance and the Effervescent Body* (Durham, NC: Duke University Press, 1993); Michael Kirby, *Happenings* (New York: E. P. Dutton, 1965); Amelia Jones, *Body Art/Performing the Subject* (Minneapolis: University of Minnesota Press, 1998). On the intersections and differences between Kaprow and Burden, see Linda Frye Burnham, "Performance Art in Southern California: An Overview," in *Performance Anthology: Source Book for a Decade of California Performance Art*, ed. Carl E. Loeffler (San Francisco: Contemporary Arts, 1980), 390–403. For an excellent overview of performance art, with an emphasis on how it changed the relationship between artist and audience and replaced the object with experience, see Sayre, *Object of Performance*.

14. Richard Meyer, "Bone of Contention," *Artforum* (November 2004): 73, 74, 249. Chicano/Chicana artists used performance not only to show the Mexican presence in the United States but to critique America's racism and isolationist pretensions. For an overview of performance art see the essays in Peggy Phelan, ed., *Live Art in LA: Performance in Southern California, 1970–1983* (New York: Routledge, 2012).

15. "Chris Burden: The Church of Human Energy; An Interview with Willoughby Sharp and Liza Béar," *Avalanche* 8 (Summer/Fall 1973): 54; Andrew McClintock, "In Conversation with Chris Burden," *San Francisco Arts Quarterly*, 5 October 2013, http://www.sfaqonline .com/2013/10/in-conversation-with-chris-burden/.

16. Howard Singerman, "Chris Burden's Pragmatism," in Burden, *Twenty-Year Survey*, 22.

17. *Chris Burden*, 214–15; Burden, *High Performance* interview, 6.

18. Malcolm Green, "Otto Mühl, 1925–2013," *Artforum*, October 2013, 59–60; Loeffler, *Performance Anthology*, 10–11.

19. Cole Matson, "Risk to Life: The Ethics of Chris Burden's 'Shoot,'" *Transpositions*, 2012, http://www.transpositions.co.uk/risk-to-life-ethics-of-chris-burdens-shoot/.

20. Bill Billiter, "Performance Art: Practice is Creating a Controversy," *Los Angeles Times*, 18 May 1983, 10.

21. Peter Plagens, "He Got Shot—For His Art," *New York Times*, 2 September 1973, 1, 3.

22. Chris Burden and Jan Butterfield, "Through the Night Softly," in *The Art of Performance: A Critical Anthology*, ed. Gregory Battock and Robert Nickas (New York: E. P. Dutton, 1984), 221.

23. Grobel, "Chris Burden," 50.

24. G. Phillips, "Interview with Chris Burden," 281.

25. Helene Winer, "Burden at Pomona," in L. Phillips., *Extreme Measures*, 162–64; Paul McMahon, "In the Front Row for Chris Burden's Match Piece, 1972," *East of Borneo*, 12 October, 2012, http://www.eastofborneo.org/articles/in-the-front-row-for-chris-burdens-emmatch-pieceem-1972.

26. On Burden's "masochism," see Kathy O'Dell, *Contract with the Skin: Masochism, Performance Art, and the 1970s* (Minneapolis: University of Minnesota Press, 1998), esp. 1–16.

27. *Chris Burden*, 54–55.

28. *Chris Burden*, 56–57.

29. L. Phillips, *Extreme Measures*, 157–58, 227.

30. Chris Burden, *Esquire*, May 1973, 165.

31. On the upheaval of this period see Andreas Killen, *1973: Nervous Breakdown: Watergate, Warhol, and the Birth of Post-Sixties America* (New York: Bloomsbury, 2006), and Philip Jenkins, *Decade of Nightmares: The End of the Sixties and the Making of Eighties America* (New York: Oxford University Press, 2006).

32. Paul Schimmel, "Other Words: Interview with Chris Burden" (October 1994/January 1996), in *Chris Burden: Beyond the Limits/Jenseits der Grenzen*, ed. Peter Noever (Vienna: MAK, 1996), 39.

33. Thomas Crow, "Mind-Body," 48; L. Phillips, "Double Bind," 18; Amelia Jones, "Bridges," 123, all in L. Phillips, *Extreme Measures*.

34. William Wilson, "This Is Art—These People Are Artists," *Los Angeles Times*, 24 March 1972, 14.

35. "Church of Human Energy," 54.

36. Melrod, "Interview."

37. Burden, *High Performance* interview, 6.

38. *Chris Burden*, 152–53.

39. L. Phillips, *Extreme Measures*, 225.

40. L. Phillips, *Extreme Measures*, 228.

41. Matson, "Risk to Life."

42. Burden, "In Conversation with Jon Bewley," 20. On the ethical implications, see Frazer Ward, "Gray Zone: Watching *Shoot*," *October* 95 (Winter 2001): 115–30.

43. L. Phillips, *Extreme Measures*, 224; Roger Ebert, "Chris Burden: 'My God, Are They Going to Leave Me Here To Die?,'" *Chicago Sun-Times*, 25 May 1975, available online at http://www.rogerebert.com/interviews/chris-burden-my-god-are-they-going-to-leave-me-here-to-die.

44. Burden, "In Conversation with Jon Bewley," 21.

45. L. Phillips, *Extreme Measures*, 228, 63.

46. Ebert, "Chris Burden."

Conclusion

1. Kenneth Silverman, *Begin Again: A Biography of John Cage* (New York: Alfred A. Knopf, 2010), 264–66; John Cage, *Empty Words: Writings, '73–'78* (Middletown, CT: Wesleyan University Press, 1981), 180–82 passim. Cage's interview about the piece is available online at https://archive .org/details/Cage_interview_and_performance_Empty_words_August_1974_A002A.

2. James Wolcott, "Review of Lou Reed, *Metal Music Machine*," *Rolling Stone*, 14 August 1975, available online at http://www.rollingstone.com/music/albumreviews/metal-machine-music-19750814. A more favorable view of the recording is Louis Pattison, "Metal Music Machine," in "Lou Reed: The Ultimate Music Guide," special issue, *Uncut*, 2014, 48–49.

3. Eliot Kidd, quoted in. Legs McNeil and Gillian McCain, eds., *Please Kill Me: The Uncensored Oral History of Punk* (New York: Grove, 1996), 259–60. Excellent on punk is Will Hermes, *Love Goes to Buildings on Fire: Five Years in New York That Changed Music Forever* (New York: Faber & Faber, 2011).

4. Norman Mailer, "The Faith of Graffiti," *Esquire*, May 1974), 77–80, 88, 154, 157–58.

5. David Steigerwald, *Culture's Vanities: The Paradox of Cultural Diversity in a Globalized World* (Lanham, MD: Rowman & Littlefield, 2004), 27–28. See also Andreas Huyssen, *After the Great Divide: Modernism, Mass Culture, Postmodernism* (Bloomington: University of Indiana Press, 1986), 170–71.

6. Very good on Koons and the unacceptable excesses of the art world is Sarah Thornton, *33 Artists in 3 Acts* (New York: W. W. Norton, 2014). On art and commerce see Pierre Bourdieu and Hans Haacke, *Free Exchange* (Stanford, CA: Stanford University Press, 1995), 104. Very useful for understanding art today is Timothy Van Laar and Leonard Diepeveen, *Artworld Perspective: Arguing Cultural Value* (Oxford: Oxford University Press, 2013).

7. Although not discussed within this book, the earthworks of artists such as Robert Smithson, Michael Heizer, and Walter De Maria, with their combination of maximalism (huge areas of land) and minimalism (in terms of form), fits perfectly into the New Sensibility as worked out by Cage. See, for example, Suzann Boettger, *Earthworks: Art and the Landscape of the Sixties* (Berkeley: University of California Press, 2002); Henry M. Sayre, *The Object of Performance: The American Avant-Garde since 1970* (Chicago: University of Chicago Press, 1989), 211–45.

8. Michiko Kakutani, "A Lucy and Ethel for an Age after Blogs," *New York Times*, 1 July 2014, C1.

9. For measured comments on Burden and when violent art may be justified, see Maggie Nelson, *The Art of Cruelty: A Reckoning* (New York: W. W. Norton, 2011), 10, 108–11.

10. Karen Finley, *A Different Kind of Intimacy: A Memoir* (New York: Thunder's Mouth, 2000), 79.

11. Cary Levine, *Pay for Your Pleasures: Mike Kelley, Paul McCarthy, and Raymond Petitbon* (Chicago: University of Chicago Press, 2013), 119–20.

12. Much has been written on the piece. A good starting point is Jerry Saltz, "Kara Walker Bursts Into Three Dimensions, and Flattens Me," *Vulture*, 31 May 2014, http://www .vulture.com/2014/05/art-review-kara-walker-a-subtlety.html.

{ INDEX }

Page numbers in bold indicate illustrations.